The Origins of
the Boxer Uprising

This volume is sponsored by
the Center for Chinese Studies
University of California, Berkeley

The Origins of
the Boxer Uprising

Joseph W. Esherick

UNIVERSITY OF CALIFORNIA PRESS
Berkeley · *Los Angeles* · *London*

University of California Press
Berkeley and Los Angeles, California

University of California Press, Ltd.
London, England

© 1987 by
The Regents of the University of California

Library of Congress Cataloging-in-Publication Data

Esherick, Joseph.
  The origins of the Boxer Uprising.

  Bibliography: p.
  Includes index.
  1. China—History—Boxer Rebellion, 1899–1901.
I. Title.
DS771.E73   1987   951'.03   86-16054

ISBN 978-0-520-06459-1 (alk. paper)

Printed in the United States of America
12 11 10 09 08
12 11 10 9 8
The paper used in this publication is both acid-free
and totally chlorine-free (TCF). It meets the minimum
requirements of ANSI/NISO Z39.48-1992 (R 1997)
(*Permanence of Paper*). ∞

For Joe and Chris

Contents

List of Tables   xi

List of Illustrations   xii

Preface   xiii

1. Shandong: Where It All Began   1

   The North China Plain. The North China Macroregion. Socio-economic Regions of Shandong. Home of the Boxers. Social Formations of West Shandong. The Geographic Distribution of the Shandong Gentry.

2. Sects, Boxers, and Popular Culture   38

   Sectarian Rebels in Shandong. Official Proscription of "Heterodox" Sects. Sectarian Rebels in the Late Eighteenth and Early Nineteenth Centuries. Sectarians and Martial Artists. Invulnerability and Possession. Boxers and Sectarians in the Late Qing. Popular Culture and Peasant Community.

3. Imperialism, for Christ's Sake   68

   The Impact of Foreign Imports. The Sino-Japanese War. Christianity and Western Expansionism. Missionary Activity in Shandong. German Catholics of the S.V.D. The Catholic Church as Imperium in Imperio. The 1890s: Christians in the High Tide of Imperialism.

4. The Big Sword Society   96

The Early History of the Armor of the Golden Bell.
The Shandong-Jiangsu Border Region.   The Armor of
the Golden Bell.   Big Swords, Bandits, and Officials.
The Big Sword Society and the Catholics.   The Uprising
of June 1896.

5. The Juye Incident   123

The Causes of the Incident.   The German Reaction.
The Impact of the Jiaozhou Seizure.

6. Guan County, 1898: The Emergence of the
   "Boxers United in Righteousness"   136

The Setting.   A History of Sectarian Activity.
The Christians.   Liyuantun.   The Dispute with the
Christians.   The Eighteen Chiefs.   The Plum Flower
Boxers.   The Struggle Renewed.   The Boxers United
in Righteousness.   1898: Christian Victory and Boxer
Dispersal.   Fall 1898: Outbreak and Suppression.

7. The Gathering Storm   167

Reform in Shandong.   The Fiscal Crisis of the State.
Natural Disasters and Civil Unrest.   Foreign Aggression
in 1898–99.   The Germans in Shandong.   Anti-
Christian Incidents in Southeast Shandong.   German
Incursions of 1899.   The Role of Yu-xian.   "Red
Boxers" in Jining.   Yu-xian's Boxer Policy.   Foreign
Response: German and American.

8. The Spirit Boxers   206

Sectarians in Northwest Shandong.   Christians in
Northwest Shandong.   Spirit Boxers: Ritual and the
Problem of Sectarian Origins.   The Transformation and
Spread of the Spirit Boxers: 1898–99.   Official Attitudes.
Patterns of Transmission and Boxer Organization.
The Social Composition of the Spirit Boxers.

9. The Inevitable Clash   241

The Spirit Boxers of Pingyuan.   Boxer Violence and
Foreign Protests.   Showdown at Gangzi Lizhuang.
The Battle at Senluo Temple.   The Official Response.
The Final Days of Zhu Hong-deng.   The Boxer Hydra
Grows.

10. Prairie Fire   271

*The Policy of the Court.   Spread Across Zhili.   Spring
1900: Escalating Conflict.   Foreign Threats and
Vacillation at Court.   The Boxers in Beijing and Tianjin.
"Declaration of War."   Siege in Beijing and Tianjin.
The Civilized World's Revenge.   Lessons.*

Epilogue: Beyond the Idol of Origins   315

Appendix: The Mid-Qing Yi-he Boxers and
the White Lotus   333

Abbreviations Used in the Notes   341

Notes   345

Glossary of Names and Terms   413

Bibliography   421

Index   441

Tables

1.	Comparison of Six Regions of Shandong	9
2.	Distribution of Provincial Degree-Holders (*Ju-ren*), Percentages by Region, 1368–1900	30
3.	*Ju-ren* Totals Along the Grand Canal, 1400–1900	31
4.	Percentages of *Ju-ren* from Counties Along the Grand Canal	33
5.	Multiple Regression of *Ju-ren* on Key Variables	35
6.	Class Backgrounds of Boxer Leaders	239
7.	Shandong Boxer Attacks by Date and County, May 1899–January 1900	259
8.	Shandong Boxer Attacks by Date and Type, May 1899–January 1900	262

Illustrations

MAPS

1. Macroregions of China   4
2. Six Regions of Shandong   8
3. Ratio of Military to Civil *Ju-ren* by County, 1851–1900   47
4. The Shandong-Jiangsu-Henan Border Region   100
5. The Guan County Exclave Area   139
6. The 1898 Yellow River Flood   178
7. The Last Days of Zhu Hong-deng, Fall of 1899   251
8. The Boxer Spread into Zhili, 1899–1900   276

FIGURES

1. "The Nine Classes"   48
2. "Gambling Outlaws in a Brawl"   49
3. Street Theatricals   64
4. Baptizing Two Shandong Villagers   78
5. Exhibition of Boxing and Acrobatics   150
6. Missionary Justice   201
7. Boxer Puppet Show   233
8. Boxer Placard   278
9. Tianjin Boxers   292
10. Attack on the Northern Cathedral   298

Preface

Few events in Chinese history are more widely known than the Boxer Uprising. The dramatic siege of the Beijing legations captured the attention of the world in the summer of 1900, and provided ample copy for journalistic sensationalism of the day and Hollywood script-writers half a century later. The "Siege of Peking" was finally lifted by an International Expedition of eight nations—including American troops fighting on Chinese soil for the first time. But the Boxers are not only important for their unusual command of an international audience. Above all they stood as a dramatic example of ordinary Chinese peasants rising up to rid China of the hated foreign presence. As such they were an important episode in the emergence of mass nationalism in China.

Although familiar to most people, the Boxer Uprising remains poorly understood. In the first place, the Boxers were not pugilists. Their "boxing" was really a set of invulnerability rituals—to protect them from the powerful new weapons of the West. Central to their rituals was the notion of spirit-possession, which was held to bring about the magical invulnerability. Boxers called down one of the gods of the popular religious pantheon, then went into a trance as the god possessed them, and rose to dance wildly and wield their swords or spears. These rituals, easily learned by young peasants from the Yellow River floodplain, were transmitted from village to village until a momentous mass movement engulfed much of northern China. The Boxer Uprising, then, was really an instance of mass shamanism, and it had more to do with the spread of certain magical techniques than the mobilization of any organization of Chinese martial artists.

A second common misunderstanding relates to the usual name for the Boxer movement: the Boxer Rebellion. The appelation is truly a misnomer, for the Boxers never rebelled against the Manchu rulers of China and their Qing dynasty. Indeed the most common Boxer slogan, throughout the history of the movement, was "Support the Qing, destroy the Foreign"—where "foreign" clearly meant the foreign religion, Christianity, and its Chinese converts as much as the foreigners themselves. In the summer of 1900, threatened with a foreign military advance on the capital, the Qing court even declared its explicit support of the Boxers. But after the movement was suppressed, both Chinese officials and the foreign powers realized that the Qing would have to continue as China's government. In order to save face for the Qing court and the Empress Dowager at its head, the fiction was created that the Boxers were really rebels, who happened to gain support from some Manchu princes who usurped power in Beijing. It was accordingly the "Boxer Rebellion," and the Qing only had to be punished for not suppressing it earlier. Despite this purely political and opportunist origin of the term, the "Boxer Rebellion" has shown a remarkable ability to survive in texts on Chinese and world history.

Confusion about the Boxer Uprising is not simply a matter of popular misconceptions. There are remarkable divergences in scholarly opinion on the Boxers. In fact, there is no major incident in China's modern history on which the range of professional interpretation is as great. This is particularly true with respect to the subject which is the focus of this book: the origins of the Boxer Uprising. As the Boxer movement was just beginning in 1899, a county magistrate by the name of Lao Nai-xuan wrote a pamphlet entitled "An Examination of the Sectarian Origins of the Boxers United in Righteousness." (Such was the full name of the Boxers, though it is often mistranslated "Righteous and Harmonious Boxers.") Lao argued that the Boxers were descended from a group linked to rebels of the millenarian White Lotus sect in the early nineteenth century. These alleged sectarian and anti-dynastic origins of the Boxers have been accepted by most scholars to this day. But there is also a strong minority position which argues that the Boxers were from the beginning a loyalist militia unit—the product of village defense forces that were operating under official sponsorship.

With professional opinion unable to decide whether the Boxers rose from sectarian rebels or loyalist militia, the uprising provides an almost irresistible challenge to the professional historian. The challenge is not simply the substantive one of determining the most plausible interpretation. The methodological difficulties which confront a Boxer researcher are also unusually great (and are, of course, one reason for the divergence of views on the substantive issues). On the Boxers we have sources derived from Chinese officials, both sympathetic and hostile to the movement; from missionaries and Chinese Christian targets of the Boxer attacks; from a few non-official observers of the Boxers (but mostly about the later stages of the movement); and from peasants in the Boxer areas interviewed sixty years after the movement by scholars in the People's Republic of China. Needless to say, the biases of all of these observers significantly color their accounts. All the usual techniques which historians employ—the identification of false accusations and bogus accounts, the seach for corroborating evidence, the granting of particular credence to information which runs contrary to the bias of the source—must be utilized to the full.

Despite these obstacles, I believe that the time is ripe for a new look at the origins of the Boxers. The last serious treatment of this subject in English was Victor Purcell's *The Boxer Uprising: A Background Study*, published in 1963. In the two decades since the publication of that volume, the Qing archives in both Beijing and Taiwan have been opened to scholars. The Institute of Modern History in Taiwan has published the voluminous *Jiao-wu jiao-an dang* (Archives on Missionary Cases) for the years leading up to the Boxer Uprising. From the People's Republic of China, there has been a flood of publications in recent years—most crucially two collections of documents from the provincial government of Shandong, the province where the uprising began. This flood shows no sign of abating. As this book was being prepared for press, the First Historical Archives (Ming-Qing archives) in Beijing announced a further collection of documents on the Boxers, soon to be published.[1]

My own research on the Boxer movement began in the fall of 1979, when I spent a year in the People's Republic of China at Shandong University and the First Historical Archives in Beijing. Without the assistance and cooperation of those two institutions, this research could never have been completed. Of particular importance were the original records of the oral history surveys done by students and faculty of the Shandong University History Department, who spread across western Shandong in 1960 and 1965–66, interviewing elderly peasants in the areas affected by the Boxer movement. A volume of excerpts from these surveys has since been published; but I was able to examine the original manuscript records of these surveys, in which the interviewers recorded the recollections of former Boxers and observers of the movement's earliest stages. These manuscript records, generously furnished to me by the Shandong University History Department, were considerably more complete than the published volume of excerpts, and were indispensable to my reconstruction of the Boxers' early history. Here, for the first time, we get something very close to a village-eye view of a major Chinese peasant uprising. When Shandong University arranged two trips to the villages from which the Boxers emerged, I was able to supplement the earlier peasant accounts with additional interviews and personal observations of the physical and social ecology of the Boxer heartland. These visits were invaluable in helping me to understand the importance of local variations in socio-economic conditions (often variation within a county) as a factor in the rise of the Boxer movement.

The sum total of this new evidence—contemporary documentation and oral history alike—not only provides more detailed insight into the local society and popular culture from which the Boxers arose; it also permits reexamination of some long-accepted interpretations of the Boxers. For example, the central problem which Purcell's *Boxer Uprising* sought to address was the alleged Boxer shift from an anti-dynastic to a pro-dynastic stance. Most subsequent textbooks and secondary accounts have followed Purcell in describing this transformation of Boxer ideology. But the recent evidence, and especially the oral histories, leave no doubt that from the very beginning the Boxers were a loyalist movement, and there never was an anti-dynastic phase.

The outline of this study is quite simple. I begin with an examination of Shandong province and the particular socio-economic conditions in the western portion of the province, on the north China plain. This was the area from which the Boxer Uprising spread—the southwest spawning the Big Sword Society (an anti-Christian predecessor of the Boxers, with distinct invulnerability rituals of its own) and the northwest producing the Boxers themselves. In chapter 2, we move from ecology and social formations to the popular culture and mentality of this region. Since so much scholarship has been devoted to the sectarian origins of the Boxers, we shall examine this question at some length—though detailed discussion of the relations between boxers and sectarians in the mid-Qing has been relegated to an appendix. In the end, however, I shall argue that the origins of the Boxers are not fruitfully sought in sectarian or martial arts groups which happened to have the same name many years before. Rather what we need to understand are the sources for the distinctive Boxer ritual repertoire, and here the key is the popular culture of the area and not the nature of some particular sectarian group. Chapter 3 completes the scene-setting with an examination of Western imperialism in Shandong, and the close link between imperialism and Christian proselytizing.

The narrative account of the rise of the Boxer movement begins with chapter 4. First we look at the Big Sword Society of the southwest, and its transformation from an anti-bandit to an anti-Christian organization. The next chapter examines the killing of two German missionaries in southwest Shandong, and the subsequent German occupation of Jiaozhou Bay on the Shandong peninsula. Chapter 6 brings us to the first mention of the Boxers United in Righteousness, who come into conflict with Christians in a difficult-to-control "exclave" of Shandong's Guan county, which, in one of those peculiarities of Chinese administrative geography, lay wholly within the neighboring province of Zhili. From there we move, in chapter 7, to an overview of economic and political conditions in Shandong in 1898–99, on the eve of the Boxer Uprising. Of particular interest are a series of anti-Christian incidents in southern Shandong, retaliatory German military expeditions sent from Jiaozhou, and the response of the new Manchu governor of Shandong, Yu-xian. Chapter 8 discusses the rise of the Spirit Boxers, the source of the distinctive possession and invulnerability rituals of the Boxer movement, and chapter 9 details the spreading violence of the Spirit Boxers and their first open conflict with the Qing authorities. With this, our tale of the origins of the Boxers is complete, and the final chapter simply completes the Boxer story, in summary form, by describing the spread of the movement across the north China plain to Beijing and Tianjin, the major incidents of anti-Christian and anti-foreign violence once the Boxers obtained official sponsorship in June and July, and finally the brutal foreign suppression by the International Expedition.

In the years that have gone into this study, I have accumulated debts to a number of institutions and individuals and it is a pleasure to acknowledge them here. The Committee on Scholarly Communication with the People's Republic of China supported my year of research in China. Its support was more than just financial, and the fine staff of that program is warmly thanked for all the assistance they rendered in making that research possible. The Wang Institute provided a generous grant to complete the research and writing of this monograph. The Center for Chinese Studies at the University of California, Berkeley, kindly helped to defray the cost of the cartography. The History Department of the University of Oregon was unusually tolerant of my frequent leaves to complete this project, and its patience is gratefully acknowledged.

The materials for this study could not have been obtained without the cooperation of Shandong University, the First Historical Archives in Beijing, the Palace Museum in Taiwan, the East Asian Library of the Hoover Institution, the Stanford University Library, the University of California Library, the Library of Congress, the Houghton and Harvard-Yenching libraries of Harvard University, the Columbia University Library, the home mission of the Society of the Divine Word in Techny, Illinois, and the Yale Divinity School. All of those institutions and their gracious staffs are warmly thanked. Professor David Buck and Gary Tiedemann provided copies of important missionary materials, and Satō Kimihiko sent documents from Japan. The assistance of these scholars, and the leads that their own research suggested, are gratefully acknowledged. Particular thanks are due to friends and colleagues in the History Department of Shandong University: especially to Xu Xu-dian, Lu Yao, Li De-zheng, and Lu Jing-qi. They were my expert guides to the sources on the Boxer movement, and always tolerant when my own approach and interpretations differed from theirs. Here in Oregon, Tom and Kathy Brady helped with the translation of a key German source; Patty Gwartney-Gibbs provided invaluable advice and assistance on statistical problems; and Enid Scofield expertly typed and corrected most of the manuscript. Ellen Laing was of great assistance in locating illustrations, and Sally Butler did a splendid job in drawing the maps. Barbara Metcalf, Phyllis Killen, and Susan Stone efficiently shepherded the work to publication at University of California Press. John S. Service expertly copy-edited the manuscript, and this was the third time I have had the privilege of working on a book with this meticulous critic and knowledgeable China hand. All of these people were quite indispensable and are warmly thanked.

A number of friends and colleagues have read earlier drafts of this monograph, and my only regret is that this work will surely fall far short of the standards they set in their generous critiques. I would like to express my warmest thanks for the thoughtful and constructive suggestions of a number of friends and colleagues. Susan Naquin kept me close to the documents and shared her considerable expertise on sectarian organization and practice. Philip Huang never let me forget the theoretical issues. Linda Grove and Elizabeth Perry reminded me of other literature and made sure I was saying what I meant. Ernest Young saved me from numerous factual errors and analytical failings; and colleagues in Asian Studies at the University of Oregon helped me to rethink and clarify the thoughts in the Epilogue. Many of the merits that this work might have are due to the careful reading and helpful criticisms of these people. The faults that remain derive from my own incurable stubbornness and persistent ignorance.

Finally I would like to thank my family, who have so patiently awaited the completion of this project. My wife Ye Wa has helped in more ways than I can count, always with unfailing good humor. My sons, Chris and Joe, have somehow survived a youth in which their father demanded so much of them, but gave so little in return—as he struggled to read one more source, or to rework one more faulty paragraph. That they not only put up with this, but actually encouraged me to press on and finish, is something for which I shall never be able to thank them enough. To them, this book is dedicated.

CHAPTER ONE

Shandong: Where It All Began

The impact of the Boxer Uprising was truly global. The political context for the uprising was significantly influenced by national trends. But in the end, the Boxers were really a *regional* movement. With the exception of a few officially inspired Boxer "militia" in such places as Shanxi, Inner Mongolia, and the Northeastern provinces of Manchuria during the summer of 1900, the movement was essentially confined to the Shandong and Zhili portions of the north China plain. Before all else, it is essential to look at the geography, the political economy and the social formations of this region—and in particular at Shandong, where it all began.

THE NORTH CHINA PLAIN

Late in the nineteenth century, an American medical missionary described a trip through the heartland of the Boxer movement:

> We were now passing through a level farming country, which appeared, as usual, thickly inhabited. At an interval of about a mile we would pass through a village of adobe houses with straw or reed roofs. These villages were usually surrounded by a decrepit adobe wall, and some even had a gate-house and heavy wooden gate. Trees grew within these village enclosures, but the plain was entirely free from any tree or shrub, every available inch of ground being taken up by the cultivation of cereals. The dreary look of all these villages made me feel home-sick. Nothing but dirty, mud-dried brick houses falling to decay everywhere, with some remnants of the red paper mottoes pasted up last New Year's time, fading and filthy, still sticking to the miserable, rotten doorways.[1]

1

Behind the prejudice and disgust displayed by a Westerner newly arrived in China, we can see here some of the most important characteristics of the north China plain: flat land, cereal agriculture, dense population, and impoverished villages. This was the alluvial flood plain of the mighty Yellow River plus a number of lesser streams that flow from the Taihang Mountains along the Shanxi border into the Gulf of Bohai. To the naked eye, the ground lies utterly flat for hundreds of miles in every direction, and the eye is not much deceived. From the point at which the Yellow River leaves the mountains of Shanxi and flows onto the plain in northern Henan, it travels 550 kilometers before it reaches the sea—and drops only 100 meters: less than 20 centimeters per kilometer. The muddiest great river in the world, its silt content reaches 25 percent. Millennia of such deposits have yielded the rich soil which makes this region one of China's most important agricultural areas. But the flatness of the plain makes drainage a major problem; and where water cannot easily be drained away, the soil grows saline and yields only the sparest of crops.[2]

The climate in this region is continental: temperatures average just above freezing during the winter months, with cold dry winds from the northwest, but the summers are hot and humid. Through most of the plain, rainfall averages less than 500 millimeters per year, and is heavily concentrated in the summer months of July and August. Along the coast and on the Shandong peninsula, rainfall is both more plentiful and more reliable, but on the plains, the variation from year to year can be considerable. Lacking any man-made irrigation network, the peasants lived wholly dependent on the heavens delivering summer rains in the right amount at the right time. All too often, the weather was not kind: too much rain would flood or waterlog the land; or too little precipitation would bring parching drought, leaving the soil hard and cracked and often covered with a thin white layer of salts risen to the surface.[3]

Though the vagaries of weather left this region prone to recurrent natural disasters, the plains had long been one of China's key agricultural regions. In fact, in the late nineteenth century agriculture was virtually the *only* source of livelihood there. Even in the 1930s, after the advent of the railway and some incipient commercialization, surveys showed roughly 90 percent (and often 95 percent) of the population classified as peasants. Though there were important areas where such commercial crops as cotton were grown, wheat, soy, millet, gaoliang (sorghum) and other subsistence grains dominated the

landscape.[4] These crops supported an extraordinarily dense population. A 1950s economic geography puts the population density
throughout the plain above 200 persons per square kilometer (over
500 per square mile), and in most regions over 300 persons per square
kilometer.[5] The population would have been somewhat less in the late
nineteenth century, but extrapolating back from 1930s figures, I
would estimate the average density in the critical western Shandong
portion of the plain to have been about 250 persons per square
kilometer.

THE NORTH CHINA MACROREGION

The vast Yellow River plain lies in the heart of what G. William
Skinner calls the "North China macroregion." In analyzing China's
cultural geography, no schema has been more influential in recent
years than Skinner's regional systems theory. He divides China south
of the Great Wall into eight macroregions: North China, Northwest
China, the Lower, Middle and Upper Yangzi, the Southeast Coast,
Lingnan (centerered on Canton) and the Southwestern region around
Yunnan and Guizhou. The North China macroregion is bounded by
the Great Wall on the north, the Taihang Mountains of Shanxi on
the west, and the Huai River drainage on the south (see map 1). By
Skinner's estimate, it was second only to the Lower Yangzi in population density (163 persons per square kilometer in 1893, as compared
to an average of 100 for the eight macroregions), but lowest in level
of rural commercialization. The unirrigated agriculture produced
little marketable surplus: the relatively uniform ecology of the north
China plain discouraged local specialization in commercial crops or
subsidiary activities within the macroregion; and the northern
winters gave peasants a long slack period in which all could engage in
handicraft production (especially spinning and weaving) for household consumption. In fact, trade in general was relatively underdeveloped in North China. There were few navigable rivers and the
cost of overland transport of grain equalled its production cost every
200 miles. As a consequence of this retarded commercialization, North
China had a lower level of urbanization than all but the substantially
frontier regions of the Upper Yangzi and the Southwest—a rather
remarkable fact given that North China was one of the oldest centers
of Chinese civilization, and the location of the national capital since
the tenth century. More than any other part of China, the North China

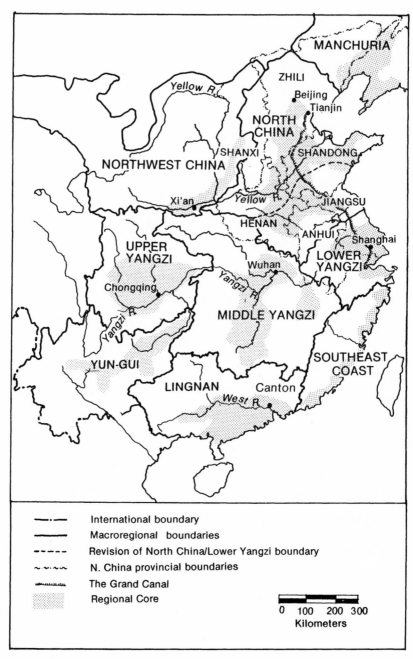

MANCHURIA

ZHILI

Yellow R.

Beijing
Tianjin

NORTH
CHINA

SHANXI   SHANDONG

NORTHWEST CHINA

Xi'an   Yellow R.   JIANGSU

HENAN   ANHUI   Shanghai

UPPER
YANGZI   LOWER
YANGZI

Wuhan

Chongqing

Yangzi R.

Yangzi R.

MIDDLE YANGZI

YUN-GUI   SOUTHEAST
COAST

LINGNAN   Canton

West R.

International boundary

Macroregional boundaries

Revision of North China/Lower Yangzi boundary

N. China provincial boundaries

The Grand Canal

Regional Core

0   100   200 300
Kilometers

Map 1.   Macroregions of China. Based on maps in G. William Skinner, *The City in Late Imperial China* (Stanford, 1977).

macroregion was a land of a few large cities and a densely populated, poor, and substantially self-sufficient rural hinterland.

China's macroregions, in Skinner's analysis, are defined by their fundamental economic independence: "The major commercial cities of the region had stronger economic links with one another than any had with cities outside the region." Within each macroregion there are densely populated lowland cores and more sparsely populated peripheries—usually lying in hilly regions that form watersheds between major river systems. The cores are not only more populated than the peripheries, they are also more fertile, better irrigated, more commercialized and served by better transport networks. In the regional peripheries, by contrast, "local society assumed its most heterodox and variegated guise," being characterized by heterodox sodalities from bandits to religious sects to secret societies and a "disproportionate number of smugglers, outcasts, political exiles, sorcerers, and other deviants."[6]

The analytic power and explanatory utility of Skinner's regional systems theory is beyond question. Perhaps especially in the Lower and Middle Yangzi, and the Lingnan region around Canton, the regional cores are substantially richer and more commercialized than the hill lands in their respective peripheries. Man-made irrigation works and waterborne transport are far better in these lowland cores. And it is unquestionably the case that the peripheries and regional frontiers have provided the base areas both for China's traditional rebellions and for her modern revolution.

But there are several respects in which North China fails to fit neatly into Skinner's model. The first problem is purely empirical and involves the southern boundary of the region. The basic definition of a macroregion requires that trade be primarily oriented to central places within the macroregion—and in North China, especially to-wards its central metropolises, Beijing and (following its growth as a treaty port in the late nineteenth century) Tianjin (Tientsin). Within North China, where even the Yellow River was barely navigable, the key carrier of such trade was the Grand Canal. This spectacular inland waterway was built to carry the tribute rice of the Yangzi valley, Henan, and Shandong to feed the capital in Beijing, but it also served as a major bearer of north–south commerce in all types of goods both on the tribute barges and on private merchant vessels. From the Yangzi port of Zhenjiang (Chinkiang), it proceeded north to the lakes on Shandong's southern border, and through Jining. Then, picking up the water of the Wen River and following earlier natural water-courses, it meandered north to Linqing on the Shandong–Zhili border. From there the canal followed the course of the Wei River flowing northeast, until it eventually reached Tianjin and the final short stretch to Tongzhou outside of Beijing.

There is no question that the Grand Canal made the boundary between the North China and Lower Yangzi macroregions extremely permeable. But these were clearly two separate economic regions and the key question is: at what point on the canal was the flow of goods primarily to and from Zhenjiang and the cities of the Lower Yangzi, and at what point was the orientation of trade primarily northward toward Tianjin and Beijing. Clearly this should be the boundary between the North China and Lower Yangzi macroregions. The line is fairly reliably established through the reports of the Imperial Maritime Customs, for goods imported through Zhenjiang moved on native boats under "transit passes" which exempted them from the collection of *likin*—a tax on domestic commerce. These transit passes listed the destination of the goods, and the reports of the Zhenjiang customs commissioners indicate that southern Shandong, at least to the point where the northern (post-1855) course of the Yellow River intercepted the canal, lay within the Zhenjiang catchment.[7] Since the transport costs would be the same for native and imported goods, we can be reasonably certain that this reflects the division of the commercial networks of the two macroregions.[8]

As we shall see below, this revision of the boundaries of the North China macroregion makes the analytical portion of Skinner's model better fit the facts. It recognizes much of southern Shandong as a periphery, appropriate for an area of widespread banditry. And since bandits, temporary laborers, and beggars from this area all tended to move southward in times of hardship,[9] this revision has them moving more properly toward a regional core rather than further out toward a periphery.

But this is only a minor factual revision of the regional systems model. Far more serious is the fact that so much of the North China core is densely populated, but scarcely commercialized except in the immediate vicinity of the Grand Canal, and poorly served by any transport beyond the wheelbarrow along rutted dirt roads. It was, in fact, less commercialized than many areas of the Shandong peninsula which are actually in Skinner's periphery—areas that also produced an inordinate proportion of the province's gentry elite. Above all, it was the plain that produced the "heterodox" practices of the Boxers—practices far more appropriate to a regional frontier. To explain these phenomena, we shall have to look for other sources of local variation beyond regional cores and peripheries and shift our unit of analysis from the North China macroregion to the province of Shandong.[10]

SOCIO-ECONOMIC REGIONS OF SHANDONG

In the summer of 1900, when advancing foreign troops threatened the Boxers besieging the Legation Quarter in Beijing, these Boxers looked for the arrival of an "old corps" (lao-tuan) from Shandong to revitalize their struggle against the alien aggressor. Shandong was the source of the Boxer magic; but the movement did not encompass all of the province. The Boxers emerged in the area north of the Yellow River, in what is usually termed "northwest Shandong" (Lu-xi-bei). The predecessor of the Boxers, the Big Sword Society, was a product of the southwest, along the border with Jiangsu and Henan. Our task here is to define the features that distinguished these areas from the remainder of the province.[11]

We may begin our survey of Shandong on the peninsula in the east. (See map 2 for the boundaries of the six Shandong regions, and table 1 for a comparison of regions by key measures.) Though the end of the peninsula is characterized by bare, long-since deforested hills and fairly rocky soils, a broad low plain stretches from Jiaozhou Bay on the southern shore to the Gulf of Bohai on the north—a plain so level that the Chinese once linked two rivers to form a canal across the entire peninsula.[12] In 1897, the Germans seized Jiaozhou Bay, on whose southeastern shore they would build the port city of Qingdao (Tsing-tao), and soon began surveying for the railway which would link the port to the provincial capital of Jinan. But the railway and the growth of Qingdao were twentieth century developments, and beyond our period of concern. In the nineteenth century, the only treaty port for foreign trade was Yantai (Chefoo), opened in 1862, which developed a very modest trade largely limited to the peninsula and Shandong's northern shore.[13]

Though the hilly end of the peninsula made this the most sparsely populated region (135 per square kilometer), the well-watered plain, where yields were among the highest in the province, was densely settled and the region as a whole accounted for 24 percent of the

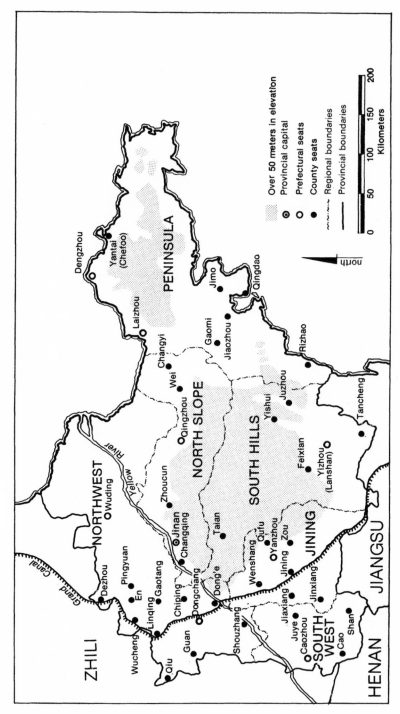

Map 2. Six Regions of Shandong

TABLE 1   COMPARISON OF SIX REGIONS OF SHANDONG

Region (number of counties)	Population per km²	Yield Index[a]	Land Rented	Non-agricultural households (percent)[b]	Disaster Index[c]	Ju-ren per 50,000 population (1851–1900)
Peninsula (17)	135	396	27.5	11.1	1.5	2.95
North Slope (15)	311	472	17.8	16.0	(190.9)	4.40
South Hills (12)	191	381	26.3	12.4	11.0	1.34
Jining (10)	291	461	20.1	11.4	106.7	2.91
Southwest (9)	312	378	23.1	(9.9)	225.1	0.81
Northwest (44)	252	367	10.6	7.1	196.7	1.85

sources: See Note 11 for a discussion of the various sources from which these data have been developed.

[a] Yield index = wheat yield + soy yield + average of gaoliang and millet yields (all in catties per mu). This figure, while most useful for comparative purposes, in very rough terms represents the number of catties of grain provided on one mu of land over two years in normal crop rotation. A catty (jin) was about one-half kilogram, and a mu one-sixth of an acre.

[b] In the Southwest, Shan county was dropped from the average as the 40,000 peasant households recorded for it (clearly somebody's wild guess) yielded an unrealistic figure of 32% non-agricultural households in the county.

[c] See note 11 on the composition of this index. The North Slope figure is inordinately high because a few areas northeast of Jinan were either covered or repeatedly flooded by the new course of the Yellow River. The rest of the region was quite free of disaster.

province's population. An early missionary visitor found "the land well-watered by rivulets, the soil rich and productive, abounding in grain, fruits and vegetables."[14] The economy was perhaps the most diverse in the province. In addition to fruit trees, the hills grew mulberry and oak trees—the latter providing the leaves for the famous pongee silk, just as the former fed the ordinary silk worm in this ancient silk-raising region. Some streams carried gold dust, which was panned by the local inhabitants, tobacco was grown as a commercial crop, straw braiding and bamboo working were important handicraft industries, and fishing was common along the coast.[15]

Though the peninsula's relative immunity to natural disasters meant that few were reduced to utter destitution, and both begging and banditry were rare,[16] there are a number of indications that society was relatively stratified here. Landlordism (27.5 percent of the cultivated area was rented) was higher than any other region, as was the production of sweet potatoes—normally the diet of the very poor.[17] Wealthier folks and town-dwellers ate and drank significantly better (often including wine with their meals), lived in tiled houses and wore fine-spun cloth.[18] A traveller through Jiaozhou was particularly impressed by the many fine houses with "high poles before their front door, indicating that some member of the family had been a mandarin."[19]

Fifteen counties along the northern slope of the central Shandong mountains, from Changyi and Wei in the east to Licheng (Jinan) and Changqing in the west, form the second region in Shandong. In many respects it closely resembled the peninsula, especially in its diversified economy. Silk production was widespread. There were large coal mines and iron founderies in Wei county, and more coal mines plus pottery and glass works in Boshan. But with much less hilly ground than the peninsula, population density was much higher (311 per square kilometer), and agriculture resembled the best that the peninsula had to offer. Streams flowing down from the hills and relatively accessible underground water made this the best irrigated region of the province; on the average, grain yields in this "exceedingly fertile" area were the highest in Shandong.

Commerce was equally flourishing. The most remarkable town was Zhoucun. Though not even a county seat, it was described as "undoubtedly the most important market place in the Province, excepting Chi-ning-chou [Jining]."[20] Zhoucun collected and distributed the silk from throughout the central mountain region.[21] The city of Wei, with 100,000 people was a "commercial and manufacturing city of considerable importance" as early as 1866,[22] and was the major entrepôt for goods from the peninsula and the treaty port of Chefoo. Between there and the capital city of Jinan, a traveller described traffic as so great as often to impede progress.[23] The contrast to the plains to the northwest was marked. Another road cut off from Wei to cross those plains in the direction of Tianjin. That road was described as "destitute of any place of importance."[24]

The peninsula and north slope were not only the most developed parts of the province, they also represented its political center of gravity. In the fifty years prior to 1900, 58 percent of Shandong's provincial degree-holders (*ju-ren*) came from these two regions—with each providing about half of that total. The northern slope's graduates, coming especially from the provincial capital and the fertile spring-watered counties to its east, were particularly out of proportion to its population. There the fifty-year total represented 4.4 for every 50,000 population—more than twice the figure for the northwest plains, and four times that of the southwest. But the peninsula was more successful in securing official positions for its gentry: fully 38 percent of the province's metropolitan officials came from the peninsula—giving that region by far the greatest political influence in the capital.

The hills of southern Shandong contrasted sharply with the north. Here was a true regional periphery. In percentage of land under cultivation (27 percent) this region was the lowest in the province. Its population density of 190 per square kilometer was lower than any area but the peninsula. With most of its land hilly, crop yields were low, though the hills also caught the summer storms, providing more dependable rainfall and making the region much less subject to natural disasters (and thus much more stable) than the western plains.[25] Still, the peasants were poor here, and there was little commerce to provide alternative employment. Silk moved across the low hills to the towns on the north slope; and in the 1890s, the region began shipping substantial quantities of peanuts south to the Grand Canal and export via Zhenjiang.[26] Some bean oil, silk, and straw braid also moved south to the Canal and eventually to Shanghai—indicating the primary economic orientation of southern Shandong toward the Lower Yangzi macroregion.[27] On the whole, however, the region was so poorly served by transport that mercantile development was slight. The same traveller of the 1860s who remarked on the bustling commercial activity north of the hills, was above all struck by the smallness of the towns and the lack of trade in the south—calling Yishui "the smallest city I have ever seen in China." [28]

The relatively retarded development of this region went together with fairly high rates of landlordism (26 percent of cultivated land—second only to the peninsula). This no doubt reflected the curvilinear relationship between landlordism and commercialization—with more patrimonial forms of landlordism in more "backward" areas, and a more purely cash-nexus rentier landlordism prevailing in highly commercialized regions. The south Shandong landlords appear to have been resident village landlords, no doubt often of a very rude and uncultured type—and thus relatively high landlordism did not go together with any gentry strength in this area. Though it included 15.6 percent of the province's population, the region furnished only 8.4 percent of the provincial degree holders—a mere 1.3 per 50,000 population over the last fifty years of the nineteenth century, one-third the ratio north of the hills.

Continuing west we come to the Jining region around the Grand Canal. With most of its land sloping gradually toward the canal, and water available from the streams flowing from the hills, this region was second only to the northern slope in agricultural productivity. Commercial crops were fairly common, as tobacco had been cultivated in the area since the early Qing; and a wide variety of fruit—peaches, persimmons, pears, apricots and dates—were sent down the canal to Jiangnan.[29] It was not, however, uniformly prosperous. The southernmost areas, where the canal skirted the Shandong–Jiangsu border, were prone to periodic flooding in the late summer and fall as the canal was unable to handle all of the run-off from the hills. When the Amherst Mission passed down the canal in 1816, they found that "whole villages, with extensive tracts of cultivated land, must have been submerged." [30] At 291 persons per square kilometer, population was extremely dense. Jining—the commercial center of the region—was the largest city in the province, with a population estimated at 150,000. A 1907 source describes Jining as "formerly a large trading center, now an industrial city, where copper, iron and bamboo articles are manufactured"—to which list we could add processed tobacco, leather goods, and pickled vegetables.[31]

In many respects, this region reflects an affinity for the Lower Yangzi quite unlike anywhere else in Shandong. Certainly most of the region's trade was with Jiangnan and the southern end of the Canal. The Jining residents regarded their city as a "little Suzhou"; with the

Grand Canal running through its center, and several scenic spots commemorating the wine-loving poet Li Bo's sojourn in the city during the Tang dynasty, the claim seems not entirely unwarranted. This was a cultured area—encompassing the ancient state of Lu, homeland of Confucius. The lineal descendants of the great philosopher continued to live in nearby Qufu, where the head of the lineage held noble rank as lord of the Confucian estate, and where an academy for the descendants of Confucius and three of his disciples produced an inordinate number of successful examination candidates. Not surprisingly, the region produced a relatively high 2.91 *ju-ren* per 50,000 population—roughly the level of the peninsula.

Further west we arrive at the southwestern corner of Shandong— basically the portion of Caozhou prefecture south of the Yellow River. In terms of its agriculture, there was little to distinguish it from the Jining region.[32] Crops were similar: wheat, soy and sorghum predominating, with smaller amounts of millet and a little cotton. Yields were a little lower—especially toward the west where the high banks of the relocated Yellow River blocked the natural drainage of the plain. With almost no hills at all, the proportion of land under cultivation and the population density were higher—in fact the highest in the province.

But in three crucial respects the Southwest differed from the Jining region. First, it was twice as prone to natural disasters— especially flooding along the Yellow River and the border with Jiangsu to the south. And in part because of this unstable environment, the Southwest, with a population roughly comparable to the Jining region, produced only one quarter as many provincial degree-holders, and three times as many bandits! With only 0.81 degree-holders per 50,000 population, the Southwest had the sparsest gentry presence of any region in the province; and Caozhou was notorious as a bandit stronghold. In fact, the low-lying marshy regions near the current course of the Yellow River provided the lair for the Song dynasty bandit gang immortalized in the novel *Water Margin* (*Shui-hu zhuan*). It was surely no accident that the Big Sword Society—whose initial function was defense against banditry— should find its origins in southwest Shandong.

HOME OF THE BOXERS

Finally, we arrive in the northwest plains, the Boxer heartland. Stretching across the entire region north of the Yellow River, and including a few counties of coastal delta south and east of the river, this was both the largest and the most populous of our regions, with 26 percent of the province's land area and the same proportion of population. This made population density about average for Shandong, over 250 persons per square kilometer (or 650 per square mile). With 93 percent of its inhabitants peasants, it was the most purely agricultural of Shandong's regions. But the area was anything but prosperous. Average yields were the lowest of any region in the province, reflecting the persistent problems of waterlogging and salinity of the soil. Even those averages probably understated the precariousness of peasant livelihood here, for the Northwest was also particularly prone to natural disasters.

When the Yellow River shifted to a northern course between 1852 and 1855, it followed the old bed of the Daqing River across western Shandong. As the dynasty fought for its life against the Taiping and other rebels, it was too preoccupied and short of funds to strengthen the embankments and protect the surrounding countryside. Consequently, especially in its lower reaches, the Yellow frequently flooded over the lower ground to its north.[33] But the problem did not become severe until about 1880, by which time gradual silting had raised the bed of the river *above* ground level through most of Shandong, and floods of terrible destructiveness became almost an annual occurrence. In 1886–87 it briefly appeared that the river gods had come to Shandong's aid as the Yellow again broke its banks in Henan and returned to a southern course. Shandong peasants were said to have resisted government requisitions of millet stalks to repair the break, while Shandong officials lobbied to let the river resume its former course. But the province's political weight was no match for that of Jiangnan and its powerful governor-general, Zeng Guo-quan. After a year's respite the breach was repaired and the river returned to continue its devastation of northwest Shandong.[34]

The shift in the Yellow River not only brought floods. It also delivered a mortal blow to interregional commerce on the Grand Canal. Crossing the Yellow River had always been the most difficult hydrologic problem on the canal. Even in its southern course, Yellow River silt had been causing major problems for travel on the canal since 1785.[35] With the shift in the Yellow River, the clear waters of the Wen, which had fed the canal between Jining and Linqing, could not pass beyond Dong'e. The only recourse was to divert the waters of the Yellow into the section of the canal between Dong'e and Linqing. This could only be done during the summer rise in the Yellow, and only for a short time as the muddy Yellow deposited enormous amounts of silt in the slow-moving canal.

The shift in the Yellow River came at a time when the Taiping rebels were occupying the lower portions of the canal, and the Yangzi valley tribute rice was already being carried to Tianjin by sea. The success of this sea route (especially when steamships were used from the 1870s), meant that the canal would never be restored to its former grandeur. By 1896, a foreign observer would write (with some exaggeration): "As a means of communication between north and south, the Canal need not be considered, as not a single vessel except the junks carrying the tribute rice ever passes." [36] Gradually the cities along its route went into decline. The prefectural capital of Dongchang was a prime example. When the Amherst mission passed through in 1816, they found it "well-built, extensive, and populous." [37] For a time after the river shifted, the city maintained its position. An 1860s traveller still found it a "very important city" with "warehouses rivalling many in Tien-tsin [Tianjin] and Shanghai." [38] But by 1897, it was "going to decay, its commerical prosperity rapidly on the wane." [39] Linqing's fall was even more dramatic, in part because it was also devasted by the nineteenth-century rebellions. From a city of 100,000 during much of the Ming and Qing, it fell to an estimated 40,000 by the late nineteenth century. Said one traveller: "The most notable feature inside the city is its emptiness." [40]

Though it was certainly the most dramatic, the Yellow River was not the only source of disasters in northwest Shandong. Lesser streams frequently met natural or human impediments to quick run-off on this flat plain, and local flooding of low-lying pockets was a recurrent problem throughout the region. [41] If there was not too much water, there was likely to be too little—for the crops here depended completely on timely rains, and north of the Shandong hills the weather was at its most unreliable. [42] A terrible drought was said to have carried off nearly two million people in 1876, and full relief did not come until several years later. [43] Ten years later, famine struck again, and "husks, chaff and leaves became part of the daily diet." [44]

Historically, the Northwest was Shandong's disaster area—but the calamities were human as well as natural. West of Jinan, an imperial highway ran north and south, entering the province at Dezhou, and passing through Gaotang and Chiping before crossing the Yellow River's northern course at Dong'e—a path which took it directly through the heartland of the Boxer movement. From ancient times, this road had carried invading armies both north and south—with the local populace always the greatest victim. The Mongol invasion passed through here—spreading a devastation shared by so much of northern China.[45] Early in the Ming (1368–1644), much of the area was devasted by the battles surrounding the Yong-le's usurpation of the Ming throne. The Gaotang gazetteer describes the destruction as so great that all the major lineages of the department date their arrival only from the mid-Ming.[46]

The Manchu invasion probably matched the Mongols in destructiveness, especially if one adds the distress brought by numerous petty rebels during the course of the Ming–Qing transition. Most cities in the area fell repeatedly to rebel forces, before the might of the Manchu armies finally restored a harsh order on what was left of the population—those few who were not killed or driven off by the rebels, the northern invaders, or the famines and epidemics which accompanied their devastation.[47] If the tax records are to be believed, some counties lost 80 percent of their population, and two-thirds of the land lay uncultivated.[48] In many areas, the government had to bring in settlers to repopulate the countryside.[49] The Grand Canal city of Linqing was probably the greatest metropolis in this region, and the Manchu invasion seems to have delivered a blow from which, in some respects, it never fully recovered. Further south—and into the Southwestern region—the Elm Forest Army (Yu-lin jun) mobilized thousands to resist the Qing, many of them famine victims who joined the army out of desperation. Their effort devastated much of the surrounding countryside, and came to an end only when a flood in the Yellow River left them with no place to flee.[50]

Though Wang Lun's sectarian uprising of 1774 (discussed in chapter 2) brought physical destruction to much of Linqing, it was a limited affair, and a minor interruption in the long peace that the Qing had brought. But the nineteenth century once again introduced Shandong to a time of troubles—and again it was west Shandong which suffered the most. On top of the Yellow River floods and the disruption of the Grand Canal came the great mid-century rebellions.

First the Taiping Northern Expedition passed through the area in 1854 after being driven back from the approaches to Beijing. Passing down the great north–south highway, the Taiping invested the city of Gaotang for much of the winter. The Mongol commander Senggerinchin finally eliminated the rebels in Chiping by surrounding them and flooding the area—leaving the local peasants once again the primary victims. In the meantime, a Taiping relief expedition had taken Linqing, the battles there leaving that great city in ruins.[51] Throughout the 1860s, the Nian rebels raided into Shandong (eventually killing Senggerinchin) first largely in the Southwest where they several times threatened to take Jining, then with considerable devastation in the Northwest, especially in 1868. These great rebellions, and the often heavy-handed efforts of the authorities to defend the old order, sparked a series of lesser uprisings and tax-resistance movements throughout the western part of the province, most notably the rebellion of White Lotus rebels allied with the martial artist Song Jing-shi, which was centered in the region west of the Canal. Few areas of the Northwest were immune from destruction in this period, though not necessarily at the hands of the rebels. The people told one traveller through this area that "they suffered quite as much from the Imperial soldiers as they did from the rebels, and at times even worse."[52]

This was the Boxer homeland: a poor agricultural region, densely populated, but particularly prone to both natural and human disasters. Many of these attributes it shared with the Southwest, which certainly suffered as much from the mid-century rebellions, and almost as much from natural disasters. Since the Southwest was the home of the Big Sword Society—the Boxer's predecessor in the anti-Christian incidents of the 1890s—we must turn now to a closer comparison of these two regions, showing how they differed from each other, and also how the two areas differed from the rest of the province. In doing so, we must shift our focus from the natural environment and local economics of these regions to their social formations.

SOCIAL FORMATIONS OF WEST SHANDONG

As we begin our consideration of western Shandong, it is worth reminding ourselves that socio-economic regions frequently transcend administrative boundaries, and that was surely the case in both our Northwest and Southwest regions. Northwest Shandong was scarcely distinguishable from the bordering regions of Zhili—which were also unbroken plain, predominantly agricultural, densely populated, and fully dependent on the same rains that watered Shandong. In fact the most systematic study of rural society in this area, Philip C. C. Huang's *The Peasant Economy and Social Change in North China* consistently treats Zhili and northwest Shandong as a single ecosystem with a similar natural environment and social structure.[53] The ecological homogeneity of the region is extremely important for this study, for it will help to explain why the Boxers spread so easily from northwest Shandong across the Zhili portion of the north China plain.

Southwest Shandong was comparable in almost all respects to the bordering counties in Jiangsu and Henan. This whole area was of course richer than northwest Shandong—and as one moved into Jiangsu it became richer still. When travellers on the Grand Canal left the marshy regions of southern Shandong for Jiangsu, they found a new "appearance of prosperity"[54] with the country "daily . . . growing more beautiful, better cultivated, and in all respects more interesting."[55] In general, both the crops and the yields of northern Jiangsu were similar to southwestern Shandong but the area was somewhat less susceptible to flooding, which was probably the main reason for its relative prosperity. Of course, now that we have moved the Lower Yangzi macroregion boundary north into southern Shandong, northern Jiangsu's prosperity also makes sense in terms of Skinner's regional systems theory, for it corresponds to movement in the direction of the regional core.

If one looked for one distinguishing feature of this southwest Shandong–northern Jiangsu region in the late nineteenth century it would probably have to be endemic banditry. Caozhou, at this time, was known as a "classic Eldorado of bandits."[56] The phenomenon was certainly not new, and in part it was the product of the complex intersection of provincial borders in this region. Caozhou prefecture had borders with Jiangsu, Henan, and Zhili provinces; and Anhui was only thirty miles away. Bandits in general did not prey on their immediate neighbors, and by striking across provincial borders it was particularly easy to escape the justice of the Chinese state, whose vertical linkages were far stronger than its capacity for horizontal cooperation.[57]

But it is clear that the banditry also had to do with the persistent victimization of this area by the Yellow River before it shifted to its northern course. The Shandong provincial gazetteer of 1736 wrote: "In records since the Song and Yuan, 50 percent of the flooding had been, if not in Cao [county] then in Shan. Since the Zheng-[de] Jia-[jing] period [1506–1567], it has been 80 percent."[58] The Cao county gazetteer described life in the region as "like sitting in the bottom of a basin. One is always fearing a deluge."[59]

There can be little doubt that this precarious existence at the mercy of the river significantly affected the character of southwest Shandong society—in part because this area was not uniformly low-lying. Some areas were repeatedly flooded, while those which escaped the floods rather prospered on the rich alluvial soil. The floods thus created victims who might turn to banditry, but also left a wealthy few who were potential targets of banditry. This wealthy elite, in part to protect itself, became increasingly militarized and tended more and more to depend on violent methods to defend its position. The 1716 Cao county gazetteer described the process in the following terms:

> The gentry were pure and the people good: such were the old customs of Cao. Then during the Ming, the Yellow River repeatedly broke its banks, and bandits ran amok. There were successive years of epidemics and the corpses of famine victims piled up on the roads. People lost the comforts of house and home, and customs changed accordingly.

The "clear laws and fair administration" of the Qing, the gazetteer obsequiously continued, had brought a restoration of the honest customs of old; but "the tendency for the wealthy to rely on cruelty and violence is well established."[60]

There is little evidence that the Qing ever broke the bandit hold on this area. Even in the middle of the generally peaceful eighteenth century, one gazetteer spoke of the Caozhou people's "tendency to fight and bring lawsuits. In the southeast [of the prefecture], there is the evil of banditry."[61] In the 1820s imperial edicts complained of growing lawlessness in the region.[62] But the problem was not only banditry. Salt smuggling was also endemic;[63] and in the late nineteenth century this became a prime area for the illicit cultivation of opium. In this it was quite unlike northwest Shandong. A traveller from Beijing in the 1870s was approaching Confucius' home in Qufu (in our Jining region) before he first sighted the opium poppy: "from this point to the old Yellow River, three hundred miles to the south, the cultivation of this plant continues at intervals the whole way."[64] Northern Jiangsu, and especially the county of Dangshan, was a prime opium-producing area.[65]

The impression one forms of the Shandong-Jiangsu-Henan border region is of an outlaw society, which sought as much as possible to live without interference from the state. The salt smuggling and opium growing were certainly illegal—but they were not only a source of livelihood for many, they also brought a necessary commodity (in the case of salt) or considerable wealth (in the case of opium) into an area where commerce had previously been quite undeveloped. Once the Yellow River shifted to a northern course, the danger of flooding passed and some areas became reasonably prosperous.[66] The banditry did not disappear with the floods, of course. The habit was too well ingrained; and public order was declining everywhere amid the nineteenth century rebellions and attendant militarization of local society. Most importantly, the prosperity of some was not the prosperity of all—more likely it provided a tempting target for outlaws. In any case, the area had long since learned to live with banditry. Maps from the early Republic show substantial walls around all but the most insignificant settlements. This was a highly militarized society which had learned to fend for itself in a fairly brutal struggle for survival of the fittest.

With banditry such an important part of southwest Shandong society, it behooves us to look for a moment into its nature, and the robbery cases (dao-an) recorded in the Board of Punishments archives in Beijing yield some interesting insights. First, Shandong as a whole was not unusually victimized by banditry. In a sample of 514 memorials from 1890 to 1897, only 25 related to robberies in Shandong. Zhili, with 114 cases (quite probably reflecting stricter security near the capital) and Sichuan with 101 far outstripped the Boxer homeland. But not far behind these leaders was Jiangsu, with 98 cases—40 of which were in the single northern prefecture of Xuzhou.[67] If we look more closely at cases from Shandong and areas on its borders, we find that though Shandong did not itself suffer inordinately from banditry, it exported a goodly number of bandits to its neighbors. In fact it had a very favorable balance of trade in banditry. Only 3 percent of the bandits caught in Shandong came from outside the province, while in heavily bandit-stricken Xuzhou, 45 percent came from outside of the province, 36 percent from Shandong alone. Along the Zhili border, 47 percent came from Shandong.

Banditry was clearly a much larger-scale business on Shandong's southern border than it was either within the province or in Zhili. In both Zhili and Shandong, bands averaged about 8 members. The Zhili bands, which specialized in highway robbery of merchants traveling across the plains, were quite well armed in the limited number of cases I examined; but in Shandong only half had any firearms at all. Along Shandong's southern border, the average band had 13 members, and two-thirds had at least one gun. But what most strikingly distinguished the cases on the southern border was the inclusion of opium in the loot stolen. Only 4 percent of the Shandong cases involved opium, and none in Zhili; while south of the border, 43 percent of the cases mentioned opium among the loot.

Clearly the widespread opium growing in this region both created an addiction that was often satisfied through a life of crime, and created a target population that had considerable wealth to steal. Society throughout this Shandong-Jiangsu-Henan border region was highly stratified, and the wealthy households were inviting targets. Jewelry and foreign (machine-woven) cloth and silk were often stolen—items rarely seen in cases from poorer regions of Shandong. In the opium growing center of Dangshan, every bandit case examined involved a take of over 100 taels (a tael was a Chinese ounce of silver), as did 16 of the 29 cases (55 percent) in the Xuzhou counties bordering Shandong. Only 10 of 49 Shandong cases (20 percent) involved such sums.

But border region banditry did not just derive from a history of natural disasters and the presence of ready targets of opportunity. A fascinating document from Shan county in Caozhou, written by some village literati in 1896, graphically describes the circumstances that pushed so many into banditry.

> The wealth of Shan is not the equal of Cao [county], but throughout the prefecture there is always enough. But the wealthy join acre after acre of land, some several thousands of *mu*, while the poor have none at all. These rich folks care only for their summer rooms or stone arches. . . . With the humanity of the past gone, how can we hope for pity for the poor? These ills are not confined to Shan: all of Caozhou is the same. Powerful families look on poor relatives or neighbors like strangers on the road. They will lend them neither cloth nor grain. They treat their tenants and hired laborers particularly cruelly, arousing a hatred so strong that these people are apt to turn to a life of danger. . . . This all tends to invite banditry. Every few weeks they will come to the door, bearing sharp knives or foreign rifles. When they repeatedly demand a loan, people are quick to assent. With things like this, how will bandits not increase day by day? If the grain of the county were equitably distributed, there would be enough to eat. But there are many without any land. None can make enough to eat through commerce, so they can only hire out their labor. But north China agriculture uses little hired labor: at most 30–40 days per year. There is no other source of food—only collecting dung. You cannot eat and drink your fill once a year. When they hear of the fun of being a bandit, who is not tempted? Some scatter to settle the frontier in Shanxi, Shaanxi, or the Northeast; or to work as hired hands in northern Anhui and Henan. But many more stay than leave.

This document then goes on to identify four sources of banditry: "(1) border towns,[68] (2) bad villages that have produced bandits for generations, (3) bankrupt households, and (4) large families with many sons." While the authors say that throughout Caozhou about half of the bandits came from outside the county, in Shan county most bandits were locals "who hide abroad while the moon is bright, and return to steal during its dark phase." The nearby provincial borders were conducive to such bandit strategies, and most of the theft was done abroad—often from hideouts in one of the neighboring provinces. Still, the bandits always kept their homes:

> The bandits of Caozhou love their native villages. . . . Though their home be only a dilapidated one-room earth-walled hut, and though they own not even the smallest piece of land, still they always return. . . . The bandits of Shan hide nearby so it is easy to return, but on their return they need a place to hide so that they will not be discovered. Their lairs are opium dens, brothels and the hang-outs of yamen runners—everyone knows of these three. But few realize that crafty *sheng-yuan* ["government students"—holders of the lowest (county) examination degree] and evil *jian-sheng* ["student of the Imperial Academy"—usually a purchased degree] also provide hiding places. Most surprisingly, so do rich households and even militia leaders. At first they do so unwillingly, hoping to protect themselves from trouble, but soon they cannot break the connection. . . . When things continue like this for some time, everyone regards it as inevitable. As a result, by now seven or eight out of ten poor and middle households have gotten themselves into this sort of trouble. This is worse than other counties. Households with only a little property first wish to avoid trouble. Then they gradually think of buying stolen goods cheaply. Soon they are fencing the loot to enrich themselves and listening for information [on potential victims] for the benefit of the thieves. It has been like this for a long time.[69]

Banditry had clearly become an integral part of the social fabric of southwest Shandong. Bandits were not just roving bands who preyed on innocent villagers. They had homes of their own, and regularly returned to them. For the vast majority, banditry was surely not a full-time job. These were peasants, who would return to their villages when there was work to do in the fields, or for festivals when they were accustomed to being with their families. Banditry was a seasonal activity, closely tied to the agricultural calendar. The Board of Punishments records show this clearly. The winter, from the eleventh to the second lunar months, was a prime time for bandits—as there was no work to be done in the north China fields in this season. But the eleventh and second months were the peaks of the winter cycle, for bandits returned home for the Chinese New Year in between. The spring was a busy agricultural season and banditry fell off markedly until the sixth month, usually beginning around mid-July. As one July 1897 account from northern Jiangsu put it: "The season when highwaymen are especially numerous and dangerous is upon us. The kaoliang [*gaoliang*, i.e., sorghum] is in its prime, and being 7 or 8 feet high and very thick affords a most convenient ambush. It is unsafe to travel alone even in daylight over lonely roads." [70] Then for two months, banditry would fall to the same low level as the spring while the fall harvest was brought in, followed by another peak in the ninth month, and a fall to its lowest point in the tenth month when cotton and corn were harvested and the winter plowing done. [71]

But our Shan county informants also focus on the intimate connection to the extensive landlordism of this area—landlordism which all contemporary references describe as considerably more extensive than the 23 percent of cultivated area shown in the Republican era figures. In the aggregate, southwest Shandong was surely better off than the Northwest, but the extremes of wealth and poverty were pronounced. That is exactly the environment in which banditry is most likely to thrive. It provides both profitable targets for bandits to prey upon, and a large population of poor young males who might be tempted to fill their stomachs with a stint in the greenwood. Equally importantly, as the document above suggests, such extremes of wealth and poverty are likely to engender the sort of resentment and hatred of the rich which would lead men to prey upon the wealthy— for there is little doubt that bandits were discriminating in their targets, and the general population had little to fear from them. [72]

Landlordism, however, was not only a source of banditry: landlords also provided the nucleus for defensive efforts against bandits. The authors of the document above were no doubt small village landlords, and what they were advocating was the organization of local militia. As we shall discuss in more detail in chapter 3, landlordism in the Southwest was not the sort of cash-nexus landlordism of the Lower Yangzi, but one which still entailed mutual patron-client obligations of the parties involved. Landlords would organize local militia, but they would also expect their tenants to join in the protection of the locality. Villages became very tight-knit communities, well-fortified against outside threats, and typically subject to the absolute rule of some leading family. [73]

The three characteristics so influential in shaping the social fabric of southwest Shandong were all absent in the Northwest. Opium was not cultivated to any extent. Except in a few counties along the Yellow River, banditry was not a major problem—especially not in the specific counties, like Chiping, from which the Boxers grew. As that county's gazetteer tellingly put it: "Before the Republic, the people didn't even know what bandits were."[74] And landlordism was almost non-existent.

The weakness of landlordism is particularly striking: only 10.6 percent of the land in this region was rented—the lowest for any part of Shandong. The most sophisticated attempt to reconstruct landholding patterns at the end of the Qing confirms these Republican figures. In a 1957 survey of 60 villages in the Northwest region, two Chinese scholars found that in the 1890s, 44 (73 percent) of the villages had no landlords renting over 50 *mu*. By contrast, on the peninsula, only 31 percent of the villages were without landlords.[75]

Philip C. C. Huang has analyzed at some length and with great insight the "persistence of small-peasant family farming" on the north China plain. There had been some large estates on the plain during the Ming, but most were devasted by the rebellions at the end of the dynasty, and the Qing made every effort to encourage a smallholder economy as the best fiscal base for a centralized imperial regime. The normal bases for significant land accumulation were exceedingly weak in this region. In contrast to the Lower Yangzi, and especially to the Canton delta, lineages never developed as corporate landowners. At most they controlled a few *mu* of burial land. Nor did commerce provide the basis for the accumulation of wealth and land. The most important commercial development was the spread of cotton cultivation beginning in the Ming. Several counties in Dongchang prefecture (especially Gaotang and En) and the area around Linqing produced significant quantities of raw cotton, but through most of the Ming this production only made the north China plain a dependent periphery to the rapidly developing lower Yangzi core: Jiangsu and Anhui merchants carried off the raw cotton, and brought finished cloth back to the north. Clearly the commercial profits did not significantly accrue to the northern plain.

In the Qing, by the eighteenth century, this relationship was substantially altered, and north China peasants began spinning and weaving their own cotton, exporting much of it to the northern frontier. But by this time, population pressure had driven north China agriculture to such an involuted state that handicraft labor in the agricultural slack season (and hiring out to wealthier farmers) only served to protect the small peasants' slender margin of subsistence, and thus perpetuate the small holder economy. Some occasionally managed to become "managerial farmers" profiting from commercial crops, but there were severe limits to the amount of land they could manage with existing technology; and within a few generations, family division under the Chinese custom of partible inheritance would reduce these larger farmers once again to smallholder status.

Huang has persuasively argued that the village-level elite in this region was not a landlord elite, but was instead predominantly composed of managerial farmers, who worked their plots, usually of 100–200 *mu*, with hired labor. Peasants spoke of "the rich" [literally: "wealth-lords" (*cai-zhu*), not "landlords" (*di-zhu*)] when they referred to the village elite.[76] Huang stresses the gap between this village elite and the "upper tier" of gentry-official elite, whose much greater wealth was necessarily based on commerce or public office.[77] I would suggest that the limited commercial potential of the northwest Shandong plain made it extremely difficult for anyone in this region to pass into that "upper tier" of the elite. Few could rise by farming alone; but the above-cited 1957 study of late Qing landlordism suggests that there were relatively few alternatives in this region. A survey of 131 "managerial landlords" from throughout the province found that in the northwest, 65 percent acquired their wealth by farming, 31 percent from commerce, and only 4 percent from public office. By contrast on the more commercialized North Slope, only 33 percent rose through farming, 58 percent through commerce, and 10 percent from public office.[78]

Huang has aptly characterized the "conjuncture of low-yield, disaster-prone dry farming with high population density that laid the basis for severe scarcity in this area."[79] Since some have associated the small number of tenant-farmers with the absence of an agrarian crisis,[80] it is essential to remind ourselves that the weakness of landlordism bespoke not the well-being of the peasantry but its pervasive poverty. The fact is, this region was simply not wealthy enough to support a substantial landlord class; or, to look at it from the standpoint of the wealthy, crops were too vulnerable to the vagaries of weather and other imponderables to warrant any investment in land in this region. The result was a generalized poverty of the peasantry of northwest Shandong. Though wealth and resources were certainly not distributed equally, the extremes were not nearly so glaring as in the Southwest. People were not so much victimized by rapacious landlords as by the very harshness of the physical environment.

It is essential to realize the extent to which poverty left peasants literally at the margin of subsistence, even in normal times. This account of daily life from the twentieth century provides a graphic appreciation of just what poverty meant on the Shandong plains:

> They live in a small humid thatched hut which usually does not let in enough light. The window is exceptionally small. Inside, all ornamentation is extremely simple. If they are a little poor, this single room serves a number of purposes. The stove, pots and bowls occupy one corner; and when they cook black smoke spreads like a thick fog until you can hardly make out a person's face. For fuel in the villages, there are only the leaves of trees or sorghum, wheat or soybean stalks.... Their food is also extremely simple. In a whole year, there are very few times when they eat any meat. Usually it is a few vegetables and coarse grain. When the wheat has just been harvested, there is a short time when they can eat vegetables and a rough sort of noodle. They do not eat all of the vegetables in their gardens. Some they take into the towns to exchange for a little grain to sustain themselves. The oil, salt and soy sauce that are used so casually in the city are to them terribly precious things. If they add some sesame oil for seasoning, they use a copper cash coin attached to a stick passed through the hole in the middle of the coin, and with this draw a drop of oil from the jar to flavor their food. Usually, they will just boil a little garlic, peppers or onions in water, and drink that for a meal. Except for weddings, funerals and the New Year festival, they rarely see any meat at all. This is true even of old people. Their normal drink is just boiled water. Sometimes they will put some bamboo or oak leaves in it just to change its color. When they are very busy, they may even drink cold [unboiled] water—not even worrying about whether it will make them sick.... Their clothes are all made from native cloth that they have woven themselves. Most are blue or black.[81]

If these were the conditions in which people lived in ordinary times, one can imagine their plight in bad years. These were truly the classic Chinese peasants of R. H. Tawney's description—standing up to their necks in water, ready to be drowned by the slightest ripple on the surface.[82] The situation was particularly severe in northwest Shandong because of the frequency of drought, flood and other natural disasters and the lack of any substantial landlord class which might provide relief to poorer relatives or neighbors—relief offered out of some Confucian sense of moral obligation or, more likely, out of fear that grain not given freely would likely be seized by those made desperate by hunger. As a result, when disaster struck this region, people were very likely simply to pick up and leave. One gazetteer speaks of people fleeing during the Ming because of high taxes.[83] An early Qing edict says that because families often had many sons and little land, "the people of Shandong easily leave their homes without a second thought."[84] In the worst cases whole villages would take to the road to beg—carrying entire families, men, women and children with them.[85]

Such mobility was not simply a product of major disasters. In normal times there was extensive movement of young males hiring themselves out as agricultural laborers. Most of this was within a village or between nearby villages, but there was also a certain amount of long-distance travel of what amounted to migrant labor. Some from northwest Shandong moved into neighboring (apparently less populated) areas of Hebei.[86] There are even reports of great bands of thousands of peasants from the Shandong–Zhili border near Dezhou travelling south to the Jining area to glean wheat from the fields,[87] an activity which was not quite hired labor—but was not quite begging either.

This long-established pattern of migration and mobility was an important aspect in the social structure of northwest Shandong villages. With people constantly moving in and out, villages were much more heterogeneous. Both in southwest Shandong and on the peninsula, single-surname villages (or villages with one clearly dominant lineage) were quite common.[88] But on the northwest plain, villages were overwhelmingly a mix of many different surnames, and it was not at all uncommon for new families to come and settle in a village—perhaps first working for a time as someone's hired hand.[89] Obviously this makes for less cohesive villages, and more acceptance of mobility among the general population. The northwest Shandong villager does not fit the stereotype of the peasant tied to his ancestral soil.

If we compare, then, northwest and southwest Shandong we find some rather fundamental contrasts. The Southwest was clearly a richer region than the Northwest—both because the soil was better and because the shift in the Yellow River left it somewhat less subject to natural disasters. Being richer, it was also able to support a fairly high rate of landlordism; the agrarian economy of the Northwest, by contrast, was dominated by owner-cultivators and agricultural laborers. The south was also a troubled border region with extensive extra-legal cultivation of opium, and endemic banditry; neither of these was true in the more peaceful north. The insecure environment of the Southwest caused villages to turn in on themselves, and become close-knit cohesive communities. The villages of the Northwest were more open, the population more mobile, and the villages more heterogeneous. People moved around in the Southwest as well, to be sure. We have seen accounts of them emigrating to the Northeast (Manchuria) or leaving more temporarily to rob or do agricultural labour south of the border—but the mobility was always *out* of the villages in this region. Few ever seemed to move in: outsiders were rarely welcome. But in the Northwest, it was much easier for outsiders to gain acceptance—and as we shall see, that was an important factor in the acceptance of those who would teach the new Boxer magic.

The differences between northwest and southwest Shandong were both numerous and fundamental—and these differences do much to account for the different natures of the Big Sword Society in the Southwest and the Boxers of the Northwest. But the two regions had one important similarity: in both the gentry was very weak. This would be critically important because the sparse orthodox Confucian gentry presence in this region was clearly one factor facilitating the spread of such heterodox rituals as were espoused by the Big Swords and the Boxers. It is essential, therefore, to account for the distribution of gentry strength in Shandong.

THE GEOGRAPHIC DISTRIBUTION OF THE SHANDONG GENTRY

The Chinese gentry were the holders of official degrees conferred by the imperial government, ideally by virtue of their having passed the examinations in the Confucian classics. Toward the end of the Qing dynasty, the sale of examination degrees became increasingly common, affording an avenue into the official elite for those with money but perhaps less capacity for book learning. But the regular path was always the examination route, and only holders of these degrees were recorded in the official gazetteers. Basically, there were three levels of examination degree: the first combined exams at the county and prefectural level, next came the provincial examination, and finally there was the metropolitan examination in Beijing—culminating in a palace examination before the emperor himself. At each level there was a quota for the number of successful candidates. As a consequence each county has a number of *sheng-yuan* (holders of the lowest degree) roughly proportionate to its population, so this degree tells us nothing about the geographic distribution of gentry. Furthermore, the *sheng-yuan* was technically only a "government student," a member of what is usually called the "lower gentry" and not yet qualified for official appointment. It was the provincial *ju-ren* degree which qualified one for official position but as the quota was province-wide, *ju-ren* were not evenly distributed across the province. Furthermore, because quotas for the *ju-ren* degree were relatively high (usually between seventy and eighty for each triennial session in Shandong),[90] they yield a larger and more representative sample than do metropolitan *jin-shi* degrees.

Since the Chinese bureaucracy was in fact quite small in size, there were always fewer posts available than there were degree-holders qualified to fill them. It is these degree-holders without official appointment that we think of as the local gentry. They would be the respected members of their communities, people who would be asked to manage public works or organize militia in times of crisis, and people with ready access to political power in the person of the county magistrate or even his superiors. Thus a substantial local gentry presence meant two things: it meant that the local elite would be chosen by its mastery of the Confucian classics and thus presumably quite proper and orthodox in its beliefs and behavior; and it meant that the local population would have spokesmen with the credentials necessary to give weight to local grievances, and to receive a favorable hearing not only at the local level, but even at provincial and national levels—for if an area produced many degree-holders, it would also produce more higher-level officials through whom influence could be exerted in the national bureaucracy.

With this introduction, we are prepared to look at the distribution of gentry across our six regions. Let us begin with the long view, and examine the distribution as it changes over the course of the Ming and Qing dynasties. Table 2 summarizes the data, giving the percentage of *ju-ren* from each region for each fifty-year period.

Several trends are evident in these figures. The most striking is the secular rise in the Peninsular and North Slope totals, and the decline in the two western regions beginning in all cases around the middle of the sixteenth century. (The period before 1550 is sufficiently distant from the Boxer Uprising as not to concern us very much. Furthermore, the 1368–1400 period is both shorter than the others, and immediately follows the expulsion of Mongol rule, and is thus sufficiently anomalous to be disregarded.) The rise of the Peninsula and the North Slope seems to reflect the progressive commercialization of this region

TABLE 2   DISTRIBUTION OF SHANDONG PROVINCIAL
DEGREE-HOLDERS (*JU-REN*), PERCENTAGES BY REGION,
1368−1900

				Region			
Year	Penin-sula	North Slope	South Hills	Jining	South-west	North-west	SW+ NW
1368−1400	12.5	26.3	10.7	10.0	8.7	32.1	40.8
1401−1450	12.5	18.5	11.7	14.5	7.4	35.7	43.1
1451−1500	12.6	15.0	6.8	13.3	8.9	43.5	52.4
1501−1550	10.6	20.0	3.8	12.6	9.9	43.5	53.4
1551−1600	15.9	23.9	3.8	10.9	6.3	39.7	46.0
1601−1650	23.9	22.3	5.7	12.1	6.0	30.3	36.3
1651−1700	26.9	23.5	3.2	12.8	7.1	26.9	34.0
1701−1750	35.4	17.6	3.9	10.6	7.8	25.0	32.8
1751−1800	30.2	19.8	6.1	10.6	6.9	26.6	33.5
1801−1850	26.6	28.0	7.1	13.7	4.1	20.8	24.9
1851−1900	29.5	28.4	8.6	11.2	3.1	19.7	22.8
(1870−1900)	31.8	27.3	8.8	10.5	2.9	18.8	21.7
(Population, ca. 1900)	24.4	15.7	15.6	9.4	9.1	25.9	35.0

SOURCE: *Shandong tong-zhi.*

from the mid-Ming on. The nineteenth century rise of the North Slope is particularly striking, and must be associated with the rise of Wei county as the leading trade center in this area. In the last half of the eighteenth century, Wei produced only 15 *ju-ren,* but in the first half of the nineteenth the figure jumped to 107.[91]

The decline of the West is equally striking. In the first half of the sixteenth century, the two western regions supplied more than half of all *ju-ren* in the province. By the end of the nineteenth century, they produced barely more than one-fifth. The fall, however, was not entirely even and the pattern suggests some of the causes. The sharpest drops tended to coincide with periods of dynastic decline and change—first in the early seventeenth century, and then in the nineteenth century. Both of these were times of natural and human disasters which, as we have seen, particularly afflicted the West. In a sense, we can see the converse of this process if we look at the

TABLE 3   *JU-REN* TOTALS ALONG THE GRAND CANAL,
1400–1900

	Years				
County	*1401–* *1500*	*1501–* *1600*	*1601–* *1700*	*1701–* *1800*	*1801–* *1900*
Jining	115	84	94	115	153
Liaocheng (Dongchang)	25	34	41	85	56
Linqing	74	102	63	25	13
Wucheng	33	21	18	13	10
Dezhou	82	82	62	74	47

SOURCE: *Shandong tong-zhi.*

Southern Hills. Here was a region relatively protected from invasion by either Manchu invaders or Chinese rebels. Its percentage of *ju-ren* accordingly rises when the West suffers its sharpest decline, from 1600 to 1650 during the Ming–Qing transition, and again during the last years of the Qing.

The decline of the Grand Canal was also a factor in the weakening of the gentry in the West, but it was particularly noticeable in the cities north of Dongchang. The hundred-year totals of *ju-ren* in the counties with major cities along the canal are given in Table 3. Clearly Jining was in fact increasing in prominence from the sixteenth century. Jining, we have argued, really belongs to the Lower Yangzi macroregion and it continued to prosper along with that region. Dongchang continued to prosper until the nineteenth century shift of the Yellow River cut off its links to the south. But Linqing declined precipitously, Wucheng steadily, and Dezhou significantly (but only in the nineteenth century).[92]

But this still does not tell the full story of the Grand Canal. It was mainly a few large cities (especially Jining, Dongchang and Linqing) whose growth was significantly stimulated by the canal—and which, accordingly, declined when the canal silted up. These were the ports where the tribute barges would stop to load and unload merchandise, and their commercial importance grew accordingly. What is striking, however, is the limited commercialized hinterland of the canal, for as we have seen above, the northwest Shandong region was in general one of the least commercialized areas of the province. Non-agricultural production was almost non-existent, transport away from the canal was overland and expensive, towns were small, and (with the exception of a few areas of significant cash-cropping in cotton) the area produced very little beyond its own immediate subsistence requirements. Even the cotton production, while an important and early form of commercialized agriculture, contributed little to the economic development of the region. It first made northwest Shandong a dependent supplier of raw materials for the Lower Yangzi; and later textile production supported only an involuted peasant handicraft production. Neither of these represented a strong economic base for a wealthy gentry elite.

One explanation for this limited commercializing function of the canal lies in the impact the canal had on the ecology of the north China plain. As early as the sixteenth century, it was observed that because the canal cut across the plain from Jining to Linqing in a north-westerly direction, its dikes blocked the natural drainage of this area, where rivers flowed to the northeast. As a result, several counties south of the canal were repeatedly flooded.[93] In the words of the great seventeenth century scholar Gu Yan-wu, "The [sage king] Yu followed the rivers to bring tribute rice. The Ming blocked the rivers to bring tribute rice."[94] In addition, the peasantry in the counties through which the canal passed were frequently summoned for corvée labor to maintain the canal, to pull the tribute barges across shallow sections or to lighten their loads by carrying the tribute rice overland.[95] We should remember that the Ming and Qing maintained the Grand Canal in order to feed the imperial capital. The Canal was not built to facilitate trade in general—much less to aid in the development of the areas through which it passed. For much of Shandong it only increased the burden of uncompensated corvée labor while bringing actual harm to the local environment.[96]

These points are important because it has often been assumed that the Canal spurred significant commercialization and economic development in western Shandong. From the changing distribution of the Shandong gentry, I would argue that, outside a few big cities, the Canal's impact may have been negative. Table 4 provides data on gentry (here expressed as percentages of the provincial total) from the area along the Grand Canal. Several things are clear. First, in all categories there is a steady decline after 1550, a date which appears to

TABLE 4 PERCENTAGES OF *JU-REN* FROM COUNTIES
ALONG THE GRAND CANAL
(In parentheses is an index taking
the 1401–1550 percentage as 100)

Area	Period			
	1401–1550	*1551–1700*	*1701–1800*	*1801–1900*
Counties along Canal: 19	25.5 (100)	19.0 (75)	15.1 (59)	12.9 (51)
Counties north of Jining: 14	19.0 (100)	13.4 (71)	10.0 (53)	6.9 (36)
Counties south of Canal: 9	10.1 (100)	6.6 (65)	4.1 (41)	3.3 (33)
All west Shandong counties: 53	49.2 (100)	38.9 (79)	33.2 (67)	23.8 (48)

SOURCE: *Shandong tong-zhi.*

represent the end of the positive contribution of the Canal. Second, in
the counties north of Jining, the decline is even sharper than it is for
our northwest Shandong region as a whole. And third, the decline is
sharpest for those counties lying on the south bank of the canal—
precisely the counties which, we were told, suffered because the canal
interfered with their drainage.[97]

The decline in the Grand Canal region was in fact but a particular
example of what was probably the basic factor in the relative decline
of western Shandong as a whole. The most fundamental problem for
agriculture in this region (other than the unchanging dependence on
timely precipitation) was waterlogging and the accompanying salinization of the soil. This problem seems to have become progressively
worse over time. The Grand Canal dikes, impeding drainage, were
only part of the problem. Of more general importance was the over-all
increase in population, which led to progressive encroachment on
marshes which used to collect excess rainwater, and on riverbeds
which had provided the natural drainage for the plain. As peasants
(often with powerful protectors) encroached on riverbeds which may
have carried water for only a few weeks each year, they might gain
fertile (and probably tax-free) land to cultivate; but the villages
upstream suffered waterlogging and periodic floods after the heavy

summer rains. Fights and lawsuits arose repeatedly from such en-
croachments, but the problem continued and the whole area slowly
declined.[98]

Clearly the decline in the gentry presence in western Shandong was
related to the unstable environment and the low level of commercialization, especially as the Grand Canal and a burgeoning population both acted to block the natural drainage of the plain and
exacerbate the waterlogging which was the principal threat to agriculture in this region. But one more interesting factor emerges if we take
all our variables and enter them in a multiple regression equation—
attempting to predict the number of gentry in a county during the
last half of the nineteenth century from various political and socio-
economic variables describing that county. The results of that multiple regression are given in table 5.

For our purposes, it is the fourth column of this table that is the
most crucial. The "R-squared" tells us what portion of a change in the
dependent variable (the number of *ju-ren*) can be accounted for by
any given independent variable. In this step-wise multiple regression,
the independent variable which best explains the number of *ju-ren* is
first entered into the equation. The second step controls for the first
variable, asks what is the next most important variable, and gives us
the "R-squared" for the portion of variation explained by the first
two variables. The third step controls for the first two variables, and
so on. In this case, we see that the number of degree holders in a given
department or county is most clearly related to the administrative
level of the locality: whether it is a provincial or prefectural seat, a
zhou (department) directly under the provincial authorities, an ordinary *zhou*, or a *xian* (county). Almost half of the variation in the
number of *ju-ren* can be accounted for by these differences in the
administrative level of the most powerful office in the county. Quite
naturally, the provincial and prefectural capitals produced a disproportionate number of gentry, for politically ambitious families were
attracted to these administrative centers.[99] If we then control for
administrative level, and enter population into the equation, we can
account for almost 60 percent of the variation, since more populous
counties tended to produce larger numbers of successful candidates.
Neither of these results is the least bit surprising.

The interesting results begin to appear at the third step in the
regression. Here we ask: if we control for administrative level and
population, what variable best predicts the number of *ju-ren*? The

TABLE 5   MULTIPLE REGRESSION OF *JU-REN* (1851–1900) ON KEY VARIABLES
(County as unit, n = 107)

Variable[a]	Metric coefficient	Standardized coefficient	t-statistic[b]	Multiple R-squared[b]	Simple correlation	Partial correlation at step three[c]
Administrative level	4.140	0.558	9.03*	0.485*	0.696	—
Population	0.00002	0.211	2.70*	0.596*	0.535	—
Number of bandits	−1.230	−0.138	2.24*	0.624*	−0.136	−0.266
Commercial tax	0.024	0.213	3.23*	0.645*	0.338	0.207
Cultivated land per capita	−3.183	−0.164	2.41*	0.663*	−0.343	−0.172
Percent of land rented	0.117	0.067	1.07	0.667	0.223	0.089
Disasters	−0.005	−0.060	0.97	0.670	−0.111	−0.127
Constant	−8.944					
R-squared	0.670					
Degrees of freedom	99					

[a] See note 11 of this chapter for descriptions and sources for key variables.
[b] Results from stepwise multiple regression. Asterisks indicate t-statistics or increments in R-squared significant at the 0.01 level.
[c] The partial correlation at step three indicates the correlation of each of the remaining variables after controlling for administrative level and population.

final column gives the partial correlation for each of the remaining variables at step 3 in the step-wise multiple regression. As we can see, the best correlation is to the number of bandits from a given county counted in the Board of Punishment archives. This proves to be a better predicter of gentry strength than any of the alternative variables, after we control for administrative level and population. Basically, the gentry were weak where banditry was widespread—the negative correlation being indicated in the signs of the metric and standardized coefficients and in the simple correlation. A number of factors might explain this correlation. The gentry were most likely to concentrate in areas that were both socially and ecologically stable— and be weak in the difficult-to-control border regions and disaster-prone plains which produced the most banditry. In short, stable areas produced gentry, unstable areas produced banditry. But the major decline in southwest Shandong gentry strength in the late Ming, and again after the mid-eighteenth century, at precisely the same time that banditry was described as increasing in the region, suggests that the two were not just related, in an inverse manner, to a certain ecological constants—they were also related to each other. The causal relationship probably worked in both directions. Strong gentry discouraged bandit activity; and bandit activity led to a gentry exodus and to the orientation of local elites more toward local self-defense than toward the scholarly path to higher examination degrees.

The next variable is the commercial tax: the best contemporary measure—but still clearly inadequate—for the level of commercialization in each county.[100] The t-statistic (as well as the relatively high simple and partial correlations) indicate the importance of commercial development as a determinant of gentry strength. It is clearly more important than cultivated area per capita,[101] the extent of landlordism, or the number of natural disasters—the last two of which are not statistically significant at the 0.01 (or even the 0.05) level.

I believe that if we had better data, the results would be considerably better than we have obtained here. In particular the disaster measure is really only a measure of flooding, and a measure of all types of natural (and human) disasters (drought, locusts, rebellions, etc.) would no doubt help to explain the sparse gentry presence in the west. Furthermore, landlordism fails to correlate closely because the Southwest and Southern Hills were areas of a quite extensive but rather backward village landlordism—rude folk whose lives were not oriented towards the examinations. The more commercial landlordism of the Peninsula was correlated to gentry strength—just as it was in the Lower Yangzi valley, the *locus classicus* of the gentry landlord.

But this regression analysis does perform one function: it confirms that in examining such questions as commercial development on the Peninsula and North Slope, and banditry in the Southwest, we have indeed identified the factors that are most important in explaining the distribution of gentry in Shandong—and in particular the weakness of the gentry in the West. That gentry weakness was a critical aspect of west Shandong life, perhaps especially in the Northwest where there were not only few gentry, but also few landlords to lend their weight to orthodoxy and stability in the area. Lacking such a gentry presence, west Shandong had a particular proclivity for heterodox activity. It is to the heterodox sectarian history of the region, and to its popular culture, that we must now turn.

CHAPTER TWO

Sects, Boxers, and Popular Culture

The context for the Boxer Uprising was not only provided by the physical and social environment of west Shandong, but also by the popular culture—or what the French call *mentalité*—of that region. Clearly the strange invulnerability rituals and spirit-possession of the Boxers would not have spread so rapidly if they had not struck some familiar chord in the popular imagination of north China peasants.

Most popular culture, of course, is formed of customs and traditions inherited from the distant past, a past which in China seems ever-present. If we plumb that past for precedents which might have conditioned peasants to accept the Boxer magic, we shall not be disappointed. Shandong, and bordering regions of Zhili and Henan, had a long tradition of heterodox religious activity, and that tradition will be our first focus of concern. The Shandong people also had a reputation as fearless fighters, and the martial arts tradition of the province was well developed. When sectarians and martial artists got together, the potential for rebellion was great, and many scholars have sought the origins of the Boxer Uprising in such combinations of the past. The focus of most past scholarship has been on the White Lotus sects, and the boxing associations that were sometimes linked to them; but clearer links to Boxer ritual are to be found in sects outside the White Lotus tradition.

More importantly, it is clear that by the end of the nineteenth century, the sects had absorbed so much from ordinary popular religion that the line between orthodox and heterodox was exceedingly difficult to draw. In the end, it was from a broad repertoire of beliefs and practices in martial arts, popular religion, and one all-important form of popular culture—the dramatic tales of local opera—that the Boxers drew their primary inspiration.

SECTARIAN REBELS IN SHANDONG

As the birthplace of both Confucius and Mencius, Shandong was the fountainhead of orthodoxy in China; but it also had a well-established reputation for heterodoxy and rebellion. In the mid-eighteenth century, one governor observed that "Shandong's evil custom of establishing sects to mislead the masses has already continued for a long time."[1] In fact, "heterodoxy" in Shandong had a history as ancient as Confucian orthodoxy. During the Zhou dynasty (ca. 1027–256 B.C.), the northern Shandong state of Qi was known for its shamans (Qi-*wu*), who practiced spirit-possession.* It is hardly surprising that such practices were much frowned upon by orthodox Confucians, whose authority was threatened by those (often women) who spoke with the voice of gods. Their suspicions were not without foundation. During the Red Eyebrows uprising of A.D. 18–27, a shamaness from this area played a prominent role as the voice through which a popular local god spoke against the ruling dynasty. At the end of the Han (202 B.C.–A.D. 220), Shandong saw another source of peasant unrest: popular Daoism. The Yellow Turban rebellion built a large following on the charms and incantations by which Zhang Jue's sect, the Way of the Great Peace (Taiping dao), healed sickness. It was the greatest religious rebellion of ancient China; in subsequent ages, Confucian officials would cite it as an example of the chaos that unchecked heterodoxy could bring. The great Tang dynasty rebellion of Huang Chao lacked any significant religious component, but it began in the same rebel-prone area along the Shandong-Henan border. And perhaps the most famous rebels of popular culture, the Song dynasty heroes of the later novel *Water Margin* (*Shui-hu zhuan*), had their base near Liangshan in southwestern Shandong.[2]

*Spirit-possession was of course fundamental to Boxer ritual, and we shall have many occasions to note such practices in China. Strictly speaking, if we follow Mircea Eliade's classic work, *Shamanism: Archaic Techniques of Ecstacy* (pp. 4–6), spirit-possession should be distinguished from true shamanism wherein the shaman's soul leaves his body and goes on a magical flight to heaven or the underworld. But it is customary to describe Chinese spirit-possession as "shamanism," and translate the Chinese term "*wu*" as "shaman" or "shamaness" and I shall follow that custom in this volume.

From the final years of the Mongols' Yuan dynasty (1264–1368), and through the Ming and Qing periods, the most important inspiration for sectarian rebellion came from the White Lotus sects. These lay sects espoused a syncretic millenarian doctrine that centered on the salvation of all true believers by the Maitreya Buddha, who would descend to earth in a time of troubles marking the end of the current kalpa. By the sixteenth century, the Eternal Venerable Mother (*Wu-sheng lao-mu*) had emerged as the principal deity of the sect: the creator of all humankind, whose concern for her children led her to send forth Maitreya on his mission of salvation. In time, the sects began to absorb from popular Daoism a repertoire of magical practices—charms, incantations, and healing rituals—which had wide popular appeal. As early as the Tang dynasty, Maitreyan millenarianism had inspired popular rebellions, and there is no doubt that by combining the millenarian message of Maitreya, the magic of popular Daoism, and the universalism inherent in the Eternal Venerable Mother creation myth, these sects had produced a potent recipe for popular rebellion. Yet it is also abundantly clear that many White Lotus believers were utterly peace-loving people (many of them older, widowed women), attracted only to the promise of salvation after leading a sincere life of ethical conduct, prayer, sutra recitation and vegetarianism. Often, indeed, such people seemed driven to rebellion only by the intense persecution of a government intent on eradicating their "heretical" practices.[3]

Shandong, and especially the broad area along the borders of Shandong, Zhili, Henan, and Anhui was an area of particularly frequent uprisings led by White Lotus sectarians. The reasons are unclear. Peasants in this area (repeatedly afflicted by either drought or flooding of the Huai and Yellow Rivers) may have felt such insecurity in their worldly existence that they were unusually open to the salvationist message of the sects. If so, White Lotus beliefs may in fact have been more common here than in other parts of the country. Alternatively, the sects (which in more prosperous areas were likely to be quite peaceful) may simply have become a convenient vehicle for organizing popular violence in an area where natural disasters often led people to rebel in defense of their livelihood. Whatever the reasons, there can be no denying the frequency of White Lotus rebellions in this area: Han Shan-tong and his son Han Lin-er began in Bozhou, northern Anhui, the rebellions that finally brought down the Yuan. The female sect leader Tang Sai-er

led the largest White Lotus rising of the early Ming on the Shandong peninsula. And near the end of the Ming, Xu Hong-ru rose
under the same banner in the southwest of the province.[4]

Xu Hong-ru's rebellion was particularly notable, for it combined
White Lotus sectarians with a martial arts group known as the Cudgel and Whip Society (Bang-chui hui). Since the primary concern of
the sects had always been religious, it was usually only their combination with other elements (brigands, frustrated scholars, men of
political ambition, uprooted peasants) in times of general social and
economic distress that produced the volatile mix for rebellion.[5] But
Xu's seventeenth-century rebellion seems to have been one of the
first in which a martial arts association combined with a forbidden
sect to produce a major challenge to the Chinese state.

OFFICIAL PROSCRIPTION OF
"HETERODOX" SECTS

The Confucian tradition held that the just ruler should, by personal
example, education, and moral suasion, lead the people to do what
is right. Rectifying people's hearts—not instituting harsh laws to
prevent wrongdoing—was the proper Confucian way. Naturally,
once Confucianism became the ideology of the Chinese state, that
state paid considerable attention to ensuring that the people conformed to Confucian norms of right thinking. In the service of
Confucian orthodoxy, "heterodoxy" was to be suppressed. The
definition of "heterodoxy" naturally changed over time. In earlier
times even Buddhism and Daoism might be attacked for their devi-
ations from the Confucian norm. But by late imperial times, most
Buddhism and Daoism had been accepted into the ruling consensus,
and the brunt of the attack was borne by various magical practices
of popular Daoism and the White Lotus sects.

The Ming law against heterodoxy, adopted verbatim by the Qing,
proscribed—against a penalty of strangulation for leaders and banishment to a distance of 3,000 *li* for followers:

> all teachers and shamans who call down heterodox gods [*jiang xie-
> shen*], write charms, [chant] incantations [to make] water [magically
> efficacious: *zhou-shui*], perform planchette and pray to sages, calling
> themselves *duan-gong* (First Lord), *tai-bao* (Great Protector) or *shi-po*
> (shamaness); and those who wildly call themselves the White Lotus
> Society of the Buddha Maitreya, the Ming-zun [Manichaean?] sect, or
> the White Cloud Assembly with their heretical and heterodox [*zuo-dao yi-*

duan] techniques; or those who hide pictures [of heterodox gods or patriarchs] and gather in groups to burn incense, meeting at night and dispersing at dawn, pretending to do good works but [actually] arousing and misleading the people.[6]

The precedents cited in connection with this law make it clear that the charms and incantations were of particular concern to the authorities, along with a phrase added later forbidding "taking teachers or transmitting to disciples" [*bai-shi chuan-tu*].[7] Mere worship, especially if the person was not engaged in spreading a sect, was either tolerated or treated fairly leniently. What was not permissible was the formation of hierarchies of masters and disciples, or the use of magic—for these were instrumental in providing the organization and the techniques for potentially subversive activity.

For a time, these prohibitions seemed relatively effective: though sectarian worship certainly continued through the early years of Qing rule, there were no significant instances of sectarian rebellion. In fact, the sectarian texts that survive from this period make a point of stressing their loyalty to the temporal authorities.[8] The "heterodox" sects seemed to be doing their best to accommodate themselves to the demands of the Confucian state. But the late eighteenth century saw the same sects again rise in rebellion. The most famous of these rebellions broke out in western China, along the Hubei-Sichuan-Shaanxi border in 1796 and dragged on until 1803. In many ways this massive rebellion foretold the onset of dynastic decline. For our purposes, however, the most important uprisings were the much smaller Wang Lun rebellion of 1774, and the Eight Trigrams uprising of 1813. Both broke out in the area of our concern, and both involved significant participation by martial arts groups. Furthermore, in both cases boxers identified as "Yi-he-quan"—the same name used by the anti-foreign Boxers of 1898–1900—were mentioned in connection with the uprising.

SECTARIAN REBELS IN THE LATE EIGHTEENTH AND EARLY NINETEENTH CENTURIES

The stubborn persistence of Shandong sectarianism was a recognized fact of the Qing era. The province was the major source of what Susan Naquin has termed "meditational sects" of the White Lotus tradition. Naquin has distinguished these from the "sutra-recitation sects" (such as the Luo Sect prominent among Grand Canal boatmen) which were characterized by a quasi-monastic, vegetarian regimen, and congregational activities in sutra halls. The "sutra-recitation sects," relying on sectarian scriptures and often maintaining buildings for congregational worship, appealed to a more literate and wealthier audience—but were also more open to discovery by the state. These factors seem to have had several consequences: such sects were more apt to be found in cities and in southern China—further from the watchful eye of Beijing; and they were less likely to be involved in subversive activity, or to include any subversive statements in their texts.[9]

The "meditational sects," by contrast, had no halls, sutras, or vows, and usually did not prescribe a vegetarian diet. They stressed instead meditation and breathing exercises (zuo-gong yun-qi), combined with the recitation of incantations. Their religious exercises were much simplified, usually a morning, noon, and evening bowing to the sun; they advocated a popular ethics often adopted from the Qing founder's Six Maxims; and they frequently engaged in healing practices. These far simpler sects were more common in rural areas of north China, and a Liu family from Shan county in southwest Shandong seems to have been a source for much of the innovation. By the late eighteenth century, many of these sects borrowed the name of, or conceived themselves as belonging to, one of the eight trigrams of the ancient Chinese divination text, the Yi-jing.[10]

Both the Wang Lun uprising of 1774 and the Eight Trigrams rebellion of 1813 were instigated by members of such "meditational sects." Wang Lun was a former yamen runner who managed to get rich as a healer in Shouzhang county of southwest Shandong. His sect was particularly noted for its fasting techniques and its boxing, and these two practices would later constitute the basis of civil (wen) and military (wu) divisions of his followers. In the close integration of boxing and sectarian activities, Wang's group closely resembled the contemporary Liu sect of the nearby Shan county, from which Wang's group may have been derived.

In 1774, two years after the arrest of several prominent north China sectarians (including the leader of the Shan county Lius), Wang began spreading rumors of the impending turn of the kalpa, and in the fall— with arrests threatened in response to these stories—he rose in rebellion. It was a small-scale and short-lived effort. Wang began with only a few hundred followers, and he managed to recruit only a few thousand more on his way through the lightly defended county seats of western Shandong to the Grand Canal city of Linqing. There the rebels occupied the Old City, and for a time used a variety of invulnerability rituals to good effect against the firearms of the besieged Qing garrison in the New City. Soon, however, the government soldiers countered with the polluting power of dog shit and urinating prostitutes, and the sect's rituals lost their efficacy. Less than a month later, the last hold-outs, resisting to the end, were burned or slaughtered in the city.[11]

The Eight Trigrams rebellion of 1813 was of considerably greater scope and complexity. Many common elements of White Lotus rebellions were present: the prominence of "meditation sects," organization according to the eight trigrams, predictions of a time of troubles and a new kalpa, and the mobilization of sectarians through master-disciple relationships. For our purposes the most significant point is the merging of some purely sectarian groups with others whose raison d'être was the practice of boxing and martial arts.

There were three principal leaders of the Eight Trigrams uprising. Lin Qing (the "King of Heaven") was a hustler who had drifted about as night watchman, gambler, healer, and holder of various odd jobs before settling down in a village south of Beijing to join and soon take over the leadership of a small White Lotus sect. In 1811, Lin made contact with Li Wen-cheng ("King of Men") who was vying for, and would soon assume leadership of, a larger network of sects in the northern Henan county of Hua and surrounding areas of Shandong and Zhili. The third leader was Feng Ke-shan ("King of Earth"), a martial artist with considerably less interest in religion but a substantial ability to recruit followers from boxing groups along the border region of Shandong, Henan, and Zhili. When a series of natural disasters and poor harvests created the appropriate social context, this combination of ambitious new sectarian leaders and martial artists provided the inspiration for revolt. Lin Qing and the others decided that the fall of 1813 would see the end of the kalpa, and they devised elaborate plans for a coordinated uprising on the 15th day of the 9th month. Lin Qing's group was to penetrate the imperial palace while Li Wen-cheng rose in Hua and moved north, absorbing on the way sectarians and boxers that Feng had informed of the impending rebellion. Lin's effort in Beijing, though it succeeded in gaining brief entrance to the palace, was quickly crushed, but Li Wen-cheng's followers held out for three months in Hua county before a bloody government suppression eliminated all resistance.[12]

SECTARIANS AND MARTIAL ARTISTS

It is clear that one of the most potent recipes for rebellion was a combination of millenarian sectarians from the White Lotus tradition and martial artists with the military skills necessary to undertake an uprising against the state. That Shandong and neighboring areas on the north China plain should frequently provide that combination was not accidental, for the area had a reputation for martial virtues as strong as its reputation for sectarianism. As early as the Song dynasty (916–1279), Shandong people were noted for being warlike and courageous.[13] The reputation seemed to strengthen over time. By the end of the nineteenth century, a Western source approvingly labeled the people of Shandong "warlike, industrious and intelligent":

> The natives of Shantung [Shandong] . . . whose overflow has peopled the rich lands of Manchuria, enjoy the finest record for both physical and moral qualities. It is from them the Chinese navy drew its best recruits; it is they who proved their prowess either as brigands or as a self-reliant and self-defended exploiters of the resources of Liaotung [Liaodong] and Manchuria.[14]

It is clear that the martial virtues of the Shandong people could work either for or against the state. From Qing times to the present, army recruiters have looked to Shandong for strong, loyal, and courageous soldiers to defend the state. But the same courage led others to a life of banditry. The Shandong people were known for their commitment to righteous justice—a commitment which could easily turn them to the sort of "social banditry" of which Eric Hobsbawm has so compellingly written.[15] This was particularly true of the western portion of the province. Repeated invasions by northern tribes encouraged the development of martial habits in self-defense; and natural and human disasters so disrupted social order that these virtues often led to a life of banditry.[16] This was, after all, the area of China's classic Robin Hoods—the Song dynasty band immortalized in the novel *Water Margin*.

The west Shandong inclination toward military pursuits is evident in a thoroughly orthodox measure: the imperial examination system. In the previous chapter we focussed on the falling number of civil *ju-ren* in the western part of the province as an indicator of a weakening gentry presence. Now we look at the ratio between military and civil *ju-ren*. Since some counties (especially prefectural and provincial capitals) produced large numbers of both types of *ju-ren*, the ratio between the two degrees is our best indicator of military as opposed to civil preferences in career patterns. What we find is that the western portions of the province consistently produced a military/civil ratio higher than the provincial average. By 1851–1900 the Northwest ratio was 1.22 to 1 and the Southwest 2.38 to 1, while the ratio for the entire province was only 0.57 to 1. Map 3 shows this pattern clearly, and it is evident that Shandong's warlike reputation was particularly applicable to its western region.[17] Furthermore, as we shall see below, it was precisely from those areas with the highest military to civil *ju-ren* ratios that the Boxers and Big Swords emerged.

It is this martial tradition of west Shandong that spawned the proliferation of martial arts groups in the area. A popular culture stressing military virtues encouraged people to study boxing and swordsmanship; and martial arts teachers were a common sight displaying their prowess in the markets of the north China plain. But what exactly was their relationship to the White Lotus sectarians? This problem is difficult to analyze because, in general, boxing groups were reported in the official documents (which provide our best window into the mid-Qing period) mainly when they were associated with prohibited sectarian activities.[18] An interesting starting place, however, is a censor's memorial of 1808—a memorial which gained prominence when it was quoted by the Zhili magistrate Lao Nai-xuan in his 1899 pamphlet urging the prohibition of the Boxers, "An Investigation of the Sectarian Origins of the Boxers United in Righteousness." The memorial discussed certain martial arts groups along the borders of Shandong, Jiangsu, Anhui, and Henan:

> In this area there are many vagabonds and rowdies (*wu-lai gun-tu*) who draw their swords and gather crowds. They have established societies of various names: the Obedient Swords (Shun-dao hui), Tiger-tail Whip (Hu-wei bian), the Yi-he Boxers,* and Eight Trigrams Sect (Ba-gua jiao). They are overbearing in the villages and oppress the good people. The origin of these disturbances is gambling. They go to fairs and markets and openly set up tents where they take valuables in pawn and gather to gamble. They [also] conspire with yamen clerks who act as their eyes and ears.

The emperor responded by ordering the strict prosecution of the leaders of such activities.[19]

---

*It is a fundamental argument of this study that any organizational link between the Yi-he quan of the mid-Qing and the Boxers of the same name in 1898–1900 is highly questionable. In order to distinguish the two, I shall use the English "Boxers United in Righteousness" (or simply "Boxers") to describe the late nineteenth century boxers, for the translation fits the meaning of the name at that time. For the mid-Qing boxers, I shall retain the transliterated Chinese name: Yi-he Boxers.

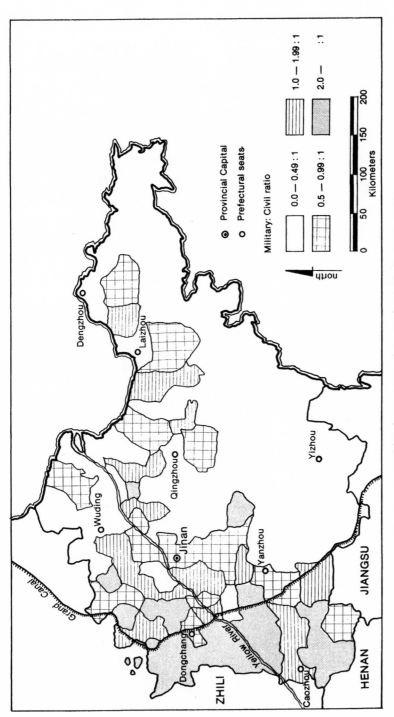

Map 3. Ratio of Military to Civil *Ju-ren* by County, 1851–1900

Legend (rotated):

Provincial Capital

Prefectural seats

Military: Civil ratio

0.0 – 0.49 : 1

0.5 – 0.99 : 1

1.0 – 1.99 : 1

2.0 – : 1

north

Kilometers

0   50   100   150   200

Labels: Grand Canal, Yellow River, ZHILI, HENAN, JIANGSU, Dengzhou, Laizhou, Wuding, Qingzhou, Jinan, Yizhou, Dongchang, Yanzhou, Caozhou

Figure 1. "The Nine Classes." Woodcut featuring a martial arts and acrobatics exhibition at a small market. From *Zhongguo mei-shu quan-ji, hui-hua bian 21: min-jian nian-hua* (Compendium of Chinese art, paintings volume 21: popular New Year's prints) (Beijing, 1985).

In general, this section of Lao Nai-xuan's pamphlet has received little attention, but it is clear that the Yi-he Boxers mentioned here had little to do with any sectarian activity. These boxers were marketplace toughs engaged in gambling, drinking, and various forms of extortion and petty crime. In the investigations that followed the imperial edict, the Yi-he Boxers were mentioned several times in this same difficult-to-control border area. Invariably they were associated with "idle vagabonds," banditry, and salt smuggling; and there was no mention of any charms, incantations or other sectarian activity.[20] These Yi-he Boxers seem to me no different from the sort of boxers the Qing court sought to eliminate in 1728. In that year, the Yong-zheng emperor issued the only imperial prohibition of boxing *per se* that I have seen. He condemned boxing teachers as "drifters and idlers who refuse to work at their proper occupations," who gather with their disciples all day, leading to "gambling, drinking and brawls."[21]

If there were boxing groups of village and market town youths who had nothing to do with sectarian religion, then there were also sectarians who were not at all involved in martial arts. The Luo Sect, and most White Lotus sects of the lower Yangzi and southeast China, seem not to have practiced boxing at all. Among the north China

Figure 2. "Gambling Outlaws in a Brawl." A nineteenth-century woodcut of a fight between partisans of two rival gambling houses, illustrating the "boxing and kicking" often associated with gambling in China. From *Dian-shi-zhai hua-bao* (Dian-shi Studio illustrated news) 13, GX 10 (1884), 7th month (Hong Kong reprint, 1983).

White Lotus sects, the Wang family of Stone Buddha Village in Luanzhou, northeast of Tianjin, had led a sect ever since the late Ming, and an extensive investigation following the group's discovery in 1815 made no mention of martial arts. This sect advocated a vegetarian diet and a strict but simple moral code modelled on Buddhist monasticism, with a distinctly pacifist prohibition on killing. Their incantations had only the moral object of aid in the escape from the "four walls of liquor, lust, wealth and anger." [22]

In general, the sects in the Beijing area seem to have shown little interest in the martial arts. Perhaps this was because proximity to the capital made such activities dangerous—though as we have seen, the legal prohibition against boxing was far less stringent than the laws against even the most pacific forms of sectarian worship. More likely, the more settled nature of the countryside in this region made martial arts less necessary than along the bandit-ridden provincial borders. With martial arts less common, the sects were less likely to absorb them into their repertoire. Lin Qing himself, when introduced to the techniques of a particularly capable fighter, is reported to have stated scornfully: "Ours is the way of the immortals, we do not use swords or weapons."[23] It was only later, after he had met the Henan sectarians and begun thinking of rebellion, that Lin invited Feng Ke-shan and another boxer to teach boxing to his key subordinates. The fact that he had to invite boxing teachers from Henan suggests that such martial artists were poorly represented among the sects of his own area.[24]

In contrast to the sects in the Beijing area, the Shan county Lius' sect—the source of many of the Eight Trigrams sects of the Henan-Shandong-Anhui border region—seems to have added the martial arts to its sectarian repertoire sometime in the late eighteenth century. The location of this sect, along the troubled southwest Shandong border, may have been one reason for the importance of martial arts. But it is also notable that references to boxing come only *after* the suppression of the sect and arrest and execution of its leaders in 1771. In fact the most consistent mention of boxing is in connection with the 1786 rising of the Eight Trigrams with the object of rescuing a young Liu imprisoned in the Shan county jail. It seems that government persecution had eliminated the more purely religious leadership of this sect, and confiscated its texts. Lacking either hereditarily sanctified leadership or textual guidance, a new leadership emerged which gave the sect a new direction. Given the need for (or, perhaps, the excuse of) rescuing the imprisoned Liu heir, it was rather natural that this group put greater stress on the martial arts. But the social context also helped. In this border region, the sort of people most likely to move into the leadership of a beleaguered sectarian assembly were young men proficient in the martial arts.[25]

In this same southwest Shandong region, also in the 1770s, Wang Lun attracted adherents by his talents as a healer and a martial artist. Though Wang's distinctive fasting practices were a new element, most scholars agree that his sect had its origins in the trigram sects initiated by the Lius. Wang seems to have systematized the inclusion of martial arts practices, dividing his adherents into "civil" (*wen*) and "military" (*wu*) disciples—the former concentrating on fasting and breathing exercises, the latter on boxing.[26] Furthermore, the boxing practiced by Wang Lun involved more than pugilistic exercise: practitioners were regularly recorded to have "learned boxing and recited incantations." Often the boxing was associated with breathing exercises. The relatively close integration of boxing into the ritual practices of the sect is clear.[27] In this respect, Wang Lun represents the polar opposite of those Beijing area sects with no martial arts at all: here we see the closest possible merging of boxing and sectarian practice—with a single leader for both types of activity. This unusually close relationship may help explain one of the surprising things about Wang's rebellion: it occurred at a time and place with no particular indication of social or economic crisis to set it off. It seems that the integral combination of martial arts and millenarian religion could itself be enough to inspire some to rebellion, even in the absence of serious ecological or political crisis.

But the 1774 uprising was not the only instance in which "civil" and "military" divisions are seen in the sects. The 1813 rebels at some point divided the eight trigrams into four "civil" and four "military" trigrams—with the boxer Feng Ke-shan in charge of the latter.[28] It was especially people like Feng who formed the link between such divisions, and Feng was said to have spread "civil and military sects (*wen-wu jiao-men*)" among known boxers along the Shandong–Zhili border.[29]

The functions of such "civil" and "military" divisions of a sect are indicated in an interesting case from the 1830s. A former member of the Li Trigram sect wished to revive the sect in southwest Shandong—the group having been inactive since the arrest of its leader following the 1813 rebellion. The reviver of the sect was able to gather some former members, but found it difficult to attract new disciples. According to the new leader,

> When one ran into stupid people, it was impossible to spread [the sect] widely. But because his son, Li Ting-biao, as well as [sect members] Lü Wan-qiu and Zhang Lun-cao, practiced boxing and cudgels, we divided into civil and military teachings. In the civil teaching they all recited incantations and did breathing exercises, and we claimed that if they had real talent, they could see the Eternal Venerable Mother. In the military teaching we taught them the techniques of boxing and cudgels.[30]

Here it is quite clear that the military practices were added to simplify the sect and make it attractive to a wider audience.

Adding martial arts to a sect's repertoire attracted not only a *wider*, but also a *different* following. It has often been observed that many ordinary White Lotus believers—perhaps even a majority—were women.[31] Females do not seem to have taken an active role in sectarian violence, so when sectarian leaders set themselves on a course to rebellion, it was important to reach a quite different audience, especially young males, and boxing was one way to accomplish that. One recruit was explicitly enjoined to recruit "young people with money," [32] and the record is replete with examples of young men who were first involved in boxing activities and then later taught the secret mantras of the sect.[33]

When boxing was used in this way, as a means of gradually involving people in a sect's activities—either for recruiting or for money-making purposes (and examples of both are seen)—the boxing group became a sort of auxiliary to the religious sect. As one censor put it: "In the past, when the White Lotus sect made trouble, many boxing sects (quan-jiao) served as their supporters (yu-yi)." [34] Studying boxing from a teacher clearly did not mean that one joined his sect: recruitment was a two-step process, and there were plenty of people who never took the second step. They learned the martial arts, but then declined to become full members of the sect.[35] In fact the loyalty of those who were primarily recruited through the martial arts appears seriously suspect. The leading boxer among the 1813 rebels, Feng Ke-shan, fled the scene once the rebellion's fortunes turned sour; and none of the boxers he recruited along the Shandong-Zhili border ever joined the uprising.[36]

The relationship of these boxing auxiliaries to sectarian groups would seem to have been at least one step removed from Wang Lun's rather close integration of civil and military followings. But there were also boxing schools, with hierarchies of teachers and disciples, which were organizationally quite independent of the sects—but which may have had incidental contact with sectarians. The best example of this again involves Feng Ke-shan. Feng's boxing master was an elderly medicine seller by the name of Tang Heng-le, who taught him Plum Flower Boxing (Mei-hua quan)—a school associated, as we shall see, with the Guan county Boxers of 1898. But when Tang heard that Feng had joined a sect, he refused to keep Feng as a pupil. When rebellion broke out some years later, Tang led his pupils to join the local militia in suppressing the sectarians.[37] Quite obviously, the Plum Flower Boxers, through Feng Ke-shan, did come into incidental contact with the White Lotus of 1813. But the main stream of the school was quite independent of (and even antagonistic to) the sectarians.

Finally, it should be noted that among boxers, master-disciple relationships were a good deal less stable than among sectarians. In the sects, to be sure, government persecution could make for considerable leadership instability. And as we have seen, the rise of such new leaders as Lin Qing and Li Wen-cheng was instrumental in turning these sects towards rebellion. But sect leadership normally changed only when one leader was arrested, or on one of those rare occasions when an upstart like Li or Lin would challenge and defeat a senior sectarian in doctrinal debate. In the martial arts, it was a normal practice for boxers to challenge each other to tests of fighting skills, with the loser then acknowledging the winner as "master."[38] This meant that even when a connection with sects existed, the hierarchy formed by generations of masters and disciples was never as strong in the martial arts groups—and their ability to persist over long periods of time with a distinct set of rituals and pugilistic techniques was quite limited.

It is clear from the above discussion that boxer–sectarian relationships could take a variety of forms. Some sects had no connections to boxers at all. There were also martial arts groups with no—or only incidental—contact with the sects, such as the Plum Flower Boxers. At the point of contact between sects and boxers, we can see two modes. One is a close connection of "civil" and "military" teachings under a single sectarian teacher such as Wang Lun. This is clearly the closest form of sectarian–boxer relationship. The more common form, however, is the final mode—with boxing groups serving as an auxiliary to the sects. Boxing could be a relatively open activity that could bring more people, especially young males, into the sectarian network; but participation in such boxing did not constitute full sect membership, and people recruited in this way tended to have only a weak loyalty to the sects.

The Yi-he Boxers of this period seem no different from these other martial arts associations. In general, their relationship to the White Lotus sectarians was incidental at best. In some cases, Yi-he Boxers were also sectarians and may have used their boxing as a means of recruiting new sect members. But in other areas, the Yi-he Boxers joined with the government and formed the basis for ad hoc militia to oppose the sectarians' rebellion. These boxers did have certain incantations that they recited in association with their martial arts, but only one third-hand reference indicates the possibility that they might have had rituals of invulnerability. Most importantly, the Yi-he

Boxers lacked the distinctive possession ritual (*jiang-shen fu-ti*) of the late-nineteenth-century Boxers. Thus, whatever their relation to the White Lotus might have been, they were certainly not the source of the Boxer movement which is our concern.*

The widespread presence of both sectarian and martial arts groups was an important part of the social environment of western Shandong. Both boxers and sectarians represented traditions of popular organization by ordinary peasants with no significant guidance or interference from the orthodox gentry elite. Such organizations accustomed people to lay leaders mastering and propagating charms and incantations with a variety of magical powers. The martial arts groups legitimized associations of young males gathering for exercise and for personal and local self-defense. All of these factors certainly made it easier for the late-nineteenth-century Boxers to find an audience in west Shandong. But they do not account for the distinctive Boxer rituals of possession and invulnerability. For these, we shall have to look elsewhere.

INVULNERABILITY AND POSSESSION

Invulnerability rituals have a long history in China. When popular rebels confronted the well-armed Chinese state, both concern for the safety of their band and the desire to enhance the bravery of men in battle led naturally to certain techniques to ensure invulnerability. Religion and magic played a natural part in this process, as the gods or Buddha were called upon to offer divine protection.[39] The need for such protection was much enhanced by the advent of firearms from the West in the seventeenth century. Several groups of late Ming rebels used magic involving the polluting power of women to stop gunfire from the walls of cities they were besieging.[40] Wang Lun seems to have been the first White Lotus rebel to use invulnerability techniques, but it is perhaps significant (given the large number of women in White Lotus sects, and the sects' relatively enlightened views on the position of women) that it was not Wang's rebels who appealed to female pollution, but the besieged government forces seeking to overcome the sectarians' magic. The magic itself, however, was quite different from that of the Boxers, and involved summoning

---

*Specialists with a particular interest in the Yi-he Boxers of the mid-Qing and their relationship to the White Lotus sects are invited to examine the discussion of these issues in the appendix to this volume.

goddesses to prevent the approach of bullets or to prevent guns from firing.[41]

For us, a particularly interesting invulnerability teaching is the Armor of the Golden Bell (Jin-zhong zhao), which appeared in connection with the 1813 Eight Trigrams rebellion. This was the original name of the Big Swords, who rose in southwest Shandong in the 1890s as a precursor to the Boxer Uprising. The basic technique— apparently a relatively difficult form of physical exercise and *gong-fu* allowing one to withstand a chop of a knife or sword—is similar enough to the Big Swords to suggest a continuity within one school. But the martial arts technique does not seem to have had more than an incidental connection to White Lotus sects.

The key example in surviving sources is one Zhang Luo-jiao, from the Eighteen Villages exclave of Guan county which will figure prominently in chapter 6. The martial arts were very popular in this frequently troubled border region; Zhang, who was a Daoist priest, first learned boxing from a relative in 1782. Eleven years later he learned the Armor of the Golden Bell from a Henanese practitioner and started teaching boxing professionally. In 1800 he joined the Li Trigram sect, but soon quit when his teacher insisted on regular monetary contributions. But Zhang maintained contacts with other teachers of religion, boxing, and healing, and learned from them. By 1813, however, he was losing his audience, and when even former pupils began to criticize his techniques as "ordinary" he was no longer able to make a living off his boxing, and began selling fried bread with his son, later turning to the practice of healing.

Other members of the Armor of the Golden Bell in this area were of a similar type—students of several varieties of martial arts, not from settled peasant families and often seemingly town-dwelling hucksters of one sort or another: a guard for a salt shop, an apparent salt-smuggler, a stone-mason who habitually interfered in law cases. Some did join sects, but their sectarian connections seem incidental to their martial arts activities. Thus the Armor of the Golden Bell, even more than the Yi-he Boxing, appears to have been a martial arts technique which was sometimes practiced by sectarians and therefore came to official notice. But in itself, it was simply a popular technique of self-defense.[42]

Though the Armor of the Golden Bell was apparently a technique of *gong-fu* similar to that practiced by the Big Sword Society, it was clearly different from the invulnerability of the Boxers themselves, which came from possession by gods. There are a few isolated examples of possession rituals among heterodox associations in the mid-Qing. The inspiration for such possession rituals was clearly the widespread practice of shamanism, especially in association with folk healing. As we have seen, in Shandong this practice can be traced all the way back to the shamans of the Zhou dynasty state of Qi. Such spirit-possession also found its way into the practices of some sects. In 1826, a Patriarch's Assembly (Zu-shi hui) was uncovered in several villages of Zhili's Baoding prefecture. Its ritual was described in the following skeptical official report:

> This society cures people's illness. It has such titles as "incense chief" (*xiang-tou*) and "horse" (*ma-pi*). The incense chief only follows along to assist. The "horse" is allowed to become a disciple of the patriarch. He burns incense and presents it, lowers his head and bows, then shakes both hands and falls on the ground saying the patriarch has possessed him. Then he removes his shirt and bares his upper body. First he does a trick with a chaff-cutting lever knife (*zha-dao*). With one hand he holds the handle and places the blade on his stomach. With the other hand he strikes the back of the knife vigorously. If he grasps the handle firmly enough, he will not be hurt. He also must be able to work with daggers, taking one in each hand and chopping the right arm with the dagger in the left hand, and the left arm with the dagger in the right hand. He also pierces [himself] with a needle, either passing it through the left cheek and out the right, or through the right cheek and out the left. All these are deceptions to cheat people. He does not really chop or pierce. He also must be able to use a whip, for all ghosts fear the crack of a whip. In addition, he must remember a few tricks (*pian-fang*) to cure illness. For example, to cure insanity he cuts a paper doll, sticks a strand of the sick person's hair to it, then burns it—saying this will send away the evil. Then he draws a charm and sticks it outside the sick person's door, saying it will keep the evil spirit from returning. These things are all only to cheat people out of their money, so [the members'] parents, wives and children have never reported it [to the authorities].

One of the arrested members of this society confessed that its practices had been passed down in his family from his grandfather, who had learned it during the Kang-xi era. The source of the society was said to be a village in Henan, near Kaifeng, from which it had by stages spread to central Zhili. But a curious belief of the assembly prevented any organizational hierachy from emerging along master-disciple lines of transmission. It was held that whenever a group wished to establish a new branch of the society, they had to steal the tablets from the patriarch's hall of some other practitioners. This clearly made it impossible to establish cordial relations between groups in different villages, for any new Patriarch's Assembly was founded on theft from earlier sectarians. Even within a given village, it was said that the members did not distinguish between master and disciple.[43] We have only one reference to this society, and given the reliance on theft to spread its practices, it is unlikely that any widespread network of Patriarch's Assemblies existed. But what is important is the existence of such practices on the north China plain—for the similarity to early Boxer ritual is remarkable: possession by gods, invulnerability, the practice of healing, even the term "horse"— which was applied to young Boxers in Pingyuan in 1899.[44] What this example demonstrates is that the basic repertoire of Boxer ritual had been practiced for some time among certain groups in north China.

A final martial arts group mentioned in the mid-Qing was the Spirit Boxers (Shen-quan), which is the same name used by the Boxers of northwest Shandong when they first appeared in the late 1890s. The principal reference to this group is in connection with a brief and abortive uprising in Zhejiang, based in a mountain village near Ningbo, in 1766. These boxers recited incantations, danced wildly, and believed themselves protected by gods (shen)—indicating some form of invulnerability ritual. Their leader claimed to be possessed by the spirit of a famous Tang dynasty general that he knew from a local opera. They worshipped Buddha but may also have had a political motive of Ming restoration. But only a few dozen people seem to be been involved, mostly from a single lineage of this mountain village.[45]

Because this incident happened at such distance—in both time and space—from the late Qing Boxers, one would not ordinarily suggest a connection between the two. But groups with the same Spirit Boxer name, and similar practices, were reported in both Henan and Zhili in the 1810s, 1820s and 1830s. Virtually all these references are extremely brief, but the ritual all seems to be of a similar type. One Zhili sectarian was said to be able to "leap straight up and do Spirit Boxing."[46] A Henanese boxer with apparently rebellious intentions leaped, danced, and was possessed by spirits who foretold coming disasters. He urged people to study his Spirit Boxing for protection against calamity, and claimed to be the Lord of the Han.[47] Finally near Beijing, members of a Red Sun Assembly (Hong-yang hui)—a White Lotus group with a substantial Daoist stress in its teachings— practiced Spirit Boxing after they met to worship, "inviting the ten patriarchs to descend and teach boxing."[48]

Though the north China references make no mention of invulnerability, the similarity of these Spirit Boxers to those of the late
nineteenth century strongly suggests a connection between the two.
In fact, as we shall see in chapter 8, when the Spirit Boxers first
appeared in the 1890s it was not so much invulnerability as healing
powers which their rituals provided—so the lack of invulnerability
rituals in the mid-Qing does not really disprove the connection. These
groups are so rarely and briefly mentioned, their numbers so small,
and their location still so distant from the western Shandong base of
the Boxers that it would be unwise to claim a definite organizational
link between the two. But that, I think, is not the point. As we shall
see below, the Boxers did not grow and spread by building on a pre-
existing organizational network. Their practices arose *de novo* in each
locality. Furthermore, in distinct contrast to the tight sectarian cohesiveness of the White Lotus groups, Boxer organization was virtually
non-existent. We should not, then, be seeking the origins of the
Boxers in terms of organizational continuity. What we need to discover is a set of rituals and practices similar to those of the Boxers—
practices that could have spread and become part of the popular
culture of north China, to be absorbed and used to new purpose by the
Boxers of the late nineteenth century.

In the Patriarch's Assembly and the Spirit Boxers, we have found
the basic components of Boxer ritual. We have not, however, found
them in any close combination with White Lotus sectarianism. The
Patriarch's Assembly, whose combination of possession, healing, and
invulnerability was closest to that of the later Boxers, seems to have
had no connection to the White Lotus at all. Two of the Spirit Boxer
groups were linked to sectarian activities—but there is no reason to
believe there was any more integral connection between the two than
we have found between other martial arts and sectarian groups. The
Henan and Zhejiang Spirit Boxers, on whom we have the most information, seem not to have had any White Lotus connection at all.

This whole consideration of the relationship between martial arts
and sectarianism must also confront the fact that the 1832 reference to
the Spirit Boxers in the Beijing area is the last reference that we have
to any of these groups until the 1890s. Yi-he Boxing was not mentioned after the 1810s. There is a whole history of mid-century rebellions lying between the events described here and the Boxer
Uprising—with the Nian and other rebels repeatedly ravaging the
western Shandong region. We need finally to turn to this period, to

see if we can detect any change in the relationship between boxers, sects, and popular culture in the late Qing.

BOXERS AND SECTARIANS IN
THE LATE QING

In the mid-nineteenth century, rebellions flared up throughout China. The pseudo-Christian Taiping rebellion established its capital in Nanjing and dominated much of the lower and middle Yangzi valley. North of them were the Nian rebels based in northern Anhui; the northwest and southwest were wracked by Muslim insurrections. With the Qing weakened by these massive uprisings, local White Lotus rebellions broke out in northern Henan, and in the hills of Zou county of southern Shandong, beginning in the late 1850s.[49] But the most serious Shandong rebellion followed the major Nian incursion into western Shandong in the fall of 1860—which brought about substantial (and unpopular) increases in land taxes to support the Qing's militia defenses.

The rebels rose in the spring of 1861 in Qiu county, in the extreme western portion of Shandong, and quickly spread through neighboring Guantao, Guan, Tangyi, and Shen counties to the south and east. After a poor harvest in 1859, the winter of 1860 had brought famine to this area. When new taxes were levied under these conditions, a series of tax protests broke out. The rebellion grew out of these protests, but there is no doubt that the leadership of the uprising lay with a network of White Lotus sectarians. They were joined, however, by a large group of martial artists under the leadership of Song Jing-shi, a professional boxer and swordsman with experience as a highway escort and armed guard for wealthy households in the area. Thus once again we have a popular rebellion combining sectarians and martial artists, and it provides a convenient insight into the nature of these two groups in the late Qing.[50]

These sectarian rebels of the 1860s seem quite different from the ones we saw in this area just fifty years earlier. Millenarian elements were much muted, and the rebels appealed instead to anti-Manchu sentiment (no doubt inspired by the Taiping and Nian), accusing the "northern barbarians" of forsaking basic Confucian virtues of loyalty and filial piety. Commoners were promised protection, while the rebels vowed vengeance against "corrupt officials and clerks."[51] In addition, the rebels relied on certain magical techniques—"scatter-

ing beans to produce soldiers, and riding a bench for a horse"—
which are frequently mentioned in the sectarian repertoire in the late
Qing.[52] Much of this was certainly a vulgarization of the sectarian
message, and represented an intrusion of the sort of sleight-of-hand
tricks in which religious charlatans specialized. On the other hand,
since it was above all the millenarian eschatology of the White Lotus
that distinguished it from ordinary Chinese popular religion, the
muting of this element probably made these sects more effective in
mobilizing popular support. And especially after the population was
subjected to the ravaging of the Qing armies, the rebels certainly
attracted popular support. According to the government troops'
Mongol commander: "The people hate the troops more than they hate
the bandits."[53] Others reported a general sympathy for the rebel
cause.[54]

If the distinctive White Lotus eschatology seemed muted among
the sectarians, Song Jing-shi and his Black Flag Army represented a
martial arts type with no perceptible religious interest at all. Song was
a professional swordsman, and while he had personal connections to
some White Lotus leaders, his followers were certainly no auxiliary to
the sectarians. Song later claimed to have joined the rebellion only
when persecuted by yamen runners following the rise of the White
Lotus; and by the summer of 1861 he had surrendered to the Qing and
offered his services against the rebels. Song's surrender was obviously
a conditional one: he kept his forces intact, resisted transfer to fight
the Nian in Henan, and finally abandoned his assignment to Shaanxi
to return to his western Shandong base and rise again in rebellion. But
he represented a type of local military adventurer quite distinct from
any sectarian tradition. Even more than in the mid-Qing, the Song
Jing-shi/White Lotus alliance joined sectarians and martial artists in a
pure marriage of convenience.[55]

Furthermore, there were surely as many boxers who aided the
government in the 1860s as joined the rebels. The local gazetteers of
this area are replete with biographies of famous boxers who died
fighting the rebels.[56] In Guantao, the Red Boxers (who had appeared
earlier in connection with the mid-Qing sectarians and would appear
again in 1899) were particularly active in fighting against Song Jing-
shi.[57] Boxing was an important skill—and an increasingly common
one in western Shandong—but it was itself politically neutral. Boxers
could join sects or join the government: which they chose was not
determined by the name or type of their boxing, but by the particu-

lar social and political situation of each individual boxer or boxing group.

More than anything, the Song Jing-shi rebellion illustrates the extent to which martial artists and sectarians had entered the mainstream of peasant life in western Shandong. The participation of martial artists on both rebel and government sides bespeaks the prominence of such people in the social fabric of the region. West Shandong in the late Qing produced ever greater numbers of military examination graduates, and military *sheng-yuan* were often the most influential men in the villages of the north China plain. Boxing was particularly popular in this area—both as a recreation for young men, and as a means of protecting one's home in an increasingly unstable countryside. But more than ever, such practices existed not as some heterodox tradition—but as part of a syncretic popular culture of the west Shandong peasantry. As the Republican era Linqing gazetteer said,

> The local people like to practice the martial arts—especially to the west of Linqing. There are many schools: Shao-lin, Plum Flower and Greater and Lesser Hong Boxing. Their weapons are spears, swords, staff and mace. They specialize in one technique and compete with one another.[58]

The transformation of the White Lotus sects was equally important. Following the Eight Trigrams rebellion of 1813, the Qing authorities vigorously suppressed sectarian activity wherever they found it in north China. Even such utterly pacific groups as the Wang family of Stone Buddha Village were devastated by arrest, execution and exile. Large networks of sectarians proved impossible to sustain, and the relentless search for sectarian literature severely depleted that link to a central White Lotus tradition. Such government persecution was certainly not capable of exterminating the heterodox sects: their rapid reemergence and spread in Republican China is proof enough of the continuing vitality of the White Lotus tradition.[59] But official persecution certainly served to alter the nature of many sects.

With sectarian literature now rarer and more dangerous to hold, the integrity of the original White Lotus theology became more difficult to maintain. Spirit-writing, or planchette, was an increasingly common source of sectarian doctrine. Two sect members would hold a stick and, possessed by some spirit (usually the patriarch of the sect) write characters in sand, thus revealing new doctrinal truths.[60] While many of the texts revealed by such planchette were completely

consistent with classic White Lotus beliefs, the practice clearly encouraged borrowing from ordinary popular religion. We see a growing importance of gods from the popular pantheon. Guan-gong began
to play an increasingly important role—perhaps in part because of his
association with loyalty to the ruling dynasty—but also certainly
because of his prominence in Chinese folk religion.[61] One common
source of new gods was the vernacular literature and opera so popular
in the countryside. The members of one sect claimed to be reincarna-
tions of the heroes of the novel *The Enfeoffment of the Gods* (*Feng-shen
yan-yi*), from which many of the later Boxer gods derived;[62] and
critics of the sects noted the influence of the *Romance of the Three
Kingdoms* (*San-guo yan-yi*), *Journey to the West* (*Xi-you-ji*, also translated as "Monkey") and other tales popular in local opera.[63] In effect,
while the persecution of the sects may have weakened them organizationally, it also brought them into closer contact with the popular
culture of the non-sectarian peasantry. When, in the context of a
much weakened Chinese state, sectarian activity began to increase
again in the late nineteenth century, it did so as but one part of an
unusually syncretic popular culture of the region.

The significance of this fusing of "heterodox" activities with popular culture is nicely illustrated by a village practice recorded by a
German missionary in southwest Shandong. He describes a custom in
the first lunar month of selecting four young men who are brought to a
temple or other appropriate place where the following poem is recited,
asking the "Monkey King," Sun Wu-kong, from the novel *Journey to
the West* to appear and demonstrate his martial prowess:

> One horse, two horses.
> Master Sun, come and perform (*wan-shua*).
> One dragon, two dragons.
> Master Sun, descend from Heaven and fight.

The four then fall on their faces until one is possessed by the Monkey
King (who is also called, in this context, "*ma-pi*" [horse]—a term we
have already seen associated with people possessed by spirits). The
possessed person is then aroused and given a sword which he swings
about, jumping over tables and benches until those presiding over the
ritual extinguish the incense which has been lit, and the possessed lad
falls to the ground exhausted.[64]

What is particularly striking about this account is that we have
here the basic Boxer ritual (minus the claim of invulnerability) de-

scribed as part of the annual cycle of festivals and customs in south-west Shandong villages. There is no mention of sectarian origins or content at all. It is clear from this that it is quite unnecessary to look for some specifically sectarian origins of Boxer practices. From their own folk customs, Shandong peasants knew of rituals calling down gods like the "Monkey King"—who would be a real Boxer favorite—to wield swords and spears in dramatic demonstrations of martial arts by possessed peasants.

POPULAR CULTURE AND PEASANT COMMUNITY

Sectarian religion in China was distinct from the popular religious beliefs of most peasants on a number of levels. Its cosmology, eschatology, and salvationist message all differed from ordinary popular religious conceptions. Furthermore, on a social level, it was a very individualistic religion: individuals joined, were promised salvation, and considered themselves distinct from the "unelect" outside the sect. As a consequence, when White Lotus sects rose in rebellion, they gathered members from a large area and acted, in general, independent of the village community. Their community was a different one: the congregation of the sect members.

Ordinary popular religion was much more closely tied to the village community. This is not to say that the community was comparable to a parish in the pre-modern West—for in general Chinese religious practice was not congregational. People did not observe a sabbath in a common service but visited temples individually in times of need (to pray for a son, a good harvest, or relief from some sickness in the family). But most north China villages had a small temple to the Local God (Tu-di shen) or perhaps to Guan-gong; and the subscriptions collected to build or repair such temples were an important community function. In times of drought, prayers for rain were also very much a community enterprise.[65] There was one paramount occasion when these temples became a focus for community activity: the temple fair, held annually at temples in larger villages or market towns. The name for these, in most of the north China plain sources I have seen, was "inviting the gods to a performance" (ying-shen sai-hui). The center of attention was an opera, supposedly performed for the benefit of the temple gods, who would be invited out and provided a front-row seat, usually under some sort of tent or parasol.

Figure 3. Street Theatricals. A large crowd watches a typical open-air opera. From Arthur E. Moule, *New China and Old: Personal Recollections and Observations of Thirty Years* (London, 1892).

Above all, these occasions were welcomed for the relief they provided from the dull monotony of peasant toil. Relatives would gather from surrounding villages. Booths would be set up to sell food and drink, and provide for gambling. The crowds and opera created an air of excitement welcome to all. But the statement of community identity provided by opera and temple was also extremely important. It is important, too, that the gods were not only part of the audience: many of the most popular dramatic characters—borrowed from novels which blended history and fantasy—had also found places in the popular religious pantheon. Since few villages had resident priests, and few peasants received religious instruction at larger urban temples, it was principally these operas that provided the substantive images for a Chinese peasant's religious universe.[66] This is why sectarian borrowing from popular theatre is so important. To the extent that sectarian groups incorporated the gods of the theatre, they brought themselves into the religious community of the village— rather than setting themselves apart as a separate congregation of the elect.

The importance of village opera for an understanding of Boxer origins can hardly be overstated. As we shall see below, the gods by which the Boxers were possessed were all borrowed from these operas. That many of the possessing gods were military figures is hardly accidental. From what little we know of the operas of west Shandong, it is clear that those with martial themes, for example those based on the novels *Water Margin*, *The Romance of the Three Kingdoms* and *The Enfeoffment of the Gods* were particularly popular. This is to be expected given the popularity of the martial arts in this area, but it no doubt helped that Jiang Zi-ya (Jiang Tai-gong), the hero-general sent down from heaven to assist the founder of the Zhou dynasty in the *Enfeoffment of the Gods*, was himself supposedly enfeoffed in the north Shandong state of Qi, and that the heroes of *Water Margin* made their base in the western part of the province.[67]

In many ways, it was the social drama of the theatre which tied together the elements of popular culture most relevant to the rise of the Boxers. Here was the affirmation of the community which the Boxers sought to protect. Here were the martial heroes who expressed and embodied the values of the young martial artists of this region. Here were the gods by which the Boxers were possessed—gods now shared by sectarians and non-sectarians alike. When the young boxers were possessed by these gods, they acted out their battles for righteousness and honor just as surely as did the performers on the stage.

The martial themes of popular culture certainly would have helped to integrate young boxers into the moral universe of north China villages. But there were also important changes in the functioning of north China villages which are likely to have tied martial artists more closely to their native communities. The martial artists that we have seen in the mid-Qing were men whose social world was outside the village community. Many led wandering lives as salt smugglers, peddlers, or professional escorts; others were primarily associated with the gambling and petty crime of market towns. But as public order disintegrated and banditry spread, first in southwest Shandong and increasingly in the northwest along the Zhili border, young men began to study martial arts to protect their families and communities.

The trend to village community defensive efforts in northwest Shandong is best illustrated by the spread in the late nineteenth century of crop-watching associations. As poverty drove large numbers of people to petty theft of their neighbor's crops, individual peasants found it necessary to watch their crops at night from tiny huts built in the middle of the fields. In time, this inefficient individual effort was superseded by collective crop-watching by an entire vil-

lage, or several adjacent villages. Meetings would be held to establish
the crop-watching association, assessments made, and then members
of the villages—invariably poor, and usually young males—hired
to watch the crops.[68] It is logical that young martial arts enthusiasts
were precisely the type most likely to be called upon for such crop-
watching duties. Thus their martial arts skills, instead of luring them
into the towns and onto the open road, now found valued use in their
own communities. Instead of a knight-errant, the young boxer might
even become a village hero.

We began this chapter with a consideration of heterodoxy—
especially of the White Lotus variety. As we conclude this discussion,
it is important to remind ourselves that it was an official Confucian
mind set that branded sects "heterodox," but the label hardly reflected a popular consensus of religious impropriety. The Qing code
branded as "heterodox" a wide range of magical and shamanistic
practices which villagers routinely relied upon. The area along the
western Shandong borders may in fact have been particularly tolerant
of "heterodox" activity: it had, after all, a long history of seditious
activity which included ancient rebellions, White Lotus sectarianism,
and martial arts associations. The latter two often came in contact, but
their relationship was less organizational than instrumental, or even
incidental: sometimes alliances of convenience, sometimes the use of
boxing and fencing to attract a wider range of followers to a sect,
sometimes the active recruitment of men with martial skills by sects
already bent upon rebellion. But what matters more than this occasional contact is the range of activities—charms, incantations,
possession, and invulnerability—which were introduced into the
popular culture of the region. They were "heterodox" only in official
eyes. To the people—especially when stripped of the unorthodox
eschatology of White Lotus millenarianism—they were quite familiar, and we have seen these same practices as normal parts of the folk
culture of Shandong.

As time went on, the line between "heterodox" practice and
ordinary popular culture became even more blurred. The sects borrowed more and more from popular religion and village drama (which
the Confucian elite also frowned upon—excluding all actors from the
official examinations). And as sects came to be known more for their
chants and spells and magical tricks, they became indistinguishable
from such common religious practitioners as itinerant Daoist priests.
These changes not only brought sectarian practice more in line with

popular culture; they also brought the sects closer to the village community. At the same time, martial artists became important members of the community as its defenders in an increasingly hostile environment.

Once these two changes had come about, the stage was set for the Boxer movement. The Boxers' "heterodox" practices—charms, spells, invulnerability, and spirit-possession—were perfectly understandable in terms of the popular culture of the west Shandong peasantry. They could, accordingly, be easily accepted by such large numbers of peasants that an enormous popular movement could spread over much of north China within a matter of a very few months. Furthermore, the integration of these new Boxers into the village community was pre-figured by measures for community defense that were already beginning in this region. That these Boxers should appear as community defenders not only helped them gain acceptance in their own villages, but also facilitated the important measure of official tolerance that the Boxers were to gain. In the late nineteenth century, officials and peasants alike were seeking new measures to defend the nation against the growing threat of Western imperialism, and that new threat provided the final precondition for the rise of the Boxer movement.

CHAPTER THREE

Imperialism,
for Christ's Sake

When the Boxers rose in arms in 1899, their most common slogan was "*Fu-Qing mie-yang*" ("Support the Qing, destroy the foreign"). The rebellious energies of these martial artists were not directed against the imperial state: their target was the foreign intruder. As such, the Boxers occupy an important place in the history of Western (and Japanese) imperialism, and Chinese responses to it. That history is, of course, extremely complex, not least because imperialism has many faces. The "foreign" which the Boxers proposed to exterminate could include "foreign people" (*yang-ren*), "foreign matters" (*yang-wu*, a term which applied particularly to the development of railways, telegraphs, ships and weapons), "foreign goods" (*yang-huo*), or the "foreign religion" (*yang-jiao*): Christianity. Any search for the social origins of the Boxer movement must include an inquiry into the impact of foreign economic penetration of China, and we shall turn to that subject first. But as will soon become clear, the initial and primary target of the Boxer movement was not foreign economic imperialism, but the "foreign religion"—the missionaries and their Chinese converts—and that subject will command most of our attention.

THE IMPACT OF FOREIGN IMPORTS

The first major impact of Western expansionism came with the "opening" of China under the barrage of British cannon fire in the

Opium War of 1839–42. But of the five treaty ports opened by that war, Shanghai was the furthest north, and for the next twenty years, the Western presence was felt almost exclusively on China's southern and southeastern coast. The "Arrow" War opened the major northern port of Tianjin (Tientsin) in 1861 and Yantai (Chefoo) on the Shandong peninsula in 1862. Only then did the north China region which was to spawn the Boxer movement begin to feel the foreign impact. The same Treaty of Tianjin which brought an end to the "Arrow" War opened the other port whose trade significantly affected the Boxer areas of western Shandong—Zhenjiang (Chinkiang), the port where the Grand Canal joined the Yangzi River. Trade through Zhenjiang did not begin until 1865, after the Qing capture of the Taiping rebels' capital at Nanjing opened the Yangzi to foreign shipping.

Much to the chagrin of Western merchants, who had pressed the second China war in hopes that additional treaty ports would at last provide great profits from the "China market," trade at these new ports was slow to expand. In the 1860s, much of Shandong was still suffering from the attacks of roving Nian bands and the even more destructive depredations of their Qing suppressors. By the time the Nian were finally suppressed in 1868, the lone Shandong port at Yantai was finding that Tianjin and Zhenjiang were eating into its markets. Isolated on the northern coast of the Shandong peninsula, and poorly connected to the interior by either overland or water transport, Yantai would never become an important center of trade.[1]

The one import which was to have any significant direct impact in the areas of Boxer activity was cotton textiles, first in the form of piece goods, then increasingly in the 1880s and dramatically in the 1890s in the form of cotton yarn. In 1882, Yantai imported only 11,288 piculs* of cotton yarn. Four years later that figure had increased five-fold to 56,726.[2] By the middle of the 1890s, despite the disruption of the Sino-Japanese War, the figure had nearly doubled again to 101,035, and in the year of the Boxer uprising itself, in 1899, it stood at 155,894 piculs.[3] The Tianjin increase was just as rapid, and the totals were even larger, from 66,946 piculs in 1889, to 269,221 a decade later—a four-fold increase. At Zhenjiang, transit dues were collected on goods passing into the interior, and the figures demonstrate the overwhelming importance of cotton textiles among the imports which served China beyond the foreign-dominated treaty ports. In 1899, in terms of

---

*A picul equaled 133⅓ pounds or 60.5 kilograms.

value, cotton yarn represented 40 percent of the goods sent inland under transit passes, and piece goods another 22 percent—the total dwarfing all other items on the list: sugar (16 percent), kerosene (8 percent), matches (2 percent), and so on.[4]

This increase in textile imports is important because the western Shandong areas from which both the Big Sword Society and the Boxers emerged were important cotton-growing areas with associated handicraft industries. In 1866, the Commissioner of Customs at Yantai had noted that native Shandong textiles were "very good and durable, and are largely used in this province."[5] Yet twenty years later, this same port reported that "the increase in its [cotton yarn's] import is said to be seriously interfering with the local industry of spinning, which affords a means of support to many poor women." And one year after that, in 1887, the same commissioner reported that "I gather that the reeling of Native Cotton Yarn in this province is almost at a standstill."[6]

The impact of foreign imports on Chinese handicraft industries has long been a subject of hot debate. Disputing "the oft-held assertion that the traditional or indigenous sector of the Chinese economy (handicrafts, small mines, junks etc.) suffered a severe decline as a result of foreign economic intrusion," Hou Chi-ming has argued that "the traditional sector existed quite well alongside the modern sector of the Chinese economy."[7] With somewhat more restraint, and considerably greater sophistication, Albert Feuerwerker has argued that while cotton spinning certainly suffered at the hands of machine-spun yarn—both imported and produced in Chinese and foreign mills in the treaty ports—handicraft weaving very much held its own, and in some places even made gains.[8]

Feuerwerker's aggregate figures are certainly very convincing, but they do not allow us to isolate the impact of machine-spun yarn on particular localities. The growth of proto-industrial weaving of machine-spun yarn in Gaoyang, Zhili—soon to become one of the most important weaving centers in North China—did little to compensate for the income lost by peasants in the cotton-growing regions of west Shandong. The detailed testimony of the American missionary Arthur H. Smith, whose post in Pangzhuang, En county, was right in the heart of the northwest Shandong Boxer area, indicates that the impact could be very great indeed. Smith's account, though lengthy, deserves citation in full:

One reads in the reports to the directors of steamship companies of the improved trade with China in cotton goods, and the bright outlook all along the coast from Canton to Tientsin and Newchwang in this line of commerce, but no one reads of the effect of this trade of expansion upon innumerable millions of Chinese on the great cotton-growing plains of China. These have hitherto been just able to make a scanty living by weaving cloth fifteen inches wide, one bolt of which requires two days of hard work, realizing at the market only enough to enable the family to purchase the barest necessities to life, and to provide more cotton for the unintermittent weaving, which sometimes goes on by relays all day and most of the night. But now, through the "bright outlook" for foreign cotton goods, there is no market for the native product, as there has always been hitherto. The factors for the wholesale dealers no longer make their appearance as they have always done from time immemorial, and there is no profit in the laborious work of weaving, and no productive industry which can take its place. In some villages every family has one or more looms, and much of the work is done in underground cellars where the click of the shuttle is heard month in and month out from the middle of the first moon till the closing days of the twelfth. But now the looms are idle and the weaving-cellars are falling into ruin.

Multitudes who own no loom are able to spin cotton thread, and thus earn a bare support—a most important auxiliary protection against the wolf always near to the Chinese door. But lately the phenomenal activity of the mills in Bombay, in Japan, and even in Shanghai itself, has inundated the cotton districts of China with yarns so much more even, stronger, and withal cheaper than the home-made kind, that the spinning-wheels no longer revolve, and the tiny rill of income for the young, the old, the feeble, and the helpless is permanently dried up. Many of the innumerable sufferers from this steady advance of "civilization" into the interior of China have no more appreciation of the causes of their calamity than have the Japanese peasants who find themselves engulfed by a tidal wave caused by an earthquake or by the sudden or gradual subsidence of the coast. Yet there are many others who know perfectly well that before foreign trade came in to disturb the ancient order of things, there was in ordinary years enough to eat and wear, whereas now there is a scarcity in every direction, with a prospect of worse to come. With an experience like this, in many different lines of activity, the Chinese are not to be blamed for feeling a profound dissatisfaction with the new order of things.[9]

The location of Smith's Pangzhuang mission, and the contemporaneity of his detailed account, make it impossible to ignore this critical testimony. Foreign imports were certainly having a major impact in the Boxer areas of northwest Shandong. But Smith may not have perceived the precise nature of the economic changes which were taking place. When I visited the Boxer villages of Pingyuan (bordering En to the east) in 1980, I was particularly anxious to ask older peasants about the impact of machine-spun yarn on the local handicraft industry. Somewhat to my surprise, the uniform response was that none had even seen the "foreign yarn" (*yang-sha*) before about 1920. In other areas I visited along the Shandong–Zhili border, the peasants, to this day, often wear clothes of hand-woven "native cloth" (*tu-bu*). Such distant recollections and contemporary observations should, of course, be used with great care; but it is significant that they are consistent with some of the specific aspects of Smith's analysis. In particular, Smith attributes the decline of handicraft weaving to the fact that "the factors for the wholesale dealers no longer make their appearance." I strongly suspect that what we are witnessing is not so much the importation of machine-spun yarn and cloth into the cotton-growing regions themselves, as the fact that these regions were losing their external markets—most of them to the north and west—which were now served directly by imports through Tianjin. The gazetteer of Nangong, just across the border in Zhili, supports this impression. After describing the widespread cultivation of cotton, the spinning by rich and poor alike, and the extensive exports to Shanxi and Inner Mongolia in particular, the gazetteer continues: "Since foreign cloth became popular, this industry has declined. Foreigners buy our cotton and make yarn and cloth, denying us any profit. Our yarn and cloth now does not leave the county. Only a little bit is sold at periodic markets."[10]

I have already described how the silting of the Grand Canal and the Yellow River's changed course and repeated flooding had left the area along the Shandong–Zhili border extremely depressed in the last years of the nineteenth century. No doubt the same lack of efficient transport which contributed to that depression also helped protect the region from the direct impact of imperialism. It is difficult, therefore, to argue that the Boxer Uprising broke out where it did because the impact of imperialism was particularly intense. Quite the contrary: almost any locale along the coast of China or in the Yangzi Valley was more directly affected by foreign economic penetration than the Boxer areas of west Shandong. But that does not mean that Western and Japanese imperialism had no economic impact on this area. Rather it seems that these regions lost crucial markets to foreign imports of cotton yarn and cloth, yet were just too isolated and too lacking in alternative resources to enjoy any of the stimulative effects that the treaty port economies sometimes generated in their more immediate hinterlands. Around Yantai, for example, some peasants were able to shift from spinning cotton to plaiting straw braid for export;[11] but in the cotton-growing plains, as Smith noted, there was "no productive industry to take [weaving's] place." As a result, these latter regions suffered the blows of foreign economic penetration without enjoying any of its benefits.

THE SINO-JAPANESE WAR

The 1890s not only brought intensified foreign economic penetration, they also saw China's humiliating military defeat at the hands of the once disdained "Eastern dwarves" of Japan. Though most of the fighting took place in Korea and the Northeast (Manchuria), the Shandong peninsula was also affected when Japan captured the port of Weihaiwei and sunk or disabled most of the Chinese fleet there. Troops were rushed northward and to the coast from the interior parts of the province. Graffiti in some inns, and the inevitable rumors of a widening conflict, indicated that some Chinese believed that the Western powers were also involved in attacking China; but there were no reports of any general anti-foreignism directly attributable to the war.[12]

The main impact of the war was indirect, but no less important. As we shall see in the next chapter, when we turn to the Big Sword Society incidents of 1896, the war's primary effect on the interior of Shandong was to strip the area of its garrison forces as more and more men were sent to the front. This left a power vacuum into which both bandits and such self-defense forces as the Big Sword Society quickly moved.[13] When the Qing troops returned in defeat, their battle tales may well have inspired hopes for invulnerability rituals such as those which the Big Sword Society and the Boxers practiced. According to the missionaries in Pangzhuang: "After the terrible fight at Ping Yang [Pyong-yang], the deserting soldiers brought detailed accounts of the terrible destructive forces of the foreign weapons, killing from unknown distances and striking terror into the souls of once brave men."[14]

Above all the war provided dramatic evidence of the Qing government's impotence and incompetence. The Great Powers were immediately emboldened to plan for "The Break-up of China"—to borrow the title of an influential book of this era.[15] In the words of the *North China Herald*—voice of the foreign business community in

Shanghai—the war put an end to "the fiction that China was a great Power whose territory could not be infringed with impunity."[16] Robert Hart worried that the Powers would "welcome a smash-up" which left them "sharing the dead intestate's estate."[17] It was such attitudes that inspired the Scramble for Concessions of 1897–98, for which the Sino-Japanese War had planted the seeds. Japan's fruits of victory included her seizure of Taiwan (the first major violation of China's territorial integrity), her successful claim to an enormous indemnity, and acquisition of the right (soon shared by all the Powers) to build factories in the treaty ports. With these, imperialism entered a new and far more dangerous phase in China, and the sense of crisis which this enhanced threat engendered formed a critical backdrop to the rise of the Boxer movement.

CHRISTIANITY AND WESTERN EXPANSIONISM

In contemporary America, where the separation of church and state is viewed as the normal (if often threatened) state of affairs, we are apt to forget that this separation is rather new in the Western world. Nowhere is this more evident than in the history of European expansionism. From the beginning, trade and Christianity formed the inextricably linked engines of Western empire-building. When Henry the Navigator initiated the great Portuguese voyages of discovery, he did so not only in search of gold and spices, but also as Grand Master of the Order of Christ. In return for the good works of the Portuguese crown, the Pope in 1514 granted to the King of Portugal the right of patronage for all of Asia. For a century, that country jealously guarded its control over all missionary activity in the East.[18] The Portuguese overseas expansion was in part an extension of the battles which finally expelled the Moors from the Iberian Peninsula. Added to the desire to circumvent the Arab stranglehold on the spice trade with the Indies, there was the hope of finding the lost Christian flock of Prester John, and thus surrounding the infidels of the Middle East. As Vasco da Gama is said to have remarked when he arrived at Calicut, he was looking for "Christians and spices."[19]

By the middle of the seventeenth century, the emergent French nation began to assert itself in Catholic missionary affairs, as Louis XIV gave support to the movement which was to result in the formation, in 1663, of the precursor to the Société des Missions Etrangères. In the nineteenth century, as the then leading Catholic power, France would assume the protectorate of all Catholic missionaries in China—often asserting herself in religious affairs when she could not challenge the British supremacy in trade.

When the Protestant powers—especially Great Britain and the United States—arrived in China in force in the nineteenth century, their interests were overwhelmingly commercial. But that did not keep missionaries from intimate involvement in the process of "opening" China to the West. Missionaries served as translators in all the treaty negotiations following the Opium War of 1839–42 and the "Arrow" War of 1856–60, and they invariably used their positions to press for the inclusion of clauses protecting their right to proselytize.[20] Yet when the missionaries proved as unsuccessful as the merchants in turning Chinese concessions into a wider market for their spiritual wares, the frustrations turned them into leading advocates of Western firepower as a means to open China still further. In 1871, the American minister Frederick Low discussed what he called the "popular course" for opening China: force. "This is regarded by most of the foreign residents here as the only sure and speedy agent for 'opening up' China. The merchants look upon the use of force as necessary to open up new resources and avenues of industry, and a large proportion of the missionaries favor it because their task will, by this means, be rendered less difficult, probably, than by the slow and laborious process of moral suasion."[21] In one of his most memorable if least enlightened judgments, the eminent American missionary and sinologue S. Wells Williams would use a briefly held diplomatic post to argue that the Chinese "would grant nothing unless fear stimulated their sense of justice for they are among the most craven of people, cruel and selfish as heathenism can make men, so we must be backed by force, if we wish them to listen."[22]

Whenever war came, the missionaries were quick to see it as an act of Providence—and if such wars appeared to be unjust attempts to open China to an illegal and immoral opium trade, that was only because God's ways are "dark and incomprehensible to our finite minds."[23] The American medical missionary Peter Parker, who would later gain notoriety as a diplomat by arguing for American colonization of Taiwan, apologized for the first Opium War in these terms: "I am constrained to look back upon the present state of things not so much as an opium or an English affair, as the great design of Providence to make the wickedness of man subserve His purposes of mercy toward China in breaking through her wall of exclusion."[24]

Though the late nineteenth century would reveal growing tensions between missionary and mercantile interests in China, the prevailing view was certainly that trade and Christianity marched together to mark the spread of Western civilization. The missionaries supported the opium wars because they were convinced that as China was opened to trade, so would she be opened to Christ. Much later, following the Yangzi Valley riots of 1891, which were spurred in part by anti-Christian propaganda from Hunan, a leading missionary was to argue that such attacks would stop only when Hunan was "humbled, and two or three of her great marts opened to foreign trade."[25] And occasionally the defenders of commerce, such as the American minister Charles Denby, would repay the compliment by casting missionaries as the servants of trade: "Missionaries," said Denby, "are the pioneers of trade and commerce.... The missionary, inspired by holy zeal, goes everywhere, and by degrees foreign commerce and trade follow."[26]

MISSIONARY ACTIVITY IN SHANDONG

To appreciate the consequences of this alliance of Christian proselytizing and Western imperialism, we must return to the area of our central concern—Shandong and its border regions, the seedbed of the Boxer movement. Though there are reports of a Nestorian bishop in Jinan under the Mongols, and of proselytizing by Odoric de Pardonne when he passed up the Grand Canal in the 1320s, active missionary work in Shandong did not begin until the 1630s, during the era of Jesuit ascendancy. At first Jesuits made periodic visits to the province from their base in Beijing. Then in 1650 the Jesuit astronomer and missionary Adam Schall introduced an Italian Franciscan to an official in Jinan; in the following year, the Italian was able to establish a permanent church in the provincial capital. At one point late in the seventeenth century, the Catholic bishop of Beijing (in whose see Shandong was now included) was compelled to operate from a base in the Grand Canal city of Linqing, and throughout this early period, Catholic conversions—said to number 1,500 in 1659—were concentrated in the northwest Shandong area.[27]

By the end of the century, according to one report, 6,638 Chinese had been baptized in Shandong, but soon the Rites Controversy soured Chinese relations with the Papacy, and in 1724 the Yong-zheng Emperor proscribed the Christian religion—while permitting missionary practitioners of such useful arts as astronomy to remain in

Beijing. Driven underground, the Church was certainly hampered in its efforts to gain new converts, but foreign priests continued to make their way secretly into the interior, and in 1765, the Church still claimed 2,471 Shandong converts.[28] Then in 1784–85, the arrest in Hubei of four Franciscans on their way to Shaanxi, which was then in the throes of a Muslim rebellion, aroused great suspicion and led to a nationwide dragnet for Catholic missionaries in the interior. The last three Italian Franciscans in Shandong were seized, leaving only two Spaniards whose field was mostly confined to the peninsular areas of the province—and the last of these died, without replacement, in 1801.[29]

It was 1844 before the French secured, from the Dao-guang Emperor, an edict of toleration for Christianity. In 1860, they gained treaty rights to travel and (via a clause surreptitiously inserted into the Chinese text of the French treaty by its missionary translator) to own land in the interior. But the Catholics did not wait for these legal niceties to return to Shandong. The province was given its own vicariate in 1839, and soon an Italian bishop had arrived to find, it was claimed, 4,000 extremely poor, widely separated faithful to whom he ministered in secret nighttime meetings. By 1849, their numbers are said to have doubled, though the figure (in another source) of 5,736 in 1850 would appear more reliable.[30] Then came the sustained growth of the late nineteenth century, to 16,850 converts in 1887, and— following the dramatic growth of the 1890s to which we shall turn presently—47,221 converts by the end of the century.[31]

In the areas bordering on Shandong, the most significant Catholic population was in the Jesuit missionary field of southeast Zhili. When this field was transferred to the revived Jesuit order in 1854, there were only about 350 Christians remaining from the earlier era of Catholic proselytizing. By 1870, that figure had grown to 20,000; and by 1896 it had doubled again to 43,736. With a bishop, seminary, and college in Xian county, this was one of the most important centers of French missionary activity on the north China plain.[32]

While the Catholics remained concentrated in the plains areas of western Shandong and Zhili, the Protestants moved slowly out of their east Shandong treaty port base of Yantai and the nearby prefectural capital of Dengzhou. By the mid-1860s, American Presbyterians, Southern Baptists, and Episcopalians, English Baptists, French Protestants, and Scottish United Presbyterians had each established missions in the area.[33] Missionary mortality was high in these early

Figure 4.   Baptizing Two Shandong Villagers. From Harry A. Frank, *Wandering in Northern China* (New York, 1923).

years, and conversions few. Of the 98 Protestant missionaries who came during the first twenty years of proselytizing, 15 died, and 43 abandoned the field—usually for reasons of health. Such progress as was made was substantially attributable to famine relief work in 1877: two-thirds of the 2,843 converts from the 1860–80 period came after the famine.[34] It was through such good works that the Protestants slowly spread their influence westward, to the Jingzhou area and to the northwest, including the En county Pangzhuang base of Arthur Smith's ministry.[35] Sometimes, the missionary correspondence leaves a grisly reminder of the Christian hopes that sprang from Chinese misery:

> Parents will sell their children and even kill them for food. The famishing dispute with the dogs over the bodies of the dead for something to sustain life. Every possible article even to the roof of the houses is sold to buy food. The bark of trees is in demand and no one can tell when the end will be. No rain has fallen here and the dust lies thick on the roads portending only continued famine. It seems to me the grandest opportunity in all the history of China to demonstrate the spirit of our religion. We can show that Christianity teaches us to love our neighbors as ourselves and to recognize all men as brethren.[36]

But even with the gains of famine relief work, Protestant progress was slow—especially in the west Shandong area which most concerns us. It was not until 1886 that the American Congregationalists established their base in Linqing, and 1890 before the Presbyterians established permanent bases in Yizhou and Jining.[37] The Protestants seemed rather more selective than the Catholics in admitting converts. As a result, their congregations grew slowly and suffered periodic purges. After ten years at Linqing, the American Congregationalists with a hospital, two doctors, and four other foreign missionaries could claim only 34 Chinese members of their congregation.[38] In Jinan in 1886, where the American Presbyterians suffered losses to the Catholics (who were more ready to take their converts' cases to court) 113 new members were baptized and 128 excommunicated.[39] The net effect of all this is that the same figures which yielded 47,221 Catholic converts (and 85 missionaries) just after the Boxer Uprising showed only 14,776 converts and 180 missionaries for the Protestants.[40] We should also remember that most of these Protestant converts were out on the Shandong peninsula, far from the areas of Boxer activity. In 1896, for example, the Presbyterians reported only 578 members in their Western Mission (which extended as far east as Jingzhou on the north slope of the mountains), as against 4,095 in their Eastern Mission.[41]

GERMAN CATHOLICS OF THE S.V.D.

Because of their smaller numbers, their relative isolation in the distant peninsular areas of the province, and their less aggressive policy in protecting converts' interests before the local authorities, the Protestants were on the whole a good deal less disruptive than the Catholics in Shandong. And of the Catholics, none were more disruptive than the new order which entered the field in the 1880s—the German missionaries of the Society of the Divine Word (S.V.D.). In 1875, Arnold Janssen had founded the S.V.D. with its home mission at Steyl, in Holland. Ironically, the Kulkurkampf in Germany prevented these staunch promoters of German national interests from basing themselves in their homeland. Undaunted, the S.V.D., whose primary purpose was missionary activity, sought to remove its missionaries from French protection and attach them to imperial Germany. The German minister in China, Max von Brandt, also favored this course, but it was not until 1886 that changes in German domestic politics increased government interest in securing the support of the Catholic Center—at which point the protection of Catholic missionary activity became politically desirable. Both the German and Italian ministers in Beijing secured the Chinese government's consent to this change in 1888, but it took another two years, and a trip to Rome by the head of the S.V.D. in China, to secure the assent of the Holy See. Even then, the Pope only gave the missionaries the choice of their own protector. While the Germans moved with alacrity to attach themselves to imperial Germany, the Italians decided that they were better off sticking with the French.[42]

The head of the S.V.D. in China from its inception until his death in 1903 was Johann Baptist von Anzer. Even in the S.V.D.'s own literature, he does not emerge as a very attractive figure. He is described as "blunt and impetuous," and even the S.V.D. Superior-General Janssen saw him as a "firebrand."[43] Arriving in China in 1879, Anzer soon made his way to Shandong. By 1882 he had secured the Franciscans' permission to assume responsibility for the bandit-ridden southern portion of the province. Three years later, a separate vicariate apostolic was established comprising the three prefectures of Caozhou, Yanzhou, and Yizhou, and the subprefecture of Jining. In the summer of 1886, upon his return from one of many trips to Europe, Anzer was installed as its first bishop. His militant nationalism set the tone for the entire mission, as in a ceremony arranged to welcome a visiting German consul, shortly after the establishment of the German protectorate:

> [T]he apostolic residence was richly decorated and there were innumerable banners, including a huge German flag, hanging from the church steeple and the buildings. The bells rang their salvo. Over the door of the house richly ornamented lettering read, "A hearty Welcome," and over the veranda, "Vivat, crescat, floreat Germania [May Germany live, flourish and grow]." The "Kaiser-Hymne" and other German songs were sung enthusiastically.[44]

But Anzer and the S.V.D. were not only aggressive nationalists, they were also aggressive proselytizers. Their methods were not such as to endear them to most Chinese. No sooner had he gained his mission field than Anzer set his sights on the city of Yanzhou—a particularly sensitive site because of its proximity to the Confucian and Mencian temples in nearby Qufu and Zou counties, and an area in which the French had apparently once agreed to refrain from active missionary work.[45] As one S.V.D. missionary later wrote,

> From the very first, Bishop von Anzer had concentrated his attention on the cities. . . . Tsining [Jining] was of special importance in the Bishop's

eyes since it was the commercial capital of the province of Shantung, and it might also be regarded as an advance post for capturing the "holy city" of Yen-fu [Yanzhou-fu].[46]

Jining was indeed successfully entered in 1891, and not long thereafter the bishop's residence was moved to that city from the small village of Poli, in Yanggu county, to which it had hitherto been confined. But the deliberately provocative struggle to establish a permanent presence in Yanzhou dragged on for ten years, from 1886 to 1896, with bitter recriminations on all sides. It was partly in order to gain a more aggressive sponsor for his efforts to enter Yanzhou that Anzer traveled to Europe in 1890 and had his mission shifted to German protection. An aggressive sponsor he certainly found. Once the German protectorate was arranged, the German consul in Tianjin embarked on a trip to Shandong. Upon arrival in Jinan, he rode directly into the courtyard of the governor's yamen to force a meeting previously denied, and then went on to Yanzhou with a guard provided by the governor, forcing his entry into the city. This provoked a near riot among the city's inhabitants, during which the consul promised to empty his revolver into the first six Chinese to advance, and to die if necessary. Fortunately, the more cool-headed local prefect succeeded in dispersing the crowd without further incident. Even this degree of German blustering did not succeed in securing a Yanzhou mission. That would not come until five years later, when the Chinese state's capacity to resist had been critically weakened by defeat in the Sino-Japanese War.[47]

The S.V.D.'s aggressive assault on Yanzhou certainly gave the order a distinctly negative reputation in southern Shandong. But the missionaries' opponents in this case were largely the gentry and those most concerned with the beliefs and rituals of the Confucian cult of the "holy city." For the villagers soon to rise up as members of the Big Sword Society, it was the missionaries' attitudes and behavior toward the Chinese people which mattered. Here too the S.V.D.'s own literature is remarkably revealing of the cultural gap which separated its members from the Chinese they had come to convert. Augustine Henninghaus, who succeeded Anzer as Bishop in 1904, arrived in Shandong in 1886. "The crudities of Chinese life," says one S.V.D. pamphlet, "revolted him." He would make "disparaging observations about the Chinese people in general."[48] When other missionaries defended the Chinese, he would counter that such ideas denied "the corruptness of paganism." Later Henninghaus himself would write that "In the central [mission] station, at Puoli [Poli] and elsewhere, a subject heatedly debated among the missionaries was that concerning the relative goodness and wickedness of the Chinese people, taken by and large." He admitted finding some missionaries' words "often betraying something akin to contempt and hatred" for the Chinese.[49]

Such contempt for the Chinese, and conviction of the corruptness of "pagan" society, led naturally to the belief that both abstract "justice" and Christian duty required foreign missionaries to intervene to defend their converts in all manner of disputes. Thus Father Henle, one of the victims of the Juye incident of 1897, was praised by another S.V.D. missionary in the following terms:

> There is no justice in China, as long as gold and silver are the chief and only arguments, and often enough the poor, innocent Christians were stretched on the rack or even condemned to death. Father Henle, therefore, tried to be on good terms with the officers and the rich and learned men, and often contrived to induce these 'friends' to pronounce a just sentence.... He became known throughout the entire mission for his prudence.[50]

Perhaps some Christians knew him for his prudence. More likely the rest of the population knew him as a phenomenal busybody. In fact the image one gets of men like Henle leaves one wondering how much time they devoted to spreading the Gospel. This same biography of Henle reports that sometimes twenty messengers would come to his office in a single day, seeking settlement of all sorts of disputes.[51]

Henle was by no means unique. In fact, he seems to have acted in accordance with explicit mission policy. According to the S.V.D. history of its work in Shandong: "The mission believed it necessary to assume the protection of the Christians. 'Wherever there are Christians, there are lawsuits,' wrote Father Anzer in his first annual report. They present delicate, dangerous, and thankless problems.... In order not to jeopardize his work, the missionary must on occasion intervene on behalf of his people. One can readily understand that occasionally dishonest persons will try to misuse the kindness of the missionary, and that sometimes the priest becomes the victim of hypocrisy."[52] Still, Anzer made it a point not to worry too much about self-styled Christians abusing the protection of the Church. "Each time the missionaries were called, they answered, and opposition served only as a stimulus to Father Anzer to make him determined to establish a station." Later, a more prudent S.V.D. missionary would note the dangers of such an indiscriminate quest for converts, which often produced congregations which were "stations of sorrow which by their bad example work much evil."[53]

THE CATHOLIC CHURCH AS
IMPERIUM IN IMPERIO

Although Anzer and the S.V.D. missionaries seem to have been unusually aggressive in their intervention in secular disputes, their behavior was not atypical. In fact it fit perfectly the classic criticism of the Catholic Church by both Chinese officials and Protestant observers. Following the "Tianjin Massacre" of 1870, the Zongli Yamen—which functioned as China's foreign ministry—attempted to regulate those missionary activities most likely to incite opposition. The American minister in Beijing, noting that "there is foundation for some of their charges," aptly summarized the lengthy Chinese document in the following terms:

> Roman Catholic missionaries, when residing away from the open ports, claim to occupy a semi-official position, which places them on an equality with the provincial officer: that they would deny the authority of the Chinese officials over native Christians, which practically removes this class from the jurisdiction of their own rulers; that their action in this regard shields the native Christians from the penalties of the law, and thus holds out inducements for the lawless to join the Catholic Church, which is largely taken advantage of.[54]

This was not simply a complaint of the Chinese officials who saw their authority slipping away. In the Shandong University surveys of older peasants from the Boxer areas, no complaint is more common than the unfair advantage Christians gained from their foreign connection—especially in lawsuits before the local magistrate. The Chiping peasants had a colloquial expression for this sort of behavior: *cheng yang-jir* (relying on foreign strength).[55] It is clear that the practice was common not only in the S.V.D. areas, but also among the Italian Franciscans of northwest Shandong and the French Jesuits across the border in Zhili. To cite just one of many reports from Protestant sources, an American missionary in Linqing wrote in 1894 that

> The Roman Catholics have for many years interested themselves not a little to speak a good word for their church members at the yamens, and as a consequence many lawsuits have been decided as they dictated. Hence it has happened that they have an unenviable reputation among

Chinese generally, and also have gained adherents who wished solely for aid in the courts.[56]

This is not to suggest that all Protestant missionaries were above such intervention in lawsuits, but all the evidence I have seen—including such complaints against the Catholics as that just cited—indicates that the Protestants were rather more sensitive than their Catholic colleagues to the dangers of this sort of behavior.[57]

Far from shunning any exercise of temporal authority, many Catholic missionaries were inclined to display the power of their religion in all sorts of mundane affairs. The structure of the Church was easily adapted to the efficient performance of its political role. If some dispute arose, the offended Christian would take the matter to the head of his parish or local priest, who would try to resolve the issue within the village or town. If that proved impossible, the priest would appeal to the foreign missionary, who had easy access to the county magistrate. If satisfaction still was not forthcoming, the missionary could take the matter to his bishop who would appeal to the prefect or governor. And if that proved unavailing, the bishop could ask his ambassador to bring the matter to the attention of the Zongli Yamen and ultimately to the emperor himself. This pattern shows itself again and again in the archives of the Zongli Yamen published in the *Jiao-wu jiao-an dang*. What strikes one repeatedly in these documents is the fact that the Catholic hierarchy was invariably faster than the Chinese bureaucratic hierarchy, as a result of which the Zongli Yamen was always on the defensive, having to respond to a version of the case first presented through the eyes of the missionary.

As the Catholic Church intervened ever more frequently in China's domestic politics and justice, it came to adopt more and more of the trappings of the Chinese bureaucratic state in the effort to legitimize its own authority.

> Thus the bishops, the spiritual rulers of the whole of a broad province, adopt the rank of a Chinese Governor, and wear a button on their caps indicative of that fact, traveling in a chair with the number of bearers appropriate to that rank, with outriders and attendants on foot, an umbrella of honour borne in front, and a cannon discharged upon their arrival and departure.[58]

Anzer seems to have been particularly taken with ceremonies which would enhance his prestige. One fellow missionary describes how, on approaching a mission station together with Anzer, "the

Christians came out with banners, tomtoms, and music to escort the Bishop." [59] The German minister cooperated fully in this effort to raise the bishop's official status in the terms of the Chinese bureaucratic hierarchy, petitioning successfully first for the granting of a button of the third rank, and later of the second rank, to honor Anzer's alleged good works in Shandong. [60]

The result of all this was to constitute the Catholic Church in China as an *imperium in imperio*. [61] The missionaries themselves were protected by the extraterritoriality provisions of the treaties. Their converts' rights to practice Christianity were also written into the treaties, and it was easy for converts to claim and missionaries to believe that the oppression of a Christian was in fact a persecution of Christianity. The Church was accordingly quick to intervene in almost any sort of temporal dispute, bringing all of its power and authority to the defense of Catholic converts. The power of the Church could be quite considerable—for it combined the freedom and flexibility which came from its structural independence of the Chinese bureaucracy with the status and authority it gained by either arrogating or acquiring by petition the symbols of legitimate power hitherto monopolized by gentry and officials. Traditional Chinese politics had no real place for pluralism. Yet here were Christian missionaries introducing a divisive pluralism to the Chinese state, and creating a structure which could stand over and against the Chinese polity, as an alternative authority system and indeed a rival for political power.

This understanding of the *political* role of the Church is essential if we are to understand the patterns of Christian conversion in China. To date, most discussion of this problem has focused on the question "Why were converts so few?" because it is a striking fact that in the century of missionary activity up to 1949, less than one percent of the Chinese population ever adopted the foreign faith. The basic reasons for this widespread Chinese rejection of Christianity are well known, and need no detailed repetition here. Christianity was not only foreign, and thus suspect for xenophobic reasons; it was also clearly heterodox—containing beliefs in miracles and salvation, and rituals of congregational worship which mixed men and women in the same church—which had led earlier emperors to link it with such proscribed sects as the White Lotus. Furthermore, most nineteenth-century missionaries—though Protestants more rigorously than Catholics—presented Christianity as an either/or alternative to Chinese popular culture. As one such missionary put it, he intended "not to engraft Christianity upon heathenism, but to uproot the one and plant the other in its place."[62] Thus conversion not only meant casting out the household's Kitchen God and ending all visits to local temples, it also meant abandoning the customary ancestor worship and participation in local religious festivals, and usually forsaking traditional wedding and funeral practices as well. Needless to say, this meant a break with both the culture of the past and the community of the present: few Chinese were willing to make it. But our point here is that some *did* make it—and probably many more either pretended (for the missionaries' benefit) to have made it, or sincerely tried (but achieved less than total success) to make the radical break. Our task now is to understand what sort of people opted to convert to Christianity.

In addressing this problem, the work of Samuel Popkin on Vietnam is instructive. Just as I have stressed the political role of the Catholic Church in China, so does Popkin stress this function in the admittedly much more powerful and successful French missionary effort in Indochina. The Catholic priest, he argues, was a "quintessential political entrepreneur," with an organization to attract adherents, administer justice, and manipulate power struggles.[63] He also argues that in order to understand the success of these and similar "entrepreneurs," the "metaphor of penetration [which] has emphasized outside initiative and the need for force to overcome collective resistance" is not entirely adequate, for it "neglects the divergence between collective and individual interests and the fact that the initiators were frequently villagers seeking outside allies in local power struggles."[64]

That Popkin's insight, with some amendment, has applicability to our Christians in Shandong is best illustrated by several Catholic congregations in the hilly regions of Yizhou in southern Shandong. The S.V.D. literature records that the process which led to the founding of these congregations began when "a large number of well-to-do farmers ... had foolishly joined one of the proscribed superstitious sects which had flourished in that mountainous district from time immemorial." The sect obviously included a well-developed invulnerability ritual for "these fanatic sectarians believed that by repeating certain charmed formulas, while burning incense and kowtowing before their tutelary idols, they could make themselves impervious to wounds of any kind, would be mysteriously preserved from the sword or spear thrusts, and even against bullets."[65] Then in 1882, a rather minor White Lotus uprising, which included only a few dozen people and was immediately put down, broke out in Chiping.[66] This provoked a wave of suppression which swept through the entire province, setting off "a reign of stark terror throughout the mountain villages" of the south.

At this point, a "man of letters" recalled the clause in the treaties guaranteeing protection of Christians. The S.V.D. account continues:

> This knowledge suggested to him the idea of becoming a Christian in order to escape persecution as a member of a proscribed sect. When he communicated this idea to others who were also in danger, the good news spread like wildfire and before long thousands of those who had belonged to the sects began requesting reception into the Catholic Church for themselves and their entire families.

Soon a representative was sent to contact the Catholic bishop in Jinan, and when the bishop referred the matter to the newly arrived S.V.D. missionaries, they saw it as "too good an opportunity to miss." Anzer hastened to the scene and before long had a wealth of new converts eager to join his church. To lead the new congregation, "an influential man who had formerly been the leader of one of the forbidden sects was formally appointed by Pro-Vicar Anzer to serve as lay leader of the new Christian community in his locality. This proved to be an excellent and fruitful arrangement."[67]

In this example, as in Popkin's scenario, the initiative clearly came from the villagers, not the missionaries; and it came for fundamentally political reasons: they needed protection. Where Popkin's model does not seem to fit is his suggestion that the political conflict is likely to involve a "divergence between collective and individual interest." Clearly the conflict here was between the state and the sectarian communities, and the new converts acted not as *individuals* but as members of an oppressed *group*. In northwest Shandong, where as I have noted earlier (chapter 1) community structures were considerably weaker, individual conversions, or conversions of only a few individuals or families in a village, were much more common.[68] Such a pattern also appears in the counties surrounding Jining.[69] But in the hills of the south, and in the border regions of the southwest, a more collective conversion pattern of whole villages seems to have prevailed. An S.V.D. source notes that "every family and every individual in the mountain village of Niusinchwang [Niuxinzhuang] accepted the Faith."[70] In Shan county, village conversions seem to have been common; and in Heze, as later informants put it, "villages with Christians or a church were almost entirely Christian, and in other villages, everybody was a non-Christian."[71]

The question then becomes, what kind of groups or communities were attracted to the Christian faith. In the example from Yizhou, the common denominator obviously was sectarian background. This is an extremely important example. As we have seen, Shandong had a long history of sectarian activity. But those sects have usually been linked to the Boxers themselves—not to their Christian antagonists. Now it appears that a substantial number of sectarians also became Christians—for the Yizhou example is far from unique. Very frequently the motive for such conversion was simply to obtain protection, and Protestants were approached as well as Catholics: "More than once in my experience, members of one of these ascetic communities, the Wu-wei keaou [Wu-wei jiao], have made proposals to be received by us as converts; their motive appearing, upon enquiry, to be simply the wish to obtain foreign protection from mandarin extortion under which they were suffering."[72] Commonly, they would seek to enter the Church "in a body with their leaders."[73] Sometimes their numbers could be very considerable indeed. A French Jesuit in southeastern Zhili wrote in the 1870s that the previous decade had seen five to six thousand White Lotus sectarians convert to Christianity.[74] In addition to its Yizhou converts, the S.V.D. reported substantial sectarian conversions in Shan county, Jiaxiang, Juye, and Wenshang.[75]

There seems little doubt that the most common motive for sectarian conversion to Christianity was the desire to escape government persecution. But we should not ignore the religious dimension of the experience. The regimen of the White Lotus sects was certainly much stricter than that required by ordinary folk religion, and it tended to orient people toward a concern for the afterlife and a quest for salvation. Some missionaries found their orientation toward a "true god" (*zhen-zhu* or *zhen tian-ye*) to be monotheistic. This—in addition to the sects' concern for the spiritual in man, for sin and a future life—helped explain why "the Christian doctrines have been very attractive to these sectaries."[76] Others noted that many of these sectarians were simply "doctrine-lovers" in search of some satisfying faith. After trying a variety of sects, they finally ended up in the Christian church.[77] Finally, in some cases, prophecies of the sect itself—as one injunction to follow "a strange man wearing white vestments"—led sectarians to the missionaries.[78]

Even in many of these more religious conversions, one suspects that state persecution and the privileged protection enjoyed by the Christians played a role. For example, Leboucq's account of the White Lotus sect whose members converted in such numbers to his southeast Zhili church leaves one with the impression of a popular cult in an advanced state of decay. Government persecution appears to have destroyed the religiously dedicated leadership, leaving the sectarians prey to a great variety of scheming charlatans. Many of the conversions to Christianity seem to have followed the exposure of particularly blatant fraud.[79] In effect, for a "doctrine-lover," Christianity was becoming a better and better deal. The old sects were degenerating under periodic government persecution, while Christianity could offer many of the same spiritual rewards, and at much lower cost in terms of official persecution.

Because the sectarians' conversion to Christianity is in such marked contrast to the linkage usually drawn between the Boxers and the White Lotus or Eight Trigrams sects, the examples we have just seen are extremely important. But the sectarians were just one of several types who were easily attracted to Christianity by the protection which it afforded. Especially in southwestern Shandong, an area noted for endemic lawlessness, it was not at all unusual for bandits to seek the protection of the Church. The oral history surveys make this charge repeatedly, one peasant stating bluntly: "At that time most of the converted Christians were bandits."[80] Often officials required to solve bandit cases within strict time limits sent out yamen runners who made indiscriminate arrests. When the priests would promise protection from such official harassment, whole villages would join the Church.[81] Occasionally the missionaries' own accounts will reveal the same pattern:

"The town [of Zhangqiao] has the reputation of being a nest of ruthless and incorrigible robbers. Many widows residing there with orphaned children mourn the loss of their husbands, caught red-handed while taking part in raids on the homes of wealthy families, and executed after undergoing terrible tortures. After the depredations of the Changkiao bandits had taxed the patience of county officials beyond the breaking point, preparations were made to raze the village to the ground and banish all of its inhabitants. When all but one of the families residing there decided to embrace the Catholic religion, the missionary pleaded effectively with the Mandarin for clemency on their behalf. Thus Changkiao escaped destruction. Tamed by their Christian faith these former brigands became law-abiding farmers and exemplary Catholics—another conquest of Divine Grace.[82]

One wonders whether the bandits' conversion was as total as this inspirational tale would have us believe.

Finally there were undoubtedly many suffering economically, who turned to the Church for financial support. That most Christians were poor goes without saying. In the words of the Chinese official: "The Catholics' clothes cannot cover their bodies. Their eating quarters are not separated from their sleeping places. They store their beds and stoves in one corner—that is how poor they are."[83] The Shandong University surveys repeatedly mention Christians who joined in order to get food that the Church would distribute.[84] This was also a common Protestant complaint against the Catholics,[85] though we have already seen what famine relief did to increase Protestant converts.

But occasionally the missionary would intervene to protect converts from economic suffering of human origin. George Stenz, whose accounts I have cited so often, tells of a group of tenants on the hereditary estate of the descendants of the Confucian disciple Zeng-zi who were much oppressed by the owner's underlings. They came to Stenz for support. When he talked to the landlord and accepted the tenants as converts, the depredations of the underlings ceased. News of this example was so compelling that soon ten nearby communities joined the church.[86] The Shandong University surveys also show how the Church could enhance a tenant's power in relation to his landlord: "In those days, if a villager had been abused by someone, he would just convert. After becoming a Christian he would not be abused. Some converted and even in years of a good harvest they would give less rent and insist that their crops had been flooded and the harvest was poor."[87]

There can be little doubt, then, that the considerable temporal powers of the Christian church had enormous impact on the type of converts that it attracted. This is certainly not to say that none converted for purely religious reasons. Far less is it to say that sectarians, bandits, and the poor could not become sincere Christians. There can be no doubt that both Catholic and Protestant congregations included substantial numbers of law-abiding and morally upright peasants. But it is also true that conversion to Christianity and especially to Catholicism was most attractive to those in need of protection—be it from the police powers of the state, the economic exactions of the landlord, or the threat of poverty and potential starvation in a hostile environment. That being the case, the converts to Christianity unquestionably included a disproportionate number of sectarians, bandits, and the poor. To the extent that this was the *imperium in imperio* which the Church was seeking to protect, it was not likely to gain a very happy reputation with the rest of the population.

THE 1890s: CHRISTIANS IN THE HIGH TIDE OF IMPERIALISM

I have argued in this chapter that an intimate link existed between imperialism and Christian missionary activity: both were part of the same process whereby Westerners sought to impose their ways on the rest of the world. I have also argued that the Catholic Church in particular acted in China as an autonomous political institution, which attracted converts by virtue of its power to offer protection and support. To the extent that these two propositions are correct, it follows that missionary success would be greatest, and conversions would come most rapidly, at such times as the imperialist forces were most aggressive in displaying their powers. For this reason, we should expect to see unprecedented growth of Christian congregations in the 1890s. We will not be disappointed.

The 1890s were of course the classic decade of imperialism throughout the world. The industrialization of France and a newly unified Germany made those two nations genuine threats to England's domination of world trade. As the free trade theories of Manchester gave way to the quest for colonial dominion, the European powers completed the partition of Africa. On the home front, the "yellow press" fanned the flames of jingoist sentiment; Rudyard Kipling was the favorite author, with his tales of imperialist conquest by tough young Englishmen bearing the "White Man's Burden." In Asia, Japan joined the colonial powers when it seized Taiwan in the Sino-Japanese War; and the U.S. soon followed suit, taking the Philippines as its prize of the Spanish-American War. In between, China was the focus of world attention as the Great Powers competed for spheres of influence in the Scramble for Concessions, and the pundits of the press debated whether or not China would continue to exist as a unified empire. Few doubted that in this context, the Powers would be treating China a good deal more roughly. In 1896, when Claude McDonald was named British Minister to China after a decade of service to the Empire in Africa, Sir Robert Hart wrote that "those of us who have succeeded so badly by treating Chinese as educated and civilized ought now to be ready to yield the ground to a man versed in negro methods and ignorant of the East."[88]

China was as much a focus of missionary energy in the 1890s as she was a focus of world politics. The two were obviously related. The missionaries easily borrowed the militant language of imperialism as they sought to "conquer the heathen" on behalf of Christ. When the Protestant missionaries in China met together in Shanghai in 1890, A. J. H. Moule asked rhetorically in one address:

> Is Christ's Church militant indeed on earth? Are we all bound to fight manfully under His banner against sin, the world and the devil? Has the Son of God indeed gone forth to war? And is our lot cast, whether missionaries or foreign residents, in this advanced post in an enemy's country, where a special assault is being delivered, not on men and political systems, but on the principalities, the powers, the rulers of the darkness of this world and the spiritual wickedness of the great, the real spiritual world?[89]

Needless to say, Moule answered all of his rhetorical questions in the affirmative. Missionaries were vital partners in the effort to remake the world to Western specifications. "Christian missions and commerce," Moule went on, "are often spoken of as the great forces which must enlighten and regenerate the world; and it is of the utmost importance that these forces should work in harmony."[90] In the United States and Great Britain, the late nineteenth century saw an alliance of progressivism and imperialism which, in the words of Arthur Schlesinger, Jr., "no doubt confirmed missionary faith in political, even in military, intervention as a means of both individual and social salvation.... 'From the muscular Christianity of the last generation to the imperial Christianity of the present day,' wrote J. A. Hobson, 'is but a single step.'"[91]

China was to be a primary target of this new imperial Christianity. By the 1880s and 1890s East Asia surpassed the Near East and South Asia as a Protestant missionary field.[92] And in East Asia, China was certainly the most important field. Sherwood Eddy of the Student Volunteers for Foreign Missions, whose slogan—"The Evangelization of the World in this Generation"—so typified the aggressive optimism of the age, would later write that "China was the goal, the lodestar, the great magnet that drew us all in those days."[93] And many indeed were drawn. The number of Protestant missionaries in China more than doubled, from a count of 1,296 in 1889 to 2,818 by 1900.[94] In the critical province of Shandong, the increase in Catholic missionaries was even more dramatic. Between 1887 and 1901 their numbers increased more than five-fold, from sixteen to eighty-five. Much of this increase came from the S.V.D.—surely the most visible Catholic example of Hobson's "imperial Christianity." Their numbers increased from just four in 1887 to forty-three in the year after the Boxers.[95]

Many of the effects of this higher stage of imperialism, and of the missionary onslaught which accompanied it, would only be seen in the latter half of the decade, after the Sino-Japanese War and the Scramble for Concessions. For these, the reader will have to await our discussion in chapters 5–7. But since the Scramble began with the German seizure of Jiaozhou Bay (Qingdao) in retaliation for the murder of two German missionaries, one may rest assured that we will find there further support for our argument that missionary activity, imperialism, and Christian conversion were all linked in a complex, interconnected dynamic. But the theme can also be illustrated in the first part of the decade when missionary incidents in the Yangzi Valley spurred the Great Powers to make ever more stringent demands on the Chinese state. As Edmund S. Wehrle says in his study of Sino-British relations during this decade: "At that moment in history world politics and missionary politics became almost completely intermixed."[96]

The trouble began in the spring of 1891, when a series of antimissionary riots swept through the lower Yangzi Valley. Then in 1895, there were anti-Christian riots in Chengdu, Sichuan, in May and June, followed by the Gutian (Fujian) massacre of eleven men, women, and children in August. Following these incidents, the British minister in Beijing threatened to use the Royal Navy against Chinese ports in an aggressive display of gunboat diplomacy which succeeded in bringing about the degradation of the former governor-general of Sichuan and six other officials, the execution of thirty-one perpetrators of the violence, and the imprisonment or banishment of thirty-eight more.[97]

Because the incidents of 1895 followed immediately upon the Sino-Japanese War, it is extremely difficult to separate the effects of those two events. But aside from the Yangzi riots, 1891 was a pretty quiet year in China, and their effect as far away as Shandong was readily discernible. On June 13, the imperial court issued a clear edict blaming the attacks on outlaws, stressing the noble motives of missionaries and the need to protect churches, and ordering the immediate resolution of all outstanding missionary cases. In July, Li Hong-zhang, then governor-general of Zhili, reported the printing and distribution of the edict for posting throughout Zhili and Shandong. On September 13, a second edict was issued complaining of the lack of action in solving outstanding missionary cases, and threatening local officials with full responsibility for any future incidents which should occur in their jurisdictions. The edicts were thoroughly one-sided, placing all blame on the opponents of Christianity, and the foreigners welcomed them as the best ever issued.[98]

The American Presbyterians soon found that with this new turn of events, long-standing property disputes in Jinan and Jining were quickly settled. They wrote that the Yangzi riots had "worked only good for us."[99] But as usual, it was the Catholics who reaped the greatest rewards. The American missionary Henry Porter in Pang-zhuang reported in 1893 that "there has been for some time past a sort of irruption of the Roman Catholics in many of the villages about us." He linked it to better official protection, and the pressure to settle disputes which had resulted from the earlier edicts. "The Roman Catholic leaders," he felt, "have been inclined to presume on the new position." The process was a typical one, and critical too was the fact that now, more than ever, the temporal power of the Church was a magnet for those seeking protection: "In the majority of cases, the movement has been under the direction of some leading man in the village who had no conception of Christian truth and no purpose but to get a little advantage over the local official and the shielding power of the Catholic Priest."[100] It may be that Porter's interpretation was overly cynical (and perhaps a bit jealous of Catholic successes), but there is no reason to doubt the basic pattern that he perceived. It fits perfectly with the dynamic of Christian penetration which we have seen throughout this chapter.

Thus, step by step, the stage was set for the outbreak of violent popular action against the Christians. China had been defeated before in war with the West, but never had she been so humbled as in the 1890s—defeated by Japan, hounded by the Western powers demanding the dismissal of officials for anti-missionary incidents, and soon to be carved up into "spheres of influence." Trade grew rapidly; the Treaty of Shimonoseki permitted foreign factories in the treaty ports;

telegraph lines criss-crossed the empire; and plans were laid for a railway system. But to the ordinary villager of north China, the unequal treaties, the gunboat diplomacy, the concessions along the coast were of little consequence. If such folk ever saw a foreigner it was certainly a missionary—and the foreign presence meant the "foreign religion." But that "foreign religion" was inextricably linked to all the other faces of Western imperialism in China. The more China was humbled, the greater the relative power of the Church. And the stronger the Church became, the more likely it was to flex its muscles—for every demonstration of Christian power attracted more converts, and served the greater goal of winning the Chinese to Christ.

But clearly there was a limit to all this. If the Chinese state was incapable of resisting the ceaseless demands of the Christians and their foreign supporters, sooner or later the "heathen" would form an organization of their own to fight back. And they did. They called it the Da-dao hui: the Big Sword Society.

CHAPTER FOUR

The Big Sword Society

My investigations reveal that the Big Sword Society is the heterodox sect, Armor of the Golden Bell (Jin-zhong zhao). Its origins lie in the distant past. Although local officials have proscribed it, its roots have never been cut. Last year the coastal borders were unsettled [because of the Sino-Japanese War], and when people heard that this sect could ward off bullets, it spread all the more, so that there was hardly a place without it. The stupid thought that they could protect themselves and their families. The crafty used it to carry out their violent schemes. Then roving bandits (*you-fei*) came from outside to stir things up and crowds gathered to cause trouble.[1]

Thus wrote the Shandong governor Li Bing-heng explaining the origins of the Big Sword Society. In the summer of 1896, the society had instigated widespread attacks on native Christians along the Shandong-Jiangsu border. Like the later Boxers, the Big Swords claimed to have rituals that made them invulnerable to bullets; and contemporary witnesses often equated the first Boxers of northwest Shandong with the Big Sword Society. So our account of the rise of the Boxer movement must begin with the Big Sword Society.

THE EARLY HISTORY OF THE
ARMOR OF THE GOLDEN BELL

Though there is mention of a "Big Sword Society" in northern Anhui in 1735,[2] we know nothing about the nature of this group, and our attention must turn to the formal name of the society which reemerged in the 1890s: "the Armor of the Golden Bell." The Armor of the Golden Bell existed at least since the late eighteenth century as a martial arts technique for achieving invulnerability. Several of its practitioners became associated with sectarian activities around the time of the Eight Trigrams uprising of 1813. There were the usual charms written on red paper, which were burned and swallowed, and spells—some of which appealed for the assistance of a patriarch (zu-shi).[3] But it seems clear that the Armor of the Golden Bell was a *technique* and not any sort of organization, and those who learned this technique, like other boxers whom we have examined earlier, had only tenuous connections to the sects.

A typical example was Zhang Luo-jiao from Ganji in Guan county, Shandong, whom we met in chapter 2. Zhang, like his father and younger brother, was a Daoist priest, and had learned boxing and certain healing methods from an in-law in 1782. Then in 1793, a teacher from Henan taught him the Armor of the Golden Bell and gave him two charms. "From the time he learned the methods (*fa*) of the Armor of the Golden Bell, he boxed and taught disciples for profit." His association with the Eight Trigrams sect came only later, in 1800, when he learned the "True Emptiness spell" (*zhen-kong zhou-yu*) from a Li trigram sectarian from the same Eighteen Villages area of Guan county. But Zhang claimed to have left the sect when his teacher kept coming to collect donations, and though a second-generation student of his was involved in the 1813 conspiracy, I have seen no evidence contradicting Zhang's claim that he had broken with the sect and was not involved in the rebellion.[4]

It would seem, then, that one hundred years before our era the Armor of the Golden Bell was an established boxing technique on the north China plain, and—as the name implies—particularly associated with invulnerability rituals, though at this time only against knives and swords. That practitioners of this technique got involved with sectarians (and thus appeared on the historical record) is without doubt. But the relationship seems to have been individual and often ephemeral. What of the Armor of the Golden Bell of the 1890s?

Li Bing-heng did call the Armor of the Golden Bell a "heterodox sect," and a wide range of informants from southwest Shandong have identified the Big Sword Society to oral historians as associated with the Kan trigram.[5] Historians in the P.R.C. remain divided on the relationship of the Big Swords to the sects—some arguing that the society's origins were clearly with the White Lotus sects; others that it

was only a group of martial artists.[6] A definitive conclusion is probably impossible at this time, but other appearances of the Armor of the
Golden Bell in north China during this decade are instructive. In the
Northeast, a captured teacher claimed to have learned the technique
from a traveling Daoist priest some years before, and confessed to
making money by teaching people to "evade weapons and the
kalpa."[7] The mention of the "kalpa" links this group quite clearly to
the millennial tradition of the White Lotus, but it is a linkage that
never appeared among the Shandong groups. One is led to believe,
therefore, that some prior connection to the White Lotus did exist,
and that the connection was reflected in the belief systems of some
groups still active in the late nineteenth century. But in Shandong, the
evidence suggests that the link had grown quite tenuous. No longer
do we see any of the key elements of White Lotus ritual: worship of
the Eternal Mother, preparation for the kalpa, or belief in the coming
of the Buddha Maitreya. To the extent that these were the defining
features of the White Lotus sect, the Big Swords did not belong. Their
function and concern were essentially military—and their "heterodox" rituals were all for the purpose of achieving invulnerability. If
in the mid-Qing, such invulnerability was particularly attractive to
those preparing for the millennium (or for a rebellion), by the late Qing,
bandits armed with firearms were so common that invulnerability
rituals now became important to those seeking only to defend their
homes and communities.

THE SHANDONG-JIANGSU BORDER REGION

The home of the Big Sword Society was southwest Shandong and
the northern corner of Xuzhou prefecture, across the border in
Jiangsu. As we have seen in our brief survey of Shandong geography
(chapter 1), it was not altogether a poor region. In particular the key
strongholds of the society in Cao and Shan counties were in areas
slightly higher than the surrounding plains, safe from the flooding
which often affected this region between the northern and southern
courses of the Yellow River. Cotton was, and continues to be, grown
extensively in the area, and it is clear that a fair degree of commercialization had occurred, no doubt stimulated by reasonably good
access to the Grand Canal.[8]

Given even moderately effective flood control, this area could have
been fairly prosperous were it not for some crucial geopolitical facts:

the southwest corner of Shandong bordered on both Jiangsu and Henan to the south (with Anhui only about fifty kilometers further south), and Zhili to the west. The administrative geography of the area was further complicated by numerous "exclaves" in southwestern Shandong (see map 4). These were small territories lying outside the borders of the county to which they belonged. We shall have more to say about such geopolitical anomalies in chapter 5, but for now it suffices to say that they were one additional factor making this a classically difficult-to-govern border region, where bandits and smugglers could easily escape arrest by slipping across borders into adjacent jurisdictions. But this border presented even more than the usual problems. In the first place, unlike most provincial borders in China (or anywhere for that matter) the boundaries did not lie along such natural barriers as mountain crests or major rivers, but on an open plain. There was, accordingly, no physical impediment to easy movement across jurisdictions. Furthermore, unlike most hilly borders, this plain was densely populated, often prosperous, and crossed by a good deal of commercial traffic. There were, accordingly, plenty of targets of opportunity for outlaw bands. Southwest Shandong was, then, characterized by an unusual combination of borderland insecurity on the one hand, and substantial prosperity amid pockets of flood-caused impoverishment on the other. This combination produced the unique political economy of the region—featuring a flourishing extra-legal economy of salt-smuggling, opium-growing, and banditry, and a community structure of tight-knit villages with landlords who were true local patrons.

In the outlaw society of the southwest, Shandong's famed martial virtues were transformed into a "Wild West" style popular culture of violence. To this day Chinese speak of the hot tempers and readiness to fight of the natives of this region. The German missionaries reflected the common view when they described the local inhabitants as "more firm of character, braver, and less cunning than the rest, but on the other hand, also more coarse and rough."[9] Another noted that "they are feared because of their aggressive disposition and inclination to fight. Quarrels, brawls, and combats are daily occurrences in Shantung, most of all in Tsaochowfu [Caozhou]."[10] Japanese observers reported similarly on neighboring Yanzhou: "Wherever you go in the city, there is hardly a place where you do not see fights."[11]

Not surprisingly, this unruly area proved particularly difficult to control during the rebellions of the mid-nineteenth century. When

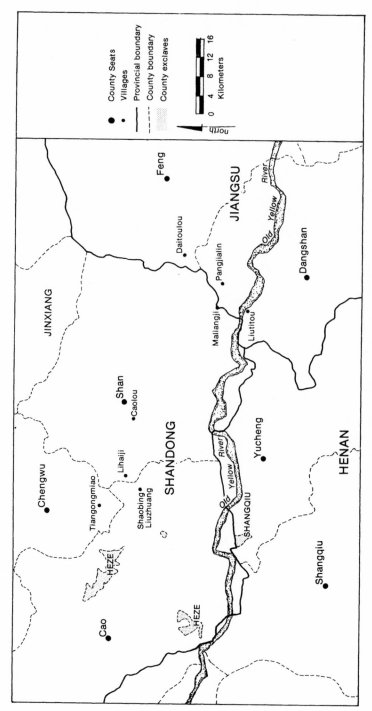

Map 4. The Shandong-Jiangsu-Henan Border Region: The Big Sword Heartland

first the Taiping and then the Nian entered the area in the 1850s, local militia organized in self defense. But soon the militia were abusing their new-found power, and a group called the Long Spears (Chang-qiang hui) rose in opposition, and increased to more than 5,000 members by 1860. All sorts of people, including many bandits, joined this organization; and eventually when the Nian attacked again, most rallied to that rebellion.[12] Even in the 1870s, which were peaceful in most of Shandong, this region had a small rebellion. A certain Zhu Zhen-guo, who made a living as a healer, claimed to be a descendant of the Ming ruling house and rose in rebellion during a prolonged drought in 1876. Poor folks from the region rallied to his banner, and he held out for almost a month before drenching rains came and his followers dispersed to return to their now cultivable fields.[13]

We have already examined, in chapter 1, the long history of ban-ditry and its integration into the structure of southwest Shandong society, but we need now to look at the specific conditions of the 1890s. Salt-smuggling had long been integral to the border economy,[14] but opium production was largely a product of the 1880s and 1890s. It was, of course, foreign trade which first introduced opium to the region, and through the 1870s Zhenjiang (the Grand Canal port which served this region) was "shown to rank first after Shanghai with regard to its opium trade."[15] By the end of the 1880s, imports began to fall off as native production increased markedly, especially in Xu-zhou.[16] In the early 1890s, Dangshan opium—product of the county in which the major 1896 Big Swords incidents occurred—was second in popularity to the Henan product in the cities of the north.[17] All this, however, was not necessarily injurious to foreign trade, for as the Maritime Customs reported as early as the 1870s: "The increase in [Zhenjiang imports destined for] Shantung is especially noticeable. One explanation given of the growth of trade in the north is that the people who have been starving over unsuccessful attempts to raise ordinary crops are now getting rich off Native Opium."[18] The expan-sion of opium production accelerated in the 1890s, as the fall in international silver prices increased the cost of the imported item, and one rather careful estimate for Xuzhou prefecture suggested that as much as one-tenth of the land was planted in poppy.[19]

With opium production expanding in an area where men were used to bearing arms and challenging the authorities, and with the Chinese state too weakened by corruption, rebellion, and foreign incursions to exert effective control, the endemic banditry of southwest Shandong was, by the 1890s, reaching epidemic proportions. Some areas had been repeatedly struck by natural disasters and especially in Dangshan, salinization and blowing sand were seriously threatening peasant livelihood.[20] When the Sino-Japanese War brought the withdrawal of local garrisons to the front, "bands of robbers began pillaging and terrorizing with reckless abandon."[21] The missionaries reported larger and more numerous bands striking even in broad daylight.[22] The "Veritable Records" for 1895 are filled with reports of major bandit attacks along the Shandong-Jiangsu-Henan border, and urgent imperial edicts commanding their prompt suppression.[23] The prefect of Caozhou, the Manchu Yu-xian—who would rise to the governorship of Shandong just as the Boxers broke out in full fury in 1899—proved exceedingly vigorous, if perhaps a bit undiscriminating, in his efforts to suppress banditry. His role there gained him notoriety in the novel *Travels of Lao Can* as something of a "butcher of Caozhou."[24]

We know a good deal less about the nature of this banditry than we would like. The documentation comes almost invariably from the side of "law and order," and it is very difficult to discern the extent to which this banditry conformed to such models as Eric Hobsbawm's "social bandit," who engaged in a primitive protest against social injustice in periods of rapid commercialization and class polarization. It is clear that bandits did not rob within their own village, and when the ties of kinship and neighborhood are added to the fact that robbery did bring resources into the local community, it is reasonable to assume that bandits could count on a degree of tacit support from their fellow villagers. It was quite natural, therefore, for some villages to be viewed as "bandit lairs," and for bandit raids to degenerate into inter-village feuds.[25] That the missionaries often became involved in such feuds, as bandits appealed for protection, we have already seen in our discussion of the S.V.D. in Shandong. But the same thing was happening to the French Jesuits across the border in Jiangsu. The history of their diocese records an amusing example of a missionary having been lured to settle in a notorious bandit lair when the robbers kindly offered their services to protect his residence. When the Frenchman left his base to preach in the surrounding villages, the bandits used the hamlet as headquarters for an extensive and lucrative fencing operation for local desperadoes.[26]

Certainly the disturbed environment of this troubled border region required a high degree of community solidarity, and that solidarity would often center about some local strongman. The area was indeed replete with powerful village magnates—in striking contrast to the paucity of such figures in northwest Shandong. Unlike the northwest, this region was rich enough to support a substantial degree of landlordism and a strong local elite. Chapter 1 has already noted the quantitatively greater extent of landlordism in the area, but equally important is the *quality* of this landlordism. In contrast to the cash-nexus landlordism of the lower Yangzi region, landlordism along the Shandong-Jiangsu border was characterized by strong ties of personal dependency on the part of tenants. Though highly exploitative, the relationship had a distinctive patron-client flavor. The Japanese agricultural economist Amano Motonosuke described in some detail the "feudal" aspects of landlordism in Cao county and Shan county as late as the 1930s. Labor services by tenants were common: washing, sending gifts, pulling carts, carding cotton, doing guard duty. Often the landlord required that the tenant periodically supply chickens, and in exchange the tenant would receive two or three plates of steamed bread (*man-tou*) at New Year. The powers of these landlords were so extensive that it was said that "they have an official's lackeys, though not an official's belly" (*you guan-chai, mei guan du-zi*).[27] Tenants were often driven like animals, so that some were known as "ox-workers" (*niu-gong*).[28]

The situation was much the same across the border in Jiangsu. One missionary reported a visit to the home of "the leading man of the section" while distributing famine relief in 1898:

> We might say to his castle, for it was surrounded with deep ditches and good walls and had two square towers, four stories high, running up above his brick dwellings. His flower-gardens, pavilions, and rare and fragrant flowers are perhaps the most beautiful in this part of Kiangsu. HE IS A VIRTUAL LORD in his neighborhood and "when he coughs half-a-dozen men stand up." At the door perhaps a hundred of his neighbors get a daily pittance. He, though the owner of 600 acres of land, is poor enough this year and the children of his own personal servants are pale and thin.[29]

The wealth of such landlords testified to the region's ability to produce a surplus sufficient for the elite to afford the extravagance of "rare and fragrant flowers," but the fortified dwellings—so different from our image of the genteel Chinese landlord in a Suzhou garden—reflected the other face of this region, its extreme insecurity. Another missionary described the situation across the border in Anhui:

Such a locality, as is well known in China, is the favoured region of lawless bands of marauders. The inhabitants live in something like a feudal state, with house and property surrounded by wall and moat, and no one goes abroad without a gun or lance, and nothing of value is transported without armed escort.[30]

Such then was the social environment in which the Big Sword Society grew and flourished in the 1890s: prosperous enough to support a strong landlord class, but with areas of poverty—especially where flooding was frequent or salinization acute. Much of the economy was based on extra-legal activities—especially salt smuggling and opium cultivation—which only enhanced the lawlessness of this border region. The local elite had long since fortified itself in walled villages, building ever more elaborate defense works against an increasingly well-armed bandit population. But when the withdrawal of Qing garrisons during the Sino-Japanese War brought an unprecedented wave of banditry, it was time to develop more effective means of self-defense. And that is precisely what the Armor of the Golden Bell promised.

THE ARMOR OF THE GOLDEN BELL

The new invulnerability technique was brought to southwest Shandong by a certain Zhao, who came from somewhere in the west—most likely from Zhili, perhaps Hejian prefecture, though he seems to have stopped in one or more places in southwestern Shandong before arriving in Shan county. One contemporary account describes this first teacher as a "wandering Daoist priest," but when he took up residence in Shan, he seems to have worked as a hired hand (*changgong*) in the village of Shaobing Liuzhuang.[31] When Zhao came is not certain. Contemporary documentary sources state that the invulnerability rituals were brought to the area only in 1894,[32] but several oral history sources say that Zhao came several decades before the 1896 uprising, and that he left well before the trouble began.[33] That Zhao was not involved in any of the militant activities of the Big Swords seems certain: he is never mentioned in any of the extant official accounts. It would seem, therefore, that his role was purely that of teacher. This separation of technical/ritual specialists (often outsiders) from the political/strategic leaders (invariably members of the village community) is not at all uncommon. One sees the same phenomenon in a twentieth-century analogue of the Big Swords, the Red Spear

Society.[34] As long as Zhao was only involved in teaching martial arts, there was no reason for the society to come to the attention of the local officials. In fact, until a local leadership group emerged, the society, as such, did not even exist.

But what exactly was Zhao teaching? Was it a set of sectarian rituals, or was it simply a boxing technique? We have earlier mentioned at least a tenuous relationship between the Armor of the Golden Bell and the White Lotus sects at the beginning of the nineteenth century, and the fact that local lore viewed the Big Sword Society as in some way associated with the Kan trigram, perhaps as its military arm. But now we must look more closely at the few sources we have on the actual rituals associated with this organization. Though several oral history sources state that Zhao fled to Shandong following the failure of a White Lotus uprising—presumably that of 1861 in southern Shandong—my suspicion is that he was strictly a martial artist, and any involvement he might have had with that uprising had little to do with sectarian beliefs.[35] But that does not mean that there was no *religious* element to his teachings. The *daotai* of Xuzhou has left us the most complete contemporary account of the ritual:

> When they study their techniques, the poor need not make an offering, but those who can, offer 6,000 Beijing cash as a gift. In the middle of the night, they kneel and receive instruction. They light lamps and burn incense, draw fresh water from a well and make offerings of it. They write charms (*fu-lu*) on white cloth. The words of the charms are vulgar and improper. There are such phrases as "Patriarch, Duke of Zhou; Immortals of the peach blossom; Golden Bell, iron armor protect my body." Those who spread the art can neither read nor write. They have others write for them. They also teach spells (*zhou*). While chanting spells they burn charms, mixing [the ashes] in water and instructing [the initiate] to kneel and drink. Then [the teacher] breathes in from above the lantern, and blows out over [the initiate's] entire body. Then he beats him with a brick and staff. After chanting the spell for three nights, one can withstand swords. It is said that after chanting for a long time, even firearms cannot harm one. It is much like breathing exercises (*yun-qi*). Where the "breath" (*qi*) moves, even a fierce chop cannot penetrate. But if one loses concentration, then the blade will enter. The simple people do not understand, and think it a magical technique.[36]

Almost all other accounts of Armor of the Golden Bell ritual are similar. They stress the recitation of spells and swallowing of charms, and then the fundamental martial arts training of pounding the body with bricks and swords (*pai-zhuan pai-dao*). Another contemporary source attributed the rapid spread of the Big Sword Society to its "use of *gong-fu* of the entire body to achieve invulnerability. Thus it is also called the Armor of the Golden Bell, the Iron-cloth Shirt (*Tie-bu shan*) or the Shadowless Whip (*Wu-ying bian*)."[37] The oral history sources are similar. They stress the beating of the body to build up resistance to injury, and the reciting of very simple spells. The operative core, then, of the Big Swords' martial arts exercises was precisely that sort of *qi-gong* or *gong-fu* that one can see practiced by Chinese martial artists and circus performers to this day.

It was the incantations and charms of the Big Sword Society that distinguished it from other martial arts schools in the region—most notably the Great Red Boxing (Da-hong quan).[38] These spells were regarded with great seriousness, and there were strict rules of secrecy. "A son does not tell his father; a father does not tell his son."[39] When they went into battle, members would wear large red protective amulets (*dou-dou* or *dou-du*) on their chests.[40] The society worshiped at least one god, "The True Martial God" (*Zhen-wu shen* or *Zhen-wu di*, also known as *Xuan-tian shang-di*), as its patriarch.[41] Some have noted this fact to link the Big Sword Society to the White Lotus, because it is said that Wang Lun, the Shandong rebel of 1774, also worshiped the True Martial God.[42] But the True Martial God was a very common god of Chinese popular religion, and particularly associated with the protection of local communities against banditry.[43] In the choice of a patriarch, the Big Swords seem much more within the spirit of conventional folk religion than any sectarian tradition.

The one fairly extensive charm which I have seen, while full of the usual obscure and ambiguous language, is also devoid of specifically sectarian content. Instead it appeals to a multitude of divine forces for assistance in achieving invulnerability. A rough and tentative translation might read as follows:

> Let the judicial officer come to the spirit's place on the charm;
> The iron clan, the Kitchen God protect my body.
> Amida's instructions pacify the three sides;
> Iron helmet, iron armor, wearing iron clothes.
> A gold-topped bronze pagoda sealed with a rock;
> Sword chops, ax slashes—I knock them away with one kick.[44]

There is no contemporary evidence to suggest that the belief system of the Big Sword Society involved calling down gods to possess one's body (*jiang-shen fu-ti*), which was such a central part of the Boxer ritual in 1899–1900. Most of the oral history record, and all of that from former participants and from the core area of the society in Cao and Shan counties, makes no mention of such a ritual. When I visited this area in 1980, and met the grandson of the principal Big Sword Society leader, a man who had helped reactivate the Big Swords to fight the Japanese during the War of Resistance, he confirmed the fact that possession was not part of the ritual.[45] Thus despite certain obvious linkages to both earlier sectarians and later Boxers, the Big Swords of the 1890s showed important differences in both belief systems and ritual. In its essence, the Big Sword Society was an association of martial artists, whose technique was aided by a rudimentary set of charms and spells which helped to provide the confidence and concentration so necessary for the *gong-fu* to succeed.

The teacher Zhao settled in the small village—perhaps sixty to eighty families—of Shaobing Liuzhuang, near the eastern border of Cao county. There his leading pupil was Liu Shi-duan. According to family tradition, Liu was 43 in 1896,[46] and had a fair degree of education, having attended school between the ages of seven and twenty *sui*.* Though he took the examination for the lowest *sheng-yuan* degree, he never passed, but purchased instead the *jian-sheng* degree, placing him at the lowest fringe of the gentry class. He was the head of the leading family in his village, and possessed better than 100 *mu* of land—quite a large holding in this fertile area, where a family could survive on a mere two *mu* per head. Back home after completing school, Liu played the role of local patron—known for his generosity, and entertaining a fairly constant stream of visitors.[47]

Sometime in his thirties, Liu learned the Armor of the Golden Bell from the itinerant Zhao, and probably in the early 1890s he began to collect disciples from his own and neighboring villages. The most notable of these were to become leaders of the Big Swords in their own villages, and they seem to have been people much like Liu himself. The one of whom we know the most was Cao De-li, a wealthy peasant in his thirties, from the Shan county village of Caolou, almost all of whose male residents joined the society. Cao's was the leading household of the village, but repeated family division had left him with far less resources than his grandfather, who had owned 300 *mu*. Cao himself probably owned about 50 *mu*, which still would have left him

*Chinese ages are counted in *sui*. A child is considered to be one *sui* at birth, and an additional *sui* is added to the age at each Chinese New Year.

with a comfortable livelihood—and certainly with the reflected glory of his family's earlier stature.[48] Peng Gui-lin, from the market town Daliji, was another student of Liu's and also a man of some substance, with 100–200 *mu* of his own and a maternal uncle who was extremely wealthy, allegedly owning over 2,000 *mu* of land.[49] In Zhouzhuang in Cao county, the Big Sword leader was the "stockade lord" (*zhai-zhu*), Zhou Yun-jie.[50]

General descriptions, in the Shandong University survey materials, of leaders and members of the Big Sword Society are basically consistent with these portraits of the most famous leaders. "The Big Sword Society's internal composition was very complex," said one peasant. "The first group was landlords and rich peasants. They joined to oppose 'bandits.' "[51] Since the object of the society was to defend against the spreading bandit scourge, it is natural that those with something to protect were the most likely to join. "The Big Sword Society was for the purpose of protecting one's home. Most members had land. Landlords also joined. The very poor didn't join, because the poor had no land—no home to protect. Big Sword Society members had to burn ten cash worth of incense each day. The poor couldn't afford this, so they didn't join."[52] But many accounts also reveal how tenants' personal dependency on landlords could draw them into the organization. "Big Sword Society members were mostly landlords and rich peasants. The very poor did not join, but tenants had to learn—in order to watch over their landlord's home."[53] According to Liu Shi-duan's son: "Both poor and rich joined the Big Sword Society. The poor joined to help their landlords watch their homes, and they could get something to eat and drink and some entertainment from their landlords."[54] One last informant gives what I think is perhaps the most cogent analysis of the class composition of the society: "Big Sword Society members were wealthy middle peasants, rich peasants, and small landlords. Large landlords did not learn [this technique]; they had their tenants learn. Most members were tenants. Those who personally controlled [the organization] were wealthy middle peasants and rich peasants."[55]

The only change I would make to this last testimony would be to add "village landlords" to the list of those who controlled the organization—and probably put that group in first place. In fact, the leaders of the Big Sword Society were probably very similar, if not indeed identical, to the authors of the 1896 "Program Respectfully Suggesting the Establishment of a Militia in Shan County," which we have cited earlier. The criticism of large landlords' engrossing, of their cruel treatment of tenants and hired laborers, and their selfish and short-sighted unwillingness to make loans even to neighbors and kinsmen sounds very much like the voice of a village landlord of moderate means, who saw the need to maintain the village community by a variety of means as a defense against spreading banditry.[56] In that published program, the means proposed was the orthodox one of "militia," but in 1895–96, the far more common and successful mechanism for defense against banditry was the Big Sword Society.

BIG SWORDS, BANDITS, AND OFFICIALS

In the spring of 1895, banditry along the Shandong-Jiangsu border had become serious enough to attract the attention of the emperor, in part because the court feared the interception of ammunition shipments to the troops then fighting the Japanese.[57] Perhaps typically, the first reports of large bandit gangs—and then of the Armor of the Golden Bell which mobilized against them—came not from local officials, who preferred to stress the orderliness of their districts, but from imperial censors. The censors, interestingly enough, were particularly worried about the "heterodox techniques" of the Armor of the Golden Bell and the Iron-cloth Shirt. But the court continued to stress the bandit danger, ordering the Shandong governor Li Bing-heng to "annihilate" the bandits, but only to "find ways to disperse" the Armor of the Golden Bell.[58] The key local official in this area was the Caozhou prefect, Yu-xian, soon to be promoted to *daotai* of all south Shandong. Yu-xian responded enthusiastically to the imperially ordered campaign against the bandits. By June, Li Bing-heng could report that Yu-xian had arrested hundreds and killed dozens. The oral histories of the area reveal a vivid popular memory of the wooden cages outside Yu-xian's yamen in which captured bandits were confined until they died of exhaustion and starvation.[59]

Credit for success in the campaign against the bandits does not belong entirely to Yu-xian. Local officials were also busy organizing militia forces,[60] and that no doubt created a pretext for the Big Sword Society to act as a legitimate village defense force. The Big Swords proved to be a potent ally in the anti-bandit campaign. The Xuzhou *daotai* left this detailed report on the society's methods:

> At this time Caozhou was suffering from banditry, and the officials and people both relied heavily on [the Big Sword Society]. Once a person

learned its techniques, the robbers would not dare oppress him. If a theft occurred, the society's members rushed in to search the robbers' nest, and were sure to seize the robber without regard to their own safety. At first they sent their captives to the officials for prosecution. Then because the officials had to treat each according to the facts of the case, and could not kill them all, the people were unhappy. Thus later they seized robbers and just killed them, and no longer sent them to the officials.

Gradually, then, the Big Sword Society moved from a close collaboration with the authorities to an arrogation of official functions. But even while recognizing this, the *daotai* praised its members brave and magnanimous spirit, and insisted that they never asked any compensation beyond food to sustain them during peace-keeping operations. If a captive pleaded for mercy, he would be released only after making a public written promise never to transgress again. The effects of all this, the *daotai* claimed, were nothing short of miraculous: "In recent years in Heze, Chengwu, Shan, Dingtao and Cao counties, there has not been a single robber. This has all been due to the power of the Big Sword Society."[61]

The Big Swords were certainly acting with well-recognized official toleration, if not outright encouragement. Though Yu-xian would later claim that "when I was Caozhou prefect, I thought their actions close to heterodoxy and strictly forbid them,"[62] the reality was no doubt closer to that reported by the Shandong governor in 1898: "Because they made no trouble, the local officials, while putting out proclamations prohibiting [the society], did not press it too closely, as it had been going on for some time."[63] The local population understood this sort of official double-talk perfectly. Because of the imperial edicts of early 1895, it had been necessary to post notices prohibiting the society. But by their actions, the officials could show their encouragement: "When the Sword Society captured outlaws and sent them to the officials, they were praised for their bravery in seizing bandits and given handsome bounties as encouragement. The members of the society were all moved, and happily aided the officials in catching bandits."[64]

When Liu Shi-duan captured the notorious bandit leader "Rice-grain Yue the Second" (Yue Er-mi-zi), the Big Swords were much praised by the authorities. It was even rumored (falsely, I believe) that Liu was rewarded with a button of the third rank.[65] It was by such actions that the people judged the officials' attitudes, and Yu-xian was certainly setting the tone. As a result, the oral history sources record very clearly that "Yu-xian did not kill [members of] the Big Sword Society; he encouraged them and used them to attack bandits." "Prefect Yu sent down a proclamation saying we should learn from the Big Sword Society and oppose banditry."[66]

The officials' attitude is hardly surprising. They had been ordered to suppress banditry, and the Big Swords were lending powerful support to the effort. Furthermore, there was nothing at all threatening in the social composition of the society: it was commanded by the natural leaders of the village communities, whose support the government had always relied upon for the maintenance of rural order. Even while claiming to have prohibited the society's heterodox techniques, Yu-xian would note that "many good and wealthy households also practice them to protect their families";[67] and Li Bing-heng would note the Big Swords' cooperation with the orthodox defenders of the local order, the militia heads, in arresting bandits and delivering them to the authorities.[68] "Even the gentry," noted the Xuzhou *daotai*, "have intercourse with them."[69] These were good, solid, property-owning villagers (Chinese yeomen, in effect) seeking to protect their families in a bandit-ridden countryside. How could local officials possibly prohibit their activities?

And so the society grew dramatically throughout 1895 and into 1896, and its activities became ever more open. In the spring of 1896, there was a spectacular celebration of their patriarch's birthday at a temple near the Shan county seat. For four days, two operas were staged simultaneously in what was certainly an enormous public relations success for the society.[70] As always, an opera brought together people from throughout the border region and provided an ideal opportunity to forge linkages among Big Sword groups in individual villages. According to local lore, Yu-xian disguised himself as a fortune-teller and attended this opera to check on the Big Swords' growing popularity. Many accounts even claim he was found out, caught, and later released.[71] If these accounts are true, the prefect certainly did nothing to check the Big Swords' growth—though he must have been impressed by their popularity. As one final indication of the society's spectacular spread, and some hint of trouble to come, let me quote again the report of the Xuzhou *daotai*, Ruan Zu-tang:

> As they spread underground and grow in secret, their party becomes steadily more troublesome; but within their own territory, they never steal, rape, or kidnap. People all praise their chivalrous spirit (*xia-yi*) and hasten to join them. Great households (*da-hu*) in the villages hire them as

guards; and even the army, counties, bureaus, and customs posts recruit them for defense. Thus they spread and proselytize more and more. They are most numerous in Shandong, next Henan, then Anhui. Xuzhou borders on Shandong and recently people [here] have joined the society. In all there are about 20,000 to 30,000.[72]

Others put their numbers as high as 100,000.[73] There is no evidence that such large numbers were linked by any unified chain of command. Rather, the Big Sword groups in any village would have one leader (usually from the leading family of the village), and he would be linked by personal or master-disciple ties to leaders in other villages. It would be through such ties that major anti-bandit operations involving several villages would be mobilized. As loose as this organization was, it made the Big Swords powerful enough so that sooner or later, they were going to cause problems. It was hardly accidental that the problems they caused involved another fast growing and independent force along the Shandong-Jiangsu border—the Catholic Church.

THE BIG SWORD SOCIETY AND THE CATHOLICS

As we seek the origins of violent conflict between village defense organizations and Christian congregations, it is always necessary to keep one eye focused on the particular local problems which activated the peasant participants, and the other eye on the more general provincial and national political situation which formed the world within which all officials and most politically active individuals operated—be they Chinese gentry or foreign missionaries. While the Big Sword Society was certainly the most dynamic force operating along the Shandong-Jiangsu border in 1895–96, on the national scene these were years of foreign and Christian assertiveness. It was, we should recall, in the summer of 1895 that the Chengdu riot and the Gutian massacres occurred. These brought unprecedented, but successful, foreign demands for the dismissal and degradation of high Chinese officials. Following this example, and the Sino-Japanese War's dramatic demonstration of Qing enfeeblement, several Western Powers began pressing the Chinese more aggressively over missionary cases. Notable among these were the Germans, who were particularly outraged over a near riot which occurred in late June 1895, on the occasion of another attempt by Bishop Anzer to gain a permanent residence in the city of Yanzhou. The threats of the German minister in Beijing reached a new height when in response to events in Yanzhou he warned the Zongli Yamen: "If your esteemed government is unable strenuously to suppress [these disturbances] and give more protection [to Christians], then my government will have no alternative but to devise methods to protect them itself."[74]

We have seen that both Chinese conversions and Christian aggressiveness in lawsuits tended to increase as the power of the foreign church was made manifest. We would expect, then, Christian missionary successes at the same time as the Big Sword Society was growing so rapidly. The coincidence was hardly accidental. Both groups were responding to the weakness of the Chinese state. The Catholic Church was essentially growing at the expense of the state—protecting converts against its police powers, or exerting its influence to dictate the settlement of lawsuits. The Big Sword Society was assuming responsibility for local defense that the state was incapable of providing. Both groups were thus certain to expand in response to the demonstrated incapacity of the Qing state in the Sino-Japanese War. Their eventual collision is hardly surprising.

We cannot, however, be content with general causes of political conflict—we must return to the particular. Here we find a variety of reasons for the Big Sword Society's shift from bandit suppression to anti-Christian activities. One simple reason, hardly unexpected given what we have seen of Catholic methods on both sides of the Shandong-Jiangsu border, was that bandits became Christians:

> In the twentieth year of Guang-xu [1894, but the date should be 1895] the Big Sword Society attacked "Rice-grain Yue the Second." He had 3,000 people with nothing to eat or wear, who stole things from the wealthy. So the Big Sword Society attacked them. After the Big Sword Society had quelled "Rice Grain Yue," Yue's followers, fearing that the rich people would arrest them, all joined the Catholic Church.[75]

Another source of conflict arose when Catholics questioned the efficacy of the Big Swords' invulnerability-bestowing rituals: "When the Catholics did not believe [the Big Swords] could resist spears and swords, and accused them of false claims, the society members became the enemies of the Catholics."[76] Each of these organizations, after all, had an important religious dimension, and the Christian antipathy toward all "pagan" beliefs made the two irreconcilable. Each, therefore, threatened the other on purely religious grounds. The successes of the Big Sword Society naturally caused people to disbelieve Catholic claims that "pagan" gods were powerless; and conversely, on a concrete psychological level, to the extent that Catholics could cast doubt on the efficacy of Armor of the Golden Bell charms, the confidence, concentration, and courage which were so much the source of the *gong-fu*'s power would be correspondingly weakened.

These factors were certainly behind the conflict between the Big Swords and the Christians, but when we focus even more microscopically on the precise incidents over which the struggles arose, we are brought once again to a picture whose most striking aspect is the struggle for power, influence, and territory. There is only one documented conflict with the Christians in which Liu Shi-duan and his closest disciple Cao De-li became directly involved. It took place in February 1896, on the border of Cao, Shan, and Chengwu counties. A pharmacist by the name of Hao He-sheng, native of Shanxi, attempting to clear his books at the end of the lunar year, went to collect a debt from a Christian convert Lü Deng-shi. Lü tried to put him off, and an argument broke out in the course of which Hao accused Lü of using his Christian status to evade his obligations. A relative of Lü's, Lü Cai, then joined the fray, accusing Hao of being a member of the White Lotus sect. Hao returned the compliment by accusing Lü Cai of joining the newly established Catholic congregation to cover up his past history as a bandit. Once this round of mutual recriminations ran its course, the three dispersed. Lü Cai, however, was not content to let the matter rest, and he went to the catechist of the local church, a certain Zhang Lian-zhu from Dongchang, and claimed that Hao had insulted the Christian religion. Zhang promptly gathered together a band of Christians armed with a variety of primitive weapons, and went to pick a fight with Hao, but never found him.

The next day was a market day at nearby Lihaiji in Shan county, and Hao went to sell his medicine. Zhang gathered his band and followed him, but Hao hid. Hearing that the Big Sword Society leader Cao De-li had also come to the market, Hao sought him out and asked his help. Cao was happy to oblige, gathered some of his men, and met the catechist on the street before a medicine shop. The owner of the shop, fearing a fight, quickly brought the two leaders inside and convinced them to bury their differences and let the matter drop. But the altercation had attracted a large crowd in the market already busy with year-end business, and the catechist Zhang apparently felt he would suffer a great loss of face by dropping a dispute which he had initiated. So he contacted another catechist from the town of Tiangongmiao, across the border in Chengwu, and made plans for a major confrontation.

The Catholics sent a challenge to Cao De-li, who was not about to refuse the invitation. He contacted Liu Shi-duan, and both of them set off for Tiangongmiao with their men. But on the way they were intercepted by the commander of the local garrison, the "stockade lord" of the town, and the magistrate of Chengwu. These three managed to dissuade Cao and Liu from any hasty action. At the same time, a German missionary who happened to be meeting with the commander met with the catechists and admonished them for their excessive zeal in protecting the faith. The two sides were induced to apologize to each other, and the affair was thus settled. But the incident had now brought the Big Sword Society and the Catholics into direct conflict—and the exaggerated Catholic reports of widespread damage to their churches (of which the local officials found no evidence) even led the German minister to intervene with the Zongli Yamen. It became necessary, therefore, to reinforce the prohibitions against the Big Sword Society—and notices to that effect were published in February, just after the Chinese New Year.[77]

The incident is most notable for its pettiness, but it seems clear that both sides were spoiling for a fight. This time it would be avoided, but only at the cost of even greater pent-up anger on both sides. The Christians had lost a good deal of face from the confrontation at the Lihaiji market; but the Big Sword Society had suffered renewed prohibition. No doubt the principal effect of the altercation was to draw the battle lines. All that wanted was another incident to renew the conflict—and that would not be long in coming.

THE UPRISING OF JUNE 1896

One key to the success of the Big Sword Society—whether in fighting bandits or Catholics—was the association's obliviousness to formal administrative boundaries. While the repressive forces of the state were hampered by an inability (or unwillingness) to cross into other jurisdictions, such was not the case with the Big Sword Society. Its power and influence transcended the divisions of the formal bureaucratic hierarchy. And in the dispute which brought the Big Swords to their ultimate demise, it was events across the border in Jiangsu which set the scene.

French Jesuits had been active in the border counties of Dangshan and Feng for only six years, but those most distant regions were far and away the most promising in their Xuzhou diocese, which in 1896 counted forty-eight parishes in all.[78] In February, at the same time that frictions were developing between the Big Swords and the Christians in Shandong, the Jiangsu Christians were experiencing problems instigated by some disgruntled lower gentry members. Red placards appeared warning that "foreigners have come to establish secretly a temple of the White Lotus sect," and announcing that "all the gentry [notables] have secretly resolved to put an end to this evil." But despite a couple of threatening mobs and abortive "arrests" of Chinese Christian leaders, things quieted down quickly when the magistrate moved to prohibit attacks on the Western faith.[79]

Then in the late spring, things heated up again in a dispute which had its origins in a long simmering controversy between the Pang and Liu lineages over rights to land in an area known as Dongtuan. The Dongtuan land lay between the two lineages' villages, Pangjialin and Liutitou, and apparently along the old course of the Yellow River, which also ran between the two. Originally belonging to the Confucian estate in Qufu, the land owed no taxes to the government, but only annual tribute of geese and ducks to the estate. Since the Nian rebellion, the official landlord's claims seem not to have been exercised. Presumably this was the result both of social disorder and of the 1855 Yellow River shift to its northern course, which left this former riverland inappropriate for raising fowl. But for ordinary agricultural uses, the alluvial soil was extraordinarily rich, and with the withdrawal of the former landlord's claims, the rights to thousands of *mu* of good land simply went to the strongest claimant. According to one peasant informant: "Whoever in the area had power could occupy and cultivate it."[80] But in fact few cultivators had adequate power for this sort of competition, so the struggles were really between rival lineages, headed by substantial landlords. Thus another local informant's version seems even more plausible: "Peasants rented and cultivated it. Then whoever was powerful, you paid rent to him."[81]

Until the 1890s, the Pangs were certainly the most powerful lineage in the area, but in 1892 their head died and the new leader, Pang San-jie, had more difficulty in maintaining supremacy. Still in his twenties, Pang was quite young to lead a lineage in this troubled territory, but he had received a little education, had devoted himself to military exercises (becoming particularly adept at archery), and had passed the military *sheng-yuan* examination. With these martial qualifications, plus a family inheritance in land amounting to at least 300 *mu*, he was certainly a fairly powerful figure. But not powerful enough. For his rivals in the Liu clan had found a new means to support their claim to the Dongtuan land: they joined the Catholic Church. Pang began to lose more than he won, and to support his power he joined the one group which seemed capable of resisting his adversaries: the Big Sword Society. In the spring of 1896, when the Lius moved in to claim the wheat in the fields, the battle was joined.[82]

On June 3, Pang San-jie led a band of about sixty Big Swords to burn the chapel at Liutitou, but the incident was minor enough so that even the local French priest, who investigated the scene together with the Dangshan magistrate on June 7, dismissed it as only a lineage feud, and left for a previously scheduled retreat. The magistrate, according to the missionary's account, attempted to visit Pang to settle the matter, but when he failed to find him, addressed a letter to him, delivered via the local gentry, suggesting that if he had a quarrel with Shandong people, he should settle it there—safely across the border. This was surely a curious suggestion, since the magistrate must have known that the quarrel was between two local lineages. Nonetheless, Pang did go to Shandong—not, however, to settle the matter, but to ask for reinforcements. His visit seems to have set off a wave of petty harassment of Christian churches and residents in Shandong,[83] but Pang's own concerns remained in Jiangsu. After rallying about 100 Shandong Big Swords at what the missionaries called his "manor" in Pangjialin, Pang set off on June 16 to attack the leading missionary residence (now without foreigners because of their retreat) at Houjia-zhuang, also in Dangshan. This time the Big Swords were joined by all sorts of local riff-raff, and together they stripped the village, and warned that more trouble was in store when further assistance arrived from Shandong.[84]

Pang San-jie and his band invested Houjiazhuang for five days, using it as a base to loot and harass Christians in fifteen neighboring villages. Non-Christians were not robbed, though wealthier households were induced to contribute animals, food, clothes, and (allegedly) opium to the Big Sword force. Meanwhile, the local officials acted quickly to protect the foreign missionaries in both Dangshan and Feng counties, evacuating them and their most valuable possessions to the well-fortified stronghold of Maqing. On June 21, Pang returned to Shandong where his band looted converts' homes in

Shan county, smashed their contents, and burned the Catholic school (*yang-xue*, "foreign school") in Xue-Konglou. Several days later, its numbers now swollen to perhaps a thousand, Pang's band returned to raid Christian homes in Dangshan on its way to the other major missionary residence, Daitaolou in Feng county. The village was deserted, but at least one resident was around who—apparently motivated by some personal grievance—was happy to identify the Christian homes, ninety-four of which were burned. The band then returned to Houjiazhuang and put many of the buildings there to the torch.[85]

Now Pang San-jie found himself at a difficult pass. He had pretty much stripped the northern Jiangsu Christians of everything they had. He was running out of targets, and running out of food as well. The Jiangsu officials were mobilizing for defense, and he surely realized that a sizeable force was moving north to deal with him. Furthermore, it was not at all clear just how committed the Shandong Big Sword Society leaders were to his cause. Liu Shi-duan had apparently assented to the despatch of his disciple Peng Gui-lin to lead the Shandong contingent in aid of Pang. But Liu himself, and his chief lieutenant Cao De-li, kept themselves safely out of the fray—perhaps somewhat chastened by their brush with the authorities in February. Pang needed to feed his troops, and so he moved back toward Shandong to the large town of Maliangji which lies directly on the Shandong-Jiangsu border. There the discipline of the band—which by now included many who were not regular members of the Big Sword Society—broke down. On June 29, salt shops, a store selling Beijing products, and a petty officials' office were looted. With this, the local militia joined the regular army's effort to suppress Pang's troublesome band. The Big Swords scattered through southeastern Shan county stealing grain and horses and seeking further support. But the ranking Big Sword leader with the force, Peng Gui-lin, was arrested by the troops sent from Xuzhou, acting in cooperation with the local militia. The other Big Swords attempted to go to his rescue, but they were defeated in the final battle—of which the most detailed account mentions only two casualties and eighteen arrests—and then dispersed into hiding or back to their homes. Pursued by the troops and local militia, thirteen more were arrested in Shan county on July 1.[86]

That was the end of the fighting, and it is important to realize how truly petty this incident was. The French Jesuits' account mentions only the attacks on the two main mission residences at Houjiazhuang and Daitaolou, and Christians' homes in sixteen other villages. They settled their losses with the local officials for only 2,000 strings of cash on June 26—*before* the final battles were even fought![87] The Germans in Shandong submitted a detailed list which showed mostly petty vandalism (roofs damaged, windows broken, altars stolen) to chapels in seventeen villages, and the burning of 119 rooms of converts' thatched huts in Xue-Konglou. Total losses in Shandong were put at 12,020 strings of cash, and Anzer finally settled for an even 10,000— after a great deal of bluster from the German minister.[88] There were no Christian casualties throughout the entire incident—either Chinese or foreign.[89] The Big Sword Society was simply flexing its muscles with demonstrative attacks on Christian churches and property. They must have scrupulously avoided threats to Christian lives, for had they wished to do so, they surely could have found human victims. The court in Beijing barely took note of the affair—and justifiably so. If one reads the "Veritable Records" for this period (and it is presumably a fair record of the view from the court), one sees incidents of "bandit" actions quite as serious as this one in Zhili, in the Northeast, and along the Guangdong-Guangxi border. And through most of 1895 and nearly all of 1896, a major Muslim rebellion raged in Gansu and Shaanxi, requiring the dispatch of troops from the capital area under General Dong Fu-xiang. The threat to domestic peace in that region absolutely dwarfed anything that the Big Sword Society was doing along the Shandong-Jiangsu border.[90]

It is only when this context is understood—both the pettiness of the incident and the relatively mild missionary response—that we can appreciate the significance of the official response. In Shandong, responsibility for the pacification of the Big Sword Society was left to Yu-xian, who had just been appointed judicial commissioner but was still in the area, and the new *daotai* in Yanzhou, Xi-liang. When the fighting stopped, the two main leaders of the society—Liu Shi-duan and Cao De-li—were still at large; and even the initiator of the incident, Pang San-jie, had escaped arrest. The main task in Shandong was to apprehend Liu and Cao, and that proved extremely easy. On July 7, the Cao county magistrate sent the militia leader Zeng Guang-huan to invite Liu to a meeting. The two men were friends, having long cooperated in bandit-suppression, so Liu went along and was promptly arrested. Yu-xian interrogated him and had him beheaded. The Shan county magistrate similarly lured Cao De-li into captivity, where Xi-liang presided over his trial and execution.[91] The demise of these two leaders would seem to display their considerable naiveté. But it also reflected the close and trusting relations the Big Sword leaders maintained both with the militia heads, their peers in the village elite, and with the local officials, with whom they had long cooperated in suppressing banditry. One should recall, too, that both Liu and Cao had avoided direct involvement in the events of June,[92] so perhaps they thought they had nothing to fear—or that they were being summoned to preside over some peaceful dispersal of the Big Sword Society. Or perhaps they went, as was often the case with leaders of Japanese peasant protests, to offer themselves in sacrifice for a cause that they knew was just. Whatever the reason, they went, and they died. And with them, for all practical purposes, died their Big Sword Society. Its members ceased gathering to practice their rituals and martial arts, and the area was quiet.[93]

Not that the society utterly disapppeared, of course. In 1897, as we shall see in the next chapter, the Big Swords were implicated in the murder of two German missionaries in the Juye incident; and there were unsubstantiated rumors of Big Sword activity along the south-west Shandong border in 1898. Finally, in 1900, when official tolera-tion of anti-Christian activity was fairly common throughout north China, there was renewed Big Sword Society activity in Yuncheng and Heze. But by then the climate had very much changed; and even then, the society's heartland in Cao and Shan counties remained quiet. As Liu Shi-duan's son put it: "After Liu Shi-duan was killed, there just wasn't any more Big Sword Society activity."[94]

If the society's quiet demise in southwestern Shandong was some-what surprising, the final resolution across the border in Jiangsu was simply extraordinary. There as in Shandong, all attention was focused on the leader, in this case Pang San-jie. An order went out for his arrest and decapitation; his elder brother was thrown in jail; much of his land was confiscated; and the local gentry were instructed to see to the destruction of his "manor." But the gentry hesitated, saying they feared revenge by the Big Swords, and the magistrate claimed he was unable to locate Pang—though most people believed he was staying quietly at home. Still, the pressure on the entire Pang lineage was troublesome and in April 1897, the heads of the lineage from eighteen villages met to devise a solution. Several days later, they presented it to the local French missionary: Father Doré was given the names of 4,000 Pangs who wished to convert to Catholicism. The next Sunday, his church was filled to overflowing with three to four hundred Pangs, including the parents and sons of Pang San-jie. The Pang elders proposed to negotiate a deal with the Church "as though with the civil authorities." Their conditions were simple: in exchange for the conversion of the Pangs, they asked only that San-jie's life be spared so that he might live in peace with his family, that his brother be released from prison, and that they be allowed to preserve their lineage hall, part of which was to be converted to a Catholic church or school.

Doré's superior, Father Gain, took the matter to the *daotai*, saying that it seemed to him a much superior settlement to the Shandong method of "cutting off influential heads." Needless to say, the *daotai* could give no explicit agreement. There was, after all, an imperial edict ordering Pang San-jie's arrest and prosecution. But he saw to it that Pang's brother was released from jail, and suggested that if San-jie would make himself scarce for a while, then it would certainly be very difficult to arrest him. With that, the deal was made. Pang San-jie left home for a time, then began returning for longer and longer visits, and soon had resumed his normal place in society. He began to attend catechism and met now and then with Father Doré. In the fall of 1897, when there were renewed threats of Big Sword Society activity in the wake of the Juye incident, Pang personally went along to provide protection for the Bishop who was making a grand tour through the diocese. And thus was the affair brought to a conclusion.[95]

By and large, the Catholics on both sides of the border were pleased with the resolution of the difficulties, but the Jesuits in Jiangsu seemed nothing short of ecstatic. And well they might be, for the conversion of the Pangs was certainly an enormous coup. More fundamentally, however, they had emerged as the victors in the struggle—having proven the efficacy of their influence with the local officials. And since, as I have stressed earlier, the success of Christian proselytizing was intimately tied to the effective exercise of Christian power, it was inevitable that more and more people would begin to turn to the Church. In discussing the aftermath of the 1896 incidents, the history of the Xuzhou diocese is remarkably frank:

> If people with lawsuits, difficulties with the courts, exaggerated taxes, quarrels over inheritance, or some other menace were afraid they did not have enough money to buy off the judges, there was still the recourse of the Catholic Church, which demanded nothing to uphold justice. But one had to be a member of the Church to claim its help. And they asked admission in groups of twenty, thirty and forty families, by entire villages

and from everywhere at once. In June 1896, when the Big Sword Society set upon Xuzhou, the number of catechumens was 3,550. In June 1897, there were 10,000; 17,000 in 1898, 26,000 the next year and over 20,000 in 1900, the year of the Boxers.[96]

The fundamental dynamic of Christian conversion was proven once again. It could only be a harbinger of more trouble to come.

That more trouble would indeed come we shall see soon enough, but I should like to return, in conclusion, to the most significant aspect of the Big Sword Society uprising: its remarkably peaceful resolution. With the arrest and execution of just thirty "outlaws," the Big Swords in Shandong were quelled.[97] From the missionaries' account, there was even greater judicial restraint in Jiangsu. Officials on both sides of the border stressed lenience. Having received an edict which directed him to "send troops to suppress (zhen-ya) and thoroughly exterminate (jiao-chu) [them] on the spot if they resist," Li Bing-heng chose to stress the final conditional phrase, replying: "This is because your imperial majesty's humanity is as [great as] Heaven's, and from the beginning, you did not wish to execute them all indiscriminately."[98] Even more notable is the Xuzhou daotai's formulation: "We should only ask if they are outlaws or not, not if they belonged to the society or not."[99] This is precisely the language that was used in an imperial decree of January 1900—a decree which is usually held to have signalled imperial toleration of the Boxers as they spread across the plains of Zhili toward Beijing.

With the Boxers of 1899–1900, that approach simply would not work. The arrest and execution of a few leaders would not stop them. But it did work in 1896 on the Big Sword Society—an organization under the firm control of the rural landlord elite, with close ties to the officials and local militia. With such an organization, the traditional method of arresting leaders and dispersing followers was very effective. The Big Sword Society was still enough within the established structures of dominance in rural society to respond to a clear indication from the officials that things had gone too far. The Boxers of 1899–1900 were quite different. Their ardor would not be blunted by a few timely executions.

CHAPTER FIVE

The Juye Incident

It was the night of All Saints' Day—November 1, 1897. Three German missionaries of the S.V.D., George Stenz, Richard Henle, and Francis Xavier Nies, had gathered at the missionary residence in Zhangjia-zhuang, in Juye county. This was Stenz's mission station, and it lay about twenty-five kilometers west of Jining. The other two men had come to visit—Henle, because he was discouraged at the slow progress of his work, and Stenz had urged him to take a break. The three did their best to raise their spirits that evening—singing songs from their childhood accompanied by Stenz's zither, and practicing the Requiem for the following day. When they finally retired, Stenz gave his own room to the two guests and moved to the servant's quarters. About an hour before midnight, shots rang out and the courtyard was filled with torches. A band of twenty to thirty armed men raced directly to the missionary's quarters, broke down the door, and hacked Nies and Henle to death. Apparently aware that they had not found the local missionary, the band burst into the sacristy and ran through the church looking for Stenz. But they had not checked the servant's quarters before the Christian villagers roused themselves to a belated defense—at which the band disappeared into the darkness.[1]

Such was the Juye incident. As pretext if not cause, it set off a chain of events which radically altered the course of Chinese history. When Kaiser Wilhelm heard of the murders five days later, he immediately dispatched Germany's East Asian naval squadron to occupy Jiaozhou Bay, on the south coast of the Shandong peninsula. The Great Powers'

Scramble for Concessions had begun. In the following months Russia would seize Dalian (Dairen) and Port Arthur on the Liaodong Peninsula in Manchuria; Britain would claim Weihaiwei across the Bohai Gulf on the northern coast of Shandong, a ninety-nine year lease of the New Territories opposite Hong Kong, and a non-alienation agreement making the Yangzi Valley her sphere of influence; Japan would extract a similar agreement making Fujian (opposite the recently seized colony of Taiwan) its sphere; while France made southwest China its sphere and obtained a leasehold on Kwangchow Bay in Guangdong. The long-feared process—referred to in Chinese as *gua-fen*, "the carving up of the melon"—was now underway.

THE CAUSES OF THE INCIDENT

In a curious way, the very importance of the incident served to obscure its causes. The Germans had been looking for a pretext to seize Jiaozhou for some time; so when the incident occurred, they concentrated on seizing the harbor and extracting the other concessions they wished from the Chinese. There was little pressure to discover who actually killed the missionaries and why. The local officials acted quickly to round up nine vagrants and local ne'er-do-wells and execute two for the crime; but no one believed that they were actually the guilty parties. Certainly the surviving missionary Stenz did not. Nor, to judge from the oral history later done on the incident, did the villagers of Juye.[2] As a result of this hasty resolution, there was never an investigation serious enough to leave concrete evidence of the cause for the killings.

The principal weakness of the government's position, devised by the lieutenant-governor Yu-xian, was its claim that a band of robbers had committed the murders. Beyond the pilfering of a few clothes from Stenz's room, there was no evidence of robbery, and in any case needless violence—especially against foreigners—was hardly part of any Chinese robber band's mode of operation. It is virtually certain that the murders represented a deliberate attack on the German missionaries.

It is not difficult to find general reasons why Juye villagers might have wished to kill the German priests. Some local informants have suggested that Henle, whose mission field was not far to the south in Yuncheng, was the target of the attack.[3] The Henle we met briefly in chapter 3, aggressively interfering in lawsuits, must certainly have made his share of enemies. In fact he seems to have been so difficult to get along with that even his own Christian congregations at one point "revolted" against him.[4]

It is more likely, however, that the band was after Stenz. He was the resident missionary and the band went straight to his room. According to Stenz, the attackers even called out his name when they failed to find him. This is certainly believable. Stenz's autobiography reveals a strikingly unattractive character, who might well have aroused murderous thoughts in the minds of those he met. He thoroughly typified the militance of the S.V.D. mission. The very first line of his autobiography reads, "On September 29, 1893, I received at Steyl the mission cross which was to be at once weapon and banner in my fight for the Kingdom of God." His racism was without disguise. His arrival in Shanghai later that year is described in the following terms:

> An entirely new world now opened before us. Crowds of slit-eyed Chinese swarmed about the harbor—prominent merchants in their rustling silks and poor coolies in ragged clothes that did not hide their filthy bodies. Confidence was not our first impression on reaching this gate of the Celestial Empire. Cunning, pride, and scorn flashed from the eyes that met our inquiring looks.

He found Chinese officials "lazy [and] procrastinating" and Chinese food frequently "unpalatable." He seemed mortified when, having forgotten his fork and spoon, he was forced, at one stop in his travels, "to use two short pieces of stick" to eat.

Such a man would not fit easily into Chinese life. For him the missionary experience was "a chain of griefs and sufferings, . . . mental trials" which produced a "sense of desertion and homesickness." The training that Stenz had received at Steyl was designed to steel him for such an experience, but the steeling was not to teach any accommodation to his Chinese surroundings. Rather, "persecution, martyrdom, death for the Faith—such was the desire of our hearts."[5] It would be going too far to suggest that such missionaries deliberately brought trouble on themselves, but we must take seriously their professions of a faith which saw death for their cause as a sign of grace. Father Nies had at one point written home: "More than once I have prayed to God for the grace of martyrdom, but most likely it will not be granted to me. My blood is not deemed red enough by God, and is still mingled with the dust of this earth."[6]

That Stenz was bound to offend many people is absolutely certain. The oral history of the incident, in addition to recording the usual missionary interference in lawsuits, punishments for alleged insults to the church, and false Christian claims for alleged thefts, accuses Stenz of more than ten rapes of local women.[7] True or not, such accusations tell something of what people thought of the man. Still, it remains unclear to this day what individual or group it was that Stenz offended enough to arouse thoughts of murder. Stenz's own account, which corresponds to one of several oral history versions, is probably at least part of the story. Consistent with S.V.D. practice throughout this region, Stenz had enrolled in his church a large number of former White Lotus members from the village of Caojiazhuang. But he had refused admission to the village headman, who was accused of having stolen and killed an ox from a neighboring town. This refusal led to a good deal of hard feelings, which were made worse because the new converts were the wealthiest families in the village, and they now refused to make the normal contributions to village festivals. The village head tried to force the Christians to pay up, but this only led to further hostilities and complaints to the local officials. Stenz was convinced that this village headman then joined the Big Swords and led them in the attack on the mission.[8]

Some local recollections of the incident are consistent with this theory, and most agree that, in some way, members of the Big Sword Society were involved. Whether this was anything like the Big Sword Society of the Shandong-Jiangsu border, with its invulnerability rituals and so forth, is not at all clear. One gets the impression of a group, bent on revenge against the missionaries, which borrowed the Big Sword Society name and reputation without paying much attention to its ritual or teachings. Furthermore, most versions seem to agree that others—including former or alleged bandits—joined in the attack on the missionaries. Of people mentioned in this regard, there are several stories of a certain Liu De-run, a former bandit who was seeking revenge against the Juye magistrate for the arrest and torture of either his daughter or his wife. For him, a major missionary incident was just a means to destroy the magistrate's official career.[9]

That is about all we can say about the origins of the incident. It probably derived from the multiple enmities which some particularly obnoxious missionaries (especially Stenz) had engendered during their years in the area—enmities complicated by intra- and inter-village quarrels. Most likely, the enemies of the missionaries found it convenient to ally with other lawless elements (some of whom may have been motivated by nothing more than the desire to embarrass the local magistrate), and to adopt at least the name of the Big Sword Society, whose anti-Christian exploits of the previous year were certainly well known. The origins of the incident were undeniably complex and obscure. But to the missionaries and the German government, it was a godsend—and they knew exactly what to do with it.

THE GERMAN REACTION

Germany in 1897 was a nation impatient for an opportunity to flex her muscles as a world power. Vigorous growth in the past decades had made her economy the strongest in continental Europe; and she had emerged as England's primary, if still distant, rival in world trade. Germany's position in China reflected her new economic strength: second to England in commercial volume, she was becoming a force to be reckoned with in shipping and finance as well. In 1890 the Deutsch-Asiatische Bank became the first non-British foreign bank in China. But Germany still did not have the requisite military capacity to defend her economic expansion in an age when even a good liberal like Max Weber recognized that "nothing but might, nothing but naked force will decide the question of foreign markets." [10] After the 1890 publication of Alfred Mahan's *The Influence of Sea Power Upon History*, it became conventional wisdom that navies would provide the "naked force" to protect world markets in the age of imperialism.

At the beginning of the decade, the German navy had slipped to fifth place in the world, far below Germany's ranking in the world economic hierarchy. Its recovery was in large part the work of Admiral Alfred Tirpitz, who forged an effective alliance with German commercial interests. Kaiser Wilhelm II, responding to more atavistic and racialist concerns for German glory, became by mid-decade an important convert to the navy's cause. In China, the key need was a coaling station, but Tirpitz was clever enough to tie his plans for a station to a more general program of economic exploitation in the hinterland of the port to be acquired. Germany had approached China with a request for a naval base in October 1895, but it was not until the following year, when Tirpitz visited China and surveyed potential sites, that the navy decided that Jiaozhou Bay on the Shandong peninsula was the place they wanted.

Jiaozhou's attractiveness as a deep-water port and its appropriateness—pointed out as early as 1882 in Richthofen's volume on his travels through Shandong—as an outlet for Shandong's considerable mineral resources were certainly the decisive factors in the port's selection. But the presence of the German missionaries of the S.V.D. was an added bonus which Tirpitz did not ignore. Bishop Anzer had long appealed for some "energetic act" which would gain some respect for Germany among the officials and people of Shandong, and he seems to have been the source of the German minister Heyking's suggestion that Jiaozhou would be an appropriate reparation for the difficulties Anzer was having in Yanzhou. Thus Tirpitz noted, in his recommendation of Jiaozhou, that Germany's occupation of the port would ease communication with western Shandong where the German missionaries were active. There was an obvious bit of politics in this move, for the Catholic Center provided the crucial block of votes which Tirpitz needed for his naval bill—and it is probably no accident that the final passage of that bill in March 1898 came with substantial support from the Catholic Center.[11]

By November 1896, Germany had essentially decided to acquire Jiaozhou, and Heyking in Beijing began looking about for an excuse to provoke an incident. The only hesitation on the German side came from a prior Chinese commitment to allow Russian ships to winter in the harbor and rumors of more permanent Russian designs on the port. But when the kaiser visited St. Petersburg in August 1897, he satisfied himself that the czar's claims were not serious. Accordingly, when news of the Juye murders reached Berlin on November 6, Wilhelm was delighted that the "splendid opportunity" had at last arrived. The czar was informed of Germany's intent to send ships to occupy Jiaozhou, and his famous reply—"Cannot approve nor disapprove"—sealed the harbor's fate. Subsequent Russian misgivings at the czar's hasty acquiescence caused the German Foreign Office to hesitate in making a permanent claim to the bay. But Wilhelm was determined to assert German power, and if his resolve needed bolstering, Bishop Anzer—who was fortuitously in Berlin at the time—was happy to provide it. As early as November 7, Anzer visited the Foreign Office to express his hope that Germany "would now use the opportunity to occupy Kiaochow." Several days later, meeting with the kaiser himself, he argued: "It is the last chance for Germany to get a possession anywhere in Asia and to firm up our prestige which has dropped. . . . [N]o matter what it costs, we must not under any circumstances give up Kiaochow. It has a future for economic development as well as industry, a future which will be greater and more meaningful than Shanghai is today."[12]

Faced with such German determination, the Qing state was utterly impotent. As was so often the case with missionary incidents, the Zongli Yamen heard of the murders from the German ambassador, on November 7, before it heard anything from local Chinese officials. The court certainly knew what was coming, for in reprimanding the Shandong governor Li Bing-heng for his slow response, the emperor noted that this would provide Germany her long awaited pretext to seize a harbor.[13] Then on November 14, German warships sailed into Jiaozhou—the Chinese garrison withdrawing without a shot. The next day, Li Bing-heng reported the assault and urged the court to fight: "Since they started the feud, we have no alternative but to resist." He proposed to raise an additional five companies of troops in Caozhou and prepare to drive the Germans off.[14] But the court immediately rejected Li's suggestion. The new recruits would be worthless in battle, and thus, "although the enemy has certainly acted arbitrarily, the court will definitely not mobilize its troops."[15] Several days later, the court again replied to Li's arguments: "The foreigners' actions rely entirely on power. If our power cannot assure victory, we will absorb a great loss." It pointed out that despite their bravery, Shandong soldiers had been repeatedly defeated in recent battles with Japan.[16]

With its navy devastated and its army in disarray following defeat in the Sino-Japanese War, with the imperial treasury virtually emptied by the indemnities which were the price of peace, the court was hardly prepared to resist Germany with force. The slim reed on which the Chinese government could rely was the traditional one of "using barbarians to control barbarians." Despite repeated defeats by the Great Powers, the Chinese empire had survived intact partly because the balance of power in Europe prevented any single power from seeking undue advantage. When Japan had claimed the Liaodong Peninsula as one prize of her victory over China, Russia, Germany, and France had combined to force its return. Now two years later, China again counted on Russia to pull her chestnuts out of the fire. Since Russia had earlier been granted wintering rights to Jiaozhou, this was not altogether a vain prospect. But the czar's telegram to Kaiser Wilhelm had greatly weakened Russia's hand, and it was not long before Germany convinced Russia that she would do better to seize a port of her own. By December, it was decided that the Russians would get their ice free ports at Port Arthur and Dalian—which in fact were far more convenient than Jiaozhou, for they could be linked up to the Trans-Siberian Railway. With that, the Scramble for Concessions, with all its momentous consequences, was made inevitable.[17]

THE IMPACT OF THE JIAOZHOU SEIZURE

The granting of naval bases along the coast and exclusive rights to mines and railroads in "spheres of influence" had enormous impact on China's national politics. These key military and economic dimensions of the Scramble for Concessions at last aroused the court to action in the Guang-xu emperor's Hundred Days of Reform in 1898. While the 1898 reforms were soon aborted, they set the themes for many of the policies actually carried out in the first decade of the twentieth century. But it would be a mistake to assume that the peasants of western Shandong shared all of the strategic concerns of the national elite. Jiaozhou, of course, was far out on the Shandong peninsula, and while German surveying for mines and railways aroused opposition and even violent conflicts, these were all in areas far from the zones in which the Boxers were soon to appear. The *direct* impact of the German incursion was therefore less than one might expect. But that does not mean there was no impact at all—for the *indirect* effects of the German actions were considerable.

As I have noted earlier, the Germans had long been seeking a port on the Chinese coast, so the Juye incident was more a pretext than a cause for the Jiaozhou seizure. But the pretext was itself an important one, for in its precise formulation it carried the logic of imperialism a critical step forward in China. In his November 6 telegram to the czar, Kaiser Wilhelm had said he was "sending [a] German squadron to Kiaochow, as it is the only port available to operate from as a base against marauders. I am under obligation to Catholic party in Germany to show that their missions are really safe under my protection."[18] In all earlier missionary incidents, though the Powers would often engage in shows of force through gunboat diplomacy, the purpose of such measures was only to compel the *Chinese* government to bring the alleged persecutors of Christianity to justice. Now it was suggested that a foreign power would *herself* act to suppress anti-Christian incidents on Chinese soil, with Germany proposing to use Jiaozhou as a "base against marauders."

This was a novel departure, and surely a major threat to Chinese sovereignty. But the German government, under strenuous pressure from Anzer, had been moving toward this position for some time. In October 1895 the German minister had threatened, in connection with disturbances in Yanzhou, that failing effective Chinese protection of Christians, "my government will have no alternative but to devise methods to protect them ourselves." [19] It was a line of argument which Heyking repeatedly used in his negotiations with the Chinese government to resolve the Juye incident. On one occasion the German minister asked the Chinese government to guarantee that incidents such as this would never recur. The ministers of the Zongli Yamen gave the honest reply that naturally they wished to prevent such incidents and would do everything in their power to prevent them, but that Caozhou was a very unruly area and it was impossible to *guarantee* that no further incidents would recur. Replied Heyking: "Since China cannot guarantee that in the future such incidents will not recur, our warships are in Jiaozhou and can help you handle the matter." The Chinese response was naturally that "this concerns the internal affairs of China, you need not interfere in it." [20] But obviously the new logic of imperialism made it quite proper for the Great Powers to intervene in other countries' internal affairs. Wilhelm II may have expressed it best in the speech delivered on December 16, as he sent his brother in command of an additional squadron bound for China:

> Make it clear to every European there, to the German merchant, and, above all things, to the foreigner in whose country we are or with whom we have to deal, that the German Michael has set his shield, decorated with the imperial eagle, firmly upon the ground. Whoever asks him for protection will always receive it.... But if any one should undertake to insult us in our rights or wish to harm us, then drive in with the mailed fist and, as God wills, bind about your young brow the laurels which no one in the entire German Empire will begrudge you.[21]

It was under the threat of such bombast that the Chinese government agreed to the most extraordinary settlement of the missionary claims. In Jining and Caozhou cities, and in the village where the missionaries were killed, cathedrals were to be constructed with government funds and the inscription over their doors: "Catholic church constructed by imperial order." In addition, the Chinese government was to build residences for the missionaries in Juye, Heze, Yuncheng, Shan, Cao, Chengwu, and Yutai counties of southwestern Shandong. Five magistrates from these counties were dismissed, and one impeached; the *daotai* was transferred; the prefect and army commander dismissed but allowed to remain at their posts.

Finally and most controversially, Governor Li Bing-heng—who had already been promoted to the viceroyship of Sichuan but was awaiting the arrival of his replacement in Shandong—was stripped of his new post, demoted two grades and barred from holding high office in the future.[22]

The punishment of Li Bing-heng was unprecedented. In 1895, the Sichuan viceroy Liu Bing-zhang was removed as a result of anti-missionary riots in the provincial capital of Chengdu. But Liu had been directly responsible and probably deliberately negligent in failing to provide for the foreigners' protection once trouble started brewing.[23] No such charge could be made against Li Bing-heng. Instead, the German complaint was the more general charge that his consistent hostility to Christian proselytizing had fostered the environment that made the attack possible.

There is no denying Li's strenuous opposition to missionary meddling, or his disdain for the quality of the converts they attracted. In 1896, in the wake of the Big Sword troubles, Li had observed: "Ever since the Western religion came to China, its converts have all been unemployed rascals [xiu-min, lit.: weed people]. They use the foreign religion as protection to bring suits for others and oppress their villages." They use the Church to avoid prosecution, and gradually the local officials, to avoid trouble, bend the law in their favor. "After a while," wrote Li in an analysis which was surely accurate, "the people's long-suppressed anger becomes unbearable. They feel the officials cannot be relied upon, and that they must vent their spleen in private disputes. Thus they gather crowds and seek quarrels, burning and destroying churches."[24] Li's proposed solution was to prohibit strictly all missionary interference in lawsuits, so that local officials would be able to decide cases involving Christians solely on the merits of the issue. His consistent opposition to German meddling, to the missionaries' exaggerated claims regarding Big Sword attacks, and to their entry into Yanzhou had earned him the unremitting hostility of the German missionaries and their minister in Beijing.[25]

Li's stubborn resistance to missionary interference, his later ties to such ultra-conservatives in Beijing as Gang-yi, and his eagerness, in 1900, to resist the Eight-Nation Expedition sent to suppress the Boxers, have earned him the reputation of a staunch reactionary.[26] There is certainly no denying Li Bing-heng's conservatism. When an imperial edict of 1895 asked for reform proposals in the wake of China's humiliating defeat by Japan, Li responded with a memorial which opposed railroads, mines, a post office, the printing of paper money, and the extension of Western education. His alternative program suggested mostly greater austerity and the elimination of corruption.[27] This was hardly a very enlightened proposal given the severity of China's problems. But even foreign observers had to admit that for all his resistance to Western-inspired innovation, he was a fearless and honest official who had done more than any other recent governor to root out corruption in Shandong. A missionary correspondent for the *North China Herald* wrote of Li under the heading "A Good Official." While confessing his reputation as being "unfriendly to foreigners and to foreign improvements," the writer observed, "he seems to be a thoroughly honest man, opposed to all trickery and malfeasance in office, and anxious to do what he can to give Shantung a fairly pure administration."[28] Even when complaints against his obstruction of Westernizing reforms became more common, the Western press still praised his "unusual honesty and economy."[29] Li's primary accomplishments were in reducing administrative expenses and efficiently managing the Yellow River dikes. When, after the Juye incident, the German minister asked why such an incompetent official could be promoted to prospective viceroy of Sichuan, the Zongli Yamen officials Weng Tong-he and Zhang Yin-huan replied: "In managing river works, Governor Li has saved over a million taels a year, and he has also raised money for the Board of Revenue, over 100,000 per year. So you cannot say he is useless. It is for this that he has been promoted."[30]

For the average villager of western Shandong, Li Bing-heng had been an unusually good governor. Not only was he doing his utmost to check Christian abuses but he was working hard to establish an uncorrupt administration, to economize on official expenditures, and to control the Yellow River. That such a "good official" would be permanently removed from high office at the insistence of a foreign power—despite the absence of any evidence indicating responsibility for the incident at Juye—was terrible and tragic testimony to the power of his foreign accusers.

Needless to say, those foreigners were delighted by the settlement of the Juye incident—and this delight was not confined to the Germans. No power had more to lose from the threatened partition of China than Great Britain; yet her minister in Beijing, Sir Claude McDonald, applauded the German move. "The effect on the security of our own people will be of the best. It seems hopeless to expect the Chinese to do their duty in protecting missionaries and discouraging anti-foreign movements unless they are forced thereto by some measure as the Germans have taken."[31] From northwestern Shandong, the American missionary Henry Porter wrote that "the German Government deserve the admiration of all right-minded men, the world over." As a result of the occupation of Jiaozhou, "a great sense of relief was felt by the foreign residents of China. . . . The immediate effect throughout Shantung province is to strengthen every form of mission work. . . . We welcome the German vigor and the German advance."[32]

There can be no doubt that these appreciations of the Germans were well-founded. At the conclusion of the last chapter, we observed that the resolution of the Big Sword Society incident in northern Jiangsu had led to even more foreign meddling and an unprecedented rate of Catholic conversions. Li Bing-heng's tenure as governor of Shandong had prevented the balance of power there from swinging too strongly in the Christians' favor. But with the removal of Li and a host of local officials in the affected area, and the occupation of Jiaozhou, the message to local officials was now clear: protect the rights of Christians at all cost. Missionaries in Linqing noted that "fear has taken hold upon the mandarin body from the Governor down." Proclamations were "scattered broadcast, free as the Gospel" attesting to the good will of the missionaries and the need to avoid incidents with them.[33] A missionary in Qingzhou called a proclamation by the new governor, Zhang Ru-mei, "much more favorable to the missionary than anything we have been accustomed to in times past."[34] In Wei county another missionary observed: "The most marked effect we see is the prestige [the Jiaozhou seizure] gives to the foreigners, a prestige that is pitiful to see. The officials seem for the time being to stand in abject fear of any complications with foreigners."[35]

The Germans were more than eager to take advantage of the leverage they had now gained. After the Juye incident, the S.V.D. missionaries got in the habit of blaming the Big Sword Society for any difficulty that arose. Their intent was clear. In the words of Governor Zhang Ru-mei: "They wish to stir up trouble in this way and let the German troops enter the interior." The result was equally predictable: the local officials leaned over backward to favor the Christians and the just mediation of disputes became impossible. Zhang gave a graphic example of the sort of situation which could arise. In the Wenshang village of Jinjiazhuang, a dispute arose over rights to a village temple. In the scuffle, one Christian was injured,

and the German missionary sent a messenger to the magistrate reporting him killed. The magistrate rushed to the scene but found the man
had suffered only an "extremely small injury." The missionary then
prepared a list of twenty persons "guilty" of the assault. They all
immediately knelt and begged to become Christians. The missionary
then praised them as "good people" who should not be prosecuted,
and presented a list of five other "guilty" villagers. These hastened to
pay the Christians a sum of 170 strings of cash, and a messenger was
sent to testify that they were no longer guilty, but that seven others
were. The magistrate then asked the local gentry leaders of the militia
to mediate. The missionary demanded that the village be fined 900
strings of cash. The magistrate, anxious for a settlement, increased the
sum, added the requirement that the Christians be given a ten-table
banquet, and the affair was at last settled.[36]

More than ever, the Catholics were able to demonstrate the power
of their church, and it is not surprising that, as the S.V.D. biography
of Father Henle states: "Another consequence of the death of the two
Fathers was an extraordinary increase of Christians. . . . The heathens,
begging to be taken into the Church, poured in on me in such numbers
that it was impossible to receive them all. . . . It was soon the same
throughout the entire mission."[37] The Protestants in the area, looking
on with some jealousy, understood the process perfectly: "The influence of the Catholic persuasion is felt in nearly all parts of the field.
Multitudes are flocking to them for the sake of 'help' in various forms,
chiefly for the 'power' that is supposed to reside in them more than in
the Protestant."[38]

The Christians, clearly, had won another round. They had brought
unprecedented humiliation on their official opponents. The protectors of the German mission now had a base in Shandong itself, a
base from which they promised to chastise any who would harm their
missionaries or converts. The officials seemed powerless to resist. But
not all were willing to accept defeat so easily. And so the conflict
would continue—and escalate.

CHAPTER SIX

Guan County, 1898: The Emergence of the "Boxers United in Righteousness"

The Boxers United in Righteousness (Yi-he quan) first appear on the documentary record of the late Qing in the spring of 1898, in connection with events in the Guan county town of Liyuantun. By the fall of that year, large bands came together in the name of the society to attack Christians in nearby villages. On their banner was the slogan: "Support the Qing, destroy the foreign." With a name and a slogan identical to the Boxer movement that swept across the North China plain in 1899–1900, the Guan county boxers have long been regarded as the source of the entire Boxer movement. As early as February 1900, a Catholic newspaper gave this version of the origins of the Boxers:

> This society has five names: Plum Flower Boxers [Mei-hua quan], Boxers United in Ri $\lrcorner$ teousness, the Red Lantern Shining [Hong-deng zhao], the Armor of the Golden Bell and the general name, Big Swords. . . . It began with the Eighteen Chiefs of Guan county, who had repeatedly destroyed the church in Liyuantun. In recent years it has spread further and further to encompass now almost all of Shandong with the object of pacifying the foreigners and eradicating their religion.[1]

The Guan county incidents, it would seem, played a critical role in the transformation of Big Swords into Boxers, and we shall have to examine the history of this area in some detail, to discover exactly what that role was.

THE SETTING

Guan county lies on the western border of Shandong, almost due west of Jinan. The people of the area had long been known for their "brave spirit and love of righteousness," as one Song geographer put it. Other early sources cited by the county gazetteer stress the poor soil which supported only a simple rural life-style and few scholars. Cotton was grown, and the county was known for its weaving; but most weaving was only for home consumption and the area produced little surplus above subsistence levels. The gazetteer estimated that in 1829, with a population quite close to that recorded for the late Qing, there averaged, after taxes, fertilizer, and labor costs, less than 2 piculs (about 120 kilograms) of grain to support each Guan county resident. Isolation and poverty did not always work to the advantage of public order, for it was claimed that the people's "stupid and direct" character made them easily misled by heterodox ideas, to which they would stubbornly cling, even following the arrest of sectarian leaders. By the 1830s, the conservative authors of a new gazetteer would bemoan the people's loss of their prized simplicity: "The young have become like knights-errant, and like to indulge in wine, and drink for pleasure. They form cliques and seek revenge."[2]

In the mid-nineteenth century, these knight-errant types, in alliance with White Lotus sectarians, joined the most important local uprising of west Shandong, the Song Jing-shi rising of the 1860s, mentioned above in chapter 2. More devastating, however, was the 1854 capture of the county seat by the Taiping during their northern expedition, and marauding by the Nian leader Zhang Zong-yu in 1863.[3] The Qing military was unprepared to protect the area from such large-scale attack. The county seat was supposed to be guarded by one lieutenant (qian-zong) with seven mounted and twenty-six infantry soldiers. Feeble as even this force would have been, by the Guang-xu era it had been reduced to the lieutenant, his assistant, and eight soldiers. The magistrate was thus compelled to raise a force of his own, numbering some twenty men.[4] Not surprisingly, the task of repelling the mid-Qing rebels and suppressing local disorder fell to local militia forces. These achieved some temporary success, and the gazetteer records laudatory biographies of their leaders. But the gentry in this region was not strong enough to generate the sort of complex militia networks of the Yangzi Valley, so well described in Philip Kuhn's work.[5] In fact, Guan county produced only two ju-ren in the last hundred years of the Qing.[6]

Guan county can justly be characterized as geographically isolated, politically weak, militarily ill-defended, and with a population increasingly restive—either in sectarian rebellion or in righteous defense of some popular cause. These characterizations can be applied all

the more to the area around the small market town of Liyuantun. This
area was known as the Eighteen Villages (*shi-ba-cun*), though it
actually contained twenty-four settlements by the turn of the century. It was a detached area or "exclave" (*fei-di* or *cha-hua-di*) of Guan
county, isolated across the Shandong border inside Zhili, more than
fifty kilometers from the county seat. Bordering this exclave to the
north were similar detached areas of Linqing and Qiu county. Scattered through the area were patches of the appropriately named
"Crooked border" (Quzhou) and Jize counties of Zhili in a carto-
graphic maze conventionally described in the Chinese sources as
"interlocking like a dog's teeth" (*quan-ya xiang-cuo*) (see map 5).[7] One
peasant from Liyuantun described the different jurisdictions which
lay within easy walking distance of his home:

> Speaking from our village, either two *li* [one kilometer] to the east or ten *li*
> to the west was Wei county. Twelve *li* to the northwest was Qiu county;
> twelve *li* to the south was Jize [Zhili]; fifteen *li* to the southeast was
> Linqing; ten *li* to the south was Quzhou; five *li* to the west were 300 *mu* of
> Guangzong [Zhili] land; and we were 130 *li* from the Guan county seat.[8]

The gazetteer of Wei county, within which many of these exclaves
were located, notes that these geopolitical anomalies had existed for so
long that their origins were unknown,[9] and none of the other gazetteers from this area offers an explanation for the exclaves. My own
presumption, from the gazetteers' summary of the administrative
history of the region, is that they came into being during the Northern
and Southern Dynasties (420–581) when this was a much contested
area and witnessed a number of changes in administrative boundaries.[10] Whatever their origins, it goes without saying that these
exclaves made the area extremely difficult to govern. In the words of
the Guan gazetteer:

> [The exclave] is separated [from the county proper] by a great distance,
> and its customs are rather peculiar. Bandits ravage everywhere, and
> commoners and Christians are mixed together. Isolated outside the bor-
> ders [of the county and province], it becomes a separate little principality.
> Even a long whip will not reach to control it, and [its residents] are
> impenetrably stubborn [if one attempts] to govern with reason.[11]

After the problems with the Christians arose, one magistrate was told
by the local residents: "Before, the prefect and magistrate repeatedly
came to calm and pacify us. They would fix a date and only when they
received permission did they dare to enter this territory."[12]

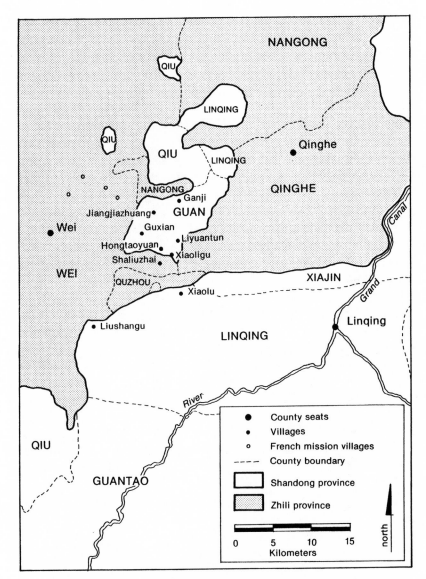

Map 5.   The Guan County Exclave Area

As the gazetteer notes, in addition to the Christians (to whom we shall turn in due course), the area was a natural refuge for bandits, at least since the end of the nineteenth century. One official from Nangong, just to the north of the exclaves, reported that despite flooding in Shandong and a few robbers coming across from that province, he had found the area peaceful on visits home in 1894 and again in 1896. But by early 1899, robbery and banditry were increasing at an alarming rate. The bands were well armed, and dared to raid even in broad daylight. Casualties were beginning to increase; seven were killed in one village. Some bands even attacked shops in the towns, and the danger had become such that "merchants dare not cross and the markets are still."[13] Though the claimed increase in banditry during the last years of the century is certainly accurate, it is not entirely plausible that things were so peaceful just a few years earlier. A missionary in Linqing, writing late in 1895, reported that this area was particularly hard hit after the west bank of the Grand Canal broke in 1895. But even without the flooding, "every year the whole section during the winter months is overrun by robbers, some mounted and others on foot, who carry things with a high hand." Suppression of these bands was made all the more difficult by the fact that "every yamen has its sympathizers with the robbers, who give information of every attempt to suppress them."[14]

But sympathizers were not only to be found among yamen underlings. It is clear that some of this border region "crime" was the sort of social banditry which enjoyed a degree of popular support. The most commonly reported incidents were highway robbery, theft from the wealthy, and the kidnapping of members of rich households.[15] Ordinary peasants did not suffer from such activities, and if the bandits spent their new-found wealth in their home villages, many stood to gain from the infusion of new money. In 1899 in Guan county, a certain Chang Wu-hua-gui (Spendthrift Chang the Fifth?) became something of a local hero, raiding widely with a band of several dozen, and sponsoring operas on his return. The county military was too weak to do anything about him, but ultimately the full force of the state was brought against him when he overstepped permissible bounds by cutting off the hand of a passing official's female attendant, in order to remove her bracelet.[16]

With banditry, kidnapping, and highway robbery becoming endemic, commerce in this area, never very strong, naturally suffered. Indeed the Guan county gazetteer notes that while the Eighteen Villages area had four markets in the mid-Qing, the 1830 gazetteer already listed two of them as no longer active, leaving only those at Liyuantun and Ganji—the latter being the administrative and cultural center of the exclave, where taxes were paid, an academy was located, and most of the petty gentry mentioned in the gazetteer lived.[17] By 1934, the two abandoned markets had revived (one becoming the major town of the area) and two more had been added for a total of six. When, in the century since 1830, this revival occurred is not at all clear. But given the state of unrest in the region, and the late Qing decline in the Grand Canal (twenty-three kilometers to the southeast, and the major transport artery), it is unlikely that any substantial recovery had occurred by the 1890s.[18] Still, compared to the rest of Guan county, the area was considered well off—and this no doubt contributed to the fierce independence of its residents.[19]

Guan county in general, and perhaps the Eighteen Villages in particular, had something of a reputation for conservatism, which befitted an area isolated from the major currents of change. In the 1930s footbinding was still common in the county; there was little enthusiasm for new schools or modern science, and only ten percent of the population was literate. These same attitudes showed themselves in the Eighteen Villages area just after the time of the Boxers, when strenuous opposition arose to the conversion of a local temple into a modern school.[20] Old traditions died hard in this region, and that is a point to keep in mind when we consider local opposition to the incursions of the Western faith.

A HISTORY OF SECTARIAN ACTIVITY

The reader will recall that our discussion of sectarian history in chapter 2 mentioned Guan county on a number of occasions. There is little doubt that this isolated county had more than its share of heterodox sects. One of the earliest documentary references to the Yi-he Boxers, in 1779, mentions a certain Yang in Guan county who is supposed to have practiced the Yi-he boxing, though the investigation failed to turn up any clear evidence.[21] And of course in 1861–63 this area was a center of the Song Jing-shi uprising, which included a number of White Lotus adherents. Both these incidents were in Guan county proper, but it is notable that the Daoist priest Zhang Luo-jiao, whom we discussed in connection with the Armor of the Golden Bell, hailed from the market of Ganji in the Eighteen Villages exclave, and he learned the White Lotus spells of the Li trigram sect from a resident of another town in the area, Guxian.[22] Thus there is no doubt that both sectarian activity and martial arts practices had long been common in Guan county proper and in the Eighteen Villages.

The gazetteer notes that from the late Qing and into the Republic, sectarian activity was on the increase. Nothing subversive was seen in this: the adherents were described as "good men and faithful women" (*shan-nan xin-nü*). But the number of sects proliferated in this period from the White Lotus, to the Green and Red Gangs (Qing-bang and Hong-bang), the Yellow Sand Society (Huang-sha hui) and the Way of the Sages (Sheng-ren dao).[23] The local history is undoubtedly correct in attributing the popularity of such sects to the county's isolation, its relatively low educational level, and the weakness of the orthodox gentry. These same factors would also enhance the authority of the boxing groups which led the attacks on the Christians. But we should not be quick to link these boxers to the sectarians of the past, for here as elsewhere, the record suggests a far closer connection between sectarians and Christians.

THE CHRISTIANS

It goes without saying that the extreme weakness of the Qing state—especially in the isolated exclaves—favored the intrusion of the Catholic Church just as it facilitated the persistence of heterodox sects. Catholic missionaries in this area followed Chinese jurisdictional boundaries in dividing their missionary fields, with the French Jesuits in Zhili and the Italian Franciscans in the Shandong exclaves. The French presence was a sizeable one, with several missionaries resident in four closely connected villages in Wei county, about ten kilometers northwest of Liyuantun. The four villages were all substantially Catholic, and when troubles broke out in 1898, and again in 1900, they became virtual fortresses with cannons and large stores of rifles and ammunition to protect their congregations.[24] In 1890 the Italians who presided over the congregations in the Eighteen Villages were based in Wucheng, some fifty kilometers to the northeast, but during the next decade a priest was stationed at Xiaolu about seven kilometers south of Liyuantun in Linqing proper. From these bases the missionaries had been phenomenally successful in attracting converts in the exclave, so that by 1900 there were chapels in at least eleven of the twenty-four villages.[25]

As for the source of these converts, the story is a familiar one. One villager described the growth of the French congregations:

> Early in the Guang-xu period, the White Lotus were active here. The county magistrate sent troops to make arrests. The French priest "Liang" told everyone, "I am a missionary. Whoever wants to join the Catholic

Church raise your hand and register. I guarantee that nothing will happen to you." Several who had joined the White Lotus raised their hands and joined the church. In this way the government troops did not arrest them.[26]

In fact, the congregation in Liyuantun began in the same way. Though the oral history accounts differ in detail, the most plausible reading suggests that in the wake of the Song Jing-shi rising, a former rebel soldier was arrested. A secret Christian in the village convinced the man's family to go to the Catholic priest, join the church, and appeal for the man's release. This was done, and with success. As a result of that example, a number of others followed suit and hastened to joined the church. By the time of the Boxer incidents, there were some twenty Catholic families in the town, mostly surnamed Wang.[27]

LIYUANTUN

We call the settlement of Liyuantun a "town" because it was fairly large, with about 300 households,[28] and hosted a periodic market on the 5th and 10th day of every ten-day portion of the Chinese lunar month. It was a multiple surname town, with Yans representing some 40 percent of the households, Wangs about 20 percent, Gaos 10 percent, and the rest a scattering of others. Even these largest surname groups were not all members of the same lineage; and kinship does not seem to have been an important source of either cohesion or divisiveness in the community. A settlement of this size would certainly have had a few permanent shops, and in addition to the larger periodic market there was a smaller market for vegetables and other local produce virtually every day. Aside from its size and commercial function, Liyuantun was not greatly different from many villages of the north China plain: its peasant inhabitants lived in mud-walled and thatch-roofed houses and supported themselves by farming, peddling, and (especially the women) spinning and weaving. They planted wheat, millet, sorghum, and cotton, and the fairly fertile soil supported quite respectable yields—often 200 catties per *mu* of millet, and over 100 for wheat but sometimes, I was told, as high as 500 in a very good year.

Predictably, this level of prosperity produced a fair degree of social differentiation in the town. The wealthiest family owned about 300 of the town's 4,000 *mu* of land, and there were at least six other households with over 80 *mu*. A few of these large landholders rented out some of their land, but far more common was the practice of hiring long- and short-term agricultural labor. At the bottom end of the economic spectrum were a few landless households, most of whom no doubt hired out as laborers, and a larger number who owned only three of four *mu* of land—supplementing their farm income from a variety of secondary occupations. The most important subsidiary occupation was peddling of vegetables, fruits, *dou-fu*, the coarse grain dumplings known as *wo-wo*, and other miscellaneous items. Some twenty families supported themselves in this way.[29]

The relative prosperity of the community also produced a fairly strong lower gentry contingent. These were not the sort of people who commanded much influence above the county level of government, but given the town's isolation, their local status was no doubt considerable. From the dispute with the Christians, we can establish that there was a total of at least six *gong-sheng*, civil and military *sheng-yuan*, and *jian-sheng* (a purchased degree) in Liyuantun. They were not necessarily from the wealthiest families. In fact one of the gentry leaders is said to have owned only about 15 *mu* of land, which he tilled with his family in addition to teaching at the academy in Ganji.

The Ganji academy was the cultural center of the entire exclave, and it was from the twenty to thirty students at the academy that the successful examination graduates would emerge. Ganji also served to link the exclave to the fiscal functions of the state, for it was there that taxes (a relatively high 500 cash per *mu*) were paid. With the most important gentry-led militia in the exclave also based here, Ganji was unquestionably the cultural, political and military center of gravity of the exclave.[30]

THE DISPUTE WITH THE CHRISTIANS

In the middle of Liyuantun, just north of the main east–west road, stood a pair of small dilapidated buildings which had once housed a temple to the Jade Emperor (Yu-huang miao) and a charitable school (*yi-xue*). According to oral tradition, the temple dated only from 1861, so it must have had a short life: during one of the rebellions of that decade it was damaged and left in disrepair. At the same time, the Christian congregation in town was growing rapidly, and in 1869 it was decided that the Christian and non-Christian residents should divide the temple property and the 38 *mu* of farmland whose rents supported the temple and school. In an agreement negotiated by three neighborhood leaders (*jie hui-shou*) and the local constable (*di-bao*), and signed by twelve neighborhood leaders, the Christians were to receive the temple property of 3.91 *mu*, and the 38 *mu* of farmland were to be divided into three sections for the "Chinese religion." This 1869 agreement was regularly challenged and never popular. In fact, some of the neighborhood leaders who signed the agreement later appear as gentry disputants of the settlement. The key point in dispute was the right to the buildings which had housed the temple to the Jade Emperor, who was, after all, the highest god in the pantheon of Chinese popular religion and a figure who should not have been lightly evicted. In 1873 and 1881, the Guan magistrate Han Guang-ding enforced temporary settlements which acknowledged the difficulty of expelling the Christians, and permitted them to use the site until they could buy another.

But the missionaries had no intention of accepting a less central location and demanded the enforcement of the original deed. In 1887 one of the Franciscans arrived with bricks, tiles, and the intention of dismantling the temple and building a proper church on the site. But after a few days of work, two lower gentry with purchased degrees (*jian-sheng*), Liu Chang-an and Zuo Jian-xun, led a mob of outraged villagers to drive off the Christians and use their building materials to reconstruct the temple to the Jade Emperor. Once again a magistrate was forced to intervene, this time the Han bannerman and *jin-shi* He Shi-zhen—one of the most popular officials in the county's history. In 1887, he was halfway through the first of three separate terms in Guan county. He would return in 1889–1894 and again in 1896–1898—dates which, as we shall see, put him in power almost every time trouble arose in Liyuantun. He was an energetic Confucian official of the old style, which fitted this area well. He vigorously supported Confucian learning, personally graded the county-level examinations and devoted himself to fund-raising for new gates and "spirit walls" for the local schools. He worked to reform abuses in tax collection, punish corrupt yamen underlings, prohibit gambling, and expel prostitutes; and when he left his post for the last time, the people of the county erected a stele in his honor.[31]

He Shi-zhen went personally to Liyuantun and confirmed that the Christians' construction work had indeed been disrupted. Liu Chang-an was punished by removal of his rank; the new temple was torn down and the property was returned to the Christians. But a final settlement was not arranged before He's term of office ended in 1888.

When subsequent magistrates were unable to resolve the matter, He was ordered back to Guan county, where he asked a gentry elder to mediate a solution. The Christians agreed to accept an alternative site for their church; Liu Chang-an agreed to buy another site and contribute to the construction of the church. He Shi-zhen and the new magistrate each added 100 taels of their own for the new Christian church. And thus, as far as the magistrate and the residents of Liyuantun were concerned, the case was resolved.[32]

The Italian missionaries and their French protectors, however, refused to accept this resolution. They claimed that the Christian villagers had conveyed the temple grounds to the missionaries and only they, not the Chinese Christians, were qualified to confirm an authoritative settlement. Magistrate He held his ground, insisting that the dispute was between two Chinese parties in the village, the Christians and non-Christians. Since the local Christians were satisfied, he would not meet with the foreign priests. A standoff continued for several years with the non-Christians, meanwhile, in possession of the temple site. Then came the 1891 riots in the Yangzi Valley and the strong imperial edict demanding the resolution of all outstanding missionary cases (see chapter 3). In January 1892 the French minister in Beijing, citing this edict, again sought to overturn the local settlement. This time the diplomatic pressure proved irresistible. Local officials told the villagers they could withstand it no longer.[33] The decade of imperialism had arrived.

Immediately after the French protest, the Dongchang prefect ordered the case reopened. The verdict was predictable: the temple site would be returned to the Christians. Now magistrate He donated 200 taels and 1,000 cash for the construction of a new temple on a different site. But the Christians sought revenge—demanding prosecution of those who had so long obstructed their efforts. This brought an escalation of the conflict. Someone (the documents only call him "an ignorant simpleton") invited a Daoist priest, Wei He-yi from Linqing. Wei had the arms of the local militia (of which one of the original gentry activists, Zuo Jian-xun, at least in 1900 and probably in 1892 as well, was the leader)[34] transferred to the temple to defend it against the Christians. With matters clearly getting out of hand, the government responded with a major show of official authority. The *daotai* of the area headed a group including the magistrate He Shi-zhen, the Dongchang prefect, the Linqing subprefect, and the magistrates of the surrounding Zhili counties of Wei, Quzhou and Qinghe to visit the site and meet with the local gentry. The officials told the gentry where their interests lay—meaning, obviously, in preserving the peace by giving in to the Christians. They persuaded the gentry to disperse their supporters, return the original site to the Christians, and dismantle the temple for reconstruction on the site for which funds had been provided. Once again a settlement seemed at hand, this time with the total victory of the Christians.[35]

Up to this point, leadership in the resistance to Christian demands clearly lay with the town's gentry. They had pressed the original suit, and pursued it from the county to the prefecture and finally all the way to the provincial capital. At the prefectural level, three of them had so vigorously protested the officials' failure to protect the rights of law-abiding residents that they were imprisoned six months for impertinence. Needless to say the expense of such a lawsuit was heavy, and several had sold property to support the cost. Liu Chang-an had been stripped of his degree. Their efforts were certainly appreciated, and the local memory of the six main gentry leaders was of "the six greatly aggrieved" (liu da-yuan).[36] But their authority was inextricably linked to the state which had conferred their degrees, and their utility was above all as an avenue to the official courts in efforts to secure a favorable judgment. By 1892 those efforts had failed—for these petty gentry could hardly match the countervailing power of the missionaries. When the officials assembled in 1892 and made clear that they would accept no further protests, the gentry quietly complied. At that point, leadership of the struggle passed to a younger and far more volatile group.

THE EIGHTEEN CHIEFS

Once the Christians regained the rights to the original temple site, they began to build their church. Soon they came under attack from a group of poor young peasants who came to be known as the Eighteen Chiefs (shi-ba kui). According to one account, the Christians fortified themselves in the church and resisted with stones and gunfire. This further inflamed the attackers, who stormed the church, injuring several Christians. The converts fled to the missionaries' residence in Wucheng and, for a time, dared not even return to till their fields. The result was a stand-off, which lasted for several years. When either side attempted to build its place of worship, the other intervened to tear it down. Finally Dongchang prefect Hong Yong-zhou ordered both sides to cease construction until a new settlement could be arranged.[37]

Who were these Eighteen Chiefs who now took up the banner of resistance? One contemporary account says that the name, and number, came from the Eighteen Villages—and from this Dai Xuan-zhi has argued that they represented the militia of the Eighteen Villages.[38] But both the oral history and documentary sources refute this notion. In fact they were all young residents of Liyuantun, mostly very poor, who took upon themselves the task of protecting the temple property. Their leaders were the relatively senior (33 *sui*) Yan Shu-qin, an accomplished martial artist of the Red Boxing (Hong-quan) school, and Gao Yuan-xiang, known locally as Pockmarked Gao (Gao Xiao-ma-zi). Yan owned only four or five *mu* of land, and had to supplement his income by peddling and ginning cotton. His two brothers (also members of the eighteen) both worked as agricultural laborers. Gao Yuan-xiang had as much as ten *mu*, and also made money milling and reselling grain he bought at the market. Only one member was a large landowner, a certain Yan Ming-jian who owned over 100 *mu*. At least three were landless, and most owned very small plots and supplemented their income by peddling or other subsidiary occupations.[39] In the wake of the 1898 disturbances, the French Minister supplied a list of eighteen names which corresponds quite well with the oral history record, and described them as "all impoverished families";[40] and the Protestant missionaries in nearby Linqing called them "of course very poor, the dregs of society."[41]

To the missionaries, this group was certainly nothing but village riff-raff; and there is little doubt that many of them struggled on after the gentry had given up the fight precisely because they had so little to lose. But they were a determined group, and even when Gao Yuan-xiang was imprisoned for two years beginning in 1895, they did not abandon the fight.[42] Still, the group was small and isolated. They knew that they could not withstand the Christians forever, and they needed allies. They turned, accordingly, to the most notable martial artist in the area, who lived about five kilometers southwest of Liyuantun, in Shaliuzhai, a large village with some 300 households belonging to Wei county. His name was Zhao San-duo.

THE PLUM FLOWER BOXERS

Zhao San-duo, also known as Zhao Luo-zhu, taught Plum Flower Boxing. The history of this school goes back at least to the Kang-xi period, when it was taught by a certain Yang Bing, from Hua county in Henan, who had passed the highest military examination with third place honors, and served in the metropolitan garrison. A second generation disciple of his was alive at the time of the Eight Trigrams uprising of 1813—in which the biggest battles were fought in Hua county. This disciple had briefly taught Plum Flower Boxing to one of the military leaders of the rising, Feng Ke-shan. This fact, plus at least one other passing mention of Plum Flower Boxing by an individual arrested in connection with sectarian unrest, has led some to link the school to White Lotus activities.[43] But what is most notable is the fact that when Feng's teacher, Tang Heng-le, heard that Feng had joined the White Lotus, he informed Feng that if he *did* join the sect he was to consider himself disowned as a disciple. And when the rebellion finally broke out, Tang and several other disciples joined the government side to assist in its suppression.[44] It seems quite clear, then, that Plum Flower Boxing was purely a school of martial arts. It had no particular connection to any subversive or sectarian tradition, and was at least as likely to lend its talents to the service of the state.

Of the nature of Plum Flower Boxing in the eighteenth and early nineteenth centuries, we know nothing. But the oral history of the Guangxu era practices is quite clear. The boxing was largely for physical and spiritual exercise, and for self-protection. Its members considered it apolitical. Practices included both inner and outer efficacy (*nei-gong* and *wai-gong*). The former involved incense burning and healing; the latter was strictly martial arts. But neither included any charmwriting, spell-chanting, possession by gods, or invulnerability rituals. The only religious element was incense burning and kowtowing, apparently to such gods of the pantheon of Chinese popular religion as Monkey (Sun Wu-kong), or "Sandy" (Sha-seng).[45] All of this remained true even after the anti-Christian members of the Plum Flower Boxing began to call themselves the "Boxers United In Righteousness." This is highly significant for our understanding of the Boxer movement's evolution, for it means that even though the final *name* of the Boxers would emerge in Guan county, this was not the source of the central rituals which defined and characterized the movement.[46]

The Dongchang prefect described the nature and purpose of Plum Flower Boxing:

> In the districts along the Zhili-Shandong border, the people are sturdy and enjoy the martial arts. Many of them practice the arts of boxing to protect themselves and their families, and to look out for each other. Great numbers practice [boxing] and it has spread widely. In Henan, Shanxi and

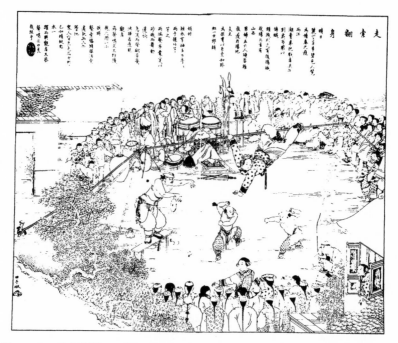

Figure 5. Exhibition of Boxing and Acrobatics. The caption explains that "professional boxers and acrobats from the rivers and lakes" (a term often associated with banditry) gather in the spring to perform for a livelihood. From *Dian-shi-zhai hua-bao* 35, GX 11 (1885), 2nd month (Hong Kong reprint, 1983).

Jiangsu there are also those who teach it, so that its name is widely known. Each year in the second or third [lunar] month there are fairs, and the boxers use this opportunity to gather and compare their techniques. They call this *"liang-quan"* ("showing off their boxing"). Thus in the countryside they are regarded as plum boxing meetings.[47]

By this theory, then, the name "Plum Flower" derives from the season in which the most famous activities of the boxers were held: their springtime boxing exhibitions at temple fairs. The society, of course, had no regular meetings, but members would often practice on market days, after sending out announcements to the surrounding villages. Furthermore, "in good times, after the wheat harvest was in and there was plenty of spare time, they would frequently stage exhibitions."[48]

Now as I have said, the most prominent local leader of the Plum Flower Boxers was Zhao San-duo. According to one contemporary account, Zhao San-duo claimed to be a fifth-generation disciple of the school, out of a total of eight to that time. While not entirely credible, the account does suggest that Zhao was a senior master of the boxing.[49] He could count, among his own and his students' disciples, some two thousand individuals—many of them conveniently employed as yamen runners, giving him valuable allies in any dispute appealed to the local authorities. Born in 1841,[50] Zhao would have been in his mid-fifties at the time the Eighteen Chiefs approached him, and a man of some stature. There is considerable debate about Zhao's wealth: the Guan county magistrate was told Zhao owned 400 *mu* and ran a store, while all the oral history sources insist that he was a poor peasant with at best 10 *mu* of land. It is clear, however, that he came from a family of some local prominence, for his grandfather was a *sheng-yuan*, holder of the lowest examination degree. A careful weighing of the evidence would suggest that Zhao hailed from a relatively humble lower gentry family which had, by this time, already fallen to an economic status only slightly better than most peasants.[51]

But if Zhao's economic status had fallen, that did not mean that his *social* status was comparable to that of most peasants. That was surely not the case. He was known for his generosity and righteousness, and loved to use his influence to right wrongs. Some of the wrongs he managed to right had been suffered at the hands of Christians, and this too served to enhance his local reputation. It was no doubt in large measure because of this reputation for righteousness and resistance to Christian wrongdoing that the Eighteen Chiefs turned to Zhao for assistance. But Zhao, at first, would not accept them, for he did not approve of their rowdy behavior. He was particularly anxious that his family and reputation not be endangered. These, assuredly, were the concerns of a man of some stature. And it was only after some pressure from his own disciples that Zhao agreed to become the teacher of the Eighteen Chiefs, and adopt their struggle as his own.[52]

THE STRUGGLE RENEWED

It is not clear exactly when Zhao got involved in the Liyuantun struggle, but his first major action came in the spring of 1897. It took a familiar form for the Plum Flower Boxers: a spring boxing exhibition. In April 1897, after the Christians again began assembling building materials for their church, Zhao staged a major exhibition right in Liyuantun itself. Though explicit anti-Christian acts and slogans were

avoided, it was designed as a clear show of force.[53] Within a matter
of days, a major conflict broke out. The Christians holed up in the
church then under construction. Then on April 27, a band, variously
numbered at 500 or 2,000 men, attacked and occupied the contested
site. The Christians counter-attacked, and in the struggle which
followed, many Christians were injured, one fatally. The church was
destroyed, Christian homes were looted, and all the Christian families
fled the area.[54]

For the moment, the Liyuantun villagers and their Plum Flower
allies held the upper hand. They had clearly won the local power
struggle; the Guan magistrate He Shi-zhen was relatively sympathetic
to their cause; and the Shandong governor Li Bing-heng, as always,
did his utmost to prevent foreign pressure from giving undue advantage to the Christians. By the fall of 1897, the authorities had endorsed
a new settlement which represented a total victory for the villagers
and their boxer allies. The officials were to buy the Christians a new
site and supply building materials for their church. The original site
was to revert to the villagers. In the official correspondence with the
foreigners, it was held that the site had been confiscated and would be
used for a charitable school for all villagers, but in fact it was used to
reconstruct the temple, and a great celebration and opera were held to
commemorate the completion of construction.[55]

But the victory was short-lived, for no sooner had the land been
recovered for the temple than the two German missionaries were
killed in Juye. The Germans seized Jiaozhou; Li Bing-heng was removed as governor, and suddenly the Christians were in the ascendancy across the province. With imperial edicts now demanding that
incidents be avoided at all costs, the missionaries pressed their case
with a vengeance. Once again, a local settlement of the Liyuantun case
was upset by political pressures originating far from that isolated
town. The Italian bishop rejected the settlement of 1897, and applied
the pressure which would soon produce the official destruction of the
temple and the return of the site to the Christians.[56]

As the conflict escalated in 1897–98, and the pendulum swung
from boxer to Christian ascendancy, important changes were occurring in the Plum Flower Boxers. For one thing, Zhao San-duo was
joined by a certain Yao Wen-qi, a native of Guangping in Zhili and
something of a drifter. He had worked as a potter in a village just west
of Linqing, and had taught boxing in the town of Liushangu, southwest of Liyuantun on the Shandong-Zhili border, before moving to
Shaliuzhai where he lived for about a year. Though Yao was appa-

rently senior to Zhao in the Plum Flower school, and thus officially Zhao's "teacher," his influence could not match that of his "student." Yao did, however, serve to radicalize the struggle, and even introduced some new recruits with a reputation for anti-Manchuism.[57] This began to bother some leaders of the Plum Flower Boxers: "Other teachers often came to urge Zhao not to listen to Yao: 'He is ambitious. Don't make trouble. Since our patriarch began teaching in the late Ming and early Qing there have been sixteen or seventeen generations. The civil adherents read books and cure illness, the martial artists practice boxing and strengthen their bodies. None has spoken of causing disturbances.'"[58] For a long time, Zhao seemed inclined to listen to such advice, but as the conflict intensified, he found that he could not extricate himself. In the end the other Plum Flower leaders agreed to let Zhao go his own way—but not in the name of the society. He was, accordingly, forced to adopt a new name for the anti-Christian boxers, the Yi-he quan.[59]

THE BOXERS UNITED IN RIGHTEOUSNESS

As we have seen, both the Plum Flower and Yi-he boxing traditions can be traced back at least to the eighteenth century. Though none of the early references suggests an identity of these two schools, that was a claim frequently made in the 1890s. As early as June 1897, an Italian Franciscan source asserted that the two schools were the same.[60] According to the Dongchang prefect, "the Plum Flower Boxers were originally called the Yi-he Boxers," and they returned to this name only in early 1898, after the officials threatened the Plum Flower Boxers with arrest should they ever again assemble.[61] One well-informed oral history source claimed that the boxers called themselves Yi-he Boxers, but outsiders called them the Plum Flower Boxers[62]—an interpretation consistent with that of the Dongchang prefect, who said the latter name derived from their springtime boxing exhibitions.

What does seem clear is that throughout their history, the Plum Flower Boxers had avoided any official proscription—in contrast to Yi-he Boxing, which had frequently been linked to heterodoxy. In the late Qing, the widespread Plum Flower Boxing practices— whether for self-protection or periodic competitive exhibitions— had not aroused any official suspicions. Thus the "Plum Flower" name was relatively safe, and the majority of its teachers wished to keep it that way. When the officials began to act against their type of boxing, they forced Zhao San-duo and his anti-Christian allies to use another name. Obviously, this had more than just nominal significance. It meant that the major boxing school of the region would not, *as an organization*, participate in the disturbances. For a brief time, the Plum Flower Boxers had allowed their name, and Zhao San-duo's network of disciples, to be used for anti-Christian purposes. But now that period was at an end, and the group which continued the struggle was far more heterogeneous, considerably more *ad hoc*, and much less subject to the discipline of the established Plum Flower master-disciple relations—or even to the authority of Zhao San-duo.

In a sense, whatever the past history of the Yi-he Boxing or its relations to the Plum Flower Boxers, in 1897–98 it was *sui generis*. Since these were the boxers who gave their name to the entire 1898–1900 anti-Christian and anti-foreign movement, it behooves us, at last, to consider what the name meant. The conventional translation has long been "the Righteous and Harmonious Fists,"[63] but "Boxers (or Fists) United in Righteousness" or "Boxers of United Righteousness" seems to fit better the popular understanding of the term. It is clear that "righteousness" was the key term—thus one official report erroneously referred to a "Righteous People's Assembly" (Yi-min hui).[64] The "righteousness" of the Boxers was clearly that *yi-qi* so valued by the heroes of China's martial arts tradition: it embodied loyalty, integrity, and a selfless altruism. The *"he"* was understood to mean "harmonized" or "unified"—almost in the sense of the homophone "合."[65] One missionary in Linqing translated "Yi-he quan" as "United Boxers,"[66] and the British minister correctly reported that "The idea underlying the name is that the members of the society will unite to uphold the cause of righteousness, if necessary, by force."[67] In essence, then, the Yi-he quan of Guan county was a group of pugilists united in righteous indignation over the usurpation of the Liyuantun temple for use by the Christian church.

It should be noted, moreover, that this was not the first time that "Yi-he" had been used in this sense in the area. In the 1860s, when militia were being organized throughout southern Zhili for defense against the Nian, Wei county organized three militia: a "Militia United in Purpose" (Zhi-he tuan), south of the city, a "Militia Worthy of Righteousness" (Pei-yi tuan) east of the city, and a "Militia United in Righteousness" (Yi-he tuan) north of the city—this last perhaps deriving its name from two villages, Yihebao and Yiheying, in the area. These militia were disbanded around 1870, and then revived in 1896 as banditry in the area increased—the last of the three under its same mid-century commander, Zhao Lao-guang, a civil *sheng-yuan*. This Zhao was no relation to Zhao San-duo; but a cousin of the latter, also a *sheng-yuan*, was vice-commander of the "Militia Worthy of Righteousness." While there is no foundation for the theory that the Yi-he Boxers of the 1890s grew from such militia units, relations between these groups and Zhao San-duo's boxers were not unfriendly, and in fact some of the militia members practiced his style of boxing.[68]

It was, then, a broad coalition that arrayed itself as the Boxers United in Righteousness in opposition to the renewed Christian assertiveness of 1897–98. The most radical and aggressive members were the Eighteen Chiefs of Liyuantun, under their leader "Big Sword" Yan Shu-qin. They were naturally the most committed to the struggle over the temple, and the most unyielding in their opposition to the Christians. Then there were the more aggressive members of the Plum Flower Boxers like the itinerant Yao Wen-qi, whose activism had frightened off the conservative Plum Flower leaders. Lending some respectability to the organization was Zhao San-duo: a man from a family with minor gentry in its past, and a noted boxing teacher with hundreds of disciples and a reputation for fearlessly upholding justice. Zhao provided contacts with friends who were petty gentry and militia leaders in the area—for this was clearly the social circle to which he belonged. In more developed areas of China, this would not have been a particularly formidable coalition. But in this isolated border region, where the geopolitical maze left the formal state so weak, this sort of loose coalition of friends, disciples and allies— many with roots in different jurisdictions—could be extremely powerful. Communication between its constituent elements was certainly far more efficient than communication between the separate administrative jurisdictions. Any official attempt to suppress these boxers could easily be frustrated by hiding with friends and allies across the maze of county and provincial borders which wound through the region. In this new Boxer coalition, the Christians had a formidable foe.

1898: CHRISTIAN VICTORY AND BOXER DISPERSAL

In their drive for victory in the Liyuantun case, the French demanded the dismissal of the popular magistrate He Shi-zhen,[69] and early in 1898 they managed to secure his resignation. He was replaced by a man with much less impressive credentials: a Jiangsu *sheng-yuan*, Cao Ti, who had purchased the *gong-sheng* degree to become eligible for office. It seems that with the district's long history of trouble, no others were willing to risk their careers by accepting appointment to Guan county. After a conference in Jinan with the prefect Hong Yong-zhou and Li Bing-heng's successor as governor, Zhang Ru-mei, Cao took up his post and traveled immediately to Ganji in the Eighteen Villages exclave, accompanied only by a single clerk and two runners.[70]

The atmosphere in the area was certainly tense. Following the German seizure of Jiaozhou and the "plentiful sprinkling of proclamations over the province," missionaries in Linqing reported with some glee that the German actions were having "good effect in making some contribution toward the cure of China's greatest evil, i.e., her stolid pride." But at the same time they admitted that in the Liyuantun area, "thousands of sympathizers have been abetting the rebellious natives, and declarations of a general rebellion in which all Christians were to be slaughtered, were rife."[71] The Dongchang prefect's report was consistent with this last interpretation: "This year [1898] in the first and second [lunar] months [22/1–22/3] there were rumors of foreign troops coming, and the Plum Boxers again gathered so that there was panic all around and both converts and people were apprehensive."[72] According to Cao Ti, when he entered Ganji, boxers were seen everywhere: "Wearing short jackets and knives, they filled the streets and alleys. Everywhere one looked, one saw their disorderly appearance." Most of the Liyuantun Christians had fled.

Cao's first task was to ease the tension, but that was not easily accomplished. Establishing himself in the Ganji academy, he assured inquirers that he wished to settle the case peacefully, and invited the local people to send representatives to meet with him the next day. No one came. Then Cao summoned the students to an examination, hosted them with tea and cakes and graded their examinations, rewarding the best candidates. But he learned little: after ten days he confessed that he still did not understand the situation. Eventually Cao managed to bribe a boxer by the name of Sixth Gao with daily payments of 5,000 cash in exchange for information on the boxers' activities; and through Gao, Cao learned that Zhao San-duo was the key boxer leader. He also learned that Zhao was particularly close to a local militia leader, Yang Chang-jun, whom he summoned and threatened with arrest if he did not bring Zhao forward. But Yang could not persuade Zhao to come, the latter refusing on the plausible grounds that he was now wanted in several provinces and had a price on his head. He was understandably doubtful that any guarantee Cao Ti might give for his safety would have any authority in the other jurisdictions of the area. In the end, Cao Ti's mission seems to have ended in failure, though his continued stay certainly upset the boxers. Fearful that the magistrate had surely not come all alone, and that well-armed troops must be hidden not far away, many of the boxers "did not dare to return to their own homes, but hid in empty rooms of the great households."[73]

By February 1898, the prefect Hong Yong-zhou took command of the effort to disperse the boxers, and his approach was quite clear. By now, the officials had come to understand that there was a significant social and political gulf separating Zhao San-duo from the lower-class activists among the Eighteen Chiefs. In addition, Hong may well have discovered that Zhao San-duo and the leader of the Eighteen Chiefs, Yan Shu-qin, did not even belong to the same school of boxing. Zhao's Plum Flower Boxing was most known for its contests and exhibitions at markets, while Yan's Red Boxing was favored by professional escorts and armed guards for wealthy households.[74] Zhao, further-more, had never been enthusiastic about accepting the Eighteen Chiefs as his disciples. There was, accordingly, an opening which Hong was fully prepared to exploit.

On February 28, Hong, claiming that Yan Shu-qin was the murderer of the Christian killed in the previous spring, led a group of braves to arrest him in Liyuantun. Hong's official report claims that he killed one boxer and wounded Yan, who was allegedly carried off, near death, by his comrades. This was apparently all a ruse. The troops in fact sympathized with the dissidents and thus fired only blanks at Yan, who was allowed to escape. Nonetheless the town was occupied, the temple torn down and the site returned to the Christians—though by this time all of them had long since fled the scene, and were living as refugees at one of the Catholic missions. Thus, for the time being, the Liyuantun issue was settled. But Hong had yet to deal with the larger problem of the boxer bands. Here he had to move carefully: "That area is adjacent to Zhili, interlocking like the teeth of a dog. The power of the local boxers and militia is quite great. It will not do to press them too closely, or we will incite another incident."[75]

Zhao San-duo clearly held the key to the situation. Hong Yong-zhou was eventually able to arrange with the local militia leaders adequate guarantees of Zhao's safety to entice him to a meeting in Ganji. There Zhao was greeted with elaborate courtesy, after which the prefect "instructed the boxer leader Zhao San-duo very clearly, and showed him that for his best interest the Plum Boxers must be dispersed, and if they ever assembled again he would be prosecuted."[76] The Guan magistrate Cao Ti leaves us a plausible record of exactly how the officials appealed to Zhao's self-interest, telling him: "Your family is said to be well off and your sons and grandsons already established. Why have you not sought to protect yourself and your family, and have instead loosed your disciples to cause trouble, even committing murder and arson? Why do you let yourself be the puppet of others?"[77] Zhao confessed that he had mistakenly taken some unruly elements into his organization as a result of the Liyuantun incidents, but now Christians had branded him a "criminal chieftain" and he had to keep his boxing followers for self-protection. When the Shandong officials promised protection, Zhao doubted the efficacy of their guarantees in Zhili, where his home was located. Finally, as a result of these negotiations, the prefect together with the Linqing subprefect and the magistrates of Guan, Wei, and Quzhou counties all assembled to offer their guarantee of Zhao's safety, if he would only disperse the boxers. The officials even traveled to Zhao's home in Shaliuzhai to hang a plaque granting him a *lin-sheng* degree at his gateway. And Zhao, in return, assembled his followers in the crossroads before the academy in Ganji and ordered them to disperse.[78]

But as we have seen, the boxers of this Shandong-Zhili border region were an extremely heterogeneous lot, and Zhao's authority was by no means assured. Furthermore, there were any number of factors serving to destabilize the situation, one of which was the presence of new troops brought in to garrison Liyuantun and other key points. Already in March it was reported: "the officer left in charge with a few soldiers has gotten into trouble. His men fell to rioting, and taking things without leave, whereupon the people rose in their wrath and took the officer prisoner, and refused to allow him to depart until he had settled their little bill for damages."[79] Throughout the spring there were reports of disturbances by the Shandong troops despatched to this region, and many people fled to the cities for safety.[80] Meanwhile in April, a notice appeared on the examination hall in nearby Daming prefecture with the following warning:

> *Notice:* The patriots of all the provinces, seeing that the men of the West transgress all limits [literally: over-reach Heaven] in their behavior, have

decided to assemble on the 15th day of the fourth moon and to kill the Westerners and burn their houses. Those whose hearts are not in accord with us are scoundrels and women of bad character. Those who read this placard and fail to spread the news deserve the same characterization. Enough. No more words are needed.[81]

Clearly there were a number of people who were unwilling to accept quietly the dispersal of the anti-Christian forces.

On the other side of this conflict, the missionaries were anxious to press to the fullest the advantage afforded by the high tide of the Scramble for Concessions. Not content to have acquired the temple site for their church, they insisted on the arrest and prosecution of their persecutors. When Hong Yong-zhou attempted to negotiate a settlement with the Italian missionary, the latter refused even to discuss monetary reimbursement. To the anti-Christian forces this was a sure sign that their adversaries would not settle until they were caught and punished. But there was one common element to the missionary and the official Chinese positions: the focus was now entirely on the Eighteen Chiefs. It was their arrest, and especially that of Yan Shu-qin, that was sought. Late in the spring, when Christians were harassed in another of Guan county's Eighteen Villages, it was the Eighteen Chiefs—not the Plum Flower Boxers or Boxers United in Righteousness—who were blamed.[82] Thus by the spring of 1898, Zhao San-duo and the core of the boxer alliance appeared to be off the hook.

This opened the opportunity for the officials to attempt another approach toward these "peaceful" boxers: to recruit them into the militia. As early as 1895, when the transfer of troops in connection with the Sino-Japanese war had left many areas ill-defended, the court had ordered the Shandong governor, then Li Bing-heng, to begin organizing local militia.[83] In December 1897, the court endorsed a memorial by the conservative official Xu Tong in favor of rural militia.[84] At a time when massive indemnities for the recent war were sorely testing the Qing budget, and army retrenchment was sought as one solution to the fiscal crisis of the state, militia were necessary to maintain public order in the face of rising banditry. In Shandong, Governor Zhang Ru-mei took militia organizing seriously. He reported, in June of 1898, that he was touring the province organizing *bao-jia* and militia groups—travels which would bring him to Lin-qing, within a few miles of the Liyuantun exclave, in July.[85] By the end of the year, the court would praise him for his successful efforts in this regard.[86] Though the purpose of these militia was primarily defense against banditry, Zhang did see a role for them in the disputes with the Christians. In May he reported:

> I have already sent deputies to the various localities to work together with the local officials to clean up the bao-jia [registers] and establish rural militia (xiang-tuan). Originally I wished to clear up the sources of banditry, but these can also be used to mediate between the people and the Christian converts.[87]

But Zhang was not really so naive as to believe that the militia would be neutral in the boxer-Christian disputes. His subordinates had already uncovered Zhao San-duo's close ties to the local militia leaders, and Zhang's own memorial of a month earlier had referred to the power of "boxers and militia" as though they were a closely linked pair. Thus Zhang's controversial recommendation on June 30 is hardly surprising:

> If we allow them [the boxers] to establish private associations on their own authority, and officials take no notice, not only will foreigners have an excuse [to protest], but in time it could become a source of trouble. Northerners are customarily willful. Their bravery and fierceness in struggle are an established custom. The techniques of these boxers, and their system of masters and disciples have had some success in protecting the countryside and capturing bandits. We should instruct the local officials to order the gentry and people to transform these private associations into public undertakings, and change the boxing braves into people's militia. This would conform to public opinion and make them easier to control, and it would seem that both people and converts would benefit greatly.[88]

In support of this recommendation, Zhang presented an erroneous and no doubt deliberately fabricated report that the boxers of the Shandong-Zhili border were derived from a militia called "United in Righteousness" which had existed in the mid-nineteenth century. This memorial has provided the key piece of evidence for the theory of Dai Xuan-zhi (first suggested by George Steiger) that the Boxers grew out of an official militia.[89] Enough, I hope, has already been said to demonstrate the error of this notion. The claim in Zhang's memorial was a politically motivated attempt to justify enlisting the more reliable of the boxers into the local militia. The fabricated history need not concern us. But the proposal to transform boxing braves into loyal militia members was a serious one. Zhang's memorial reveals the source of this recommendation to be his lieutenant governor Zhang Guo-zheng and his judicial commissioner, none other than Yu-xian.

Given Yu-xian's earlier support of the Big Sword Society in southwest Shandong, it is easy to see why he might have favored enrolling boxers in a militia which would be both a defense against bandits and an effective counterweight to the Christians.

How many boxers, if any, were actually enrolled in militia bands we do not know. It is unlikely that much was done during the busy agricultural season of the summer. But it is also true that the agricultural cycle served to quiet the struggles against the Christians, as the opponents were all busy in the fields.[90] Zhao San-duo was certainly inactive; that much is certain. Whether he had been bought off with money and honors, as the accounts above suggest, or had simply gone into hiding (perhaps even leaving the area), as the local defenders of his memory insist,[91] is impossible to say. But we should keep in mind the settlement which was reached with Pang San-jie in northern Jiangsu following the Big Sword uprising of 1896. While the officials were not able to drop the charges against Pang, they agreed to stop pressing him if he simply made himself scarce for a time. It is quite possible that a similar understanding was reached with Zhao. Whatever the ingredients of the truce during the summer of 1898, it was a peace that could not last.

FALL 1898: OUTBREAK AND SUPPRESSION

In his handling of the Guan county incidents, Governor Zhang Ru-mei's principal advisor was his judicial commissioner Yu-xian, whose reputation for handling anti-Christian incidents had been considerably enhanced by his successful suppression of the 1896 Big Sword Society uprising. Throughout his career in Shandong, Yu-xian would approach the boxer troubles from the perspective of his experiences in southwest Shandong. It would be the fatal flaw of his policy. Along the Shandong-Zhili border in 1898, the damage would be relatively slight; but with several Christian deaths, the incident was certainly more serious than that of 1896. And the *reason* for the policy's failure is particularly significant. The Big Sword Society had been a relatively disciplined organization: its innermost rituals secret, its master-disciple relations clear, and its domination by members of the village elite complete. It was possible, therefore, for Yu-xian to tolerate the society when it was primarily involved in combatting banditry, and later, when its behavior went beyond acceptable bounds, to terminate the Big Swords promptly by executing their leaders.

In Guan county, the government saw Zhao San-duo and the local militia leaders as the key to any peaceful solution. Its approach assumed that if an agreement could be reached with them, they would enforce it on the boxer bands: thus the elaborate ritual whereby Zhao dispersed his boxer followers, and the government's subsequent attempt to enroll them in the militia. The problem was that the boxers of this region were a much more heterogeneous group than the Big Sword Society of the southwest, and Zhao's authority was not secure. Some adherents, like Yan Shu-qin, did not even come out of the Plum Flower Boxing tradition; and Zhao himself had been forced by the other Plum Flower leaders to disassociate himself from that school, so he could hardly rely on his authority as a senior teacher of Plum Flower Boxing. The key roles of the Eighteen Chiefs and the wandering potter Yao Wen-qi demonstrated that the leadership of the established village elite was by no means secure. The government, of course, hoped to split Zhao San-duo and the militia from these elements, and concentrate the brunt of its suppression on the Eighteen Chiefs. Had this been an area like southwest Shandong, where strong landlords and tight village communities made for village leaders who could enroll their tenants in the Big Sword Society, that approach might have worked. But such was not the case along the Shandong-Zhili border. While the approach worked better than it would a year later in northwest Shandong, it was still less than a total success.

In the fall, after the harvest was in, rumors began to circulate that the Shandong officials were planning further arrests.[92] The rumors were probably accurate, for on September 28 Governor Zhang had received a message from the Zongli Yamen informing him that only the arrest of the anti-Christian leaders stood in the way of settling the Liyuantun case. Probably in the next month, two were arrested: Yan Shu-qin's elder brother, and another of the Eighteen Chiefs, a thirty-four year old tenant farmer by the name of Yan Shi-he.[93] It was in this context that a group of soldiers stationed at the missionary residence in Xiaolu, Linqing, crossed the border into Zhili and, probably in the course of searching the village, took some beef from Shaliuzhai, Zhao San-duo's home base.[94] This was all the provocation the more radical boxers needed. Convinced that the Christians intended to press their dispute to the end, the boxers took the offensive. In this decision, the lead was taken by Yao Wen-qi, the potter-cum-boxer, whose mobile life had led him from his home in Guangping prefecture to Linqing and finally to Shaliuzhai, where he had been living for about a year. But Yao needed Zhao San-duo's help. When the latter proved reluctant to give it, Yao together with the Eighteen Chiefs bundled off Zhao and his entire family on the night of October 25 and forced him to take up the attack.[95]

For the next few days, boxers gathered by the hundreds at various points in the exclave area, and to the south along the border of Shandong and Zhili proper. The group from Shaliuzhai first moved north, harassing Christians and destroying two of their homes in a village northwest of Liyuantun on the 26th.[96] In the next few days, more bands mobilized and moved generally southward, passing through Hongtaoyuan, which had a large Christian population, and destroying a church and several houses in Xiaoligu, both in the Guan county exclave, before heading on south to the border of Shandong and Zhili proper.[97] Meanwhile, rumors spread of a planned attempt to rescue prisoners from jail—most likely Yan Shu-qin's brother and the other arrested member of the Eighteen Chiefs.[98] The boxers borrowed forty or fifty horses from supportive villagers; and they raised flags with their slogan, which a French missionary translated "Obeissance aux Tsing, mort aux Européens,"[99] and an American rendered "Up with China and down with the foreigners."[100] It was certainly "Fu-Qing mie-yang" or "Zhu-Qing mie-yang" ("Support the Qing, destroy the foreign") and thus the first appearance of the slogan that was to be so universal in the Boxer movement.[101] But the Qing clearly could not tolerate this sort of "support," and the officials hastily summoned troops from Linqing in Shandong and Daming in Zhili.

The use of force, however, was not the government's preferred tactic. According to the Zhili governor, the magistrates of Guan, Qiu, and Wei counties, together with representatives of higher officials,

> ordered the militia heads and gentry directors (shen-dong) of the three counties to go forward to enlighten the people to sincerity and public-spiritedness, and to make them aware of the pros and cons. They strenuously reasoned with the boxers. Zhao Luo-zhu [i.e., Zhao San-duo] then publicly kowtowed to Yao Luo-qi [i.e., Yao Wen-qi] and the boxer crowd, and asked them to disperse and return to their homes. The boxers were deeply repentant and on the 17th and 18th [October 31 and November 1] they dispersed in small groups and returned home.[102]

Subsequent defenders of Zhao's memory deny that he heeded this gentry plea to disperse his followers,[103] but in fact such an action would have been totally consistent with Zhao's cautious approach and his repeated hesitation to get involved in the Liyuantun struggle.

The springtime dispersal of the boxers had gained at least a summer of quiet. But this dispersal failed as soon as it began. As the boxers headed back to their homes, some passed through Hongtaoyuan where the Christians "assaulted them verbally." Yao Wen-qi and some of the more radical types became extremely unhappy, and banded together again on the night of November 2. Early the next morning, some seventy or eighty boxers attacked the Christians of Hongtaoyuan, burning the church and seven houses and killing two or three Christians. Then they moved off in the direction of the Christian villages to the north of the Wei county seat. But the French missionaries there had been organizing a large and well-armed militia of their own—eventually totaling 477 men in the four principal villages. These were to prove unassailable, but the nearby village of Disankou was attacked around noon on the third, and Christian homes looted and burned. By the following day, however, Qing troops had assembled once again, and they attacked the boxers at Hou-Wei village, killing four and capturing nineteen including Yao Wen-qi. Yao's head was removed the next day, and hung on display in Hong-taoyuan.[104]

This battle marked the end of the 1898 disturbances, but neither the officials nor the troops were anxious to use their overwhelming military superiority against the anti-Christian forces. In the battle of the fourth, many of the government soldiers simply fired into the air, and sought to avoid injury to their adversaries. There seems to have been little pursuit of the boxer remnants, who once again fled to the south. There, back on the Shandong-Zhili border, Zhao San-duo was once again at their head. When the government promised amnesty to all but Zhao, and local gentry came to persuade fellow villagers to return home, Zhao again dismissed his band and traveled north into hiding in central Zhili.[105] Meanwhile, "The peaceful boxers were enrolled in the militia in order better to keep in touch."[106]

This would not be the last word from the boxers of this exclave region. The two most important leaders, the supremely cautious Zhao San-duo and the more activist Yan Shu-qin of the Eighteen Chiefs, were still at large. In 1900, after the Boxers had spread over much of the north China plain, and the court in Beijing had sanctioned their anti-foreign activities, these two men rose again—Zhao operating mostly in the same area around the Guan exclaves, and Yan Shu-qin moving north into Wucheng along the east side of the Grand Canal. The separate actions of the two groups suggest that Zhao still wished to keep his distance from his intemperate, plebian ally. When in the fall of 1900, Yan was arrested and taken off to Linqing to be executed, Zhao did not try to intervene.[107] But Zhao's career was still not over. Again he went into hiding, emerging finally in the summer of 1902 when the military *ju-ren* Jing Ting-bin led the local militia to protest the government's failure to grant tax relief to Guangzong county in a year of severe drought. This time Zhao got involved in a disturbance with clear anti-government overtones, and it was his final undoing. Betrayed by another military *ju-ren*, he was arrested and starved to death in jail. His head was cut off, and hung outside the Wei county seat. And so, after years of unrest, the checkered career of one of the first boxer leaders came to an end.[108]

But these events take us beyond our period of primary concern. In the year following the 1898 disturbances, peace returned to the Eighteen Villages. As late as November 1899, a Protestant missionary would report receiving a "cordial welcome" in the now garrisoned village from which the boxers had first emerged—presumably Liyuantun.[109] By that time the Boxers were spreading rapidly over northwest Shandong, but this area was again quiet. The critical question, of course, is how much the Guan county events up to 1898 contributed to the spread of the Boxers elsewhere. But that is a question with no easy answers.

The protracted struggle over the Liyuantun temple has received such attention in previous scholarship on the Boxers, and has been told here in such detail, because this was unquestionably the point at which the "Boxers United in Righteousness" emerged on the historical scene as anti-Christian activists. This was also the point at which the dominant Boxer slogan, "Support the Qing, destroy the foreign" emerged. Quite understandably, many scholars have taken these as clear evidence that the Boxer movement began here. In some sense, that argument is certainly correct. The Eighteen Villages of Guan county achieved a considerable notoriety in 1898–99, and news of their long struggle against the Christians undoubtedly spread widely in both official reports and the gossip of the market place. Without doubt, the name "Boxers United in Righteousness" was adopted in northwest Shandong in 1899 because of the fame which the Guan county boxers had given to that appellation.

But the adoption of the name did *not* mean the spread of any organization. That most certainly did not occur—for the rituals of the two areas were utterly different. The Boxers United in Righteousness of Guan county had no invulnerability rituals at all, no possession, no charms, no spells. The religious content of their boxing exercises was almost non-existent. It was unquestionably this lack of anything approaching heterodox religious practices which made the officials so lenient in their treatment of these boxers, and so ready to recruit them into the militia. With their market-place boxing exhibitions, these were the least secretive boxers of all. That unquestionably helped to legitimize them, and allowed them to struggle on for so many years in opposition to the Christians. Those struggles certainly enhanced their reputation, but the spread of that reputation to northwest Shandong can in no way explain the nature and content of the later Boxer movement. That had to come from somewhere else. We will seek those origins in a moment, but first we must turn to the larger social and political context for the events of 1899, as storm clouds gathered over the troubled province of Shandong.

CHAPTER SEVEN

The Gathering Storm

January 22, 1898, was Chinese New Year Day. Late in the afternoon, the sky over Beijing blackened in a total eclipse of the sun. It was not an auspicious sign, and the mood in the capital was one of "general gloom and depression."[1] The omens were not all of heavenly origin. The Scramble for Concessions was proceeding at full speed, and the Great Powers seemed poised to complete the "carving up of the melon." China would never be the same again, and 1898 showed that clearly enough.

While in the Guan county exclaves local tensions between boxers and Christians were building toward violent conflict, on the national level the imperial state was wracked by political controversy of a very different sort. This was the year of the Guang-xu emperor's "One Hundred Days of Reform," and the rising influence at the court of the visionary reformer Kang You-wei. Kang espoused a unique blend of New Text Confucianism and Western-inspired modernization. He managed to find in the Confucian classics justification for fundamental reform in the direction of constitutional monarchy and state-supported modernization similar to that of Meiji Japan. A stream of imperial edicts called for changes of the examination system to stress practical studies; the reorganization and modernization of the army and navy; the establishment of bureaux to promote agriculture, industry, and commerce; the founding of an office to translate Western books; the broadening of the right to memorialize the emperor; the abolition of sinecure positions; and a host of other lesser matters. For many conservative officials, the reforms went too far too fast; on September 21, a coup d'état returned the reins of power to the Empress Dowager. The Emperor was confined in seclusion; Kang You-wei fled into exile; and some of his closest disciples and allies in Beijing, the "Six Martyrs," were arrested and executed.

The dramatic events at court commanded the attention of Beijing, the treaty ports, and most of the centers of power in the provinces. To many, China was at last—after the successive shocks of defeat by the Japanese and the Scramble for Concessions—rising from her lethargy to embark on a thorough-going program of reform. As early as 1895, Kang You-wei had induced a number of high officials to join his short-lived Society for the Study of National Strengthening (Qiang-xue hui); and in 1898 similar study societies sprouted in major cities. In the treaty ports, Chinese journalism suddenly came of age. While in 1895 there had been only twelve newspapers and eight periodicals (the latter all missionary-linked), three years later there were twenty newspapers and thirty-five magazines, almost all of them "liberal in tendency." [2] When the editor of one of these papers, Kang You-wei's most famous disciple, Liang Qi-chao, was invited to head a new school in Hunan, that province became the most prominent (and radical) example of reform at the provincial level. By the spring of 1898, the Hunan reforms had aroused the vigorous opposition of senior gentry in the province, and there, as in Beijing, one saw a polity pitching wildly from radical reform to conservative reaction.

Though these events have properly dominated the historiography of 1898, we should not assume that the provinces simply mirrored the political swings of the capital. In Shandong, radical reform was never a serious issue. The concerns of the province were the traditional ones of finances, taxes, natural disasters, and rising banditry—plus one newly added threat: the Germans based in Qingdao. The distinctly local nature of the problems in Shandong requires emphasis because the Boxer Uprising is too often regarded as simply the culmination of a swing from reform to reaction, led by the court in Beijing. The background for the final outbreak of the Boxer movement is not to be found in the new conservatism of the court, but in the growing crisis in Shandong itself, and in the policies which the new governor Yu-xian devised to meet it.

REFORM IN SHANDONG

Some modernizing reforms had of course been undertaken. Most prominently, the telegraph line linking Shanghai and Tianjin was built through western Shandong in 1881, with branches linking Jinan, Jining, and Taian. Basically following the route of the Grand Canal, the line went directly through the heart of the later Boxer areas, so it is particularly notable that there is no evidence of popular opposition or complaints that the geomantic balance (*feng-shui*) of the area was being disturbed.[3] During the 1880s and 1890s, lines were extended to prefectural and many county seats—again with no evidence of popular opposition.[4] The relatively peaceful manner in which the telegraph was accepted in Shandong suggests that the local population did not view the introduction of foreign-derived technology as particularly threatening, though the telegraph would certainly prove important in speeding official response to the growing Boxer crisis. The modernization of communications was extended to the postal service in 1897, when the Imperial Maritime Customs assumed operation of the China Imperial Post—first between the treaty ports, and gradually extending to a network criss-crossing the interior.[5]

The only other significant Shandong reform effort was the construction of an arsenal outside of Jinan. Completed in 1876, it was primarily engaged in manufacturing ammunition, though it did repair and even assemble a few rifles. In 1897–98, spurred by the German threat on the peninsula, the arsenal underwent a major expansion.[6] But that was really the extent of "self-strengthening" in Shandong. In 1895–96, the conservative governor Li Bing-heng opposed private efforts to open mines on the peninsula—claiming they were unprofitable and bound to fail, putting large numbers of unruly miners out of work and likely to cause trouble.[7] Even during the heady days of 1898, there was little sign of significant reform activity. The greatest stir was caused by the edicts calling for the conversion of temples into schools. There was some preparation for such reforms—but they came to nought once the conservatives regained power in the capital.[8] The only administrative change was the establishment in September 1898 of a Foreign Affairs Bureau (Yang-wu ju) to handle relations with the Germans, boundary questions around the new concessions, customs service, mines, railways and missionary matters.[9] Change was certainly coming to Shandong, but it was not coming very fast. Above all the province remained preoccupied with quite traditional concerns: most notably, finances and natural disasters.

THE FISCAL CRISIS OF THE STATE

Shandong had always been a surplus-producing province for the Qing, its tax revenues outstripping local expenditures enough to allow the province annually to forward roughly 1.2 million taels to support the central government and poorer provinces.[10] Provincial reports to the Board of Revenue from the early 1890s show few signs that Shandong was having any difficulty meeting its obligations, except in years when extraordinary expenditures were necessary to contain flooding on the Yellow River.[11] The Sino-Japanese War changed all this. First there was the cost of supporting additional troops to defend this strategic and vulnerable province.[12] To a Shandong budget which had been officially balanced at about 3.2 million taels,[13] well over a million taels was added to pay for coastal defense, and in 1894 Shandong was allowed to keep one-half of the amount normally forwarded to Beijing and other provinces.[14] When the war ended in 1895, Shandong was able to disband many of its forces and save on military expenses, but with Japanese forces continuing to occupy Weihaiwei and both Russia and Germany openly eyeing Jiaozhou as a potential naval base, there were real limits to the cuts that could be made in defense expenditures. In addition, the province was saddled with an annual obligation of 390,000 taels to repay the debt incurred to meet Japan's substantial war indemnity.[15]

As a result, in the final years of the nineteenth century, Shandong governors regularly pleaded fiscal insolvency and appealed to the court for some release from their obligations to the central government. Li Bing-heng even courageously protested against the extravagant expenditure of scarce resources for the reconstruction of the Empress Dowager's pleasure gardens at the Yuan-ming-yuan.[16] But there was no avoiding the increased cost of government (and especially defense) in this period, and there is some evidence that to meet these expenses, additional burdens were placed upon the farming population. When the government attempted to raise funds to repay the indemnities with "Bonds to Manifest Confidence" (zhao-xin gu-piao), there were complaints that in some areas of Shandong forced exactions were made based on a household's landholdings.[17] Salt taxes were increased in 1897 to raise an additional 300,000 taels.[18] And in the Linqing area, the subprefect was rewarded for his successes in tax collection, and then resisted demands for the customary reduction in taxes following the poor 1895 harvest. As a result, peasants in the disaster-stricken western part of the subprefecture were reported to be in a "state of insubordination" by early 1896. In the words of a local missionary, "[An] insurrectionary spirit [is] manifest everywhere. . . . It shows in miniature what is to be the result if the Central Government attempts to pay its war debt by laying heavier burdens upon the people."[19]

Budget balancing and the transfer of the burden to the tax-paying peasantry were aided by a steady decline in the price of silver in the 1890s. In Tianjin, a tael of silver exchanged for 3,286 cash in 1891, which was roughly the level of the early 1880s. By the spring of 1898, a tael was worth less than 2,200 cash.[20] In Shandong, peasants paid their land tax in copper cash, with conversion rates fixed at a period when cash were much less valuable. In 1896, in response to complaints from the powerful gentry of eastern Shandong, where taxes were collected at rates as high as 5,800–5,900 cash per tael, Li Bingheng set a uniform rate for the entire province of 4,800 cash per tael.[21] Li portrayed this as a reduction in the tax burden, but that was not necessarily the case in the western parts of the province. It still meant converting silver taxes to cash at a rate roughly twice the market rate. And throughout the province, since the cash-silver exchange rate continued to decline for the rest of the 1890s, landowners found their taxes fixed in terms of a currency whose value was steadily increasing. In real terms, peasant taxes increased year by year, with predictable costs in peasant livelihood and popular discontent.

The decline in the price of silver was one factor which helped local and provincial officials meet the greater costs of defense and indemnities: the taxes collected in cash could be exchanged on the market for ever larger sums of silver taels—the currency in which the state's obligations were set. But this fortuitous assistance from falling international silver values was not without cost. Petty officials and army men found their silver-based salaries inadequate to support their families. Officials with more leverage found a ready opportunity for corruption—as they pocketed the difference between their fixed obligations and revenues which were rising in terms of silver.[22]

The other principal means of balancing the provincial budget was to reduce the military budget by disbanding as many of the corrupt, decrepit, and ill-trained traditional forces as possible. There were five major types of troops in Shandong in the late Qing. Green Standard troops, whose full complement including the governor's brigade was 17,148 men, were far and away the most numerous. In addition, there were garrisions of Manchu bannermen at Dezhou and Qingzhou; military colonies at Dezhou, Linqing, and two points near the tip of the peninsula; patrols for the Yellow River and Grand Canal, whose major responsibility was flood prevention and dike repair; and "braves" (yong-ying) recruited on the model of the regional armies of the mid-nineteenth century.[23] The bannermen were, in one historian's words, "demoralized . . . , indigent, [and] addicted to opium,"[24] but it was not politically feasible to effect any savings by dismissing them. In 1897, the small military colonies in Dezhou and Linqing were abolished, but substantial savings required reductions in the Green Standard forces and the "braves."

In 1897, Li Bing-heng reported that emergency recruitment during the Sino-Japanese War had brought the total number of coastal and internal defense forces in Shandong to some 30,000; but that 16,000 braves and 1,900 Western-drilled troops (lian-jun) of the Green Standard had already been disbanded.[25] Li proposed a further 50 percent reduction in the next five years; in 1898, Zhang Ru-mei reported that 30 percent had already been dismissed. Fears of unrest consequent upon the Yellow River flood of 1898 temporarily halted plans to dismiss the last 20 percent.[26] Nonetheless, considerable savings were realized by all this troop reduction. Li Bing-heng reported total defense costs for 1895 as close to 2 million taels, while in late 1899, Yu-xian submitted a detailed report of Shandong's military expenses totalling only 1.46 million taels.[27]

There can be little doubt that many of these reductions were made only on paper: the soldiers had long since died without replacement while their names were kept on the rolls so officers could pocket the salaries. Others were old, weak, decrepit, or addicted to opium and quite useless for either national defense or domestic peacekeeping.[28] Still, the troop reductions must inevitably have diminished the coercive forces of the state in western Shandong. Few, if any, savings were attempted in coastal defense.[29] With the Germans in Jiaozhou, it was not possible to diminish troop strength on the peninsula. Thus the savings were all realized from the forces in the interior, and the river and canal patrols. Some destabilizing effect on western and southern Shandong was unavoidable. When the local forces were disbanded in southern Shandong early in 1898, the missionaries in Yizhou felt "elements of danger" in a situation which found them "without a defender except the petty military officer, who is left with a couple of secretaries and an umbrella bearer."[30] As the Boxer disturbances increased in 1899, the governor repeatedly noted how thinly defense forces were spread in the interior.[31] Reductions in river patrols left fewer men on the dikes and contributed to the disastrous Yellow River flood of 1898 (see below).[32] Finally, all troop reductions not only weakened the forces of "law and order," but also cast forth large numbers of "dispersed braves" (*san-yong*) who often had no means of support beyond the use of their military skills in lives of crime and banditry.[33]

This was the context for the revived interest in militia organizing in 1897–98. With the need both to cut total military expenses and to concentrate the remaining funds on modern forces for national defense, much of the traditional peacekeeping role of the Chinese military was to be assumed by locally organized militia. It is important to stress that both conservatives and reformers favored this policy. In Beijing, besides the conservative Xu Tong, who urged the establishment of militia in December 1897,[34] the reformer Zhang Yin-huan and even Kang You-wei himself favored local militia as the basis for a citizens' army.[35] In Shandong, both the moderate governor Zhang Ru-mei and his conservative successor Yu-xian encouraged militia organizing.[36] But even Yu-xian should not be seen as an uncritical supporter of any and all militia forces. In the summer of 1899 he impeached two gentry members in Zhucheng accused of "using their power to intimidate others, gathering crowds to coerce officials, and forcibly collecting contributions of grain and cash from the people."[37] In the light of later charges that Yu-xian organized boxers as militia to resist the foreigners, it is significant that the American missionaries in Yizhou believed Yu-xian impeached the Zhucheng gentry because the latter intended to use their force to resist German railway building on the peninsula.[38] Whether or not this particular report is true, the facts are clear that the militia organizing of the late 1890s was not part of some anti-foreign plot by conservative elements. It was an idea supported by officials of all political stripes in an effort to keep the peace while reducing military expenditures to balance the budget.

NATURAL DISASTERS AND CIVIL UNREST

With the Yellow River—"China's sorrow"—cutting across the alluvial plain of western Shandong, this portion of the province suffered repeatedly from floods. At other times, when the summer rains failed, the soil of this dry and unirrigated land hardened and cracked into a barren expanse which peasants would not even attempt to cultivate. Natural disasters such as these made life bitter and precarious on the north China plain, but the peasants did not always passively accept their fate. From the Red Eyebrows of the Han dynasty to the Nian rebels of the Qing, major natural disasters had been followed by massive rebellions which shook the very foundations of the established order. In the final years of the nineteenth century, Shandong and bordering regions of Jiangsu, Henan, and Zhili were again struck by flood and famine—and their impact on the Boxer uprising is unmistakable.

In the south, along the Shandong-Jiangsu-Henan border, the distress started earliest and was most prolonged. By the winter of 1898–99, it had spawned a significant local uprising in Henan. The main problem in this region was flooding, as the rivers flowing south from the mountains of Shandong all drained into the same low-lying area along the southern course of the Yellow River and repeatedly inundated vast stretches of farmland. Inevitably, in this troubled border region, natural disasters and popular distress fed the ranks of the already substantial outlaw population. In 1896, in addition to a tidal wave which brought destruction to the coastal prefecture of Haizhou, the runoff from heavy rains produced widespread flooding in the interior sections of northern Jiangsu. "As a consequence," wrote a missionary correspondent, "HIGHWAY ROBBERIES are the order of the day, the bolder of the country folk 'taking to the road' to make up what is lacking in the field."[39]

The following year was just as bitter for northern Jiangsu. For two years, an area 200 miles square along the Shandong border had suffered severely damaged crops and prices rose sharply: "Food stuffs have not been as dear since the great famine of 1834."[40] Lawlessness increased, with "armed desperadoes who literally prowl everywhere."[41] Further south in Qingjiangpu, the missionaries reported: "During the ten years that foreigners have been in the city there has never been so much robbery as now—the whole vicinity is terrorized."[42] Though southern Shandong was also affected in 1897, with Yizhou reporting shortages of wheat and "an alarming increase of highway and village robbery,"[43] the situation was still better than in Jiangsu. But that only served to attract a potentially troublesome refugee population. In the winter of 1897, the resident foreigners reported: "At this season the roads are usually filled with refugees going South, but this year the movement is reversed, and hundreds of wretched families are to be met making their way northward."[44]

The year 1898 brought no relief whatsoever. Now all the signs of prolonged famine began to appear. "Children are sold or given away."[45] Anything edible was consumed: "The elm trees were stripped of their bark, the lower leaves of the willows stripped of their leaves, and caterpillars and snails were eaten when they could be gotten."[46] The crisis attracted the urgent attention of the central government, always fearful that famine would bring about disruptive vagrancy and increased banditry.[47] But the sorely strapped national budget could not support expensive relief measures, and with taxes already remitted in the famine district, the local governments had no resources at their command. The situation was so desperate that as a money-saving measure, one north Jiangsu magistrate allowed 284 prisoners to die in the county jail between February and October 1898.[48]

By 1898–99, southeastern Shandong began to be affected. Its refugees joined northern Jiangsu peasants in the annual trek south along the Grand Canal—a route which had become a "highway of death and misery."[49] In the same southeastern area which would produce the first anti-foreign attacks of 1898–99, missionaries reported an almost complete failure of crops from drought and caterpillars.[50]

In this situation, some violent popular reaction was almost inevitable, and there were several recorded incidents from early 1898. In one, a group from Shandong crossed the border into Jiangsu where they raided a village and carried off thirty of its members in a dispute over borrowed grain. This was not particularly surprising on this troubled frontier, except for the fact that the Shandong contingent was led by the magistrate of Yi county, who was soon dismissed for having acted on the basis of false testimony. It was, in essence, an instance of "official banditry" and a fair indication of the state losing its grip on the troubled border region, and becoming more a tool than a regulator of local society.[51]

A more serious incident arose in the summer of 1898 when the salt smuggler Tong Zhen-qing from Xiayi, Henan, along the border of Shandong and Jiangsu, rose up in a fairly classic instance of what Elizabeth Perry has called "predatory" rebel behavior. Tong led a band of three to four hundred northward, carrying small red flags with unspecified "seditious words," "to steal grain and cattle and send it back to eat." That much was surely a traditional response to the utter destitution of this region. But Tong added a new element which was particularly troubling to the officials still reeling under the impact of the Scramble for Concessions: he announced his intent to "smash Western learning." Indeed one reason for his northward thrust in the direction of Shandong was allegedly to ally with the Big Sword Society. But the effort failed when Shandong and Henan forces quickly surrounded Tong in a town on Shan county's southern border, capturing him and many others, killing about a dozen, and dispersing the remainder.[52]

The anti-foreign element made Tong's brief rising notable, but the bloodiest action in this area arose from the old Nian base area of Guoyang in northern Anhui. The rising apparently began with an attempted government crack-down on salt smuggling,[53] and quickly grew into a rebellion of tens of thousands under a certain Pimpled Liu (Liu Ge-da). The leaders had long operated along the Anhui-Henan-Shandong border and soon invested the old Nian stronghold of Yimenji. Famine victims rallied to their cause by the thousands, and soon most of Guoyang county had fallen to the rebels, who announced plans to head northward into Shandong, again supposedly to ally with the Big Sword Society. Then, in neighboring Dangshan in Jiangsu, another force rose up under a flag with a "couplet about destroying the Catholics."[54] It was all certainly the greatest threat to the peace that this area had seen in some time—and far surpassed the magnitude of the Big Sword Society disturbances of 1896. But the government assembled overwhelming military force from the surrounding provinces, and by the end of January 1899, within a month of the first violence, the rebellion was suppressed—though not without enormous destruction and loss of life.[55]

Though the Shandong side of the border saw no incidents as serious as this Guoyang uprising, there is no question that the same conditions led to sizeable outlaw gangs in that province as well. In the summer of 1898, the Shandong governor Zhang Ru-mei reported an incident along the border of Lanshan and Fei counties in southern Shandong:

> [The Shandong-Jiangsu border] has always been a place where bandits come and go. This year the spring rains were late and grain prices rose. In addition it was a time of troop reduction and consolidation. Dispersed braves and habitual outlaws from elsewhere ... combined with unemployed vagrants into a mob of several hundreds.... Armed with foreign

rifles and weapons, they plundered neighboring villages on the pretext of borrowing grain, and extorted horses, weapons and ammunition.[56]

As with the incidents across the border in Henan, these bandits were suppressed as soon as their activities became too threatening; but the outlaws seemed to be getting bolder. The most shocking incident occurred in late July 1899—the dangerous season when the sorghum stood high along the sides of the road and provided ready cover for desperate men. A lieutenant-colonel (*can-jiang*) Yue Jin-tang, who had been instrumental in capturing Tong Zhen-qing in 1898, was ambushed and killed by bandits he was pursuing in Shan county. It was certainly not common practice for bandits to challenge the Qing military directly, much less kill an important local officer. Thus the incident stood as a clear reminder that the combination of successive years of natural disasters and a state weakened by cut-backs in the military was leaving local officials in an extremely vulnerable position.[57]

All of this trouble along the Shandong-Henan-Jiangsu border was certainly more than a little disturbing—but it paled in comparison to the devastation of the Yellow River flood of 1898. On August 8, as the river rose following heavy summer rains, "China's Sorrow" burst its banks in Shouzhang, flooding south and east to cover 400 villages as the waters swept through Yuncheng to the Grand Canal. But this break was not enough to relieve pressure further downstream, and the south bank again broke below Jinan sending a broad flood north-east to cover 1,500 villages in an area of some 2,600 square miles. Finally and most disastrously, the north bank broke at Dong'e pro-ducing a vast lake extending through Chiping, where the "Spirit Boxers" would soon be stirred to activity, and on to cover some 3,000 square miles of farm land in northwest Shandong before it finally flowed into the sea. In all, thirty-four counties were affected by the flood, and millions were driven from their homes to seek refuge on dikes or any other high ground they could find (see map 6).[58]

The missionary correspondents of the *North China Herald* did not exaggerate when they called it the "most widespread and disastrous flood since the Yellow River returned to Shandong some forty years ago," and "MORE APPALLING AND DISASTROUS than any within living memory."[59] Foreigners traveling to Jining in the south, and from the American mission station at Pangzhuang to Jinan in the north, reported an endless expanse of water in which one could

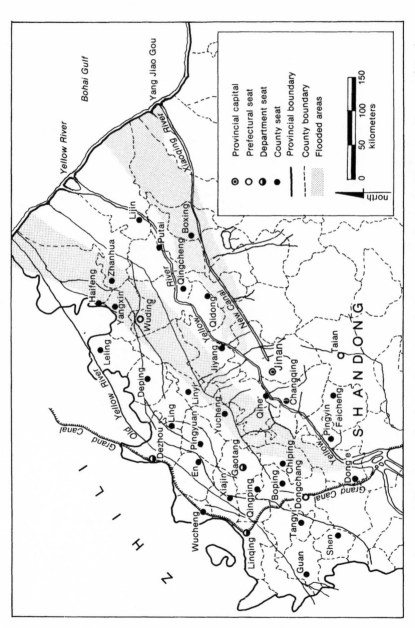

Map 6. The 1898 Yellow River Flood. Based on a map in Inspectorate General of Customs, *Reports of Trade at the Treaty Ports of China,* 1898.

hardly distinguish the river from the fields.[60] In many areas north of the river, the autumn crops were virtually a total loss. As the rains continued into September, the water was extremely slow to recede, and many peasants were still huddled on the dikes eating leaves, bark, or weeds fully three months after the flooding began.[61] Others set off in small family or village groups to beg through the winter in more prosperous areas—usually "preserving their self-respect and conducting themselves in an orderly manner," and insisting that they were "fleeing famine" (*tao-huang*), not "begging" (*tao-fan*).[62]

What made this human suffering particularly tragic was the fact that the 1898 flood was not simply another natural disaster: it had human and political causes as well. During his tenure as Shandong governor, Li Bing-heng had always paid careful attention to the maintenance of the Yellow River dikes. His collected memorials are filled with accounts of preparations for the high waters of summer, and impeachments of minor officials who had failed to prevent breaks and even embezzled official funds. According to one censor's report, Li would spend six months of the year on flood control, and he managed to avoid any major floods during his tenure in office. By contrast, Li's successor, Zhang Ru-mei, never spent a day on the dikes. While Li had kept enough straw and other materials on hand to cope with four risings of the river, Zhang ran out in one big flood.[63] When the flood did come, the governor was unusually slow to organize effective relief.[64]

Zhang, of course, had plenty of other things to worry about in 1898—in particular, the Germans in Jiaozhou. Because of the foreign threat (and also the threat to public order brought about by the other natural disasters and the disbanding of soldiers) Zhang had spent the summer of 1898 touring the province inspecting not dikes, but local militia. The crisis brought on by the Scramble for Concessions had diverted Zhang's attention from the traditional concerns of a Shandong governor. But it is also true that it was precisely a conservative Confucian official like Li Bing-heng who would be most likely to devote himself to an activity like flood control. Less anti-foreign officials were perhaps better qualified to deal constructively with the new threat of imperialism, but they were not necessarily the most likely to concentrate on a matter of far greater importance to the west Shandong peasantry: taming the Yellow River.

But Zhang's responsibility for the flood went beyond the matter of different priorities. When complaints about his handling of the riverworks began to surface, the court ordered a full investigation into charges of nepotism, corruption, and malfeasance in office. Though the investigation, as was typical, found the most serious charges unfounded, it did discover enough evidence of nepotism, favoritism, and protection of corrupt subordinates to bring about Zhang's dismissal and demotion in the spring of 1899.[65]

A second official implicated in the disastrous flood was one Zhang Shang-da, a former Jinan *daotai* whom Li Bing-heng had removed in 1897 for corruption in his handling of the river works. But Zhang Shang-da had gotten along well with the Catholic missionaries, and throughout early 1898, in connection with the Guan county troubles, the French had been pressing for his return. Eventually he was brought back—and given, of all things, flood prevention as his first duty. Though investigators found no evidence of Zhang's responsibility for the 1898 flood, they were forced to admit that his reputation was "extremely bad," and the belief prevailed that this official, brought back at foreign insistence, was through his incompetence and corruption responsible for the great flood.[66]

It would be ludicrous to suggest any necessary connection between pro-foreign officials and incompetence at river management. But it was an undeniable fact that Li Bing-heng's successors were far less diligent and less successful than he in taming the Yellow River. Thus it is not at all surprising that when Zhang Ru-mei was dismissed for his failures in connection with the Yellow River flood, the court should turn to someone much more in the mold of Li Bing-heng. And it was these considerations which led to the fateful appointment of the conservative Manchu Yu-xian to succeed Zhang Ru-mei in the spring of 1899.[67]

This chronicle of Shandong history on the eve of the Boxer disturbances suggests something of a fateful conjuncture. The central dynamic of the Chinese nation and the court in Beijing took the form of a swing from radical reform to conservative reaction—both forces, in their separate ways, responding to the unprecedented new threat from the West and Japan in this classic decade of imperialism. When the Scramble for Concessions threatened China's sovereignty and territorial integrity, the reformers promoted a far-reaching program of economic, social, and political modernization on a Western model—a program designed to protect China from the imperialist menace. The conservatives, on the other hand, feared that alien ideas and institutions from the West would undermine the Qing state and Confucian culture. Both parties recognized that the challenge of imperialism was the overriding issue of the day.

The view from Shandong—and especially from the folks in the countryside—was rather different. Though the fiscal crisis of the state, brought about by the new imperatives of defense and indemnity payments, was certainly part of a dynamic originating in the confrontation with imperialism, the fundamental problems for Shandong officials were quite traditional: natural disasters and popular unrest. And the men and measures most effective in dealing with these problems were from the traditional Confucian mold. Li Bing-heng may have been conservative and anti-foreign, but he vigorously rooted out corruption and efficiently contained the destructive potential of the Yellow River. The organization of local militia may have been quite useless for defending the nation, but it had long been the most effective means of controlling local disturbances. And thus in the spring of 1899, the court turned to another conservative official to govern Shandong. Yu-xian's appointment should not be understood as part of the national struggle between reformers and conservatives. Yu-xian had long served as an official in Shandong, and his selection was a response to the particular problems of that province—not to the national debate over conservative versus reformist responses to imperialism. The irony and the tragedy was that once in power, Yu-xian was immediately confronted with a series of new threats from the Germans in Jiaozhou. Appointed to handle the age-old problems of natural disasters and local unrest, the new governor found himself preoccupied with the new problem of imperialism.

FOREIGN AGGRESSION IN 1898–99

The Scramble for Concessions had ushered in a new era in the international relations of the Chinese empire. The settlement of the Juye incident included Chinese accession to German demands for extensive punishment of local and provincial officials for little more than alleged antipathy to foreign activities. The German seizure of Jiaozhou and the subsequent moves by Russia, Britain, France, and Japan to carve out their own "spheres of influence" positioned the great powers either to complete the "carving up of the melon," or to use their new leverage to press fresh demands on a hopelessly weak and divided Manchu court.

The situation was precarious precisely because it was so new. For decades, as the European powers competed throughout the world for trade, influence, and territory, the sovereignty and territorial integrity of the Chinese empire were assumed to be inviolable. The Sino-Japanese War, ending in the cession of Taiwan and the Liaodong Peninsula to Japan, made that assumption obsolete—although the Triple Intervention of Russia, Germany, and France forced the return of Liaodong to China, thus keeping the continental empire momentarily intact. But the Scramble for Concessions ended China's brief respite, and it was unclear just how much "influence" the Great Powers intended to demand in their newfound "spheres" or, indeed, in imperial governance generally.

Economic advantage was not really an issue in 1899: trade was booming for everyone. The Imperial Maritime Customs annual report was the most sanguine ever: "The Foreign trade of China during the year 1899 was characterized by an astonishing development, and merchants, both Foreign and Native, made handsome profits in almost every branch.... [T]he year beat all previous records and showed an advance without precedent." Much of the advance was in the north, where the new Beijing-Hankow Railroad had been opened as far as Baoding. Along its route had developed a "flourishing trade which was formerly undreamt of."[68]

But not all was peaceful and calm along the railway, largely because of conflicts between foreigners and Moslem troops under the command of Dong Fu-xiang. Dong had been summoned to the capital region in the summer of 1898 to beef up the defenses of Beijing in the face of the new foreign threat. In July, on the way to this new assignment, Dong's troops damaged churches in Baoding. Then on September 30, the day of the mid-autumn festival, there were three separate minor attacks on foreigners in Beijing. The powers quickly summoned extra guards for their legations, but this only heightened tensions and helped bring about a further incident between Dong's troops and railway workers near the Marco Polo Bridge. Though knowledgeable foreigners did not take them seriously, rumors circulated in Beijing on October 23 that "the troops are to act tomorrow when all foreigners in Peking are to be wiped out and the golden age return for China."[69] Finally the powers demanded that Dong's troops be removed from the capital area, and, predictably, this foreign ultimatum was accepted. Growing foreign intolerance of even petty anti-foreign incidents was making it impossible for the dynasty to plan freely for the defense of Beijing—although the foreign protests against Dong's troops had of course convinced many Chinese that these were precisely the men needed to protect the capital.[70]

Early in 1899, the focus shifted from the capital region to the Powers' newly acquired foreign concessions. In February, Russian troops killed forty-seven and injured fifty-one in a tax dispute in Liaodong. In the following month, the Germans launched a punitive expedition (which we shall examine in detail below) in retaliation for minor harassing of Germans in southeastern Shandong. Then in April, the British killed several Chinese in disputes arising from their absorption of the New Territories opposite Hong Kong.[71] In the midst of all this, the Italians decided to join in the Scramble for Concessions, demanding rights to Sanmenwan on the Zhejiang coast. Italy dispatched warships to threaten the Chinese, and in Shandong troops were put on alert to guard against seizure of islands off the peninsula.[72] For once, the Qing was not to be browbeaten. In March, the view from Beijing was that "by all accounts the Chinese this time are more likely to fight than to give way."[73] In November the court issued a clear edict warning provincial officials that if it came to war "not only must the word 'peace' not escape from your mouths, but it must not even remain in your hearts."[74]

Tension was growing throughout China in 1899, and perceptive observers like Robert Hart in Beijing clearly saw the storm clouds on the horizon. On May 28 he wrote his agent in London:

> I have been worried—I can't tell you how much!—by the troubles of China. British doings at Kowloon have been very aggravating: Russian demand for Peking-railway has been a thunderbolt: German action and military movements in Shantung have outraged the people: and everywhere there is a feeling of uneasiness spreading.... [T]here are lots of rowdies among every thousand men and the proof that their own Govt. is weak, as shown by the inroads of foreigners, will encourage their natural rowdyism, while, instead of seeing superior civilization in the foreigner, they will regard him as simply another rowdy and chip in for their share of what disorder can wring from weakness. Some Chinese say that revolt and disorder are fast coming on—that the rioters will wipe out every foreigner they come across—that, regardless of consequences every province will follow suit and such anarchy and bloodshed follow that for years and years industry and commerce will all disappear: how will that suit the west?[75]

In the end, the Boxer troubles were not to be quite this severe (nor were they simply the work of "rowdies"!). But there is no denying the accuracy of Hart's sense of impending crisis.

THE GERMANS IN SHANDONG

This national context is important, for imperialism was a threat to the entire nation, and officials were part of an imperial bureaucracy responding to national as well as local issues. But the Boxers were a regional movement and their origins were in Shandong. We must turn, therefore, to the working out of the new imperialist threat in Shandong—and that meant above all the Germans. German actions were aggressive and peremptory from the very beginning. The Germans intended to reap every possible benefit from their new sphere of influence, and were not to be bound by the niceties of treaty provisions or international law. Even before the Sino-German treaty was signed on March 6, the European power demonstrated its intent to interfere in official appointments throughout the province. On February 22, the German minister presented an ultimatum demanding the removal of the *daotai* in Yanzhou within forty-eight hours, failing which Germany would herself remove the man by force. The Qing quickly complied.[76] Such actions so effectively intimidated local officials that they were loath to complain against German misdeeds. As part of the effort to force Chinese compliance with her demands, German troops had occupied the county seat of Jimo, just northeast of Jiaozhou Bay. During the occupation they had desecrated an image in the Confucian temple. This naturally outraged the local gentry, but the magistrate and governor twice denied that any damage had taken place before a strong imperial edict forced an investigation which disclosed the damage and the official cover-up.[77]

In the immediate area of the Jiaozhou Bay leasehold, the establishment of German administration of course brought new land surveys, revision of tax registers, and enforced purchase of land for use by the colonial administration. Conflicts inevitably arose; and when they did, German justice was swift and severe. When some survey markers were removed in February 1899, a naval datachment was sent to confiscate cattle from twelve suspected villages. The villagers protested, and two were shot and killed in the ensuing confrontation.[78]

But German activity was not confined to the Jiaozhou area. No sooner had the leasehold been acquired than prospectors fanned out across the province looking for exploitable mineral resources. Governor Zhang Ru-mei protested that the treaty provided only for mineral rights by Sino-German firms within thirty Chinese *li* of the two proposed railway lines—north and south of the central Shandong mountains—which were to link Qingdao to its hinterland. Since the route of the railways had yet to be established, and the German firms had invited no Chinese participation, as required by the treaty, Zhang insisted that the mineral explorations cease. But he received scant support from the Beijing government, and the Germans paid no heed to either the governor or the treaties.[79]

For our purposes, the most important activity was in south Shandong around Yizhou. In March 1898, the German chargé d'affaires passed through the region on his way from Beijing to Qingdao and was described as "awe-inspiring" as he paraded along in full uniform. A railway agent followed in April,[80] and there was an unending stream of prospectors looking for coal. "Agents of the German syndicates are daily among us," reported an American missionary, adding that they usually stayed in the German Catholic mission—thus underlining, for the local population, the intimate connection between missionaries and foreign economic penetration.[81]

ANTI-CHRISTIAN INCIDENTS IN SOUTHEAST SHANDONG

We have observed on a number of occasions the linkage between Christian proselytizing and Western imperialism. Whenever the Western powers successfully asserted their "rights" in China, the Christians were certain to follow suit. In Guan county, both an increase in conversions and new Christian assertiveness followed inevitably from the German-imposed settlement of the Juye incident. Throughout this entire region, 1898 was a good year for the Christians. Their star was in the ascendant. A Protestant missionary in northern Jiangsu wrote what might stand as the classic statement on politics and religion in China. He described, late in 1898, a new threat to peasant well-being, which had been added to the ever-present burdens of over-population, natural disasters, and "an unspeakably corrupt officialdom":

> But now another and comparatively new source of oppression has been added in the person of the Catholic priest and his followers. It is well-known that the foreign priests behave and act generally more or less in the style of native officials, and the natives know, often by sad experience, that these priests represent power.... The general principle of action seems to be, let a Chinese be but a Catholic and he shall have the protection of his foreign priest, which means foreign power. His lawsuits are taken up and put through to his advantage, and to the disadvantage of his less fortunate heathen neighbor.[82]

The problem was certainly not new, but by 1898 foreign power was so much more pervasive in China that a new stage seems to have been reached. The same pattern certainly applied to southern Shandong, but there was a significant new twist to the Christian-commoner conflicts in this area. The incidents of 1898–99 are analyzed in a lengthy report by Peng Yu-sun, the *daotai* in Yanzhou, whose relations with the Germans were quite cordial.[83] Peng began by noting that "After settling the [Juye] incident, the number of churches increased; converts became more numerous; and Christian conflicts steadily flared up."

He went on to discuss a particular cause of ill-feeling: Christian abuse of the practice of levying fines on village miscreants. At the outset, there was nothing unusual in this: Chinese custom favored privately negotiated settlements to local disputes as a way of avoiding costly and complicated lawsuits at the officials' yamen. It was common to agree upon a fine which would be collected from the party judged to be at fault. When the Christians first adopted this custom, they asked for straw mats for prayers. As these were cheap, they were usually given without complaint. Then the Christians began to assess feasts. As Peng explained: "In the villages, enjoying wine together to cast off difficulties and dissolve anger remains close to the old custom. Thus when they first fined feasts, the people still reluctantly agreed." Then the Christians began to transform this custom, whose function was to reknit community bonds and reaffirm common values in an always welcome feast. They turned it into a ritual to publicize their own superior status and power. Sometimes they did away with the feast altogether, and collected "converted feasts" (*zhe-xi*), i.e., the money that a feast would have cost. Not only did this eliminate all of the social function of the feast, but it opened the door for steadily escalating demands in cash. Alternatively, the Christians would demand a feast but would hold it in the church. The priest would force the fined "offenders" to serve each dish to the Christians on bended knee, while drums and firecrackers announced the Christian victory to all. By turning rituals of community solidarity into occasions for the open flaunting of Christian power, the Catholics of southern Shandong were fostering a tremendous reservoir of popular resentment.[84]

When one adds to this new Christian assertiveness the anxieties caused by the occupation of Jiaozhou, the steady stream of German prospectors, and the famine conditions which were now affecting southeast Shandong as well as northern Jiangsu, the result is certainly a region ripe for trouble. Soon the local population began to fight back, and in late 1898 and early 1899, anti-Christian incidents spread quickly from east to west across southern Shandong. This series of incidents, large and small, formed an important background to the full-scale Boxer movement which was growing simultaneously in northwest Shandong, and would break into the open soon after the suppression of the disturbances in the south. But the southeast Shandong incidents were not themselves part of the Boxer movement: there is no record of martial artist involvement at this stage. Nor is this unexpected. The area of southeastern Shandong along the coast—and in particular Rizhao where the most important incidents occurred—was an area of significant gentry strength. In the words of one German missionary: "Much more attention is given to study here than in the West [of the province]: the Itsehao [Rizhao] pupils always show to the best advantage in the provincial examinations." [85] Judging from the military to civil *ju-ren* ratio, which was lower in this area than in any other part of the province, the southeast and south hills had a very weak martial arts tradition. Not surprisingly, the anti-Christian incidents of this region were very much of the traditional variety—often inter-communal conflicts with a significant degree of behind-the-scenes manipulation by the local elite.

The incidents seem to have begun when George Stenz, the same intemperate German missionary who had been the intended victim of the Juye murders, became embroiled in an argument in the Rizhao market town of Jietouzhuang early in November 1898. Stenz apparently threatened to call in German troops unless an alleged tormentor of his Catholic charges was turned over, and aroused such a ruckus that a mob carried him off and held him for a few days, inflicting a number of minor injuries. At the same time, Christian converts of the American Presbyterians along the Rizhao-Juzhou border were attacked: their church was burned and several homes were looted. In both cases, there are indications that it was the Christians who provoked the incidents. The American missionaries believed that their attackers came from a village from which a public feast had recently been exacted, and, even while appealing to the American consul for assistance, confessed that their own converts had been "in several matters, more or less in the wrong." [86] The same men viewed the S.V.D. converts' troubles as the product of "more or less justifiable anger against the aggressions of the Catholics." [87]

But the rapid spread of the incidents was also due to a prevalent rumor that, following the Empress Dowager's coup in Beijing, an edict had been issued calling for the expulsion of the foreigners and their converts.[88] In fact, the rumor was quite false, for the Empress Dowager had actually issued two edicts shortly after the coup stressing the obligation to protect missionaries and prevent any untoward incidents.[89] But the force of a rumor bears no necessary relation to its accuracy, and in this case rumor fed on anxiety created by the new German presence at Qingdao and popular resentment over the aggressions of Christian converts.

Throughout November and December, attacks on Christian converts, especially the more numerous Catholics, spread slowly eastward to Juzhou, Yishui, and Lanshan. Then following a lull in January, incidents picked up again after the Chinese New Year, spreading south to Tancheng and further east to Fei county. Though most of the incidents seemed to involve harassing, looting, and occasionally burning Christian churches and homes, others were considerably more serious and, in all, thirteen Christians died.[90] The wave of attacks was extremely effective in checking the Catholic influence, which had been growing since the German seizure of Jiaozhou Bay. Foreign observers saw this clearly enough. The Germans, wrote the Americans in Yizhou, "must do something of a very striking and decisive character if their prestige in their chosen sphere of influence is to be maintained."[91]

GERMAN INCURSIONS OF 1899

The S.V.D.'s Bishop Anzer could not have agreed more. Following the release of the kidnapped missionary Stenz, Joseph Freinademetz, the second in command of the S.V.D. in Shandong, hurried to Rizhao and concluded a quick resolution of the incident. But Anzer refused to recognize his lieutenant's agreement and insisted on 25,000 taels for Stenz's injuries, to be used to construct a church in the county. When this was granted, the German minister in Beijing, Heyking, refused to accept even this resolution; and Anzer himself began playing a double game. While Stenz, recuperating in Qingdao, wrote inflammatory articles for the Catholic press in Germany, Anzer pressed both Heyking and the German governor of the Qingdao colony, Captain Paul Jaeschke, for direct military intervention to teach the Chinese a lesson—but Anzer never told Jaeschke that he had already negotiated a settlement of the Rizhao case.[92] By March, with troubles continuing in southern

Shandong, Anzer had convinced Jaeschke of the need for a punitive expedition, and the latter sent out three men to reconnoiter the area around Yizhou. In Lanshan county, on March 22, these three were surrounded by a curious and possibly hostile crowd. The foreigners opened fire, killing three, then escaped with their belongings after the village head intervened to halt the conflict. All the casualties had been on the Chinese side, but the Germans seized on the incident as an excuse for military intervention.[93]

On March 29, having received approval from Berlin, Captain Jaeschke dispatched two units from Qingdao. After landing on the southeast coast, one moved rapidly inland to the site of the Lanshan incident, burned thirty-nine houses to the ground and returned to the coast. The second unit, guided by the missionary Stenz, occupied the city of Rizhao and demanded an acceptable settlement of all outstanding missionary cases. Finally on May 25, they returned to Qingdao, but not before a group of German soldiers shot and killed one more villager in an incident which the Chinese say began as an attempted rape of the murdered man's wife.[94] On their return, the Germans took with them five gentry hostages from Rizhao, while Anzer repaired to Jinan to negotiate a comprehensive settlement of all missionary cases in his south Shandong diocese.[95]

The alliance of missionaries and imperialism had clearly reached a new stage. In the 1890s, the European powers proved quite willing to resort to gunboat diplomacy to coerce the Qing government to render verdicts favorable to Christian converts and missionaries. But up to this time, the foreigners had always exercised their power *indirectly*—relying on the duly constituted Qing officials to enforce the agreement. After the German seizure of Jiaozhou, there was the added threat that the powers would undertake their own enforcement (see chapter 5). Now that threat was made real. And it was made real by men convinced that the economic penetration of Shandong was linked to the success of the missionary enterprise. Jaeschke wrote that he favored the military expedition "less because of the missionaries than because of our economic interests." And Heyking saw the latter as building on the success of the former: "With the development of our economic undertakings in Shantung, we will have to create a 'clientele' from within the native population. . . . For this the Christian congregations are our first good source. . . . So the violence against them and the efforts to drive them out can't be viewed calmly."[96]

This was the context in which, on April 11, 1899, Yu-xian took up the seals of office as the new governor of Shandong. He may have been chosen because he was better suited than his predecessor to handle the problems of natural disasters and civil unrest. But they were no longer the main threat to the province's stability. The problem now was controlling the Germans and their Christian allies.

THE ROLE OF YU-XIAN

Yu-xian's role in the growth and spread of the Boxer movement is one of the most controversial questions in the historiography of the uprising. Correctly perceiving his conservative and even anti-foreign views, Western (and some Japanese) studies have conventionally mirrored contemporary missionary and diplomatic accounts in viewing Yu-xian as a critically important sponsor of the Boxers. In the most extreme versions of this interpretation, Yu-xian becomes almost the *creator* of the Boxer movement, and the Boxers themselves ignorant, superstitious, manipulated peasants.[97] Before 1949, Chinese studies of the Boxers put forth a similar interpretation, but in obvious reaction to these views, Boxer studies in the P.R.C. have commonly pointed to Yu-xian's earlier role in bandit-suppression in Caozhou, and in putting down the 1896 Big Sword uprising, and painted him as a cruel suppressor of the Boxers as well.[98] Between these two polar views there are any number of plausible alternatives; but no consensus yet exists on Yu-xian's role, and the problem is not subject to easy resolution.

Any careful consideration of the Manchu governor's policies is complicated by the fact that after foreign pressure forced his dismissal in December 1899, Yu-xian emerged much more clearly as a defender of the Boxer cause. A substantial number of contemporary, but invariably second-hand, accounts name Yu-xian as instrumental, in the winter of 1899–1900, in convincing the conservative Manchu princes and ministers in Beijing that the Boxers were a force that could be used to check foreign meddling in Chinese affairs.[99] With the support of these same officials, Yu-xian was appointed governor of Shanxi in March 1900. At that post in the summer of 1900, following the Qing declaration of war against the foreign powers, he encouraged the formation of Boxer bands and carried out a brutal anti-Christian and anti-foreign policy. Most notably, on July 9, he rounded up forty-four men, women, and children from missionary families, foreigners whom he had invited to the provincial capital, and had them executed—to which massacre he soon added seven more turned over by a local magistrate. Though he justified his actions as necessary to calm popular fears of foreign plotting, he clearly revealed himself as a man capable of the utmost cruelty in a hopeless attempt to drive the foreigners from China.[100] Quite naturally, following the occupation of Beijing by the Eight Nation Expedition in August 1900, Yu-xian appeared near the very top of the powers' "most wanted" list. Thus, on February 13, 1901, the Empress Dowager was forced to order his execution as part of the price of peace.[101]

Because of his actions in 1900, it is tempting to see Yu-xian as consistently and rabidly anti-foreign and likely to support such anti-Christian forces as the Boxers. But it is extremely dangerous to read back into 1899 the policies he followed during the summer of 1900, when war had already been declared against the foreign powers. As to Yu-xian's lobbying with the Manchu princes on behalf of the Boxers, the accounts are all imprecise, second-hand, and open to question as quite possibly politically motivated. To the extent that these reports are plausible, they describe the views and actions of an official whose career had just been cut off in mid-course at the insistence of foreign powers. Yu-xian's policies as governor of Shandong must be judged on the basis of the record of 1899. Fortunately, that record is fairly complete; and it reveals a policy developing step by step in a constantly shifting context—a policy whose flaws were as much the product of misperception as of malice.

Yu-xian was a Manchu of the Yellow Banner, the holder of the purchased *jian-sheng* degree—the lowest possible qualification for an official career. His father had been a minor official in Guangdong, and presumably relying upon his family's wealth, Yu-xian purchased the rank of prefect in Shandong in 1879. Though in 1899 he referred to twenty years as an official in Shandong, his first regular post seems to have come only in 1889 when he was appointed acting prefect of Caozhou—a posting which was regularized two years later. Here Yu-xian distinguished himself in the suppression of banditry—though his efforts in retrospect seem more notable for their cruelty than their success. We have already examined this stage of Yu-xian's career: his role first in supporting the Big Sword Society's anti-bandit activities, and then in suppressing the society itself and executing its leader Liu Shi-duan, after the society turned violently against the Christians (see chapter 4). There is little question that Yu-xian rose to prominence on the basis of the reputation he built as prefect of Caozhou—a reputation for efficient, incorrupt administration and quick, if sometimes brutal, execution of justice. In 1895 (even before the Big Sword Society uprising broke out), he was promoted to *daotai* of the entire south Shandong area, based in Yanzhou. In the following year he rose to judicial commissioner of the province, and in 1898 briefly served as acting lieutenant governor under Zhang Ru-mei before being transferred out of the province that fall, to the same post in Hunan. Probably before he ever arrived in Hunan he was reassigned to a military post in Jiangsu, then ordered back to Shandong to replace governor Zhang Ru-mei in an edict of March 13, 1899.[102]

Virtually all of Yu-xian's official career had been within the province of Shandong—and he was particularly familiar with the problems of the troubled southwest. In fact, on the basis of his handling of the Big Sword Society in 1896, he became, while judicial commissioner, the provincial expert on martial arts groups in conflict with Christians. It was he who, in the spring of 1898, was sent to investigate reports of renewed activity by the Big Sword Society in Caozhou. He found no foundation for the reports, and accused the Catholics of causing trouble by levying fines in money or banquets and falsely accusing their enemies of being Big Swords. His detailed report was not remarkably xenophobic, even suggesting at one point that the Catholics would do well to study the methods of their Protestant counterparts.[103] Shortly thereafter, Yu-xian made the preliminary report on the difficulties with the Guan county boxers, including the controversial recommendation that the Plum Flower Boxers be recruited into a local militia (see chapter 6).

As noted above, Yu-xian's appointment as governor was based upon his reputation for tough, efficient administration, and his previous success in flood control—the key area in which Zhang Ru-mei had failed. The American missionaries in Jinan had to admit that the people of Shandong remembered Yu-xian as "a very just official and as being a terror to thieves and robbers"—who were certainly a growing threat following the natural disasters of the last few years.[104] But the Germans were not at all happy with his selection, their minister in Beijing protesting as soon as it was made.[105] For his part, Yu-xian was not at all happy with the Germans. On his first day in office, he memorialized the throne on the subject of the German attacks on Lanshan and Rizhao. He had passed through Yizhou (of which Lanshan is the prefectural county) shortly after the incident occurred, and he observed that while the populace was patient and enduring in the face of German aggression, they could not be expected to "await death with folded arms."[106]

From the very moment he took office, Yu-xian was embroiled in the crisis engendered by Germany's new forward policy in Shandong. First, of course, the Yizhou cases had to be solved; and once the gentry hostages had been taken in Rizhao, Anzer repaired to Jinan to negotiate a settlement. Anzer drove a hard bargain, rejecting all of Yu-xian's attempts to claim indemnification for Chinese lives and property lost in the German incursions, and finally settling on a figure of 77,820 taels in late June.[107] While these negotiations were going on, troubles were brewing in Gaomi on the peninsula, along the route of the railway the Germans were building to Jinan. Conflicts with villagers brought repeated German protests and ultimately direct action. In June, marines were sent to occupy Gaomi city, and on July 5, German troops, retaliating against a stockaded village from which a few shots had been fired, killed thirteen and injured eight Chinese.[108] Meanwhile, on the north side of the peninsula, the Germans engaged in a series of landing exercises near Dengzhou—leaving Yu-xian always guessing as to their true intentions and very much concerned over the thinness of Chinese defenses in this region.[109]

The one consistent theme in Yu-xian's reaction to these German provocations was his insistence that if Germany was to demand indemnification for every Christian property loss, and for every threat or minor injury to a German, then China should be entitled to demand indemnification for Chinese deaths and the destruction of property in Lanshan, Rizhao, Gaomi, and wherever else the Germans had acted in a peremptory manner.[110] Obviously believing that China should begin to treat Germany as she in turn treated China, he suggested that the Zongli Yamen instruct the Chinese minister in Berlin to demand the replacement of the German military officials in Qingdao.[111] The approach was obviously doomed to failure. The Germans had no intention of putting *any* value, much less an equal value, on the lives of heathen Chinese; nor were they about to undercut their influence in Shandong by disciplining their military officers in the field. The result, clearly, was that Shandong entered the summer of 1899 with tensions high and a number of complex questions awaiting solution. They would have to wait for some time. In the middle of July, Yu-xian set off to inspect the dikes along the Yellow River, and he would not return to Jinan until September 7.[112]

"RED BOXERS" IN JINING

While conflicts between Yu-xian and the Germans were building on a number of fronts, the series of anti-Christian incidents which had begun late in 1898 in Rizhao, on the southeast coast, was continuing an inexorable spread westward. The German incursions into Rizhao and Lanshan had brought the troubles in that region to an end, but as news of German excesses spread, resentment against their missionaries and converts grew. Yu-xian reported from the southwest in July that "the gentry and people everywhere are outraged at the Germans' unprovoked murder and arson." [113] No doubt most of this tidal spread of news, rumor, and resentment was carried from town to town by merchants, peddlers, and uprooted elements from this south Shandong area which was annually swept by waves of refugees and casual laborers in search of work or relief. But there were others to spread the news who were more directly the product of the German aggressions. Late in the fall of 1899, missionaries in Linqing reported the passage of a "curious army [of] families of the middle class, small farmers" from regions bordering on the German occupation, who had traveled through south Shandong and were passing on west toward Shanxi to escape the unwelcome Western presence.[114]

The final major disturbances of south Shandong broke out in Jining and the neighboring county of Jiaxiang. It was a logical breeding ground for trouble. Lying immediately east of Juye, site of the 1897 incident which had brought on the new level of German intervention in Shandong, Jining was now the seat of the S.V.D. vicariate, and Jiaxiang had become a major new field of missionary activity.[115] The subprefecture was probably not very well governed, its head being impeached later in 1899 for being drunk in court, making arbitrary arrests, and extorting funds from villages wishing tax exemption on account of poor harvests—a practice known locally as "buying a disaster" (*mai-zai*).[116] Economic conditions were not particularly bad in this region in 1899, but that may even have worked to the disadvantage of public order—attracting refugees from the disaster-stricken area along Shandong's southern border. The key ingredients of the volatile new mixture were detailed in a remarkable report by the *daotai* of all south Shandong, Peng Yu-sun.[117]

Peng first pointed to the increased assertiveness of the Catholic population since the Juye incident, and in particular their growing inclination to use fines and banquets to lord it over their adversaries.[118] It was resentment of this sort of Christian behavior that spurred the growth of boxing groups:

> These [factors] are the source of the rise of the Red Boxers (Hong-quan) and other boxing groups. The Big Sword Society has long existed in Caozhou. Because they disliked the name as infelicitous, they changed it to Red Boxer, United in Righteousness [here written with the characters 義合], Charm Boxing (Jue-zi) or Red School (Hong-men). The names multiplied, and they studied [boxing] techniques. Their methods include promising the gods not to covet children or wealth. They swallow charms and chant spells to be able to resist guns and swords. The main charms with which they dazzle people are very common, wild, and heterodox. They say they are protecting themselves and their families, but secretly they certainly seek to feud with the Christians. They spread the practices everywhere, the same in every village. Because it is simple and easy to learn, it can rouse the common people as surely as beating a drum.

The involvement of boxing groups in the Jining area clearly distinguished this stage of the anti-Christian movement from the incidents in the southeast during the winter and spring. Given the proximity of this area to earlier loci of Big Sword Society activity, Peng's linking of the boxing groups to that organization is at least plausible. Yet no other accounts mention any boxing school in this area other than Red Boxing and I suspect that he included United in Righteousness Boxing because of its prominence the previous year in Guan county. The other names were presumably popular or variant names of the Red Boxers. Red Boxers were clearly the most important new ingredient in the Jining disturbances, but Peng's account of their origins is not necessarily reliable. Red Boxing was an established school quite distinct from the Big Sword Society.

Oral history accounts make it clear that Red Boxers did not, in general, engage in such religious practices as swallowing charms, burning incense, or chanting spells, and did not have any invulnerability ritual. They were, instead, strictly a martial arts school which had long been active in villages along the Shandong-Jiangsu border.[119] Still, at least in northern Jiangsu, there seems to have been some merger of the groups as early as 1897, with members of the Sword Society adopting the Red Boxing or Great Red Boxing name and organizing, as they originally had, for defense against banditry, which had become rampant in that area following successive years of national disasters. The ritual of these boxers was very similar to that of the Big Sword Society: on joining, one paid 2,000 cash to the teacher and presented a yellow paper inscribed with "the spirit tablet of our patriarch" (*zu-shi lao-ye zhi shen-wei*). Charms were scribbled on paper, burned, and swallowed; and incense was burned before tablets (presumably of the patriarch) while initiates did breathing exercises in what was called "receiving the gods" (*jie-shen*).[120] It would appear that the position of the boxing teachers was a very important one, their authority being supported by their special relation to the school's patriarch. The hierarchic organizational principle of the school was thus reinforced by the nature of its ritual.

The two named leaders of the newly active boxer organizations in Jining were both outsiders. The first, Shao Shi-xuan, was identified only as a "weed person" (*xiu-min*), the conventional official term for individuals, often itinerants, who live on the margins of the law. Shao hailed from Feng county in northern Jiangsu, where the earlier merger of Big Swords and Red Boxers was noted, and it was probably he who brought the boxing techniques to the Jining area.[121] The second leader was a discharged soldier from Juye, Chen Zhao-ju, no doubt a direct product of economizing in the military. Those who spread the new boxing were, then, of that mobile class of marginal men—drifters and hucksters who moved from town to town seeking their livelihood from whatever they could hustle on the edges of a predominantly sedentary peasant society. And their success with the new boxing came quickly: "hundreds joined at a shout" throughout the southwest.

The next crucial factor, according to Peng, was the formation of local militia, which as we have seen had been encouraged by officials since Zhang Ru-mei's initiatives of 1898, and was certainly warranted by the rising banditry of 1898–99. Peng was quite precise in arguing that in the Jining area this provided a convenient cover for the boxers to organize for essentially anti-Christian purposes:

> At that time there was an order to organize militia. [Officials] were to rely on public-spirited initiative. Without thorough investigation, all were regarded equally. The idea was to lodge troops with the peasantry (*yu-bing yu nong*) to guard against [foreign] insult. Thus there were proclamations stating that practicing [boxing] techniques to protect oneself and one's family is not prohibited by statute. Petty people could work their will, and had nothing to fear. The local officials completely ignored this [danger]. But if one tested the wind, [one could see] that the great villains and abhorrent people could easily mix among them. [The militia] contained good and bad; the true and false were not distinguished. They did not realize that of those who studied these techniques, only one or two in a

hundred were law-abiding citizens. Most were unemployed vagabonds hiding in the woods and fields, and relying for their sustenance on blackmailing Christians. They trusted to their membership in the [boxing] society for protection, scorning the law and seeking selfish profit.... At first they gathered in cliques of threes and fives; then they formed bands of tens or hundreds, carrying weapons and behaving violently.

The situation threatened to degenerate into a Hobbesian world of unrestrained feuding and communal strife. "The rabble of the markets joined, but could not follow on an empty stomach." So they made pretexts to extort money, kidnap for ransom, burn and loot. Christians fled their homes, but then commoners were attacked for harboring them. The boxers lived off the land: "When they stop, they are given wine and food; on the road they extort dry provisions"— which probably reflected a good deal more popular support for the boxers' anti-Christian cause than Peng was willing to admit. Still, it does seem clear that violent, private justice was becoming so commonplace that even the line between boxers and Christians was sometimes blurred: "There are even Christians harboring grudges who secretly combine with boxer societies to harm their own kind and thus express their private hatred."[122] Given the lack of effective official action to suppress the spreading violence, Peng wrote that he "honestly fear[ed] that the basic danger now is not foreign insult but internal rebellion."

This, clearly, was Peng's greatest concern and the reason for his extraordinary report. He noted that he had repeatedly informed his superiors (which could only mean Yu-xian) of the dangerous situation, but the response was always inadequate. Then Peng delicately made his plea for a more coherent (and obviously tougher) official policy toward the boxer bands: "In officialdom, the practice is to value consensus. When the great officials' opinions are in discord, the subordinate functionaries' actions become incoherent. [Communication between] superior and inferior is obstructed." Quite clearly local magistrates were taking their cue from the governor, who was not inclined to pursue a tough policy against the boxer bands, and Peng Yu-sun, the *daotai* of the region, felt powerless to control threats to domestic peace. He was appealing to the court to direct Yu-xian to take a harder line against boxers.[123]

Peng Yu-sun's report is a critical commentary on spreading boxer activity in southwest Shandong. His analysis, pointing to the provocation of Christian misdeeds and the spread of boxer activity under the protective mantle of officially sanctioned militia, is both balanced and convincing. His direct suggestion that Yu-xian's attitude was instrumental in permitting the spread of boxer bands impels us to take seriously all the missionary complaints against the Manchu governor. Yet we must also hear Yu-xian's side of the story—not merely from a liberal conviction that one must "listen to both sides," but because in this case Yu-xian's policy worked. By the end of the summer he had quieted the Red Boxers of the southwest and restored the region to peace—a peace which would last clear up to the summer of 1900 and the imperial declaration of war against the powers.[124]

YU-XIAN'S BOXER POLICY

Harassment of Catholics in the Jining area began in the spring of 1899, often by groups calling themselves the Big Sword Society.[125] But a significant escalation of violence came around June, bringing protests from the missionaries and the German minister in Beijing. Reports from Anzer indicated that "outlaws of the association (hui-fei) even claim that they are acting on word from the Shandong governor."[126] This accusation was not new in 1899. In March, before Yu-xian took up the seals of office, American missionaries in Yizhou were told by a friendly magistrate: "There is an understanding from the Governor down (if not up, also) that while talking nice things to our faces, they are to do nothing whatever toward putting down the riots or settling the riot cases. The word has gone out that the Christians are to be assumed to be the aggressors in every instance."[127] As we have seen, there was a widespread popular belief in the southeast in the winter of 1898–99 that an imperial edict had sanctioned efforts to expel the foreigners. But the Jining incidents were the first in which martial arts groups claimed to be acting with official approval, and the German officials in Beijing were quick to protest, suggesting with their usual bombast that Germany might be forced to protect her own missionaries and even remove Yu-xian as governor.[128]

Yu-xian's reply to the German reports denied some of the incidents, but admitted many others—mostly extremely petty incidents, many essentially turning the tables on the Christians and assessing them for banquets.[129] By late July, Yu-xian reported the more serious problem presented by the Red Boxers under Shao Shi-xian and Chen Zhao-ju. Proclamations had been posted prohibiting such activities and troops sent to "punish the leaders and disperse the followers."[130] Yu-xian himself briefly detoured from his survey of the riverworks to travel to Jining on July 22. There he conferred with Peng Yu-sun, the Jining subprefect, and magistrates of three affected counties. It was clearly an extremely important conference, for the themes in Yu-xian's report on it were echoed in almost all of his subsequent reports on boxer disturbances.

The key to the problem, Yu-xian telegraphed to Beijing, was that Christian persecution of ordinary villagers had forced the latter to study boxing in self-defense. This would have been a process rather different from the first appearance of the Big Sword Society in 1895, where the defense was at first against bandits and only later against Christians. But it would not have differed much from what we saw in the Guan county exclaves, where the aggrieved villagers turned to the Plum Flower Boxers to protect their temple from the Christians. In any case, while stressing the initially defensive nature of the villagers' turn to boxer organizations, Yu-xian confessed that three kinds of problems arose. In some cases, "outlaws among the boxers" wormed their way into local militia and aroused mobs to forcibly recover fines levied by the Christians. There were "also Christians who combine with boxing outlaws to steal Christian grain and goods and secretly split it." Finally there were outright outlaws who assumed the boxer name to attack both Christians and commoners.[131]

It is quite clear that Yu-xian was in basic agreement with Peng Yu-sun in the substance of his analysis. This should not surprise us, for Peng was the senior official with whom Yu-xian conferred in Jining. The differences in their interpretations were largely matters of degree. Yu-xian perceived merely minor harassment; Peng saw the threat of "internal rebellion." Yu-xian was particularly unwilling to acknowledge any unprovoked persecution of Christians. Earlier in the spring he had gone so far as to claim: "There really have not been cases of mistreating Christians. I know this clearly from what I have heard and seen in more than twenty years as an official in Shandong."[132] But in general, the two officials agreed that the heart of the problem lay in peasants' defensive responses to the post-Juye Christian aggressiveness, the appearance of the new boxer bands, the entry of "outlaw" elements into these bands, and the absorption of unruly boxer elements into the local militia. The real difference between the two officials lay in their proposed remedies for this new threat.

Both men were acting within the context of an imperial policy that remained ill-defined. As we have seen, tensions in 1898–99 over incidents with Dong Fu-xiang's troops and over the Italian demands for their own concession had produced a considerable stiffening of imperial resistance to each new foreign encroachment. But the court was anxious to temper Yu-xian's obvious distaste for the foreigners. Following the German occupation of Rizhao, a secret edict warned him: "If [they] are completely wild and arbitrary, it certainly will not do to give way on every point, or there will be no end to it. But even more will it not do to display rudeness, lest the dispute be started by us."[133] A month later, the court allowed Yu-xian to recall a previously impeached military officer whom the governor had worked with while Caozhou prefect, but warned Yu-xian that the man was not "particularly well versed" in foreign affairs, and that Yu-xian should himself try to see the large picture and "not stick to a one-sided fixed opinion."[134] Clearly the court had doubts about Yu-xian's judgment in foreign affairs, so that whatever impact might be ascribed to the Manchu governor's boxer policy, it was not a simple reflection of reactionary trends in a court now dominated by the Empress Dowager.[135]

At the heart of Yu-xian's policy there were two implicit themes: villagers must be permitted to organize some countervailing power to balance that of the Catholic Church; and a uniform standard must be applied to aggressions against Chinese and Christians alike. With regard to the first, Yu-xian perceived clearly the link between increased imperialist pressure on China and the new conflicts between Christians and commoners:

> I observe that discord between commoners and Christians in Shandong has existed for some time. The reason is that many Christians are not good people. Twenty years ago, it was common for ordinary folks to despise Christians, but they did not mistreat them. Later, they became strong and we weak, so that everywhere Christians began persecuting commoners. Recently, their sect has daily grown more violent. Once one joins, one can rely on the church for protection and do as one wishes in the countryside, making fish and meat of the good people and even coercing officials.[136]

A constant theme of Yu-xian's reports on the Jining incidents is the complaint that Christians were regularly taking the law into their own hands—not only in imposing fines, but even in arresting those who opposed them, and holding them in churches until a fine could be collected.[137] The boxers were only a popular response to this privatization of justice—either administering a crude justice of their own, or recovering the fines that the Christians had imposed. At one point Yu-

Figure 6. Missionary Justice. According to this photo's caption, "the missionaries had tied up this thief to stew in the sun for a few days," a typical instance of Christian missions taking justice into their own hands. From Harry A. Frank, *Wandering in Northern China* (New York, 1923).

xian claimed that the boxers were only recovering improperly imposed fines. "They never take anything belonging to another. If there should be one or two youths who get angry and take things to pawn, they [the boxers] quickly ask someone to return it."[138] Sometimes boxers would content themselves with shows of force—practicing their boxing near the churches or even using the churches as a boxing ground.[139] As long as boxers confined themselves to these defensive activities—acting only as a counterweight to the autonomous power of the Catholic Church—Yu-xian was prepared to tolerate them: "In my area we have already checked accurately," he informed the Zhili governor-general in August. "All peaceful [boxing] for self-defense we do not prohibit. But if they kidnap for ransom and loot, then we send troops to seek them out and arrest them."[140] And this was indeed the policy which Yu-xian followed. Thus in September he was able to report the arrest, interrogation, and execution of the Red Boxer leader Chen Zhao-ju, whose aggressive attacks even on non-Christians had clearly overstepped permissible bounds. In addition two "outlaws from an association" were killed in Shouzhang and ten more arrested in nearby counties.[141] When boxers went beyond the legitimate bounds of self-defense, Yu-xian was clearly prepared to suppress them vigorously.[142]

The second theme implicit in Yu-xian's policy was the conviction that anti-Christian incidents should be weighed in the context of German actions elsewhere in the province. He was painfully aware that reports of anti-Christian incidents were often grossly exaggerated—a fact that missionaries themselves would admit once a crisis had passed. That seems clearly to have been the case in Jining and Jiaxiang. A detailed report on the incidents in Jining revealed no damage to property, only a long series of extortions (all allegedly recovering fines) of Christians, and an even longer series of false Christian claims.[143] In Jiaxiang the cases were far more varied, usually extremely petty, and often little more than family quarrels complicated by the fact that one party was a Christian.[144] There were no deaths or even injuries reported by the missionaries in the negotiated settlements of these cases, and they paled by comparison to the German troops' killing of Chinese in Lanshan, Rizhao, Jimo, and Gaomi. Yu-xian's sense of justice told him that if he was to press vigorously the prosecution of boxers guilty of petty harassment of Christians, then Germany should be forced to make reparations for her troops' actions.[145] But the logic of imperialism had little to do with any abstract sense of justice, and all his complaints against German excesses naturally came to nought.

The Germans in Shandong, for their part, were not particularly inclined to act with more restraint following the incidents in the south. In October, near Taian, three Germans ran a Chinese carter off the road when he failed to allow them to pass. When the man protested, they beat him to death and proceeded on their way. Neither Yu-xian nor the local populace could have been pleased by the Germans' refusal to consider any reparation.[146]

Yu-xian's genuine concern that the punishment fit the crime made him extremely reluctant to adopt the more vigorous anti-boxer policies favored by Peng Yu-sun. But he was also concerned, in what was already a very volatile situation, not to stir up even more trouble by an overly hasty reaction. As he said in early July, "The boxers in that area are very numerous, and the local officials dare not act hastily for fear of provoking an incident."[147] With local defenses weakened by repeated troop disbandment, and numerous famine refugees in southern Shandong posing a potential threat to public order, Yu-xian moved very cautiously. He urged the boxers to disperse, or allowed them to enroll in gentry-controlled militia, arresting only those clearly guilty of criminal acts. The result was recorded in a report from Bishop Anzer in early August: thanks to the governor's protection, Jining had returned to peace.[148] Disturbances would continue in neighboring areas for another month or so, but soon they ceased as well. The final westward spread of these disturbances saw a revival of the Big Sword Society from Caozhou harassing Christians across the border in Zhili. Again, Yu-xian's policy was a lenient one, but the Zhili authorities were quick to apply force, and by October that area too had returned to peace.[149]

The bottom line was that at the end of all these disturbances in southern Shandong, Yu-xian's policy worked—just as it had worked earlier with the Big Sword Society. Damage to Christian property was minimal, and during Yu-xian's tenure in office, there had been no loss of life, either Christian or foreign. Eventually the boxers in the area were dispersed, peace returned and lasted throughout the south. Why was this so? The answer, I believe, lies both in the social structure of the area, and in the nature of the boxer bands. Like the Cao and Shan county area where the Big Sword Society was active in 1895–96, the Jining area was a prosperous agricultural region. The landlord-gentry presence was, if anything, even stronger than in Caozhou. Though the boxers may have gained entry to the militia, control remained with the gentry. Thus at one point the German missionaries claimed that it was the "Jining gentry and militia heads" who were stirring up the trouble with the Christians.[150] Similarly, one of the leaders of the Caozhou Big Swords active at the Zhili border was identified as a licentiate (*fu-sheng*).[151] This was a group toward which Yu-xian's lenient policy of persuasion could be effective.

But there were also boxer bands which came under the control of ex-soldiers like Chen Zhao-ju. Toward them a more forceful policy was necessary—including even violent suppression. Since these were outsiders in an area of stable and prosperous villages, much of the local population was willing to see them sacrificed. Furthermore, the ritual of the Red Boxers of this region had not gone beyond that of the earlier Big Sword Society with its charm-swallowing and incense-burning before an altar to the sect's patriarch. The religious nature of the ritual remained fundamentally hierarchic: the authority of the boxer leaders derived from that of the patriarch. Once Yu-xian had successfully arrested the leaders, it was relatively easy to disperse the followers. Such had been the case with Liu Shi-duan in 1896, and such it was with Chen Zhao-ju in 1899.

In fact, one can almost imagine Yu-xian contentedly patting himself on the back for his successful handling of the crisis through the summer of 1899. He must surely have been aware that another band of boxers, the Spirit Boxers (Shen-quan), was beginning to act up in the Northwest. But he no doubt believed that his now tested methods could handle them as well. He could hardly have been more mistaken.

FOREIGN RESPONSE: GERMAN
AND AMERICAN

There were foreign as well as domestic protagonists in this drama, and the impact upon them of the south Shandong incidents was as important as the impact on Yu-xian. Germany, surprisingly, was somewhat chastened by the experience. Robert Hart reported from Beijing that "the Germans don't want any trouble in Shantung and they find military promenades very expensive."[152] The reaction of Admiral Tirpitz in Berlin was particularly significant. Tirpitz was the secretary of state of the Naval Ministry—the chief architect of Germany's naval development, and of the establishment of the Jiao-zhou colony. The events of early 1899 had convinced him that the missionaries were a "serious danger" to the development of the

German sphere of influence. "There is no doubt," he wrote to the Jiaozhou governor, Jaeschke, "that the uproar in Shantung was caused by the Catholic missionaries in general, and the provocative behaviour of the Chinese Christians in particular." Though the missionaries must be treated well, "this must not reach the point where the governor [of Jiaozhou] becomes their blind tool."

Most importantly, Tirpitz assured Jaeschke that he and the Foreign Ministry were agreed that henceforth Germany would "only demand guarantees for the rights and interests of its own citizens. . . . This does not include the Chinese Christians." The embassy would no longer "even as a matter of form [present] the demands of injured Christians. . . . How much less can one speak of armed intervention." Tirpitz was particularly irate to have learned that Anzer had pressed for the punitive expeditions of March and April while withholding from Jaeschke word of his resolution of the Rizhao case. And he expressed his determination that the German forces in Jiaozhou would not become "supernumeraries for the missionaries."[153]

Thus by fall of 1899, not only had Yu-xian's policies quieted the Red Boxers of southern Shandong, but the German missionaries operating in the region were put on notice that the German government did not look kindly upon their disruptive activities. As a result, southern Shandong ceased to be a flashpoint of Sino-foreign conflict.

Unfortunately, by the fall of 1899, trouble was building elsewhere. Yu-xian had quelled the Red Boxers of the South, but he had yet to deal with the "Spirit Boxers" of the Northwest. They were operating outside of the German sphere of influence, where the Catholic missionaries were Italians (under French protection) and the Protestants mostly Americans. The Americans were the more important, for they had been affected by the south Shandong events as well. When Washington finally got around to assessing the proper response to such incidents, its reaction was quite different from Berlin's. Instead of reining in its local representatives, the U.S. State Department reprimanded its minister, Conger, for failing to demand punishment of local officials in the area where the anti-Christian incidents had occurred.[154] Thus just as the crisis was building in northwest Shandong, and as the American missionaries in Pangzhuang began crying for vigorous foreign intervention, Conger received instructions encouraging him to a more aggressive defense of missionaries and their Chinese converts. The stage was thus set for the full-scale disturbances of the fall of 1899, when the "Spirit Boxers" would ignite the movement soon to spread across the north China plain.

CHAPTER EIGHT

The Spirit Boxers

While official attention focused on the anti-Christian incidents in southern Shandong, another movement was slowly spreading in the northwest. For some time, a group calling itself "Spirit Boxers" had been recruiting followers in the poor villages on the broad plains north of the Yellow River. Their rituals were significantly different from those of their southern brothers, containing for the first time the distinctive invulnerability ritual of possession by gods (*jiang-shen fu-ti*). By early 1899 they were already beginning to organize around anti-Christian principles, and soon they would adopt the name of the Guan county militants: Boxers United in Righteousness. Recruiting in local markets, and training openly in village "boxing grounds" (*chang*), there was nothing secret about these boxers. In the "Spirit Boxers" we see the rituals, the gods derived from popular literature and opera, the name, and the organizational form which were to characterize the Boxer movement for the remainder of its history. Here, at last, were the "true" Boxers.

The sphere of activity of the "Spirit Boxers" roughly corresponds to the diamond-shaped area bordered by the Grand Canal on the north- and southwest, the Yellow River in the southeast, and the present route of the railway from Jinan to Dezhou (not yet built at the time of the Boxers) on the northeast. Chiping county was the most important center, and from there the Boxers spread their anti-Christian message north and east to Gaotang, En, Pingyuan, Yucheng, and Changqing counties.

This entire area lies in the flat floodplain of the Yellow River. The Kang-xi edition of the Chiping gazetteer could have characterized the whole region with its reference to "infertile land and poor people."[1] Especially in pockets where the land is slightly sunken, the soil—difficult to drain and prone to waterlogging—is highly saline.[2] Still, the population was generally quite dense. Arthur Smith estimated that around his mission in En county there were 531 persons per square mile.[3] With a dense population on poor soil, most villagers in this region were extremely poor—"so poor," wrote Smith, "as to be barely able by the hardest toil to keep the wolf from the door."[4] Above all, these peasants were dependent on the vagaries of the weather. In years when the spring saw no rain, the winter wheat crop was likely to fail; and the summer crops were utterly dependent on the rains of July and August. "Without rain," says the Pingyuan gazetteer, "nothing grows when planted."[5] A year of drought could send a family to ruin. And drought or other natural disasters were virtually a way of life in this region. The same Pingyuan gazetteer (from the Qian-long era) gives the most complete listing: sixteen years with droughts, six with floods, and six with other assorted disasters in the first hundred years of the Qing: an average of roughly one disaster every three years.[6]

The unstable ecology of the area meant that a large proportion of the population, at one time or another, would periodically take to the road to survive natural or human disaster. We have noted earlier the severe depopulation of this area at the time of the Manchu invasion, and the smaller but still severe shock of the Taipings' northern expedition and the Nian rebellion. The gazetteers suggest that much of this population loss was from flight rather than wartime casualties. This history made the people of the area unusually ready to leave their native villages in times of trouble—and meant that the population was a good deal more mobile than one normally expects of a peasant society. The Pingyuan gazetteer put a characteristically unsympathetic interpretation on the phenomenon: "They [the Pingyuan peasants] are customarily negligent and [wish] only to escape with their lives. They have few savings, and thus it is easy for them to flee."[7]

In areas where the soil was only slightly saline, it was suitable for growing cotton, and a fair amount of cotton was grown in this region, especially in En, Gaotang, and Chiping. This, then, was one of those areas where handicraft spinning and weaving for a wider north China market were affected by the importation of machine-spun yarn. The

Republican era gazetteer for Chiping notes that many women lost a source of livelihood with the importation of the foreign yarn;[8] already in 1906, according to Gaotang's brief gazetteer, imports of foreign cloth exceeded exports of the local product.[9] We have noted earlier Arthur Smith's account of the deleterious effect of yarn imports on villagers around his Pangzhuang mission (see chapter 3).

Running straight through this area in a north-south direction— from Dezhou, through the capitals of En, Gaotang, and Chiping, and on to the Yellow River at Dong'e—was the "official road" (*guan-lu*) linking Beijing to the cities of the lower Yangzi. Though it certainly could not rival the Grand Canal, this thoroughfare carried a fair amount of commerce and official traffic before the advent of the railway,[10] plus the sizable mobile population of these plains: smaller merchants, peddlers, itinerant healers of body or spirit, migrant laborers, and vagrants cast off from their native village by some natural or personal catastrophe. As we shall see, it is likely that when the Spirit Boxers spread out of Chiping in the direction of Pingyuan (where they would have their first major confrontation with the authorities), they travelled along this road.

In general, however, this was not an area of significant mercantile activity. Cotton was the only major commercial crop, and it was carried overland in the direction of Jinan and the Shandong peninsula.[11] The area produced little else of great commercial importance. There were of course local markets, and even a few larger towns along the main roads, but most visitors to the area described even the county seats as village-like with thatched-roof houses, and a population still primarily engaged in agriculture.[12]

Given the poor soil and underdeveloped commerce, it should not surprise us that substantial landlords were rare in this region. According to the Industrial Gazetteer figures from the 1930s, 95 percent of the peasants were owner-cultivators in En county, 90 percent in Chiping, 78 percent in Gaotang, 75 percent in Changqing, 66 percent in Pingyuan, and 63 percent in Yucheng. Even these relatively low figures for Pingyuan and Yucheng do not necessarily indicate widespread landlordism, for both of those counties record a relatively high 10 percent of the rural population as agricultural laborers.[13] In general, as the Shandong University oral histories show, large landholders in this region usually owned only 70–80 *mu* of land and cultivated it with hired laborers. Reported two informants of their home in Chiping: "There were no large landlords. There were not even any with over 100 *mu* of land."[14]

With neither agricultural nor mercantile foundations for a comfortable, leisured elite, members of the regular gentry were few and far between in this poor dust-driven area of the north China plain. Of all the counties in this area, only Changqing had more than ten *ju-ren* in the half-century before the Boxer Uprising—and it is likely that most of the Changqing degree-holders came from the wealthier half of the county east of the Yellow River. The Chiping gazetteer lists a few luminaries from the sixteenth century, but the county seems never to have recovered from the devastations of the Manchu invasion. Its first Qing *jin-shi* appears only in 1770, and the remaining notables from that era were only lowly licentiates, school teachers, doctors, or militia leaders.[15] This is probably typical of the region as a whole.[16] There was, however, an additional reason for the particular weakness of the Chiping gentry at the end of the nineteenth century.

In 1882, Chiping was hit by a major flood, but the magistrate insisted on collecting taxes at the usual rate. Enraged by this violation of customary concern for peasant subsistence, the people engaged in brief (but unsuccessful) tax resistance. Soon a handbill appeared proposing a boycott of the local examinations scheduled for 1883. It worked: when the exams were held, no one showed up. The prefect threatened to retaliate for this insolence, warning that such a boycott could cause men of Chiping to be excluded for ten examination sessions. In the end, ten men were induced to attend the exams, and the case was considered closed. But not a single man from Chiping earned the *ju-ren* degree for the next twenty years—which the locals noted was almost exactly ten examination sessions.[17] Thus in Chiping—the county which was to become the most important Spirit Boxer base—the degree-holding elite was numerically unusually weak, and the aspirants for that status were no doubt significantly alienated from the Qing establishment.

Lacking the "civilizing" guidance of a strong gentry elite, the residents of this region were not known for their Confucian gentility. Said the Kang-xi edition of the Chiping gazetteer: "The temperament of the Chiping [people] has long been called truculent." Perhaps not wishing to insult the locals too much, the compilers of the gazetteer were quick to add that at least "they know to fear the law." The area was also noted for its gambling and, to our considerable interest, its vulgar popular religion.[18] The Republican gazetteer added that the locals were "quick to fight," and apt to rise in righteous anger to external stimuli—certainly an accurate characterization of the Boxers of this county.[19] The Pingyuan gazetteer from the mid-eighteenth century painted a similar picture of the local population: "If one word does not agree with them, they suddenly wave their fists and start screaming, and then go to the yamen to state their grievance."[20]

There is, of course, no reason to interpret the fighting spirit of west Shandong peasants as inherently threatening to the Qing state. We should recall our plot, in map 3 (chapter 2), of the ratio of military to civil degree-holders in the counties of Shandong. This measure of thoroughly orthodox military inclinations shows some of the highest ratios in just those west Shandong counties from which the Boxers emerged.

SECTARIANS IN NORTHWEST SHANDONG

The ecology of northwest Shandong was obviously an ideal breeding ground for sectarian societies. With basic subsistence regularly threatened by natural and human disasters, and without the presence of a strong Confucian elite to see to the ethico-religious propriety of the peasantry, many villagers turned to one of the numerous sects in search of religious or personal solace—some no doubt attracted to what Richard Shek has described as the "egalitarian tone" and "ethical radicalism" to be found in these popular religions,[21] some with a more political radicalism in mind.[22] We have already had several occasions to consider the relationship between such sects and anti-Christian martial arts groups, and now we must return to that theme to consider any possible relationship between the sectarians of northwest Shandong and the Spirit Boxers. In the course of this consideration we shall see a number of familiar themes—most notably the frequent conversion of sectarians to Christianity—but there are also a few new elements in this region, some of which suggest a possible connection between boxers and sectarians.

As we have said in chapter 2, the relationship of sects, boxers, and popular rebellion was complex and constantly changing. But there was a general and logical tendency for sectarians, following the failure of rebellion and in the context of stringent official repression of heterodox sects, to return to a more apolitical search for salvation. In general, this was the state in which most of our sects found themselves in the final decades of the nineteenth century. There were exceptions, of course. In 1882 in Chiping, which was said to be full of White Lotus adherents at the time, several dozen sectarians set out with a donkey and a drum, armed with knives and spears, to attempt an uprising that was suppressed by yamen runners as soon as it began. Though the incident attracted a certain amount of official attention, the local memory of it stressed its tragi-comic nature, as seen in this little ditty—regrettably unrhymable in English:

> You don't giggle and I won't laugh:
> Wuguantun had White Lotus.
> They had no rifles; they had no guns.
> They just had spears and vegetable knives.[23]

But the 1882 Chiping rising was a brief and exceptional occurrence. In general, the missionaries were probably not far wrong when they observed that "the political purpose of the sects in the north has been largely lost sight of."[24]

Following the great famine which struck northern Shandong in 1877–78, ever greater numbers turned to the various sects. The people, wrote one missionary, were forsaking their "old moorings" and even burning (no doubt in punishment) the idols in some temples. "Religious societies have been formed, some secret, some open. They are blindly feeling after a good thing they have failed to find."[25] Accounts of these sects do not differ markedly from those elsewhere, but there are several elements which deserve particular mention.

First, there was an undeniable tendency toward the "vulgarization" of sectarian doctrine and ritual. We have noted this process earlier (chapter 2), as the inevitable by-product of official persecution of White Lotus sects following the 1813 Eight Trigrams rebellion. But the tendency seems particularly pronounced in the late nineteenth century. Many sect leaders engaged in various types of legerdemain: for example the popular scattering of beans which would turn into soldiers,[26] or riding stools as horses—a technique employed by the sad band in Chiping in 1882.[27] Some certainly exploited sect members for pecuniary advantage. Most interestingly, there was the increasing prominence of gods from popular novels and operas, most notably *The Enfeoffment of the Gods*, which would also supply many of the Boxer deities.[28] Though there were undoubtedly sectarians who clung more closely to the classic doctrines of the White Lotus tradition, a large number in the late nineteenth century were drawing much closer to the popular culture of north China villages.

Second, it was very common for sectarian leaders to attract their first followers by their talents as healers—a scenario which we shall see repeated by the Spirit Boxers. One of the Pangzhuang missionaries described how a certain Big Belly Li (Li Da-du-zi) began by curing various illnesses. "With the healing art he soon began to combine judicious preachings of himself and of his doctrines. To these he further added the gymnastics of the military Pakua [Eight Trigrams] sect, and thus easily gathered both pupils and disciples."[29] It was logical enough for a sect leader to look after both the spiritual and physical health of his flock, for the common belief in the unity of one's physical and spiritual being made the combination of medical and religious practice quite natural. (It was not entirely accidental, one might note, that the American missionaries in this area also turned to medical practice as the preferred means for spreading their faith.)

Finally we must note several important aspects of an abortive uprising in 1869 in Chiping. A certain Sun Shang-wen was a self-professed advocate of the Li Trigram sect. He had prepared flags with the slogans "Prepare the Way on Behalf of Heaven" (ti-tian xing-dao) and "Kill the Rich and Aid the Poor" (sha-fu ji-pin)—two fairly standard rebel slogans, but the former was also used by the Boxers in this region. Sun gained his followers by practicing healing, and added others to his band by claiming his intention to set off to steal salt. Most notably, when giving orders to his subordinates, Sun claimed to be possessed (jia-shen fu-ti).[30] Despite widespread shamanism in Shandong, possession was not a normal part of sectarian ritual. But the link between these two traditions had been made at least once in Chiping, some thirty years before the Spirit Boxers were to spread from the same region on the basis of quite similar rituals of healing and possession.

It should be clear, however, that the logic I am suggesting stops well short of claiming any organizational connection between sectarians and boxers. On the contrary, the record, here as elsewhere, shows far closer organizational links between sectarians and Christians. We have noted earlier that the American mission in En county began after missionaries were invited to the area by a delegation of sectarians who sought them out in Tianjin to escape the extortions of the yamen runners. The delegation was apparently composed of followers of the then deceased Big Belly Li, and the tale of Li's sect provides an interesting model for understanding the complex relationship between sectarians, boxers, and Christians.[31]

Big Belly Li was a seer from "the south" (probably Henan)—the unfailing source, the American missionary Porter tells us, for "the weird, the strange, the marvellous or unknown." Li had amazing prophetic powers, which were supposed to derive from an extra eye hidden in his massive stomach. As we have noted above, he added to his religious preaching a certain amount of healing and the martial arts of the Eight Trigrams. Around 1861—which would be just after the successful Anglo-French assault on Beijing and the humiliation of the Qing court—Li developed an interest in Christianity and annotated a "Four Character Classic" which he had adopted from a Catholic text. Apparently convinced that the West bore the new truth to China, he left his followers with instructions to follow the Europeans when they appeared.

The old man's injunction had some effect, for as we have noted, it was one of his followers who first attracted the missionaries to En county. But the old man had been unable to train a worthy successor to lead his sect. Following common sectarian practice, Li had attempted transmission through his son,[32] but the young man only became a "professional boxer, having taken up the less difficult of his father's professions." The younger Li had "scores of pupils," but was apparently ignorant of his father's religious teachings, and gradually the two grew farther and farther apart. With their estrangement came the estrangement of the previously united religious (or "civil") and military branches of the movement. In the end, the religious sect fell apart with the death of Big Belly Li.[33]

Apparently the history of Big Belly Li's sect was not unusual, for all accounts of these sects by the Pangzhuang missionaries mention the clear division between religious and military groups. In another article, Porter notes that the civil (*wen*) sects sought to "preserve the spirits and nourish their vital energy" (*cun-shen yang-qi*) through meditation. "The Wu, military sects, hope to secure the same by their more active works—T'i T'ui Ta Ch'uan [kicking and boxing], gymnastics, incantations, charms, finger twistings, incense offerings and like well known methods." The martial sects had little religious interest, but their members were probably more numerous than the purely religious sectarians.[34]

It seems clear from the missionaries' accounts that the converts they drew from the sects came from the religious side—as one would surely expect. The strict ethical regimen (often involving a prohibitionism which the Protestants praised highly), the relative monotheism (with the "Eternal Venerable Mother" as the high god), the concern for an afterlife, and the need to prepare for "world-destroying cataclysms" which looked much like the Last Judgment were all important aspects of the religious sects, and they made the Christian doctrines at least outwardly familiar.[35] But once the martial arts groups became divorced from any religious teaching, they appealed to a different audience, and one sees no accounts of these boxers converting to Christianity.

It would be attractively simple to conclude that the religious sectarians became Christians and the martial artists became Spirit Boxers—but history, unlike physics, has no rule to equate simplicity, elegance, and truth. Here the truth was surely far more complex. That many Christians came from the sects is undeniable; but the Spirit Boxers had a number of different sources. Our investigation so far is enough to suggest that the sectarian tradition of northwest Shandong included several elements—the worship of gods from popular literature, possession by spirits, healing, and martial arts—which soon became integral parts of the Spirit Boxer repertoire. But these elements were hardly unique to the sects. To put the matter simply, the Boxers grew from the popular culture of the Shandong plains, and the sects were an important part of that culture.

CHRISTIANS IN NORTHWEST SHANDONG

Before turning to the rise of the Spirit Boxers themselves, we need to introduce their adversaries, the Christians. The most famous Christians in this region were the Congregationalists of the American Board at Pangzhuang in En county. Headed by the missionary-author Arthur Smith and the doctor Henry Porter, the Pangzhuang mission had been established in 1880 after several years of visitation from Tianjin, especially during the famine of 1877–78. Many of the initial converts came from former sectarians or from the beneficiaries of famine relief work; but the commitment of these was often thin, and large numbers fell away or went over to the Roman Catholics in the early 1890s.[36] Medical work soon became one of the most important concerns of the Pangzhuang station, and the peasants were said to be impressed by the "Spirit and Ghost Power of the Jesus Doctrine."[37] Still, Protestant numbers grew very slowly, from some 300 members (all in En county) at the founding of the mission, to only 631 on the eve of the Boxer troubles.[38] The overwhelming majority were concentrated in En county, and it was only in 1897–98 that the Protestants had their first opening in Chiping—with five old women, at least one a sectarian for fifty years, as their foundation.[39]

The Catholics were far more numerous, and, as usual, most of the anti-Christian sentiment was directed at them. Unfortunately their numbers and distribution are more difficult to specify. All in this area were under the Italian Franciscan mission in Jinan, but there were no resident missionaries in the immediate Boxer area. The closest Italian priests resided at the Hanzhuang mission station in Yucheng and Shi-er-li-zhuang in Wucheng, and toured their parishes from those bases. From the oral history sources one can count a minimum of fourteen churches in Pingyuan, and a draft history of Chiping lists seventeen, so in these two crucial areas of Boxer activity, Catholic churches were fairly numerous—though most were little more than ordinary peasant homes converted to religious purposes.[40]

In contrast to southwest Shandong, one rarely saw large-scale village conversion to Christianity in the northwest. That kind of village solidarity was rare here. In most cases, only a few village members would convert—usually less than a dozen. Often it was the poor who would join, taking advantage of loans and other support from the church.[41] In another common pattern, village outsiders would join the church—either folks who had recently moved to the village, or people who were, for some reason, on the outs with the village leadership. The oral histories record several instances of Christians who joined the church to protect themselves against village despots.[42] Having joined the Christians, such people usually became even more isolated from the village majority: in several instances the community even refused to let Christians drink from the village well.[43]

Such Christians may have been outcasts in their own villages, but once connected to the church they were not without recourse. The oral histories record the usual litany of complaints against Christians abusing their power in lawsuits, or extorting fines and banquets from fellow villagers—one classic case involving an agricultural laborer who forced his employer to serve him a feast.[44] As elsewhere in Shandong, these problems were coming to a head in the late 1890s: Christians were rapidly becoming both more numerous and more obstreperous. We have seen the pattern so often, there is no need to detail it further here. It is time now to pass to the anti-Christians, the Spirit Boxers, and to trace their origins.

SPIRIT BOXERS: RITUAL AND THE PROBLEM
OF SECTARIAN ORIGINS

The Spirit Boxers first appeared in the area of Changqing west of the Yellow River, probably around 1896. Separated from the county seat by the river, these martial artists went officially unnoticed so long as they were not disturbing the peace—which they certainly were not doing. Unfortunately, the same official oblivion which allowed the group to spread has denied us contemporary records of their earliest activities, so we are entirely dependent on oral history sources, with all their usual shortcomings, especially with regard to dates. But calculating the date from the informants' ages at the first appearance of the Spirit Boxers, the consensus is clear that villagers were learning this type of boxing by 1896 or 1897 at the latest. Almost immediately the practice spread westward to Chiping, with most informants giving the same years as the time of first appearance there. Ordinarily one would be extremely reluctant to date any distant event from oral testimony given more than sixty years later. But this was precisely the area swept by the great Yellow River flood of 1898, and a large number of informants specified that the Spirit Boxers were active for at least one year before the flood.[45]

In this earliest stage, there was no anti-Christian dimension to Spirit Boxer activities. They taught only the simplest ethical principles, the most common being "respect your parents, live in harmony with your neighbors" (xiao-jing fu-mu, he-mu jia-xiang)—phrases originating in the Six Maxims of the first Ming emperor, adopted by the Qing, and long used by north China sectarians. In addition there were injunctions against covetousness, lust, drink, and taking advantage of the weak or young.[46] Healing was an important function of the boxing practitioners, and it was clearly an important drawing card for the Spirit Boxers: many joined in order to cure some illness or physical deformity. Others joined simply to protect their families (kan-jia) or to avoid being taken advantage of.[47]

References to the earliest activities of the Spirit Boxers concentrate on these utterly peaceful and protective activities, and most of their ritual was equally simple and unthreatening. In contrast to sectarian groups which tended to meet unobtrusively (if not indeed secretly) at night, or to the Big Sword Society, which zealously guarded its secret charms of invulnerability, the Spirit Boxers established public boxing grounds and practiced openly in the villages. As a result, even non-members could observe their activities and we have a rather good record of their rituals.

What was most striking about Spirit Boxer ritual was its simplicity. The members would bow to the southeast—apparently in the direction of Peach Flower Mountain (Tao-hua shan) in Feicheng, where there were six caves filled with a variety of gods from the popular pantheon. There would be some chanting of simple spells; charms were written on paper, burned, and the ash then drunk with water; and in some cases incense was burned. But there is no record of any initiation fee or regular dues as in the case of the Big Sword Society of the southwest, with which the Spirit Boxers were often equated. In fact, in many respects, the Spirit Boxers appear as poor cousins of the Big Sword Society. We cited above (chapter 4) reports that the poorest villagers could not afford the Big Sword Society's regular charge for ritual incense. By contrast, the Spirit Boxers often did away with incense burning altogether.[48]

The most distinctive feature of Spirit Boxer ritual was spirit-possession. Whether the aim was invulnerability (which seems to have been added later when they began contesting Christian power) or healing (more important in the early stages), possession by gods was the means: the Spirit Boxers "did good deeds and cured sickness; they were possessed and cured sickness."[49] The missionaries, who first took note of the Spirit Boxers late in 1898, were unequivocal about the importance of the ritual of possession. After tracing the origins of the northwest Shandong boxers to the Guan county and Caozhou anti-Christian militants, Henry Porter noted the change as the boxing practices spread to the Chiping area: "At that time there was added a new element which has caused the rapid spreading of the assemblies. The emissaries who went about to stir up the interest of people pretended to be possessed of a demon." Elsewhere, Porter compared the Spirit Boxers to the German Turners, saying that they "add a kind of spiritism to their gymnastics. They suppose that their trainer is a medicine [man]. The fellows, mostly young men, practice under him and fancy themselves under the influence of a spirit. In this condition they pretend that nothing can harm or injure them."[50]

In southeast Zhili, to which the Spirit Boxers (then known as the Boxers United in Righteousness) had spread by 1899, one of their most inveterate foes was the Wuqiao magistrate Lao Nai-xuan—whose theory of the White Lotus origins of the society we have noted above. Lao was equally convinced that the possession ritual was at the heart of the Spirit Boxer danger. In an official proclamation, Lao warned:

> You should know that although the practice of martial arts for self-protection is not forbidden in the statutes, the school of Boxers United in Righteousness, with its calling down gods and chanting charms, is really a heterodox sect. They are utterly different from the usual practitioners of the martial arts.[51]

The standard format for the possession ritual involved kowtowing to the southeast, burning incense, and performing a simple purification ritual of drinking clear water. Then the boxer would usually sit on a chair on top of a table, and call upon his "teacher" to "come down from the mountain" (*qing lao-shi xia-shan*). With his eyes closed, the boxer would slowly go into a trance, begin wavering about and breathing rapidly until he finally went into a frenzy of possession by his god. Each boxer would be possessed by a particular god, and that god would, in effect, become part of the individual's identity.[52] Virtually without exception, the possessing gods were the heroes of popular literature and theatre: the "Monkey" Sun Wu-kong, his sidekick "Pigsy" (Zhu Ba-jie), Guan-gong (the God of War), Zhou Cang and Zhao Yun from the *Romance of the Three Kingdoms*, Mao Sui (a clever strategist of the Warring States era), Sun Bin (a one-legged warrior of the same period), Yang Jian (warrior in the novel *Enfeoffment of the Gods*), et cetera. These were, in Arthur Smith's words, "the deified heroes of extinct dynasties . . . the knowledge of [whose deeds] had been everywhere diffused and popularized by the all-pervasive theatrical representations and the equally universal story-teller."[53] Not surprisingly, the great majority of them were martial deities.

It is essential to stress that in all important respects it was this fundamental boxer ritual which would characterize the movement for the remainder of its history. The same possession by the gods of popular literature and theatre would be noted repeatedly by observers in Tianjin and Beijing. Once the International Expedition had occupied Beijing and Chinese leaders began to assess the full extent of the tragedy which the movement had brought about, it was typical to place the blame on the ignorant peasants of north China who had received no more than an "education by novels"—usually in the form of popular operas.[54] It was these gods who promised divine or magical relief from distress; and it was natural that villagers would seek literally to identify with them as Spirit Boxers.

The influence of popular culture on peasant consciousness and, by extension, on peasant uprisings is not at all surprising. Scholars have traced some aspects of Taiping ideology to popular novels, and Taiping commanders on occasion borrowed military strategems from that literature.[55] To the Qing authorities, the link between novels and popular unrest was so obvious that there were several understandably futile attempts to suppress such "subversive" literature.[56]

The association of shamanistic possession with popular uprisings also had a long tradition. As noted in chapter 2, the pre-imperial state of Qi in northern Shandong was particularly known for its female shamans. One of these was also instrumental in the Han dynasty revolt of the Red Eyebrows.[57] Among the Taiping, of course, both Hong Xiuquan and Yang Xiu-qing used their ability to be possessed by pseudo-Christian spirits as an important source of religious authority. Even within the White Lotus tradition, the orthodox White Lotus followers of the Song master Mao Zi-yuan would complain during the Yuan dynasty that the sect was being subverted by those claiming authority by all sorts of heresy including "inquiring into the minds of ghosts in the manner of shamans, or claiming the descent of Maitreya or saying that divinities have possessed them."[58]

But what differentiated Spirit Boxer ritual from all of these earlier forms was the mass character of the possession. It was not just the leaders who were possessed, using their unique access to the gods as a divine source of authority. The Boxers were peculiarly egalitarian in their possession ritual: any young man with a pure heart could be possessed. Furthermore, consistent with usual shamanistic practice for exorcism or communication with the dead, the possessed person would be associated with one particular spirit who would always come to possess him. As the contemporary accounts make clear, the popularization of the possession ritual was fundamental to the Spirit Boxer appeal: it held out the promise that ordinary men could assume, for a time, the attributes of gods. For the poor peasants of northwest Shandong, that was an extremely attractive promise.[59]

But where did this Spirit Boxer ritual come from? Were these boxers an offshoot of martial arts groups associated with the White Lotus? The theory of the White Lotus origins of the Boxers was first propounded by Lao Nai-xuan in 1899, and it has remained the dominant view in successive generations of scholars of the Boxer movement both in China and abroad.* Lao's theory was put forth more in the form of assertion than argument. He simply cited early

---

*See also chapter 2 and the appendix for a discussion of Lao Nai-xuan's theory as it applies to the early nineteenth century relationship of sects and boxers.

nineteenth-century memorials linking groups called "Boxers United in Righteousness" to the White Lotus or Eight Trigrams sects, and stated that the Boxers of the 1890s were the same thing.[60] Later, determined to stress the rebellious intentions of the Boxers, Lao resorted to increasingly lame arguments to explain away the lack of evidence for such intent. First he claimed: "The distant origins of the rebellious heterodoxy which has been passed down are known only to the leaders and the unscrupulous bravoes who join their conspiracy. It is not only outsiders who are unaware, even those who are enticed into joining the sect do not know the full story."[61] Here, it seems, was a band of rebels who were ignorant of their own rebellious purpose. Most implausibly, Lao argued that the anti-Christian activities of the Boxers were just a "trick to mislead the masses," and a cover for their real subversive intent.[62]

In its original version, Lao's theory has been pretty much discredited. As Arthur Smith noted, "identity of name is by no means proof of identity of origin,"[63] and several scholars have made detailed studies of Lao Nai-xuan's evidence and concluded that his theory shows more about his own political hostility to the Boxers than it does about historical reality.[64] It is certainly true that among contemporary observers it was usually those most hostile to the Boxers—including Christians—who were most apt to argue for the White Lotus origins of the group.[65] It was a convenient way to condemn the Boxers, and it was certainly a good way to dissuade the authorities from any thought of supporting the anti-Christian militants. In P.R.C. historiography, of course, the White Lotus link has performed exactly the opposite function—linking the Boxers to a "progressive" rebel tradition. There have been several quite sophisticated studies in this vein, usually based on some similarity or analogy between Boxer and White Lotus beliefs.[66]

But in the end, the notion that the Boxers grew from organizational and ideological roots laid down by White Lotus sectarians seems fatally flawed. One of the attractions of the theory was the explanation it provided for the Boxers' ability to mobilize so many people so quickly: they simply called up existing sectarian networks. Yet it is quite clear from the oral history sources (and implicit in much of the documentary record) that virtually all the Spirit Boxers were newly recruited to the organization. Furthermore, the Spirit Boxers were everywhere regarded as something new on the village scene: people could recall when they first appeared. Most notably, we have already mentioned that Chiping in particular was an area where the White Lotus was long active and well known. The popular perception of the Spirit Boxers was that they were a distinct group. The oral history record is virtually unanimous in this regard: "The Boxers United in Righteousness also had no connection to the White Lotus. The White Lotus was completely a heterodox teaching." "The White Lotus sect and the Spirit Boxers were not the same family. The White Lotus sect could summon the wind and rain, and ride benches like horses."[67]

The peasants of Chiping knew the White Lotus in a rather debased form: as magicians and bench-riders. They saw no connection between such people and the Boxers. If we define the admittedly syncretic tradition of north China sectarianism by more fundamental characteristics, the distinction between that tradition and the Spirit Boxers becomes quite clear. Among the various aspects of sectarian belief, the most fundamental were a concern for salvation and a belief in the Eternal Venerable Mother as the agent of that salvation.[68] Yet neither the documentary nor the oral history record mentions the Eternal Venerable Mother among the extensive pantheon of Boxer gods. With the central defining characteristics of White Lotus belief missing, it is impossible to support the notion that the Boxers were an offshoot of the White Lotus sects.

More fundamentally, any approach to the origins of the Boxers which focuses on their *organizational* roots would seem to be quite misdirected, for if the Boxers had one fundamental weakness it was surely in the area of organization. The sectarian networks were characterized by clear master-disciple relationships and the hereditary transmission of sect leadership within certain families into which the coming Maitreya would be incarnated. Both of these elements gave the sects remarkable staying power and the ability to survive centuries of official persecution.[69] The Boxers were a totally different phenomenon: they rose seemingly from nowhere, spread extremely rapidly, and then disappeared utterly from the historical stage. Our explanation of their origins must be consistent with this history of the movement—and the theory of White Lotus origins is not.

How then are we to understand the origins of the Spirit Boxers? Regrettably, a definitive answer to this question could only be given by the person who first introduced the boxing rituals to northwest Shandong—and we do not even know who he was. The best that can be offered is a general hypothesis consistent with the facts presented above. I would suggest that the Spirit Boxers were a new group, initiated by some boxing master who combined, from a variety of different sources (possibly including the mid-Qing Spirit Boxers seen in chapter 2), a number of familiar elements: possession by spirits, healing, martial arts, kowtowing in a particular direction, burning incense, chanting spells, and drinking charms. Somewhat later, the Spirit Boxer possession ritual was held to confer invulnerability. All these elements were familiar to the villagers of northwest Shandong. Given the long history of both martial arts and sectarian activity in this area, the arrival of a new group which combined elements of those two traditions was nothing particularly out of the ordinary.

We should not, however, assume that the Spirit Boxers rose only from the sectarian and martial arts traditions. The gods which possessed the Boxers were familiar to peasants whose most important sources of culture and entertainment were the operas and story-tellers' tales glorifying the exploits of these mythic heroes.[70] And certainly there was nothing distinctly sectarian about kowtowing or burning incense. In the late nineteenth century, the line between popular religion and sectarian worship was growing thin—and much of the Spirit Boxer ritual derived from sources which were not at all sectarian. We should remember, after all, that the popular memory of the Spirit Boxers clearly distinguished them from previous sects, and from the White Lotus in particular.

The very eclecticism of the Spirit Boxers suggests that we should regard them as deriving from the popular culture of northwest Shandong—a popular culture which included a substantial amount of sectarian belief and practice. The most original contribution of the Spirit Boxers was their possession ritual—though, as we have seen in chapter 2, other parts of the country had witnessed possession rituals in groups practicing martial arts, including some who called themselves "Spirit Boxers." Closer to home there was the Chiping sectarian leader of 1869 who claimed to be possessed. Most importantly, shamanistic possession was common enough in Shandong so the Boxers would have known it without the sects. But the Spirit Boxers turned it into something different: by making divine possession widely accessible to ordinary peasants they were offering something new, something fundamental to their appeal. Still, the appeal of the ritual was not enough. We must remember that the Spirit Boxers had been active in the Chiping–western Changqing area for about two years before their explosive expansion and turn to anti-Christian activities began in the winter of 1898. To explain that expansion and transformation, we must turn to the social and political context of the time.

THE TRANSFORMATION AND SPREAD OF
THE SPIRIT BOXERS: 1898–99

Sometime late in 1898 the Spirit Boxers underwent a transformation. They began threatening Christians; they came to be associated
with and called the "Big Sword Society" or (by the spring of 1899) the
"Boxers United in Righteousness"; invulnerability became an important object of their rituals; and they spread rapidly beyond their
initial base in the Chiping-Changqing area. Most notably, they spread
northward along the official highway, first to Gaotang, and from
there, by the spring of 1899, to Pingyuan and En counties.[71] By the
fall, there were hundreds of boxing grounds in villages throughout
the region. A letter from a former magistrate on the Shandong peninsula, written as he passed through the area, is interesting: "The road
passed through Chiping. The area is bitterly poor, but in hundreds of
villages they are studying United-in-Righteousness Boxing."[72] Apparently two things struck the traveller through this area: its poverty
and its boxers.

The poverty must have been particularly notable in 1899, for in
August–September 1898, the great Yellow River flood had devastated
this area. The ground in Chiping is slightly higher north and west of
the city, and the flood waters stopped just east of the county seat, but
the rest of the county lay submerged for much of the fall. In most
villages, the fall harvest was lost and the ground was too wet to plant
winter wheat.[73] In Changqing, much of which is even lower, the
situation was certainly much the same. This was precisely the area of
earliest Spirit Boxer activity: Changqing west of the Yellow River, and
the southern and eastern portions of Chiping. With the flood came a
major transformation of the Boxers. In the words of one Chiping
informant: "There were Spirit Boxers [here] before the flood, but they
only studied [boxing] and established a boxing ground. After the
flood they started acting up [nao-qi-lai le]."[74]

The flood of 1898 was also a key factor in the spread of the Spirit
Boxers. Said one Gaotang peasant: "In the 24th year of Guang-xu
[1898], the Yellow River broke its banks and there was a great flood.
Right after the water went down, the Spirit Boxers rose up. Every
village set up a [boxing] ground."[75] It is likely that the flood forced
some boxers to flee the Chiping-Changqing area, and these refugees
brought their new teaching with them. Floods of this magnitude are
also inevitably followed by epidemics—cholera in particular. Since
one of the most important practices of the Spirit Boxers was curing

disease, the flood certainly gave them an excellent opportunity to use their talents. Finally, of course, the severe physical and mental distress associated with a natural disaster of this magnitude provides an environment which has always been conducive to the spread of popular movements or beliefs promising some relief or escape from the cares and confines of normal life—and by promising the ability to take on the attributes of gods, the Spirit Boxers certainly promised such escape.

At the same time, an identifiable Spirit Boxer leadership was emerging in Chiping—headed by Zhu Hong-deng, soon to become the most famous of all Shandong Boxer leaders, and the monk Xin-cheng ("Sincere Heart"), who was known in the documentary sources by the name "Ben-ming." Zhu seems to have been born in Sishui, in southern Shandong, in a family that had fled natural disasters in Changqing in the 1860s. Sometime in the early 1890s, Zhu returned by himself to live with his maternal uncle in Dalizhuang (Big Li Village) in Chang-qing, just a few kilometers north of the Yellow River.[76] In 1965, an old peasant gave this account of Zhu Hong-deng in Dalizhuang:

> Zhu Hong-deng's nickname was "Little Zhu" [pronounced and some-times recorded as "Little Pig"]. He was a good kid. When he came to this village he was about 32 or 33 *sui*. He came here and learned Spirit Boxing and learned it very well. After he went to the west [to Chiping], some of the Spirit Boxers gave him the name Zhu Hong-deng.... This fellow Zhu Hong-deng wasn't very tall. His whole face was covered with black pockmarks. His body was very stout, very fat. He practiced Spirit Boxing here for four or five years. He was a very good person. He often cured people's illnesses or boils and took no money. Here in this village, Zhu Hong-deng practiced Spirit Boxing at night and during the day he worked for others. When he worked for others, they took care of his food. He was very good at contacting and organizing the masses. Everyone in the vil-lage liked him a lot.[77]

Other accounts generally support this picture. Zhu was a poor, landless agricultural laborer who had come to Big Li Village from the outside to live with his uncle. Sometimes he sold peanuts to make ends meet;[78] sometimes he was forced to beg.[79] It was apparently after he came to Big Li Village that Zhu learned Spirit Boxing—possibly from the monks at the Cloud Zen Temple (Yun-chan si) just southwest of the village.[80] There is, in any case, fairly general agreement that Zhu learned his Spirit Boxing in Changqing, and thus he was not himself the original teacher who brought the practice to the area. Further-more, in this early period, Zhu used his skills mostly to cure illness—

and all recollections of this early stage of his activities stress his role as a popular village healer.

It seems that it was probably early in 1899 that Zhu moved to Chiping, living with fellow boxers south of the county seat—and moving from village to village on the basis of recommendations from other Spirit Boxers.[81] Meanwhile, the monk Xin-cheng was emerging as the main Spirit Boxer leader in the north of the county. Xin-cheng's base would be the town of Liulisi ("Glazed Temple") which lay directly on the Chiping-Gaotang border. He was born Yang Zhao-shun or Yang Shun-tian in Yangzhuang (Yang Village), about two kilometers north of Liulisi. A sickly child, he was sent to the care of the monks at Ding Temple (Dingsi) about ten kilometers to the east in Yucheng. There he learned boxing, grew to be big and strong, and acquired the nickname "Goose" (E).[82]

Contemporary sources suggest that Xin-cheng may have been responsible for the addition of invulnerability rituals to the Spirit Boxer regimen. The magistrate who replaced Lao Nai-xuan in Wuqiao first describes Zhu Hong-deng largely as a sectarian leader. Then he continues: "Zhu's friend, the monk Yang, was also good at boxing and accepted [Zhu's] teaching. He said he could withstand guns with his flesh. Those who were taken in by this regarded him as a god."[83] A source somewhat closer to the scene was the magistrate who passed through Chiping in the fall of 1899. This is the version he heard:

> There are two Boxer leaders: "Red Lantern" (Hong-deng) and "Sincere Heart" (Xin-cheng). . . . "Sincere Heart" is a Buddhist name; his original name was Zhou Zhen-jia—a monk of the Western Temple (Xisi). Of the two, Sincere Heart's abilities are greater. As a youth, he studied Shaolin Boxing. In swordsmanship and the "flower spear" he is thoroughly trained. Whenever he competes with the Boxers, even ten or more men cannot approach him. He boasts that "my whole body has qi-gong [lit.: "breath-efficacy"]; I can resist spears and guns. When the hard and precious [Buddhist guardians] possess my body, the foreigners cannot oppose me."[84]

Zhu Hong-deng and Xin-cheng obviously had a significant impact on the transformation of the Spirit Boxers; and Xin-cheng may even have introduced the invulnerability rituals which were to become a Boxer trademark. While accounts of the early Spirit Boxers in Changqing all stress the link between possession and healing, in Chiping statements such as this (from a former Boxer) are more common: "Once possessed, you become a Spirit Boxer and can be invulner-

able."[85] The shift in Spirit Boxer focus from healing to invulnerability certainly bespoke a new militance of the group, with much
more potential to disturb public order. Furthermore, as poor itinerant
boxing practitioners, men like Zhu and Xin-cheng had little to lose
should trouble arise, and they represented a particularly volatile type
of leadership. Certainly the authorities thought them so—at least
after trouble *did* break out in the fall. At that time, they became convenient scapegoats for some officials, who were quite prepared to
throw the book at them. The Pingyuan magistrate accused Zhu of
being both a Ming pretender and a sectarian preaching a coming
millennium. Xin-cheng was referred to as "Ben-ming" (originally of
the Ming), which was held up as further evidence of subversive purpose. Regrettably, much of the literature on the Boxers has relied
quite uncritically on this account and concluded that Zhu Hong-deng
and his group were originally anti-Qing Ming loyalists.[86]

The oral history record is quite clear, however. Villagers from
throughout the region record the Spirit Boxer slogan, at least from the
time of their attacks on Christians in 1899, to be "Revive the Qing,
destroy the foreign" (*Xing-Qing mie-yang*) or "Protect the Qing, destroy the foreign" (*Bao-Qing mie-yang*).[87] Nor does the oral history
record support the claim that Zhu foretold the coming of a millennium
in 1900.[88] Zhu and Xin-cheng were a new type of leader—and the
invulnerability rituals and anti-Christian message of the Spirit Boxers
under them certainly had the potential for stirring unrest. But we
should by no means conclude that their target was the official order:
that would completely misunderstand the nature of the Spirit Boxers.
Like the Big Swords and the Guan county boxers before them, their
target was the Christians, not the dynasty.

Where did their anti-foreignism come from? For several years the
Spirit Boxers had peacefully practiced boxing without any threat to
the local Christian population. What inspired the change? My hypothesis would be that the inspiration came from the various anti-
Christian movements that we have been considering in previous
chapters: from the Big Sword Society, from the Boxers United in
Righteousness of Guan county, and from the anti-Christian activists
of southern Shandong in 1898–99. Clearly, ever since the Sino-
Japanese War, and especially since the German occupation of Qingdao, anti-Christian sentiment was becoming quite commonplace in
Shandong. It would not have been difficult for the Spirit Boxers to
adopt it as their new cause.

The perception at the time was fairly uniform: the anti-Christian activists were derived from the Big Sword Society and/or the Guan county boxers. The Pingyuan magistrate Jiang Kai mentioned both sources as possible.[89] When Henry Porter returned from a December 1898 trip to Chiping, he called them "'The Boxers' or the Big Sword Society" and also linked them to the Guan county boxers.[90] The Christian press equated the Boxers United in Righteousness with the Armor of the Golden Bell, the Iron-cloth Shirt, the Red Lantern Shining, the Plum Flower Boxing, and the Big Sword Society— with the latter sometimes treated as a general name for all such invulnerability-conferring boxing.[91] And there is this extremely interesting confession from a boxer captured in Yucheng in January 1900: "Previously I had studied Spirit Boxing. Recently I studied [the techniques of] the Big Sword Society from Yang De-sheng and Liu Tian from Caozhou."[92]

The oral history record is also rather clear in asserting the identity of these variously named practitioners of invulnerability. In the words of one of many informants: "The Boxers United in Righteousness, the Spirit Boxers, The Big Sword Society and the Red Lantern Shining were all the same thing."[93] A more precise and plausible statement noted: "The Big Sword Society [members] did not call themselves the Big Sword Society. Internally they called themselves Spirit Boxers. The name Big Sword Society came because outsiders saw them carrying big swords, so they called them the Big Sword Society."[94] As in the southwest, "Big Sword Society" was a name applied by outsiders—a kind of generic term for martial artists, especially those with some invulnerability ritual. Just as the real name of the southwestern group was "Armor of the Golden Bell," so the real name in the northwest was the "Spirit Boxers."

But by mid-1899, the name "Spirit Boxers" was being replaced by "Boxers United in Righteousness"—the name of the Guan county boxers. Especially in Pingyuan, which only began to see its first boxers at this time, the oral history record usually refers to the latter name. By contrast, there were people in Chiping who had only heard of Spirit Boxers and never of Boxers United in Righteousness.[95] Clearly the reputation of the Guan county boxers, after their battles with the Christians in the fall of 1898, had reached this northwest Shandong area—and when the Spirit Boxers turned to anti-Christian activities, they adopted the name of the Guan county militants.

The essential point, however, is that the Spirit Boxers were certainly not a transplanted version of either the Big Sword Society or the Guan county Boxers United in Righteousness. They had their own ritual including, most prominently, possession by gods, and they had been present in the area before they ever turned to anti-Christian activities. The Spirit Boxers surely adopted the name "Boxers United in Righteousness" from the Guan county boxers—but as we have seen, those boxers did not even have an invulnerability ritual. The two were ritually utterly distinct. It seems most likely that just as the Spirit Boxers were turning to anti-Christian activities as part of the general Sino-foreign crisis of 1898–99, news of the Guan county militants spread via the usual marketplace grapevine. The Spirit Boxers adopted their felicitous name—but maintained their own distinctive ritual.

Similarly, it is likely that the Big Sword Society was part of the inspiration for the notion of invulnerability. They were already famous both for their anti-Christian activity and for their techniques of invulnerability. But it is unlikely that any genuine practitioner of the Armor of the Golden Bell came to northwest Shandong from Caozhou: the Spirit Boxer invulnerability ritual was entirely different from that of the Golden Bell, which involved an extensive period of *gong-fu* practice and no reliance on possession. Among the Spirit Boxers, there was no mention of the distinctive Big Sword training by "beating with bricks and swords." The Spirit Boxer ritual was much simplified and even vulgarized. Thus while the Big Sword Society usually referred to "impenetrability to swords and spears" (*dao-qiang bu-ru*), and occasionally to "avoiding spears (or guns) and swords" (*bi qiang-dao*),[96] the northwest Shandong boxers often referred to "*stopping up* guns" (*bi-pao*),[97] a technique which often amounted to preventing (presumably by pre-arranged ruse) a gun from firing in the first place.

In sum, then, as the Spirit Boxers turned to anti-Christian activities, they derived inspiration both from the Big Sword Society and from the Boxers of Guan county—but that inspiration was not in the form of direct transmission of rituals (much less any organizational tradition or discipline). The growth and development of the Boxers is not to be understood in organizational terms but in terms of the social and political context from which they grew—in this case, a context of massive natural disaster, growing foreign threat and concomitant Christian aggressiveness, anti-Christian activity elsewhere in the province, and a government which was increasingly willing to look the other way as ordinary villagers sought their own way to counter Christian abuse of power.

OFFICIAL ATTITUDES

Through the summer of 1899, the attitudes of officials in northwest Shandong reflected the policies of governor Yu-xian, which we discussed in some detail in the previous chapter. So long as boxing bands did not engage in violent disturbances of law and order, they were to be tolerated as a legitimate form of village self-defense. In this regard, it was the implementation of this policy by the Chiping magistrate, Yu Xian,* which was the most crucial—for that county was the center of Spirit Boxer activity.

Yu Xian was a Han bannerman and a *jin-shi*, only the eighth holder of this highest degree to serve as Chiping magistrate since 1800. He seems to have been an unusually capable official: in the summer of 1899, he was one of six Shandong officials commended by the governor for particular merit; when he left office he was commemorated by a tablet to his "virtuous governance"; and villagers in the 1960s still remembered him as a "good official" (*qing-guan*).[98]

His policy toward the Christian-Boxer troubles was to stay as even-handed as possible, and to do all he could to mediate disputes and prevent violence. In large measure, he was following the lead of his predecessor, who in December 1898 had prohibited sword-making—an obvious means of limiting lethal violence by the "Big Swords."[99] But he also tended to bend with the wind, and by the late spring of 1899, with Yu-xian now governor, the Chiping magistrate's efforts to mediate were being interpreted as signs of support for the Spirit Boxers. Most notable was an incident in the large village of Zhang-guantun, where in settlement of a dispute between Christians and Boxers, the former were required to stage an opera—which the latter used as an opportunity to show off their boxing and invulnerability. Yu Xian personally attended the celebration. According to one account: "Magistrate Yu even went to watch the opera and praise the Spirit Boxers! At that time the Spirit Boxers were at their height. They went to every village. Magistrate Yu even gave awards to the Spirit Boxers."[100] In Chiping as in the southwest, officials were beginning to

---

*The magistrate's name was written with different characters from the governor's, but the pronunciation was the same. To distinguish the two, I have eliminated the hyphen from the romanization of the former.

tilt against the Christians—or at least to a more sympathetic mediation of disputes with the Christians. But they were also generally successful in preventing violence: the Zongli Yamen archives of missionary incidents reveal no foreign protests against either the officials or the Boxers in northwest Shandong at this time.

In his retrospective account, the Pingyuan magistrate Jiang Kai claims that he made repeated attempts to suppress the Boxers only to be frustrated by the governor. But the contemporary record shows Jiang's policy to be very close to the tolerant provincial norm. Most importantly, like his colleagues in the southwest, he attempted to enroll the Boxers in the militia. According to Jiang's own report:

> Previously boxing teachers from elsewhere boasted of their talents and bravery, and young villagers, being ignorant, were moved by them to gather in groups and study boxing. Their intent was to protect each other. This magistrate observed the situation and had the strong enrolled in the militia, in order not to lose the aspect of self-protection. The weak would respectfully keep their station. They would not themselves do anything to cause unexpected offense.[101]

From all accounts, we must conclude that any such attempt to enroll Spirit Boxers in the militia must have failed utterly, and Jiang's own report indicates that he left many Boxers ("the weak") alone—hoping that they would cause no trouble. Certainly the main Boxer groups remained quite distinct from any officially sanctioned militia.[102] But Jiang Kai's testimony is important, for it shows that throughout the summer of 1899, a relatively tolerant official policy prevailed toward the Spirit Boxers, even among officials who would later prove quite hostile to the movement. There can be little doubt that this type of official toleration was another important factor facilitating the spread of the Boxer movement.[103]

PATTERNS OF TRANSMISSION AND BOXER ORGANIZATION

If we are to explain how the Boxers spread so rapidly first through northwest Shandong and ultimately across the entire north China plain, we shall have to understand how the Spirit Boxer practices were transmitted from village to village. The question involves more than just the propagation of Boxer ritual; it touches on the much larger question of the networks that link peasants living in separate village communities.[104]

The basic unit of Boxer organization was of course the boxing ground (*quan-chang* or simply *chang*). Later on, when Boxers entered the large cities of Beijing and Tianjin, an "altar" (*tan*) would define a given Boxer headquarters and the unit that it commanded,[105] but in the villages of Shandong that term was not used. The boxing ground would be established in an open area of a village, sometimes at a local temple, or in a large house (perhaps in its courtyard)—but the activities would be open for all to see. There would normally be only one boxing ground per village, so each ground was associated with a particular village, but men from a village without a ground of its own might join that of a neighboring village. Thus the separate village boxing grounds were not reflections of any exclusive village community. If anything, the relative openness of the boxing grounds reflected the relative openness of the village communities in this region.

Each village's boxing ground would have a leader and usually a second in command, known as "Senior Brother-Disciple" (*da shi-xiong*) and "Second Brother-Disciple" (*er shi-xiong*). The ordinary members would know each other as "Brother-Disciples" (*shi-xiong*).[106] All of these translations are awkward, but the critical meaning is that all were brothers by virtue of having studied from the same boxing master. In general, the master-disciple relationship seems to have been far weaker than in most schools of boxing—largely because the ritual was so easily learned, and all who learned the ritual became equally divinely possessed. Thus the individual boxing grounds maintained a good deal of organizational independence, and within each ground—although there was a clear leader and often a second in command—all the members were regarded as "brothers." Leadership within a boxing ground, and the title "Senior Brother-Disciple," simply passed to whoever was the most skilled in the boxing techniques. That was the extent of the hierarchy.[107]

The most common way for Spirit Boxing to spread from village to village was for young men from one village to hear of the practice nearby, and to go watch the performance out of curiosity—"to watch the excitement" (*kan re-nao*) as the informants often said, using the same term that would describe a visit to a busy market or an opera.[108] Being impressed, they would invite one of the more accomplished practitioners to establish a boxing ground in their own village. Thus it was common for the boxer teacher in any village, at least in the initial stage, to be an outsider.

With landlordism rare in northwest Shandong, most landless peasants survived by working as agricultural laborers, frequently outside their own village. Sometimes these agricultural laborers, with their relatively mobile lifestyle, became the means of transmission of Spirit Boxer practices. Here is how one former Boxer described the establishment of the boxing ground in his village:

> I did magic boxing with Xie Dian-yuan, Xie Yan-xiu, Xie Si-jian, and Xie De-chang. At that time, Xie De-yuan [presumably a brother of the last] came back from working [*gan-huo*] and said "Playing at Spirit Boxing is really good stuff." I said, "If it's good stuff, let's do it." So we did it. We did it for three or four months, and soon there were lots of us. I was only eighteen *sui* at the time.[109]

Certainly aware of the attractiveness of the public display of their skills, the Spirit Boxers often showed off their talents at periodic markets or temple fairs. In doing so, they were of course continuing a common pattern for all manner of theatrical and magical performances—and there was a great deal of theatre in the Boxers' rituals. Here indeed was a group which was building upon the ordinary activities and symbolism of peasant culture—the gods of popular opera, the excitement of local fairs, the feats of magic which could thrill any audience—and creating a quite extraordinary popular movement. The ruling elite was not unaware of the thin line separating the ordinary from the extraordinary, and was particularly suspicious of fairs which brought the two together. The Chiping gazetteer from the Republican era listed fairs as the first of several evil customs that should be restricted—and then went on to note the significant fact that in a two-to-three-month period every spring and summer, there were no less than fifteen or sixteen fairs held in the area south of the city.[110] This, of course, was precisely the area from which the Boxers spread, and the time of year at which their growth was most rapid in 1899.

The fact that the Christians also used the markets and fairs as an opportunity to attract converts sometimes made the Boxer exhibitions particularly explosive. A missionary in Jizhou, across the border in Zhili, records a band of "United Boxers" expelling the Christian volunteers preaching at a local fair in June 1899, and then proceeding to use the theatre stage to spread their own anti-foreign message to a "huge crowd" for three more days.[111] In the competition for a mass audience, the Boxers would always out-draw the Christians.

Figure 7. Boxer Puppet Show. Though much of this drawing reflects Western racist caricature, the close link between Boxer beliefs and popular theatre is accurately presented. From *Illustrated London News* 117:3201 (25 August 1900).

Fairs such as these would draw crowds from considerable distances—often more than a full day's journey of thirty or more kilometers. As such, they were an ideal way to spread Boxer practices
beyond just a few neighboring villages, and outside a local marketing
community. We should recall that the Big Swords used an opera and
fair to spread their fame in the southwest. But another common way
for the practices to spread was through the affinal networks that
linked peasant families and villages. This account from Pingyuan
shows such a pattern:

> There was a woman from Gaotang by the name of Wu. She came to
> Liuzhuang as the wife of Liu Wei-ling. Her brothers often came to see her,
> and they spread the word that the Boxers United in Righteousness could
> cure illness and do good works, and that one could study boxing and
> guard one's home. So the villagers believed in the Boxers United in
> Righteousness and Ma Zhao-lin established a boxing ground.[112]

The establishment of a boxing ground required at least the tacit
consent of the village leadership. By and large, the practitioners of the
new Spirit Boxing were young men in their teens and early twenties,
and if their elders forbade it, they could be prevented from establishing a boxing ground. In fact this often happened. One village head in
Pingyuan is said to have declared: "Whoever wants to join, we don't
want in our village." [113] In cases where the Boxers did *not* establish
a boxing ground in a village, the most common explanation was that
the village head or elders did not permit it.

From all appearances there was no real organization linking the
various boxing grounds. Certain individuals, such as Zhu Hong-deng
or Xin-cheng, were recognized as having superior abilities, and when
large-scale conflict with the Christians came in the fall they were able
to rally Boxers from a wide area to join the struggle. Furthermore,
when some group of young men decided to establish a ground in their
village, they would naturally seek the best teacher they could find—
but there is no evidence of any established hierarchy of Boxer units.
Within the individual units, at least in the early stages of the movement, there were clear attempts to maintain some discipline around
the basic Spirit Boxer commitment to good works and proper treatment of fellow villagers.[114] But between the units, functional independence was the rule. For example, much has been made of Zhu
Hong-deng's red costume and red flags (seen in the fall battles described in the next chapter)—often taken as evidence of a connection

to the Li Trigram of the White Lotus Eight Trigram sect.[115] But the record is quite clear that the Spirit Boxers appeared under flags of many colors: red, yellow, black, blue/green, and white.[116] They were committed to the same principles. They shared a common ritual. They were, in that sense, surely a single "movement." But to all intents and purposes, they had no organization. Hierarchy and authority were not part of the Boxer world—and this showed as much in the spontaneous manner in which the movement spread as in the egalitarianism of their possession ritual.

THE SOCIAL COMPOSITION OF THE SPIRIT BOXERS

It remains, finally, to consider just who joined the Spirit Boxers. What was the social composition of these Boxer bands, and what was the social background of their leadership? To the first question, some answers are clear enough: the Spirit Boxers were young and male. Jiang Kai says they were all around 20 *sui*, and many oral history accounts refer to them as "children" as young as twelve or thirteen, though more commonly in their late teens. Chiping even had a group of adolescents known as the "Baby Brigade" (*wa-wu dui*).[117] They were invariably male, and the Boxer discipline in its strictest form prohibited sexual contact or even looking twice at a woman— apparently out of fear that the female's polluting *yin* would destroy the efficacy of the invulnerability ritual.[118] Thus when, later in 1900, especially in the Beijing-Tianjin area but also in Chiping, young women (also teenagers) began to participate in the anti-foreign movement, they had a separate organization of their own, the Red Lantern Shining (*Hong-deng-zhao*).[119]

If the Spirit Boxers were relatively uniform with respect to age and gender, the same cannot be said of their economic background. Certainly the vast majority were poor peasants and agricultural laborers: in this region that is what most young men were. Furthermore, as time went on—and especially when Boxer activity flared up again in Shandong in the summer of 1900—there was a tendency for poor, unemployed vagrants to join the movement, many no doubt opportunistically seeking momentary gain at the expense of the Christians.[120] But the fact that an initial object of the Spirit Boxers was the protection of one's home indicates that many boxers came from established property-owning peasant households.[121]

There is considerable evidence that the Spirit Boxers represented something close to a cross-section of peasant society in northwest Shandong. There is no question that even members of prominent families joined. The inveterate foe of the Boxers, Lao Nai-xuan, had to admit: "In all the boxer bands, there are people from titled lineages and wealthy families mixed in. They are not all unemployed vagrants." [122] In the words of the Taian prefect: "Most practitioners are sons and younger brothers of peasant families. There are even some from literate families of comfortable circumstances. They are not all worthless outlaws." [123] The oral histories confirm this picture. Though many informants stress that most Boxers were poor, others note that "the Spirit Boxers paid no attention to rich or poor." Thus, said an informant from the Pingyuan village where the penultimate conflict with the authorities would come: "In our village, there were no poor people in the Spirit Boxers." [124]

It would be very difficult to argue that the social composition of the Spirit Boxers distinguished them markedly from the rest of the population. But the nature of their leadership was rather special. For in striking contrast to the landlord leadership of the Big Sword Society, or the established local eminence of Zhao San-duo, leader of the Guan county boxers, the Spirit Boxer leaders were often itinerants or poor villagers. If they came from wealthier families, they were usually families very much on the decline. This was particularly true of the earliest Boxer leaders. In their poor and simple origins, the main leaders in this region—Zhu Hong-deng and the monk Xin-cheng— were quite representative of these early Spirit Boxer leaders. Let us look at a few others.

Next to Zhu and Xin-cheng, the most prominent Boxer leader in Chiping was Yu Qing-shui from the north of the county. Yu may have owned a little land, but he made his living selling vinegar and working for a wealthy uncle, whom he is said to have greatly feared. About thirty at the time of the Boxers, he had a wife and possibly a daughter, but no other family, and was described as "a little like a vagabond (liu-mang)." He had long practiced boxing before he took up Spirit Boxing in the spring of 1899. One gets the sense of a distinctly poor cousin from a fairly well-off lineage who finally found a meaningful identity with the Boxers. One of the most common Chiping rhymes told of Yu Qing-shui as a "a hero, in yellow riding pants and a red plumed hat" riding a white (or red) horse with a red-tasseled spear.[125] With the Boxers, Yu Qing-shui had finally made a name for himself.

Yu resembled several other village-level leaders who were clearly from families on the decline. "Wang Shang-xuan," reported a villager in eastern Chiping, "was the Spirit Boxer leader in our village. He was a peasant—very poor. He used to push a cart with kindling and straw and peddle for a living. His father was a teacher, who raised six children. They had only 4.8 *mu* [of land] at that time."[126] Another village leader was the son of a former jail warden in the county seat. But he was himself very poor, with only ten-odd *mu* of often-flooded land.[127] One of the Yucheng leaders was actually a military *sheng-yuan*, but he had become addicted to opium. Despite moderate landholdings of 30–40 *mu*, his family was very much on the decline.[128]

In an early Boxer village, one leader was a tenant and native of another village, a second was a noodle-seller.[129] In another there were three leaders—two very poor, one from a bankrupt landlord family.[130] One fairly prominent associate of Zhu Hong-deng had a small plot of land and made ends meet by selling cooking oil. A fellow villager's description of this fellow is interesting:

> Liu Tai-qing came from our village. Outside he was very famous. But he had no talent—he couldn't box. He spun cotton at home. But in the city they thought he had great talent. He wasn't tall. . . . Liu was very stupid— he couldn't learn. Even when the teacher told him, he couldn't do it. Later the teacher gave up teaching him.[131]

The poor, the outsider, even the young man despised in his own village could rise to prominence as a Boxer leader. The attraction and the opportunity for many downtrodden young men was obviously enormous.

On the other hand, there were certainly cases where leaders came from the established village elite. This seems to have been more common as the Boxers spread north out of Chiping—perhaps because by that time official toleration of the movement was fairly clear, and such people had less to fear in joining the Spirit Boxers. In Gaotang, the most notable Boxer leader was Wang Li-yan. Wang was a literary man, a village teacher with a love of gambling. He ran a clothing store and, according to his cousin, sold Beijing goods and "foreign cloth." Locally he was known as "Minister Wang" (Wang Cheng-xiang) and, like so many of these Boxer leaders, often wore a yellow riding jacket—which was, of course, supposed to be granted by imperial grace for extraordinary military service. Wang was an older man, with failing eyesight by this time, and he served more as a record keeper and perhaps as a strategist for the boxers than as a practitioner of the Spirit Boxing.[132] Further north in Yaozhancun, the town on the highway from which the Boxers spread to Pingyuan, the head was a certain Wang Ming-zhen, a wealthy owner of 110 *mu* who established a boxing ground to protect his home.[133] And in Pingyuan itself, virtually all of the major Boxer leaders (whom we shall meet in the next chapter) were prominent village leaders: substantial owner-cultivators (often with 70–80 *mu*) and usually military *sheng-yuan*, *li-zhang* (sub-bureaucratic functionaries responsible for tax-collection and general order in several villages), or village heads.[134]

Kong Ling-ren of Shandong University, based on more complete data than I have seen, has made a comparative analysis of the class background of northwest Shandong Spirit Boxer leaders, Guan county boxers, and Big Sword Society leaders from the southwest. The results are in table 6.

What is particularly striking about this table is the proportion of tenant/agricultural laborer leaders in the northwest Shandong base of the Spirit Boxers, in comparison to the southwest Shandong base of the Big Sword Society. I suspect that if Kong had been able to distinguish early and later Boxer leaders (difficult to do with oral history sources), she would have found an even stronger representation of these poorer leaders, and far fewer landlords. We have already noted that in the Pingyuan boxing grounds which were established later, leadership of the Spirit Boxers seems to have passed to wealthier village leaders. But this is even more the case if one includes (as Kong certainly has) the Boxer leaders who emerged only in the summer of 1900. The two most prominent landlords among the Boxer leaders, both with gentry backgrounds, were He Hu-chen in Chiping and Shi Yan-tian in Pingyuan—and both seem to have been active only in 1900.[135]

The picture that emerges of the Spirit Boxers during their most volatile stage of expansion is of a very diverse leadership of itinerants, monks, poor peasants and agricultural laborers, and a few village leaders. What this suggests, I believe, is that class stratification in the rural areas of northwest Shandong had not produced a distinct, powerful landed elite. A militant boxing association would not necessarily be controlled by the rural elite as was the case in the landlord-

TABLE 6   CLASS BACKGROUNDS OF BOXER LEADERS

	All Shandong		SW Shandong		NW Shandong		Guan county	
	Number	*Percent*	*Number*	*Percent*	*Number*	*Percent*	*Number*	*Percent*
Landlords	20	22.5	8	33.3	10	27.0	2	7.1
Owner-cultivators	34	38.2	12	50	9	24.3	13	46.4
Tenants or agricultural laborers	22	24.7	1	4.2	13	35.1	8	28.6
Craftsmen	4	4.5	—	—	—	—	4	14.3
Merchants or peddlers	5	5.6	2	8.3	3	8.1	—	—
Veterinarians	1	1.1	—	—	1	2.7	—	—
Itinerants	3(?)	3.4	1	4.2	1	2.7	—	—
Actors	1	1.1	—	—	—	—	1	3.6
TOTALS	89	100	24	100	37	100	28	100

SOURCE: Kong Ling-ren, "Shi-jiu shi-ji-mo Shandong de she-hui jing-ji yu Yi-he-tuan yun-dong," *Shandong da-xue wen-ke lun-wen ji-kan* 1980.1: 20–22.

dominated southwest. In an area with a very weak gentry elite, the village leadership was neither closely tied to the government and official orthodoxy, nor clearly differentiated from the ordinary villagers. Furthermore, this was a very mobile society—and outsiders could be welcomed as boxing leaders in the villages here.

The mobile and socially fluid nature of northwest Shandong society was not only reflected in the social composition of the Boxers and their leadership, it was also reflected in Boxer ritual—and all these aspects were clearly related. I have stressed several times the egalitarian nature of Boxer possession ritual. Let me conclude by citing the Taian prefect on the relationship between this ritual and Boxer leadership:

> I have heard that in this boxing sect, when on any given day they call the gods and recite their spells, the one who is possessed by the heterodox god is the leader, and the others go according to his orders. On another day, this may change. Thus you can see there is not a fixed leader.[136]

This was surely an exaggeration: there were certainly some relatively permanent Boxer leaders. But the point is nonetheless well taken. The possession ritual's capacity to give anyone the identity of a god gave the Spirit Boxers the capacity to make anyone a leader. This was a movement which would not be easily controlled: not by the officials, not by the leaders themselves. In particular it would not respond to Yu-xian's policy of arresting the leaders and dispersing the followers—no matter how well that policy had worked elsewhere. The governor's experience with militant martial artists had all been in southwest Shandong. But the open, fluid village structure, the mobile peasantry, the underdeveloped landlordism and weak gentry all made northwest Shandong very different from the southwest. The Spirit Boxers reflected that difference. As their practices spread rapidly from village to village, full-scale conflict with the authorities would not be long in coming.

CHAPTER NINE

The Inevitable Clash

In the spring and summer of 1899, the Spirit Boxers spread through northwest Shandong and across the border into Zhili. Boxing grounds were established in countless villages, and petty harassment of Christian converts became increasingly common. As foreign (and especially American) protests mounted, local officials moved belatedly and ineffectively to control the anti-Christian militants. By the fall, the conflict came to a head in Pingyuan. A minor village dispute escalated dramatically when local Boxers sought assistance from Zhu Hongdeng in Chiping. Zhu's boxers faced off against troops dispatched from Jinan, and the Spirit Boxers fought their first major battle against government forces. In the following weeks, Spirit Boxers raided Christian households and churches throughout the region, until Zhu and other Boxer leaders were arrested and later executed in the provincial capital. By then, however, the Pingyuan events had electrified the north China plain—and polarized debate at the capital. The Boxers, now usually calling themselves "Militia United in Righteousness" (Yi-he tuan), spread all the more rapidly—and the Boxer movement was fully underway.

THE SPIRIT BOXERS OF PINGYUAN

The Spirit Boxers had been active in Pingyuan since the spring of 1899, the practices having spread northward from Chiping and Gaotang. They were concentrated in the southwest of the county, and

across the Majia River which marked the border with En county
(see map 7 below). Even by the depressed standards of northwest Shandong, this was a poor area: the soil unusually saline—often utterly
uncultivable—and the villages widely dispersed. Several of the earliest Boxer villages were right on the Pingyuan-En border, which was
also the border between Jinan and Dongchang prefectures and thus
particularly difficult to control.[1] Most of Pingyuan's Catholic converts were concentrated in this southwest corner of the county, and
the American missionaries in Pangzhuang noted that "lawsuits have
been particularly intense" in that area—with Catholic interference in
legal proceedings arousing considerable resentment.[2] Though Protestant converts would soon find themselves caught up in the growing
anti-Christian movement, the primary Boxer animus was directed at
the Catholics.[3]

The Boxer leaders of this area seem all to have been men of some
power and influence in their communities. One of the earliest was
Zhang Ze, from the village of Beidi on the Majia River. Zhang was a *li-
zhang* and a military *sheng-yuan*, who owned 70–80 *mu* of land. With a
violent temper and a coarse mouth, he ruled his village with an iron
hand: people spoke of the community as "King Zhang's court."[4] The
other key Boxer leader, and the man who would summon Zhu Hong-
deng to Pingyuan, was Li Chang-shui of Gangzi Lizhuang. Li's grandfather had been quite wealthy, with some 400 *mu* of land. Family
division had left Li himself with a good deal less—but still better than
70 *mu* of land and a small flour mill. According to the Pingyuan
magistrate, Li Chang-shui was a *li-zhang*. He was certainly a man of
some influence, over fifty years old at the time, and a student of the
martial arts even before he took up Spirit Boxing.[5] In addition, the
magistrate mentions two more military *sheng-yuan* and two village
heads who were in league with the Spirit Boxers,[6] which indicates a
substantial degree of support from the village-level elite in Pingyuan.

BOXER VIOLENCE AND FOREIGN PROTESTS

By May 1899, the first Christian complaints against Boxer activities
came to the attention of the Pingyuan magistrate, Jiang Kai. Jiang was
a *gong-sheng* from Hubei, who had served for three years as subprefect
of Juzhou in southeast Shandong. Taking up the seals of office in
Pingyuan only late in April 1899, Jiang immediately found himself in
the thick of a mounting crisis. His handling of events was by all

accounts inept. Governor Yu-xian accused him of being "naturally dilatory," with a tendency to try to patch over any problems which arose.[7] The missionaries were no more kindly disposed. According to a Catholic newspaper, when the Boxer troubles first arose, Jiang "was still asleep in bed, one lamp lit, smoking away." The Protestants at Pangzhuang called him "incompetent."[8]

Jiang's own testimony acknowledges that, in May, when the first complaint came from a Christian nephew of Zhang Ze, he ignored it—as the nephew was said to be a contrary sort who got along with no one in the village. Then a Catholic priest came from Yucheng to press the case, and Jiang went to investigate. He discovered minor damage to two buildings that the Catholics used for worship. He gave money to the local constable (di-bao) to have the damage repaired, and then summoned the son of the military sheng-yuan Wang Zhi-bang, who was said to be the local head of the Boxers United in Righteousness. Jiang first warned the son (who was also a military sheng-yuan) that events in Juye and the southwest—where Jiang had served in his last post—showed that anti-Christian incidents only led to settlements increasing the number of churches in an area. The gentry, said Jiang, should understand this and endeavor to prevent such incidents. The advice had little effect. Then Jiang warned of the heterodox nature of the spells and charms used by the Boxers, and the extreme punishment to which sponsors of heterodox rebellion would be subjected. Wang apparently had second thoughts and returned to urge his father to avoid further problems.[9]

In the following month there was a second complaint against Zhang Ze—this time that he had stolen some animals from a Christian. Jiang Kai investigated, found no grounds for the complaint, conferred with the Catholic priest and thus ended the matter.[10] According to Jiang's later account, the fact that the Boxers got away with no punishment for these early incidents only emboldened them, and they practiced their invulnerability rituals all the more widely:

> They claimed swords could not injure or bullets penetrate. In practice, some got broken arms, others wounds in their chests. But it was claimed that these people's techniques were imperfect, and they continued to practice. Some said that in fact the authorities were secretly behind [the movement].[11]

Jiang mentions this last point as part of a consistent criticism of Yu-xian's lenient policy toward the Boxers, but the magistrate himself certainly furthered the impression of official sympathy when he sought to enroll some of the stronger Boxers in the militia.[12]

The Boxer practices became even more popular during the summer, and by September incidents began to escalate. Though the record is mixed, the weather may have had something to do with this. A number of oral history accounts from this area deny that the 1899 harvest was poor; and the spring wheat harvest was in fact quite good.[13] But the summer rains failed throughout the north China plain. Yu-xian reported a poor fall harvest and noted that many of the "lazier" peasants were not even trying to plant their winter wheat.[14] Arthur Smith put a slightly more charitable interpretation on the matter:

> The drought was great and practically universal. For the first time since the great famine in 1878 no winter wheat to speak of had been planted in any part of northern China.... The ground was baked so hard that no crops could be put in, and at such times the idle and restless population are ready for any mischief.[15]

Jiang Kai certainly saw trouble coming early in the summer, and by the fifth lunar month (June 8–July 7) he petitioned the governor for a prohibition of the Boxers. For a long time, no response came, only feeding the popular belief that the governor approved of the Boxers United in Righteousness—as they were now generally known in Pingyuan. When the governor's reply finally came in the seventh month (August 6–September 4), it showed his basic failure to understand the difference between the Spirit Boxers of the northwest and the martial arts groups he had previously encountered in the southwest. He equated the Pingyuan Boxers with the Red Boxers in the southwest under Shao Shi-xuan—with whom he had dealt just a month earlier (see chapter 7). What most bothered Jiang Kai was the governor's failure to stress the heterodox nature of the boxing:

> If such a grave governor's order, written with such enthusiasm, never once acknowledged that [the Boxers] belong to the Li Trigram of the Eight Trigrams, how were the simple people to know heterodoxy? They were united in their hatred of the converts. Their resentment of the foreigners had risen to a public fury. Once the governor's order came down they worshipped Zhu Hong-deng like a god.[16]

By this time, the Italian missionaries had already brought their troubles to the attention of the French minister in Beijing, who on August 25 complained to the Zongli Yamen about renewed threats from the Big Sword Society, as the missionaries routinely called all anti-Christian militants in Shandong.[17] On September 10, the father of a Pingyuan Catholic was robbed by local Boxers including Zhang Ze, and then got into an argument with his village head—also, it seems, a Boxer sympathizer. The father died in frustration and anger over the incident, and his son accused the Boxers of killing the old man. Jiang Kai went to investigate, found clear evidence of burglary but no evidence of wounds to the eighty-year-old father. He arranged with Zhang Ze and other Boxers for the return of clothing and pilfered items, and closed the case. Meanwhile, the Catholics had complained of arson, theft, and murder all the way up to the French minister— who addressed the complaints to the Zongli Yamen, which in turn asked Yu-xian for details. The report Yu-xian received from Jiang Kai on September 24 went out of its way to play down the incident. Boxers were never mentioned, and the theft at the Christian home— clearly acknowledged in Jiang's retrospective account—was explicitly denied in his report to the governor. As a result, Yu-xian became even more convinced that the Catholics were grossly exaggerating the severity of petty incidents.[18] But Jiang Kai was playing a dangerous double game, for at the same time he was reporting all quiet to the governor, he was telling an Italian missionary that Pingyuan was too full of outlaws to allow him to visit—and soon, of course, this was duly reported to the French minister, the Zongli Yamen, and back down the Chinese hierarchy.[19]

The En county magistrate Li Wei-xian's response was far more forceful and effective. Boxer activity became even more pronounced in the eighth month—perhaps in part because the weather prevented the wheat planting which would normally have occupied peasants at that time. Faced with a growing crisis, and responsible for the safety of the Pangzhuang missionaries who were now making alarmist reports to the American Consul in Tianjin, Li, on September 13, went personally to report to the provincial authorities in Jinan. He arranged for the dispatch of a cavalry contingent, which arrived on the 22nd. The Pangzhuang mission was given protection, constables and village heads were called together, and En county returned to some semblance of peace and order.[20]

The same could not be said of Pingyuan. Petty attacks on both Protestant and Catholic converts increased around the time of the Mid-Autumn Festival (September 19). Churches were vandalized; Christians were ordered to renounce the foreign religion or pay a ransom; homes were looted; but there was as yet no violence against individuals. Though Jiang Kai began to arrest the offending parties—and reported optimistically on the success of his efforts to Yu-xian—it is clear that matters were getting out of control.[21] As the troubles spread, the American missionaries continued their urgent appeals for the protection of Chinese converts through the Consul in Tianjin—and these were routinely forwarded to Yu-xian by the Commissioner of North Ports (and governor-general of Zhili) Yu-lu.[22]

SHOWDOWN AT GANGZI LIZHUANG

Gangzi Lizhuang lies about 10 kilometers due south of the Ping-yuan county seat. It is actually divided into two villages, called Front (Qian) and Back (Hou) Gangzi Lizhuang—with a broad expanse of uncultivable saline land between the two. The former was a village of only about forty households, and the home of the Boxer leader Li Chang-shui. It was not a particularly cohesive village, being divided into three clear sections (which are now production teams): the west Lis, the Yangs, and the east Lis. Li Chang-shui was a west Li, and among the east Lis was a Christian of moderate circumstances, Li Jin-bang. The latter owned almost as much land as Li Chang-shui's 70–80 *mu*, had a hired hand, and ran a small wine shop. The two Lis had quarreled some years earlier over the return of land that Jin-bang had mortgaged to Chang-shui, but the events of 1899 were not necessarily the product of this private feud. The issue was obviously Li Jin-bang's Christianity, which left him isolated in his own village: "He did not drink from the same well."[23]

On September 17, Li Chang-shui and other Boxers looted Li Jin-bang's home. Jiang Kai sent runners to arrest the thieves, but the officers were scared off by the Boxers. Five days later, taking advantage of the show of force by the cavalry which had passed through on the way to En county, Jiang again sent runners under one Chen De-he who arrested six men from Gangzi Lizhuang. On the 26th, the cavalry was transferred from En to Pingyuan and toured the affected villages. Li Chang-shui had fled, but some of the stolen goods were located in his and other Boxers' homes and returned to the Christians. Once again Jiang Kai reported optimistically on the prospects for peace. Several days later, he posted a "strict and just" gubernatorial proclamation prohibiting the establishment of boxing grounds, and expected no further trouble. The governor's comments on these reports indicated considerable skepticism that things were as quiet as Jiang was reporting—but the provincial troops were apparently withdrawn.[24]

On October 9, Jiang Kai learned that when Li Chang-shui had fled, he had gone to Chiping to ask assistance of Zhu Hong-deng and now the two had returned and gathered a force of several hundred Boxers who camped in the fields around Gangzi Lizhuang. As usual, this large Boxer band had no particular organization. Zhu had come with only about ten men of his own. The others had gathered when handbills were sent out to Pingyuan and En county boxing grounds, calling the local Boxers to assemble. The Boxers forced the local Christians to feed them, held two converts in ransom for the release of the six arrested villagers, and demanded that the runner Chen De-he be turned over to them for punishment. The situation was grave, and on the 11th, Jiang Kai led several dozen braves and runners to arrest the Boxer leaders. He received a quite unexpected reception: there was Zhu Hong-deng, dressed in red pants and a red cap, and flying red flags, with his troops arrayed for battle. On the flags was the slogan "Under Heaven, the Boxers United in Righteousness; Revive the Qing and destroy the foreign" (Tian-xia Yi-he-quan; Xing-Qing mie-yang), and the names of two local Boxer leaders: Sun Zhi-tai, from En County, about whom we know nothing, and "Wang Zi-rong," which may be an error for Wang Zhi-bang.[25] Together with some monks and Daoist priests among them, the Boxers bowed to the southeast and prepared to resist. Several government soldiers galloped through the village, and then, after some minor skirmishing, two young Boxers burst forward and cut down the magistrate's flag-bearers. According to local lore, Jiang Kai turned to his chief runner, Chen De-he, and asked, "Which is faster, a horse or sedan chair?" Chen put him on a horse, and the magistrate fled. The Boxers thus had their first clear victory over an official bent on suppressing them.[26]

Jiang Kai now found himself in an utterly untenable position. In his reports to the governor, he had consistently downplayed the Boxer-instigated incidents in Pingyuan—and now he had a major challenge to his authority, which could only be met with the aid of additional armed support from Jinan. Such a request for troops was surely going to undermine what little credibility Jiang still had with the governor; and it was also certain to isolate him from the local population. No sooner had Jiang returned to the city than four village heads appeared at his yamen to urge him not to call for troops, saying this would surely force Zhu Hong-deng into outright rebellion. According to these village leaders, Zhu had only come to force the release of the six men arrested on September 22. The kidnapping of Christians was only to ransom the six; and the stealing from Christians was only "because they [the assembled Boxers] have nothing to eat." Though these rural leaders insisted that they were not themselves Boxers, their sympathy with the Boxer demands was unmistakable.[27]

It was not only the rural elite of Pingyuan which supported the Boxer demands. On the night of the confrontation at Gangzi Lizhuang, Jiang Kai was visited by three of his subordinates in the county administration, led by the District Director of Schools, Xu Bing-de. Xu's *ju-ren* degree was superior to the magistrate's *gong-sheng* and he had been in Pingyuan for ten years. The other two functionaries had also served in the county for a number of years and had a familiarity with the local scene that Jiang, in only his sixth month in Pingyuan, certainly lacked. In a poor county like Pingyuan, there was essentially no local gentry elite, and these petty officials acted in the usual gentry role—as intermediaries between the magistrate and the commoner leaders of the villages. The officials supported the village leaders' call for the release of the six peasants, and further suggested that Chen De-he, the runner who had made the arrests, be taken into custody himself.[28] Jiang resisted this suggestion adamantly, and would consistently defend Chen De-he—who, after all, had only been carrying out the magistrate's orders. But the other officials were probably quite correct in perceiving the runners as a focus of local resentment. Four years earlier a Pingyuan magistrate had been impeached and removed from office for listening to evil runners who extorted from and imprisoned guiltless citizens.[29] Chen De-he had been a runner in Pingyuan for some time, and it is unlikely that he was innocent of such crimes himself.

Clearly local public opinion was entirely on the side of the Boxers, and the last thing the people wanted was a visit by troops from the capital—with the violence that was sure to result. But with the countryside now virtually under Boxer control, Jiang Kai had no choice. On October 12, he petitioned the governor for the dispatch of troops. In his usual dilatory fashion, Jiang sent the request by post, but on the same day the En county magistrate urgently cabled for troops, which arrived after a forced march on October 15 or 16. The troops were led by the Jinan prefect Lu Chang-yi, and an officer from the provincial command, Yuan Shi-dun—a cousin of Yuan Shi-kai, the trainer of north China's army who would soon begin a rise to

prominence in which he would succeed Yu-xian as Shandong's governor, be promoted to viceroy of Zhili and, after the fall of the Qing,
become President of the Republic of China.[30]

Once in Pingyuan, Lu Chang-yi took command. Having heard, on
the road to Pingyuan, rumors of bribery by Chen De-he, he immediately took the runner into custody. Then after perusing the local
archives on the various anti-Christian cases, he conferred with Xu
Bing-de and the other long-time Pingyuan officials. Xu in particular
acted as an intermediary between the prefect and the crowd which
had gathered about the yamen. Lu wanted to go personally to Gangzi
Lizhuang, and a *sheng-yuan* in the crowd volunteered to prepare the
way. At the same time, someone was sent to the village to post the
governor's proclamation prohibiting the Boxers—but it was immediately torn down. On the 17th, as arranged, Lu went to meet the *sheng-
yuan* intermediary at a village halfway to the Boxer stronghold. On the
way he was told by another rural *sheng-yuan* that since the arrival of
the troops from Jinan, robberies had proliferated in the area. When he
finally met the intermediary, Lu discovered that Zhu Hong-deng and
the Boxers had already left Gangzi Lizhuang. Continuing on to the
village, he found the community well fortified, with a large foreign-
style cannon and a pile of warm ashes of Boxer charms—but no
Boxers.[31]

The fact is, nobody was anxious for a fight. Zhu's departure from
Gangzi Lizhuang was at the request of the village elders.[32] They had
no desire to involve their community in further trouble. Zhu Hong-
deng himself did not wish to confront the authorities. On the evening
of the 17th a government scout who had been captured by the Boxers
returned with this message from Zhu: "I have given up Gangzi
Lizhuang, so now it belongs to the two great officials. But if they keep
pressing me, and end up losing face themselves, do not blame me!"[33]
Finally Lu Chang-yi himself sought to mollify the Boxers: he had
already arrested Chen De-he, and now he released the six villagers
whom Chen had seized—though they had all admitted participating
in the robbery of the Christians.[34] Despite these efforts at compromise,
the battle was not to be avoided.

THE BATTLE AT SENLUO TEMPLE

When Zhu Hong-deng and his Boxer legions left Gangzi Lizhuang,
they headed northwest in the direction of En county, stopping at
Senluo Temple, on the east (i.e., Pingyuan) bank of the Majia River.

Lying just outside the large village of Zhifang, through which passed the main east-west road between the county seats of Pingyuan and En, the temple was an imposing structure. With its foundation on the outer dike of the river, about five meters above the surrounding plain, the temple commanded a clear view all the way to the walls of Pingyuan. It was probably the size and strategic value of the temple that drew the Boxers there, but it was also directly on the way to the American missionary station at Pangzhuang, and soon urgent appeals from that quarter led to the dispatch of troops to En county and the Pangzhuang mission.[35]

On the morning of October 18, there were between 1,000 and 1,500 Boxers gathered at the temple. The village of Zhifang had no Boxers of its own—the village head having prohibited the practice—and the Boxers were kept outside. Many got their morning meal from the periodic market at Zhangzhuang, across the river in En county. From Pingyuan the officials first sent out two village heads from the Majia River area to try to pacify the Boxers, but the attempt was without effect: they may never have even reached the Boxer force. Then Yuan Shi-dun set out with twenty cavalry and a company of infantry (probably 400–500 men). A scout preceded the commander, announcing his approach; and the Boxers, arrayed under the flag "Revive the Qing, destroy the foreign," sent someone to greet him. But Yuan interpreted the message from Zhu's force as a "War Note" (zhan-shu) and opened fire. The Boxers, armed only with swords, spears, a few primitive hunting rifles, and a couple of antique cannons, attacked with all the fearless bravery that their youth and supposed invulnerability afforded. The official forces, for their part, carried only single-shot rifles, and were unable to reload quickly enough. Three were killed and ten wounded by the fierce Boxer onslaught, and the rest fell back in pell-mell retreat.

Considerably shaken by the ferocity of the Boxer attack, the official forces paused to regroup. Soon reinforcements came from the cavalry sent ahead to En county. When these forces counter-attacked, the Boxer casualties were substantial: twenty-seven killed, including the En county Boxer leader Sun Zhi-tai, according to the official account; thirty to forty according to most local accounts. One Daoist priest who was accused of aiding the Boxers was beheaded. But Zhu Hong-deng and the other Boxers fled west or south, Zhu himself returning to Chiping. Finally, when the battle was over, the elders of Zhifang sent representatives to meet the official forces and plead their innocence of any involvement in the struggle. Among them was the father of a

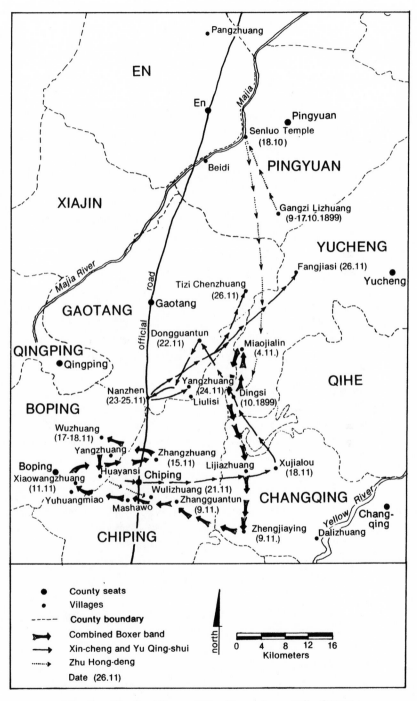

Map 7.   The Last Days of Zhu Hong-deng, Fall of 1899

village *sheng-yuan* who fell to his knees before the government troops. Thinking him a Boxer engaged in a possession ritual, the soldiers shot him dead. This old man was the final casualty of the day—though there was still some minor looting as the troops searched the village for concealed Boxers.[36]

The effect of this first major battle between the Boxers and Qing troops was as complex as any aspect of the Boxer movement. But in the end, the battle was certainly a watershed. It brought the Boxers inescapably to public and official attention—and it eventually provided an impetus for the movement far greater than the battle's outcome would seem to warrant. Locally, the battle finished the Boxers: the large number of Boxer casualties convinced the Pingyuan and En county peasantry that the invulnerability rituals did not work. Until revived under official inspiration in the summer of 1900, the Boxer movement in these counties was dead.[37]

Further from the scene, however, it is clear that a very different version of events circulated—and the escape of Zhu Hong-deng meant that the most important Boxer leader survived to capitalize on the reputation his forces had gained, especially for the initial rout of the government troops. When he returned to Chiping after the battle, Zhu was carried about in an elaborate sedan chair, and people who knew him from this period portray him very differently from the short man with the pockmarked face and little ability described by those who knew him before. "Zhu Hong-deng was an official," recalled one informant.[38] Said another who witnessed the Senluo battle: "Zhu Hong-deng was a civil *xiu-cai* and a farmer."[39] Many who saw his return to Chiping recall an impressive figure, all in red, in a sedan chair with the slogan, "Revive the Qing, destroy the foreign."[40]

The appearance of this slogan as early as the Gangzi Lizhuang confrontation in Pingyuan was no doubt even more important than the exaltation of Zhu Hong-deng's reputation—for as we have seen, a strong leadership structure was not one of the Boxers' characteristics. Zhu himself would be arrested within a month of the Pingyuan battle—and the Boxer movement easily survived that setback. But during the course of the confrontations in Pingyuan, the Boxers United in Righteousness acquired a direction which was to shape the rest of their history. The "Revive the Qing, destroy the foreign" slogan was certainly symbolic of this direction—and the concrete meaning of "foreign" would gradually expand from a focus on the "foreign religion" to an opposition to foreigners and foreign things in general. Though the Guan county Boxers had a similar slogan, it was in Pingyuan that the slogan gained major prominence—just as the Boxers were coming into conflict with Qing troops.[41]

The contradiction of fighting Qing troops under a "Revive the Qing" flag is in fact not very surprising. History is replete with examples of rebels who conceived themselves as loyal to the monarch; and the Boxers were not even rebels. Their aim was to restore the sovereignty and revitalize the energies of the Qing—conceived as the representative of Chinese tradition and Chinese culture—and to rid China of the foreigners and their religion. They had no fundamental quarrel with the Qing, or with any Chinese officials for that matter. When Zhu Hong-deng left Gangzi Lizhuang he warned the officials not to press him, and he certainly took no offensive moves against the Qing authorities. If anything, the Boxers hoped that the officials would support their crusade. One Christian account claims that prior to the Senluo battle, the Boxers invited the Jinan prefect to join them;[42] and several observers explain the pacific Boxer overtures to the officials on the eve of the battle by the fact that "at that time, the Militia United in Righteousness was already cooperating with the officials."[43]

The use of the term "Militia United in Righteousness" is also significant, for the battle at Senluo Temple marked the first appearance of the term "Yi-he *tuan*." In general, when specifically asked, Pingyuan informants said that the militants called themselves "Yi-he *quan* [boxers]," not "Yi-he *tuan* [militia]." But one Zhifang informant explicitly says that at the time of the battle, they were called "Yi-he tuan."[44] More critical evidence comes from the contemporary petition of the *sheng-yuan* whose father was accidentally killed in the battle. He refers to the battle as between government troops and "militia-people" (*tuan-min* or, elsewhere, *tuan-zhong*).[45] Shortly after the battle, Christians began receiving menacing invitations from (in the missionaries' translation) "The Liu Lin harmonious Boxer levy."[46] This "levy" was almost certainly a translation for "*tuan*." By calling themselves "militia" rather than "boxers," the militants were quite consciously distancing themselves from the tradition of proscribed martial arts sects, and associating themselves with the orthodox tradition of village self-defense. The fact that Jiang Kai, and more recently the governor in his proclamations, had branded the "Boxers United in Righteousness" a heterodox sect must surely have played a role in encouraging this change of name.

But as the ultimate conflict with the authorities showed, the aim of "reviving" or "supporting the Qing," the hope of cooperating with the officials, and the desire for orthodox legitimacy as a local militia force most assuredly did not indicate an unconditional respect for the authority of the established state administration. Quite the contrary, the basic political thrust of the Boxer movement was the arrogation of official functions by young militants convinced that the authorities were not doing enough to expel the foreign menace. In December 1899, the leading Boxer foe, Lao Nai-xuan, cited this interpretation of the slogan "Support the Qing, destroy the foreign:" "The Westerners oppress us terribly. The state (*guo-jia*) cannot resist them, so the people themselves resist them." This was utterly improper in Lao's eyes—like a son picking a fight on behalf of his father—but the interpretation was highly significant for it explicitly recognized that what the Boxers were doing was undertaking, on behalf of the Chinese people, actions which the state was incapable of performing.[47]

This was reflected in the most basic patterns of Boxer behavior. In general, at this stage, the Boxers did not simply loot Christian homes. They would fine Christians, or require them to feed the Boxer army on the move, or demand that Christians either renounce the faith or pay a ransom. An "attack" on a Christian home would be preceded by an announcement in the form of an official summons, as this one issued in Pingyuan just after Zhu Hong-deng's arrival: "Exalt the Manchus [Qing?], Down with the foreigners, Kill the foreigners. The Universal Boxer Society demands your presence upon the seventh of the ninth month [October 11]. Refusal to obey this summons means the loss of your head."[48] If the Qing officials would not, or could not, put the Christians in their place, then the Boxers would do it for them.

In all of these respects, the events in Pingyuan—and especially the battle at Senluo Temple—represent a watershed in the development of the Boxer movement. The movement now had the slogan— "Revive" (or more commonly later "Support" [*fu*]) "the Qing, destroy the foreign"—under which it would fight to the end. It had adopted a new name—"The Militia United in Righteousness"— which was soon to become its orthodox appellation. And though coming into dramatic and costly conflict with the authorities, the Boxers had displayed a cautious effort to avoid any direct affront to the local officials. All of these elements no doubt served to enhance the Boxers' reputation, but the spread of the Boxers was also aided by the actions of the Qing officials in dealing with this unusual new movement.

THE OFFICIAL RESPONSE

No social movement develops according to a dynamic purely of its own making. Its evolution is always subject to the influence of established authorities and other independent actors beyond the movement itself. Sometimes these external influences may inhibit a movement's growth, sometimes they may promote it. In the case of the Boxers, especially given their desire to act on behalf of Chinese sovereignty (and, if possible, in cooperation with Chinese authorities), the response of the Chinese state was extremely important. The official response to the battle at Senluo Temple clearly played a key role in the development and spread of the Boxer movement. This response had two parts: dealing with Zhu Hong-deng and the other Boxers who had escaped after the battle, and dealing with the civil and military officials involved in the incident. Let us treat the second of these first.

The first action taken was the removal of the Pingyuan magistrate, Jiang Kai. He was temporarily replaced by a Han bannerman (and affinal relative of the governor) one week after the battle took place. As we have seen, Jiang Kai had no defenders in any camp, and his handling of the crisis was extraordinarily inept. Particularly inexcusable from the governor's standpoint was Jiang's consistent downplaying of the troubles in his reports to Jinan, until events finally overwhelmed him and he had to summon troops to enter a situation already highly inflamed. Yu-xian memorialized to have Jiang removed and permanently barred from office, and the advice was accepted.[49]

But for some people, the removal of Jiang Kai was not enough. On November 3, the censor Wang Chuo (from Zhucheng, in southeast Shandong) memorialized on the Pingyuan incident: his was in fact the first memorial on the subject to reach the court. Wang gave a rather exaggerated version of events, stressing the excesses of the local runners and the inept handling by Jiang Kai. But he also raised questions about Yuan Shi-dun's initiation of the battle at Senluo Temple, and looting and arrests by his troops after the battle.[50] Yu-xian's initial reports to the Zongli Yamen had not mentioned Yuan Shi-dun at all, but now the governor's hand was forced. While generally defending the officer as honest and brave, he admitted that Yuan had not been able to control his troops: some looting had occurred, and innocent people had been injured. Here, of course, the most important victim was the father of the local *sheng-yuan* whose case was reported to the governor following the investigation prompted by Wang Chuo's memorial.[51] In response to Wang's accusations, Yu-xian recommended that Yuan Shi-dun be stripped of his command, and the court accepted the recommendation.[52]

In a context where many people saw the governor as supporting the Boxers' anti-foreign cause, the removal of Jiang Kai and Yuan Shi-dun was widely interpreted as punishment of those who had acted forcefully to suppress the movement. As one Christian source put it: "The outlaws misunderstood and thought [the officials'] crime was attacking outlaws, and so they boasted: 'Governor Yu protects us, so who is to stop us?'"[53] There is little doubt that this was indeed a misunderstanding of Yu-xian's position, but it was a widely shared misperception—among both Boxers and Christians. The Pangzhuang missionaries thought the Senluo battle should have ended the movement, but the officials' reaction to the incident made it "evident that the Manchu Governor of Shantung was not unfriendly to the [Big Sword] society." This so inflamed the missionaries that they wrote to the *North China Herald* that an extension of the German sphere of influence "will be welcomed . . . by the now numerous foreigners *en masse.*"[54]

Yu-xian's handling of the Pingyuan crisis became the basis for a foreign campaign blaming the Manchu governor for the entire Boxer movement, a campaign which would ultimately force his removal from office.[55] There is certainly no question that the Boxers—at least in areas sufficiently distant from the battle to be ignorant of the casualties actually suffered—were emboldened by the dismissal of the two officials. But it would be a mistake to understand Yu-xian's policy as unqualified support for the movement. In fact, his fundamental policy toward the Boxers remained what it had always been: arrest the leaders and disperse the followers.

When Jiang Kai first reported on the confrontation at Gangzi Lizhuang, Yu-xian's rescript warned: "Fights between the people and Christians must not be treated as cases involving outlaws. The key is educating and dispersing [the Boxers.]"[56] After the battle of October 18, Yu-xian ordered the arrest of Zhu Hong-deng and the other leaders of the disturbances, but he was careful to treat the other participants as good citizens and to distinguish them from the "bandits." "The Christians oppress the common people so much that the masses have risen in discontent. Bandits have taken advantage of the situation to burst forth."[57] Yu-xian made it clear that he included many Boxers among the guiltless common people. In his final memorial on the Shandong situation he wrote: "You cannot say for sure that some of these boxers have not been deceived. There are also boxers who have nothing to do [with these incidents]. Thus you cannot indiscriminately label boxers as anti-Christian." [58] He was also quick to respond positively to the Boxers calling themselves "militia," reviving the claim (first seen in connection with the Guan county incidents) that the Militia United in Righteousness had begun in the mid-nineteenth century, and using that term, rather than *Boxers* United in Righteousness, in memorials to the throne.[59]

Above all, Yu-xian was anxious that the anti-Christian incidents not be allowed to drive a wedge between the state and the people— and he was convinced that only a liberal policy toward the Boxers could maintain the loyalty of the Shandong peasantry. As a result, he seems to have issued what the missionaries called "INSANE ORDERS not to have the soldiers kill any one." [60] Many soldiers were no doubt quite pleased to act under such orders, for at least two of Jinan's companies had been recruited by Yu-xian while he was prefect in Caozhou, and were reputed to be full of Big Sword Society members.[61] Whether pro-Boxer sentiment within the army or orders from Yu-xian provided the cause, this much is clear: following the battle at Senluo Temple, no significant effort was made to pursue and suppress Zhu Hong-deng's band. Not surprisingly, Zhu and the other Boxer leaders soon led their forces forth on another even greater round of anti-Christian attacks.

THE FINAL DAYS OF ZHU HONG-DENG

Following the battle of Senluo Temple, the Pingyuan Boxer force scattered, most to return to their homes. Zhu Hong-deng returned to the south. He went to Ding Temple (Dingsi), in Yucheng near the Chiping and Changqing borders, where Xin-cheng had been a monk. There he joined Xin-cheng, Yu Qing-shui, and other Boxer leaders who had assembled following news of the battle. As the leaders debated their next move, Boxer activity stopped. With the exception of two minor cases of extortion in Changqing, there were no anti-Christian incidents anywhere in the area for two full weeks. Zhu and his comrades waited and watched the government's reaction to the events in Pingyuan. Their first realization was surely that nobody was pursuing them. Soon they must have learned of Jiang Kai's dismissal.

Perhaps they also learned of the investigation into the Senluo battle which would ultimately lead to Yuan Shi-dun's dismissal. In any case they certainly realized that Yuan's approach of militarily confronting the Boxers had been reversed. It was in this context that, early in November, Zhu Hong-deng, Yu Qing-shui, and Xin-cheng set out with a substantial band to raid Christian households in Yucheng, Changqing, Chiping, and Boping.[62]

The movements of this Boxer band are indicated in map 7. The Boxers first went north, on November 4, to rob and burn the homes of Christians in Yucheng—and in the process killed a non-Christian gatekeeper, who became the first civilian casualty of Boxer violence. Then they moved south into Changqing, and west into the southern part of Chiping, thus traversing the earliest stronghold of Boxer activity. On the ninth, they seized and executed a Catholic "teacher," the first Christian casualty of the movement. Then they proceeded west into Boping where theft, extortion, kidnapping for ransom, and arson against Christians continued.[63]

The confessions of Zhu Hong-deng and Yu Qing-shui recorded in the official version of events claim that the band learned, in Boping, of the governor's intention to be lenient towards the Boxers if they peacefully dispersed. Accordingly they divided their spoils and headed home, but on November 15 were attacked by Catholics as they passed by Zhangzhuang, north of the Chiping county seat. Hard pressed by the Christians, the Boxers counterattacked, burned most of the village, killed two and wounded three Christians, and then decided that they were "riding a tiger" and dispersal was impossible.[64]

Neither the oral history accounts nor the pattern of Boxer violence summarized in tables 7 and 8 is fully consistent with this interpretation. There was no interruption of Boxer incidents before the confrontation at Zhangzhuang. On the contrary, twenty-two Christians in four villages of Chiping and Boping were looted on November 14, the day before the Zhangzhuang incident. According to one oral history source, the Boxers had attacked one village in the morning before arriving at Zhangzhuang; and they did not come in a manner which indicated dispersal: "When they burned Zhangzhuang, they were carrying flags and [some] wore silk. It was just like an opera."[65] On the other hand, it is true that the incident at Zhangzhuang was initiated by the Catholic village.

One of the key weaknesses of Yu-xian's policy was his failure to recognize that by reining in the coercive forces of the state, he in effect

TABLE 7 SHANDONG BOXER ATTACKS BY DATE AND COUNTY, May 1899–January 1900

County	Date[a]							County totals
	May 5–Oct. 4 (148 days)	Oct. 5–18 (14 days)	Oct. 19–Nov. 2 (15 days)	Nov. 3–14 (12 days)	Nov. 15–27 (13 days)	Nov. 28–Dec. 7 (10 days)	Dec. 8–Jan. 5 (29 days)	
Guan								
victims	1	—	—	—	—	—	—	1
villages	1	—	—	—	—	—	—	1
Pingyuan								
victims	5	24	—	—	1	—	—	30
villages	4	4	—	—	1	—	—	9
En[b]								
victims	4	1 (1)[b]	—	—	—	—	2	7 (1)[b]
villages	1	1	—	—	—	—	1	3
Shen								
victims	8(4)	—	—	—	—	—	—	8 (4)
villages	2	—	—	—	—	—	—	2
Changqing								
victims	—	—	2	2	3	—	28 (11)	35 (11)
villages	—	—	2	2	3	—	11	18
Yucheng[c]								
victims	—	—	—	5 (1)	11	6 (1)	5	52 (6)
villages	—	—	—	1	6	3	2	17

continued on next page

TABLE 7 (continued)

County	Date[a]							County totals
	May 5–Oct. 4 (148 days)	Oct. 5–18 (14 days)	Oct. 19–Nov. 2 (15 days)	Nov. 3–14 (12 days)	Nov. 15–27 (13 days)	Nov. 28–Dec. 7 (10 days)	Dec. 8–Jan. 5 (29 days)	
Chiping								
victims	—	—	—	83	40	—	1	124
villages	—	—	—	14	18	—	1	33
Boping								
victims	—	—	—	12	50 (12)	—	4	66 (12)
villages	—	—	—	4	14	—	3	21
Qingping								
victims	—	—	—	—	4	1	—	5
villages	—	—	—	—	3	1	—	4
Gaotang								
victims	—	—	—	—	15 (2)	3 (1)	1 (1)	19 (4)
villages	—	—	—	—	7	3	1	11
Qihe (3)[c]								
victims	—	—	—	—	—	19	3	29 (1)
villages	—	—	—	—	—	4	1	6
Liaocheng								
victims	—	—	—	—	—	—	23 (4)	23 (4)
villages	—	—	—	—	—	—	4	4

	1	2	3	4	5	6	7	Total
Tangyi								
victims	—	—	—	—	—	—	22 (2)	22 (2)
villages	—	—	—	—	—	—	4	4
Pingyin								
victims	—	—	—	—	—	—	17 (1)	17 (1)
villages	—	—	—	—	—	—	5	5
Xiajin								
victims	—	—	—	—	—	—	5 (1)	5 (1)
villages	—	—	—	—	—	—	1	1
Feicheng								
victims	—	—	—	—	—	—	1 (1)	1 (1)
villages	—	—	—	—	—	—	1	1
Dong'e								
victims	—	—	—	—	—	—	1	1
villages	—	—	—	—	—	—	1	1
TOTALS								
victims	18	25	2	102	124	29	113	
non-Christian	4 (22%)	1 (4%)	— (0%)	1 (1%)	14 (11%)	2 (7%)	21 (19%)	
villages affected	8	5	2	21	52	11	36	
counties affected	4	2	1	4	7	4	13	
TOTALS/DAY								
victims	0.12	1.79	0.13	8.50	9.54	2.90	3.90	
non-Christian	0.03	0.07	—	0.08	1.08	0.20	0.37	
villages	0.05	0.36	0.13	1.75	4.15	1.10	1.24	

SOURCES: Yuan Shi-kai, GX 25/12/19 (19/1/1900), JWJAD 6.1: 488–498, supplemented with data from Jiang Kai, YHT, vol. 1; AJ, 8-20, 205–206, 219, 245–247, 348–350.

[a] The periodization is based on the Chinese lunar calendar. The first period represents the 4th through 8th months. October 18 was the date of the Senluo Temple battle; the Zhangzhuang incident occurred on November 15.

[b] The figures in parentheses represent the number of non-Christians among the victims.

[c] The totals for Yucheng and Qihe come from AJ, 247 and 219, and are greater than the totals by period.

TABLE 8   SHANDONG BOXER ATTACKS BY DATE AND TYPE[a]
May 1899–January 1900

Type of incident	Date							County totals
	May 5–Oct. 4 (148 days)	Oct. 5–18 (14 days)	Oct. 19–Nov. 2 (15 days)	Nov. 3–14 (12 days)	Nov. 15–27 (13 days)	Nov. 28–Dec. 7 (10 days)	Dec. 8–Jan. 5 (29 days)	
Vandalism								
Christians	4	—	—	1	2	1	19	27
Non-Christians	—	—	—	—	—	—	—	—
ALL per day	0.03	—	—	0.08	0.15	0.10	0.66	
Theft (all)								
Christians	6	24	—	79	48	21	62	240
Non-Christians	4	1	—	—	4	1	9	19
ALL per day	0.07	1.78	—	6.58	4.00	2.20	2.45	
Theft: grain								
Christians	4	24	—	11	5	16	18	78
Non-Christians	4	1	—	—	—	—	—	5
ALL per day	0.03	1.79	—	0.92	0.38	1.60	0.62	
Extortion								
Christians	4	—	2	12	47	5	12	82
Non-Christians	—	—	—	—	9	—	4	13
ALL per day	0.03	—	0.13	1.00	4.31	0.50	0.55	
Kidnapping								
Christians	—	—	—	6	4	—	3	13
Non-Christians	—	—	—	—	—	1	3	4
ALL per day	—	—	—	0.50	0.31	0.10	0.21	

Arson								
Christians	—	—	—	20	92	—	9	121
Non-Christians	—	—	—	1	9	—	1	11
ALL per day	—	—	—	1.75	7.77	—	0.34	
Injury								
Christians	—	—	—	—	3	—	—	3
Non-Christians	—	—	—	—	—	—	6	6
ALL per day	—	—	—	—	0.23	—	0.21	
Deaths								
Christians	—	—	—	1	2	1	1	5
Non-Christians	—	—	—	1	1	1	—	3
ALL per day	—	—	—	0.17	0.23	0.20	0.03	
TOTALS								
Incidents								
Christians	18	48	2	130	203	44	124	
Non-Christians	8	2	—	2	23	3	23	
Incidents per day								
Christians	0.12	3.43	0.13	10.8	15.6	4.4	4.28	
Non-Christians	0.05	0.14	—	0.17	1.77	0.3	0.79	

SOURCES: Yuan Shi-kai, GX 25/12/19 (19/1/1900), JWJAD 6.1: 488–498, supplemented with data from Jiang Kai, YHT, vol. l; AJ, 8–20, 205–206, 219, 245–247, 348–350.

[a] For each time period and type of incident, the first row records the number of Christian victims; the second row, non-Christian victims; the third row, the total number of victims per day.

When any attack is recorded as affecting "XX Christian [or commoner] and others," the attack is counted as affecting two victims, that being the median number of victims in the sample.

Often after enumerating the number of victims of a major action (theft, arson, etc.), the document will note "and kidnapped Christian[s]" or "and robbed Christian[s]," with no specification of number of victims. In such cases, only one victim of the second action is counted.

encouraged the competing Christian and Boxer factions to look after their own defense. It was inevitable that, if the Christians felt inadequately protected by the government, they would undertake to protect themselves. In En county, the Pangzhuang mission was always fairly well guarded by the local magistrate, but Dr. Porter also took measures of his own. In his words,

> We went at once into camp, unfurled the American flag, gathered a strong force of Christians about us as guards, borrowed native guns, purchased powder in considerable quantity, and prepared for any emergency that might suddenly come upon us.[66]

The Catholic mission stations in Wucheng, Yucheng, and Pingyin were also extremely well armed with modern repeating rifles.[67] Late in October, the Pingyuan Christians were reported by the French ambassador to be "going out to repulse the Big Sword Society."[68] It was this sort of action that provoked the major confrontation at Zhangzhuang.

Zhangzhuang was the leading Catholic center in Chiping, and almost entirely Christian. The local magistrate had provided it with a small guard of five mounted soldiers. On the morning of November 15, when the Christians observed a small Boxer force resting in a nearby temple, they attacked, together with the five soldiers. Soon Yu Qing-shui arrived with a large number of Boxers, drove off the soldiers, and burned the village.[69]

The burning of Zhangzhuang represented another turning point for the Boxer movement. Two days later, in Boping, the Boxers fell to quarreling among themselves over the division of spoils. Zhu Hong-deng was injur_d in the fracas and headed south by himself, while Xin-cheng and Yu Qing-shui went east to Changqing before they too split up. With the Boxers now more dispersed, incidents occurred more frequently, and over a wider area. As we see from table 7, an average of four villages per day were affected by Boxer actions in the thirteen days after the Zhangzhuang battle, as against 1.75 villages per day in the twelve days prior to the battle. The post-Zhangzhuang period also marked the beginning of Boxer actions in Qingping and Gaotang. The dispersal of the Boxer force obviously affected Boxer discipline, and there was a major escalation of violence against non-Christians. Prior to the Zhangzhuang confrontation, incidents involving non-Christians averaged less than one every ten days. But in the period immediately following the battle, such incidents averaged better than one per day. Oral history accounts frequently speak of the degeneration of the Boxers in their later stages, and that process surely began with the battle at Zhangzhuang.[70]

There was also a certain fatal inevitability in the attacks on non-Christians. As Lao Nai-xuan observed: "In Chiping, they even robbed common people. Since there were so many, and they had nothing to eat, they had no way to feed themselves except by robbery."[71] Table 8 shows that from the beginning, the Boxers had made grain a key object of their expropriations from the Christian population—but now that population was pretty well stripped clean. The Boxers, perforce, became a good deal less discriminating in their choice of targets. Non-Christian victims of theft, extortion, and kidnapping for ransom became increasingly numerous as the Boxers sought any means to support their band. This had dire consequences. In the words of one informant: "When the Big Sword Society was robbing Christians, the officials let them. Later, when they stole from the rich, the officials began arresting them."[72] It is doubtful that the dynamic was quite that simple, but there is no question that the spreading Boxer attacks, the ravaging of non-Christians, and the scale of the Zhangzhuang incident itself finally forced Yu-xian and the authorities to act.

Following the Zhangzhuang incident, the Boxer force moved west back into Boping. On November 17th, Zhu was resting at the pig-slaughtering ground of Huayansi, which was having its market on that day, while the Boxers were looting Christian homes in nearby Little Zhangzhuang. When they returned, there was a dispute over the division of spoils: "In a moment it flared up like a dog fight. Some of the Spirit Boxers wanted to kill Zhu Hong-deng, scaring him so that he went and hid in his sedan chair." During the fight Zhu was wounded in the head.[73] Several oral history accounts say the dispute was between members of the larger "left platoon" and the smaller "right platoon," which protected Zhu.[74] But we know from Yu Qing-shui's confession that Yu had also proceeded to the Huayansi area on the 17th, and then on the following day went (together with Xin-cheng, it seems) some thirty kilometers clear across Chiping to Changqing.[75] The likely interpretation is that the dispute at Huayansi involved the bands of Zhu Hong-deng on the one hand, and Yu Qing-shui and Xin-cheng (both from the northern Chiping-Gaotang area) on the other.

This was the beginning of the end for the Chiping Boxers. The authorities were now getting serious about arresting the leaders and dispersing the followers. The task proved not difficult at all. Learning of the dispute at Huayansi, troops sent from Jinan pursued Zhu to southeast Chiping where, in Wulizhuang on November 21, a Boxer friend identified Zhu as he attempted to escape through the fields wearing peasant clothes and carrying a shit-basket over his shoulder.[76] Three days later, Xin-cheng was surrounded and seized while asleep back at home in southern Gaotang. There was still a substantial force of several hundred Boxers under Yu Qing-shui occupying the town of Nanzhen on the Gaotang-Chiping border. But in the final days of November, Yu made the mistake of taking money, cotton, animals, and carts from several wealthy non-Christians, including two lower gentry members. The Boxer leader in nearby Liulisi turned against him and gave him over to the authorities. With that, all three major Boxer leaders were in custody.[77] Soon they were taken to Jinan, where they would be executed in December. With their arrest, Boxer activity in Chiping and Boping came abruptly to an end.

THE BOXER HYDRA GROWS

Tactically, Yu-xian's policy worked brilliantly. He had every reason to expect that just as his arrest of the Big Sword Society leaders in 1896 had stopped that uprising, so would the swift surgical strikes seizing Zhu Hong-deng and the other Spirit Boxer leaders bring this most recent chapter of anti-Christian violence to a close. But the Spirit Boxers were not the same as the Big Sword Society of the southwest; and nothing showed this more clearly than the contrasting results of Yu-xian's arrest-and-disperse policy in the two cases. Against the Spirit Boxers, Yu-xian's policy was a strategic disaster. Table 7 tells the story.

Following the arrest of the main Boxer leaders, the movement came to a temporary halt in Chiping and Boping. But within a month, new Boxer activity broke out in Qihe, Liaocheng, Tangyi, Pingyin, Fei-cheng, Xiajin, Dong'e, and the areas of Changqing south of the Yellow River. Villages were attacked at a rate of better than one per day —higher than at any time other than the height of Boxer activity in the tenth lunar month (November 3–December 2). The Boxers were showing their most fundamental strength: whenever one leader was arrested or cut down, they could generate a new one at a moment's notice, and that person would revive the movement in some new location.

There was also a significant escalation in the villages targeted for attack. At first, the Boxers had victimized small groups of Christians isolated in the villages across the plain. The November 15 attack on Zhangzhuang was the first assault on a fortified Catholic village. The success of this attack perhaps emboldened the Boxers to turn against the local bases of the Christians' power: the mission stations of the foreigners themselves. We have already noted how well-armed and fortified the missions were, and it is hardly surprising that the Boxers initially shied away from such outposts as Pangzhuang, with its extensive guard and American flag flying prominently overhead. Pangzhuang, in fact, would remain untouched. The Senluo battle had finished the Boxers in that area, and the Protestants were not the prime Boxer target in any case. But in December, the senior Boxer leader Wang Li-yan directed an attack on the Catholic mission in Yucheng; and another assault was launched against a Pingyin mission south of the Yellow River. Both of these would withstand the Boxer attack, but the incidents indicated the Boxers' attempt to rid the region of the hated foreign presence.[78]

As the movement spread, it also tended to evaporate in its original heartland. In general, the movement did not revive where it had once been suppressed: just as the Senluo battle ended the movement in Pingyuan and En, so did the arrest of Zhu and others quell the movement in the Chiping area. Only in the very different context of the summer of 1900 would Boxers reemerge in these areas. The clearly demonstrated opposition of the authorities (together with the failure of the Boxer invulnerability) was enough to end what was, after all, fundamentally a loyalist movement. In most cases, such cutting off of a peasant uprising at its base would end the movement—or at least reduce its adherents to the status of roving bandits. But that was not the case with the Boxers. Suppressed in one locale, the movement quickly sprouted new leaders elsewhere. The anti-foreign cause was so popular, the Boxer ritual so easy to learn, and the promise of invulnerability so tempting that before long someone in a neighboring county would spread the Spirit Boxer magic and rally peasants to attack the noxious foreign religion. The very logic of the movement guaranteed that its suppression in one area meant its reemergence eleswhere.

The Boxers would clearly not be terminated by arresting leaders and dispersing followers. Yu-xian's policy was obviously inapt, and the Manchu governor's position was becoming increasingly untenable. As anti-Christian incidents spread throughout northwestern

Shandong, missionaries and diplomats began clamoring for his removal, and threatening dire consequences if it was not speedily ordered. By late November, the missionaries at Pangzhuang were in daily contact with the American consuls in Tianjin and Yantai, and at one point the latter (in a bit of bluster) threatened to protect the missionaries himself if the governor would not do it—a line reminiscent of the German actions in the southeast some months earlier.[79] Following the Boxer attack on the Catholic mission in Yucheng, the American Protestants in Jinan wrote to the *North China Herald* placing full blame on the governor and offering their view that "When such puny men can pose as Governors, we think it high time for some Power to take charge of the country and really rule it."[80]

The French and American ministers in Beijing flooded the Zongli Yamen with protests against the continuing Boxer incidents, and it eventually caved in to their complaints. On December 1, the Yamen cabled Yu-xian on the latest visit from the U.S. envoy: "The American minister has not been a habitual meddler. It seems that his words are not without cause."[81] Finally on December 5, the American minister, Conger, "suggested the necessity and propriety of [Yuxian's] removal." On the very next day, the governor was summoned to the capital and Yuan Shi-kai appointed in his place.[82]

But Yuan Shi-kai hardly arrived with a mandate to reverse Yuxian's tolerant policy toward the Boxers. On December 26, the very day that he took office in Jinan, a Hanlin scholar memorialized with a cogent analysis interpreting the rise of the Boxers as a response to increased conversions and Christian aggressiveness following the dismissal of Li Bing-heng. He then went on to claim that over a hundred innocent civilians had been killed in the battle at Senluo Temple, and urged that Yuan Shi-kai be restrained from relying on military means to suppress the Boxers—lest the result of the Pingyuan incidents be even greater conversion to Christianity. The court accepted the analysis of the memorial, and forwarded it to Yuan with an edict endorsing the suggested policy.[83]

On the following day another memorial came to the defense of the Boxers, again tracing the origins of the movement to the German seizure of Jiaozhou, and linking the Boxers to the tradition of militia defense:

> The local officials, paying no heed to right or wrong, consistently protect the Christians and put down the people. Thus denied the opportunity to sue [in court], they are forced to organize militia to protect themselves and

their families. . . . These sword societies and boxing societies are simply the other side of the coin from militia. When they break the law they are bandits; when they behave themselves they are good citizens.

The censor appealed to the Confucian principle of "taking the people as the foundation," and suggested using these "militia" to defend the realm. He particularly warned that Yuan Shi-kai, in part because of his kinship to Yuan Shi-dun, was inclined to pursue a policy of military suppression of the Boxers. This was strongly condemned: "We spend several millions of cash each year to support our soldiers, yet they do not protect us against the foreign barbarians but only slaughter the common people."[84] The court was not yet prepared to go so far as endorsing boxer militia units, but it issued an edict to Yuan Shi-kai affirming that "repression and dispersal" should be the basic policy toward the Boxers, and above all Yuan "must not go straight out to attack and annihilate (*jiao-ji*) them."[85]

Yuan Shi-kai was distressed and angry that such attacks should come with such unseemly haste, before he had even begun to act as governor. He was convinced that Yu-xian's lenient policy was responsible for the spread of the Boxers, but now he was constrained to act according to principles quite similar to those of his predecessor.[86] When he published a proclamation and issued a general order to local officials immediately after assuming office he stressed only the protection of churches guaranteed by treaty, the cost of missionary incidents, the certainty of punishment of any who attacked Christians, and the Christians' obligation to obey the law and not rely on the church to gain favor in lawsuits. The documents reported to the central government were in fact quite even-handed. Another notice, seemingly *not* reported to Beijing, did prohibit boxing societies, but even Yu-xian had eventually been forced to take that action.[87]

In this context, it is not surprising that the dismissal of Yu-xian in early December, and the arrival of Yuan Shi-kai near the end of the month, brought little change in the pace of Boxer incidents. In fact, it was shortly after Yuan took up office that the first foreigner fell victim to the Boxers: on December 31, 1899, the British missionary S. M. Brooks was killed in Feicheng by a band that included both locals and militants from north of the Yellow River. Brooks was rather foolishly travelling alone in a region known to be troubled by the "Big Sword Society," and when confronted on the road he apparently attempted to fight the men accosting him. Wounded in the initial encounter, he was finally killed only after he sought to escape. All accounts of the incident picture it as a good deal less than a premeditated attack—but the fact is, a foreign missionary had been killed in Shandong for the first time since the Juye incident, and that was a significant escalation of Boxer violence.[88]

After the first weeks of 1900, Boxer violence in Shandong began to taper off, but it is likely that the weather and the Chinese New Year celebrations were as important a factor here as Yuan Shi-kai's slightly firmer treatment of anti-Christian militants. As Yuan reported in mid-January: "Shandong is blanketed with a great snow, and those with any property have dispersed and returned home."[89] Above all, what happened in Shandong after Yuan's arrival was very close to what happened in Pingyuan after the Senluo battle, or in Chiping after the arrest of Zhu Hong-deng and the other Boxer leaders. In those cases, the movement was halted in a couple of counties, only to spring up in the surrounding areas. Now the Boxers would be checked in Shandong, only to rise up again in neighboring Zhili.

The battle in Pingyuan and the flurry of anti-Christian incidents that engulfed northwestern Shandong in the fall of 1899 marked the final maturation of the Boxer movement. Their simple rituals of possession and invulnerability had reached their final form. They had their slogan—"Revive the Qing, destroy the foreign." They began to rename themselves the "Militia United in Righteousness." Popular support for their anti-Christian cause was extremely widespread, and the official reaction to the battle at Senluo Temple indicated that as high as the court in Beijing, there were many who favored the Boxers over the troops sent to suppress them. Finally the nature of the movement was such that a policy which stressed arresting leaders and dispersing followers could never succeed—for the Boxers could regenerate leaders with incredible speed, and assemble new followers with the greatest of ease. The movement had now reached its flashpoint. The events in Pingyuan provided the spark. The prairie fire would follow.

CHAPTER TEN

Prairie Fire

The focus of this study is the origins of the Boxer Uprising. Having traced those origins to the point at which the Boxers burst onto the national scene, we have essentially completed our tale. On the other hand, we are now (as the Chinese phrase has it) "riding the tiger," and it is difficult to dismount gracefully, abandoning our Boxer tiger just as he is poised to rage across the north China plain. We must finish the Boxer story, but abandon our microscopic approach. Much of the ground has been covered before and is far less controversial than the question of the Boxers' origins. As a consequence, this chapter will rely more heavily on the secondary literature in the field. The focus, however, will be on various continuities with the patterns and processes we have been examining in the preceding pages.

These continuities are worth stressing because in a few short months the Boxer movement took on an appearance quite removed from the ragtag band of poor Shandong peasants who followed after Zhu Hong-deng harassing local Christians. By June of 1900 the Boxers were streaming into the national capital by the thousands, blocking a foreign relief expedition, besieging the foreign legations, provoking a full-scale war with the Great Powers, and winning formal sponsorship by the Chinese court. Throughout this period of spectacular spread and growth, the Boxers' ritual remained basically unchanged; their loyalist and anti-Christian purpose developed into a broader anti-foreignism only at a very late stage; and the manner in which they spread their practices from village to village across the north China plain essentially replicated the process by which the movement had spread in northwest Shandong. Our task now is to describe that spread of the Boxer prairie fire—and the continuing inadequacy of the official measures to contain it.

THE POLICY OF THE COURT

On January 11, 1900, the court issued a crucial edict on the anti-Christian disturbances:

> Recently banditry has flared up in various provinces and anti-Christian incidents have broken out repeatedly. Some commentators have called the guilty parties "outlaw associations" [hui-fei] and requested strict punishment. But we observe that there are differences even among associations [hui]. The law certainly cannot tolerate those unlawful sorts who form bands and alliances, relying on their numbers to incite trouble. But those law-abiding citizens who practice various arts to protect themselves and their families, or who unite the people of their villages to protect their neighborhood are simply observing the righteous duty to keep watch and render mutual assistance. Local officials who do not distinguish between [these two types], who carelessly listen to rumors and regard all as outlaw associations, who implicate whole families and slaughter indiscriminately so that there is no distinction between good and evil and the people become agitated and confused—these officials only add fuel to the fire and drive the fish back into deep water.

The edict went on to insist that officials adjudicate all cases involving Christians with an even hand, in order to "lead the masses to obedience," "solidify the base [of the state] and produce [peaceful] relations with the foreign powers." It concluded with this critical instruction: "Local officials, in handling such cases, are only to ask if those involved are outlaws or not, whether they incite trouble or not. They are to pay no attention to whether or not they belong to some association, or whether or not they are Christians."[1]

The edict represented the court's response to the flurry of memorials that had followed the Pingyuan incident and the Brooks murder, criticizing Yuan Shi-kai's alleged "extermination" policy in Shandong. A number of censors argued that a firm policy attacking the Boxers would only force people to join the Christian church, and "once the people have been forced into the church, they are all foreigners [yang-min] and no longer belong to the dynasty."[2] "If there were an incident," asked one memorial, "would they resist the enemy for us, or conspire against us for the enemy? One need not be brilliant to figure that out." [3] In the growing polarization of the north China countryside, many officials were unwilling to allow Christians to organize in a foreign-dominated church, while denying others the right to assemble in self-defense. In essence they favored Yu-xian's policy of allowing boxers to organize, as long as they did not provoke violent incidents—and we should recall that that policy had twice worked, with both the Big Swords and the Red Boxers in southwest Shandong.

In terms of Chinese political theory, however, the court's action represented a radical departure. Chinese law had always prohibited private associations of individuals, regarding such assemblies as potential sources of subversion. The prohibition on "privately establishing associations and alliances" had been renewed following the 1898 coup, to eliminate the "study societies" (*xue-hui*) which had flourished during the brief period of reform. As recently as December 1899, this prohibition had been restated, and rewards offered for arrests of members of south China secret societies like the Triads (Tian-di hui), revolutionary organizations like Sun Yat-sen's Revive China Society (Xing-Zhong hui) or anti-Christian organizations like the Big Sword Society.[4] Now the Boxers were being told that they had, in effect, a right of association—as long as they did not use those associations to break any other laws.

Clearly extraordinary circumstances led to this shift in basic imperial policy. In part, these circumstances were the growing national crisis following the Great Powers' Scramble for Concessions, and the Christian-commoner conflicts that ensued—not only in Shandong, but also in such faraway places as Sichuan and Hubei, where other groups were quite independently raising equivalents to the Boxer slogan "Support the Qing, destroy the foreign."[5] But there was also a serious political crisis in the capital, where the court was gravely divided between reactionary supporters of the Empress Dowager and men still loyal to the more progressive Guang-xu emperor. Ever since the coup of September 1898, the Empress Dowager's group had the clear upper hand. As time went on, leadership of this group passed to a small and bitterly anti-foreign clique of Manchu princes. Late in 1899, the veteran statesman Li Hong-zhang, who for decades had dominated the politics of north China, departed to become governor-general in Canton and one more moderating influence on the court was lost. By January 1900, the Empress Dowager and her most sycophantic supporters were ready to make their move.

The son of this group's most prominent member, Prince Duan, was named heir apparent to the throne—an unprecedented move in the Qing political system, and one which was widely interpreted as foreshadowing the formal deposition of the Guang-xu emperor. When the ministers of the foreign powers all indicated their displeasure by refusing to attend a celebration in honor of the new heir, the anti-foreign animus of the princes was further strengthened.[6]

This, then, was the context in which the January 11 decree was issued. A xenophobic group was in the ascendant at court, and their natural sympathies for the Boxer cause were certainly strengthened when Yu-xian arrived in the capital at about this same time. When he met with the princes, the former Shandong governor certainly defended the loyalty and righteousness of the Boxers, and there is some evidence that he may have attested to the efficacy of the Boxer invulnerability magic—something that would have appealed to those seeking ways to neutralize the superior weaponry of the West.[7] But we should not overstate the degree of official toleration of the Boxers, for less than two weeks after the famous January 11 edict, the court ordered the Shandong and Zhili officials to strictly prohibit the Boxers United in Righteousness—an order which the Zhili viceroy Yu-lu printed and posted throughout the affected areas of the province.[8]

The debate at court was not really over whether or not to tolerate the Boxers. The issue was whether local officials should disperse the society with a policy of pacification (*fu*), or use military force in a policy of annihilation (*jiao*). In this the court consistently opposed the policy of annihilation—arguing that it would only incite wider unrest. As late as May 1900, when the Boxer disturbances were reaching truly threatening proportions, the court still cautioned Yu-lu against the excessive application of military force.[9] And the court continued to muddy the issue by defending, in general terms, the right of villagers to organize in self-defense, even while holding to its policy of proscribing Boxers United in Righteousness.[10]

As a result of this division and confusion at court, any official proclamation prohibiting the Boxers was met by popular skepticism and resistance. The divisions at court were widely known, and the Boxers and their sympathizers simply dismissed any prohibition of Boxer activities as issuing from the anti-Boxer officials, and not representing the true will of the throne. Furthermore, the low regard most people had for late Qing officials supported the common belief that any anti-Boxer proclamation was the result of foreign bribing of the issuing official.[11] It was in this context—politically confused and legally contradictory—that the Boxers continued their spread across Zhili in the direction of Beijing.

SPREAD ACROSS ZHILI

In May 1900, Yu-lu, governor-general of Zhili, described the expansion of the Boxer movement in his jurisdiction:

> The Society of Boxers United in Righteousness began in Shandong. Those who spread its boxing were all homeless vagrants. They claimed that by carrying charms and reciting chants they could call down gods to possess their bodies so that swords could not pierce them nor guns wound them. They travelled about misleading the simple villagers, taking teachers and transmitting to disciples, establishing [boxing] grounds and altars where they gathered to practice. The gods they worship are mostly taken from historical novels. They assemble in an unreasonable manner and [preach] heterodox nonsense.[12]

Allowing for the inevitable disparaging comments of disapproving officials, Yu-lu's description is not far from the truth—and certainly establishes the fact that we are dealing here with the same Spirit Boxing, with possession rituals and invulnerability beliefs, that had its origin in northwest Shandong.

In fact, anti-Christian Boxer activity had spread into Zhili in 1899, at the same time that it was spreading across northwest Shandong. This was all part of the great north China plain. The ecology and social formations were basically uniform, and peddlers and agricultural laborers moved frequently and naturally across the borders of these two provinces. The initial extension of Boxer activity to Zhili was part of the same process of expansion described for Shandong in the last two chapters. The most affected areas were in Hejian prefecture, adjacent to the Boxer regions of northwest Shandong. As early as the spring of 1899, the Boxers were preaching their message at a large temple fair in Zaoqiang, evidently protected by the "phlegmatic and opium-besotted" magistrate, who would be removed early in 1900 for allowing a local boxing teacher ready access to his yamen.[13]

In many of the Zhili boxing centers, the initial teachers came from Shandong. Some came on their own; others were invited by local villagers who crossed the border in search of masters of the new boxing. Shandong teachers were apparently involved in the spring 1899 incidents described above, and later in neighboring Gucheng

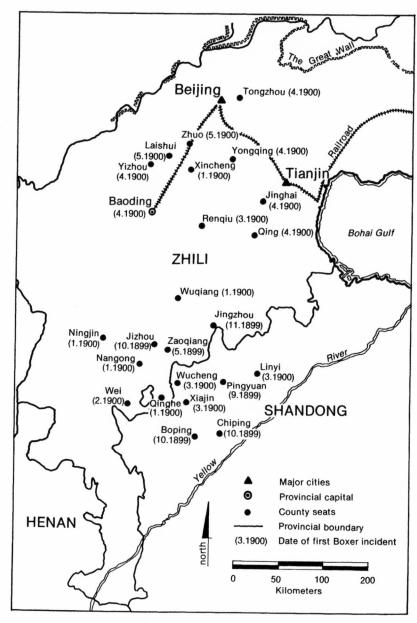

Map 8. The Boxer Spread into Zhili, 1899–1900

and Xian county, in Xincheng, and in substantial numbers among the Boxers in Tianjin.[14] Often the teachers were Buddhist monks or Daoist priests—itinerant types, with no families to bind them to a given locality, and men familiar with the world of magic and mystery which was so central to the Boxer appeal.[15] But it is essential to recognize that while a few teachers brought the Boxer practices from Shandong, there was no widespread movement of whole Boxer bands from Shandong to Zhili. In each new locality, the Boxers were overwhelmingly local youths, and the battles they fought were with the Christian congregations in their immediate neighborhoods. Only in the final phases of the movement, as the Boxer practices spread to the outskirts of Beijing, did Boxers from central Zhili leave their native villages and set forth in hundreds of small bands, heading for the national capital.[16]

As seen above, temple fairs could provide the Boxers an opportunity to spread their possession ritual and anti-foreign message, and Boxers also tended to gather at local market towns where larger populations and plenty of traffic from neighboring villages provided a ready audience. Their boxing grounds were usually established at large local temples—spacious areas for their activities and convenient roofs for the itinerants to sleep under.[17] Placards and handbills advertised the Boxers' cause—especially when they needed to assemble large groups from surrounding communities for some confrontation with local Christians. Men from all walks of life were attracted to the boxing grounds, but in this overwhelmingly agricultural area, the vast majority of new Boxer recruits were peasants. What most impressed contemporary observers was their tender age: "They are all youths in their teens," reported Yu-lu.[18] Others called them "children" of ten years and older;[19] or recorded the oldest as barely twenty, the youngest not yet ten.[20]

After the Zaoqiang incidents in the spring of 1899, troubles next arose in Jingzhou, on the Shandong border north of Dezhou, and in neighboring Wuqiao, where the local magistrate was Lao Nai-xuan, author of the famous pamphlet linking the Boxers to the White Lotus sect. Beginning in November, a familiar pattern of Boxer activity ensued: boxing groups calling themselves the Militia United in Righteousness spread throughout the countryside, organizing under the banner "Support the Qing, destroy the foreign." Petty frictions with Christians grew worse, a few Christians were kidnapped for ransom, then some churches were burned, wounding a few of the converts. By mid-December there had been fourteen incidents in the five counties

Figure 8. Boxer Placard. In addition to the usual pro-Qing and anti-foreign sentiments, this placard particularly warns of the harm that will come to those who collaborate with the enemy. Courtesy of the Chinese Historical Museum, Beijing.

around Jingzhou. As both Catholic and Protestant missionaries issued cries of alarm to their consular authorities, troops were sent from the provincial forces and before long a battle had broken out in which thirty Boxers were killed and eighty captured, including several leaders who were promptly executed. At about the same time, several lesser battles were fought further north in Xian county, where a French bishop resided, with the casualties again on the Boxer side.[21]

A few weeks later, a band of about a hundred Boxers from Shandong joined local Boxers to attack Christians in Wuqiao, burning a church and several homes. Lao Nai-xuan summoned the provincial troops, and nine Boxers were killed and a dozen or so seized. Lao used the opportunity to demonstrate the ineffectiveness of the Boxer magic—inviting one of the leaders to call down his god before chopping his head off.[22] These rather brutal measures essentially brought the disturbances to a close—but they also brought a flurry of protests from pro-Boxer officials in the capital, including one censor from Shandong who accused Lao Nai-xuan of being a Christian who insulted the gods to whom the local people were praying for relief from the prolonged drought.[23] Another urged the destruction of Lao's misguided pamphlet and made the telling observation: "The officials of the two provinces [Zhili and Shandong] who come to Beijing mostly say that the Society of Boxers United in Righteousness is a branch of the heterodox sects and should be exterminated. The gentry of the two provinces say they are good people seeking to protect themselves and their families and not plotting rebellion."[24]

In a sense, the events in Jingzhou and Wuqiao were a repetition of what had happened a few months earlier in Pingyuan. The Boxers were temporarily quieted in one area but still spread inexorably across the plain. The telegraphic correspondence of the Zhili governor-general's office shows clearly the steady northwestern spread of the Boxer incidents—bringing them ever closer to the court in Beijing. From October 1899 through January 1900, the incidents concentrated in the counties around Jingzhou directly on the Shandong border. February was basically quiet (with the exception of an alarm near the Guan county exclave further south) as most peasants were preoccupied with Chinese New Year celebrations. In March, incidents resumed further north, in the counties east of Baoding. April brought a major confrontation near Baoding, the intensification of Boxer activity along the new railroad between Baoding and Beijing, and the first serious incidents around Tianjin. By May, the Boxers were fully mobilized on the outskirts of Beijing, and the most serious battles with Qing troops occurred.[25]

It is essential to stress the still very limited nature of the Boxer attacks. In May, the American minister in Beijing could report that "in no case as yet have the 'Boxers' attacked any American mission or disturbed any property in the towns or villages where they are stationed";[26] and one Baoding missionary wrote home that "little of note has happened in our routine life" and made no mention of the Boxers.[27] In part, these reports reflected the fact that the Boxer animus was still primarily directed against the Catholics—and the American Protestants were relatively secure.[28] Still, for all the harassment of Christians, and despite the few cases of arson, the Boxers seem to have killed only one person (a non-Christian in Wuqiao) before the spring of 1900, while suffering at least fifty deaths at the hands of government troops. The Boxers were by no means on a bloodthirsty rampage by this point. On the government side, despite all the tolerant edicts from the court, the provincial troops in Zhili were pursuing the Boxers with considerable vigor, and inflicting substantial casualties. But nothing had happened to reduce the tension between the Boxers and the followers of the foreign religion, and the spring would see a significant escalation of the violence.

Despite the petty nature of most Boxer harassment, the northward direction of the Boxers' spread was highly significant. It reflected the purpose embodied in their rallying cry: "Support the Qing, destroy the foreign." There were Christians scattered across the north China plain, and the Boxers would have found plenty of victims had the movement spread southward toward Henan. But it did not. Instead the teachers who transmitted the Boxer magic seemed always to move north—drawn inexorably toward the capital and the Qing court they sought to support, and toward the centers of foreign power in the Beijing legations and the Tianjin concessions. Most Boxer violence was perpetrated by local villagers against local Christians, but everyone recognized that it was powerful foreign support that allowed the Christians to work their mischief. To end that mischief, the foreigners would have to be confronted at the seats of their power. And that is where the movement headed.

SPRING 1900: ESCALATING CONFLICT

When Boxer incidents revived following the Chinese New Year, they both broadened in extent and increased in severity. The 7,000 modern troops that Yuan Shi-kai had brought to Shandong when he assumed the governorship had kept that province fairly peaceful during the winter months. Then in March, Yuan reported, "I called the troops together for training, and outlaws took advantage of their absence to cause disturbances anew."[29] Large Boxer bands reemerged to harass Christians along the Grand Canal in Xiajin and Wucheng, and around Linyi, just east of the original Boxer homeland; and dozens of petty cases sprang up throughout the northwest.[30] But the main spread continued northward—and as the Boxers increased in number and Christians armed in self-defense, the severity of the conflicts steadily increased.

One major factor contributing to this escalation of violence was unquestionably the prolonged and severe drought across much of the north China plain. Significantly, the area along the Zhili-Shandong border got a substantial penetrating rain in early April, sending the peasants back to the fields to plant the spring crops and quieting things down considerably.[31] But the rest of Zhili was not so fortunate. In the words of the American minister, Edwin H. Conger:

> The present conditions in this province are most favorable to such a movement [as the Boxers]. The people are very poor; until yesterday [May 7] practically no rain has fallen for nearly a year, plowing has not been and can not be done, crops have not been planted, the ground is too dry and hard to work in any way, and consequently the whole country is swarming with hungry, discontented, hopeless idlers, and they . . . are ready to join any organization offered.[32]

Even after serious conflicts between Boxers and government troops broke out in mid-May, the British minister, MacDonald, would report that "I am convinced that a few days heavy rainfall, to terminate the long-continued drought . . . would do more to restore tranquility than any measures which either the Chinese Government or foreign Governments could take."[33]

Any natural disaster is a grave threat to peasant survival, but in psychological terms, drought is certainly the most difficult to endure. It has no perceptible natural cause, nor any human remedy. Floods come from breaks in dikes: one can affix blame for the breaks, and take measures to repair them. Floods recede, and may even leave fertile sediment for a new crop to be planted. But peasants can do nothing to fight a drought but wait, and pray for rain. Waiting makes men restless—especially young men—and it is no great surprise that many young men filled their idle days by going to watch the Boxers practice, becoming interested, and joining the new association. And praying: when prayers are not answered, people begin to ask why. The Boxers had a ready answer: the Christians had offended the gods. Early in 1900, a missionary recorded the following placard, which had been "posted everywhere in the North of China, including cities, towns and villages":

> On account of the Protestant and Catholic religions the Buddhist gods are oppressed, and the sages thrust into the background. The law of Buddha is no longer respected, and the Five Relationships [of Confucian ethics] are disregarded. The anger of Heaven and Earth has been aroused and the timely rain has consequently been withheld from us. But Heaven is now sending down eight million spiritual soldiers to extirpate these foreign religions, and when this has been done there will be a timely rain.[34]

And thus resentment of the Christians increased—and with it support for the Boxers, until county after county reported boxing grounds as numerous as "trees in a forest," and sympathy for the Boxer cause appeared almost universal in the villages of the north China plain.

With Boxer activity increasing, the Christians naturally began arming in self-defense—and with aid from the missionaries, this inevitably left the Christians with far better weapons than the Boxers, who rarely carried more than spears, swords, and perhaps a few old muskets. The contradictions between the two groups were intensifying to the extent that the smallest incident could spark a major confrontation. That is precisely what happened near Baoding in April. A certain Zhang Luo-di from Big Zhang Village asked a Christian bowl-mender from nearby Jiangzhuang to mend a flint for him, and then refused to pay the bill. When the Christian went to collect, the two got into an argument with much cursing back and forth, presumably including an appropriate array of insults and accusations against Christians and Boxers alike. The next day, the bowl-mender returned with thirty fellow Christians and a much expanded bill: a five-table feast, repairs for the church, 100 strings of cash, and enrollment of Zhang's whole family in the church. In the next few days, the Christians came five times to press their demands, the final time arriving well armed and provoking a skirmish in which one of the Zhangs was killed and three were wounded. The Zhangs immediately retaliated and led a large band of villagers and Boxers to attack Jiangzhuang. In the attack, on April 21, the church and ten Christian houses were burned, but the human casualties were all on the Boxer side: at least twenty killed by well-armed Christians firing from the roofs of their houses.[35]

News of this incident spread quickly, and the Boxers between Baoding and Beijing became all the more inflamed. Magistrates travelled regularly to the provincial capital in Baoding to request more troops to maintain order, but as early as February the commander there complained that he had only 200 men left to maintain order and protect the mission stations in the capital.[36] Incidents were breaking out everywhere, and there simply were not enough troops to go around.

The critical breaking point came less than a month later in Laishui, about halfway up the railway from Baoding to Beijing. The incident that set things off is worth recording because it bears so many similarities to Boxer-Christian controversies we have seen throughout this study. Some thirty years earlier, during the Tong-zhi reign, there had been six sectarians in Gaoluo village. The village head, one Yan Lao-fu, reported them to the authorities, upon which they promptly became Christians. As the years passed, the Christians seemed to concentrate at one end of the village, so that by the 1890s there were a North and a South Gaoluo village, with Christians concentrated in the south. Serious trouble only began in 1899 when a conflict arose over an opera which was staged, as always, at a central crossroads in the southern village—a spot now directly in front of one Christian's home. As was the usual practice, a tent was set up to house the gods from the village temple, who were of course brought to watch the performance. The Christians took offense at these pagan deities on their doorstep, and went and abused the gods and knocked over their tablets. The villagers retaliated by ransacking the Christians' church.

In the lawsuits that followed, the Catholic bishop in Baoding intervened with the investigating official, and in the end a harsh judgement was imposed on the non-Christians and especially on Yan Lao-fu, who was identified as the ringleader. Yan was clearly a man of some substance. His son was a *sheng-yuan*, and both the local constable (*di-bao*) and temple head were his relatives. The 250 tael fine was something he and his kin were apparently prepared to accept. But the feast to be offered to the Christians and their local priest and the kowtow Yan was to perform in presenting it were more than he could stand. Some acceptably subservient apology was apparently offered, however, for the dispute was resolved in the Christians' favor. As a result, "The Christians became even more oppressive, and within half a year increased to over twenty families."[37]

Yan and his kin were clearly bent on revenge, however, and when the Boxers arrived in the area in the spring of 1900, someone was sent to a neighboring county to invite a couple of teachers to establish a boxing ground in the temple of the northern village. The ground had been established only ten days (a good sign of how quickly the "boxing" could be learned) when Boxers were invited from all around to prepare for action against the Christians. This brought immediate Christian complaints to the magistrate, who on May 12 went to the village with four runners to investigate. He was immediately surrounded by Boxers, briefly detained, and then forced to beat a hasty retreat. That same night, the Boxers went into action—burning the church and all the Christians' homes, killing all the members of some thirty Christian families and dumping their bodies in the wells.[38] When deputies sent from Baoding arrived with twenty soldiers two days later, the Boxers were still assembled in such numbers that they dared not enter the northern section of the village. When they finally entered the next day, the authorities were met with a complete stonewall: the fires in the southern village had been started by lightning, and nobody knew where the Christians had gone.[39]

In the next few days, Colonel Yang Fu-tong took charge of suppressing the Boxers. He managed to close the boxing ground in the village temple on May 15; but the Boxers immediately reassembled and when he returned the next day several hundred Boxers waited in ambush. The battle, however, went entirely in favor of the well-armed regular troops, and about sixty Boxers were killed. Two days later, the Boxers and troops met again, and about twenty were captured. By this time, the incident had aroused Boxers throughout the region, and they assembled by the thousands to try to rescue their arrested colleagues and gain revenge against the government forces. On the 22nd, they had their moment, as Yang was caught in another ambush and killed with a couple of his men.[40]

The impact of Colonel Yang's death was enormous. The Boxers were tremendously emboldened, and their power and influence increased greatly. The local gentry were terrified by the potential dangers of a movement willing to initiate open hostilities with imperial soldiers. But when they urged the Boxers to disperse, they found that the movement was beyond any possible control by the local elite: the Boxers paid no heed.[41] In fact, in the next few days, the Boxers occupied the city of Zhuozhou, took full command of the city gates, and began attacking stations, bridges, and telegraph lines along the railroad between Zhuozhou and Beijing. The court, for its part, was unwilling to provoke further attacks on its thinly spread military forces, and thus ordered its troops to avoid hostilities.[42] But one reason the Qing forces were so weak was because it was only at this very late stage that troops from the Western-trained Military Guards Army (Wu-wei jun) were diverted from their primary duty—the defense of the capital against foreign threats—to the suppression of the professedly loyal Boxers.[43]

FOREIGN THREATS AND VACILLATION AT COURT

A great many factors contributed to the rapid escalation of Boxer activity in Zhili during the spring of 1900. First there was the drought. Then there was the continuing division of opinion in the court, which many interpreted as imperial support for the Boxers' cause. In Zhili, this division was reflected at the highest level of provincial government. The governor-general, Yu-lu, was certainly doing his best to suppress the Boxers—though this rather mediocre official's best was little more than a reactive series of telegrams dispatching troops to put out the brush fires being kindled across the province. Yu-lu was also hampered by the fact that as Commissioner of Northern Ports, he spent most of his time in Tianjin; and the key officials in the provincial capital—to whom most local magistrates repaired for direct oral instructions when troubles broke out in their jurisdictions—were themselves bitterly divided in their attitude toward the Boxers. The financial commissioner (who was the ranking official and often called the lieutenant governor) favored forcible suppression, but the key decisions often rested with the judicial commissioner, Ting-yong, a Manchu member of the imperial clan, who was clearly sympathetic to the Boxers and resolutely opposed any effort to eliminate them by military force.[44]

Zhili's relative shortage of troops to maintain order also facilitated the Boxers' spread in the province. When the troubles first broke out in Jingzhou in the winter of 1899, a force of a little over two hundred men was sent to suppress the Boxers. In Laishui, as we have seen, the officials at first had only twenty men; and Yang Fu-tong, when he was overwhelmed, commanded a force of only seventy. Furthermore, all of these forces were part of the old Anhui Army—raised during the war against the mid-century Taiping and Nian rebels, brought to Zhili by Li Hong-zhang, and only recently given some rudiments of modern training and superior weaponry. The best trained forces in the province were the Military Guards Army under Rong-lu. It was a division of this army that Yuan Shi-kai had led to Shandong, and which he used to keep order there. Following the death of Yang Fu-tong, another contingent of this army, under Nie Shi-cheng, was finally committed to action against the Boxers. But the belated commitment of this modern force was in part because of the reluctance of even anti-Boxer officials to divert troops from the defense of the capital at a time when the foreign threat was very real.

Since the beginning of the year, the Great Powers had made clear their disapproval of the Qing handling of the Boxer troubles. Great Britain, France, Germany, and the United States had joined in an identic note protesting the January 11 decree defending the right of peaceful villagers to assemble in self-defense. They repeatedly demanded, in notes and meetings with the Zongli Yamen, publication in the semi-official *Beijing Gazette* of a decree banning the Boxers. They vehemently criticized the routine honor given Yu-xian on the occasion of his imperial audience in January, and protested even more strenuously when in mid-March he was appointed governor of Shanxi. More and more, these foreign protests took the form of veiled threats that the Powers would consider taking action on their own if the authorities could not protect missionaries and their converts. By the middle of April there were two British, two Italian, one French, and one American warship drawn up before the Dagu forts protecting the approaches to Tianjin and Beijing, in a none too subtle naval show of force.[45]

Predictably, this sort of Great Power bullying only strengthened the resistance of the anti-foreign element in the capital, and the court vacillated wildly as it was buffeted by these two contrary forces. In April, following the naval demonstration, it finally published an edict in the *Beijing Gazette* prohibiting the Boxers. But then two days later, it repeated the language of the January 11 edict tolerating peaceful associations formed in self-defense.[46] In May, the court gave serious consideration to a memorial from a censor (again a native of Shandong) who recommended recruiting the Boxers into a popular militia, and rejected the idea only when both Yuan Shi-kai and Yu-lu registered their strenuous objections.[47]

As the court vacillated, the simmering crisis turned into a raging conflagration. In the final weeks of May, the confrontations in Laishui were quickly followed by the Boxer occupation of Zhuozhou and the first destruction of the railway line. The first Boxer attacks on the railway had been on the Beijing-Baoding line, and were no doubt motivated in part by the desire to block the approach of Chinese troops sent to suppress the movement. But on May 28, the Fengtai station on the Beijing-Tianjin line was burned, and the foreigners in the capital feared that their last link to the coast would be cut. Accordingly the ministers decided to call up the legation guards (as they had in 1898) and so informed the Chinese. There was no treaty justification for such a move, but the Zongli Yamen eventually agreed as long as the numbers were limited to thirty men for each mission. On the 31st, the guards arrived by train: 75 Russians, 75 British, 75 French, 50 Americans, 40 Italians, and 25 Japanese. (Fifty Germans and 30 Austrians would come the following days.) The Powers clearly had no intention of adhering to limits set by the Chinese. Meanwhile, the threat of still more serious measures by the Powers was clear, as by early June, twenty-four foreign warships had gathered offshore.[48]

Such precipitous foreign action only made matters worse. On May 29, following news of Yang Fu-tong's death and the destruction along the railway, the court had ordered that officials should, if Boxers resisted orders to disperse, "annihilate as the situation requires."[49] It was the first time in 1900 that an edict had used the term "annihilate" (*jiao*) in connection with the Boxers. But the following day, after the Powers had announced their intention to call up the guards, the court beat a quick retreat and said that its policy was none other than the long-ineffective one of "rigorously arresting the leaders and dispersing the followers." All reference to "annihilating" Boxers was quickly dropped, and on June 3 the court explicitly warned *against* annihilating Boxers.[50] The foreign action only succeeded in strengthening the pro-Boxer faction at court—as is evidenced by the surfacing once again of the proposal to enlist the Boxers into the nation's armed forces.[51]

News of the foreign intervention probably helped to precipitate the first attacks on foreigners since the death of the British missionary Brooks in December 1899. French and Belgian engineers working on the Beijing-Baoding railway attempted to escape to Tianjin by boat after the railway was cut. They were constantly harassed by Boxers who, though dreadfully out-gunned and suffering heavy casualties of their own, eventually killed four of the thirty-six foreigners. On June 1, the day after and somewhat north of the attack on the engineers, two English missionaries were killed in Yongqing.[52] Now the movement was clearly widening into something much larger than just an attack on the foreign religion: the foreigners themselves (and not just missionaries) were also under attack.

By early June, the seriousness of the crisis was clear for all to see. For the first time, officials from outside of north China entered the debate. The powerful Yangzi Valley viceroys, Zhang Zhi-dong in Wuhan and Liu Kun-yi in Nanking, and the director of railways and telegraphs, Sheng Xuan-huai, all called for an immediate military suppression of the Boxers to forestall intervention by the Powers.[53] But the court remained characteristically undecided on what to do. This time it essentially followed both the pacification and the annihilation policy at the same time. Two grand councillors sympathetic with the Boxers, Gang-yi and Zhao Shu-qiao, were sent to pacify them and persuade them to disperse—an attempt which predictably came to nought.[54] At the same time, Nie Shi-cheng's modern-trained troops were sent to guard the railway and soon engaged the Boxers in several major battles. Though his machine guns killed hundreds of Boxers, Nie's men suffered many casualties of their own—80 men killed or wounded in one battle alone. In the end, the overwhelming support for the Boxer cause in the surrounding countryside—support that was often increased by the inevitable mistreatment of innocent villagers by undisciplined soldiers—forced Nie to retreat and invest the town of Yangcun on the Beijing-Tianjin railway.[55] Meanwhile the court issued increasingly urgent edicts indicating that any Boxers who resisted orders to disperse were surely outlaws and should be dealt with as such.[56]

But the court never got the opportunity to follow through on these edicts. On June 10, at the urgent request of the British minister, MacDonald, Admiral Edward Seymour set out from Tianjin with an international force of two thousand men to protect the Beijing legations. Seymour decided to repair the railway as he advanced. His slow progress allowed the Boxers ample opportunity to harass the column, so that soon it was bottled up between Tianjin and Beijing and eventually forced to beat a troubled retreat—finally arriving back in Tianjin only on the 26th after a loss of 62 killed and 212 wounded. This precipitate foreign incursion, unlike the earlier summoning of the legation guards, had not been sanctioned by the Chinese and caused great alarm at court. On the 13th, Yu-lu was ordered to resist the foreign advance, but in fact no troops were committed until June 18, following the foreign storming of the Dagu forts. Much of the credit for stopping Seymour belonged to the Boxers, and their reputation increased enormously.[57]

On June 16 and 17, two extraordinary mass audiences of princes and metropolitan ministers were held before the Emperor and Empress Dowager. As always, the issue was pacification versus annihilation. But the issue on which the debate turned was a significant one. Yuan Chang, a minister of the Zongli Yamen who would soon be executed for his anti-Boxer convictions, was expounding his view that the Boxers were only rioters whose magic was not to be relied upon when the Empress Dowager interrupted him: "Perhaps their magic is not to be relied upon; but can we not rely on the hearts and minds of the people? Today China is extremely weak. We have only the people's hearts and minds to depend upon. If we cast them aside and lose the people's hearts, what can we use to sustain the country?"[58] No one on either side of the debate could dispute the fact that popular support for the Boxers was almost universal in the countryside. To turn on the Boxers was to risk losing the support of the people—at a time when a direct military threat from the foreigners made that support particularly critical.

But this phrasing of the question also highlighted the unique problems that the Boxer Uprising posed—especially for those intent on suppressing it. In the first place, it was almost axiomatic that the hearts and minds of the people were with the Boxers. Even in Shandong, where Yuan Shi-kai was doing everything he could to convince the people that the Boxers were a heterodox and potentially rebellious force, a local magistrate would report: "If one person speaks of the wrongs of the Boxers, his family will meet disaster; if one household resists the Boxer ravages, the whole village will suffer annihilation. . . . From scholars to simple villagers, they believe that if foreigners can be exterminated, there is nothing wrong with the Boxers."[59] And in Zhili, not only were the Boxers everywhere, but they were often being fed and aided by villagers as they went about their task of destroying the railroad and extirpating Christians.[60] Secondly, by arguing that the support of the people was necessary to sustain the country, the court—though certainly basing its thinking on ancient Confucian principles—was endorsing a principle as radical as any that the 1898 reformers had enunciated before their unfortunate demise.

The fact that the people's hearts and minds were with the Boxers made it particularly difficult for those advocating a policy of military suppression. From the time of Lao Nai-xuan's initial pamphlet, a regular refrain of the anti-Boxer group was the heterodox connections and rebellious intent of the Boxers United in Righteousness. By this time, even leading patrons of the Boxers like Gang-yi would admit that "they burn charms and speak of gods descending, much like the heterodox sects." But he insisted that they were neither riotous nor disloyal. Indeed, they had met him, when he went to reason with them, by kneeling along the road with hands clasped in greeting.[61] The Boxers were heterodox, perhaps, but still loyal. This was a much easier message for the court to accept than that of the anti-Boxer faction: it had to argue (against all the evidence) that the Boxers were indeed disloyal, while admitting that these "disloyal" Boxers nonetheless enjoyed the overwhelming support of the people. That was a difficult enough message for the court to accept, but it was still not the end of the problem, for the pro-Boxer group also held that if a policy of military suppression was followed, the loyalist Boxers would certainly resist (as in fact they had, following the Laishui incidents) and the court would have a full-scale rebellion on its hands.[62]

In other words, both sides' analysis of the situation agreed that a policy of military suppression would leave the dynasty faced with a popularly supported rebel force with roots in villages throughout northern China. The only difference was that the anti-Boxer group argued that these Boxers were rebellious all along, while the pro-Boxer group argued that they would be *made* rebellious by the very act of suppression. With a foreign military force whose objectives were quite unclear advancing toward the national capital, the court was not anxious to spark such a rebellion by aggressively suppressing the Boxers. By June, the Boxer movement had grown to such dimensions that the court's options for dealing with it had essentially been foreclosed. "Pacification" was really the only route to take.

THE BOXERS IN BEIJING AND TIANJIN

Retrospective accounts mention young men practicing boxing in Beijing by the end of 1899, but it is not clear that these were really the same as the Spirit Boxers then active in Shandong. It was not until the spring of 1900 that identifiable Boxers United in Righteousness began to appear, first in the back alleys, and then with increasing brazenness in the busy commercial districts of the capital.[63] At the same time, Boxers were organizing in the towns along the Grand Canal west of

Tianjin. By June, Boxers from the countryside were streaming into both Beijing and Tianjin by the thousands. The large numbers of Boxers roaming through the capital certainly had a major influence both on the deliberations at court, and on the Great Powers concerned for the protection of their legations. It behooves us, therefore, to interrupt our narrative for a moment, and examine the background, ritual, and behavior of the Boxers in the capital region. Rather plentiful contemporary source material also provides an opportunity to see how the Boxer movement might have changed since its origins in Shandong.

On June 20, a minor official in the capital left this account of the first major influx of Boxers:

> Tens of thousands of Boxers [*tuan-min*] have come from all parts in the past few days. Most seem to be simple country folk who make their living by farming. They have neither leaders directing them nor potent weapons. They provide their own travelling expenses and eat only millet and corn. Seeking neither fame nor fortune, they fight without regard for their own lives and are prepared to sacrifice themselves on the field of battle. They come together without prior agreement, a great host all of one mind. They wish only to kill foreigners and Christians and do not harm the common people. From this perspective, it seems that they are fighting for righteousness.[64]

The clearest difference between the Beijing Boxers and their predecessors was the fact that most were not locally recruited: these Boxers came from the outside, and especially from the surrounding countryside. The same was true of Tianjin. A 1958 survey found that 70 percent of the identifiable Boxers were peasants.[65] They came into Beijing and Tianjin in small groups of five or ten young men—forty or fifty at the largest—carrying banners inscribed with "Support the Qing, destroy the foreign," or "Militia United in Righteousness, carry out the Way on behalf of Heaven," with their village of origin sometimes noted as well. From May, the roads of central Zhili were filled with such groups, all headed north toward the capital.[66] Once in the cities, they took up lodging in temples or vacant inns, or sometimes the homes of wealthy sponsors, and there they were joined by many of the poorer classes of the cities. There were peddlers, rickshaw men, sedan chair carriers, yamen runners, and craftsmen of all types—leather workers, knife-sharpeners, iron workers, barbers, and masons. A certain number of the urban underclass joined—beggars, dismissed soldiers, salt smugglers, criminals, and homeless

Figure 9. Tianjin Boxers. This photo of Boxers captured by U.S. forces in China reveals the darkly tanned peasant faces and the youth of most Boxers. Courtesy of the Library of Congress.

vagrants—but more of these at later stages, after the court gave explicit support to the Boxers, and joining became a way to get a free meal. Many soldiers joined the Boxers—especially those from Dong Fu-xiang's army, which was noted for its anti-foreign sentiments. And around Tianjin and south of Beijing in particular, boatmen and trackers on the canal—men thrown out of work by the new railroads—joined the Boxers in great numbers, and provided an important part of the leadership in the Tianjin area. In all, the popular (and primarily peasant) quality of the Boxer movement continued right into its high tide in the capital region.[67]

The spirit-possession which formed the distinguishing feature of Boxer ritual also continued fundamentally unchanged. According to one detailed account from Beijing, a spot for the ritual is chosen, called an "altar" (*tan*) in the urban areas, presided over by a master called "Senior Brother-Disciple." He calls together young men who declare their intentions, vow to maintain a vegetarian diet and especially to avoid "pollution by women." In addition, "they are not permitted to steal or covet wealth." The disciples then approach the altar, burn incense and swear an oath, and the master presents them with paper charms. They tie on the turbans they have brought with them and the master recites a spell over them which is called "receiving the magic" (*shang-fa*).

> The person then falls to the ground as though sleeping. After a while he rises and kowtows to the southeast. Then his eyes open wide and he pants from the mouth. His strength [*qi-li*] rises through his body. Picking up his weapons he dances wildly and his power is greatest. He practices three times a day. When the magic is exhausted [*fa-jin*], his strength is expended. This is called "shedding the magic" [*xie-fa*]. Then he is completely exhausted and much weaker than normal. Those whose technique is best cannot maintain the power for a full day. If their party claims more, in fact there are no such people. Most can sustain it only for a few hours.[68]

Clearly we are dealing here with a fairly classic form of spirit-possession, and the abnormal, crazed nature of the possessed Boxers is repeatedly mentioned by observers. According to another eye-witness: "Suddenly their faces got red and their eyes stared straight ahead as though they were having an epileptic fit. Foam dripped from their mouths as they shouted out, while their fists flew and their feet kicked."[69] That the ritual was based upon common Chinese conceptions of spirit-possession is indicated by the fact that one could, inadvertently, become possessed not by the usual gods and heroes known from popular opera but by unwanted, wandering ghosts suffering from some past wrong who were searching for a body to inhabit.[70]

Possession by wandering ghosts indicates one of the major problems of the Boxer ritual: its basically unpredictable and uncontrollable nature. But it is also clear that a good master could guide the trance, through what was essentially hypnotic suggestion. In one account, the youths when possessed would fall to the ground, then leap up and fight fiercely "as though drunk, or in a dream," having assumed the identity of the god who possessed them and often calling out his name. Then the teacher tapped one youth on the back or the head and called out his real name. "Suddenly he woke up, standing there like a wooden chicken. He had utterly forgotten his boxing magic and was like a completely different person from when he was fighting." [71] For such hypnotic suggestion to work, the simple faith of these usually uneducated village youths was important. According to one observer, only "simple and uneducated children could learn. If one had a little learning, the spirit would not possess him." [72] This form of boxing was not for skeptical intellectuals.

The gods who descended to possess the Boxers were the same heroes of popular culture seen in Shandong. Above all they came from the vernacular novels *Romance of the Three Kingdoms, The Enfeoffment of the Gods, Water Margin,* and *Monkey. The Enfeoffment of the Gods* was a particularly important source, for it combined historical figures of the eleventh century B.C. founding of the Zhou dynasty with a tale of defending the three religions (Buddhism, Daoism, and Confucianism) against heresy. The popularity of Monkey, Pigsy, and Sandy, who guard the Tang dynasty monk Xuan-zang on his pilgrimage to India in the novel *Monkey,* also presumably relates to their role as protectors of the Buddhist faith. Quite naturally, the possessing spirits tended to be military heroes—the most frequently noted being Guangong (the God of War), Zhang Fei, Zhang Huan-hou, and Jiang Tai-gong. These were all heroes that any Chinese knew from village operas or storytellers of the market place; and many of them, such as Guangong, had long since found their way into the pantheon of Chinese popular religion. [73]

Spirit-possession was clearly the key to this particular form of "boxing" and the invulnerability which was supposed to accompany it. It did not take very long to learn. We have already seen how in Laishui the Boxers had learned enough in a week to set out and avenge themselves against their Christian neighbors. Masters stressed the ease with which their magic could be learned, but the amount of time required varied from place to place. One Shandong master promised that the techniques could be learned in a day; another said seven or eight days; and a third more rigorous teacher claimed 103 days but still noted that it was "much easier than the Armor of the Golden Bell." [74]

As conflict with government and foreign troops became more common, Boxer casualties increased. To maintain morale it was important to explain these failures of the invulnerability ritual. Some boxing masters seemed to have some medical talent and could treat wounds, claiming that the individual was only tired. But if the wound was serious, it was almost invariably attributed to a violation of Boxer discipline. Most commonly the individual was said to have stolen some object found on his body.[75] Such explanations are a tribute to the Boxer leaders' efforts to maintain discipline, and those efforts are also attested in accounts of the rules Boxers were to live by:

> Do not covet wealth.
> Do not lust after women.
> Do not disobey your parents.
> Do not violate Imperial laws.
> Eradicate the foreigners.
> Kill corrupt officials.
> When you walk on the streets, keep your head lowered,
>   looking neither left nor right.
> When you meet a fellow member, greet him with hands
>   clasped together.[76]

By all accounts, these efforts to maintain discipline were very effective in the early stages of the movement: looting or injury to non-Christians was almost non-existent, and when order finally broke down in Beijing, it was almost always the imperial troops and not the Boxers who were guilty.[77]

In all of these respects—members drawn from the young and the poor, spirit possession, easily learned spells, and invulnerability rituals—the Boxers demonstrated a fundamental continuity with their earliest days in Shandong. But in other respects, the movement displayed new customs and practices not seen in its earlier stages. For one thing, whereas in Shandong, the first Boxers simply set out in ordinary peasant garb, by the time they approached the capital, a fairly distinctive boxer "uniform" had emerged—or rather several uniforms:

> They wear red turbans wrapped around their heads with charms stuck inside, red belly-charms [dou-du], red leggings and red around their arms with white charms on their wrists. Others have yellow turbans. Some have a red robe and a black bandana. These are called the black corps, and the red and yellow all praise them, telling everyone "They are the toughest."[78]

The red and yellow uniforms were by far the most common, and by and large they were worn by groups which associated themselves with the *kan* and *qian* trigrams. This appearance of trigram association was also a new development, and some scholars have interpreted it as an indication of Eight Trigrams Sect influence. While this is possible, there were plenty of non-sectarian sources for this trigram association, and it is significant that contemporary sources only mention the *kan* and *qian* trigrams, while in the Eight Trigrams Sect of the early nineteenth century it was the *zhen*, *kan* and *li* trigrams which were the most important—with the *li* trigram, absent in 1900, most closely associated with the White Lotus–allied boxers of the earlier period.[79] Whatever the origins of these trigram organizations, these identifications, with their associated colored turbans, do indicate an impulse toward a fairly basic level of organization as the peak of the Boxer movement was reached.

In general, however, organization above the level of the individual unit was never a strength of the Boxer movement. By and large, each individual Boxer unit (a village Boxer group, or an "altar" in the cities) acted independently. Often new altars were set up by a particularly famous teacher in an area, and this produced networks which could be mobilized when a battle was at hand. But usually the Boxers gathered, practiced, worshipped, and slept in the temples or shrines where their own altar was located, and were not under the discipline of any overarching federation.[80] This lack of any coordinated leadership was one of the most striking aspects of the Boxer Uprising. It stemmed, of course, from the fundamentally egalitarian nature of Boxer ritual, which gave everyone the attributes of divinity. Central leadership was thus effectively precluded. But the loyalist purpose of the Boxers made such leadership quite unnecessary. They had come to support the Qing and resist the foreigners, not to provide an alternative hierarchy to the reigning dynasty.

When the Boxers first entered Beijing and Tianjin, the focus of their animus remained the Christians. Above all it was Christian homes and churches that were attacked and burned. Gradually, however, and most likely under inspiration from anti-foreign elements in Beijing officialdom, the attack broadened to include all foreign things: lamps, clocks, medicine, matches, or any object of alien origin. People were threatened with death if they kept foreign goods in their homes, and shops selling articles of foreign origin became the target of arson.[81]

The repertoire of Boxer magic at the height of the movement was considerably expanded from the basic charms of invulnerability seen during its early phases. Probably much of this magic was learned from the religious specialists who were prominent in the spread of the movement through Zhili, or from magicians who practiced at markets and fairs. They claimed to be able to summon comrades from hundreds of miles away by burning a notice and calling to them. Feeding the multitude of Boxers gathered in Beijing was a major problem, and for this there were pots of gruel which could be kept always full, no matter how many ate from them.[82] But the most important magic involved fire, which was the Boxers' primary offensive weapon. Sometimes fires were started by drawing a charm on the ground with a sword or spear and calling out "fire." [83] But the most common magic was that which confined fires to Christian dwellings and churches. The Boxer charms would protect innocent neighbors' dwellings, and fire brigades were prevented from extinguishing flames which would seek out only the foreign believers and foreign goods. Unfortunately, on June 16, the magic failed in the crowded business and entertainment district in the southern section of Beijing, and a conflagration which lasted all day and night consumed 1,800 shops and several thousand dwellings.[84]

The usual explanation for such failures is significant for the insight it gives into the Boxer belief system. Women were usually blamed for undermining the Boxer magic with their inherent pollution.[85] Later, during the siege of the Northern Cathedral in Beijing, this same explanation would recur. Thousands of Catholics, including many women, had fled to the Cathedral for refuge. When after weeks of attacks by explosives, fire, and all other means at their disposal, the Boxers were still unable to take the church, they explained their failure by the polluting influence of the women inside: "There are dirty things oppressing our magic, so we cannot advance." The women inside were accused of exposing themselves and waving "dirty things" from the walls causing the spirits to leave the Boxers' bodies. Such sexist notions of female pollution are extremely important, though not at all unexpected among the adolescent males who filled the Boxer ranks. But what is particularly significant is the Boxer answer to this pollution: a female unit of their own, the Red Lanterns Shining (Hong-deng-zhao). Said the besiegers of the Northern Cathedral: "We have to await the Red Lantern Shining before we can advance. The Red Lanterns are all girls and young women, so they do not fear dirty things." [86]

Reliable accounts of the Red Lanterns are extremely difficult to come by. They are mentioned in many places, usually (as in Beijing) as a group heard of or awaited, but rarely seen. Their magic was believed to be extremely powerful: they could walk on water, fly through the air, set fire to Christians' homes, or attack the enemy's ships at sea and

Figure 10.   Attack on the Northern Cathedral. In the center, young women
of the Red Lanterns are protected from the crossfire of the opposing forces.
From V. M. Alexeev, *Kitayskaya narodnaya kartina: Dukhovnaya zhizn
starogo Kitaya v narodnykh izobrazheniyakh* (The Chinese folk picture: the
spiritual life of old China in folk graphic art) (Moscow, 1966).

stop up their guns. These were powers far beyond anything claimed
for the Boxers, and reflected the fact the women, though polluted (or
perhaps, *because* polluted), possessed extraordinary powers. But reliable accounts of actual Red Lantern units are almost all derived from
Tianjin, where their most prominent leader was the Holy Mother,
Lotus Huang (Huang Lian sheng-mu), daughter of a boatman imprisoned for some transgression against the foreigners and herself a
young prostitute. It is unclear what the young women who joined the
Red Lanterns did, though retrospective accounts mention support
work in tending wounded Boxers and sewing and cleaning. Still, their
very existence indicates that during the confusion of the Boxer high
tide, some young women also found an opportunity to escape the
confines of Confucian patriarchy and join in mysterious and no doubt
exciting activities with their peers, outside of the home.[87]

Given the essential autonomy of individual Boxer bands, communication between the different groups was all-important, and here the
most important innovation of the Beijing-Tianjin boxers was the
extensive use of wall posters to spread their message. These would be
posted outside the Boxer altars or on prominent street corners, and
were an important addition to the Boxer propaganda effort. Often

these notices were in a sort of doggerel verse, and the following
example gives something of their flavor:

> Divinely aided Boxers,
> United-in-Righteousness Corps
> Arose because the Devils
> Messed up the Empire of yore.
>
> They proselytize their sect,
> And believe in only one God,
> The spirits and their own ancestors
> Are not even given a nod.
>
> Their men are all immoral;
> Their women truly vile.
> For the Devils it's mother-son sex
> That serves as the breeding style.
>
> And if you don't believe me,
> Then have a careful view:
> You'll see the Devils' eyes
> Are all a shining blue.
>
> No rain comes from Heaven.
> The earth is parched and dry.
> And all because the churches
> Have bottled up the sky.
>
> The god are very angry.
> The spirits seek revenge.
> *En masse* they come from Heaven
> To teach the Way to men.
>
> The Way is not a heresy;
> It's not the White Lotus Sect.
> The chants and spells we utter,
> Follow mantras, true and correct.
>
> Raise up the yellow charm,
> Bow to the incense glow.
> Invite the gods and spirits
> Down from the mountain grotto.
>
> Spirits emerge from the grottos;
> Gods come down from the hills,
> Possessing the bodies of men,
> Transmitting their boxing skills.
>
> When their martial and magic techniques
> Are all learned by each one of you,
> Suppressing the Foreign Devils
> Will not be a tough thing to do.

Rip up the railroad tracks!
Pull down the telegraph lines!
Quickly! Hurry up! Smash them—
The boats and the steamship combines.

The mighty nation of France
Quivers in abject fear,
While from England, America, Russia
And from Germany nought do we hear.

When at last all the Foreign Devils
Are expelled to the very last man,
The Great Qing, united, together,
Will bring peace to this our land.[88]

This common Boxer placard illustrates a number of important points. There is the initial focus on the Christian heresy, which is blamed for the continuing drought. The Boxer possession ritual is described as the manner in which the gods will descend to wreak their revenge on the foreigners. There is the broadening of the target of attack from just Christians to the railways, telegraph, and steamships associated with the foreign presence. And finally there is the denial of heterodox White Lotus connections, and the affirmed loyalty to the Qing.

Without a doubt, this placard reflected the beliefs and hopes of most Boxers in the Beijing-Tianjin area, but not all placards were of this sort. In particular, there were a number of wall posters recorded in the Beijing area containing language which almost certainly derived from one of the sectarian religions, and others containing subversive anti-Qing messages. Many of these notices are said to be the results of planchette rituals in which possessed people wrote on sand with a stick—which had become a common source of sectarian texts during the nineteenth century. Others were said to transcribe the text on steles dug from the ground. The references were almost always obscure: "two, four, add one five" was a phrase that appeared in several placards, and it is usually interpreted to refer to the 15th day of the 8th lunar month—a traditional date on which the Mongols (and by analogy, the Manchus) were to be attacked. Another placard referred to the "moon and sun shining on me," which was probably a call for the return of the Ming dynasty—the character for "Ming" combining the characters for "sun" and "moon." Some spoke of an approaching calamity (jie), which may have meant the White Lotus millennial belief in the end of a kalpa (also a "jie"). And finally some foretold that a "true lord" would soon emerge, which might have had a religious sectarian meaning or a secular anti-dynastic meaning, but was subversive in either case.[89]

The fundamentally loyalist behavior of the Boxers, and the consistency of that behavior with their proclaimed desire to "Support the Qing, destroy the foreign" convince me that few if any of these sectarian or subversive notices should be attributed to the Boxers. None of the subversive notices contained any indication that they were issued by the Boxers, and very few even mentioned the Boxers. But the notices are nonetheless extremely significant. When the court granted the right of peaceful assembly to the Boxers in January 1900, the language of the edict extended the same tolerance to all associations. Especially when the Boxers began actively mobilizing in Beijing and Tianjin, the general breakdown in public order allowed other more subversive groups to spread their message as well, and the anonymous wall poster proved an extremely convenient vehicle. It is unlikely that these trends went unnoticed by the authorities as they weighed their options in June 1900.

The loyalist origins of the Boxers were beyond question, but their primary commitment was to the eradication of the Christian and (especially recently) the foreign presence in China. They had long since shown their willingness to resist Qing troops who interfered with their anti-Christian crusade, and now they had carried their campaign to the nation's capital where they acted without paying the slightest heed to imperial prohibitions of their behavior. In Tianjin, they were even more high-handed, forcing officials to get out of their sedan chairs and remove their caps in respectful subservience to passing Boxer bands.[90] With the country still reeling from the series of foreign policy disasters that had followed the Sino-Japanese War, and the imperial court now in utter disarray, the fate of the dynasty was none too secure. There were surely some at court who realized that if they mishandled the Boxer crisis, they might force the Boxers into alliance with elements whose intent was more clearly anti-dynastic. Popular rebellion against the dynasty was certainly not out of the question. Contemporary Chinese sources were reluctant to speak openly of this threat, but even foreigners clamoring for strong action to put down the Boxers admitted that faced with such measures, the Boxer movement "would doubtless turn its energies and direct them to rebellion against the Throne."[91]

"DECLARATION OF WAR"

We left our narrative at the point of the court conferences of June 16 and 17, and the latter was surely the crucial day. On that day, both sides moved decisively toward war, though the Qing move was somewhat more tentative. At court on the 17th, the Empress Dowager read from an alleged four-part ultimatum from the foreign Powers: a designated residence was to be prepared for the emperor; all revenues were to be collected by the Powers; and all military affairs were to be consigned to foreign control. The fourth point was not read, but was later revealed to be a demand that imperial power be returned to the emperor. The ultimatum was a forgery by Prince Duan (who had been appointed President of the Zongli Yamen on June 10), but it had its intended effect. The Empress Dowager declared dramatically: "Today they [the foreign Powers] have opened hostilities, and the extinction of the nation is before us. If we fold our arms and yield to them, I will have no face before my ancestors when I die. Rather than waiting for death, is it not better to die fighting?" With that the issue was sealed. Several ministers, and Yu-lu, who was directly confronting the foreign troops in Tianjin, had protested that China had been unable to defeat even one Power in past conflicts, and stood little chance of withstanding a united expedition of all the Great Powers now. But the debate had now escalated to a question of the Empress Dowager's honor, and such practical objections had no effect.[92]

But the issue was really sealed by the foreign attack on the forts at Dagu early on the morning of the same day. The situation in Beijing was deteriorating rapidly. On June 11, Sugiyama Akira, secretary of the Japanese legation, had been shot down near the railway station by troops from Dong Fu-xiang's army. The foreigners in the capital were already taking matters into their own hands. On the 15th and 16th, marines set out from the legations to rescue native Christians, shooting some forty Boxers during a sortie on the latter date.[93] Telegraphic communication between Beijing and the coast had been cut following Seymour's ill-starred foray in the direction of the capital, and rumors were flying wildly. Meanwhile, the British consul in Tianjin reported that "the [Chinese] city is practically in the hands of the Boxers and the mob," and there was considerable anxiety over the safety of the foreign concession.[94] Though Dagu was peaceful enough for the ladies of the foreign community to enjoy a pleasant game of tennis on the afternoon of the 16th, the Powers felt compelled to issue an ultimatum for the surrender of the forts the next day—and then seized them an hour before the time was up.[95]

News of the foreign ultimatum only reached Beijing on June 19, and convinced the court that war was inevitable. Emissaries were sent to order the evacuation of the foreign legations within twenty-four hours. But the diplomats in Beijing were understandably concerned for their safety en route to the coast—a concern heightened the next day when the German minister, Baron Clemens von Ketteler, was shot dead by a Chinese soldier on his way to an appointment with the Zongli Yamen. The other ministers were convinced they were safer in the legations; and with that the siege of the legations began. On the 21st, the court received an extremely misleading memorial from Yu-lu, mentioning the battle at Dagu but not the outcome, and stressing the cooperation of Boxers and imperial troops in resisting the foreigners. The court read this as a report of Chinese victories and on the 21st issued its "declaration of war." On the same day orders were issued to enlist the Boxers into the official militia, and Gang-yi and two other Manchu noblemen were ordered to take charge of managing Boxer affairs.[96]

The Qing "declaration of war" was a decidedly curious document. It was not a formal communication issued to the foreign Powers, but just one of a flood of edicts coming from the court. It blamed the foreigners for initiating the hostilities, praised the resistance of the "righteous soldiers" to this aggression, and asserted that it would not be difficult to overcome the aggressors and restore the nation's prestige. Officials were warned against retreat or traitorous activities, but there was not even a clear statement that a state of war existed.[97]

The impact of this "declaration of war" essentially depended upon the attitude of the provincial authorities in each area, and was perhaps the supreme example of how far regional autonomy had proceeded in nineteenth-century China. Officials in south China, led by the Yangzi viceroys Zhang Zhi-dong and Liu Kun-yi, decided to base their actions on an edict of June 20 ordering provincial officials to act "according to conditions in your provinces. You should be practical in each matter as you consider how to protect your territory so that foreigners cannot work their will."[98] With the director of railways and telegraphs, Sheng Xuan-huai, acting as the key mediator in Shanghai, agreement was reached with the foreign consuls to keep the Yangzi region out of the conflict: the Chinese officials would suppress anti-foreign disturbances and the Powers would avoid any dispatch of troops to the area.

Soon Li Hong-zhang in Canton joined the understanding, as did the other officials in south China.[99]

In Shandong, the province where the whole movement started, Yuan Shi-kai's sympathies were surely with the southern viceroys, but the Boxers were still strong enough and the court close enough to force him to a more ambiguous position. Above all, he preserved his independence of action—resisting the court's appeals to send troops against foreign invasion, and rejecting the southern officials' suggestion that he march north to remove the reactionaries from court. Within Shandong, he escorted all foreign missionaries to the safety of Yantai and Qingdao, and protected the major mission stations with his troops. But he was unable to prevent a substantial flare-up of renewed Boxer activity (in all over 300 Christians were killed), and he acceded to imperial pressure by issuing orders encouraging Christians to renounce their faith. Toward the Boxers, his fundamental policy was rather simple: they were ordered to proceed to the Beijing-Tianjin area to resist the foreigners; and any who remained in Shandong were disloyal "outlaws" who faced a bloody suppression—thousands being killed by Yuan's troops in one northwest Shandong operation.[100]

The greatest spread of Boxer activity and anti-foreign and anti-Christian violence was in the provinces surrounding the capital—all of which were under the control of Manchu officials who proved responsive to edicts ordering the mobilization of Boxers to resist foreign aggression and Christian complicity with it. It was at this point, and in these areas, that massive violence against Christians and foreigners really occurred. Prior to the "declaration of war" only nine foreigners had lost their lives—and only one (Brooks in Shandong) prior to the May 31 summoning of the legation guards. But now, with substantial official encouragement and complicity, a major bloodbath would begin.

West of the capital was Shanxi, where Yu-xian had been appointed governor in March. Up to the time of the declaration of war, there was very little Boxer organizing in the province; but with a little encouragement from the governor, thousands rallied to the cause during June. Early in July, Yu-xian called missionaries to the capital allegedly for their protection, but then on July 9, he personally supervised the execution of 44 foreign men, women, and children. Further executions and officially inspired killings brought the toll to about 130 foreigners and 2,000 Chinese Christians in Shanxi, by far the highest toll in Western lives in any province.[101]

Boxers from Shanxi and Zhili also spilled over into Inner Mongolia, where they received support similar to that seen in Shanxi. Christians turned their large churches into veritable fortresses, and resisted under the direction of their missionary leaders. Before long, Manchu-led troops joined the Boxers in pitched battles with the Christians. One of the larger churches was overwhelmed and in all some 3,000 Christians (mostly Catholics) died. Among foreigners, 40 Protestants and 9 Catholics died—which meant that the total for Shanxi and Inner Mongolia accounted for over three-fourths of all foreign deaths.[102]

The Northeast (Manchuria) was an area of intense imperialist rivalry between Russia and Japan. The Russians were engaged in extensive railway building throughout the area, and popular resentment of these incursions was added to the usual grievances against Christians and missionaries. The Boxers' ritual had spread to the Northeast by the spring of 1900, but it was only after the declaration of war that the Boxers and Manchu troops began ripping up the railroad to block the anticipated Russian advance, and launching major assaults against the Christians. These actions, of course, only brought about the Russian occupation of the entire northeast region.[103]

Certainly the greatest loss of life, and the fiercest struggles between Christians and reasonably spontaneous Boxer bands, occurred in Zhili, where the Boxer base had been building for some time. But it was only with the declaration of war, and the official sanctioning of Boxer activities, that widespread killing of the hated Christians occurred. The Catholics retreated to their larger mission bases where, well-armed by their missionary leaders, they were usually able to hold off Boxer attacks. In the capital of Baoding, 15 Protestant missionaries decided to stay on in June when the officials promised protection. But after the declaration of war, with Yu-lu on the front in Tianjin and the telegraph cut, the anti-foreign judicial commissioner Ting-yong was the ranking official, and he allowed the Boxers to sack the mission compound and kill the missionaries there. Still, this loss was minor compared to the native Christians (especially Catholics) of whom thousands certainly perished.[104]

The only other province where significant Boxer activity occurred was Henan, where another Manchu (the brother of Yu-lu) was governor. Isolated Boxers had apparently been present on the border with Shandong since 1899, but widespread organizing and attacks on churches only occurred after June 1900. The Catholics were long established and relatively numerous in Henan, so the usual resentments were undoubtedly present. Boxer actions, once the officials permitted them, were largely directed at destroying churches, and few Christian (and no foreign) lives were lost.[105] Other provinces saw anti-Christian disturbances in the summer of 1900, the most serious being a militia-led mob action in Zhejiang. The militia had mobilized in response to an uprising by a vegetarian sect which had occupied two nearby county seats. The mob believed the Christians to be in league with the sect, and killed eleven missionaries in the city of Quzhou. While such incidents certainly indicated the ease with which popular anti-Christian violence could break out when people believed the court supported their cause, they clearly bore no direct connection to the Boxer movement.[106]

This brief catalogue of anti-Christian actions illustrates the tremendous escalation of violence following the court's "declaration of war." The examples of Shanxi, Inner Mongolia, and Zhili's Baoding also make it clear that most of the foreign deaths were either official executions or very directly instigated by particularly anti-foreign officials. In the early stages of relatively spontaneous Boxer activity, the scale of violence was generally limited to crimes against property. Christian deaths began to escalate only in the spring of 1900, following a substantial number of Boxer deaths at Christian hands. But the real violence—and especially the violence against foreigners—occurred only when the movement ceased to be under purely popular direction, when Manchu officials decided to use the movement for their own xenophobic ends.

SIEGE IN BEIJING AND TIANJIN

In Beijing, the big story was of course the siege of the legations, which continued with varying degrees of intensity for fifty-five days. But the siege was largely carried on by regular troops under Rong-lu and Dong Fu-xiang, and the former ensured that it was never pressed home. The Chinese remained in a basically defensive posture throughout; and though they fired about 4,000 shells at rather close range, they caused a total of only fourteen casualties. The gunners seemed to be deliberately aiming high. The siege was significantly loosened in late July, and fruit and vegetables were sent through the lines as the court briefly sought a negotiated solution to the crisis. This ended in early August when the hard-line former governor of Shandong, Li Bing-heng, returned to the capital to attempt a final rallying of the Boxers against the advancing international expedition. Li's return provoked a stepped-up bombardment of the legations.[107]

Meanwhile, the Boxers were busy elsewhere. When the court announced its intention to resist foreign attacks on the capital region, it began to enlist the Boxers into an imperially sanctioned corps. On June 23, Gang-yi and Prince Zhuang were appointed to command this Boxer force. Boxers were supposed to register at the Prince's mansion. Eventually 30,000 Boxers were reported enrolled under these two Manchu commanders, with many more under Prince Duan. By all accounts, this imperial sponsorship attracted a number of undesirable opportunists to the Boxer cause: members of the urban lumpenproletariat seeking little more than a ready meal, and wealthy urbanites who joined in order to protect their positions of privilege. The initially quite strict Boxer discipline became more lax. The Boxers demonstrated that imperial sponsorship would not necessarily subject them to imperial authority; several high officials (some quite sympathetic to the Boxers) found their homes ransacked and their persons threatened by self-willed Boxer bands. The Boxers also exhibited a certain leveling instinct by forcing contributions from the population based on the wealth of each family.[108]

Besides patrolling the capital and urging people to hang out red lanterns and bow to the southeast, the Boxers concentrated most of their energy on the siege of the Catholics' Northern Cathedral. This was the last remaining church in the city, and some 10,000 Boxers joined in the siege of over 3,000 Christians and 40 French and Italian marines. But regular troops offered little assistance to the Boxers here, and the Boxers were without any effective offensive weapons. A number of attempts to mine the compound's walls took a toll on the Christians inside, but the Boxers (their magic neutralized by the female pollution of the church) suffered even more from the foreign rifles, and in the end were unable to take the cathedral.[109]

For our interest in the relationship of the Boxers to sectarian religions, one of the most significant events of the Beijing summer was the Boxers' arrest and execution of some seventy White Lotus sectarians in July. Their leader, a certain Zhang who worked in a cash assaying shop, wrote charms and cured illness. He also engaged in two common forms of late-nineteenth-century sectarian magic: cutting out paper men, and scattering beans to become soldiers. According to one account: "Because of the military emergency, he urged people to join his sect and burn incense in order to avoid the calamity (*jie*) of warfare. Because people all seek the auspicious and avoid misfortune, they followed his sect in untold numbers." These followers were described as "simple, stupid people"; but the group apparently had gotten close enough to preparing an actual uprising to have named an emperor, empress dowager, empress and concubines, heir apparent, and several civil and military commanders.[110]

The description fits perfectly all accounts of White Lotus sectarianism in this period: belief in an approaching calamity, the use of certain standard magical techniques, and the preparation of an alternative political hierarchy to assume power after the chaos and rebellion which would mark the end of the kalpa. What is of course significant is that the Boxers recognized this sectarianism as utterly different from their own ritual and as both subversive and dangerous. The gulf separating Boxers and White Lotus continued right up to the end.

Tianjin presented a picture not wholly different from Beijing. The large foreign community fortified itself in the foreign concessions, protected by a force initially composed of about 2,000 troops and steadily reinforced from the sea by the rail line which was, with some effort, kept open to Dagu. In the Chinese city, the Boxers were a powerful force, patrolling the streets and (as we have seen) forcing imperial officials to treat them with respect. While many Beijing Boxers were at least nominally enrolled in forces commanded by the Manchu Princes and noblemen, the Tianjin Boxers seem to have preserved a greater independence and produced several leaders of their own (most, significantly, natives of Shandong) capable of rallying thousands of Boxers in different Boxer altars subject to the general influence of a "headquarters altar" (*zong-tan*).

But the battles around Tianjin were largely conventional, with well-armed Chinese troops of the Military Guards Army arrayed against a foreign force composed largely of Japanese and Russians. The Boxers launched a few attempts to storm the concessions, but their only offensive weapon was fire and despite considerable displays of bravery, they fell in great numbers before the foreign guns. After a series of lesser battles in which the foreign forces seized key Chinese positions, a full-scale allied attack on the Chinese city of Tianjin was launched on July 13. After a day of fierce fighting, the city fell, the Chinese defenders and most of the Boxers having fallen back at the last moment. Most of the population had fled, and wisely so, for "at first everyone was shot indiscriminately." For several days, the city was simply given over to the foreign troops to loot and plunder.[111]

THE CIVILIZED WORLD'S REVENGE

After the fall of Tianjin there was a slight lull in the fighting. For some time, the court had been receiving fairly encouraging reports from Yu-lu on the resistance to the foreigners, stressing the effective cooperation of Boxer and regular army units. But now Tianjin was lost, and in the battle China had lost one of its best generals (and a firm foe of the Boxers), Nie Shi-cheng, and as many as three thousand of his men. Furthermore, Yu-lu now reported that in response to repeated imperial decrees, he had contacted the principal Boxer leaders in Tianjin to arrange joint resistance to the foreign force. But "those Boxers are too wild and difficult to train. On the pretext of enmity to the Christians, they loot everywhere and have no intention of attacking the foreign troops." When the battle came, the Boxers scattered without a trace.[112] While allowing for some anti-Boxer bias in this report, it does seem true that most Boxers preferred to confront the more vulnerable native Christians, and it was extremely difficult to use them against the regular forces of the invading army. Chastened by the loss of Tianjin, and repeatedly urged by the southern viceroys to negotiate an end to the conflict, the court moderated its policy significantly: the shelling of the legations stopped; letters were sent asking the United States, France, and Germany to help resolve the conflict; and Li Hong-zhang was ordered to assure the foreign Powers of the safety of their legations.[113]

The lull lasted for a while, as the Powers waited for a sufficient force to assemble in Tianjin for the assault on the capital, but there would be no negotiated settlement. On July 26, Li Bing-heng arrived in Beijing and immediately rallied the court to a final valiant resistance. All talk of compromise was stifled when two high ministers, opponents of the Boxers and advocates of some accommodation with the Powers, were executed on July 28, and three more killed in early August. Meanwhile, an allied expedition of over 20,000 men, half of them Japanese and most of the rest Russian and Indians under British command, set off from Tianjin on August 4, in sweltering summer heat. Only two battles of any consequence were fought along the way to Beijing, with the Japanese leading the way each time. With his forces crumbling under him, Yu-lu committed suicide at Yangcun on the 6th. From Beijing, Li Bing-heng led a hastily assembled force for a last-ditch stand to defend the capital, but most of his men scattered when faced with the overwhelmingly superior foreign armies, and Li took poison and died on the 11th. Three days later, the walls of Beijing were stormed and the siege of the legations relieved. The Empress Dowager led the court in flight, which would end several months later in Xi'an. And Beijing, like Tianjin before it, was left for the armies and missionaries of the "civilized nations" to wreak their terrible revenge.[114]

The march to Beijing had met only minimal resistance from Chinese forces, but the civilian population along the way suffered terribly as the advancing forces put village after village to the torch and left a great swath of destruction in their wake. Once in the capital, everyone joined in the looting: troops of all nationalities (though the Europeans were the worst, and the Japanese the best-behaved), and missionaries who would later justify their activities in articles with such delightful titles as "The Ethics of Loot." Patrols passed through the city, and then into the surrounding countryside to seek out and shoot Boxers, as a result of which (in the words of the American commander): "It is safe to say that where one real Boxer has been killed since the capture of Pekin, fifty harmless coolies or labourers on the farms, including not a few women and children, have been slain."[115] In October, an expedition was sent to Baoding, to rescue several missionaries imprisoned there and punish the officials and inhabitants for those who had died earlier. Judicial Commissioner Ting-yong (who had handed the city over to the foreign forces) and two others were given a summary trial and executed. Meanwhile outside Beijing, troops went out on "punitive picnics" to punish, by looting, rape, and arson, suburban villages suspected of harboring Boxers.[116]

By this time, of course, the court had long since prohibited the Boxers and sent out edicts for their strict suppression, and it was this combination of imperial prohibition and enormous and frequently indiscriminate slaughter by foreign troops which finally brought the movement to an end. Needless to say, the methods did not leave the citizenry any more favorably disposed toward foreigners; but the folly of magically protected resistance of the Boxer variety was now clear for all to see.

The court and the nation, of course, still had a price to pay, and the Powers would make it an enormous one. The negotiations leading up to the Boxer Protocol were long and tortuous, but the end was a foregone conclusion. With the foreign Powers occupying Beijing, they were bound to get their way. The most intense negotiations were over the punishments to be meted out to pro-Boxer officials. The Powers demanded death for eleven of these, and in the end settled for the execution of Yu-xian, and the deaths of Prince Zhuang and four others by suicide. Of the others, Li Bing-heng and Gang-yi were already dead. Of the key ministers, only Prince Duan was permitted to live his life out in exile in Xinjiang. Of the other terms, the 450,000,000 tael indemnity stands out for its enormous size—more than four times the annual revenue of the Beijing government and an even one tael for each Chinese subject. It was to be paid over thirty-nine years at 4 percent annual interest, the annual payments representing about one-fifth of the national budget.

From the standpoint of national security, the military provisions of the treaty were equally significant. The Dagu forts were to be destroyed, and foreign troops stationed at key points along the approaches to the national capital. There was to be a permanent and substantial legation guard in Beijing, and for two years China was not permitted to import any arms.[117] The court had been made a military hostage and fiscal purveyor for the foreign powers. It would take more than one revolution before China would escape from the subservient position that the imperialist coalition imposed on her for the impertinence of the Boxer Uprising.

LESSONS

The lessons of the Boxer Uprising were both domestic and international. The "Siege of Peking" and the Eight-Nation International Expedition captured the attention of the world, which was certainly awakened to the intensity of Chinese resentment of the foreign presence in China. By and large, that resentment was passed off as the ignorant reaction of a proud but fundamentally uncivilized people. There were some, however, who saw the unmistakable signs of an emerging Chinese nationalism, and the significance of that nationalism was not lost on sensitive observers. Together with the international rivalries evident ever since the Scramble for Concessions, and made all the more clear during the suppression of the Boxer Uprising (above all by the Russian occupation of Manchuria), that emerging Chinese nationalism essentially ended any thoughts of "carving up the [Chinese] melon." Instead, a consensus developed behind the American approach of keeping an Open Door, giving all Powers equal access to China's markets and resources, and preserving China's "territorial integrity."

But the domestic impact of the Boxer Uprising was even more important. The immediate effect was clearly disastrous for China: the terms of the protocol made that clear to everyone. Accordingly the question became: who was responsible? In the numerous accounts of the "Boxer catastrophe" two villains emerge: reactionary Manchu princes and officials, and ignorant, superstitious peasants. The Boxer episode thoroughly discredited the conservative policies which had reversed the 1898 reforms. The last decade of the Qing would be one of dramatic reform activities: the abolition of the examination system and the establishment of new schools, administrative and military modernization, the encouragement of industry and mining, and a program for a gradual transition to constitutional monarchy and local self-government. But it was not only conservative policies that were discredited. The extraordinary prominence of Manchus among Boxer supporters both in Beijing and in the provinces caused many to quietly question the capacity of that group to guide China through these times of crisis. In the following decade, suspicion of the Manchu capacity to rule would fuel the movement for constitutional government and finally the 1911 Revolution which brought to an end over 260 years of Qing rule.

More fundamentally, however, the Boxer Uprising would leave the Chinese elite extraordinarily fearful of any involvement of the ordinary people in the political affairs of the nation. The man who gained more than anyone as a result of the Boxer Uprising was Yuan Shi-kai. His bloody suppression of the Boxers in Shandong had saved that province from further foreign interference and gained him important foreign admirers as well. In December 1901, he was appointed governor-general of Zhili and Commissioner of Northern Ports, taking charge of military and foreign affairs in north China. Yuan Shi-kai would dominate the final years of the Qing, and the early Republic as well. His approach to government would stress military modernization, administrative centralization, and bureaucratic rationalization. Constitutionalism, insofar as Yuan approved of it, was to be built on a tightly circumscribed electorate based on the old gentry elite. There was no place for the common people in Yuan Shi-kai's polity, and any stirrings on their part would most likely be met with the swift and brutal application of military force.

Yuan Shi-kai is important, because his rise was so closely linked to the Boxer Uprising, and his political influence so clearly authoritarian. But Yuan Shi-kai was not alone in fearing the threat from the unwashed masses. The urban reformist elite, and even many revolutionaries, shared his distrust of China's vast peasant majority. The Boxers had shown what could happen if the masses were once unleashed—and few were willing to risk an attempt to turn their fury to the cause of remaking China. Not until Mao Ze-dong went down to investigate the peasant movement in Hunan in 1927, and saw there the potential for a great storm sweeping over China, would anyone really dare to light the spark and start another prairie fire.

Epilogue:
Beyond the Idol of Origins

In *The Historian's Craft*, Marc Bloch wrote of the historical profession's obsession with "The Idol of Origins"—the "explanation of the very recent in terms of the remotest past." Taking the history of Christian practices as his example, he wrote:

> A knowledge of their beginnings is indispensable to understand, but insufficient to account for, the actual religious phenomena. To simplify our problem, we must postpone the question as to how far the creed, identical in name, is the same in substance. Even assuming our religious tradition entirely unchanging, we must find reasons for its preservation.... Now, wherever fidelity to a belief is to be found, all evidences agree that it is but one aspect of the general life of a group. It is like a knot in which are intertwined a host of divergent characteristics of the structure and mentality of a society. In short, a religious creed involves the whole problem of the human environment. Great oaks from little acorns grow. But only if they meet favorable conditions of soil and climate, conditions which are entirely beyond the scope of embryology.[1]

This advice is particularly apt for an inquiry into the origins of the Boxer Uprising. All too often, historians have looked to the "remotest past," where they have found, in association with the White Lotus sect, boxing groups which were identical in name to the Boxers of 1899–1900 but in this case quite different in substance. At best, these historians have succumbed, in Bloch's terms, to the "danger of confusing ancestry with explanation."[2] (At worst, the ancestry they discovered was merely an accidental identity of name.) As this study has argued, an understanding of the rise of the Boxers must be sought in a detailed analysis of the contemporary environment—the structure and mentality of society in west Shandong, and the shape of provincial, national, and international politics on the eve of the twentieth century.

The problem is well illustrated by a comparison to the Ghost Dance of the Sioux Indians, which spread rapidly (and tragically) just a decade before the Boxers arose in China. The ancestry of the Sioux Ghost Dance is easily traced to the Paiute prophet Wavoka, who had traveled to heaven on January 1, 1889 (the day of a solar eclipse), and seen there a vision of paradise to come. The sources of his vision can also be traced, especially to the Shakers of the Pacific Northwest, where Wavoka had worked picking hops around the Puget Sound. Wavoka preached the imminent coming of a millennium in which the white man would be swept away as the Indians rose to the heavens with sacred feathers, later descending together with their ancestors to reinhabit the earth. But his teachings were entirely peaceful, and included a strong component of Christian ethics which enjoined against fighting of any kind. This was not unexpected of a man who had grown up with a white family and, like many Paiutes, worked for a white man in a relationship which (while no doubt economically exploitative) was at least amicable.

As other tribes heard of Wavoka, emissaries traveled to Nevada to meet the prophet, and quickly the Ghost Dance spread: to the Arapaho and Shoshoni in Wyoming, the Cheyenne in Oklahoma, and the Sioux in the Dakotas. In the course of the Ghost Dance, trances were induced and people traveled to see their ancestors in heaven and get a taste of the paradise to come. The new religion found thousands of adherents throughout the American West, but led to trouble only among the Sioux. This largest of the North American tribes had suffered most from the eradication of the buffalo herds upon which their livelihood had depended, and the forced abandonment of a life honoring warfare and hunting in favor of a sedentary reservation existence. Recent decades had seen repeated reduction in the size of their reservations as white farmers, ranchers, and gold-diggers demanded more and more of the Sioux lands. The final 1889 Land Agreement had been particularly unpopular, and the situation was not helped by scorching summer winds which destroyed most crops in 1890, a federally-mandated reduction in Indian rations despite evidence of hunger and some starvation, and a census that many feared would bring further cut-backs.

This was the context in which the Ghost Dance spread to the Sioux; but in picking it up they introduced important new elements of their own. Wavoka had shown visitors wounds on his hands and feet, which were interpreted as the result of his crucifixion as (or like) Christ. Tribes like the Cheyenne ascribed these wounds only to persecution by "people"; but the Sioux held the white man responsible. The millennium that the Sioux envisioned explicitly entailed the extermination of the white man. Finally, the Sioux introduced the Ghost Shirt into the dance, and it was believed to make its wearer invulnerable to the white man's bullets. Tensions between Indians and whites heightened as the Ghost Dance grew in popularity among the Sioux and gained a powerful sponsor in Sitting Bull, hero of the 1876 victory over General Custer at Little Bighorn. Eventually the Indian agents and the U.S. Army moved to suppress the dance. The ill-conceived effort soon led to the shooting of Sitting Bull and the tragic massacre at Wounded Knee.[3]

The Ghost Dance is interesting to us because it entailed both trances and invulnerability rituals, and it clearly expressed a longing among the North American Indians for a world once again free of the much hated white man. There is, accordingly, much in the movement that is quite reminiscent of the Boxer Uprising itself. It can serve to remind us that the peasants of north China were not the only ones who wished for a world free of Caucasian intrusion, and hoped that invulnerability rituals would help to bring that world about. (Other examples could be found in the Cargo Cults of Melanesia, or the Maji-Maji of East Africa.)[4] But my purpose here is not only to note the Ghost Dance's ritual and functional similarity to the Boxers. Of primary interest is the methodological point that we learn little about the *origins* of the Sioux outbreak of 1890 by tracing the Ghost Dance to Wavoka. The Dance was not simply imported wholesale. The creative impulse did not end with Wavoka. The Sioux transformed the Dance to give it meaning in their particular predicament, and it was that transformation which made the Dance a source of violent unrest. The origins of the unrest must be sought in the reasons for the Dance's transformation, and those reasons are to be found in the particular local social, economic, and political conditions of the Sioux in 1889–90.

Our approach to the origins of the Boxer Uprising has been similar. Above all, it has been necessary to explore, in the most systematic and minute way possible, the social, economic, and political conditions in the local areas from which the Boxers (and their Big Sword Society predecessors) emerged. Most students of Chinese social history recognize that, given the country's size and regional diversity, generalizations about China as a whole are fraught with danger. Regional and provincial studies have become increasingly common. But that may not be enough. Shandong's population of some thirty-seven million at the turn of the century was roughly equivalent to that of France; its land area was greater than England and Wales. Such a province is itself too large and diverse for meaningful generalization, and much of our effort has been devoted to describing the characteristics of regions within Shandong which were significant in shaping the evolution of the Boxer movement. At times, as in our discussion of the Guan county exclaves or the flood-afflicted regions of Chiping and their relation to the Spirit Boxers of 1898–99, we have found that distinctions have to be made even *within* counties if we are to appreciate fully the context within which Chinese peasants lived.

Our analysis of the socio-economic environment has entailed a careful review of agricultural productivity, commercialization, natural disasters, social formations, degrees and forms of stratification, strength of the orthodox elite, and the extent of banditry in the areas from which the Boxers and Big Swords arose. These phenomena were not simply examined as *background* for the social movements under examination, but as *preconditions* for the specific form that these movements took. At the heart of the argument has been the idea that the more tightly organized, secretive, village-elite-led Big Sword Society in some way *reflected* the social structure of southwest Shandong, with its strong landlord elite and tight-knit village communities. Similarly, the Spirit Boxers of the northwest, with their mass possession ritual, openly practiced and easily learned, and the ability to reproduce leaders with ease and accept them even if they were outsiders to the community, reflected the relatively undifferentiated society and open villages of northwest Shandong. Thus the local social environment not only facilitated the rise of these new organizations, but influenced the form that they would take.

The close "fit" of both Boxers and Big Swords with the social formations from which they grew was in part due to the consistently loyalist purposes of the two organizations. No social movement can avoid being shaped by the social structures and cultural values of the region from which it grows. But the constraints on the Boxers and Big Swords were particularly severe precisely because they sought to operate *within* the confines of the established order. The Big Swords at the outset worked closely with the local officials and militia to combat rising banditry. The Boxers' goals were summed up in the slogan "Support the Qing, destroy the foreign." It is movements of this type which, in contrast to radical millenarian movements with a vision of a totally new social order, should reflect most closely the local society from which they emerge.

It should be clear, however, that what we mean by this "reflection" is not some reductionist principle whereby one can derive and predict the nature of a social movement from the social enviroment that spawns it. Rather our point is the much more modest one that the social environment will *constrain* the possible forms that a social movement might take in any given area. Thus I would argue that the Spirit Boxers could never have taken hold in southwest Shandong— for the strong local landlord elite would not have permitted a movement capable of generating an endless number of alternative leaders and likely to grow beyond the range of local elite control. Despite the fact that imperialist penetration was much more marked on the Shandong peninsula and North Slope (especially after the Germans began surveying for their mines and railroad), neither Spirit Boxers nor Big Swords were likely to emerge in these areas. The martial subculture was weak and the civil gentry strong; banditry was not a problem to encourage local defense forces; natural disasters were rare; and a moderate commercialization and diversified economy left fewer peasants threatened with a genuine subsistence crisis.

What the local socio-economic environment did was to limit the options for social movements: certain types were possible, others were not. The strength of the local elite was a particularly critical factor. A weak elite obviously left more options open; a strong elite would either have to be coopted (with certain inevitable consequences for the nature of the movement), or directly confronted (giving the movement a certain class-struggle character). The cohesiveness of the village community was also critical. Strong, cohesive communities are only likely to get involved in fundamentally defensive struggles. The Big Swords were an example of this, and so, in all likelihood, were their twentieth-century counterparts the Red Spears.[5] On the other hand, small and weak communities (like the Hakka communities of Guangxi where the massive nineteenth-century rebellion, the Taiping, began), or discontented members of internally divided communities (like the poorer peasants and displaced persons of the Yangzi Valley who joined the Taiping as they swept through) were more likely to join aggressive attacks on the existing social system. Though the Boxers of the north China plain never launched attacks of this order, they were clearly (especially as they spread toward Beijing and Tianjin) a good deal less defensive than the Big Swords, and this certainly reflected the more mobile peasantry and the less cohesive villages of this region.

It is clear, however, that the structure of local society cannot, by itself, explain the outbreak of a major social movement. The historian of social movements is fundamentally concerned with explaining an "event." She or he must bridge the gap between structure and event—between the relatively static structures defined in the language of economics, sociology, and anthropology, and the dynamic process of historical change. In our case, we must explain how and why, in the last years of the nineteenth century, the society of west Shandong suddenly spawned these dramatic anti-Christian and anti-foreign movements.

The usual approach to this problem is fairly simple. Either exogenous forces or internally generated contradictions are seen as producing some crisis in the system. Then a new idea (in peasant societies, frequently a religious doctrine) and new organizations emerge to lead a social movement which can be seen as a response to the crisis, perhaps even promising a resolution to the particular difficulty that the affected population faces. Much of the logic of our argument follows this form. The new stage which imperialism reached in the last years of the nineteenth century made missionaries and native Christians a much more aggressive and disruptive force. This was particularly so after the Qing defeat in the Sino-Japanese War and the 1897 German seizure of Jiaozhou Bay. Soon villagers began organizing in self-defense. First the Big Swords and then the Boxers emerged to combat the Christians and their foreign backers—the Boxers with a particularly attractive and explosive set of possession and invulnerability rituals.

But if our explanation is not to rest entirely on exogenous variables, we must go one step further. We must ask: how did the new and volatile beliefs and rituals of the Boxers gain a following among the peasants of the north China plain? The Boxers did not merely activate longstanding sectarian networks and turn them against the Christians: we have found the old theory of White Lotus origins to be quite without foundation. Only in the case of the Guan county Boxers is there evidence that a pre-existing boxing society was mobilized to attack the hated converts. The Spirit Boxers in particular—and they were the most important, for they were the "real" Boxers—were a new creation of the northwest Shandong peasants. Every village that picked up the rituals of possession and invulnerability was learning the "boxing" for the first time. How was this Spirit Boxing able to find a place in the structure of north China village life and quickly mobilize peasants in a massive popular uprising?

The heart of my argument has been that it was the popular culture of the west Shandong peasants which provided the link between structure and event. In theoretical terms, this popular culture plays the same functional role as the *habitus* of which Pierre Bourdieu writes. In discussing the origins of collective action, Bourdieu (in the inimitable style of French social theory) describes how "a *habitus*, understood as a system of lasting, transposable dispositions ... integrating past experiences, functions at every moment as a *matrix of perceptions, appreciations, and actions* and makes possible the achievement of infinitely diversified tasks, thanks to analogical transfers of schemes permitting the solution of similarly shaped problems."[6] It was the Boxers' "analogical transfer" of a peasant *habitus* of possession rituals and heroic theatrical narratives that allowed them to mobilize peasants for the struggle against the foreign religion.

I shall return to the Boxers presently, but first I would like to argue for the general applicability of this method by suggesting how it might be applied to another great social movement of modern Chinese history, the Taiping Rebellion. I would hold that the method not only proves to be heuristically valuable, but that it also provides an understanding of the origins of the Taiping that is slightly different from the conventional account.

The Taiping Rebellion was inspired by Hong Xiu-quan, a young teacher from the Canton delta region, who had suffered a mental breakdown following failure in the prefectural examinations of 1836. While ill, Hong had a vision in which he traveled to heaven, and was charged by God to return to earth and cast out the demons, purge the world of wickedness, and lead the people to a paradise of peace and brotherhood. Hong's vision had clearly been inspired by a Christian pamphlet he had read, and the Christian elements of the vision were strengthened in later contact with missionaries in Canton. It was 1843 before Hong read the pamphlet again and understood the meaning of his vision, and in the following year he set forth to spread his message.

So much attention has been given to Hong's vision and its impact on the rebellion that it is sometimes forgotten that when he left home, Hong first traveled south into the Canton delta, twice passed through Canton, and wandered for some time east and north of the city without finding any sort of audience. Only when he headed up the West River and into Guangxi did he at last find a following for his teachings.[7]

Between his first visit to Guangxi in 1844 and the outbreak of the rebellion six years later, Hong in fact spent more time at home near Canton than he did in the Guangxi hill country—but it was in Guangxi that his teachings took root and the rebellion broke forth. Clearly, as Bloch reminded us, "Great oaks from little acorns grow. But only if they meet favorable conditions of soil and climate." What were the favorable conditions in southeastern Guangxi? In general, they are well known: sharply rising population, commercialization of the economy along the rivers linking the area to Guangdong, epidemics and natural disasters, unemployment from recently closed silver mines, banditry in the hills and piracy on the rivers, a plethora of restive secret societies, opium and salt smuggling, and perhaps above all a population deeply divided between Zhuang minority tribes, established Han residents (Punti), and "Guest people" (Hakka)—a linguistic minority who had come later to the area and inhabited smaller, poorer upland villages. Hong was himself a Hakka, and it was from this group that most of his original followers were drawn.[8]

Here clearly were preconditions not present on the Canton Delta. But why were these people particularly attracted to the God-worshipping Society (Bai shang-di hui) which Hong and his lieutenants established in the Guangxi hills? The conventional answer to this question has always stressed the appeal of Hong's pseudo-Christian millenarian teaching. Here is the classic exogenous element and mobilizing ideology, and one cannot gainsay its importance. Like most Chinese millenarianism (and in contrast to most other Christian-inspired millenarianism),[9] the stress was more on surviving an impending disaster than on welcoming an imminent paradise. Both elements were of course present, but it is significant that Hong is described as having "taught people about being eaten by serpents and tigers [if they did not believe] and about avoiding disasters and sickness."[10] In 1836, and again in 1847, rebels influenced by White Lotus millenarianism had risen on the Hunan-Guangxi border,[11] and it is quite likely that Hong's disaster-avoidance message was understood as essentially similar to this indigenous Chinese millenarianism.

It is, however, the *positive* appeal of Hong's message that is most striking, for there we see the mirror-image of the strife-torn Guangxi society. By the end of the 1840s, conflicts between Hakka and Punti had reached a state of virtual civil war. It was village against village, and clan against clan—with the less numerous, more dispersed and poorer Hakka very much at a disadvantage. Hong was clearly sensitive to the distress caused by such strife, and addressed the problem directly, attacking the parochialism in which "even within one province, prefecture or county, this township, this village, or this clan hates that township, that village or that clan. The ways of the world and the minds of men having come to this, how can they do other than oppress one another, steal from one another, fight one another, kill one another and thus perish altogether."[12]

To replace this unending warfare, the Taiping promised a world in which all were one family, equally the sons and daughters of God. They promised a "Heavenly Kingdom of Great Peace"—to translate directly the full name of the Taiping regime—and it was understandably appealing. But it was appealing in the specific context of Guangxi (and especially southeast Guangxi) society. Life was not necessarily all peace and harmony in the Canton delta, but the established structures of village and kin were at least stable enough to prevent any great flood of converts to Hong's alternative vision. And the Taiping were, above all, an alternative vision. To the extent that doctrine was decisive, they gained a following in Guangxi not because of any fundamental compatibility with the structure of communal conflict—but because they promised relief from it.[13]

One can still ask, however: just how decisive was this newly imported doctrine? There can be no question that Hong Xiu-quan's Christian-inspired vision of an ascent to heaven, and his subsequent studies of Christian texts, were of critical importance in defining the ideology of the Taiping Rebellion. Evidence of how seriously the Taiping leaders took their religion is overwhelming: they published a wide variety of pamphlets and tracts; they set up a state examination system based on the Taiping teachings; they were so insistent that secret society bands (Triads) submit to the discipline required by Taiping ideology that most of these potential allies quickly left the fold; and when Westerners came to the Taiping capital in Nanking they were closely questioned on aspects of Western Christianity which would confirm Hong's vision. The role of Hong's vision and beliefs in shaping the Taiping movement has been so clear that they have quite properly been the focus of significant scholarly attention.[14]

The critical importance of Taiping ideology to the movement's leaders does not, however, necessarily apply to the rank and file. On the contrary, it is likely that religious doctrine both meant *less* to ordinary followers, and was understood in new ways more consistent with local structures of belief. It is clear, for example, that for many, religion had little or nothing to do with their adherence to the movement. When outright battles developed between Hakka and Punti villages in 1849–50, the God-worshipping Society emerged as the only effective organization protecting the Hakka. Often the outnumbered Hakka were driven from their homes and fled to join the God Worshippers. As one contemporary source put it: "They willingly submitted to any form of worship in order to escape from their enemies, and received the necessary supplies, which they were now destitute of."[15]

Before the God-worshipping Society could effectively protect the beleaguered Hakka villagers, it had to achieve a certain strength of its own, and it is likely that the initial appeal was religious. In assessing that religious appeal we would do better to follow the anthropologists and focus on ritual and symbolism, and avoid overstating the theological concerns of the movement's peasant followers. In the first place, we must recognize that many (perhaps most) of the original followers were seeking the usual benefits of folk religion. If we read the prayers set forth in the Taiping "Book of Heavenly Commandments" (*Tiantiao shu*), we see an attention to the sorts of practical concerns that most poor Hakka peasants would have. The grace to be said at meals asked for food and clothes, and freedom from disasters. There were prayers to be said at birth, at the traditional one-month celebration for a young infant, for house-building, family division, and of course the avoidance of illness. This last is perhaps most interesting for it is phrased in terms of classic Chinese religious healing: "If a demon should invade and harm me, I earnestly beseech our Heavenly Father and Great God to greatly exert your divine majesty and seize the demon and destroy it."[16] In the enthusiasm of the newly formed God-worshipping Society, there were numerous miracles: "The dumb began to talk and the insane to recover." In fact, in the earliest years of the movement, Hong was so devoted to doing good works that "the officials and troops also considered him a man of virtue and did not fight him."[17]

Particularly important for our purposes is the period from 1848 to the summer of 1849 when both Hong and his closest follower, Feng Yun-shan, were absent from the God Worshippers' Guangxi base. This was the period during which the movement grew to the point that it was capable of defending the Hakka, and thereby attracted additional followers. The following account describes what Hong and Feng discovered when they returned to Guangxi in the summer of 1849:

> They now learned, that, during their absence in Kwang tung, some very remarkable occurrences had taken place in the congregation of the God worshippers, which had brought disorder and dissension among the brethren. It sometimes happened that while they were kneeling down engaged in prayer, the one or the other of those present was seized by a sudden fit, so that he fell down to the ground, and his whole body was covered with perspiration. In such a state of ecstacy, moved by the spirit, he uttered words of exhortation, reproof, prophesy, &c. Often the words were unintelligible, and generally delivered in verse. The brethren had noted down in a book the more remarkable of these sayings, and delivered them to the inspection of Hung Siu-tshuen [Hong Xiu-quan].[18]

Clearly the God Worshippers were going into ecstatic trances and behaving precisely in the form of south Chinese shamans, even down to the point of speaking in verse. The most important of those possessed was Yang Xiu-qing, who was already emerging as the effective leader of the Taiping—Hong's own role being substantially confined to religious matters. Yang was possessed by the Holy Ghost and in this state was able to effect miraculous cures of the sick. Here the shamanistic role was reproduced in its entirety.

One of the paradoxes of any revolutionary movement (and the Taiping, with their wholesale attack on Confucianism, were most assuredly revolutionary) is that it must maintain its vision of a radically transformed society, and at the same time sufficiently adjust to the norms of conventional social behavior to make the revolutionary vision both understandable and acceptable to a mass audience. Without their Christian-inspired millennial religion, the Taiping would never have produced the inspired and disiplined army that came so close to toppling the Qing. Yet without some means of making that religion comprehensible to a peasantry utterly unfamiliar with Christian eschatology, the rebellion could never have gotten off the ground. I would argue that for the Taiping, this dilemma was resolved by the fact that much of their religious behavior could be understood in terms of ordinary Chinese folk religion.

There is one further point. As the account above shows, the sort of mass spirit-possession seen in the God-worshipping Society in 1848–49 led to "disorder and dissension." For the Taiping to carry out their revolutionary design and realize the Heavenly Kingdom, a disciplined organization with clearly established lines of authority would be necessary. This meant that access to divine authority would have to be controlled. That was precisely the role that Hong played on his return. Hong's own spiritual primacy was never questioned, and he decreed that only two of the possessions during the previous year had been genuine—Yang Xiu-qing's by the Holy Ghost and one other future Taiping king's possession by Jesus. The others, Hong decided, had been possessed by demons—a perfectly acceptable solution, for possession by unwanted or malevolent ghosts and spirits was a normal part of Chinese folk belief. Thus without denying the reality of the possessions which people had observed, Hong interpreted them in such a way that his and his closest lieutenants' primacy was assured. Religious authority was centralized and the stage was set for the rebellion to break forth in earnest.

The contrast between this account of the rise of the Taiping and the conventional version is obvious. The focus is removed from Hong Xiu-quan and the source of his doctrine in Christian and classical Chinese texts, and placed upon the peasants who rallied to his sect. China, like any peasant culture, had innumerable teachers, prophets, or just plain madmen preaching a variety of new cults and doctrines. It is far less important to know where they got their ideas than to understand how their ideas attracted an audience. Nor should the relationship of cult-founder and audience be seen as purely unidirectional. The members of a new cult—especially one which developed into a broad-based social movement—were not simply passive followers. The way in which they *understood* the cult's message may not have been identical to the way in which the founder taught it. What is important is to explore the popular understanding of a movement or cult: what the movement *meant* to its members. Therein lies the explanation of its appeal.

As we seek the clues to that popular understanding, we are immediately led to the realm of popular culture and religion. The study of popular culture is one of the liveliest fields of historical research today—though the sources (especially those generated by the Inquisition) are far richer in European history than anything yet discovered for the China field.[19] This sort of study is important not only because it tells us about the world which most of the population inhabited, but also because it provides an insight into patterns of ritual, belief, and behavior which peasants could creatively adapt in the praxis of the situational moment. "[C]ultural categories acquire new functional values ... [and] cultural meanings are thus altered." [20] Among the God Worshippers of Guangxi, the traditional spirit-possession of Chinese folk religion was transformed from a ritual of healing and communication with ancestors to a source of legitimation for a dynamic millenarian rebellion.

The similarity of all of this to the Boxers is obvious. They too had their mass spirit-possession. But they differed from the Taiping in not limiting popular access to divine power. The loyalist logic of the movement did not require a centralized revolutionary authority. Their purpose was to provide a myriad spirit-soldiers to drive out the foreigners and protect the Qing. They required (and produced) no generals or emperors of their own.

The Boxer link to popular culture was even more obvious than the Taiping's. As we have repeatedly argued, the Boxers were not a reactivated and reoriented branch of the White Lotus sect, but a new ritual complex that was easily learned and spread rapidly across the north China plain. To argue that the Spirit Boxers were created *de novo* is not to say that they arose *ex nihilo*. The crucial elements of Boxer ritual were put together from a repertoire of martial arts and folk religious practices that were familiar to most north China peasants. We do not know who put the various elements together, but the origins of the separate components seem relatively clear. The notion of invulnerability had been present in such martial arts groups as the Armor of the Golden Bell, at least since the eighteenth century. It was an extension of the sort of *qi-gong* that one can see performed on the stage to this day. Long practice and arduous physical training can teach people the intense concentration and muscle-tightening techniques that enable practitioners to withstand sword chops or even steady pressure against the stomach and chest with a pointed instrument. These practices were first revived and popularized by the Big Swords, and their regimen of "striking with bricks and swords" was certainly part of the toughening process that prepared one's body to withstand an attack with weapons. Even at the stage of the Big Swords, the regimen was greatly simplified, the time in training shortened and the invulnerability extended to the exaggerated claim that guns could be withstood as well as swords and spears. (It is my guess that this extension of the invulnerability claims was facilitated by the fact that the Chinese word for "gun" [*qiang*] is the same as the word for spear.) The Spirit Boxers carried the simplification process one step further, providing a ritual that could be learned in a few days and claiming that invulnerability would come from spirit-possession.

The notion of spirit-possession was also familiar to any Chinese peasant. Most notably, illness was caused by possession by malevolent ghosts, and cured by shamans who were possessed by more powerful gods who could capture or drive away the offending ghost. The fact that the earliest function of the Spirit Boxers was to cure illness indicates that they were closely tied to this tradition.[21]

Invulnerability and spirit-possession were the two hallmarks of the Boxer ritual. All that remained was to adopt the name Boxers United in Righteousness, and to direct their attacks against the Christians. The name was almost certainly borrowed from the Guan county Boxers, whose long resistance to Christian aggression spread their name and fame across the north China plain. The Spirit Boxers picked up this new name at the same time that they adopted their anti-Christian mission. Their anti-Christianity is both the hardest and the easiest part to explain: hard, because we can point to no specific incident initiating the anti-Christian attacks; easy, because peasants everywhere had grievances against the Christians, and in 1898–99 attacks on Christians had been spreading throughout Shandong province (and indeed throughout the nation). It would be more surprising if an active, popular peasant movement like the Spirit Boxers did *not*, at some point, turn its aggressive potential against the Christians.

The above discussion has been phrased in reference to the person or persons who put the Spirit Boxer ritual together. But in fact that is not the critical question. As I have argued with respect to the Taiping, what is important is to explore the popular understanding of a movement or cult: what the movement meant to its members. Therein lies the explanation of the movement's appeal.

The popular understanding of the Boxer ritual was also, as we have indicated above, likely to have been in terms of shamanistic behavior. The popularity, on the north China plain, of both martial arts and sectarian groups with a familiar repertoire of charms, spells, and magical tricks prepared the people to accept this new form of Spirit Boxing. But there was another major influence on Boxer practices, which may have had even greater impact on popular understanding of the movement, and that was the theatre. Most of the gods by which

Boxers were possessed were known from the operas performed at temple fairs (usually in the spring), or at other occasions for village celebration. The operas were based on vernacular novels (or sometimes vice versa) in which the line between the heavens and the mundane world was often unclear and frequently crossed. *The Romance of the Three Kingdoms* (which provided the "God of War" Guangong, as well as his comrades Zhang Fei and Zhao Yun) is in fact a historical novel, whose human protagonists were only later elevated to the status of gods in the popular religious pantheon. *Water Margin* was another historical novel, which had the added attraction of being based in western Shandong. *Journey to the West* (translated as "Monkey") provided the very popular gods "Monkey," "Sandy," and "Pigsy." Though the story was based on an actual journey to India by the Tang dynasty monk Xuan-zang, the elaboration was entirely fictional and contained the important element of the "Monkey" and his friends with their divine powers coming to the aid of those in the mundane world. This is even clearer in *The Enfeoffment of the Gods*.

The Enfeoffment of the Gods provided some of the most popular Boxer gods: Jiang Zi-ya (Jiang Tai-gong), Yang Jian, and Huang Fei-hu. Jiang Zi-ya had been sent down from heaven (the term used was "down from the mountain" [*xia-shan*], the same term the Boxers used), to assist the Zhou kings to overthrow the last corrupt and evil ruler of the Shang in the eleventh century B.C. The novel describes a number of fierce struggles of Jiang and his colleagues against a variety of evil and heterodox spirits defending the Shang.

I would suggest that it was especially operas like *The Enfeoffment of the Gods* which provided the "narrative context" for the actions of the possessed Boxers. Trances are a very dangerous state—both for the individual and for the community. People's bodies are possessed by spirits and subject to the spirits' control: in many cultures, the spirits "capture" the individual. It is accordingly important that certain accepted cultural constructs—myths—define the ways in which spirits will behave, and it is these myths which provide the "narrative context" for the behavior of the possessed.[22]

In our case, the narrative context was provided by the operas which were such a central part of folk culture in village China. When Boxers were possessed by a certain god, they behaved as they had seen that god behave in the operas: "Pigsy" would even root about in the dirt with his nose, and the various martial figures would always grab the weapon appropriate to the possessing god. The similarity to the crowded excitement of an opera was such that some observers thought passing Boxer bands with their flags and bright clothes looked just like an opera.

Anthropologists have often stressed the link between ritual and theatrical performance.[23] In the case of Boxer ritual, the link was particularly direct. Spirit Boxer rituals were always openly performed, and people were attracted to them by the same "hustle and bustle" (re-nao) that drew people to the operas of temple fairs. When they left behind their mundane lives and took on the characteristics of the god that possessed them, the Boxers were doing what any good actor does on stage. It is probably no accident that it was in the spring of 1899, after the usual round of fairs and operas, that the Boxers' anti-Christian activity really began to spread in northwest Shandong; and in 1900 it was again the spring which saw the escalation of Boxer activity in Zhili. On some occasions the Boxers even took over the opera stage, and performed from the same platform that provided their gods.[24]

There is no strict functional division between religion and theatre in Chinese society. (The Chinese would certainly not have understood the opposition between the two that the English and American Puritans saw.) Not only are operas filled with historical figures deified in the popular pantheon, but they provide the primary occasion for collective religious observances. Most Chinese folk religion is an individual or at most a family affair. There is no sabbath and people go individually to temples to pray when they have some particular need. The main collective observance is the temple fair and opera—normally held on the birthday of the temple god. The term for these on the north China plain is "inviting the gods to a performance" (ying-shen sai-hui). The idols are brought out from their temple, usually protected by some sort of tent, and invited to join the community in enjoying the opera. Thus the theatre provides an important ritual of community solidarity—which is of course one reason the Christians' refusal to support these operas was so much resented.

Because such an important religious function took this theatrical form, ritual was capable of moving from a strictly prescribed form of religious behavior to that less controlled and potentially innovative or even revolutionary form of "social drama." The actor, whose function is to entertain and to move an audience, is always given more room for individuality and creativity than is the religious ritualist. When the Boxer ritual became theatrical performance, it too gained this creative potential. Old ideas, old gods, old values were given radical new potential. Inspired by a hope for a world free of Christians, free of Western missionaries, the Boxers made the world their stage, and acted out a social drama of their own creation. The terrible drought of 1900 increased the fervor of their convictions, and though their wish was not to be, they wrote a remarkable chapter in the history of China and the world. In the continuing drama of modern China, the Boxer role will not easily be forgotten.

Appendix: The Mid-Qing Yi-he Boxers and the White Lotus

The full Chinese name for the famous Boxers of 1898–1900 was Yi-he quan, Boxers United in Righteousness. The first appearance of this name in the historical record was in connection with the Wang Lun uprising of 1774; and boxers of the same name were linked by investigating officials to the Eight Trigrams rebels of 1813. Because of these earlier links, opponents of the late Qing Boxers accused the anti-Christian activists of being descendants of a known heterodox sect. Lao Nai-xuan's famous 1899 pamphlet, "Investigation of the Sectarian Origins of the Boxers United in Righteousness," was little more than a reproduction of official documents from this earlier period. To this day, Lao's linking of Boxers and sectarians remains at the center of the debate on the organizational origins of the Boxers. Though a fundamental argument of this volume is that we cannot understand the origins of the Boxers by looking to some distant group which happened to have the same name, there are still important issues surrounding the relationship of the mid-Qing Yi-he Boxers and the White Lotus sectarians. So much earlier scholarship has been devoted to this question that I feel compelled to state my own understanding of the evidence.

The debate, as I have said, begins with Lao Nai-xuan's pamphlet. Two memorials are cited in that pamphlet. The first relates to a group of market-town boxing toughs along the Shandong-Jiangsu-Anhui-Henan border in 1808. We have discussed this group in chapter 2, and as it had no relationship to sectarian organizations, there is no need to return to it here. The second document cited by Lao Nai-xuan is the more critical one, for it is a long memorial by Na-yan-cheng, who had directed the suppression of the 1813 Eight Trigrams rebellion. The memorial, from late in 1815, was on the occasion of the discovery of the Clear Tea sect (Qing-cha men) of the Wang family of Stone Buddha Village (Shifokou)—a family with a sectarian history dating back to the Ming dynasty.[1] The memorial summarized Na-yan-cheng's findings on all sects uncovered in connection with the 1813 rebellion, mentioning among them the Yi-he-men quan-bang (United in Righteousness School of Boxing and Cudgels), which was identified as one of many schools descended from the Li Trigram sect.[2]

Beyond citing these two documents from the early nineteenth century, Lao Nai-xuan made no attempt to describe the precise relationship between the sects and the Yi-he Boxers. Nor did he attempt to demonstrate the relationship between the mid-Qing Yi-he Boxers and the Boxers at the end of the century. He merely noted that the latter also had charms and chanted incantations, called upon the gods to possess them, and claimed invulnerability. Though he made no attempt to document the practice of similar rituals by the Yi-he Boxers of the mid-Qing (and he would have been hard put to do so), he claimed that these practices were enough to demonstrate the heterodox heritage of the movement and urged that it be suppressed.[3]

This simple pamphlet by a county magistrate of declared hostility to the Boxer movement has remained the center of controversy in scholarship on the origins of the Boxers ever since. Initially, that debate focused on the events of the 1890s, but in recent years a number of works have appeared treating the Yi-he Boxers of the mid-Qing in some detail. Most of these are based on very much the same sources—published collections of documents on the 1813 uprising and archival materials from Taiwan and Beijing—but a remarkable polarity of views persists. Many hold that the additional documentation supports the Lao Nai-xuan theory of a close connection between the sects and the Yi-he Boxers; others read the same evidence very differently, and see these boxers as part of a martial arts tradition with only incidental connections to the sects.[4]

One reason for the complexity of the problem and the enduring diversity of views is the nature of the documentation. Since the Qing code included no explicit prohibition of boxing (despite a Yong-zheng edict against it), the Yi-he Boxers (like all other mid-Qing martial artists) tend to appear in surviving documents only when some connection to prohibited sects can be claimed. The surviving documentation thus has a built-in bias which tends to emphasize sectarian-boxer links. In addition, since the punishable offenses were sectarian, not pugilistic practices, the official documents on the Yi-he Boxers lack specific information on the nature of the boxing itself.

The first known mention of Yi-he Boxers occurs in connection with the Wang Lun rebellion of 1774. Because boxing had played such a prominent role in Wang's sect, the authorities became extremely suspicious of any form of boxing at all. Throughout western Shandong, officials prohibited such martial arts, and even men training for the military examinations halted their practice.[5] In En county in northwest Shandong, two boxing leaders, Li Cui and Guo Jing-shun, were arrested for suspicious behavior. Though these two died under torture, the arresting officials claimed to have discovered that:

> Li Cui had once taken Li Hao-ran of Linqing as a teacher and had learned from him the White Lotus teaching. [Li Cui] changed the name to Yi-he Boxing and with Guo Jing-shun from the same [En] county, took pupils, taught the sect, chanted incantations and practiced boxing (*song-zhou xi-quan*).

The incantations used by the boxers included the names of two boxing masters from Guan and Shen counties south of Linqing. They were identified as Li Hao-ran's teachers—and were possibly the originators of this school of boxing.

Li Cui was apparently a man of some substance, for he had purchased a *jian-sheng* degree. He was accused of having traveled to Linqing in September (when the rebels occupied part of the city), but if he did go he certainly returned quickly. His pupils were found only to have "learned boxing and chanted incantations."[6]

This En county incident seems to have set the authorities looking specifically for Yi-he Boxers—and the effort produced a number of false accusations over the next few years. Not long after the En county arrests, one captured rebel falsely accused a number of village boxers from Linqing of being rebels. The accused were in turn arrested, but protested that although they had learned boxing either from their fathers and grandfathers, or from neighbors, "we have never entered any sect, and know nothing of the name Yi-he Boxing." The officials concluded that the accused "indeed had not entered a sect and joined the rebels, or learned Yi-he Boxing."[7]

In the next twelve years there were at least three additional cases in which men were charged with being Yi-he Boxers, all along the Shandong-Zhili border not far from Linqing. Again the charges were found to be false, so in the end no confessions from practitioners of this boxing were obtained. But the accusations refer to the "Yi-he Boxing heterodox teaching," and indicate a widespread perception that accusing people of Yi-he Boxing would bring dramatic attention to the charge, and even link the accused to the Wang Lun rebellion.[8] Still, there is no evidence linking this Yi-he Boxing to Wang Lun, much less suggesting that it was a name for Wang's own form of boxing. On the contrary, it seems that it was just one of several schools of boxing which had been practiced for some time. According to one document: "There has long been the custom of practicing boxing and cudgels in Shandong, and thus there are such names as Yi-he Boxing and Red Boxing."[9] Nonetheless, the belief persisted that this boxing was somehow linked to Wang Lun. Following the 1813 uprising, further accusations appeared including one more from the Linqing area mentioning garbled names of several boxing groups. One Plum Flower Boxing teacher was said to have 3,000 disciples, and according to the accusation: "In several places south of Linqing city, they are all the Yi-huo [sic] boxing sect, which is actually Wang Lun's boxing sect."[10]

It is regrettable that we have no further information on the Yi-he Boxing of this period, for the language of the documents on these cases comes closest to suggesting a boxing group with some clearly sectarian content or association. One might conclude that the Yi-he Boxers did exist as a martial arts group with some heterodox rituals, but the government was simply incapable of finding any. However, the government proved quite efficient in most of its sectarian investigations of this period, and we should not exclude the possibility that it was simply Wang Lun's dramatic combination of boxing and sectarian doctrine that made officials suspicious of *all* boxing groups. It is certainly true that the next time the Yi-he Boxing appeared on the historical record, its sectarian content was much diluted.

This next appearance came in 1808, with the edict condemning this and other groups active on the Shandong-Jiangsu-Anhui-Henan border. This was the first document cited by Lao Nai-xuan, and we have discussed it above. Here there was no indication of any sectarian connection, and the Yi-he Boxing was associated above all with semi-criminal drifter and gambling elements in the towns of this region. Though none of the documents gives any information on the techniques of this boxing, the Tiger-Tail Whip (which was proscribed at the same time) did have a series of magical spells which were supposed to allow one to overcome an opponent from a distance of thirty paces.[11] This same technique had been attributed to the Guan county Yi-he Boxers of 1778.[12]

The final appearance of the Yi-he Boxing was in connection with the 1813 Eight Trigrams, and the examples here are those alluded to in the second document of Lao Nai-xuan's pamphlet. There were actually two Yi-he groups mentioned in the Na-yan-cheng memorial cited by Lao, but one had nothing to do with boxing. An "Yi-he school sect" (Yi-he men-jiao), apparently related to the Li Trigram, was active in the Qingzhou area, along the Grand Canal south of Tianjin. It practiced meditation and breathing exercises; some of its teachers did healing; it had a text which the authorities found lacking in any heterodox content; it included a large number of women among its adherents; but it used no charms or other forbidden magic, and took no part in the 1813 rebellion. It was, in short, a typical pacific White Lotus sect with neither martial arts nor seditious activities. It is worth noting largely because it reminds us that very different groups could use similar names.[13]

The crucial examples of sectarian–Yi-he Boxing contact in the 1810s come from the area along the Grand Canal, south and west of Dezhou, in northwest Shandong. Here there are several clear examples of boxing groups associated with sectarians of the Li Trigram. One man selling turbans at a temple fair in En county from the 1780s into the 1800s belonged to the Li Trigram and practiced healing. His family had passed the techniques of Yin-Yang Boxing from father to son, relying on it for self protection.[14] Two other recognized sectarians practiced something called Six Reclining Boxing (Liu-tang quan). According to one, "In the sixth year of Jia-qing [1801] I took Zhou De-qian as a teacher and learned Six Reclining Boxing. [He] also passed on the Bai Yang teaching to me."[15] The second practitioner was Guo Wei-zheng (or -zhen), from Gucheng, on the Zhili side of the canal. Guo learned the boxing from a relative, and then later was introduced into the Li Trigram sect by another teacher.[16] Finally there are two accusations of sectarians practicing Yi-he Boxing—one this same Guo Wei-zheng.

It is important to stress that none of the people involved in this boxing actually participated in the 1813 uprising. They all had some sort of connection to Song Yue-long, the boxing leader from Dezhou. In 1812, a sectarian living in the region had invited the Henan boxing leader and "King of Earth" of the 1813 rebels, Feng Ke-shan, to meet Song. After a match which resulted in Song acknowledging the superiority of Feng's boxing, Song was introduced into the Li Trigram. During the next year, Song became Feng's most important contact and used his boxing to recruit men into the sect. But when

Feng returned in the fall of 1813 to inform Song of preparations for the uprising, Song claimed he had too few followers to rebel. Accordingly, it was decided that he would await Li Wen-cheng's march north from Henan and join the rebellion at that point. In the end, none ever moved into action. The connection of these people to the 1813 rebellion is then marginal at best—but they were unquestionably linked to White Lotus sects.[17]

The Yi-he Boxing mentioned in the Na-yan-cheng memorial cited by Lao Nai-xuan was from this group. It involved two individuals, Ge Li-ye and his great-uncle Ge Wen-zhi, whom Song Yue-long counted among his followers.[18] Ge Li-ye was a poor homeless carter from Gucheng with no immediate family. According to Li-ye's confession, Ge Wen-zhi was "a military branch disciple of Liu Kun's Old Heavenly Gate Sect (Lao tian-men jiao), spreading and practicing Yi-he Boxing and Kicking (Yi-he quan-jiao)." In the fall of 1813, Ge Li-ye was recruited into the sect, and taught the distinctive eight-character mantra of the White Lotus. Told of the impending uprising, he was urged to recruit wealthy young men.[19] Unfortunately, this is all we know about the boxing in this case. Liu Kun had been introduced into the White Lotus only in the summer of 1812, by the same sectarian who had arranged the meeting of Feng Ke-shan and Song Yue-long, but his confession makes no mention of boxing or of Ge Wen-zhi as a disciple.[20] While it is quite likely that Ge Wen-zhi did indeed practice Yi-he Boxing, it may well be that his great-nephew (who was only brought into the sect at the last moment) was misinformed about the source of this boxing and its relationship to the sects.[21]

The second example follows more closely the normal pattern of sect-boxing relationships in this area. According to the confession of one Lü Fu from Dezhou: "During the 17th year of Jia-qing [1812], he took the previously executed Guo Wei-zhen as a teacher, burned incense and made offerings of tea. [Guo] taught him to recite incantations and called it the Li Trigram sect. [He] also passed on the Yi-he Boxing."[22] We know from his own confession that Guo Wei-zheng also practiced the Six Reclining Boxing, and that his Li Trigram teaching had been learned much earlier from another teacher. One of Guo's disciples had a copy of the sectarian scripture "The Cycle of the Three Buddhas" (San-fo lun), which indicates a fairly serious religious interest.[23] While it is clear that Guo was both a boxer and a sectarian, it is unlikely that there was any organizational connection between his Yi-he Boxing and his religious sect, and it was certainly not the only form of boxing that he practiced.

These two cases are the only ones from this area—and they form the heart of the case usually made for the link between Yi-he Boxing and the White Lotus sects. In my mind, the link is rather weak. While there is no doubt that several of these boxers were also sectarians, the link tended to be tenuous—with the sectarian component coming late and being weakly held. Guo Wei-zheng may have been an exception: he had joined the Li Trigram sect in 1798, but the fact that he practiced several types of boxing makes his connection to the Yi-he school something less than a total commitment. If we consider the various possible modes of sect-boxer relationship, the linkages here seem slightly more than an incidental connection. But if the Yi-he Boxers were an auxiliary group to the White Lotus sects, serving as an avenue for recruitment, they were only one of several boxing groups which had that same function.

If these cases from the Dezhou region form the heart of the case for the sectarian origins of the Boxers, those arguing against this view would seem to have a better case from Jinshan county in southwest Shandong. Throughout this area, there was a well-established network of sectarians belonging to the Li Trigram. They recited the eight-character mantra, made regular contributions to a sect leader, and had chants and songs for the avoidance of calamities. In the fall of 1812, Xu An-guo, from Changyuan in southern Zhili, came as a representative of Lin Qing and Li Wen-cheng's Eight Trigrams to recruit sectarians in this region. Xu was successful in persuading the Jinshan leader Cui Shi-jun of the superiority of his Zhen Trigram teaching, apparently by stressing the virtues of its meditation and disaster-avoidance techniques. By the spring of 1813, Xu informed his recruits of the coming kalpa, and the process of preparing for it (and for rebellion) began.[24]

This process was interrupted in the fall of 1813 when the energetic acting magistrate Wu Jie began the investigations which ultimately uncovered the sect and precipitated the 1813 rebellion in Henan and Zhili.[25] Crucial in the investigations and arrests were two runners of the county yamen who were Yi-he Boxers. This should not surprise us, for the 1808 imperial edict on the Yi-he Boxers in this region had explictly noted their "conspir[ing] with yamen clerks who act as their eyes and ears."[26] For boxers frequently involved in gambling and other forbidden activities, such contacts within the official establishment were extremely important. But the sectarian leader Cui Shi-jun was also actively courting these same people, inviting all the yamen runners to a banquet in the seventh month.[27] Somewhere in the process of recruitment and competition (or perhaps long before) the Yi-he Boxers became "mortal enemies of the sectarian outlaws." According to Wu Jie, the two groups were like "fire and water."[28]

In his campaign against the sectarians, Wu Jie decided that the Yi-he Boxers were an extremely useful ally, and he posted proclamations recruiting "red-blooded youths" from the organization to join the local military for the campaign against the sectarians. The language of the proclamation is significant, for it began by noting that this type of boxing had been prohibited, and members who joined the local forces were to "rid themselves of their old habits, and thoroughly reform their past errors." They were to "change from the heterodox and return to the orthodox."[29]

There is no question, then, that despite the antagonism between the Yi-he Boxers and the White Lotus sectarians, the boxers themselves were also considered "heterodox." It is also clear that despite their antagonism to the White Lotus, these boxers were not easily made into pawns of the government. Late in 1813, the Shandong governor noted rising banditry in the southwest of the province in the wake of the sectarian rising. Among the bandits he noted that Yi-he Boxers and the Red Brick Society (Hong-zhuan hui) were most numerous. "Some claimed to be rebels and burned and robbed in the villages; others passed themselves off as militia and robbed peaceful citizens."[30]

In all likelihood, the "heterodoxy" of the Yi-he Boxing came from the fact that they used spells and incantations in their rituals. We have noted that as early as the time of the Wang Lun uprising, the Yi-he Boxers in this southwest Shandong region were called the "Yi-he Boxing heterodox sect"—an epithet usually not added to descriptions of the boxers who emerged in the Dezhou area in connection with the sects of 1813. The 1808 prohibition of these boxers also branded them "heterodox." Regrettably we know very little about Yi-he ritual which would allow us to define the nature of that heterodoxy, but there is one reference to Jinshan boxers which is extremely suggestive. A blacksmith arrested in 1814 confessed that in 1804 he had studied martial arts in Jinshan. He himself learned the use of a pig-butchering knife and not any boxing technique, but he was told of his instructor: "Meng is an Yi-he Boxer. They have incantations. There are four sentences: iron helmet, iron armor, iron chain mail, and so forth." [31] While this reference is isolated, third-hand, and ten years after the events reported, it strongly suggests not only the use of magical spells, but also some form of invulnerability ritual.

If nothing else, this survey of sources on the Yi-he Boxers of the mid-Qing should help explain why there is such division of opinion on the relationship between these boxers and the White Lotus sectarians. The record is indeed contradictory. But I believe it also suggests a solution. An approach simply based upon organizations' names—with the assumption that all groups which called themselves Yi-he Boxers were the same thing—is unlikely to be very fruitful. In different periods and different places, groups with the same name behaved in very different ways. More important than what a group of boxers called itself is what that group did, and in this respect I believe the record suggests the following.

Yi-he Boxing emerged sometime in the late eighteenth century, and while it had no direct contact with Wang Lun's rebellion, it did involve some use of magical incantation which made it anathema to the authorities. It spread along the borders of western Shandong, where it became popular among underworld figures involved in a variety of activities, from gambling to salt smuggling, prohibited by the authorities but not necessarily unpopular with the local residents. Its martial arts skills (possibly including invulnerability rituals) led some officials to use the group against the sectarians of 1813, and antagonism between the boxers and White Lotus sometimes made this possible. But the independence of the martial arts groups was never fully lost, even when recruited into local militia units.

This picture, I believe, easily fits all the cases except those from the Dezhou area. For those, it seems to me that several possibilities exist. Most probably, these were also independent boxer groups—by now organization-ally quite divorced from those of the southwest—which formed temporary relationships with White Lotus sectarians, just as the boxers of the southwest formed a temporary relationship with the government *against* the White Lotus. The looseness of martial arts organizations generally, with boxers often switching teachers and adding new techniques, makes it quite possible that boxers in different areas could go quite different ways. But it is also possible that these were two utterly different boxing schools. "Yi-he" was in fact quite a common name. We have already noted a pacific meditation sect, unconnected to the boxers, which had the same name. And a glance at any detailed map of northwest Shandong will reveal villages called Yi-he scattered across the plains. It is thus possible that two completely different groups of boxers came up with the same name—those in southwest Shandong more active among gamblers and yamen runners, those in the northwest entering into closer relationships with the White Lotus sects.

But if this is an adequate picture of the mid-Qing Yi-he Boxers, what does it tell us about the relationship to the Boxers of 1898–1900? Most significantly, we must note the lack of any mention of the distinctive Boxer possession ritual (*jiang-shen fu-ti*) of the late nineteenth century, and the single and problematic reference to invulnerability. Negative evidence is of course dangerous, but we should remember the terms of the Qing law on heterodoxy cited at the beginning of chapter 2. The very first line prohibited "teachers and shamans who call down heterodox gods [*jiang xie-shen*]." Given the concern in official documents to extract confessions and gather evidence in terms of the official code, it is almost inconceivable that these boxers could have practiced shamanistic possession without some mention by the authorities.

The implications of this seem to me quite clear: whatever they were, the Yi-he Boxers of the mid-Qing were ritually distinct from the late Qing Boxers. I would argue that those who have attempted to trace origins by following a common *name* have been following a false trail. The proper approach, I believe, is that taken in this monograph: seeking the source of rituals and practices, and seeking it more in contemporary popular culture than in distant sectarian organizations.

Abbreviations Used
in the Notes

ABC   American Board of Commissioners of Foreign Missions [Congregationalist] papers. Houghton Library, Harvard University.

AJ   *Shandong Yi-he-tuan an-juan* (山東義和團案卷). Edited by Zhong-guo she-hui ke-xue-yuan jin-dai-shi yan-jiu-suo, jin-dai-shi zi-liao bian-ji-shi (中國社會科學院近代史研究所近代史資料編輯室). Jinan: 1980.

BFM   Presbyterian Church in the U.S.A., Board of Foreign Missions, Correspondence and Reports, China, 1837–1911. (Microfilm)

CASS   Chinese Academy of Social Sciences.

C : IGC   China: Inspectorate General of Customs. *Returns of Trade and Trade Reports.*

CBOC   *Chou-bi ou-cun* (籌筆偶存). Edited by Zhong-guo she-hui ke-xue-yuan, jin-dai-shi yan-jiu-suo (中國社會科學院近代史研究所) and Zhong-guo di-yi li-shi dang-an-guan (中國第一歷史檔案舘). Beijing: 1983.

CR   *Chinese Recorder and Missionary Journal*

DASL   *Yi-he-tuan dang-an shi-liao* (義和團檔案史料). Edited by Gu-gong bo-wu-yuan Ming-Qing dang-an-bu (故宮博物院明清檔案部). Beijing: 1959.

DG   Dao-guang reign (1821–1850) 道光

FRUS   United States Congress. House of Representatives. *Papers Relating to the Foreign Relations of the United States.*

GX   Guang-xu reign (1875–1908) 光緒

GZD   Gong-zhong-dang 宮中檔 (Palace memorial archive). National Palace Museum, Taiwan.

I.G.   John King Fairbank et al., eds. *The I.G. in Peking: Letters of Robert Hart of the Chinese Maritime Customs, 1868–1907.* Cambridge, Mass.: 1975.

JFJL   *Qin-ding ping-ding jiao-fei ji-lüe* (欽定平定教匪紀略). N.P.: 1816; Taibei reprint: 1971.

JNCBRAS   *Journal of the North China Branch of the Royal Asiatic Society*

JQ   Jia-qing reign (1796–1820) 嘉慶

JWJAD   *Jiao-wu jiao-an dang* (教務教案檔). Edited by Zhong-yang yan-jiu-yuan jin-dai-shi yan-jiu-suo (中央研究院近代史研究所). Taibei: 1977, 1980.

LFZZ   Jun-ji-chu lu-fu zou-zhe (軍機處錄復奏折). First Historical Archives, Palace Museum, Beijing.

LBH   Li Bing-heng (李秉衡). *Li Zhong-jie gong (Jian-tang) zou-yi* (李忠節公 (鑑堂) 奏議). Liaoning: 1930.

MQ   Ming-Qing archives (First Historical Archives). Palace Museum, Beijing.

NCH   *North China Herald*

NYC   Na-yan-cheng (那彥成). *Na-wen-yi gong zou-yi* (那文毅公奏議). N.p.: 1834, Taibei reprint, 1968.

QDDASLCB   *Qing-dai dang-an shi-liao cong-bian* (清代檔案史料叢編). Edited by Ming-Qing archives section of the Palace Museum. Beijing: Zhong-hua, 1979.

QL   Qian-long reign (1736–1795) 乾隆

QSL	*Qing shi-lu* (清實錄)
SDDC	*Shandong Yi-he-tuan diao-cha zi-liao xuan-bian* (山東義和團調查資料選編). Edited by Shandong da-xue li-shi-xi jin-dai-shi jiao-yan-shi (山東大學歷史系近代史教研室). Jinan: 1980.
SD Survey	The original manuscripts from which the above title was selected—usually bound by county. Cited if the interview was not published in SDDC.
SDJDSZL	*Shandong jin-dai-shi zi-liao* (山東近代史資料). Edited by Shandong-sheng li-shi xue-hui (山東省歷史學會). Jinan: 1961.
SDSZZL	*Shandong sheng-zhi zi-liao* (山東省志資料). Jinan: irregular periodical.
SDXF	Shandong xun-fu dang-an (山東巡撫檔案). First Historical Archives, Palace Museum, Beijing.
SJSDA	*Song Jing-shi dang-an shi-liao* (宋景詩檔案史料). Edited by Guo-jia dang-an-ju Ming-Qing dang-an-guan (國家檔案局明清檔案館). Beijing: 1969.
TZ	Tong-zhi reign (1862–1874) 同治
XF	Xian-feng reign (1851–1861) 咸豐
YHT	*Yi-he-tuan* (義和團). 4 vols. Shanghai: 1951.
YHTSL	*Yi-he-tuan shi-liao* (義和團史料). Edited by Zhong-guo she-hui ke-xue-yuan jin-dai-shi yan-jiu-suo (中國社會科學院近代史研究所). Beijing: 1982.
YLSL	*Yi-he-tuan yuan-liu shi-liao* (義和團源流史料) Edited by Lu Jing-qi (陸景琪) and Cheng Xiao (程嘯). Beijing: 1980.
YZ	Yong-zheng reign (1723–1735) 雍正

Notes

PREFACE

1. A paper previewing this publication was kindly sent to me by Philip Huang. The collection appears to include previously unpublished sections of the Shandong governor's archive that I saw in Beijing, plus documents previously seen in the Taiwan-published *Jiao-wu jiao-an dang*, as well as some documents from private collections that I have not seen. Most pleasingly, the paper introducing the collection presents an analysis of the Boxer origins closer to my own than any article I have previously seen in Chinese. (See Cheng Xiao and Zhu Jin-fu, "'Yi-he tuan dang-an shi-liao xu-pian' chu-tan," paper prepared for the conference commemorating the sixtieth anniversary of the First Historical Archives, October 1985.)

CHAPTER ONE

1. Robert Coltman, Jr., *The Chinese, Their Present and Future: Medical, Political and Social* (Philadelphia: F. A. Davis, 1891), 40. Coltman was passing through Pingyuan county in Shandong at the time.
2. Amano Motonosuke, *Santō nōgyō keizairon* (Dairen: 1936), 2–6; Hou Jen-zhi, *Xu tian-xia jun-guo li-bing shu: Shandong zhi bu* (Beiping: Harvard-Yanjing Institute, 1941), 57–58.
3. Amano Motonosuke, 6–15; Sun Jing-zhi, *Hua-bei jing-ji di-li* (Beijing: Science Press, 1957), 119.
4. Zhang Xin-yi, "Shandong-sheng nong-ye gai-kuang gu-ji bao-gao," *Tong-ji yue-bao* 3.1 (January 1931): 20–45; Zhang Xin-yi, "Hebei-sheng nong-ye gai-kuang gu-ji bao-gao," *Tong-ji yue-bao* 2.11 (November 1930): 1–56.
5. Sun Jing-zhi, 15.
6. G. William Skinner, "Regional Urbanization in Nineteenth-Century China," and "Cities and the Hierarchy of Local Systems," in *The City in Late*

Imperial China, ed. G. William Skinner (Stanford: Stanford University Press, 1977), 211–249, 275–351. Quotes from pp. 283, 322.

7. China: Inspectorate General of Customs, *Reports of Trade at the Treaty Ports* (hereafter cited as C:IGC), passim, but especially 1876, 92–93; and maps in 1875, 120 f.; 1876, 120 f. Transit passes were not used in the north, as northern likin (easily evaded by commerce that moved largely overland) was lower than the cost of the pass. Thus we have only qualitative statements from the northern ports on the extent of their trade. But the Tianjin commissioner did note that following the opening of Zhenjiang after the Taiping Rebellion, the Yangzi port was beginning to serve markets in Henan and northern Anhui formerly served from Tianjin (C:IGC, 1871–1872, 34–35.) A later commissioner would note only "the northern portions of the provinces of Shantung and Honan" as the area served by Tianjin. (C:IGC, 1880, 258.)

8. It appears that Skinner's boundary has been placed just south of the Huai because this is the center of a "periphery" defined by lower population density. In fact, I suspect that this "periphery" represents only the sparsely populated marshy floodplain of the Huai.

9. Zhang Ru-mei to Liu Kun-yi, [GX 24]/9/26, in *Shandong xun-fu dang-an*, First Historical Archives, Beijing (hereafter cited as SDXF), incoming and outgoing telegrams.

10. It must be admitted that much of the reason for shifting to a provincial unit of analysis is purely practical: it was the administrative area on the basis of which socio-economic data were collected. Often, however, we are as much interested in social conditions elsewhere on the north China plain, and where data permit I shall discuss those conditions beyond the borders of Shandong.

11. Some comment is in order on sources, which may be divided into quantitative and qualitative records. The latter, largely nineteenth-century travellers' tales and gazetteers, I shall cite individually at appropriate points in the text. The quantitative sources warrant a more general introduction. During the course of this research I have developed a data base with a number of variables for each county in Shandong, and this data base represents the foundation for all quantitative analysis in this study. Unless specifically noted otherwise, all quantitative data mentioned below come from this data base. (Persons interested in inspecting or using the raw data are invited to contact the author.)

The population figures represent my best estimate, from a variety of Republican period sources (deflated to adjust for the twentieth-century growth of such cities as Qingdao, Chefoo, and Jinan), of county populations at the turn of the century. The key sources are the *Zhongguo shi-ye-zhi: Shandong-sheng* (Shanghai: International Trade Office of the Ministry of Industry, 1934), which includes 1933 figures, plus Interior Ministry figures for 1928 (incomplete) and Shandong Civil Affairs Bureau figures for 1930; household and peasant household estimates in Zhang Xin-yi, "Shandong-sheng nong-ye gai-kuang gu-ji bao-gao"; and Guan Wei-lan, *Zhong-hua min-guo xing-zheng qu-hua ji tu-di ren-kou tong-ji-biao* (Taibei, 1955), whose population figures actually derive from Zhang Yu-zeng and Liu Jing-zhi,

Shandong zheng-su shi-cha ji ([Jinan?]: Shandong Printing Bureau, 1934). My first choice was to use Guan Wei-lan, which is also Skinner's source, correcting it only for obvious copying errors. But especially along the Qingdao-Jinan railway, Guan's estimates are significantly higher than the others, and while they may correctly reflect the situation in the 1930s, they seem inappropriate for our purposes. In cases where Guan's figure seemed inordinately high, I adopted an appropriate medium range figure from the *Shi-ye-zhi*.

County areas (for population densities) come from Guan Wei-lan. Cultivated area generally follows the estimate in the *Shi-ye-zhi*; but Zhang Xin-yi's estimates were also consulted and sometimes used, as were those in Nong-shang-bu, *Nong-shang tong-ji-biao, 1918* (Beijing: Ministry of Agriculture and Commerce, 1922). In general the procedure was to adopt the best estimate considering percentages of cultivated land in surrounding topographically similar counties. Agricultural output, crop distribution patterns and crop indexes were based on Zhang Xin-yi, though his figures for peanuts and tobacco are taken to be substantial increases over the late nineteenth century levels, and most of the area in those crops is assumed to have been planted in millet.

Estimates of the extent of landlordism (more precisely: the percentage of cultivated land that is rented) are based on figures in the *Shi-ye-zhi*; John Lossing Buck, *Land Utilization in China, Statistics* (Shanghai: University of Nanjing, 1937); Jing Su and Luo Lun, *Qing-dai Shandong jing-ying di-zhu de she-hui xing-zhi* (Jinan: Shandong-sheng Xin-hua shu-dian, 1959); and 1930 figures from the Ministry of Agriculture and Mining in Amano Motonosuke, *Santō nōgyō keizairon*. Most of these sources provide figures for the number of owners, owner-tenants, and part tenants which I have converted into a single estimate for percentage of land rented using the procedures introduced in my article "Number Games: A Note on Land Distribution in Prerevolutionary China," *Modern China* 7.4 (1981).

Gentry strength in each county has been measured by the number of *ju-ren* listed in the Ming and Qing examination records in the *Shandong tong-zhi*. The count of metropolitan officials from each county includes all Beijing officials listed in the *Da-Qing jin-shen quan-shu* for the fall of 1879, and the *Da-Qing Jue-zhi quan-lan* for the fall of 1889 and 1899. The commercial tax quotas are the "miscellaneous" taxes in silver listed in the 1899 edition of this same source.

Measures of the incidence and severity of natural disasters have been developed from data in the First Historical Archives (Ming-Qing archives) in Beijing. Two measures were used. The first is an attempt to measure the incidence of natural disasters, their severity, and the number of villages affected in each county for the years 1892–1895. Four memorials list the number of villages suffering total, 80%, 70%, 50–60%, "relatively heavy," and "relatively light" loss of crops, and corresponding tax remissions or delayed collection. I have multiplied the number of affected villages by the percentage of crop loss to produce a "disaster index" for each county. The sources are four memorials by Li Bing-heng, GX 20/12/13 (Hu-ke ti-ben, GX 20, no. 21), GX 21/11/29 (GX 21, no. 27), GX 22/8/7 (GX 22, no. 25), GX 23/4/21

(GX 23, no. 25). A second, and rather less useful measure, simply counts the number of times between 1868 and 1899 that taxes in a county were remitted on account of natural disasters. Li Bing-heng, GX 21/11/19 (Hu-ke ti-ben, no. 27) provides figures on 1868–1891. The four memorials above (for which only remissions [for losses 50% or greater], not postponements, are counted) cover 1892–95; and the *Da-Qing shi-lu* (Mukden, 1937; hereafter cited as QSL), 398:10a–10b, 413:6a–6b, 435:22b, 456:3a, covers 1896–1899. (N.B. The Shi-lu records are essentially an abbreviation of long memorials such as those cited on 1892–95. The counties are listed in order of the extent of remission [and severity of disaster]. Counties are listed in a conventional order [the same order followed in all official publications] within each level of remission. Thus, although the counties appear as one unbroken list, the "code" can be broken by noting when the list of counties returns to the top of the sequence, indicating the beginning of the next lower level of remission. In my count, I have eliminated those counties whose taxes were only postponed, not remitted, to make them consistent with the other sources.) I should note that while these data are useful in identifying counties affected by severe natural disasters, they are much better at identifying areas of major flooding than they are in indicating reduced harvests from drought—a perennial problem in the northwest. Ideally, the imperially mandated semi-annual crop reports should indicate reduced harvests due to drought. Unfortunately, by the late Qing, these were handled in an absolutely routine fashion in Shandong (in contrast to Zhili under Li Hong-zhang) and virtually without exception, every county reported "slightly over 50%" harvests for every year from 1890–1898. It is, however, notable that it was on the peninsula that several counties, especially Ye and Jiaozhou, regularly reported 60% harvests. (For an example, see Zhang Ru-mei, GX 23/12/20 [Hu-ke ti-ben, GX 23, no. 24].)

Finally Board of Punishment records were examined, and 107 memorials read on bandit incidents in Shandong and bordering counties in Jiangsu, Henan, Anhui, and Zhili. These produced 171 alleged bandits from Shandong, in 49 Shandong cases and 58 from bordering prefectures. Their distribution by county was recorded, and other information on the timing of incidents, size of bands, type of weapons and loot was tabulated which I shall refer to when we discuss the question of banditry. All of these data come from *Xing-ke ti-ben* (*dao-an*, robbery) from the 1890s, found in the First Historical Archives in Beijing. For a typical example see Zhang Yue, GX 16/9/24 (GX 16, no. 108).

12. Shi Nian-hai, *Zhong-guo de yun-he* (Chongqing: History Press, 1944), 139–140.

13. See Chapter 3, pp. 69–73.

14. J. A. Danforth, 21/10/1861, Presbyterian Church in the U.S.A., Board of Foreign Missions, Correspondence and Reports, China, 1837–1911 (microfilm, hereafter cited as BFM), reel 196.

15. John Markham, "Notes on the Shantung Province, being a Journey from Chefoo to Tsiuhsien, the City of Mencius," *Journal of the North China Branch of the Royal Asiatic Society* (Hereafter: JNCBRAS) 6 (1869–1870): 1–5;

R. F. Johnston, *Lion and Dragon in Northern China* (London: John Murray, 1910), 59, 162–166; Alex Armstrong, *Shantung (China), A General Outline of the Geography and History of the Province; A Sketch of its Missions and Notes of a Journey to the Tomb of Confucius* (Shanghai: Shanghai Mercury, 1891), 4–14, 56–83.

16. R. J. Johnston, 74, 158. A twentieth-century survey of counties in Shandong also consistently noted the absence of banditry on the peninsula. (Zhang Yu-zeng and Liu Jing-zhi, 651–727.)

17. In Sun Jing-zhi's description of Shandong's agricultural regions, he notes (pp. 134–135) that the peninsula in the mid-twentieth century produced 41.8 percent of the province's sweet potatoes.

18. Zhang Yu-zeng and Liu Jing-zhi, 651–727. Although these might seem common enough distinctions, Zhang and Liu do not make them about western Shandong.

19. A. Williamson, "Notes on the North of China, Its Productions and Communications," JNCBRAS 4 (1867): 59. Dengzhou was another important center of gentry power: Armstrong (p. 61) found it "chiefly noted for the pride of its broken-down aristocracy."

20. Armstrong, 52. Cf. Jing Su and Luo Lun, *Qing-dai Shandong jing-ying di-zhu di she-hui xing-zhi* (Jinan: Shandong People's Press, 1959), 18–24.

21. C:IGC, 1899, II:81–82.

22. C:IGC, 1866, 81.

23. Markham, "Notes on Shantung," 6–13.

24. C:IGC, 1866, 81.

25. Sun Jing-zhi, 119.

26. Peanut exports through Zhenjiang from southern Shandong and northern Jiangsu increased from 61 piculs in 1888 to 558,933 in 1897. (C:IGC, 1897; II:206–207.)

27. Armstrong, 55.

28. Markham, "Notes on Shantung," 22–25. Cf. Armstrong (p. 55) on the only prefectural capital in this region, Yizhou, which was described as "not at all a rich city."

29. Jing Su and Luo Lun, 34–36.

30. Henry Ellis, *Journal of the Proceedings of the Late Embassy to China* (London: John Murrary, 1817), 261. Cf. John Francis Davis, *Sketches of China* (London: Charles Knight, 1841), 1:257–259.

31. L. Richard, *Comprehensive Geography of the Chinese Empire and Dependencies*, M. Kennelly, trans. (Shanghai, T'usewei Press, 1908), 84; Jing Su and Luo Lun, 10–18. By the late 1880s, the Zhenjiang customs reports were noting the substantial importation of old iron into southern Shandong, and Jining was surely the main receiver. In 1892–93, flint stones begin to appear prominently—suggesting that much of the production may have been of weapons for the troubled region on Shandong's southern border. (C:IGC, 1889, II:216–217; 1893, II:262.)

32. This is the one area where my regions differ significantly from those of Sun Jing-zhi, whose five agricultural regions (pp. 130–135) combine my Jining and Southwest regions.

33. Jona. Lees, "Notes on a Journey from Tientsin to Chi-Nan Fu," *Chinese Recorder and Missionary Journal* (hereafter: CR) 1.6 (October 1868): 101–102.

34. *Changqing xian-zhi* (1935), 1:25a–25b; *Qihe xian-zhi* (1933), *shou-juan*: 12b–16a; Richard Simpson Gundry, *China, Present and Past; Foreign Intercourse, Progress and Resources; the Missionary Question, etc.* (London: Chapman and Hall, 1895), 364–376; Coltman, *The Chinese*, 32–57; Amano Motonosuke, 34–35.

35. Shi Nian-hai, 158–159. In this year, the Huai River, whose clearer waters were used to keep the Yellow River away from the southern entrance to the canal, was too low on account of drought in its upper reaches. As a result the Yellow backed up into the catch basins used to collect the Huai and funnel it toward the canal. When the Yellow receded, the basins were so silted up as to effectively preclude future cleansing action by the Huai.

36. W. R. Charles, "The Grand Canal of China," JNCBRAS 31 (1896–1897): 102–115. Cf. Shi Nian-hai, 160–161, 171–175; Sun Jing-zhi, 121; Harold C. Hinton, *The Grain Tribute System of China (1845–1911)* (Cambridge, Mass.: Harvard University Press, 1956).

37. Davis, *Sketches of China*, 242.

38. Williamson, "Notes on the North of China," 59.

39. F. H. Chapin to J. Smith, 13/11/1897, American Board of Commissioners of Foreign Missions Papers. Houghton Library, Harvard University (hereafter cited as ABC), 16.3.12, vol. 18, no. 46.

40. Armstrong, 67. On Linqing's earlier prosperity and estimated population, see Jing Su and Luo Lun, 3–10.

41. The Chiping gazetteers contain repeated references to "local strongmen" (*tu-hao*) in neighboring Yucheng banding together to block the streams dredged to drain water from Chiping—actions which Chiping apparently lacked the political clout to overcome. See *Chiping xian-zhi* (1710), 107; (1935) 12:17a–19b; Cf. ibid., 2:12b–13a, 3:77a–77b.

42. Sun Jing-zhi, 131–132; Zhang Yu-zeng and Liu Jing-zhi, 431–650.

43. C:IGC, 1877, II:251; 1879, II:258, 269–271.

44. J. H. Laughlin and Kuo Tsy King, "Narrative of the Presbyter of Shantung, 1888–1889," n.d., BFM, reel 207.

45. *Pingyuan xian-zhi* (1749; Taibei reprint, 1976) 9:9a–12b; *Chiping xian-zhi* (1710; Taibei reprint, 1976), preface: 3a.

46. *Gaotang xiang-tu-zhi* (1906; Taibei reprint, 1968), 63–65.

47. A summary of Chiping's Kang-xi era gazetteer (pp. 104–106) is typical for this area: 1368: city seized by rebels; 1641: locusts, famine and epidemics, nine-tenths of the population dies and the fields lie abandoned; people eat each other; 1643: city seized; 1646: rebels seize the city; 1647–49: unceasing warfare; 1650–1651, 1655: Yellow River floods. Cf. *Gaotang xiang-tu-zhi*, 31–33.

48. *Chiping xian-zhi* (1710), 123–124, 157–158; *Changqing xian-zhi* (1835), 5:2a. Compare this to Shan county in the Southwest, where only 13 percent of the population was dropped from the tax rolls. (*Shan xian-zhi* [1759], 3:2a–2b.)

49. *Gaotang xiang-tu-zhi*, 61; *Qihe xian-zhi* (1737), 3 : 1b–4b.

50. *Guancheng xian-zhi* (1838) 10 : 11a–11b; Jing Su and Luo Lun, 2–5. The figures on *ju-ren* from Linqing tell an interesting story: from 1450 to 1650, the department averaged 47.25 degree-holders for every fifty-year period. From 1650–1900 (though the provincial *ju-ren* quotas increased significantly), it averaged only 11.6.

51. Shandong da-xue li-shi-xi, *Shandong di-fang-shi jiang-shou ti-yao* (Jinan: Shandong People's Press, 1960), 42–44; *Gaotang xiang-tu-zhi*, 33–35; *Chiping xian-zhi* (1935; Taibei reprint, 1968), 11 : 17a–17b.

52. Markham, "Notes on Shantung," 13. Liu Kwang-ching, "The Ch'ing Restoration," in John K. Fairbank, ed., *The Cambridge History of China*, vol. 10: *Late Ch'ing, 1800–1911, Part I* (Cambridge: Cambridge University Press, 1978), 464–477, gives a good summary of this period. Kanbe Teruo, "Shindai kōki Santōshō ni okeru 'danhi' to nōson mondai," *Shirin* 55.4 (July 1972): 78, shows clearly the concentration of tax-resistance movements in the northwest region.

53. Philip C. C. Huang, *The Peasant Economy and Social Change in North China* (Stanford: 1985). Sun Jing-zhi; Zhang Xin-yi, "Hebei-sheng nong-ye gai-kuang gu-ji bao-gao," *Tong-ji yue-bao* 2.11 (November 1930): 1–56; Zhili-sheng shang-pin chen-lie-suo, *Di-yi-ci diao-cha shi-ye bao-gao shu* (Tianjin, 1917), Regions 7 (Grand Canal) and 8 (Southern Zhili), give rather complete descriptions of the predominantly agricultural and relatively depressed state of the Shandong-Zhili border region in the early Republic.

54. Ellis, *Journal of an Embassy*, 267.

55. Davis, *Sketches of China* 1 : 263.

56. George M. Stenz, *Life of Father Richard Henle, S.V.D., Missionary in China, Assassinated November 1, 1897*, trans. Elizabeth Ruff (Techny, Illinois: Mission Press, 1915), 35.

57. See Huang Chun-yao, *Shan-zuo bi-tan* (Changsha: Commercial Press, 1938), 3, for a Ming reference to banditry on the southern border. The *Shan xian-zhi* (1929), 20 : 30a, also explains the banditry in terms of the nearby borders, referring to a time sometime prior to the 1855 shift in the Yellow River.

58. Cited in Hou Ren-zhi, 57.

59. *Cao xian-zhi* (1884), 4 : 11b. In general, the Cao and Shan county gazetteers are more preoccupied with flooding and river works than any I have ever seen. In addition to those already cited, see *Cao xian-zhi* (1716), and *Shan xian-zhi* (1759).

60. Cited in *Cao xian-zhi* (1884), 1 : 17a–17b. (The original passage is unfortunately almost completely illegible in the 1716 gazetteer that I examined.)

61. *Shan xian-zhi* (1759), 2 : 77b.

62. Edict of DG 6/3, QSL, [DG] 96 : 22a–23a, cited in Kobayashi Kasumi, "Kōsō, kōryō tōsō no kanata—kakyū seikatsu no omoi to seijiteki shūkyōteki jiritsu no michi—" *Shisō* 584 (1973): 244; Zhong Xiang, DG 14/1/8, in Lu Jing-qi and Cheng Xiao, *Yi-he-tuan yuan-liu shi-liao* (Beijing: People's University, 1980; hereafter cited as YLSL), 108.

63. One author even blamed the banditry on smuggling. Caozhou, he wrote, "appears to be constantly in a state of rebellion, on account of dissatisfaction caused by the salt monopoly which the Government exercises." (Reverend Miles Greenward, letter of 17/4/1878, in Armstrong, 126.)

64. J. Edkins, "A Visit to the City of Confucius," JNCBRAS, 8 (1874): 79.

65. See chapter 3 for more detail.

66. The *Cao xian-zhi* (1884), 7:1b, put it nicely: "Cao was spared its anxiety over [becoming] fish."

67. All figures below are from Xing-ke ti-ben in the First Historical Archives in Beijing. This sample counted the province of origin of all robbery-related memorials for three months (different months in each successive year) in the years 1890 to 1897.

68. These border towns are a striking feature on detailed maps of this region. Elsewhere, on the Shandong-Zhili border for example, the boundary tends to wind around villages. Here, people seem to have deliberately put their villages on a border, presumably in order to escape jurisdiction from either side. I regard these towns as another example of the "outlaw" character of this region, and its inhabitants' attempt to live, as much as possible, beyond the reach of the Chinese state.

69. "Shan-xian zun-zha yi-ban tuan-lian zhang-cheng," quoted in Satō Kimihiko, "Shoki giwadan undō no shosō—kyōkai katsudō to taitōkai," *Shichō*, 1982.11:49–51.

70. N. Jiangsu correspondence, 27/7/1897, in *North China Herald* (hereafter: NCH) 59:309 (13/8/1897). For a Shandong story on the "usual winter crop of ROBBERIES WITH VIOLENCE" see NCH 58:339 (26/2/1897).

71. The raw figures from the cases I saw are:

1st month	9	7th month	5
2nd month	21	8th month	6
3rd month	6	9th month	15
4th month	6	10th month	3
5th month	5	11th month	13
6th month	15	12th month	9

72. Prosper Leboucq, *Associations de la Chine: Lettres du P. Leboucq, missionaire au Tché-ly-sud-est, publiées par un de ses amis* (Paris: F. Wattelier et Cie [ca. 1880]), 296. Philip Billingsley, "Bandits, Bosses, and Bare Sticks: Beneath the Surface of Local Control in Early Republican China," *Modern China* 7.3 (1981) provides a useful introduction to banditry in Republican China, and a taste of an excellent forthcoming book. His study seems to indicate that as banditry became more widespread, and especially as the large armies of "soldier-bandits" appeared, common people were more likely to suffer along with the rich.

73. Williamson, *Journeys* 1:214, comments on the "more and more fortified" villages he found as he passed into the southern part of Shandong.

74. *Chiping xian-zhi* (1935), 11:20a.

75. Jing Su and Luo Lun, Appendix I. I have recomputed their raw data on the basis of my regions. Significantly, 67 percent of the villages in the Southwest had at least one landlord, but the sample there is very small (only six villages).

76. In the Shandong University Boxer surveys, peasants regularly speak of cai-zhu, even when the interviewers seemed to be asking for landlords. Japanese investigators from the South Manchurian Railway Company surveyed a village from the heart of the Boxer region in the 1940s, and their report gives a good example of life there. There were no landlords, and villagers tended to speak only of "cai-zhu." When asked why there were no landlords in the village and few in the county, one of the village representatives said: "The rich do not trust the poor, so instead of renting the land, most use hired labor to cultivate their own fields." Clearly the mentality of the village rich was still that of a farmer intent on closely supervising production on his land. (Niida Noboru et al., ed., Chūgoku nōson kankō chōsa (Tokyo: Iwanami, 1981), 4:401.

77. Huang, Peasant Economy, passim, but esp. 53–120, 169–201.

78. Jing Su and Luo Lun, Appendix II. The figures for the peninsula resembled the North Slope: 41% from farming, 50% from commerce, 9% from office. In other areas, the sample was too small to be really meaningful.

79. Huang, Peasant Economy, 65.

80. I am thinking especially of Ramon Myers, The Chinese Peasant Economy: Agricultural Development in Hopei and Shantung, 1890–1949 (Cambridge: Harvard University Press, 1970). From the other end of the ideological spectrum, the Jing Su and Luo Lun study sees the substitution of managerial farming for "feudal" landlordism as accompanying commercialization and agrarian capitalism. Though that may have been occurring on the North Slope, where their best data come from, I do not see that as the process in northwest Shandong.

81. "Lu-xi nong-fu sheng-huo de yi-ban," Da-gong ri-bao, 8/7/1934, cited in Amano Motonosuke, 188–190. For a similar but somewhat less graphic nineteenth-century description of the northwest Shandong peasants' diet, see Coltman, The Chinese, 131–132.

82. R. H. Tawney, Land and Labor in China, (Boston: Beacon Press, 1966), 77.

83. Gaotang xiang-tu-zhi, 24.

84. Yong-zheng edict cited in Kataoka Shibako, "Minmatsu Shinsho no Kahoku ni okeru nōka keiei," Shakai keizai shigaku 25.2/3:90.

85. Leboucq, Associations, 265–267.

86. Wang You-nong, "Hebei Ningjin nong-ye lao-dong" in Feng He-fa, Zhong-guo nong-cun jing-ji zi-liao xu-bian (1935; Taipei reprint: 1978), 2:781–782.

87. Kataoka, "Minmatsu shinsho no Kahoku," 85.

88. R. F. Johnston, Lion and Dragon in China, 134.

89. Huang, Peasant Economy, 91–94, 255–256, shows how frequently agricultural laborers came from outside the village.

90. By regulation, the examinations were scheduled once every three years, but from the middle of the Qian-long reign (from 1750 on) special examinations by imperial favor were regularly added: twenty in the last century and a half of the system's operation. As a result, exams in fact averaged about one every two years (72 exams in the years 1751–1903).

91. Though one might suspect that the rise of the Peninsula and the North

Slope reflected an eastward shift in Shandong's population, this was not the case. The best estimate we have of the Ming population distribution (Liang Fang-zhong, *Zhongguo li-dai hu-kou, tian-di, tian-fu tong-ji* [Shanghai: People's Press, 1980], 214–216) differs little from that of the late Qing in the relative sizes of regional populations. In addition, every mention I have seen of Ming population shifts within Shandong is from the east to the west: *Yucheng xiang-tu-zhi*, 20a–20b; Shandong da-xue li-shi-xi, *Shandong di-fang-shi jiang-shou ti-gang*, 31–32.

92. In reading these raw figures we should keep in mind that the total number of *ju-ren* in Shandong increased by 32 percent between the fifteenth and nineteenth centuries.

93. Huang Chun-yao, *Shan-zuo bi-tan*, 3.

94. Gu Yan-wu, *Ri-zhi-lu*, 12:34a, cited in Hou Ren-zhi, 33.

95. Ayao Hoshi, *The Ming Tribute Grain System*, translated and abstracted by Mark Elvin (Ann Arbor: University of Michigan Center for Chinese Studies, 1969), 93, 98.

96. Chi Ch'ao-ting makes this point in *Key Economic Areas in Chinese History as Revealed in the Development of Public Works for Water-Control* (London: George Allen and Unwin, 1936), 142–143.

97. Included in these counties are not only those southwest of the canal below Linqing, but also southeast of the canal above Linqing: these were not so much harmed by blocked drainage as by periodic flooding when excess water in the canal was released in their direction, and by the raised water table which increased salinization of the soil.

98. Hou Ren-zhi, 37–38, 48–49, 139, 146.

99. One can easily assign an ordinal rank to each county based on the highest administrative office located in the county seat, but the regression equation required a numerical value. In order best to reflect the extent to which gentry strength could be predicted by administrative level, each level was given a dummy numerical value reflecting the average number of *ju-ren* from counties of that level throughout the entire Qing period.

100. It should be noted that the total data set included over sixty variables for each county. A number of different regressions and correlation tests were run on every promising variable. The multiple regression presented here represents the results of the most significant computer run. For measures of commercialization, regressions were also run using the number of markets in each county, and the number of markets in relation to population and land area. In each case, the correlation was lower than the correlation to the commercial tax. A multiple regression using twentieth century figures for the percentage of population who were peasants (essentially an index of *non*-commercialization) did yield marginally better results than the commercial tax variable: a multiple R-squared at the fourth step of 0.655 ($t = 3.01$) vs. 0.645 ($t = 2.43$) for the commercial tax. The difference was so small, however, that I opted to use the commercial tax variable, which was an authentic nineteenth century statistic, contemporaneous with the *ju-ren* statistics.

101. The simple correlation of *ju-ren* to cultivated area per capita is

interesting. The correlation is negative (shown by the simple R of −0.343). That is, there were more gentry where there was *less* cultivated land per capita. In effect, this variable is another indirect measure of commercialization. It is not simply a measure of more productive land supporting a denser population, for an index of acre yields was tested as an independent variable and proved not to be significantly correlated. What the cultivated area per capita probably measured was a combination of more productive land and/or the availability of non-agricultural sources of income supporting a greater population on the available land.

CHAPTER TWO

1. Ka-er-ji-shan, QL 9/9/5, in Lu Jing-qi and Cheng Xiao, ed., *Yi-he-tuan yuan-liu shi-liao* (Beijing: Chinese People's University, 1980), 3. (Hereafter this source is cited as YLSL.)

2. Suzuki Chūsei, *Chūgokushi ni okeru kakumei to shūkyō* (Tokyo: Tokyo University Press, 1974), 1–47.

3. Daniel Overmyer, *Folk Buddhist Religion: Dissenting Sects in Late Traditional China* (Cambridge, Mass.: Harvard University Press, 1976) is the best English introduction to the White Lotus sects, proposing a phenomenological approach to the sects and downplaying their frequent involvement in rebellions. Chan Hok-lam, "The White Lotus-Maitreya Doctrine and Popular Uprisings in Ming and Ch'ing China," *Sinologica* 10.4 (1969): 211–233 is a much less adequate survey stressing the White Lotus involvement in "seditious activities." Susan Naquin, *Millenarian Rebellion in China: The Eight Trigrams Uprising of 1813* (New Haven: Yale University Press, 1976), 7–60, gives an excellent introduction to the White Lotus sects of the Qing. In Japanese, see Suzuki, *Kakumei to shūkyō*, 66–124, 152–232; and Suzuki Chūsei, *Shinchō chūkishi kenkyū* (Tokyo: Ryogen Bookstore, 1952 [reprinted 1971]), 104–121. The classic Western work on these sects, strenuously (and no longer convincingly) arguing that it was only government persecution which drove sectarians to rebellion, is J. J. M. De Groot, *Sectarianism and Religious Persecution in China: A Page in the History of Religions*, 2 vols. (Amsterdam: Johannes Muller, 1903).

4. Suzuki, *Kakumei to shūkyō*, 70–76, 94–95, 107–115; Overmyer, 98–103; Chan Hok-lam, 214–218.

5. This is the central theme of Suzuki, *Kakumei to shūkyō*.

6. *Da-Qing hui-dian shi-li*, 766 : 7–8. De Groot, 1 : 137–148 reproduces and translates (rather inadequately) the Qing law. "*Duan-gong*" and "*tai-bao*" were both Daoist lay adepts. Susan Naquin informs me that the former were "live-in-the-world" Daoists, and my own oral history research in Jiangnan has taught me that *tai-bao* practiced the "soft" art of treating disease-causing ghosts to a feast and inviting them to leave. This contrasted to the more elaborate rituals of Daoist priests (*Dao-shi*) who would actually capture and deport ghosts.

7. This phrase was added following the Eight Trigrams uprising of 1813 (*Da-Qing hui-dian shi-lu* 766 : 10). The same edict added the Eight Trigrams

and the Bai-yang Sects to the list of proscribed groups. All the precedents on this law are in *juan* 766.

8. Daniel L. Overmyer, "Attitudes Toward the Ruler and State in Chinese Popular Religious Literature: Sixteenth and Seventeenth Century *Pao-chuan*," unpublished paper, May 1983.

9. Susan Naquin, "The Transmission of White Lotus Sectarianism in Late Imperial China," in *Popular Culture in Late Imperial China*, D. Johnson, A. Nathan and E. Rawski, eds. (Berkeley: University of California Press, 1985). The relatively pacific and law-abiding nature of the sutra-recitation sects is one reason why scholars like De Groot and Overmyer, who have based their work on the texts (*bao-juan*) of these sects, have tended to stress the non-rebellious nature of White Lotus sects generally.

10. Naquin, "Transmission." For further detail on the Liu family of Shandong, see Naquin, "Connections Between Rebellions: Sect Family Networks in Qing China," *Modern China* 8.3 (July 1982): 337–360. For many of the original sources, see YLSL, 11–13, 27–29.

11. Susan Naquin, *Shantung Rebellion: The Wang Lun Uprising of 1774* (New Haven: Yale University Press, 1981); Satō Kimihiko, "Kenryū san-jukyūnen Ō Rin Shinsuikyō hanran shoron," *Hitotsubashi ronshū* 81.3 (1979): 321–341.

12. Susan Naquin, *Millenarian Rebellion in China*, is an exhaustive study of this uprising.

13. Wolfram Eberhard, "Chinese Regional Stereotypes," *Asian Survey* 5.12 (1965): 604.

14. Archibald R. Colquhoun, *China in Transformation* (New York: Harper and Brothers, 1898), 271.

15. E. J. Hobsbawm, *Primitive Rebels: Studies in Archaic Forms of Social Movement in the 19th and 20th Centuries* (New York: Norton, 1965; original: 1959); Eric Hobsbawm, *Bandits* (New York: Dell, 1971).

16. Huang Ze-cang, *Shandong*, 102–103.

17. See Chapter 1, note 11 for sources. For military *ju-ren*, I have counted only Han Chinese, eliminating the large number of Manchu bannermen selected from the Dezhou and Qingzhou garrisons.

18. On this general question of boxer-sectarian connections, there is a clear division in the literature, perhaps best illustrated by the contrast between the work of Susan Naquin, who tends to treat boxing, like healing, as one element in the repertoire of "meditational sects"; and Suzuki Chūsei (*Kakumei to shūkyō*, esp. 69–70, 204–218), who argues that martial arts groups are socially and organizationally distinct from religious sects, and that it is precisely the alliance of these two in times of trouble that produced the periodic popular rebellions of Chinese history.

19. Edict of JQ 13/7/14 (4/9/1808) in Lao Nai-xuan, "Yi-he-quan jiao-men yuan-liu kao" (1899), YHT, 4:433.

20. See memorials of Zhao Wei-tong, JQ 16/10/29; and Tong-xing, JQ 16/11/11, 17/3/9, 17/8/11, in YLSL, 34–39. The closest thing to a mention of sectarian activity is the fear expressed in Tong-xing's first memorial that the Boxers, prohibited and allegedly underground since the edict of 1808,

"might because of years of neglecting their proper livelihood, again revert to their old tricks, and even establish a sect [or teaching] of some name (*xing-li jiao-ming*)."

21. Edict of YZ 5/11/28 (9/1/1728), *Dong-hua lu*, YZ 5:50a–b.

22. *Na-wen-yi gong zou-yi* (1834, Taibei reprint: 1968), *juan* 42, *passim*. (Hereafter this source is cited as NYC.) *Qing-dai dang-an shi-liao* 3:1–90. Cited passage from Fang Shou-chou, JQ 21/3/8, in *Qing-dai* 3:72.

23. Dong Guo-tai confession in Dong Gao, JQ 18/10/16, *Qing-ding ping-ding jiao-fei ji-lüe*, To-jin et al., eds. (Beijing: 1816; Taibei reprint: Cheng-wen, 1971), 11:25. (Hereafter this collection is cited as JFJL.)

24. Niu Liang-chen confession, in Dong Gao, JQ 18/12/26, JFJL 29:4a–b. I have seen only two references to sect-related martial arts in the Beijing area: a man who claims to have studied boxing from a White Lotus leader in his village when a teenager. The sect (the Da-cheng sect, later renamed the Rong-hua Assembly) seems not to have been involved in the 1813 uprising, and was only uncovered in 1815. Its teachings involved urging people to do good, which was often expressed in terms of two of the Qing founders' Six Maxims: "foster unity and harmony in village life; respect and obey your parents." I have some doubts about the confessor's claim to have studied boxing with this sect: he may have been seeking the lighter punishment the law prescribed for such activities. (Liu Cheng-er confession, in Na-yan-cheng, JQ 20/6/10, NYC, 38:61b–62a.) See *juan* 38 *passim* for more on this sect. The second reference is to the Spirit Boxers which we shall treat below.

25. See documents on the Liu family in YLSL, 11–13, 27–29. The documents I have seen here indicate some problems with Naquin's unquestionably useful distinction between "sutra-recitation" and "meditation" sects. She treats the Lius as the origin of many of the latter type of sect. This organizational line of descent is certainly important, but it also seems clear that the Liu sect itself changed character after the arrests of 1771. Before that time, the sect did have texts, some of its leaders had purchased official degrees and offices, and there is no mention of either martial arts or seditious purpose. In effect, the government persecution seems to have transformed a "sutra-recitation" sect into a "meditation sect" with a substantial martial arts interest. The initially distinct nature of sectarian and martial arts traditions in this area is also suggested in the following statement from a 1740 memorial: "The people of Henan are simple yet strong-willed. If they are not studying boxing and cudgels, prizing bravery and fierce fighting, they believe in heterodox sects, worshipping Buddhas and calling on gods." The two elements, martial arts and heterodox beliefs, are clearly alternatives, not linked elements of a single tradition. Ya-er-tu, QL 5/1/17, *Kang-Yong-Qian shi-qi cheng-xiang ren-min fan-kang dou-zheng zi-liao* (Beijing: Zhong-hua, 1979), 620.

26. YLSL, 22; Naquin, *Shantung Rebellion*, 186; Sato Kimihiko, "Kenryū sanjukyūnen," 326–327.

27. See YLSL, 14–21, for numerous references to "*xue-quan nian* [or *song*] *zhou*" and "*xue-quan yun-qi*" among Wang Lun's followers.

28. Niu Liang-chen confession, Na-yan-cheng JQ 19/2/10, JFJL, 42:18a;

Feng Ke-shan confession, Board of Punishments JQ 18/12/12, JFJL, 25:1a–1b; Song Shu-de confession, [JQ 18?]/12/2, YLSL, 75.

29. Tong-xing, JQ 19/3/23, in YLSL, 65–66.

30. Jing-e-bu, DG 16/9/13, YLSL, 113.

31. Na-yan-cheng, JQ 18/12/17, 18/12/29 in NYC, 33:4a–4b, 15a–16a. See also Naquin, *Millenarian Rebellion*, 41–42, 151, 219, 299–300.

32. Ge Li-ye confession, JQ 20/9/3, NYC, 38:73b–74a.

33. For a series of examples, see YLSL, 64–66.

34. Qing-pu, JQ 19/10/14, YLSL, 72.

35. For boxers who refused the step of joining the sects and their 1813 rebellion see Na-yan-cheng, JQ 20/6/22, NYC, 20:8a; Tong-xing, JQ 18/12/6, JFJL 23:39a–42b; Tong-xing, JQ 19/3/23, YLSL, 65–66; Zhang Xu, JQ 19/8/16, Gong-zhong-dang (National Palace Museum, Taiwan) 16303. For an example from 1784, see Jiang Sheng and Liu E, QL 48/12/7, Gong-zhong-dang 46730.

36. Naquin, *Millenarian Rebellion*, 87–88, 106–108, 215.

37. Tang Heng-le confessions, JQ 18/12/16 and 26, YLSL, 2, 63–64; Na-yan-cheng, JQ 18/12/14 and 19/1/5, NYC 32:39a–39b, 43a.

38. It is in this way that Feng Ke-shan became the teacher of Song Yue-long and brought that Shandong boxer and many of his pupils into his orbit. See Feng's confession in Dong Gao, JQ 18/12/11, JFJL, 24:22a–22b. For the continuation of the practice in later martial arts tradition, see Chen Bai-chen, *Song Jing-shi li-shi diao-cha-ji* (Beijing: People's Publishing House, 1957), 17, 240.

39. Overmyer, *Folk Buddhist Religion*, vii, mentions the use of the character for "Buddha" on the jackets of sectarian rebels as early as 1338.

40. Suzuki, *Kakumei to shūkyō*, 129–130.

41. Naquin, *Shantung Rebellion*, 59–60, 100–101, 191–192n; Satō, "Ken-ryū sanjukyūnen," 332–334.

42. See Zhang Luo-jiao confessions (the first partially repudiated later) in Na-yan-cheng memorials of JQ 20/6/22, 20/9/5 and 20/12/17, NYC 40:6b–9b, 18b–20b, 21a–29b; Guo Luo-yun (a pupil who later turned against Zhang), ibid., 20/5/25, 40:3b–6a; Zhang Wu, ibid., 20/5/4, 40:1a–3a; Liu Yu-long, ibid., 21/2/9, 40:29–33a. Note that Na-yan-cheng's memorial containing Zhang's third confession gives two lists of pupils: one of the Li Trigram Sect, one of the Armor of the Golden Bell. The two were clearly regarded as independent organizations. Naquin, *Millenarian Rebellion*, 30–31, also discusses this group and provides some details on invulnerability from sources I have not seen. Among participants in the 1813 rebellion, Xu An-guo, according to one report, knew the techniques of the Golden Bell. (Qin Li confession, JQ 19/11/14, YLSL, 74.)

43. Na-yan-cheng, DG 6/6/16, NYC 70:14–21 (also in YLSL, 100–103). This group was first pointed out by Hu Zhu-sheng, who observed the close similarity to Boxer ritual. ("Yi-he-tuan de qian-sheng shi Zu-shi-hui," *Li-shi yan-jiu* 1958.3:8.)

44. Jiang Kai, "Pingyuan quan-fei ji-shi," YHT 1:354.

45. Xiong Xue-peng, QL 31/3/2, YLSL, 5–8, and other sources in YLSL,

8–11. Chen Zhan-ruo, "Yi-he-tuan de qian-shi," *Wen-shi-zhe* 1954.3:20–21, was the first to link these Spirit Boxers to the late nineteenth century Boxers.

46. Zhang Xu, JQ 19/1/20, YLSL, 65.

47. Yao Zu-tong, DG 1/2/19, YLSL, 94–96.

48. Qi-ying, DG 11/12/25, 12/1/17, YLSL, 105–106.

49. See K. C. Liu, "The Ch'ing Restoration," *The Cambridge History of China*, vol. 10: *Late Ch'ing, 1800–1911*, Part I, John K. Fairbank, ed. (Cambridge: Cambridge University Press, 1978), 463–469.

50. Edict of XF 11/2/20; Qing-sheng, XF 11/2/26; Lian-jie, XF 11/3/5, *Song Jing-shi dang-an shi-liao* (Beijing: Zhong-hua, 1959; hereafter cited as SJSDA), 1–4; *Guan xian-zhi* (1934), 1565. Though the scale and duration of this uprising far exceeded either the Wang Lun or Eight Trigrams uprisings of the mid-Qing, we still lack a competent study of it. A lengthy history was published in the P.R.C., based in part on oral history sources: Chen Bai-chen, *Song Jing-shi li-shi diao-cha ji* (Beijing: People's Publishing House, 1957). The author was a playwright, and the oral history survey was for the purpose of writing a movie about Song Jing-shi which would be a counterpart to a movie about the west Shandong beggar-turned-philanthropist Wu Xun, which Mao Ze-dong had severely criticized for its reformist message. In fact Song Jing-shi had first been "discovered" by an earlier investigation team including Mao's wife, Jiang Qing, which was gathering material for a critique on the Wu Xun film. (For a summary of the events which led to the discovery of this peasant rebel hero, see Fox Butterfield, "The Legend of Sung Ching-shih: An Episode in Communist Historiography," *Papers on China* 18 (1964): 129–148.) Historians in China have often mentioned Chen Bai-chen's book to me as an example of the abuse to which oral history material can be put. I have accordingly relied on it only sparingly in this account, which should be read as a very tentative effort to sketch the outlines of an extremely complex rebellion. A recent article on the rebellion, which seems to me to rely uncritically on the Chen Bai-chen volume, is Benjamin Yang, "Sung Ching-shih and His Black Flag Army," *Ch'ing-shih Wen-t'i* 5.2 (December 1984): 3–46.

51. "Proclamation of Yang Tai," included in Sheng Bao, XF 11/4/28, SJSDA, 31–32.

52. *Guan xian-zhi* (1934), 1566; Chen Bai-chen, 84n. Cf. Prosper Leboucq, *Associations*, 163–164.

53. Senggerinchin, TZ 2/4/22, SJSDA, 289–290.

54. Leboucq, *Associations*, 29–30.

55. See Sheng-bao, XF 1/6/21, SJSDA, 63–66, which includes Song's original surrender note; *Guan xian-zhi*, 1568–1572; Chen Bai-chen, *passim*.

56. *Chiping xian-zhi* (1935), 3:22a–22b, 39a, 41a; *Guan xian-zhi* (1934), 877–878.

57. *Guantao xian-zhi* (1935), 8:34–35; cited in YLSL, 115–116.

58. *Linqing xian-zhi*, "Li-su zhi" (Customs), cited in Satō Kimihiko, "Giwadan (ken) genryū—hakkekyō to giwaken," *Shigaku Zasshi* 91.1 (1982): 75–76. Cf. *Chiping xian-zhi* (1935) 12:90a–92a.

59. See Li Shi-yu, *Xian-dai Hua-bei mi-mi zong-jiao* (Chengdu: 1948) for a

survey of White Lotus sects in the twentieth century.

60. Overmyer, *Folk Buddhist Religion*, 185; Chao Wei-ping, "The Origin and Growth of the Fu Chi," *Folklore Studies* 1 (1942): 9–27.

61. Huang Yu-pian, "Po-xie xiang-bian" (1834) in *Qing-shi zi-liao*, vol. 3 (Beijing: Zhong-hua, 1982), 30, 69. Overmyer, "Attitudes Toward the Ruler and State," 28–29, notes far earlier incorporation of Guan-gong.

62. Jing-e-bu, DG 16/9/13, YLSL, 113–114.

63. Huang Yu-pian, "Po-xie xiang-bian," 30, 31, 38, 57, 59, 69, 72; NYC, JQ 20/6/1, 40:1a–8a.

64. Georg M. Stenz, *Beiträge zur Volkskunde Süd-Schantungs* (Leipzig: R. Voigtlander, 1907), 47–49.

65. Niida et al., *Chūgoku nōson kankō chōsa* 4:419, 433, 439, 458. (This Japanese survey is of a village in En county, northwest Shandong.) Cf. Arthur Smith, *Village Life in China: A Study in Sociology* (New York: Fleming H. Revell, 1899), 169–173.

66. C. K. Yang, *Religion in Chinese Society: A Study of Contemporary Social Functions of Religion and Some of Their Historical Factors* (Berkeley: University of California Press, 1961), 82–86; Arthur Smith, *Village Life in China*, 54–69, which provides an interesting account of village theatre as observed in northwest Shandong. For references to the importance of "inviting the gods to a performance" in this area, see Zhang Yu-zeng and Liu Jing-zhi, 436, 443, 549. An interesting recent study is Charles Albert Litzinger, "Temple Community and Village Cultural Integration in North China: Evidence from 'Sectarian Cases' (*Chiao-an*) in Chihli, 1860–95," Ph.D. dissertation, University of California at Davis, 1983.

67. All of the characters mentioned by Smith in his discussion of village theatre were drawn from either the *Three Kingdoms* or *Enfeoffment* (*Village Life*, 57). On the popularity of *Water Margin* tales in west Shandong see Zhong-guo qu-yi yan-jiu-hui, ed., *Shandong kuai-shu Wu Song zhuan* (Beijing: Writers' Press, 1957), 339–347.

68. Leboucq, *Associations*, 165–172; Smith, *Village Life*, 161–167. One Shandong missionary, with a characteristic lack of charity, described the watchman hired as "usually some idle, worthless fellow in the village (not infrequently a thief he is)." Charles R. Mills, 21/4/1873, BFM, reel 197.

CHAPTER THREE

1. C:IGC, 1870, 11; 1874, 22; 1875, 80–81.

2. C:IGC, 1886, II:54.

3. C:IGC, 1899, II:75.

4. C:IGC, 1899, II:262.

5. C:IGC, 1866, 77.

6. C:IGC, 1886, II:41; 1887, II:43.

7. Hou Chi-ming, *Foreign Investment and Economic Development in China, 1840–1937* (Cambridge, Mass.: Harvard University Press, 1965), 218, 178.

8. Albert Feuerwerker, "Handicraft and Manufactured Cotton Textiles in China, 1871–1910," *Journal of Economic History* 30.2 (June 1970): 338–378.

9. Arthur H. Smith, *China in Convulsion* (New York: Fleming H. Revell, 1901), 1 : 90–91. In this book on the Boxer Uprising, Smith, as a missionary, is clearly concerned to direct attention from the religious to the economic causes of Chinese anti-foreignism. This may account for the rather dramatic and possibly overstated picture that he draws. But he is clearly not just engaged in *ex post facto* rationalizing. In his *Village Life in China* Smith had already observed (p. 276) that "Within the past few years the competition of machine twisted cotton yarns is severely felt in the cotton regions of China, and many who just managed to exist in former days are now perpetually on the edge of starvation."

10. *Nangong xian-zhi* 3 : 17–18, cited in Shandong da-xue li-shi-xi, ed., *Shandong Yi-he-tuan diao-cha bao-gao* (Jinan: Zhong-hua, 1960), 40.

11. C : IGC, 1887, II : 43. It should be noted that this sort of development, mostly in the area of treaty ports, of new home industries for export is the basis for Hou Chi-ming's argument that the net impact of foreign trade on handicrafts may not have been negative.

12. On the graffiti, see Yizhoufu correspondence, NCH, 56 : 599 (17/4/1896); on rumors, see Annual report of the Linqing station to 31/3/1895, ABC 16.3.12, vol. 15.

13. E. J. Edwards, *Man from the Mountain* (Techny, Ill.: Mission Press, n.d.), 95.

14. Annual Report, Pangzhuang station, to 31/3/1895, ABC 16.3.12, vol. 15.

15. Lord Charles Beresford, *The Break-up of China, with an Account of its Present Commerce, Currency, Waterways, Armies, Railways, Politics and Future Prospects* (New York: Harper and Brothers, 1899).

16. NCH, 56 : 557–58 (10/4/1986).

17. Hart to Campbell, 24/2/1895, in *The I.G. in Peking: Letters of Robert Hart, Chinese Maritime Customs, 1868–1907*, edited by John K. Fairbank et al. (Cambridge, Mass.: Harvard University Press, 1978), 2 : 1010 (hereafter cited as I.G.).

18. Columbia Cary-Elwes, *China and the Cross, A Survey of Missionary History* (New York: P. J. Kennedy & Sons, 1957), 123–126.

19. Arthur Schlesinger, "The Missionary Enterprise and Theories of Imperialism," in *The Missionary Enterprise in China and America*, ed. John K. Fairbank (Cambridge, Mass.: Harvard University Press, 1974), 342, citing Carl Cipolla, *European Culture and Overseas Expansion*, 99.

20. Kenneth Scott Latourette, *A History of Christian Missions in China* (New York: Macmillan, 1929), 274–77.

21. Frederick Low to Hamilton Fish 10/1/1871, in *Papers Relating to the Foreign Relations of the United States*, House of Representatives, 42nd Congress, 2d session, Executive Document 1, pt. 1, 84 (hereafter cited as FRUS).

22. Samuel Wells Williams, *Life and Letters*, 257, 268, cited in Stuart Creighton Miller, "Ends and Means: Missionary Justification of Force in Nineteenth Century China," in *The Missionary Enterprise in China*, ed. John K. Fairbank, 261.

23. T. L. McBryde, cited in Miller, "Ends and Means," 254.

24. Miller, "Ends and Means," 254.

25. NCH, 47:498 (9/10/1891).

26. T. J. McCormick, *China Market* (Quadrangle, 1966), 66; cited in Schlesinger, "The Missionary Enterprise," 345.

27. John Thauren, *The Mission Fields of the Society of the Divine Word, I: The Missions of Shandong, China; with a General Introduction to China and the Catholic Missions There*, trans. Albert Paul Schimberg (Techny, Ill.: Mission Press, 1932), 32–36; John J. Heeren, *On the Shantung Front: A History of the Shantung Mission of the Presbyterian Church in the U.S.A., 1861–1940 in its Historical, Economic and Political Setting* (New York: Board of Foreign Missions, 1940), 35–36; Cary-Elwes, *China and the Cross*, 111–114; Latourette, 111.

28. Heeren, 35–36.

29. Bernward Willeke, *Imperial Government and Catholic Missions in China during the Years 1784–1785* (St. Bonaventure, N.Y.: Franciscan Institute, 1948), 106–110, 130–33, 160.

30. Latourette, 232; *Album des Missions Catholique: Asie Orientale* (Paris: Société de Saint-Augustin, 1888), 100–101; Heeren, 36, for the figure of 5,736.

31. CR 20.3 (March 1899): 138, 141; *Maritime Customs Decennial Reports 1891–1900*, I:125. For similar figures see Latourette, 320.

32. Latourette, 319, where a second (and less credible) figure for 1870 is also given: 9,000 converts; *Album des Missions Catholique*, 116.

33. Heeren, 40–44.

34. Rev. Hunter Corbett, "The Work of Protestant Missions in the Province of Shantung," CR 12.2 (Mar/Apr 1881): 87–90.

35. John L. Nevius, "Mission Work in Central Shantung," CR 11.5 (Sept/Oct 1880): 358; Arthur H. Smith, "Sketches of a Country Parish," CR 12.4 (July/Aug 1881): 252–254.

36. Albert Whiting, 13/3/1877, BFM, reel 202.

37. Heeren, 78–81; H. P. Perkins, "Report on the Lin-ch'ing Station," 30/4/1896, ABC 16.3.12, vol. 15.

38. Annual Reports of 1895 and 1896, 31/3/1895 and 30/4/1896, in ABC 16.3.12, vol. 15.

39. Heeren, 72–73.

40. China, Imperial Maritime Customs, *Decennial Reports, 1891–1900*, I:125. These figures are for 1901, but the Catholic figures agree closely with those cited (supposedly for the time of the uprising) in the Catholic Publication *Quan-huo-ji*, in *Shandong jin-dai-shi zi-liao* 3:192–93, 305. Since the Catholics suffered more than the Protestants from Boxer attacks, one suspects that the Catholic/Protestant ratio was even larger on the eve of the uprising. In addition, one should note an attrition of Protestant missionaries. Heeren's figures (p. 86) show 205 Protestant missionaries in 1878.

41. Jinanfu correspondence, NCH, 57:1011 (11/12/1896); Qingzhou-fu correspondence, NCH, 57:1100 (24/12/1896).

42. John E. Schrecker, *Imperialism and Chinese Nationalism: Germany in Shantung* (Cambridge, Mass.: Harvard University Press, 1971), 11–13; Henri

Cordier, *Histoire des Relations de la Chine avec les Puissances Occidentales, 1860–1900* (Paris: Germer Baillière, 1901–1902), 3 : 72–89; Chao-Kwang Wu, *The International Aspects of the Missionary Movement in China* (Baltimore: Johns Hopkins Press, 1930), 87–98.

43. Edwards, *Man from the Mountain*, 11.

44. Cited in Schrecker, 13.

45. Schrecker, 12, claims that the French Treaty of 1860 banned missionary activity around Yanzhou, but I have been able to find no such clause in any published copy of the treaty. Nonetheless, the German missionary accounts refer to a French agreement to limit missionary activity in the area. (See, e.g., George M. Stenz, *Life of Father Richard Henle, S.V.D., Missionary in China, Assassinated November 1, 1897*, trans. Elizabeth Ruff [Techny, Ill.: Mission Press, 1915], 79.)

46. Stenz, *Twenty-five Years in China, 1893–1918* (Techny, Ill.: Mission Press, 1924), 17; Edwards, *Man from the Mountain*, 83–5.

47. Stenz, *Life of Henle*, 79–84; Edwards, 86–95. The Chinese documents on this long case stretch through JWJAD, 5.1, 5.2 and 6.1.

48. Edwards, *Man from the Mountain*, 66.

49. Quoted in Clifford J. King, *Man of God: Joseph Freinademetz, Pioneer Divine Word Missionary* (Techny, Ill.: Divine Word Publications, 1959), 96–97.

50. Stenz, *Life of Henle*, 88.

51. Ibid., 102.

52. Thauren, 58.

53. Ibid., 56–57.

54. Frederick Low to Hamilton Fish, 20/3/1871, in FRUS (1871), 98.

55. Zhu Yuan-ze, in Shandong da-xue li-shi-xi Zhong-guo jin-dai-shi jiao-yan-shi, ed., *Shandong Yi-he-tuan diao-cha zi-liao xuan-bian* (Qi-Lu, 1980), 107 (hereafter cited as SDDC).

56. F. H. Chapin to J. Smith, 11/1/1894, ABC 16.3.12, vol. 18.

57. Articles in the *Chinese Recorder* frequently discussed this issue during the 1890s and displayed both Protestant sensitivity to the problem and evidence of at least occasional Protestant abuses. See especially 27 (1896) *passim*; 30.6 : 261–268; and 30.7 : 328–335 (June and July 1899).

58. Smith, *China in Convulsion*, 48. It should be stressed that this describes the situation before the edict of March 15, 1899, which in effect granted bishops a rank equal to that of governors. For a vivid description of a French bishop's triumphal procession through northern Jiangsu in 1897, see Renaud, 203–208. For villagers' later recollections, see SDDC, 105–107.

59. Stenz, *Twenty-five Years*, 23. A similar incident is described on p. 25.

60. JWJAD, 5.1, Nos. 725 (3/3/1893), 727 (9/3/1893), and 728 (20/3/1893) summarized on p. 42; 753 (1/11/1894) and 754 (22/11/1894), 574–75.

61. This phrase has been much used to describe the Catholic Church in China. For a contemporary example, see the letter of W. E. Soothill in NCH, 63 : 579–80 (18/9/1899). Note the judicious use of the same phrase by the eminent missionary-historian Kenneth Latourette in *History of Christian Missions in China*, 279–80.

62. T. P. Crawford, cited in Irwin T. Hyatt, *Our Ordered Lives Confess: Three 19th Century Missionaries in East Shantung* (Cambridge, Mass.: Harvard University Press, 1976), 23.

63. Samuel Popkin, *The Rational Peasant: The Political Economy of Rural Society in Vietnam* (Berkeley: University of California Press, 1979), 188–193.

64. Ibid., 34.

65. King, *Man of God*, 70–71.

66. King's account (pp. 71–72) makes it much larger, "about 1000," and places it in 1881, but his identification of "Cheping" as the site makes it virtually certain that this is the rising in the spring of 1882 recorded in *Chiping xian-zhi* (1935), 11 : 3a–3b; QSL, 147 : 12b–13a; and NCH 9/6/1882.

67. King, *Man of God*, 72–78.

68. This is clear from the Shandong University survey materials.

69. Stenz, *Twenty-five Years*, 40–41.

70. King, *Man of God*, 81.

71. SDDC, 50.

72. C. E. Moule, "Some Remarks on a Recent Correspondence in the North China Herald," CR 6.2 (March-April 1875): 133. Professor David Buck was the first to point out this pattern of sectarian conversion to Christianity in the period leading up to the Boxers, and he was instrumental in leading me to the S.V.D. sources which document the trend. See his "Christians, White Lotus and the Boxers in Shandong: A New View of Their Interconnections," unpublished paper, 1979.

73. J. L. Nevius, "Methods of Mission Work," letter VIII, CR 17.8 (August 1886): 301–2.

74. Leboucq, *Associations*, 31–32.

75. Stenz, *Twenty-five Years*, 38–41, 146; King, *Man of God*, 118–119.

76. Porter, "Secret Sects," II, CR 17.2 (Feb. 1886): 65–69. See also Daniel H. Bays, "Christianity and the Chinese Sectarian Tradition," *Ch'ing-shih Wen-t'i* 4.7 (June 1982): 33–55.

77. A. H. Smith, "Sketches," II, CR 12.5 (October 1881): 329 ff., 335 ff. Cf. YLSL, 170–171.

78. Stenz, *Twenty-five Years*, 39–40. For another example: H. D. Porter, "A Modern Shantung Prophet," CR 18.1 (January 1887): 16–18.

79. Leboucq, *Associations*, 34–41.

80. Liu Han-chen, SD Survey: Yuncheng/Heze.

81. Yang Shou-qin, SDDC, 46–47; cf. 50.

82. King, *Man of God*, 119–120. See also R. G. Tiedemann, "The Geopolitical Dimension of Collective Rural Violence, North China 1868–1937," unpublished ms. (1979): 31 and note 93.

83. Wang Wang-geng (Jining sub-prefect) cited by Yu-xian, GX 25/11/29 (31/12/1899) JWJAD, 6.1 : 479 (No. 721).

84. E.g., SDDC, 36, 49.

85. See CR 12.5 (Sept.–Oct. 1881): 318; 28.2 (Feb. 1897): 96; 30.10 (Oct. 1899): 481.

86. Stenz, *Twenty-five Years*, 54–55.

87. Ren Ke-li et al., SDDC, 53.

88. Hart to Campbell, 19/1/1896, I.G., 2 : 1048. For the warm welcome

given MacDonald by the British community in China, see NCH, 56:76, 557–58, 590, 612–615 (17/1/1896, 10/4/1896, 17/4/1896).

89. A. J. H. Moule, "The Relation of Christian Missions to Foreign Residents," in *Records of the General Conference of the Protestant Missionaries of China* (Shanghai: American Presbyterian Mission Press, 1890), 23–24.

90. Ibid., 27.

91. Schlesinger, "The Missionary Enterprise," 355. The quote from Hobson is from *Imperialism*, 216.

92. James A. Field, "Near East Notes and Far East Queries," in Fairbank, ed., *The Missionary Enterprise in China and America*, 33–37.

93. Cited in Paul Varg, *Missionaries, Chinese and Diplomats: The American Protestant Missionary Movement in China, 1890–1952* (Princeton: Princeton University Press, 1958), 3.

94. Edmund S. Wehrle, *Britain, China and the Antimissionary Riots, 1891–1900* (Minneapolis: University of Minnesota Press, 1966), 12, citing Latourette, 406, and McIntosh, *Chinese Crisis and Christian Missionaries,* 89–90.

95. CR 29.3 (March 1899): 138, 141; *Maritime Customs Decennial Reports, 1891–1900*, I, 125. See also discussion in note 40.

96. Wehrle, viii.

97. Ibid., 24–28, 82–95.

98. JWJAD, 5.1:75–77; Wehrle, 32–33.

99. P. Bergen, 2/11/1891, BFM, reel 208. See also G. Reid, 7/12/1891, on same reel.

100. H. D Porter to J. Smith, 7/8/1893, ABC 16.2.12, vol. 20:167.

CHAPTER FOUR

1. Li Bing-heng, GX 22/6/24 (3/8/1896), DASL, 1:4.

2. Zhao Hong-en and Zhao Guo-lin, YZ 13/run 4/10, in YLSL, 3.

3. See Chong-lu memorial, n.d. YLSL, 87–88.

4. Na-yan-cheng, JQ 20/11/20, YLSL, 84–85. See also Naquin, *Millenarian Rebellion*, 30–31.

5. SDDC, 12–18.

6. Two professors from Shandong University have given the best defenses of these respective views: Lu Yao, "Lun Yi-he-tuan de yuan-liu ji qi-ta," *Shandong da-xue wen-ke lun-wen ji-kan* 1980.1:37–38, arguing for the sectarian connection; Xu Xu-dian, "Yi-he-tuan yuan-liu chu-yi," ibid., 1980.1:24–25, arguing against it.

7. Yu-lu, GX 18/12/3, YLSL, 126–128. Cf. ibid., 128, 131–132.

8. Huang Ze-cang, *Shandong*, 231–233.

9. Stenz, *Life of Henle*, 35–38.

10. Thauren, *Missions of Shantung*, 31.

11. *Shina shōbetsu zensho, Santō*, 294. For a similar report on Caozhou, see p. 327. Lest one think such judgments only reflect foreign prejudice, see Ji Gui-fen to Yao Song-yun, 13/10/1899, SDJDSZL, 3:191; Peng Yu-sun, GX 25/8/26 (30/9/1899), JWJAD, 6.1:443.

12. "Chang-qiang hui-fei ji-shi," in SDJDSZL, 1:262–268.

13. *Heze-xian xiang-tu-zhi*, 13b. This incident can also serve as a reminder of the dangers of uncritical reliance on oral history sources, for several accounts make the Big Sword Society the actors in this rebellious drama. (See SDDC, 7, 33.) One of these accounts puts the main Big Sword leader Liu Shi-duan himself at the leadership of the incident, and some historians in the P.R.C. have quite unconvincingly used this as evidence of Liu Shi-duan's own anti-dynastic intentions. (See SDDC, editors' introduction, 1; Lu Yao, "Lun Yi-he-tuan," 38.)

14. Elizabeth J. Perry, *Rebels and Revolutionaries in North China* (Stanford: Stanford University Press, 1980), 60–62, 104–107.

15. C:IGC, 1879, II:79.

16. C:IGC, 1889, II:159.

17. C:IGC, 1891, II:22.

18. C:IGC, 1875, 135.

19. Li Wen-zhi, ed., *Zhong-guo jin-dai nong-ye-shi zi-liao* (Beijing: San-lian, 1957), 1:459–462. Ding Shu-li, a merchant from Shan county, said that there, large landowners with 100 *mu* would plant 8–10 *mu* in opium. Mrs. Shang and Zheng noted opium as the key cash crop of the poor (SD Survey, Shan county).

20. Gui-jun, GX 21/5/2 in Hu-bu ti-ben No. 2649: Zhao Shu-qiao, GX 23/2/16, ibid., No. 2663.

21. Edwards, *Man from the Mountain*, 95.

22. Stenz, *Life of Henle*, 90.

23. QSL (GX), 363:1a–9a, 14a; 365:1a–1b, 9b; 367:4a–4b.

24. Liu T'ieh-yun, *The Travels of Lao Ts'an*, trans. Harold Shadick (Ithaca: Cornell, 1952), 45–70. See also Li Bing-heng memorial, GX 21/jun 5/1 (23/6/1895) in QSL, 369:1b–2a; NCH, 56:123 (24/1/1896) and 56:165 (31/1/1896).

25. Stenz, *Life of Henle*, 71, 90; *Twenty-five Years*, 73; NCH, 62:61, 289 (16/1/1899 and 20/2/1899).

26. Rosario Renaud, *Suchou, Diocèse de Chine*, vol. 1 (1882–1931), (Montreal: Editions Bellasmin, 1955), 195–197. I am indebted to Gary Tiede-mann for supplying me with a copy of this source.

27. Amano, *Santō*, 206. Note also the reference to tenants and agricultural laborers doing guard duty in Cao county in Liu T'ieh-yun, *The Travels of Lao Ts'an*, 47.

28. *Shan xian-zhi* (1929), 1:42b–43a.

29. N. Jiangsu correspondence, NCH, 60:929 (30/5/1898).

30. NCH, 58:836 (7/5/1897).

31. Su Yu-zhang, SDDC, 23, gives Zhao's name as Zhao Jin-huan, and says he came from Hejian, stopping in Yanggu. Wan Guang-wei, SDDC, 7–8, confirms much of this, and says Zhao worked as a hired hand. Gary Tiede-mann ("Geopolitical Dimensions," 29, 32) has discovered contemporary German sources which give Zhao's name as Zhao Tian-ji, a name confirmed by new documents announced from the Beijing archives. (Cheng Xiao and Zhu Jin-fu, 11.) The Xuzhou *daotai*, Ruan Zu-tang, while mentioning no names, says the initiators of the new technique came from Guide in Henan.

(Liu Kun-yi, GX 22/6/18, JWJAD, 6.1:150–151.) For the Daoist priest reference, see Li Bing-heng, GX 22/5/12, JWJAD, 6.1:144.

32. Liu Kun-yi, GX 22/6/18, JWJAD, 6.1:150–151.

33. Liu Kong-jie (Liu Shi-duan's son), SD Survey, Shan, has his father learning from Zhao twenty years before the rising; Wan Guang-wei, has Zhao in the area some fifty years before 1896 (ibid.; cf. SDDC, 7–8).

34. Tanaka Tadao, *Kakumei Shina nōson no jisshōteki kenkyū* (Tokyo: Shuninsha, 1930), 242–245; Baba Takeshi, "Kōsōkai—sono shisō to sho-shiki," *Shakai keizai shigaku* 42.1 (1976): 71–72.

35. SDDC, 6, 7. My skepticism over the relation of Zhao to the White Lotus is enhanced both by the lack of specifics in the claims, and by the fact that the sources are not local peasants but, on the one hand, a survey by the Shandong provincial museum whose sources are unspecified, and on the other, a member of the Shan County Political Consultative Conference. The views of both could well be politically inspired.

36. Ruan Zu-tang, cited in Liu Kun-yi, GX 22/6/18, JWJAD, 6.1:151.

37. *Shandong shi-bao*, 11/9/1896, SDJDSZL, 3:183–4.

38. See the many informants cited in SDDC, 14–18.

39. Gao Shi-cai, SDDC, 15. Gao was a former member of the Big Swords. Cf. Song Chong-xing, SD Survey, Yuncheng.

40. Liu Han-chen, SDDC, 17; also Liu Shan-di and Yang Jian-bang, SD Survey, Yuncheng.

41. Chu Feng-yun, SDDC, 56; Liang Yu-chun, SDDC, 17; Chen Hua-chen et al., SDDC, 13.

42. Satō Kimihiko, "Kenryū sanjukyūnen," 89, 96. On Wang Lun, see Naquin, *Shantung Rebellion*, 39.

43. C. K. Yang, *Religion in Chinese Society*, 152–155.

44. Li Xing-hong and Qin Ya-min, "Guan-yu 'Da-dao-hui' shou-ling Liu Shi-duan de bu-fen qing-kuang" (manuscript provided during November 1980 visit to Shan county). The Chinese text of this charm is as follows:

法官請到符神位，鐵宗神灶保護身。
彌陀訓字鎮三邊，鐵盔鐵甲穿鐵衣。
金頂銅塔石頭封，刀剁斧砍一脚踢。

45. The informant was Liu Hui-min, grandson of Liu shi-duan. There are two passing references to "spirits descending" (*xia-shen*) in the printed Shandong University survey materials (SDDC, 17), but both are from people at most ten years old at the time of the rising, and relatively educated, so that one suspects their information may be based on accounts they had read of Boxers elsewhere, or perhaps of Big Swords who later adopted the Boxer ritual. In any case it is not at all clear that *"xia-shen"* refers to possession. Finally, a piece of negative evidence: the German source cited at note 64 in chapter 2 describes possession by the "Monkey King" in southwest Shandong. It was published in 1907, well after the Big Sword disturbances, and written by a man (George Stenz) well acquainted with the Big Swords—who once tried to kill him. Had these possession rituals been shared by the Big

Swords, Stenz would have almost certainly have noted it in one of his many publications.

46. Interview with Liu Hui-min, 22/11/1980.

47. Liu Kong-jie, Shi-duan's son, and Liu Qing-yue, SDDC, 8, 9; interview with Liu Hui-min; Li Bing-heng, GX 22/5/12 (22/6/1896), JWJAD, 6.1:144.

48. Cao Jing-wen, De-li's grandson, has the most complete and credible account (SDDC, 8–9); Cai Jing-qin (SDDC, 9) puts Cao's holdings at 50–60 *mu*; Cui Gui-zi (SDDC, 8) puts them at 33. It is interesting that an informant from the county seat believed Cao a landlord with over 100 *mu*—probably not true, but in keeping with the norm for many Big Sword leaders. (Zhang Ri-shu, SD Survey, Shan County.)

49. Jiang Zhi-ye and Fan Lian-zhong both in SDDC, 28.

50. Dong XX, SDDC, 31.

51. Hou Gong-bei, SD Survey, Yuncheng/Heze.

52. Cai Jing-qin, SDDC, 20–21. Li Zhao-xiang says the poor did not join, because they could not afford their food and weapons (SD Survey, Shan County).

53. Su Yu-zhang, SDDC, 20.

54. Liu Kong-jie, SD Survey, Shan county.

55. Wu Meng-zhou, SDDC 19–20. In keeping with the general preference in the P.R.C. to stress poor peasant participation in such progressive movements as the anti-Christian Big Swords, the editors of this published version have rearranged the sentences in this account, placing the third sentence first. I have restored the order of the original.

56. See Satō Kimihiko, "Shoki giwadan," 49–50.

57. Edict, GX 21/3/1 (26/3/1895), QSL, 363:1a–1b.

58. Edicts of GX 21/3/4 (29/3/1895) and GX 21/4/1 (25/4/1895) citing memorials by Guan Ting-xian and Jiang Shi-fen, QSL, 363, 4a–4b; 365, 1b–2a. In the second of these edicts, the court does order the "eradication" of the heterodox society, but this is in response to Jiang's report that their leader Liu (presumably Liu Shi-duan) had led an attack on Suizhou in Henan. Since in the next month, Li Bing-heng reported that this attack was led not by Liu, but by the bandit "fifth Xie, the Blindman," Li presumably felt justified in following the earlier more lenient line toward the alleged sectarians. (Li Bing-heng, GX 21/5/1, YLSL, 130–131.)

59. Li Bing-heng, GX 21/jun 5/1 (23/6/1895), QSL 369, 1b–2a; SDDC, 75–77. See also the description of the cages and Yu-xian's cruelty in Liu T'ieh-yun's novel *Travels of Lao Ts'an*, 44–70.

60. *Shan xian-zhi* (1929), 4:5b–6a.

61. Ruan Zu-tang report in Liu Kun-yi, GX 22/6/18 (28/7/1896), JWJAD, 6.1:151.

62. Yu-xian, cited by Zhang Ru-mei in GX 24/5/3 (21/6/1898), JWJAD, 6.1:240–241.

63. Zhang Ru-mei, GX 24/3/21 (11/4/1898), JWJAD, 6.1:222–223.

64. Ruan Zu-tang, GX 22/6/18, JWJAD, 6.1:150–151.

65. Ibid., 152 reports the rumor.

66. Liu Chang-ru and Zhang Zong-fen, SD Survey, Yuncheng/Heze.

Similar comments are to be found from many informants in these surveys (e.g., Wan Guang-wei, Shan county), but regrettably the editors of the published volume have chosen to paint Yu-xian (presumably because of his established reputation as a reactionary) as a cruel oppressor of the Big Sword Society (SDDC, 6). Consequently none of these comments are to be found in the published version.

67. Yu-xian, cited in Zhang Ru-mei, GX 24/5/3, JWJAD, 6.1:240–241.

68. Li Bing-heng, GX 22/5/12 (24/6/1896), JWJAD, 6.1:144.

69. Ruan Zu-tang, JWJAD, 6.1:152.

70. Ibid., 152; Shandong shi-bao, 11/9/1896, in SDJDSZL, 3:183–184; SDDC, 10–11. The patriarch's birthday was on the third day of the third month.

71. Liu Qing-yue, Wu Yuan-han, Zhang Qi-he, SDDC, 9–10, 12, and several others in the original Shan county survey.

72. Ruan Zu-tang, JWJAD 6.1:151. Ruan's typical claim that of all areas, the Big Swords were least numerous in his jurisdiction should be taken with a grain of salt.

73. Shandong shi-bao, 11/9/1896, SDJDSZL, 3:183.

74. Brandt, GX 21/8/18 (6/10/1895), JWJAD, 5.2:604–605. On the Yan-zhou incidents, see esp. JWJAD, 5.2:590–591, 595–596.

75. Su Yu-zhang, SDDC, 22.

76. Shandong shi-bao, 11/9/1896, SDJDSZL, 3:183. Cf. Stenz, Twenty-five Years, 78.

77. Li Bing-heng, GX 22/5/12 (22/6/1896), JWJAD, 6.1:140–146. This long memorial includes the joint report of the magistrates of Cao, Shan, and Chengwu and the report of the expectant subprefect Qin Hao-ran who went in plainclothes to make a secret investigation.

78. Renaud, Suchou, 180, 206, 209, 211–212.

79. Renaud, Suchou, 173–175.

80. Su Gui-fang, SDDC, 25–26. Cf. Han Zhen-huan et al., SD Survey, Dangshan, Pei, and Feng counties.

81. Zhang Ri-shu, SDDC, 23.

82. Renaud, 176; SDDC, 23–26. Li Bing-heng, GX 22/6/24 (3/8/1896), DASL, 1:4. Li's memorial inexplicably calls Pang a bannerman, but this is surely an error. Pang's landholdings may have been even greater than indicated here. One unpublished oral history source (Su Gui-fang, SD Survey, Dangshan, Pei, Feng counties) says he had 8,000 mu.

83. German chargé, GX 22/5/21, JWJAD, 6.1:149.

84. Renaud, 176–179. The magistrate's curious letter, which may have been composed to confuse the missionary, is quoted in a letter from the local missionary Gain to Havret, 22/6/1896, cited on p. 179.

85. Renaud, 177–180; Liu Kun-yi, GX 22/5/25 (5/7/1896), DASL, 1:2; Li Bing-heng, GX 22/6/24, DASL, 1:4–5. Ruan Zu-tang in Liu Kun-yi, GX 22/6/18, JWJAD, 6.1:152. Renaud, Liu Kun-yi, and Ruan Zu-tang put the Big Sword numbers at about 1,000; Li Bing-heng mentions 400 to 500. A confused report in the North China Herald, said to originate with the Xuzhou daotai, mentions a figure of 3,000. (NCH, 57:107 [17/7/1896].)

86. Renaud, 180; Li Bing-heng, GX 22/6/24, DASL, 1:4–5. A much sketchier report by Liu Kun-yi mentions over one hundred "bandit" casualties in the first battle (June 29), and 80–90 on the following day. (Memorial of GX 22/5/25, DASL, 1:2.) While Li Bing-heng's report of only two killed is perhaps incomplete, Liu's numbers do not seem credible in the light of Li's more detailed report. For oral history recollections of the incident, see SDDC, 25–27.

87. Renaud, 184–186. It should be noted that the missionaries were less concerned with the amount of the indemnity than with the chance to gain a residence in Xuzhou and several county seats—in which endeavor they succeeded as a result of these negotiations.

88. Heyking to Zongli Yamen, GX 22/10/6 (10/11/1896), JWJAD, 6.1:164–166; Li Bing-heng, GX 23/2/19 (11/3/1897), ibid., 186. The Sino-German negotiations over this affair stretch over pp. 148–187 of this volume and conclude with the German minister asking that Anzer be granted the honor of wearing the peacock feather for his goodwill in accepting the settlement.

89. Renaud, 187.

90. QSL (GX), *juan* 369–396, *passim.*

91. Li Bing-heng, GX 22/6/24, DASL, 1:5. SDDC, 29. A local gentry member is said to have led the arrest in Shan county, and opposed the general sentiment that the Big Swords leader there should be pardoned. (*Shan xian-zhi* [1929] 12:25b.)

92. In fact Liu never even acted against Christians in Gao village just a few paces from his home. As a Big Sword follower of Liu explained, "they never picked on us." Gao Shi-cai, SD Survey, Shan county.

93. Ibid., 29; *Shandong shi-bao,* GX 22/8/5 and GX 22/10/2, SDJDSZL, 3:184, 302.

94. Liu Kong-jie, SDDC, 33.

95. Renaud, 201–207. This tale, documented with correspondence from the missionaries involved, would seem to give credence to Yu-xian's claim that some Big Swords (apparently in Shandong) left to join the Christians. Cited in Zhang Ru-mei, GX 24/5/3 (21/6/1898), JWJAD, 6.1:240–241.

96. Renaud, 200–201.

97. Li Bing-heng, GX 22/11/9 (13/12/1896), JWJAD, 6.1:170–171.

98. Imperial edict GX 22/5/23 (3/7/1896); Li Bing-heng memorial GX 22/6/24, DASL, 1:1, 5–6.

99. Ruan Zu-tang in Liu Kun-yi, GX 22/6/18, JWJAD, 6.1:152.

CHAPTER FIVE

1. Stenz, *Life of Henle,* 119–123; *Twenty-five Years,* 82–85. "Juye jiao-an diao-cha," SDJDSZL, 3:30–33.

2. Stenz, *Life of Henle,* 130–131; *Twenty-five Years,* 90–92; SDJDSZL, 3:27–45. Unfortunately the documents which would best state the official position, from the Zongli Yamen archives, are inexplicably absent in the JWJAD volumes. All we have is a single Zongli Yamen memorial (1/12/1897)

in Lian Li-zhi and Wang Shou-zhong, eds., *Shandong jiao-an shi-liao* (Jinan: Qi-Lu, 1980), 187–189.

3. SDJDSZL, 3:32.

4. Stenz, *Life of Henle*, 109; cf. 78.

5. Stenz, *Twenty-five Years*, 7, 9, 20, 25, 34.

6. Cited in Stenz, *Life of Henle*, 140.

7. SDJDSZL, 3:29–30.

8. Stenz, *Life of Henle*, 127–128; *Twenty-five Years*, 79–90. Cf. SDDC, 39–40, 43.

9. SDJDSZL, 3:32, 42, 44. R. F. Johnston, *Lion and Dragon in Northern China*, 58, has another version of the revenge-against-the-magistrate theme.

10. Cited in Langer, 429–430.

11. Schrecker, 1–30; Langer, 429–439. Schrecker's study of German policy and the Jiaozhou seizure is the basis for much of the discussion in this section.

12. Cited in Schrecker, 33.

13. Edict, GX 23/10/16 (10/11/1897), QSL, 410:10a.

14. Li Bing-heng memorial, GX 23/10/21 (15/11/1897), DASL, 1:9–10. Li's proposal to raise the troops in Caozhou seems curious, as that prefecture was the farthest in Shandong from the invading force in Jiaozhou. The suspicious might imagine that he was thinking of former Big Sword Society members from that region, but this was in fact a favorite place to recruit soldiers—given the militant reputation of the prefecture—and Li's reference to Caozhou may reflect no more than an established preference of army recruiters.

15. Edict GX 23/10/23 (17/11/1897), DASL, 1:10.

16. Edict GX 23/10/26 (20/11/1897), QSL, 411:17a.

17. Langer, 445–480. The change in the Russian position from Chinese supporter against the Germans to seeker of concessions for herself is evident in her ambassador's conversations with the Zongli Yamen, in QDDASLCB, 3:162–181.

18. Cited in Ralph A. Norem, *Kiaochow Leased Territory* (Berkeley: University of California Press, 1939), 29.

19. Heyking to Zongli Yamen, GX 21/8/18 (6/10/1895), JWJAD, 5.2:604–5.

20. Memorandum of conversation between Heyking and Prince Gong et al., GX 23/11/9 (2/12/1897), QDDASLCB, 3:173.

21. Cited in Langer, 459.

22. Edict of GX 23/12/23 (15/1/1898) in QSL, 413:13b–14a; Zongli Yamen memorial of same date and edict of GX 24/1/11 (1/2/1898) in Lian Li-zhi and Wang Shou-zong, 194–95.

23. Edict, GX 21/8/11 (29/9/1895), QSL, 374:9a–9b; Wehrle, 82–86, 90.

24. Li Bing-heng, GX 22/6/24 (3/8/1896), DASL, 1:6.

25. See, e.g., Li Bing-heng, GX 22/11/19 (23/12/1896), and Heyking, GX 22/12/3 (5/1/1897), in JWJAD, 6.1:170–171, 173–177; Li Bing-heng, GX 21/9/23 (9/11/1895), GX 22/2/26 (8/4/1896), JWJAD, 5.2:620, 6.1:133. Heyking, 2/12/1896 meeting with Zongli Yamen, QDDASLCB, 3:173.

26. For the Catholic view, see "Quan-huo-ji," in SDJDSZL, 3:207–209.

27. Li Bing-heng, GX 21/9/16, in *Li Zhong-jie gong zou-yi* (Liaoning, 1938), 10:3b–10a.

28. NCH, 56:755 (15/5/1896).

29. NCH, 58:1091 (18/6/1897).

30. Memo of conversation with Heyking, QDDASLCB, 3:171. Heyking's reply was caustic (if regrettably accurate): "I fear that he has not saved enough to pay for the reparations to us."

31. MacDonald to Salisbury, 1/12/1897, cited in Wehrle, 102.

32. Henry D. Porter, "The German Mission in Shantung," n.d. [spring 1898], in ABC 16.3.12, no. 191.

33. NCH 60:409–410 (14/3/1898).

34. NCH 60:227 (14/2/1898).

35. J. A Fitch, January 1898, BFM, reel 213.

36. Zhang Ru-mei, GX 24/3/21 (11/4/1898), JWJAD, 6.1:222–23.

37. Stenz, *Life of Henle*, 131.

38. J. Murray, from Jining, 5/12/1898, BFM, reel 214.

CHAPTER SIX

1. *Hui-bao* no. 153 (2:422), GX 26/1/22 (21/2/1900) in SDSZZL, 1960.2:118. Cf. Yu-lu to Yuan Shi-kai, GX 25/12/9 (9/1/1900) in Lin Xue-jian, ed., *Zhi-Dong jiao-fei dian-cun* (1906; Taibei reprint: Wen-hai, n.d.), 1:60b–61a. Among recent scholars, Dai Xuan-zhi has argued in his *Yi-he-tuan yan-jiu* (Taibei: Wen-hai, 1963) that the Boxers originated in this area.

2. *Guan xian-zhi* (1934), 126–133.

3. Ibid., 720–721, 1367–1376, 1558–1573.

4. Ibid., 237–238.

5. Philip Kuhn, *Rebellion and Its Enemies in Late Imperial China: Militarization and Social Structure, 1796–1864* (Cambridge, Mass.: Harvard University Press, 1970).

6. *Guan xian-zhi* (1934), 336–7.

7. For documentary mention of the exclaves and the number of villages in each (officially each 18), see Zhong-guo she-hui ke-xue-yuan, jin-dai-shi yan-jiu-suo, ed., *Shandong Yi-he-tuan an-juan* (Jinan: Qi-Lu, 1980), 138, 461 (hereafter cited as AJ). For oral history accounts, and various versions of which villages comprised Guan's "18 villages," see SDDC, 261–264.

8. Gao Jing-shi, SDDC, 262.

9. *Wei xian-zhi* (1929), 2:15a.

10. For the shifting jurisdictions of this area, see *Dongchang fu-zhi* 1:3–15; *Guangping fu-zhi, juan* 2. The most plausible explanation I heard from residents of the area during my visit in June 1980 was that some ancient magistrate had fled to the Guan eighteen villages area and successfully held out there against some local disturbance. As a result, the area was added to the Guan county jurisdiction.

11. *Guan xian-zhi* (1934), 103. Cf. Lin Chuan-jia, 259–260.

12. Cao Ti, "Gu-chun cao-tang bi-ji," Zhong-guo she-hui ke-xue-yuan, jin-dai-shi yan-jiu-suo, ed., *Yi-he-tuan shi-liao* (Beijing: CASS, 1982), 1:268 (hereafter cited as YHTSL).

13. Sun Chao-hua, GX 25/1/30, Ming-Qing Archives, *lu-fu-zou-zhe* (hereafter: LFZZ) GX 25:75/6. Jizhou, to which Nangong belonged, seems to have been one of the worst departments for banditry. See the repeated mention of the department in the QSL (GX), 367:8a; 370:3a–3b, 10b–11b; 373:13b–14a; 438:13a–13b.

14. Linqing correspondence, NCH, 56:445 (20/3/1896), 56:84 (17/1/1896).

15. See reports in NCH, 56:445; 56:679 (1/5/1896); 57:918–919 (27/11/1896); 58:341 (26/2/1897).

16. *Guan xian-zhi* (1934), 1577.

17. See *Guan xian-zhi* (1934), 880, 899, 915–16. Three of the six mentioned exclave notables came from Ganji, also known as Zhongxingji. The other two were lesser individuals, recorded only as "filial and righteous."

18. *Guan xian-zhi* (1934), 222–224.

19. Cao Ti, YHTSL, 1:267.

20. *Guan xian-zhi* (1934), 151, 1454–1456.

21. YLSL, 23–25.

22. Na-yan-cheng JQ 20/11/20, YLSL, 84–85. In this memorial Gu-xian (固獻) is rendered "固賢", but the references to Ganji (rendered "甘集") and the village in which Zhang served as priest, Wangshigong (王世公, here rendered 王士公)—all of which are in the exclave—remove any doubt that these activities were in the Liyuantun area.

23. *Guan xian-zhi* (1934) 152–153.

24. Guo Dong-chen, SDDC, 275.

25. Zhang Yue, GX 16/4/4, JWJAD, 5.1:464–465; Guan magistrate, GX 26/10/10, AJ, 453–454.

26. SD Survey, Zhao San-duo, 11–12.

27. Yu Zhong-hai and Gao Jing-shi, SDDC, 254–257; Zhang Yue, GX 16/4/4, JWJAD, 5.1:464–465.

28. Zhang Yue, GX 16/4/4, JWJAD, 5.1:464–5.

29. Interviews in Liyuantun, 10/6/1980. The SD Survey (Zhao San-duo, p. 3) and *Shandong Yi-he-tuan diao-cha bao-gao*, 38–39, based on information from Yu Zhong-hai, an 81-year-old villager in 1960, claim that 28 landlords owned 80 percent of the village land. The largest was said to own over 3,000 *mu*. When, during my visit, I asked the oldest surviving peasants (in their 70s and 80s), they found these claims laughable. The figures above are based on these men's recollection of the holdings, at the time of the informants' earliest memory, of the landlords named by Yu Zhong-hai.

30. Interview in Liyuantun; SD Survey, Zhao San-duo, 3–5; SDDC, 255–256; Guo Dong-chen, "Yi-he-tuan de yuan-qi," SDDC, 333; *Guan xian-zhi*, 880.

31. *Guan xian-zhi*, 455–61, 648–649, 723–724.

32. French minister Lemay to Zongli Yamen, GX 15/11/8 (30/11/1889), JWJAD, 5.1:458–460; Zhang Yue, GX 16/4/4 (22/5/1890) which includes He Shi-zhen's report, ibid., 464–466. Guo Dong-chen, "Yi-he-tuan de yuan-qi," SDDC, 327–28; *Shandong Yi-he-tuan diao-cha bao-gao*, 46.

33. Yu Zhong-hai, Li Lao-shen, and Li Ji-zeng, SDDC, 254–255.

34. Guan magistrate's report, 11/6/1900, AJ, 447.

35. French Minister Lemay to Zongli Yamen, GX 17/12/16 (15/1/1892),

JWJAD, 5.1 : 522; Fu-run, GX 18/5/6 (31/5/1892), ibid., 528–529; Guo Dong-chen, "Yi-he-tuan de yuan-qi," SDDC, 327–328; Yu Zhong-hai, SDDC, 254–255.

36. Guo Dong-chen, "Yi-he-tuan de yuan-qi," SDDC, 327–328, 333; Zhang Lan-ting, Gao Yuan-chang (son of one gentry leader), SDDC, 255–256.

37. Guo Dong-chen, "Yi-he-tuan de yuan-qi," SDDC, 327–328, and a slightly fuller version of this in "Zhao San-duo zi-liao," 4, 7–9; Zhang Ru-mei, GX 24/10/4 (17/11/1898), JWJAD, 6.1 : 279–80; F. M. Chapin to J. Smith, 16/5/1892, ABC 16.3.12, vol. 18, no. 18. Chapin claims "a few" Christians were killed in this incident, and Guo Dong-chen dates the death of one "Lame Wang" (Wang Que-zi) in 1892—but I suspect a death would have brought more missionary protests in JWJAD and that "Lame Wang" was the same as the Wang Tai-qing killed in 1897 (see below).

38. Hong Yong-zhou, cited in Zhang Ru-mei, GX 24/4/29 (17/6/1898), JWJAD, 6.1 : 238; Dai Xuan-zhi, 15–16.

39. Wang Huai-ling, Yu Zhong-hai, and Zhang Lao-he, SDDC, 259–260, and Yu in *Shandong Yi-he-tuan diao-cha bao-gao*, 46–47. These oral history sources contain a full list of the Eighteen Chiefs and the property and occupations of most. This evidence is corroborated by the fact that when the Qing began confiscating property in the wake of the 1900 uprising, they found the two leaders Yan and Gao to be propertyless, and seized a total of only 3.196 *mu* in Liyuantun, out of some 140 *mu* from boxers in three of the Eighteen Villages of Guan county. (Guan magistrate's reports received 1/12/1900 and 3/2/1901, AJ, 455, 464.) The confession of Yan Shu-qin's brother Shu-tang gives the former's age as 39 *sui* in 1898. (Cited in Zhang Ru-mei, GX 24/10/2 [15/11/1898], JWJAD, 6.1 : 270–271.)

40. French Minister to Zongli Yamen, GX 24/5/27 (15/7/1898), JWJAD, 6.1 : 245. It should be noted that this document was certainly available to Dai Xuan-zhi when he wrote his book attempting to prove the militia origins of the Boxers. His deliberate ignoring of this evidence raises some questions about his methodology.

41. Linqing correspondence, NCH, 60 : 465 (21/3/1898).

42. Yu Zhong-hai, SDDC, 260; Yan Lao-wen, SD Survey, Zhao San-duo, 22.

43. The most thorough attempt to link these references all the way to the Guan county events of the 1890s is Li Shi-yu, "Yi-he-tuan yuan-liu shi-tan," *Li-shi jiao-xue*, 1979.2 : 20–21. Another is Lu Yao, "Yi-he-tuan yun-dong chu-qi dou-zheng jie-duan de ji-ge wen-ti," *Zhong-guo jin-dai-shi lun-wen-ji* (Beijing: Zhong-hua, 1979), 676–7. Susan Naquin, *Millenarian Rebellion*, 31, mentions Plum Flower Boxing as one of the schools taught by the sects, apparently based on the document reproduced in YLSL, 73.

44. Tang Heng-le confessions, JQ 18/12/16 and 18/12/26, YLSL, 2, 63–64. See also the discussion in chapter 2.

45. Wang Jun, SDDC, 279; Guo Dong-chen, SDDC 264–5; Hou Chun-jing, SDDC, 267; Xing Dong-chun, SDDC, 267; Yi Lao-quan, SDDC, 267.

46. It is notable (though too little noted) that none of the contemporary documentary sources on the Guan county boxers makes any reference to

invulnerability rituals. The only original documentary reference to invulnerability is in the 1934 Guan county gazetteer (pp. 1574–1576) but this is unquestionably the result of confusing the Boxers United in Righteousness of 1897–98 and those who spread over north China in 1899–1900. In fact, it seems that when the Boxers returned to the area in 1900, some brought the new rituals with them. (Yu Zhong-hai, SDDC, 268.)

47. Hong Yong-zhou report, cited in Zhang Ru-mei, GX 24/4/29 (17/6/1898), JWJAD, 6.1:236.

48. Zhang Lao-he, SDDC, 265–66; cf. Zhang Ru-mei, GX 24/5/12 (30/6/1898), DASL, 1:15.

49. Cao Ti, "Gu-chun cao-tang bi-ji." If Yang Bing was indeed the patriarch in the Kang-xi era, this would imply generations of about 35 years up to Zhao San-duo. That is not very plausible. See below for a more plausible oral history account of 16 or 17 generations.

50. Luo Cheng-lie, "Zhao San-duo, Yan Shu-qin ling-dao de Yi-he-tuan fan-di dou-zheng," paper presented to Shandong Historical Association, 1979, 5 (citing a tablet discovered near Zhao's home).

51. The magistrate, Cao Ti (YHTSL, 1:268), says that his information came from one of his clerks, who in turn got it from a boxer leader by the name of "sixth Gao," which leaves plenty of room for exaggeration and error. Guo Dong-chen, who served as an aide to Zhao, is particularly vehement and precise in insisting that Zhao was a poor peasant: "Guo Dong-chen de qin-bi hui-yi," Shandong da-xue wen-ke lun-wen-ji, 1980.1:155–156; "Yi-he-tuan de yuan-qi," SDDC, 332. The issue of class background is such an important issue in the P.R.C. (especially to Zhao's descendants) that the local Public Security Bureau arranged an investigation in 1977, which again yielded unanimity for Zhao's humble status—though it is notable that of 11 old peasants surveyed, 7 were Zhaos. They observed that the village head, Zhao Lao-hang, who came from a different branch of the Zhao lineage, owned three or four hundred mu, and Cao Ti's informant may have confused this man and Zhao San-duo (Zhao Lao-zhu). (Survey notes by Lu Jing-qi, 20–21/12/1977, loaned to me by the author.) The stakes involved in the assignment of class categories are so important in the P.R.C. that one must be extremely wary of choosing such testimony over documentary evidence. But in this case, I am inclined to believe that the magistrate was misinformed. Yet it is equally improbable, given Zhao's considerable local prestige, that he was only a poor peasant. Most plausible is a missionary report from 1899 which called him a "small landlord." (Wettswald, in Lettres de Jersey 19.1 [Jan. 1900], cited in Tiedemann, "Geopolitical Dimensions," 34.)

52. Guo Dong-chen, SDDC, 269–270; "Yi-he-tuan de yuan-qi," SDDC, 328–329.

53. Guo Dong-chen, "Yi-he-tuan de yuan-qi," SDDC, 328–9. This printed source places the exhibition on GX 22/2/22 (4/4/1896), but earlier manuscript versions of Guo's recollections give the date as the spring of 1897, which better fits the documentary record. (Guo Dong-chen, "Zhao San-duo zi-liao," 11; also part 2:3–4.)

54. Linqing correspondence, 30/4/1897, in NCH, 58:863 (14/5/1897);

French Minister to Zongli Yamen, GX 23/6/27 (26/7/1897) JWJAD 6.1 : 192. It should be noted that the NCH source terms the Plum Flower Boxers a "successor" of the White Lotus, but for reasons explained above, I am not inclined to accept this. In fact it seems that the Christians, in order to discredit their rivals, often tried to link them to the White Lotus—an unusual twist, given the background of many Christian converts. Even in the oral history sources, it is usually Christians who link the Boxers to the White Lotus. See Hu De-qing, and Hu Xiu-lan, both of Xiajing, SDDC, 292–293. The NCH correspondent also claims three Christians were killed, but this is corrected in NCH, 59 : 1129 (24/11/1897). That the Christian injuries were real enough is attested by the report of the Protestant hospital in Linqing to which they fled for treatment. (E. R. Wagner, "Annual Report of Medical Work, Lin Ching Station," May 1897, ABC 16.3.2, vol. 15.)

55. Guo Dong-chen, "Yi-he-tuan de yuan-qi," SDDC, 329. Linqing correspondence NCH, 59 : 654–655, 1129 (8/10/1897 and 24/12/1897); Zongli Yamen, GX 23/11/29 (22/12/1897), GX 23/12/23 (15/1/1898), JWJAD, 6.1 : 195, 197–198.

56. Zhang Ru-mei, GX 25/3/21 (11/4/1898), JWJAD, 6.1 : 222. It should be stressed that Zhang makes the connection to the Jiaozhou seizure explicit.

57. On Yao Wen-qi, see Yu-lu, GX 24/12/12 (23/1/1899), JWJAD, 6.1 : 301; Li Jiu-zi, SDDC, 314; Ren Lao-tong, SDDC, 317–318. Guo Dong-chen, a key source on this entire incident, has consistently argued that the early boxers were anti-Qing Ming-restorationists in the classic tradition of nineteenth century secret societies. Part of his argument surrounds two boxers who lived with a blind Daoist priest in Yongnian, who were introduced into the struggle by Yao Wen-qi. This is at least plausible, but there is no reason to believe that their own beliefs influenced the boxing organization as a whole. An even less credible claim is that Guo carried on correspondence on Zhao's behalf the content of which was anti-Manchu, and that it was a doctor with the Qing army who persuaded Zhao to change his slogan from "Expel the Qing, destroy the foreign" to "Assist the Qing, destroy the foreign" (Zhu-Qing mie-yang). No other evidence supports the claim that the Guan county boxers were ever anti-Qing, and Guo's ultimate position that Zhao was "secretly" anti-Qing is both quite unverifiable and of questionable significance to any assessment of the political aims of the movement which Zhao led. (Guo Dong-chen, "Zhao San-duo zi-liao," 3, 16, 47; part 2 : 4, parts of which are reproduced in SDDC, 313–14; Guo, "Yi-he-tuan de yuan-qi," SDDC, 328, 334–5.) Guo's testimony has nonetheless been the basis for claims in some P.R.C. historiography that these earliest Boxers of Guan county were initially anti-Manchu (e.g., Shandong shi-fan xue-yuan, "Shandong Yi-he-tuan fan-di ai-guo yun-dong," Yi-he-tuan yun-dong liu-shi zhou-nian ji-nian lun-wen-ji [Beijing: Zhong-hua, 1961], 98).

58. Li Jiu-zi, SDDC, 315.

59. Ibid.; Guo Dong-chen, "Yi-he-tuan de yuan-qi," SDDC, 334–335; SDDC 264–265. Qing reports stress official proscription of the Plum Flower Boxers, and pressure on Zhao San-duo to disperse them, as the reason for the

name change to Yi-he quan. Hong Yong-zhou, cited in Zhang Ru-mei, GX 24/4/29 (17/6/1898), JWJAD, 6.1:236.

60. De Marchi to A. Gerard, 31/5/1897 from the French legation archives, cited in Tiedemann, "Geopolitical Dimensions," 34.

61. Hong Yong-zhou, cited in Zhang Ru-mei, GX 24/4/29 (17/6/1898), JWJAD, 6.1:236.

62. Zhang Lao-he, SDDC, 265–66.

63. The new *Cambridge History of China*, vol. 11, part 2:117 reflects this convention. It is consistent with George Steiger calling the Yi-he tuan the "Righteous and Harmonious Band" in the first serious scholarly work on the subject in English (*China and the Occident* [New Haven: Yale, 1927], 134). Chester Tan translates the term "Righteous Harmony Fists" (*The Boxer Catastrophe*, 36), which corresponds to Purcell's "Righteous Harmony Boxing" (*The Boxer Uprising*, 163).

64. Zhang Ru-mei, GX 24/4/3 (22/5/1898), DASL, 1:14. This is corrected by the Hong Yong-zhou report cited by Zhang on GX 24/4/29 (17/6/1898), JWJAD, 6.1:236.

65. See Wei You-xue, SDDC, 266.

66. H. P. Perkins to Conger, 25/11/1899 in FRUS, 1900, 83.

67. MacDonald to Salisbury, 31/1/1900 in Parliamentary Papers, *China (No. 3) 1900*, 13. Cf. the oral history accounts in SDDC 126–127 saying "'Yi-he' meant 'of one mind (*tong-xin*),'" and a Beijing source in YHT, 2:183.

68. Guo Dong-chen, "Qin-bi hui-yi," 155–56. Cf. Lu Yao, "Lun Yi-he-tuan," 49–52. Lu and Guo both had access to a 1923 Wei county gazetteer which I have not seen, but which mentions these militia groups.

69. Lebon to Zongli Yamen, GX 23/12/15 (7/1/1898) JWJAD, 6.1:196.

70. *Guan xian-zhi*, 724–725. Cao Ti, "Gu-chun cao-tang bi-ji," YHTSL, 1:267–268. Cao's account was written in 1927, well after the events occurred. It is extremely melodramatic, and not entirely trustworthy. Sometimes it is simply wrong: for example he places most of the action in Liyuantun itself, though it is clear from his mention of the academy and tax-collection that he must have been in Ganji. Nonetheless, when corroborated by other materials, it remains an invaluable source on the incidents of 1898.

71. H. P. Perkins, "Report of the Lin-ching Station for the year ending April 30, 1898," ABC 16.3.2, vol. 15.

72. Hong Yong-zhou, cited in Zhang Ru-mei, GX 24/4/29 (17/6/1898), JWJAD, 6.1:236.

73. Cao Ti, 267–268; Linqing correspondence, 4/3/1898, NCH, 60:464–5 (21/3/1898). Cao Ti's account goes on to describe his success in dispersing the Boxers, but the NCH source is clear that Cao's initial solo effort failed. The documentary record in JWJAD and the oral histories all stress prefect Hong Yong-zhou's primary responsibility for the dispersal which finally took place. Thus in the portions of Cao's account cited below, I am assuming that he was accompanying Hong on a separate mission.

74. Xiao Lao-tai, SDDC, 267.

75. Zhang Ru-mei, GX 24/3/21 (11/4/1898), JWJAD, 6.1:221. On the ruse

allowing Yan to escape, Guo Dong-chen, "Yi-he-tuan de yuan-qi," SDDC, 329.

76. Hong Yong-zhou, cited in Zhang Ru-mei, GX 24/4/29 (17/6/1898), JWJAD, 6.1:236.

77. Cao Ti, 269.

78. Cao Ti; Li Ji-zeng, SDDC, 272; Zhang Lan-ting, SDDC, 255; Ren Lao-tong, SDDC, 272; Linqing correspondence, 4/3/1898, NCH, 60:464–5 (21/3/1898). According to this last source, prefect Hong offered Zhao "such honor and wealth as no one in this whole region possesses." That no doubt overstated the case, but it was probably a fair reflection of Hong's approach.

79. Linqing correspondence, 18/3/1898, NCH, 60:570–571 (4/4/1898).

80. See various reports in JWJAD, 6.1:86 (Nos. 115, 117); 90–91 (No. 125); 250 (No. 274).

81. P. Isoré, "La Chrétienté de Tchao-kia-tchoang sur le pied de guerre," Chine et Ceylon 1:106–108. These handbills are also noted in Zhang Ru-mei, GX 24/4/29 (17/6/1898), JWJAD 6.1:237–238.

82. French Minister, GX 24/4/26 (14/6/1898), JWJAD, 6.1:234–235; Zhang Ru-mei, GX 24/4/29 (17/6/1898), JWJAD, 6.1:237–238. For other such documents focusing on the Eighteen Chiefs, see ibid., 232–234; 243–245.

83. QSL, GX 21/4/18 (12/5/1895), 366:6a.

84. QSL, GX 23/11/25 (18/12/1897), 412:15b.

85. Zhang Ru-mei, GX 24/5/12 (30/6/1898), DASL, 1:15; Linqing correspondence 18/7/1898, NCH, 61:204 (1/8/1898).

86. QSL, GX 24/10/12 (25/11/1898), 431:12a–12b.

87. Zhang Ru-mei, GX 24/run 3/28 (18/5/1898), DASL, 1:13–14.

88. Zhang Ru-mei, GX 24/5/12 (30/6/1898), DASL, 1:14–15.

89. Dai Xuan-zhi, Yi-he-tuan yan-jiu, 5–19; George N. Steiger, China and the Occident, 129–146. The most effective refutations of Dai's argument are Sasaki Masaya, "Giwadan no kigen," Pt. II, Kindai Chūgoku, 1977.7, 124–5, 132–4; and Lu Yao, "Lun Yi-he-tuan," 49–52.

90. Linqing correspondence, NCH, 60:1,113 (27/6/1898).

91. Guo Dong-chen, "Yi-he-tuan de yuan-qi," SDDC, 329. An earlier version of this in "Zhao San-duo zi-liao," 16, says that Zhao traveled north-ward into central Zhili at this time.

92. Yao Wen-qi confession in Yu-lu, GX 24/12/12 (23/1/1899), JWJAD, 6.1:301–304. The rumors are dated in the ninth lunar month (Oct. 15–Nov. 13).

93. Zhang Ru-mei, GX 24/10/2 (15/11/1898), JWJAD, 6.1:270–71. This document does not give the date of the arrests, but the context suggests that it was prior to the hostilities which broke out in late October.

94. Shandong governor to Caozhou commander, GX 24/9/14 (29/10/1898), SDXF in Chou-bi ou-cun (Beijing: CASS, 1983), 711 (hereafter cited as CBOC); Wan Pei-yin cable, received GX 24/9/20 (3/11/1898), Lin Xue-jian, 1:3b–4a.

95. Wan Pei-yin cables, received GX 24/9/20 (3/11/1898), Lin Xue-jian, 1:2a–4a; and Yao Wen-qi confession, JWJAD, 6.1:301–304. The latter gives October 26 as the date Zhao was carried off.

96. Report of Cao Ti and the Linqing subprefect Wang Shou-ming, cited

in Zhang Ru-mei, GX 24/12/5 (16/1/1899), JWJAD, 6.1:297–8. This report, based on Cao's inspection, put the attack in Chenjiazhuang. Guo Dong-chen, SDDC, 270, puts the attack in Chiangjiazhuang, which is immediately adjacent to Chenjiazhuang. Guo also claims (improbably, as the missionaries made no such claim) that one convert was killed.

97. Ibid. Both sources reflect the southward movement. Zhang's memorial dates the attack on Xiaoligu on October 30. Wan Pei-yin (received GX 24/9/20 [3/11/1898], Li Xue-jian, 1:3b–4a) has a detailed description of the movement of the boxer bands, but his Longshanggu (龍上固) is certainly an error for Liushangu (留善固), a large village (market town?) in Linqing, directly on the Zhili border.

98. Wan Pei-yin, received GX 24/9/20 (3/11/1898), Liu Xue-jian, 1:2a.

99. Isoré, 106.

100. E. E. Aiken to Judson Smith, 10/11/1898, ABC 16.3.12, vol. 17, no. 71. Cf. the report of "a flag in favor of the Government." (Linqing corresp. NCH, 61:950 [21/11/1898].)

101. Guo Dong-chen, SDDC, 313; "Yi-he-tuan de yuan-qi," 329, gives both versions of the slogan on the flags.

102. Yu-lu, GX 24/12/12 (23/1/1899), JWJAD, 6.1:301–2. Cf. *Daotai* Wan Pei-yin's report to Yu-lu, received GX 24/9/23 (6/11/1898), Lin Xue-jian, 1:7a–7b; Zhang Ru-mei to Yu-lu, GX 24/9/21 (4/11), ibid., 1:5a. During this effort to disperse the Boxers peacefully, Cao Ti anxiously requested that no more troops be sent to the area, and even claimed that the incident in Xiaoligu on October 30 had been nothing more than a Christian burning his own home in order to try to provoke trouble. (Guan to Governor, GX 24/9/17 [31/10/1898] SDXF in CBOC, 689.) On Nov. 2, Cao Ti reported the Boxers dispersed. (CBOC, 689.)

103. Guo Dong-chen, SDDC, 270. It is true that the official accounts are all unusually protective of Zhao San-duo, and perhaps a little questionable on that account. One small point that makes me believe Yu-lu's account is its reference to the commander from Daming leaving a few cavalry and returning to his base after the Boxers dispersed. Had the Boxers *not* dispersed, the troops would certainly not have left the area; and I can think of no reason for the officials fabricating a story which tends to make them appear too quick to assume that quiet was restored.

104. Yu-lu, GX 24/12/12 (23/1/1899), JWJAD 6.1:301–304 (this gives 15 as the number captured); Zhang Ru-mei, GX 24/12/5 (16/1/1899), ibid., 297–8; Wan Pei-yin, received 24/9/27 (10/11/1898), Lin Xue-jian, 1:10a–11a; Isoré, 106–113.

105. Guo Dong-chen, SDDC, 270–271; "Yi-he-tuan de yuan-qi," 329–30, 335; Li Jiu-zi, SDDC, 272.

106. Wan Pei-yin, received GX 24/9/27 (10/11/1898), Lin Xue-jian, 1:10a–11a.

107. Guo Dong-chen, "Zhao San-duo zi-liao," 39–40. The oral history of these 1900 battles is given in SDDC, 275–308; and Guo Dong-chen, "Yi-he-tuan de yuan-qi," SDDC, 330–332, 335–337. For documentary references, see AJ, 138–140, 354, 375–7, 379–382, 449–451, 462.

108. Guo Dong-chen, SDDC, 308–309, "Yi-he-tuan de yuan-qi," 331–332.

109. F. H. Chapin to Judson Smith, 23/11/1899, ABC, 16.3.12, vol. 18, no. 64. See also E. A. Aiken, Linqing Station report for the year ending 30/4/1899, ABC, 16.3.12, vol. 16.

CHAPTER SEVEN

1. Hart to Campbell, 23/1/1898, I.G., 2:1149.
2. Ernest Box, "Native Newspapers," NCH, 61:736–738 (17/10/1898).
3. C:IGC, 1881, II:4, 25 and map.
4. Zhang Yu-fa, 2:500–502.
5. NCH, 58 (1897) *passim*; Zhang Yu-fa, 2:495–497.
6. Zhang Yu-fa, 1:385–390.
7. Li Bing-heng, GX 21/11/11 and 22/1/24 (26/12/1895 and 7/3/1896), *Li Zhong-jie gong zou-yi* (hereafter: LBH), 10:26b–29a (798–803), 11:1a–3a (553–857).
8. See NCH, 61:339 (22/8/1898); JWJAD, 6.1:260–62, 266–68.
9. Zhang Yu-fa, 1:321–322.
10. With few systematic figures on Shandong's budget for this period, I have had to reconstruct this figure from several sources. An 1891 memorial from Zhang Yue (GX 17/6/16, Hu-bu ti-ben, No. 2619) lists 1,091,000 taels in obligations to Beijing and other provinces that Shandong was at least partially in arrears on. In 1895, Li Bing-heng reported that one-half of the funds remitted would only support Shandong's defense requirements for three months at the rate of 200,000 taels per month. (Li Bing-heng, GX 21/9/12 [29/10/1895], LBH, 10:2a–3a [749–751].) The 1.2 million figure that Li's statement implies is consistent with statistics cited in Zhang Yu-fa (1:341–342) which show local expenses of 1,202,717 taels for 1892, and local plus remitted expenditures of 2,378,571 for 1895.
11. See, e.g., Hu-bu memorial, GX 19/4/4 (19/5/1893), Hu-bu ti-ben (Agriculture) No. 25; Li Bing-heng, GX 22/11/22 (26/12/1896), Hu-bu ti-ben No. 2659; also Zhang Yu-fa, 1:341–343.
12. Li Bing-heng, GX 23/6/16 (15/7/1897), LBH, 15:4a–5b (1111–1114).
13. Zhang Yue, GX 17/6/16 (21/7/1891), Hu-bu ti-ben No. 2619 (on 1887); Fu-run, GX 18/11/19 (6/1/1893), Hu-bu ti-ben No. 2630 (on 1888); Li Bing-heng, GX 22/11/22 (26/12/1896), Hu-bu ti-ben No. 2659 (on 1892). There is an extreme, and to me unexplainable, discrepancy between these figures and those in Zhang Yu-fa (1:341–342, citing *Wan-guo gong-bao* and a 1903 memorial), which report 1892 revenues as 1,570,492 plus 67,902 piculs of grain; and 1895 revenues as 2,585,338 taels. It was of course normal for officials to underreport revenues, but one would expect them at least to report consistently. When they do not, we are logically impelled, as here, to accept the larger figures.
14. Li Bing-heng, GX 22/4/1 (13/5/1896), LBH, 12:3a–4a (907–909).
15. Li Bing-heng, GX 22/7/10 (18/8/1896), LBH, 12:22a–24a (945–949).
16. Li Bing-heng, GX 22/4/1 (13/5/1896), LBH, 12:1a–3a (903–907). For

other claims of a bare treasury, see QSL 388:8a; Shandong governor to Zongli Yamen, [GX 25]/6/17 (24/7/1899), SDXF, telegrams; governor to Xing-bu (?) [GX 25]/11/19 (21/12/1899), SDXF, outgoing telegrams, No. 168.

17. Edict of GX 24/7/5 (21/8/1898), QSL, 423:4a–4b.

18. Li Bing-heng, GX 23/2/12 (14/3/1897), in LBH, 14:8a–9b (1057–1060).

19. Linqing correspondence (24/1/1896), in NCH, 56:275 (21/2/1896).

20. C:IGC, 1898, II:31; 1899, II:32. This second source gives a figure for 1898 of 2,080, but this is apparently a different tael, for the 1892 figure in this report is given as 3,100, while it was 3,263 in the series reported in 1898. Assuming a constant ratio between the two taels, the 1899 figure would be 2,189 according to the 1898 series.

21. Edict of GX 22/5/2 (12/6/1896) QSL, 390:26; Li Bing-heng, GX 22/7/28 (5/9/1896), LBH, 14:1a–2a (1043–1045). *Chiping xian-zhi* (1935), 7:6a (1075).

22. Linqing correspondence, NCH, 60:273 (21/2/1898); 60:113 (27/6/1898).

23. Zhang Yu-fa, 1:379–383.

24. K. C. Liu, "The Military Challenge: The North-west and the Coast," *Cambridge History*, vol. 11, 205.

25. Li Bing-heng, GX 23/6/16 (15/7/1897), LBH, 15:4a–5b (1111–1114).

26. Edict of GX 23/3/4 (5/4/1897), QSL, 402:3a–4a; edicts of GX 24/3/30 (20/4/1898) and 24/9/24 (7/11/1898), QSL, 416:21b, 430:12a. It seems, however, that when Yuan Shi-kai became governor in the winter of 1899, he completed the planned 50% reduction, for in 1901 he reported total reductions in force between 1870 and 1900 as 10,318 men, which would imply a 50% reduction after 1895. (Zhang Yu-fa, 1:382.)

27. Li Bing-heng, GX 22/8/28 (4/10/1896), LBH, 12:33a–34a (967–969); Yu-xian to Hu-bu, [GX 25]/10/27 (29/11/1899), SDXF, outgoing telegrams. As an indication of the distribution of forces in Shandong as the Boxer uprising broke out in earnest, Yu-xian's report is worth summarizing in tabular form:

Type of unit	Number of men	Annual cost (taels)	cost/man
Bannermen	2,130	129,100	60.6
Coastal defense	11,300	508,000	45.0
Interior peacekeeping	7,300	317,000	43.4
Yellow River guards	11,853	221,600	18.7
Grand Canal guards	3,800	178,000	46.8
Officers' salaries, artisans, ammunition and construction	—	110,000	
Totals	36,383	1,463,700	

28. Edict of GX 24/1/30 (20/2/1898), QSL 414:21a–21b.

29. Both Li Bing-heng's memorial of 1896 and Yu-xian's of 1899 (cited in note 27) list the cost of coastal defense as roughly 500,000 taels.

30. Yizhoufu correspondence, NCH, 60:659 (18/4/1898). This report refers to the disbanded forces as "militia" but the timing and context

indicates that they must have been either "defense braves" or Green Standard units.

31. Yu-xian drafts of GX 25/5/2 (9/6/1899), GX 25/10/1 (3/11/1899) and GX 25/10/29 (1/12/1899), CBOC, 4, 38–40, 45–48.

32. In 1895 Li Bing-heng reported that the despatch of troops to the coast contributed to flooding in that year. (Edict, GX 21/3/2 [27/3/1895], QSL 363:2b.)

33. QSL, GX 24/12/10 (21/1/1899), 435:14a–14b. Muramatsu Yuji has argued this point at some length. *Giwadan no kenkyū* (Tokyo: Gannando, 1976), 10–14, 45–49. Yu-xian's reports on summary executions in the first 3 quarters of 1899 explicitly identify 23 of the 31 victims as "roving braves." (Statements of account [*qing-dan*] with receipt dates of GX 25/8/28, 10/25 and 12/23 [2/10 and 27/11/1899, 23/1/1900], LFZZ, GX 25, No. 75/76.)

34. QSL, GX 23/11/25 (18/12/1897), 412:15b.

35. Guo Ting-yi, 2:1019; Lo Jung-pang, 112.

36. On Zhang, see chapter 6; on Yu-xian, QSL, GX 25/10/24 (26/11/1899), 453:11b.

37. Edict of GX 25/6/6 (13/7/1899), DASL, 1:30.

38. Yizhou correspondence, NCH, 63:325–326 (14/8/1899).

39. Qingjiangpu correspondence, NCH, 57:919 (27/11/1896); NCH, 57:475 (18/9/1896).

40. N. Jiangsu correspondence, NCH, 59:740 (22/10/1897); Board of Revenue, Jing-xin et al., GX 23/10/22 (16/11/1897), Hu-bu ti-ben, No. 2640.

41. N. Jiangsu correspondence, NCH, 59:1129–1130 (24/12/1897).

42. Qingjiangpu correspondence, NCH, 59:1130 (24/12/1897).

43. Yizhoufu correspondence, NCH, 59:617 (1/10/1897).

44. Yizhoufu correspondence, NCH, 59:1083 (17/12/1897).

45. N. Jiangsu correspondence, NCH, 60:660 (18/4/1898).

46. Ibid., NCH, 60:929 (30/5/1898).

47. See repeated mention in QSL 417:7a–7b and 15a–15b; 421:3b–4a; 433:2a; 435:10b–11a.

48. N. Jiangsu correspondence, NCH, 62:170–171 (30/1/1899).

49. W. N. Crozier, 4/5/1899, BFM, reel 212.

50. W. O. Elterich, 23/12/1899, BFM, reel 213.

51. QSL, GX 24/2/23 (15/3/1898), 415:15a–15b.

52. Zhang Ru-mei, GX 24/6/17 (4/8/1898), GX 24/7/29 (14/9/1898), DASL, 1:17–19; Shandong governor to Caozhou general Fang Zhi-xiang, GX 24/6/11 (29/7/1898) and to Henan governor Jing, GX 24/6/13 (31/7/1898), SDXF, telegrams; CBOC, 702–703.

53. N. Jiangsu correspondence, NCH, 62:171 (30/1/1899).

54. N. Jiangsu correspondence, NCH, 62:247 (9/2/1899).

55. The fullest account of this rising is the joint memorial of Yu-zhang, Liu Kun-yi, and Deng Hua-xi, GX 25/1/30 (11/3/1899), LFZZ, GX 25, No. 9A. Liu Kun-yi has a second memorial (GX 25/9/7 [11/10/1899]) in 9B of the same archive. QSL has several references: 435:13a–13b, 15a–15b; 436:3b–4a; 437:12a–13a. For accounts of the death and destruction in the aftermath, Dr. George King, NCH, 63:131–132 (17/7/1899); W. N. Crozier, 4/5/1899, BFM, reel 212.

56. Zhang Ru-mei, GX 24/5/12 (30/6/1898), DASL, 1:16.

57. Yu-xian to Liu Kun-yi, GX 25/6/27 (3/8/1899), SDXF, outgoing telegrams, no. 177; Yu-xian to Zongli Yamen, GX 25/7/4 (9/8/1899), ibid., no. 194; Yu-xian memorial, GX 25/7/22 (27/8/1899), LFZZ GX 25, no. 75/76.

58. QSL, GX 24/7/6 (22/8/1898), 423:7a–7b; F. H. Chalfant, NCH, 61:1081–1082 (12/12/1898).

59. Wei county correspondence, NCH, 61:858 (7/11/1898); Qingzhou correspondence, NCH, 61:583 (26/9/1898).

60. Stenz, *Twenty-five Years*, 96–98; Henry Porter, *Mary H. Porter*, 29.

61. Henry Porter, NCH, 61:872–873 (7/11/1898); NCH, 61:1156–57 (19/12/1898).

62. F. H. Chalfant, NCH, 61:1081–1082 (12/12/1898).

63. Hu Fu-chen, GX 25/3/7 (16/4/1899), LFZZ, GX 25, 52–53.

64. QSL GX 24/11/4 (16/12/1898), 433:3b–4a; GX 24/11/7 (19/12/1898), 433:8a; GX 24/12/22 (2/2/1899), 436:10a–10b. Zhang Ru-mei had been warned of unusually high water upstream on the Yellow. See Shaanxi governor-general, GX 24/6/5 (23/7/1898), CBOC, 700.

65. QSL, GX 24/12/4 (15/1/1899), 435:4b–5a; GX 25/3/20 (29/4/1899), 441:4a–4b. While such findings of corruption were quite common and often politically motivated, in Zhang's case they were quite plausible. After a relatively brief and undistinguished career, Zhang was wealthy enough in 1898 to purchase 100,000 taels of Bonds to Manifest Confidence and contribute 10,000 taels for famine relief—generosity for which his three sons were rewarded with official positions. (*Peking Gazette* 22/10/98, trans. NCH, 63:871 [30/10/99].) He certainly stood in glaring contrast to the scrupulously parsimonious Li Bing-heng.

66. QSL, GX 23/3/23 (24/4/1897), 403:6b; GX 24/7/24 (9/9/1898), 425:6a–6b; GX 24/12/6 (17/1/1899), 435:6b–7a; GX 25/3/20 (29/4/1899), 441:5a. On the French pressure, see Pinchon, GX 24/4/11 (30/5/1898), JWJAD, 6.1:232–233; Zhang Ru-mei, GX 24/6/7 (25/7/1898), ibid., 248–249; Zongli Yamen, GX 24/4/12 (31/5/1898), CBOC, 687.

67. On Yu-xian's abilities in flood control and their role in his appointment see *Qing-shi lie-zhuan* 62, cited in Li Hong-sheng, 1; *Qing-shi* 7:5058.

68. C:IGC, 1899, 1:1.

69. Robert Hart to Campbell, 23/10/1898, I.G., 2:1175.

70. Ibid., 13/11/1898, 1177. On the whole series of incidents surrounding Dong Fu-xiang, see Steiger, 108–112; Muramatsu, *Giwadan no kenkyū*, 19–20; Conger to Hay, 1/10/1898 and 3/11/1898 plus enclosures, FRUS, 1898, 226–239; QSL, 420:6a–6b; 429:13a.

71. Guo Ting-yi, 2:1040, 1042, 1043, 1044.

72. Yu-xian drafts to local commanders and Yu-lu, GX 25/10/1 (3/11/1899), CBOC, 38–40.

73. Hart to Campbell, 19/3/1899, I.G., 2:1191.

74. Edict GX 25/10/19 (21/11/1899), DASL, 1:37–38. On the Italian demands and the Qing reaction, see Steiger, 114–127; Muramatsu, 55–56.

75. Hart to Campbell, 28/5/1899, I.G., 2:1197.

76. Guo Ting-yi, 2:990.

77. QSL, 417:5a, 9a; 418:1b, 9b–10a; CBOC, 685–687.

78. Schrecker, 63.

79. Schrecker, 87–90.

80. Yizhoufu correspondence, NCH, 60:841 (16/5/1898).

81. W. P. Chalfant, 5/10/1898, BFM, reel 214; cf. Yizhoufu correspondence, NCH, 61:292, 949–50 (15/8/1898 and 21/11/1898). Of course when local officials suggested the connection of missionaries to Western economic penetration, the preachers were certain to complain. When the new prefect to Yizhou proposed as a topic for examination essays "The use by Western Countries of the preaching of Doctrine as a means of spying out [the conditions of] other countries," the American missionaries were quick to protest. (Yizhoufu correspondence, NCH, 60:364 [7/3/1898].)

82. N. Jiangsu correspondence, NCH, 62:17 (9/1/1899).

83. In 1897, when the Germans had demanded the removal of Yao Xi-zan, they had requested that Peng be appointed in his place. (Guo Ting-yi, 2:990.)

84. Peng Yu-sun, GX 25/8/26 (30/9/1899), JWJAD, 6.1:443–444. Cf. Zhang Ru-mei, GX 25/3/3 (12/4/1899), JWJAD, 6.1:327–328.

85. Stenz, Twenty-five Years, 99–100.

86. Charles A. Killie, Wallace S. Faris, and William P. Chalfant to U.S. Consul Fowler (Chefoo), 29/11/1898, in FRUS, 1899, 155.

87. C. A. Killie, 9/1/1899, BFM, reel 214; cf. W. O. Elterich, 7/4/1899, BFM, reel 213. For Stenz's own dramatic account of his kidnapping, see Twenty-Five Years, 99–113. Stenz, however, is curiously silent on the causes of the incident. For that, see Zhang Ru-mei, GX 25/2/1 (12/3/1899), GX 25/3/3 (12/4/1899), JWJAD, 6.1:316–319, 327–328.

88. This rumor is reported in a letter of 16/11/1898 from Wm. P. Chalfant in NCH, 61:1058 (5/12/1898); Killie, Faris, and Chalfant to Consul Fowler, 29/11/1898, in FRUS, 1899, 155; Heyking to Zongli Yamen (citing Anzer), GX 24/12/1 (12/1/1899), JWJAD, 6.1:292–393; Hui-bao, GX 25/10/2, SDSZZL, 1960.2:132.

89. QSL GX 24/8/21 (6/10/1898), 428:1a–1b; GX 24/9/2 (16/10/1898), 429:2a–2b.

90. Yu-xian to Zongli Yamen, GX 25/5/15 (22/6/1899), CBOC, 7; and CBOC, n.d. 36–37 for casualties. Most of our information on these incidents comes from the American missionaries in Yizhou, which the American minister in Beijing, after checking with the German and French legations, judged to be based on "exaggerated reports made by the natives" (Conger to Hay, 8/2/1899, FRUS, 1899, 154). See FRUS, 1899, 154–178; BFM, reel 214; NCH, 61:1058, 1189 (5/12/1898 and 24/12/1898); 62:115, 169, 288, 478, 580–81, 669–670 (23/1/1899, 30/1/1899, 20/2/1899, 20/3/1899, 3/4/1899, 17/1/1899). For a Catholic reference, Thauren, Missions of Shandong, 47–49.

91. Yizhoufu correspondence, 10/1/1899, NCH, 62:169 (30/1/1899).

92. Schrecker, 94–95; Stenz, Twenty-five Years, 115–120; JWJAD, 6.1:292–3, 301, 305, 311.

93. Schrecker, 96; Zhang Ru-mei, GX 25/2/24 (4/4/1899), JWJAD, 6.1:323.

94. On this attempted rape/murder case, see extensive correspondence in JWJAD, 6.1:356–362, 375–377, 425–431.

95. Schrecker, 96–98. For the Chinese documentation in the Lanshan and Rizhao incursions, see DASL, 1:21–24; JWJAD, 6.1:330–347, 364–371. On the negotiated settlement see CBOC, 7–9, 12–13, 15–17, 25–26. There is also extensive telegraphic correspondence relating to the missionary incidents and German incursion in SDXF, but most of this is repeated in the published correspondence.

96. Both citations from Schrecker, 95.

97. See, for example, Immanuel Hsu's treatment of the Boxers in *The Cambridge History of China*, vol. 11, esp. pp. 118–119. For similar Japanese treatments, see Muramatsu Yuji, 89–90, 123; and especially Sasaki Masaya, "Giwadan no kigen," part 3, 174–177.

98. For a relatively sophisticated argument along these lines, see Lu Yao, "Yi-he-tuan yun-dong," 683–684. It is notable that at the 1980 Conference on the History of the Boxer Movement, there were three papers reversing this earlier view and praising Yu-xian for his support of the Boxers. (Chen Zai-zhen, "Lun Yi-he-tuan yun-dong shi-qi de Yu-xian"; Li Hong-sheng, "Yu-xian yu Shandong Yi-he-tuan"; Qi Chang-fa, "Lun Yu-xian.") Those by Chen and Li are particularly impressive, but they lead us back to an interpretation which is very close to the standard Western view—in part through uncritical reliance on foreign and Christian sources, the most important of which is "Quan-huo-ji," in SDJDSZL, 3:209–214.

99. Sheng Xuan-huai, GX 26/9/2 (24/10/1900), DASL, 2:727–728; Yuan Shi-kai letter to Yuan Shi-lian, his brother, n.d. (late 1900), SDJDSZL, 3:226–227; "Jing-shan ri-ji," YHT, 1:60 (but see Purcell, 272–284, on problems regarding the authenticity of this source); Luo Dun-rong, "Quan-bian yu-wen," in *Geng-zi quan-luan zi-liao*, ed., Zuo Shun-sheng (Taibei reprint, n.d.), 109–110.

100. See Yu-xian's matter-of-fact report of his action in a memorial of GX 26/6/14 (10/7/1900), DASL, 1:281.

101. The edict accused him of believing in the Boxer techniques while governor of Shandong, recommending the Boxers in Beijing, and killing Christians in Shanxi. (Edict, GX 26/12/25 [13/2/1901], DASL, 2:939.)

102. Li Hong-sheng, "Yu-xian," 1–2. The only error I have noted in Li's fine capsule biography of Yu-xian's early career is his following the *Qing-shi-gao* in calling Yu-xian a *Han* bannerman. The various *Jin-shen quan-shu* make clear that Yu-xian is a Manchu.

103. Yu-xian report cited in Zhang Ru-mei, GX 24/5/3 (21/6/1898), JWJAD, 6.1:240–242. See also Zhang Ru-mei, GX 24/3/30 (20/4/1898) and GX 24/run 3/28 (18/5/1898), DASL, 1:12–14.

104. Jinan correspondence, 10/4/1899, NCH, 62:814 (8/5/1899).

105. Heyking to Zongli Yamen, GX 25/3/13 (22/4/1899), JWJAD, 6.1:347. The *North China Herald* also opposed the appointment: 62:814 (17/4/1899).

106. Yu-xian to Zongli Yamen, GX 25/3/2 (11/4/1899), SDXF.

107. Yu-xian to Zongli Yamen, GX 25/5/15 and 5/28 (22/6 and 5/7/1899), SDXF; Yu-xian memorial GX 25/6/10 (17/7/1899), DASL, 1:30–31.

108. Schrecker, 104–111; Ge Zhi-jia and Zhang Cheng-lian to Yu-xian, incoming No. 42, GX 25/5/18 (6/7/1899), Yu-xian to Zongli Yamen, GX 25/6/3

(21/7/1899), No. 91, SDXF. SDXF is filled with telegraphic correspondence on the troubles along the railway, but these two reports are perhaps the most crucial. See also CBOC, 9–12, 20–21, 30–31.

109. Yu-xian to Zongli Yamen, No. 23, GX 25/4/18 (6/6/1899), SDXF; GX 25/5/2 (20/6/1899), CBOC, 3.

110. See, inter alia, Yu-xian to Zongli Yamen, GX 25/5/15 (22/6/1899), GX 25/6/10 (17/7/1899), and GX 25/6/9 draft (16/7/1899), CBOC, 7–8, 17–18, 21–22; Yu-xian, GX 25/6/20 (27/7/1899), JWJAD, 6.1:403–407.

111. Yu-xian to Zongli Yamen, No. 92, GX 25/6/3 (10/7/1899), SDXF.

112. On July 18, Yu-xian cabled Jaeschke that he would be unable to meet a representative to negotiate the Gaomi incidents because he was leaving to inspect the river (outgoing No. 95), and the excuse was repeated several times later in July. Yu-xian announced his return in No. 104 to the Zongli Yamen, GX 25/8/3 (7/9/1899), SDXF.

113. Yu-xian to Zongli Yamen, No. 174, GX 25/6/19 (26/7/1899), SDXF.

114. Linqing correspondence, 24/11/1899, NCH, 62:1212 (18/12/1899).

115. Stenz, *Twenty-five Years*, 93.

116. Wu Hong-jia, GX 25/12/21 (21/1/1900), LFZZ, GX 25, no. 75/76. The impeachment was unsuccessful, the magistrate, Wang Wang-geng, being found "arbitrary" in only one case. (QSL, 457:7b–8a.)

117. Peng Yu-sun, GX 25/8/26 (30/9/1899), JWJAD, 6.1:443–446. The document is unique in the Shandong materials in being a direct report from a *daotai* to the Zongli Yamen. Normally a *daotai* would report through the governor, but in this case, Peng's obvious differences with Yu-xian impelled him to take the unusual step of voicing his concerns directly to the central authorities.

118. One Presbyterian missionary noted some Protestants' adoption of the practice, and his opposition thereto. (J. A. Fitch, 27/11/1899, BFM, reel 214.)

119. Li Xiang-tian, Su Yu-zhang, Liu Chang-ru and Liang Yu-chun, SDDC, 14–17.

120. *Yi-wen-bao*, Nos. 1686 and 1688, 30/6/1897 and 7/7/1897. I am indebted to Professor Lu Yao for his copies of these sources.

121. Elsewhere a report by Peng and Wang Wang-geng (Jining sub-prefect) says Shao was from Xiao county (No. 51, GX 25/5/28 [5/7/1899], SDXF)—but all accounts agree the school spread from Jiangsu. Yu-xian, GX 25/6/19 (26/7/1899), JWJAD, 6.1:402, gives Shao's name as Yu-huan.

122. Though this accusation may seem a bit far-fetched, it is twice repeated by Yu-xian (Yu-xian to Yu-lu, received GX 25/7/17 [22/8/1899], Li Xue-jian, 1:22b–23a; Yu-xian to Zongli Yamen, No. 192, GX 25/6/23, SDXF). One Protestant missionary speaks of Catholics turning the anti-Christian bands against Protestants, in hopes of bringing more foreign pressure on the court in Beijing. (J. Murray, 7/9/1899, BFM, reel 214.)

123. One of the ironies of the rift between Peng and Yu-xian is the fact that just a few months prior to Peng's long report, Yu-xian had defended him against a censor criticizing Peng's closeness to the foreigners and had even resisted an imperial edict suggesting that Peng be reassigned to another area. Yu-xian, GX 25/5/2 (9/6/1899) and 25/5/26 (3/7/1899), DASL, 1:25–27.

124. Even in the fall of 1900, a Chinese Protestant pastor in Jining reported that despite many alarms, "seven parts in ten are false" and the area was "all quiet." (Sing Yu-fu to Z. H. Laughlin, n.d., BFM, reel 214.)

125. J. Murray, 7/9/1899, BFM, reel 214.

126. German chargé to Zongli Yamen, GX 25/5/18 (25/6/1899), JWJAD, 6.1 : 382.

127. Charles A. Killie, 27/3/1899, BFM, reel 214. In the summer, this official was forced to resign, apparently for his overly harsh treatment of those who were harassing Christians. (Yizhou correspondence, NCH, 63 : 170 [24/7/1899].)

128. Chargé to Zongli Yamen, GX 25/5/18 (25/6/1899), JWJAD, 6.1 : 383. The yamen immediately telegraphed Yu-xian of this German threat. (Zongli Yamen to Yu-xian, No. 29, GX 25/5/1899, SDXF.)

129. Yu-xian, GX 25/5/30 (7/7/1899), JWJAD, 6.1 : 383, 386–388.

130. Yu-xian, GX 25/6/19 (27/6/1899), JWJAD, 6.1 : 402. Cf. CBOC, 19. It should be noted that Peng Yu-sun admitted that this was precisely Yu-xian's policy. Thus there is no disagreement on the facts—only on whether punishing leaders and dispersing followers was adequate to deal with the problem. (See Peng's GX 25/8/26 [30/9/1899], JWJAD, 6.1 : 445.)

131. Yu-xian to Zongli Yamen, No. 192, GX 25/6/23 (30/7/1899), SDXF. Compare this to Yu-xian's cable to Yu-lu, received GX 25/7/17 (22/8/1899), Lin Xue-jian, 1 : 22b–23a.

132. Yu-xian, postscript to GX 25/3/21 (30/4/1899), DASL, 1 : 24.

133. Edict, GX 25/3/1 (11/4/1899), DASL, 1 : 22.

134. QSL, GX 25/4/5 (14/5/1899).

135. In this regard, I would differ with the interpretation in Schrecker, 92–93, as well as all the standard histories which simplistically link the rise of the Boxer to the domination of the court by conservative Manchu officials.

136. Yu-xian, postscript to GX 25/3/21 (30/4/1899), DASL, 1 : 24.

137. Yu-xian, GX 25/8/21 (25/9/1899), JWJAD, 6.1 : 438–439.

138. Yu-xian, GX 25/11/19 (31/12/1899), JWJAD, 6.1 : 479.

139. Yu-xian to Zongli Yamen, No. 90, GX 25/6/2 (9/7/1899), SDXF.

140. Yu-xian to Yu-lu, received GX 25/7/17 (22/8/1899), Lin Xue-jian, 1 : 22b–23a.

141. Yu-xian, 25/7/26 (31/8/1899), GX 25/8/21 (25/9/1899), JWJAD, 6.1 : 425, 438–439; Yu-xian to Zongli Yamen, No. 200, and to Jining sub-prefect Wang, No. 201, both of GX 25/7/17 (22/8/1899), SDXF.

142. Yu-xian would later claim that after events got out of hand in the southwest, he issued eight proclamations prohibiting "establishing grounds for the practice of boxing." (GX 25/11/4 [6/12/1899], DASL, 1 : 39.) The telegraphic correspondence in SDXF bears this out—showing the frequent dispatch of troops to suppress and disperse boxers beginning in late June.

143. Nine of the incidents did in fact occur, though in five cases the amount was less than the Christians claimed to have paid. In seven cases the Christians never paid the "fines" anyway; nine more were incidents that never occurred; and five more either did not involve Christians or involved no losses. Yu-xian, based on the report of the Jining sub-prefect, GX 25/11/19 (31/12/1899), JWJAD, 6.1 : 478–484. See also CBOC, 12, 688.

144. In one case, a Christian and his nephew got into a dispute over the income from a boat whose use they shared. Three cases involved conflicts between members of the Gao lineage in the village of Gaojiahai, Yu-xian, GX 25/7/1 (6/8/1899), JWJAD, 6.1 : 402, 418–423.

145. Yu-xian, GX 25/6/20 (27/7/1899), JWJAD, 6.1 : 403–407; postscript to GX 25/6/10 (17/7/1899), DASL, 1 : 32. A number of other officials echoed Yu-xian's insistence that equal weight be given to the loss of Chinese and German lives. Cf. Zhang Ru-mei, GX 25/3/15 (24/4/1899), and 3/17 (26/4) JWJAD, 6.1 : 348–349, 349–355 (this latter including a letter to the German Prince Henry on the subject); Hu Fan-chen, GX 24/2/10 (2/3/1898), DASL, 1 : 11.

146. Yu-xian, GX 25/9/19 (21/10/1899) and 25/9/24 (28/10/1899) and Ketteler reply, GX 25/9/26 (30/10/1899), JWJAD, 6.1 : 455–456, 463–466.

147. Yu-xian to Zongli Yamen, no. 90, GX 25/6/2 (9/7/1899), SDXF.

148. Zongli Yamen to Yu-xian, no. 162, GX 25/7/1 (6/8/1899), SDXF.

149. See Lin Xue-jian, 1 : 15b–26b.

150. Zongli Yamen to Yu-xian, no. 59, forwarding a complaint from Anzer, GX 25/5/29 (6/7/1899), SDXF.

151. Pang Hong-shu, Daming *daotai*, received GX 25/7/16 (21/8/1899), Li Xue-jian, 1 : 21a–21b.

152. Hart to Campbell, 4/6/1899, I.G., 2 : 1198.

153. Tirpitz to Jaeschke, 27/6/1899, cited in Schrecker, 101–103.

154. Acting Secretary of State Alvey A. Adee to Conger, 24/8/1899, FRUS, 1899, 175–176.

CHAPTER EIGHT

1. *Chiping xian-zhi* (1710), 123.

2. Huang Ze-cang, *Shandong*, 182–184, contains a number of references to the persistent waterlogging problems in this area.

3. A. H. Smith, "Estimating the Population of China," CR 24.1 (January 1893): 29–30.

4. A. H. Smith, *China in Convulsion*, 1 : 11.

5. *Pingyuan xian-zhi* (1749), 3 : 20a.

6. Ibid., 9 : 8a–8b.

7. Ibid., 2 : 13b.

8. *Chiping xian-zhi* (1935), 9 : 2a.

9. *Gaotang xiang-tu-zhi* (1906), 135–138.

10. *Chiping xian-zhi* (1935), 2 : 49b–50a, 9 : 2a–2b.

11. *Gaotang xiang-tu-zhi*, 135.

12. See, for example, the descriptions of Pingyuan in *Shina shōbetsu zenshi: Santōshō*, 243; and Huang Ze-cang, 177–178.

13. *Zhong-guo shi-ye-zhi: Shandong-sheng*, B53–57.

14. Ding Han-chen and Yan Rui-pu, SD Survey, Chiping (1960), 22.

15. *Chiping xian-zhi* (1935), 388–468.

16. The *Gaotang xiang-tu-zhi*, 67–68, estimates the department's population according to the traditional categories in 1905 and comes out with 3.4

percent of the population in the gentry (*shi*) class (as against 87.0 percent peasants, 1.3 percent craftsmen, and 8.4 percent merchants). This figure would have to include all *sheng-yuan*, civil and military, and would be close to the national average. (See Chang Chung-li, *The Chinese Gentry*.) The 1749 Pingyuan gazetteer (3:4a–4b) has 622 adult males (3.76 percent of the total) exempt from taxes because of gentry status of *sheng-yuan* or higher. These figures show that despite the lack of success in the provincial and national examinations, local quotas for lower degrees guaranteed that this region would still have its fair share of licentiates.

17. *Chiping xian-zhi* (1935), 11:2b–3a, 1498–1499.

18. *Chiping xian-zhi* (1710), 117–118.

19. *Chiping xian-zhi* (1935), 2:20a–20b.

20. *Pingyuan xian-zhi* (1749), 2:13b.

21. Richard Shek, "Millenarianism without Rebellion: The Huangtian Dao in North China," *Modern China* 8.3 (July 1982): 322, 329.

22. F. H. James, writing on "The Secret Sects of Shantung" (p. 196), found that "some appear to be almost entirely political," and some "almost, if not altogether religious."

23. Yang Guang-tai, SDDC, 129. See also other accounts on 128–129 of this source; *Chiping xian-zhi* (1935), 11:3a–3b; QSL, 147:12b–13a; NCH 9/6/1882. R. G. Tiedemann, "Geopolitical Dimensions," 26 and note 78, cites some additional missionary sources on the White Lotus in Chiping which I have not seen.

24. H. D. Porter, "Secret Sects of Shantung," part 1, CR 17.1 (January 1886): 3. J. Edkins, writing specifically of the Dezhou area, claimed that "the White Lily sect exists as a religion without any political importance whatever." ("Religious Sects of North China," CR 17.7 [July 1886]: 251.)

25. J. S. Whiting, writing of the Pingyuan area, 18/7/1878, BFM, reel 200.

26. Leboucq, *Associations*, 163–164.

27. Yang Guang-tai, SDDC, 129.

28. H. D. Porter, "Secret Sects of Shantung," part 1, CR 17.1 (January 1886): 4; part 2, CR 17.2:71.

29. Henry D. Porter, "A Modern Shantung Prophet," CR 18.1 (January 1887): 15.

30. Ding Bao-zhen, TZ 8/11/9 (11/12/1869), YLSL, 118.

31. Porter, "A Modern Shantung Prophet," 12–21. See also Arthur Smith, "Sketches of a Country Parish," part 1, CR 12.4 (July–August 1881): 248–250.

32. For examples and analysis of this practice see Susan Naquin, "Connections Between Rebellions: Sect Family Networks in Qing China," *Modern China* 8.3 (July 1982): 337–360.

33. Porter, "A Modern Shantung Prophet."

34. H. D. Porter, "Secret Sects of Shantung," part 1, CR 17.1 (January 1886): 7. Cf. Arthur H. Smith, "Sketches of a Country Parish," part 1, CR 12.4 (July–August 1881): 246–247.

35. These points were often made by the missionaries, but see especially Porter, "Secret Sects," part 2, CR 17.2 (February 1886): 66–69.

36. "Pangchuang Station Report, 1892–93," "Annual Report of the Pangchuang Station, year ending April 1, 1894," both in ABC 16.3.12, vol. 14.

37. "Annual Report, Williams Hospital, 1890," ABC 13.3.12, vol. 14.

38. A. H. Smith, "Sketches of a Country Parish," part 2, CR 12.5 (September–October 1881): 342–343; NCH, 59:696–697 (15/10/1897).

39. Porter to J. Smith, 24/1/1898 and 13/1/1899, ABC 16.3.12, vol. 20, nos. 185 and 192.

40. SD Survey, Pingyuan, *passim*; Zhang Shu-pu, SD Survey, Gaotang; *Wo-xian jin-dai-shi* (manuscript, Chiping Cultural Bureau), 52–53; Li Wei-xian report, received GX 25/8/25 (29/9/1899), AJ, 3.

41. Ma Xi-cheng, Li Yan-he, Liu Zhi-bang, Wang Wen-rong, SD Survey, Pingyuan, 30, 45, 63; Zhang Zhen-bei et al., SDDC, 101–103.

42. Li Zhao, Su Ting-jia, and Zhang An-dao, SD Survey, Pingyuan, 10, 36, B-60.

43. Li Ming-ying, SD Survey, Pingyuan, 7.

44. Zhu Yuan-ze, SD Survey, Chiping (1960), 109. SDDC, 97–112 contains a long selection of complaints against Christian abuse of power.

45. Most of the testimony is reproduced in SDDC, 85–92. I have seen a few additional datings of the Spirit Boxers' first appearance in the original survey materials and they agree with the published oral histories (e.g., Wang Xue-cheng, Yang Zhao-kuan, Xu Guang-ye, Xu Guang-lin, and Xu Guang-jie, SD Survey, Chiping [1960], 21, 30, 53.) The earliest datings are in 1893–94, a few are in 1894–95, and the largest number are 1896–97—especially the more plausible datings by the number of years before the flood.

46. See SDDC, 192–194, for these slogans or minor variations on them. Additional references to these are found in Li Xi-han, Zhu Yong-cai, and Li Qing-jiang, SD Survey, Changqing (courtesy of Professor Lu Yao).

47. SDDC, 96–97, 120, 202. The Pingyuan surveys in particular mention the importance of healing: Wei Qing-chen (42), Hou Shan-quan (B-3), Li Jin-zhi (B-17), Ma Zhen-jia (B-19), Ren Jin-jian (B-20). For somewhat later documentary records see Jinan prefect, received GX 26/6/11 (7/7/1900), Ling magistrate, received GX 26/10/28 (19/12/1900), AJ, 146–147, 341.

48. Lu Yao, "Yi-he-tuan yun-dong," 677–679, discusses and interprets the southeast kowtow in some detail. CBOC, 148 (GX 26/2/7 [7/3/1900]) provides a contemporary source linking the Boxers to the Peach Flower Mountain caves. SDDC, 199–203, provides most of the oral history accounts on ritual.

49. Liu Hong-zao, SD Survey, Pingyuan, B-33.

50. Henry D. Porter to J. Smith, 14/10/1899 and 13/1/1899, ABC 16.3.12, vol. 20, nos. 197, 192. (This second letter by Porter is the first mention of the Spirit Boxers by the Pangzhuang missionaries. It was written after Porter visited Chiping on a trip from which he returned by Christmas of 1898.)

51. Lao Nai-xuan, proclamation of 27/10/1899, YHT, 4:482.

52. A report by Zhang Xun (GX 26/8/1 [25/8/1900], AJ, 65) notes a group of boxer leaders who used the names of the gods that possessed them as nicknames (*bie-hao*).

53. Smith, *China in Convulsion* 1:169. My description of early Boxer ritual is derived from Jiang Kai, "Pingyuan quan-fei ji-shi," YHT, 1:354, and from the oral histories. Unfortunately the published version of the latter (SDDC, 199–204) contains only a small sample of this rich record: the original Chiping and especially Pingyuan surveys contain much more. For a particularly interesting and unusual account by a former boxer who claimed to be possessed by as many as six different "teachers," see Hou Shan-quan, SD Survey, Pingyuan, B:1–3. In 1900, Yuan Shi-kai would describe Boxer organization and ritual in Shandong. Though his elaborate version of Boxer organization seems unfounded, his list of Boxer deities conforms to other sources (memorial of GX 26/4/21 [19/5/1900], DASL, 1:93).

54. See, for example, Wu Yong, "Geng-zi xi-shou zong-tan," YHT, 3:463. On Boxer ritual in the Beijing-Tianjin area, see Jerome Ch'en, "The Nature and Characteristics of the Boxer Movement—a Morphological Study," BSOAS, 23.2 (1960), esp. 298–304; Ichiko Chūzō, "Giwaken no seikaku," in *Kindai Chūgoku no seiji to shakai*, enlarged edition (Tokyo: Tokyo University Press, 1977), 291–292; and chapter 10.

55. Vincent Shih, *Taiping Ideology: Its Sources, Interpretation and Influence* (Seattle: University of Washington Press, 1967), 285–296.

56. Hsiao Kung-ch'uan, *Rural China: Imperial Control in the Nineteenth Century* (Seattle: University of Washington, 1960), 241.

57. Suzuki Chūsei, *Kakumei to shūkyō*, 5, 43.

58. Ibid., 57.

59. Kobayashi Kazumi ("Giwadan no minshū shisō," in *Kōza Chūgoku kingendaishi 2: Giwadan undō*, 243–245) has written with particular insight and eloquence about the liberating and egalitarian aspects of Boxer ritual— and in particular compares it to the hierarchical command implicit in the Taiping belief system. On a more mundane level, it should be noted that there could be disadvantages in taking on the attributes of certain gods. A number of informants in the Jinan area describe young men possessed by Pigsy being told to root about in the dirt looking for food—and doing so! (Jia Hong-qing, Chen XX, Zhao Hong-xiang, SD Survey, Jinan, 115, 126, 127.)

60. Lao Nai-xuan, "Yi-he-quan jiao-men yuan-liu kao," YHT, 4:431–440.

61. Lao Nai-xuan, report of 9/12/1899 in "Geng-zi feng-jin Yi-he-quan hui-lu," YHT, 4:467.

62. Lao Nai-xuan, "Quan-an za-cun," YHT, 4:454. See also his "Yi-he-quan jiao-men yuan-liu kao," YHT, 4:438–439.

63. Arthur Smith, *China in Convulsion* 1:154. Cf. Purcell, 148.

64. The most famous attack on Lao's theory is Dai Xuan-zhi's *Yi-he-tuan yan-jiu*, 1–5, but Dai's alternative militia theory of origins is equally flawed. A carefully considered Japanese review of Lao's theory is Sasaki Masaya, "Giwadan kigen," part 1, 144–168.

65. See, e.g., *Hui-bao* (a Catholic paper), no. 176 (GX 26/4/14), in SDSZZL, 1960.2:122.

66. See, e.g., Li Shi-yu, "Yi-he-tuan yuan-liu shi-tan," 18–23; Lu Yao, "Lun Yi-he-tuan," 36–61; Cheng Xiao, "Min-jian zong-jiao yu Yi-he-tuan jie-tie," *Li-shi yan-jiu*, 1983.2:147–163.

67. Ding Han-chen, Ke Meng-bei, SDDC, 130, 129. Cf. Xie Jia-gui, a former Boxer, in SD Survey, Chiping (1966B), also cited in "Shi Bin" [Lu Jing-qi], "Shandong Chiping, Pingyuan yi-dai Yi-he-tuan diao-cha-ji," *Wen-wu* 1976.3:10. Only two informants assert a link between the White Lotus and Boxers—one was born the year the Spirit Boxers were active in Chiping, one was at most seven years old at the time. (Zhang Han-yu and Sun Yong-chang, SDDC, 130–131.)

68. Susan Naquin (*Millenarian Rebellion*, 9–14), virtually takes the Eternal Venerable Mother as the defining deity of the White Lotus Tradition. See also Overmyer, *Folk Buddhist Religion*, 135–145.

69. Naquin, "Connections Between Rebellions."

70. It might be noted that one village leader of an early Boxer band in Chiping was a tenant particularly known for his love of opera. (Lin Can-zhi, SDDC, 89.)

71. Jiang Kai, YHT, 1:353. The oral history sources make clear that the immediate source of teachers for the Pingyuan Boxers was Gaotang. (Liu Ruo-qi, Wang Jin-ting, Liu De-cheng, Duan Xue-liang, SDDC, 92–94; Zhang An-dao, SD Survey, Pingyuan, 35.)

72. Ji Gui-fen, letter of 13/10/1899, in SDJDSZL, 3:191.

73. *Chiping xian-zhi* (1935), 9:92, 11:26a–26b; H. D. Porter to J. Smith, 13/1/1899, ABC 13.3.12, vol. 20, no. 192; Yu Xun-chen, and Fan Ting-hua, Chiping survey, 21, 42–43. Local cadres in Chiping were extremely helpful during my June 1980 visit in explaining the topography of the county.

74. Zhang Shun-xiu, SDDC, 91–92; Cf. Chen Ting-xian, 92; Fan Ting-hua, SD Survey, Chiping, 39–42.

75. Chen Ting-xian, SD Survey, Gaotang.

76. Zhu's regrettably (and suspiciously?) brief confession gives Sishui as his home. (Jinan report, GX 25/11/1 [3/12/1899], AJ, 19.) The oral history sources indicate that he returned to Changqing from somewhere in the area of Sishui. (Lu Jing-qi, "Shandong Chiping, Pingyuan yi-dai," 3, summarizes the oral history record.) At least two contemporary sources record Zhu as coming from Changqing, one specifying Li Family Village (Lijiazhuang) in that county. (Jiang Kai, YHT, 1:354, which specifies Li Family Village, and lists Chiping as an alternative home; *Hui-bao*, no. 146 [GX 25/12/10], in SDSZZL, 1960.2:112.)

77. Li Lian-wu, SDDC, 135–136. The published version of this account appears to have been somewhat edited. I have not seen the original, but in the records of other interviews with Li Lian-wu he appears much less clear-headed about the details of Zhu's history. Most notably, though on one occasion he states that Zhu learned Spirit Boxing in Changqing, on two other occasions he says that Zhu had already studied Spirit Boxing at the time of his arrival. (SD Survey, Qihe, 89, 104. See also discussion below.)

78. Li Lian-wu, SDDC, 136.

79. Kong Zhao-chun, SD Survey, Qihe, 69.

80. Li Lian-wu, SDDC, 136 (but see note 77, above); Kong Qing-ping, SDDC, 138.

81. Lu Jing-qi, "Shandong Chiping, Pingyuan yi-dai," 3; cf. Yang Yong-si, Dong Yu-yao, Zhao Hong-zhu, SDDC, 139–142.

82. Jinan prefect's report on Xin-cheng's arrest and confession, received GX 25/11/1 (3/12/1899), AJ, 19–21; Lu Jing-qi, "Yi-he-tuan yun-dong zai Shandong de bao-fa ji qi dou-zheng," *Yi-he-tuan yun-dong liu-shi zhou-nian ji-nian lun-wen-ji* (Beijing: Zhong-hua, 1961), 72; "Shandong Chiping, Ping-yuan yi-dai," 4; Nie Xi-guang, Yang Yong-han, SDDC, 216, 217.

83. Zhi Bi-hu, YHT, 4:443.

84. Ji Gui-fen to Yao Song-yun, 13/10/1899, in SDJDSZL, 3:191–192. Obviously this source is not entirely reliable. It has Xin-cheng's real name wrong (and also Zhu Hong-deng's)—and it incorrectly identifies the latter as "coming from a rich household in this county." But it probably reflected the common view in Chiping that Xin-cheng was the abler of the two. Judging from the oral histories, many in Chiping were not at all impressed with Zhu Hong-deng: "Zhu Hong-deng was a short fellow; his face was covered with pockmarks. He had no ability: couldn't read, couldn't use a sword or spear." (Liu Chang-hua, SD Survey, Chiping, 64; cf. SDDC, 141.) "A face full of big black pockmarks.... From the looks of him he couldn't do anything." (Zhao Zhan-ting, SD Survey, Chiping, 75.) By contrast, Xin-cheng was described as having extraordinary *gong-fu*. He was called "the bronze-headed monk" for his ability to withstand blows to the skull. (Yang Yong-han, SDDC, 217.)

85. Xie Jia-gui, SDDC, 200.

86. It would needlessly belabor the point to cite all the accounts based on Jiang Kai's self-serving report, but two particularly influential English works must be noted. Jerome Ch'en writes that "it is impossible to deny that Chu Hung-teng did claim to be a descendant of the Ming ruling house"; and he finds it "very hard for [him] to have raised the slogan of 'Supporting the Ch'ing and Driving out the Foreigners' as ascertained by Chinese Communist historians." ("The Origin of the Boxers," in· *Studies in the Social History of China and Southeast Asia*, ed. Jerome Ch'en and Nicholas Tarling [Cambridge: Cambridge University Press, 1970], 76.) Even more problematic is Victor Purcell's book, which not only misreads parts of Jiang Kai's text (mistaking an analogy for an identity, and saying that Zhu's real name was Li Wen-qing—identical to that of the Eight Trigrams leader), but also insists that since Zhu's group was certainly anti-Qing, the Boxers' alleged change from an anti-dynastic to a pro-dynastic stance must have taken place after Zhu's defeat. (Purcell, 197–222.) Unfortunately, Zhu Hong-deng was no more anti-dynastic than any of the other martial arts groups of the 1890s. Thus both Purcell's attempt to date the alleged change from an anti-dynastic to a pro-dynastic stance by reference to Zhu Hong-deng's defeat, and indeed the whole point of his book—to analyze the "anti-dynastic to pro-dynastic" shift—are based on a fundamental misconception.

87. SDDC, 208–213, has dozens of references to these slogans. There are no accounts of Ming loyalism. Even the name Ben-ming for Xin-cheng appears primarily in hostile official documentary sources.

88. Jiang Kai's claim is repeated by Zhi Bi-hu, in what seems clearly a derivative account. (YHT, 4:443.) These are the only two references to millenarian beliefs among the Boxers—and since both come from sources anxious to condemn the Boxers for sectarianism, I do not consider them reliable. Perhaps the closest the oral histories come to suggesting a millennium is the widespread mention of a popular ditty, which went something like this (see SDDC, 213–214 for several different versions of this rhyme):

二四加一五，再苦不算苦。
天下紅燈照，那時才算苦。

Two, four, add one five;
Even worse would not be bad.
When all under Heaven is the Red Lantern Shining,
That will be the time when things are really bad.

The opening line, which is probably a reference to the fifteenth day of the eighth month—a day with anti-Mongol and anti-Manchu associations—has been interpreted by some as showing an anti-Manchu orientation in the Boxers. (See Lu Yao, "Lun Yi-he-tuan," 39–40.) But one should note that one Chiping informant interpreted the opening line as referring to the Yellow River flood of the 6th month (1 + 5) of Guangxu 24 (1898). (Zhou Mao-tong, SD survey, Chiping [1966A].) Whatever the sense of this first line, the whole poem is more likely to have been told *about* the Boxers than *by* them; and what it presumably meant was that no matter how chaotic anti-barbarian struggles (or floods) had been, they were not as bad as the Boxers. The reference to the Red Lantern Shining—a term for later female Boxers, but including the "Hong-deng" from Zhu's name—also suggests that this little poem first appeared well *after* the initial Boxer unrest.

89. Jiang Kai, YHT, 1:353.

90. H. D. Porter to J. Smith, 13/1/1899, ABC 16.3.12, vol. 20, no. 192. See also Porter's "Twelfth Annual Report of the Pang-chuang Station, Year Ending April 30, 1900," ABC 16.3.12, vol. 16.

91. *Hui-bao*, nos. 146, 153 (GX 25/12/10 and 26/1/22); *Wan-guo gong-bao*, no. 132 (GX 25/12), all in SDSZZL, 1960.2:112, 114, 118.

92. Yucheng report received GX 25/12/30 (30/1/1900), AJ, 245.

93. Yu Han-chen, SDDC, 123. See others, SDDC, 122–125.

94. Yang Yu-shan, SDDC, 120. Cf. Li Liu-shi, and Jia Lun-yuan (a former Boxer), Pingyin survey courtesy of Lu Yao; and Jiang Kai, YHT, 1:354.

95. This pattern is fairly clear in the accounts published in SDDC, 120–126.

96. *Shandong shi-bao*, GX 22/8/5, SDJDSZL, 3:183.

97. Yuan Ting-jie, Hou Shan-quan, SD Survey, Pingyuan, B1–3, 22; Dong Yu-yao, SDDC, 203.

98. Edict of GX 25/5/13 (20/6/1899), QSL, 444:11a; *Chiping xian-zhi* (1935), 8:14b–15a, 69a; Ke Meng-bei, Fan Ting-hua, SDDC, 145, 165.

99. H. D. Porter to J. Smith, 13/1/1899, ABC 16.3.12, vol. 20, no. 192. Yu

Xian was appointed to the first of his two terms in Chiping in the twelfth month of GX 24 (January 12–February 9, 1899). (*Da-Qing jue-zhi quan-lan,* summer 1899, ting: 66.)

100. Yang Yong-si, SDDC, 143. See other accounts on 143–146.

101. Jiang Kai report received GX 25/9/2 (6/10/1899), AJ, 6–7; also cited in Yu-xian, GX 25/9/8 (12/10/1899), JWJAD, 6.1:452.

102. SDDC, 127–128.

103. This was the conclusion of Ji Gui-fen, letter to Yao Song-yun, 13/10/1899, SDJDSZL, 3:191–192.

104. The following discussion is based upon the Shandong University surveys of the Boxers in this area. It would be excessively tedious to footnote every particular statement here, so I shall restrict my notes to direct quotes and particularly important issues.

105. Jerome Ch'en, "Nature and Characteristics," 297.

106. Ibid., 296. For Shandong references to these terms, see Jiang Kai, YHT, 1:354; Wang Zhao-lan, SD Survey, Chiping (1960), 72; Liu Yue-xiang, SDDC, 195.

107. Xie Jia-gui (a former Boxer), SD Survey, Chiping (1966B).

108. See, for example, Wei Qing-chen, and Guo Bing-fu, SD Survey, Pingyuan, 42, 44–45; Shi Dong-dai, SD Survey, Chiping (1960), 2.

109. Xie Jia-gui, cited in Lu Jing-qi, "Shandong Chiping, Pingyuan yi-dai," 4. The Boxer leader Yu Qing-shui also studied from an agricultural laborer from outside his village. (Yu Huai-zhi, SD Survey, Gaotang.)

110. *Chiping xian-zhi* (1935), 2:29a. Lao Nai-xuan also noted the similarity between Boxer demonstrations at markets and the usual array of dramatic and magical exhibitions. (Lao Nai-xuan, "Quan-an za-cun," YHT, 4:453, 471.)

111. William H. Rees, letter of 8/6/1899, in Purcell, 286.

112. Liu De-cheng, SDDC, 93.

113. Yan Yin-xiang, SD Survey, Pingyuan, B-22. For other examples, see Pingyuan survey, 68, 69, B-18, B-24; SDDC, 188–189.

114. SDDC, 194–199, gives examples of Boxer discipline.

115. See Purcell, 215; Lu Yao, "Lun Yi-he-tuan," 39.

116. SDDC, 119–120.

117. Jiang Kai, YHT, 1:354; SDDC, 117–118. The Zhili governor-general said the boxers there were "all youths in their teens." (Yu-lu, GX 26/4/19 [17/5/1900], DASL, 1:91.)

118. SDDC, 192–194, esp. Yang Yong-han and Yang Guang-fu.

119. On the Red Lantern Shining in Chiping, see SDDC, 131–135; Chiping report GX 26/run 8/15 (8/10/1900), AJ, 404.

120. In January 1900, Yuan Shi-kai reported that Boxers with any property and employment had dispersed and only "brigands and roving outlaws" remained. (Memorial of GX 25/12/13 [13/1/1900], DAZL, 1:59.) In the fall of 1900, when the Jiyang magistrate reported on attempts to confiscate Boxer property, he explained that most were "extremely poor shiftless fellows" with little or nothing to seize. (Jiyang report, received GX 26/9/16 [7/11/1900], AJ, 235.) The Changqing (present Qihe) and Chiping surveys

also show a popular perception of a degeneration of the Spirit Boxers as outlaw elements began to join. (SD Survey, Qihe, 57–65; Chiping [1960], 54–55.)
See also Linqing correspondence (21/9/1899), NCH 63:710 (9/10/1899).

121. Zhou Hai-qing, "Lun Yi-he-tuan zu-zhi de yuan-liu ji-qi fa-zhan,"
Po yu li 1979.6:35, makes exactly this point.

122. Lao Nai-xuan, 1901, YHT, 4:452. See also his report of 9/12/1899,
ibid., 470.

123. Taian prefect's report, received GX 26/1/10 (9/2/1900), AJ, 485.

124. Liu Sheng-yun, SD Survey, Pingyuan, 18, 23. Cf. SDDC, 113–116.

125. SDDC, 218–220, and Yu Huai-zhi, ibid., 162–163; Licheng report,
received GX 25/11/17 (19/12/1899), AJ, 8–9.

126. Yu Xun-chen, SD survey, Chiping (1960), ff. 21.

127. Cui Zheng-yan et al., SD survey, Chiping (1960), 35–36.

128. SDDC, 234–235.

129. Lin Can-zhi, SDDC, 89.

130. Wang Heng-sheng, SDDC, 116.

131. Yang Yong-si, SD Survey, Chiping (1966A). Cf. Liu Dao-zeng, Liu
Jin-dou, SDDC, 140.

132. SDDC, 222–224; Wang Jin-yue, SD Survey, Gaotang; Yucheng report, received GX 26/1/11 (10/2/1900), AJ, 245. The survey reports indicated
that Wang's motivation in aiding the Boxers may have been personal: his
son become a Catholic and he wished to punish the young man.

133. Li Gong-you, SDDC, 97.

134. Jiang Kai, YHT, 1:353, 355; SDDC, 231–234.

135. On these two, see SDDC, 185, 193, 232–233, 242–243. It would be
nice if we could distinguish clearly which Boxer leaders were active in
1898–1899, and which only in 1900; but most of the village leaders are only
mentioned in the oral history surveys, and it is simply impossible to date
leaders systematically from such retrospective accounts.

136. Taian prefect's report, received GX 26/1/10 (9/2/1900), AJ, 485.
Compare this missionary comment on the lack of any clear leaders: "Were
there a leader of real power to come forward with a gift for organizing, the
danger would be great; but no such man has appeared." Linqing correspondence (21/9/1899), NCH, 63:710 (9/10/1899).

CHAPTER NINE

1. The physical description of this area is based on my visit in June 1980.
Both Jiang Kai (YHT, 1:353) and the En magistrate Li Wei-xian (report
received GX 25/8/25 [29/9/1899], AJ, 3) stress the concentration of activity
at the borders—each, of course, suggesting that the Boxers came from the
other county.

2. H. D. Porter to J. Smith, 14/10/1899, ABC 16.3.12, vol. 20, no. 197. SD
survey, Pingyuan, *passim*, also locates the churches in this area.

3. *Hui-bao*, no. 146, GX 25/12/10, in SDSZZL, 1960.2:112–113. Later,
the Pangzhuang Protestants would be visited by two Boxers leaders who
"wanted the foreign teachers to be assured that they only intended to make

it uncomfortable for the Romanists." (H. D. Porter to Friends, 13/11/1899, ABC 16.3.12, vol. 20, no. 201.)

4. Jiang Kai, YHT, 1:353; Wei Chuan-chen and Zhang An-dao, SDDC, 115, 233–234.

5. Jiang Kai, YHT, 1:355; Li Wen-gui and Li Sheng-yun, SD Survey, Pingyuan, 12, 17–27. Jiang puts Li's age at over seventy, but this seems unlikely; the oral histories say fifty and note that he fled to Manchuria after the Boxers, and returned over twenty years later—unlikely for a man already seventy.

6. Jiang Kai, YHT, 1:355. One Pingyuan informant indicated that "at first it was [composed of] the wealthy, later, the poor." (Xu Da-min, SD Survey, Pingyuan, 73, 74.)

7. Yu-xian, GX 25/10/6 (8/11/1899), DASL, 1:34. On Jiang Kai's previous official career, see Da-Qing jin-shen quan-shu, summer 1898.

8. Hui-bao, 2:367, GX 25/12/10 in SDSZZL, 1960.2:113; NCH, 63:1121–1122 (4/12/1899).

9. Jiang Kai, YHT, 1:353. Whether the two Wangs truly withdrew from support of the Boxers is unclear. Their names still headed a missionary list of Pingyuan Boxer leaders in October. (Pinchon to Zongli Yamen, GX 25/9/5 [9/10/1899], JWJAD, 6.1:451.) Jiang's appeal to a lowly military sheng-yuan as a representative of the "gentry" (he uses the term shen-dong) is an indication of how weak the orthodox civil-examination elite was in this area.

10. Jiang Kai, GX 25/9/2 (6/10/1899), AJ, 6–7.

11. Jiang Kai, YHT, 1:354.

12. Jiang Kai, GX 25/9/2 (6/10/1899), AJ, 6–7.

13. SD Survey, Pingyuan, B-12, 16, 28; Qihe, 16; Yu-xian to Zongli Yamen, GX 25/5/2 (9/6/1899), No. 44, SDXF.

14. Yu-xian to Zongli Yamen, GX 25/9/24 (28/10/1899), No. 131, and 10/9 (11/11), No. 135, SDXF. Cf. letter to Bishop Marchi, GX 25/10/1 (3/11/1899), CBOC, 41.

15. China in Convulsion, 1:219. Cf. the reports in C:IGC 1899, II:30–31, 55; NCH, 63:665–666 (2/10/1899).

16. Jiang Kai, YHT, 1:355. Jiang follows Yu-xian in calling Shao Shi-xuan Shao Yu-huan.

17. Pinchon, GX 25/7/20 (25/8/1899), JWJAD, 6.1:424. The report has come from the missionary "Fu-tian-de" who had visited En county from Wucheng on August 20. (Li Wei-xian [En magistrate] report, received GX 25/8/25 [29/9/1899], AJ, 3.)

18. Jiang Kai, YHT, 1:355; Pingyuan magistrate's report, received GX 25/8/20 (24/9/1899), AJ, 2–3. This same report is cited in Yu-xian, GX 25/8/25 (29/9/1899), JWJAD, 6.1:441–442.

19. Pinchon to Zongli Yamen, GX 25/8/30 (4/10/1899), JWJAD, 6.1:446–447.

20. Li Wei-xian report received GX 25/8/25 (29/9/1899), AJ, 3–5; H. D. Porter, "Twelfth Annual Report on the Pang Chuang Station, for the year ending April 30, 1900," ABC 16.3.12, vol. 16; Pangzhuang correspondence, 25/9/1899, in NCH, 63:759 (16/10/1899).

21. Jiang Kai and [Zhu] Jing-rong report received 25/8/28 (2/10/1899), AJ, 5–6; Jiang Kai, YHT, 1:355. See also Arthur Smith's description of the ransom Christians were forced to pay, and his admission that "few dwellings [were] burned and no lives taken." (*China in Convulsion* 1:175–176.)

22. See the telegraphic correspondence between Yu-lu and Yu-xian in Lin Xue-jian, 1:26b–34a (84–99); NCH, 63:665 (21/10/1899).

23. Li Wen-gui, Li Ming-du, and Li Sheng-yun, SD Survey, Pingyuan, 12–13, 18–22, 27.

24. Jiang Kai reports and Yu-xian rescripts, GX 25/8/28 (2/10/1899) and GX 25/9/2 (6/10/1899), AJ, 5–7. Cf. Jiang Kai, YHT, 1:355–356.

25. *Hui-bao*, no. 146, GX 25/12/10 (10/1/1900), in SDSZZL, 1960.2:113. An earlier issue (GX 25/11/4 [6/12/1899], in ibid., 117) lists Wang Zhi-bang's name in connection with the Pingyuan incidents. Cui Ming-quan, SDDC, 212.

26. Jiang Kai, YHT, 1:356; Jiang Kai reports received GX 25/9/10 (14/10/1899), GX 25/9/12 (16/10/1899), AJ, 11–13; Li Zhao, Li Lu-ming, SDDC, 153–154; Li Sheng-yun and Cui Yan-zhong, SD Survey, Pingyuan, 25, B-n.p.; Lu Chang-yi report received GX 25/9/15 (19/10/1899), AJ, 13.

27. Jiang Kai, YHT, 1:357. One of the rural leaders, Shi Yan-tian was a *li-zhang* and military *sheng-yuan* from Huayuan, on the Pingyuan-En border. In 1900, he would be invited by the local authorities to head a Militia United in Righteousness, and later executed for having done so. (SDDC, 232–233.)

28. Jiang Kai, YHT, 1:357.

29. Edicts of GX 21/5/25 (17/6/1895) and GX 21/7/4 (23/8/1895), QSL, 368:7a, 372:2a. For Jiang Kai's further defense of Chen, see YHT, 1:360, 362.

30. Jiang Kai, YHT, 1:357–358; Jiang Kai report received GX 25/9/12 (16/10/1899), AJ, 12–13; Lu Chang-yi report received GX 25/9/15 (19/10/1899), AJ, 13–14. Jiang Kai's day-by-day retrospective account in YHT puts Lu's arrival on the 15th. Lu's more contemporary account says the 16th.

31. Jiang Kai, YHT, 1:358.

32. Li Ming-ying and Li Zhao, SD Survey, Pingyuan, 7, 9.

33. Jiang Kai, YHT, 1:359.

34. Ibid., 359; Lu Chang-yi report received GX 25/9/15 (19/10/1899), AJ, 13–14.

35. Jiang Kai, YHT, 1:358. The physical description is based on my visit of June 1980.

36. Jiang Kai, YHT, 1:359; Yu-xian, GX 25/11/14 (26/12/1899), DASL, 1:41–42; Ren Yu-jun, Liang Zhen-qing, Sheng Yuan-qing, SDDC, 155–159; Ren Yu-xin, Xing Feng-lin, Ren Yu-he and Chen Yu-xi, Yuan Ting-jie, Zhuang Wen-bin, Peng Yuan-qing, SD Survey, Pingyuan, 57–67, B-22, 24, 29. Lu Jing-qi ("Shandong Chiping, Pingyuan yi-dai," 7–8) gives a somewhat glorified, but still useful, account of the battle at Senluo Temple.

37. Zhang An-dao, Li Yu-zhen, Li Jin-zhi, SD Survey, Pingyuan, 36, B-17, 22.

38. Liu Yu-ling, SD Survey, Chiping (1960), 65.

39. Ren Yu-he, SD Survey, Pingyuan, 61.

40. SDDC, 150–151, contains a collection of rhymes in praise of Zhu Hong-deng. See also SD Survey, Chiping (1960), 2, 16, 20.

41. SDDC, 208–213, contains a large number of oral history accounts of this slogan. See also note 24, above.

42. *Hui-bao*, no. 146, GX 25/12/10 in SDSZZL, 1960.2:113.

43. Chen Yu-xi, SD Survey, Pingyuan, 66–67. Cf. Zhuang Wen-bin, ibid., B-29.

44. Ren Yu-jun, SDDC, 158.

45. Pingyuan report, received GX 25/10/23 (25/11/1899), AJ, 17. See also Lu Yao, "Lun Yi-he-tuan," 53–54.

46. H. D. Porter to Friends, 13/11/1899, ABC 16.3.12, vol. 20, No. 200.

47. Lao Nai-xuan, report of GX 25/11/7 (9/12/1899), YHT, 4:470. Lao inexplicably renders the Boxer slogan as "Support the Chinese dynasty, destroy the foreign religion" (*Fu Zhong-chao, mie yang-jiao*). For an interesting and highly theoretical interpretation of the "Support the Qing" slogan, see Kobayashi Kazumi, "Giwadan no minshū shisō," 251–256.

48. H. D. Porter to Friends, 23/10/1899, ABC 16.3.12, vol. 20, No. 198. This is apparently the same summons mentioned in an October 28 telegram from Pangzhuang, cited in NCH, 63:963 (13/11/1899). There the Boxers are called "The Imperial Righteous Harmony Boxers."

49. Yu-xian memorial GX 25/10/6 (8/11/1899) and edict of GX 25/10/18 (20/11/1899), DASL, 1:36–37. Yu-xian rescript on Lu Chang-yi report received GX 25/9/19 (23/10/1899), AJ, 14. On Jiang's replacement, Jiang Kai, YHT, 1:360.

50. Wang Chuo memorial, GX 25/10/1 (3/11/1899), DASL, 1:33.

51. Pingyuan report, received GX 25/10/23 (25/11/1899), AJ, 16–18.

52. Yu-xian memorial, GX 25/10/6 (8/11/1899) and edict of GX 25/10/18 (20/11/1899), DASL, 1:36–37. Criticism of Yuan Shi-dun continued into January 1900, often on the basis of highly exaggerated hearsay reports of extensive civilian casualties in the Senluo battle. It seems that such criticism was often an indirect means of attacking Yuan Shi-kai, by then governor of Shandong. (See DASL, 1:50, 53, 55.)

53. *Hui-bao*, GX 25/12/10 (10/1/1900), in SDSZZL, 1960.2:114. Jiang Kai (YHT, 1:355) attributes an almost identical boast to Big Sword Society members among two companies of troops that Yu-xian had earlier recruited in the southwest, and places the event before the fall battles with the Boxers. While the presence of such Sword Society members in the military is certainly likely, I am more inclined to believe the newspaper account that the Boxer boasts of support from the governor came after the battle at Senluo Temple.

54. NCH, 63:1121–1122 (4/12/1899). Cf. H. D. Porter, "Twelfth Annual Report of the Pang-chuang Station for the year ending April 30, 1900," ABC 16.3.12, vol. 16.

55. For a reasonably complete statement of the missionary case against Yu-xian in Shandong, see "Quan-huo ji," in SDJDSZL, 3:193–194; Smith, *China in Convulsion* 1:181–182.

56. Yu-xian rescript to Pingyuan report received GX 25/9/12 (16/10/ 1899), AJ, 13.

57. Yu-xian to Yu-lu, received GX 25/10/6 (8/11/1899), Lin Xue-jian, 1:32a.

58. Yu-xian, GX 25/11/4 (6/12/1899), DASL, 1:40.

59. Yu-xian draft memorial of GX 25/10/29 (30/11/1899), CBOC, 43–45.

60. West Shandong correspondence, NCH, 63:1269 (27/12/1899). Cf. H. D. Porter to Friends, 13/11/1899, ABC 16.3.12, vol. 20, no. 200.

61. Jiang Kai, YHT, 1:355. On the recruitment of these troops, see LBH, 8:7b–8a; CBOC, 18–19; DASL, 1:191. On Boxers in the army, cf. Smith, *China in Convulsion,* 1:179.

62. Yu Qing-shui confession in Licheng report, received GX 25/11/17 (19/12/1899), AJ, 8.

63. For oral history accounts of the execution of the Catholic teacher and other Boxer activities in this area, see SD Survey, Chiping (1960), 3–4, 21 ff., 27, 31, 56, 62–70.

64. Ibid., 8–9; Zhu Hong-deng confession in Jinan report, received GX 25/11/1 (3/12/1899), AJ, 20.

65. Huang Ke-chuan, SD Survey, Chiping (1960), 76–77.

66. H. D. Porter, "Twelfth Annual Report of the Pang-chuang Station for the year ending April 30, 1900," ABC 16.3.12, vol. 16. In addition, when the officially provided cavalry guard was once ordered withdrawn, Porter took command of those soldiers and provided them with Remington rifles. (H. D. Porter to Friends, 23/10/1899, ABC 16.3.12, vol. 20, No. 198.)

67. Yuan Shi-kai, postscript to GX 25/12/13 memorial (13/1/1900), DASL, 1:60.

68. Zongli Yamen to Yu-xian, GX 25/9/22 (26/10/1899), SDXF.

69. SDDC, 160–162.

70. In the peasants' terms, the Boxers "went bad" (*huai-le*), and the example usually given was that they began robbing and extorting money from non-Christians. (Liu Wen-tang, Wang Xu-mei, Wang Zhi-yuan, SD Survey, Qihe, 5, 20, 23.) Arthur Smith also reports Boxer attacks on commoners in December, resulting in villagers resisting and even punishing such behavior. (Arthur Smith to Conger, 30/12/1899, ABC 16.3.12, vol. 20, no. 202. Cf. Smith, *China in Convulsion* 1:177–178.)

71. Lao Nai-xuan, 1901, YHT, 4:451.

72. Wang Xu-mei, SD Survey, Qihe, 20.

73. Shi Dong-dai, SD Survey, Chiping (1960), 2–3, quoted in part in SDDC, 146–147; Zhao Ting-cai, Chiping (1960), 21.

74. SDDC, 118–119, 148.

75. Licheng report, received GX 25/11/17 (19/12/1899), AJ, 8–9.

76. Ma [Jin-shu] reports, received GX 25/10/19 (21/11/1899) and GX 25/10/24 (26/11/1899), AJ, 15–16, 18–19; Liu Jin-dou, Yang Cun-kui, Chen Dian-jia, SD Survey, Chiping (1960), 59, 60, 74–75.

77. Licheng magistrate's report, received GX 25/11/17 (19/12/1899); Ma [Jin-shu] report, received GX 25/10/24 (26/11/1899), AJ, 8–9, 18–19; Gao-tang magistrate's report, GX 25/11/X, CBOC, 705–706. The troops had been

explicitly instructed to arrest the leaders "by ruse" and they succeeded quite remarkably in doing so. (Yuan Shi-dun report, received GX 25/10/17 [19/11/1899], AJ, 14–15.) For oral history accounts of Luo Hui-ying turning in Yu Qing-shui following the latter's robbery of a wealthy commoner, see Hao Da-jiang, and Yu Huai-qin, SDDC, 162, 218. A near-contemporary documentary reference is in CBOC, 174 (GX 26/2/23 [23/3/1900]).

78. Yucheng report, received GX 26/1/11 (10/2/1900), AJ, 245; *Hui-bao*, GX 26/1/22 (21/2/1900), in SDSZZL, 1960.2:118; SDDC, 166–170, 175–177.

79. H. D. Porter, "Twelfth Annual Report of the Pang-chuang Station for the year ending April 30, 1900," ABC 16.3.12, vol. 16; U.S. Consul "Fa-le" to Yu-xian, GX 25/10/13 (15/11/1899), SDXF.

80. Jinan correspondence, 4/12/1899, in NCH, 63:1264 (27/12/1899). The governor, for his part, was not about to be moved by such threats and stuck to his convictions on the nature of Boxer-Christian troubles. He reported the Yucheng attack to the Zongli Yamen as an ambush of the Boxers by well-armed Christians, and stressed the casualties on the Boxer side. (Yu-xian to Zongli Yamen, No. 159, GX 25/10/27 [29/11/1899], SDXF.) Other Yu-xian telegrams in this archive (e.g., to British Consul in Chefoo, GX 25/11/12 [14/12/1899]) repeat the wishful claim that the Boxers had already dispersed.

81. Zongli Yamen to Yu-xian, GX 25/10/29, No. 237 [sic: error for 137], SDXF archive.

82. Conger to Hay, 5 and 7/12/1899, FRUS, 1900, 77–78, 84.

83. Zhu Zu-mou memorial, GX 25/11/24 (26/12/1899), and edict of same day, DASL, 1:42–44.

84. Huang Gui-jun memorial, GX 25/11/25 (27/12/1899), DASL, 1:44–45.

85. Edict of GX 25/11/27 (29/12/1899), DASL, 1:46.

86. Yuan Shi-kai letters to Xu Shi-chang, GX 25/12/6 and 16 (6 and 16/1/1900) in *Jindai shi ziliao*, 1978.2:18–21.

87. Yuan Shi-kai, GX 25/12/19 (19/1/1900), JWJAD 6.1:472, 485–488. This report makes no mention of the prohibition on boxing societies, which is noted in CBOC, 140 (GX 26/1/29 [28/2/1900]) as having been issued at roughly the same time.

88. Yuan Shi-kai, GX 26/2/15 and 3/16 (15/3 and 15/4/1900), DASL, 1:65–77, 75–77; SDDC, 172–175.

89. Yuan Shi-kai, GX 25/12/13 (13/1/1900), DASL, 1:59.

CHAPTER TEN

1. Edict, GX 25/12/11 (11/1/1900), DASL, 1:56.

2. Wang Pei-you, GX 25/12/9 (9/1/1900), DASL, 1:53. (Wang was a Shandong native, from Pingdu.)

3. Gao Xi-zhe, GX 25/12/5 (5/1/1900), DASL, 1:49.

4. QSL, GX 24/9/25 (8/11/1898), GX 25/11/24 (26/12/1899), 431:12a–13a; 455:11b–12a.

5. Liao Yi-zhong, Li De-zheng, and Zhang Xuan-ru, *Yi-he-tuan yun-dong shi* (Beijing: People's Press, 1981), 24–26, 88. In Sichuan the slogan was

"Follow the Qing [*shun-Qing*], destroy the foreign"; in neighboring Hubei, it was "Protect the Qing [*bao-Qing*], destroy the foreign."

6. Ibid., 14–17; Li Chien-nung, *The Political History of China, 1840–1928*, 171–173.

7. Luo Dun-rong, "Quan-bian yu-wen" in Zuo Shun-sheng, *Keng-zi quan-luan zi-liao* (Taibei, n.d.), 109–110; Sheng Xuan-huai, GX 26/9/2 (24/10/1900), and edict of GX 26/12/25 (13/2/1901), DASL, 2:727–728, 939. The closest direct evidence of Yu-xian's belief in the Boxer invulnerability magic comes in a telegram to Yu-lu following the arrest of Zhu Hong-deng and the monk Xin-cheng. "They seem," he said, "to have magical powers and heterodox techniques to ward off spears and swords." (Lin Xue-jian, 1:33b–34a [98–99].)

8. Yu-lu, GX 26/3/10 (9/4/1900), DASL, 1:72–73. Note also the court's full endorsement of a long memorial in which Yuan Shi-kai described his policy for handling anti-Christian disturbances. Yuan Shi-kai memorial and imperial rescript, GX 25/12/13 (13/1/1900), DASL, 1:56–60.

9. Edict, GX 26/4/24 (22/5/1900), DASL, 1:97. For discussions of the division in the court, see Liao Yi-zhong et al., 150–156; Dai Xuan-zhi, *Yi-he-tuan yan-jiu*, 64–69.

10. Edicts, GX 26/3/18 (17/4/1900) and GX 26/3/22 (21/4/1900), DASL, 1:80, 82.

11. Shanghai Mercury, *The Boxer Rising: A History of the Boxer Trouble in China* (1900; New York reprint: Paragon, 1967), xii. See also letters from William H. Rees, 8/6/1899 and 13/10/1899, in Purcell, 288–289.

12. Yu-lu, GX 26/4/19 (17/5/1900), DASL, 1:90.

13. See correspondence from members of London Missionary Society, in Purcell, 285–288; Yu-lu to Gao Can-lin, GX 25/4/11 (20/5/1899) and Gao's reply, GX 25/4/15 (24/5/1899), in Lin Xue-jian, 1:15a–15b (61–62); Yu-lu, GX 26/2/26 (26/3/1900), DASL, 1:69; H. D. Porter, "Twelfth Annual Report of the Pang Chuang Station for the year ending April 30, 1900," ABC 16.3.12, vol. 16; Liao Yi-zhong et al., 108–109.

14. Liao Yi-zhong et al., 106–107, 164–166; Ai Sheng, "Quan-fei ji-lüe," YHT, 1:444; SDDC, 191–192; Yucheng report received GX 26/1/24 (23/2/1900), AJ, 250.

15. Liao Yi-zhong et al., 107; Lin Xue-jian, 1:47a–47b (125–126), 64b–65a (160–161), 70a–70b (171–172); Ai Sheng, "Quan-fei ji-lüe," YHT, 1:463; Zhu Fu, "Geng-zi jiao-an han-du," YHT, 4:378.

16. Li Zong-yi, "Shandong 'Yi-he-tuan zhu-li xiang Zhili zhuan-jin' shuo zhi-yi," *Jin-dai-shi yan-jiu* 1979.1:303–319.

17. For examples, see Sawara Tokusuke and "Ou-yin," "Quan-shi za-ji," in YHT, 1:251; Ai Sheng, in YHT, 1:460; Zhu Fu, "Geng-zi jiao-an han-du," YHT, 4:372.

18. Yu-lu, GX 26/4/19 (17/5/1900), DASL, 1:91.

19. Sawara and "Ou-yin," YHT, 1:244; cf. 239, 240, 250, 251.

20. Ai Sheng, YHT, 1:460.

21. Lin Xue-jian, 1:31a–51a (93–133); Lao Nai-xuan, "Quan-an za-cun,"

YHT, 4:473–474, 480–481; *Hui-bao,* nos. 140–145, GX 25/11/21–12/3, SDSZZL, 1960:2, 129–130.

22. "Lao Nai-xuan zi-ding nian-pu," YHTSL, 1:416–417; Lin Xue-jian, 1:57b–60a, (146–151).

23. Guan Ting-xian, GX 26/5/14 (10/6/1900), DASL, 1:122–124.

24. Hu Fu-chen, GX 26/3/29 (28/4/1900), DASL, 1:83–84.

25. Lin Xue-jian, *passim.*

26. Conger to Hay, 8/5/1900, FRUS, 1900, 121.

27. C. R. Hodge, 10/5/1900, BFM, reel 212.

28. J. A. Miller, 5/1/1900, BFM, reel 212; Shanghai Mercury, *Boxer Rising,* xii, 9.

29. Yuan Shi-kai, GX 26/2/18 (18/3/1900), DASL, 1:68–69.

30. Ibid.; Qihe reports received GX 26/1/16 and 26 (15 and 25/1/1900) AJ, 207–209; Linyi report GX 26/3/21 (20/4/1900), AJ, 284–285; CBOC, 126–225 *passim,* esp. 190–191 (GX 26/3/1 [31/3/1900]).

31. Zhang Lian-fen, GX 26/3/7 (6/4/1900), Lin Xue-jian, 2:12b.

32. Conger to Hay, 8/5/1900, FRUS, 1900, 122.

33. MacDonald to Salisbury, 21/5/1900, in Great Britain, Parliamentary Papers, *China, No. 3 (1900): Correspondence Respecting the Insurrectionary Movement in China* (hereafter cited as "BPP, *China (3) 1900*"), 105. Cf. the Baoding missionary observation: "Oh that God would send rain. That would make things quiet for a time." (Shanghai Mercury, *The Boxer Rising,* 9.)

34. Shanghai Mercury, *The Boxer Rising,* ix–x. For similar notices, see Smith, *China in Convulsion* 1:200; Dai Xuan-zhi, 88, 91.

35. Zhili Provincial Commissioners (Judge and Financial Commissioner), GX 26/3/24 (23/4/1900), in Lin Xue-jian 2:19a–20a (209–211). This report puts Boxer-Zhang casualties at 20+. A British report (Carles to MacDonald, 2/5/1900, BPP, *China (3) 1900,* 106) puts the number at 70 Boxers and one Christian.

36. Zhili Adjutant (*zhong-xie*), GX 26/1/18 (17/2/1900), Lin Xue-jian, 2:1b–2a (174–175).

37. Ai Sheng, "Quan-fei ji-lüe," YHT, 1:448.

38. The French missionaries claimed that sixty-eight were killed (Zongli Yamen to Yu-lu, GX 26/4/17 [15/5/1900], Lin Xue-jian, 2:34b–35a [240–241]), but it is unclear how they arrived at that figure. Ai Sheng says over thirty families (YHT, 1:448). The authorities on the spot reported twenty to thirty deaths, but were unable to find any Christians to testify as to who was missing. (Zhu Fu, "Geng-zi jiao-an han-du, YHT, 4:371.)

39. Zhu Fu, YHT, 4:363–374; Ai Sheng, YHT, 1:448.

40. Zhu Fu, YHT, 4:373–391; Ai Sheng, YHT, 1:448–452.

41. Zhang Lian-fen, GX 26/4/28 (26/5/1900), Lin Xue-jian 2:48a–b (267–268).

42. Ai Sheng, YHT, 1:453–455.

43. Yu-lu to Nie Shi-cheng, GX 26/4/17 (15/5/1900), Lin Xue-jian 2:30b (232).

44. Liu Chun-tan, "Ji-nan ji-bian ji-lüe," YHTSL, 1:308–311, 316.

45. Muramatsu, *Giwadan no kenkyū*, 115–122; Wehrle, 148–157.

46. Muramatsu, *Giwadan no kenkyū*, 122; edict, GX 26/3/15 (14/4/1900), DASL, 1:80.

47. Zheng Bing-lin, GX 26/4/3 (1/5/1900), Yu-lu, GX 26/4/19 (17/5/1900), and Yuan Shi-kai, GX 26/4/21 (19/5/1900), DASL, 1:84–85, 90–95; edict on Zheng's memorial in YHT, 4:12–13.

48. MacDonald to Salisbury, 10/6/1900 in BPP, *China (3), 1900*, 1–3; Conger to Hay, 21/5/1900, 2/6/1900, 8/6/1900, FRUS, 1900, 127–133, 143.

49. Edict, GX 26/5/2 (29/5/1900), DASL, 1:105–106.

50. Edict, GX 26/5/3 (30/5/1900), DASL, 1:106; Muramatsu, *Giwadan no kenkyū*, 179–180.

51. Zhao Shu-qiao, GX 26/5/3 (30/5/1900), DASL, 1:109–110.

52. DASL, 1:114, 116; Steiger, 204–207.

53. Zhang Zhi-dong, GX 26/5/4 (31/5/1900), Sheng Xuan-huai, GX 26/5/9 (5/6/1900), Liu Kun-yi, GX 26/5/12 (8/6/1900), DASL, 1:112, 117–118, 121.

54. Muramatsu, *Giwadan no kenkyū*, 155–157; Gang-yi, GX 26/5/18 (14/6/1900), DASL, 1:137–140.

55. Liao Yi-zhong et al., 134–142; Ai Sheng, YHT, 1:453; edict, GX 26/12/6 (25/1/1901), DASL, 2:945.

56. DASL, 1:119–141.

57. Seymour to Admiralty, 29/6/1900, and Tratman to Admiralty, 29/6/1900, BPP, *China (3) 1900*, 84–85; Edicts of GX 26/5/17 and 20, DASL, 1:142, 145; William J. Duiker, *Cultures in Collision: The Boxer Rebellion* (San Rafael, California: Presidio Press, 1978), 77–81, 87–89.

58. Yun Yu-ding, "Chong-ling chuan-xin-lu," YHT, 1:47–48.

59. Yucheng report, received 11/7/1900, AJ, 267.

60. Liao Yi-zhong et al., 139–140. Since the pro-Boxer party is usually (and not inaccurately) regarded as reactionary, it is important to recognize that the anti-Boxer position was also conservative and profoundly anti-democratic. This shows clearly in the writings of Lao Nai-xuan, who argued that allowing "righteous people" to act on behalf of the state was like letting a son settle the affairs of, or press a private feud on behalf of a father. In response to those who said the Jia-qing prohibitions of the Yi-he quan were a thing of the past, he replied: "The glorious ancestral instructions should be followed for ten thousand generations." (Lao Nai-xuan, 1901, in YHT, 4:453, 457. Cf. 451.)

61. Gang-yi, GX 26/5/18 (14/6/1900), DASL, 1:137.

62. Zai Lian, GX 26/5/20 (16/6/1900), DASL, 1:146. Cf. Baoding commander, GX 26/5/4 (31/5/1900), Lin Xue-jian, 3:28b–29a (328–329).

63. Wu Hong-jia, GX 26/5/12 (8/6/1900), DASL, 1:121; Yuan Chang, "Luan-zhong ri-ji can-gao," YHT, 1:347.

64. Zhong-fang, "Geng-zi ji-shi," in *Geng-zi ji-shi* (Beijing: Zhong-hua, 1978), 15.

65. Nankai da-xue li-shi-xi, "Yi-he-tuan shi yi nong-min wei zhu-ti de fan-ti ai-guo zu-zhi," in *Yi-he-tuan yun-dong liu-shi zhou-nian ji-nian lun-wen-ji*, 261.

66. Sawara and "Ou-yin," YHT, 1:250.

67. Nankai da-xue, 261–263; Liao Yi-zhong et al., 50–53; Dai Xuan-zhi, 73–74; Zhong-fang, "Geng-zi ji-shi," 11–12, 16; Ai Sheng, YHT, 1:459.

68. Yuan Chang, YHT, 1:346.

69. Sawara and "Ou-yin," YHT, 1:251. Cf. 239, 243; Zhong-fang, 12.

70. Sawara and "Ou-yin," YHT, 1:239, 240.

71. Ibid., 239. Cf. 240. Missionary observers noted the likelihood of hypnotic trances (Shanghai Mercury, Boxer Rising, 1, 5–6); and Dai Xuan-zhi interprets all Boxer possession in these terms (25–31).

72. Ai Sheng, YHT, 1:460.

73. Sawara and "Ou-yin," YHT, 1:240, 243, 251; Zhong-fang, "Geng-zi ji-shi," 18; "Tianjin yi-yue-ji," YHT, 2:142; Ai Sheng, YHT, 1:444, 456, 460. For an excellent analysis, see Jerome Ch'en, "The Nature and Characteristics of the Boxer Movement—a Morphological Study," Bulletin of the School of Oriental and African Studies 23.2 (1960).

74. Ai Sheng, YHT, 1:460; Sawara and "Ou-yin," 238 (one day), 251 (7–8 days).

75. Yuan Chang, YHT, 1:346.

76. "Tianjin yi-yue-ji," YHT, 2:142.

77. Zhong-fang, "Geng-zi ji-shi," 17, 18, 23–24.

78. Yuan Chang, YHT, 1:345.

79. Zhong-fang, "Geng-zi ji-shih," 20, 24, 28. On the early Eight Trigrams, Naquin, Millenarian Rebellion, 90. Liao Yi-zhong et al., 40–41, notes oral history evidence for other trigrams, especially the zhen and li in the Tianjin area, and makes the argument for a White Lotus connection.

80. Liao Yi-zhong et al., 41–46.

81. Zhong-fang, "Geng-zi ji-shi," 12–13; Shanghai Mercury, Boxer Rising, 89–91; Dai Xuan-zhi, 91–92.

82. Zhong-fang, 12; Guan He, "Quan-fei wen-jian-lu," YHT, 1:470.

83. Yuan Chang, YHT, 1:345.

84. Zhong-fang, 12–14.

85. "Tianjin yi-yue-ji," YHT, 2:142.

86. Zhong-fang, 17. Cf. 28. These notions of female power and pollution will be familiar to readers of Mary Douglas's Purity and Danger, An Analysis of Concepts of Pollution and Taboo (London: Routledge and Kegan Paul, 1966).

87. Song Jia-heng and Pan Yu, "Yi-he-tuan yun-dong-zhong de fu-nü qun-zhong," Shandong da-xue xue-bao, 1960.2:54–60; Liao Yi-zhong, 46–47; Jerome Ch'en, "Nature and Characteristics of the Boxer Movement," 298, 303; Sawara and "Ou-yin," YHT, 1:272; Guan He, YHT, 1:469–470, 487; Yuan Chang, YHT, 1:346; Arthur Smith, China in Convulsion, 2:662–3. The Red Lanterns did apparently later spread to Shandong: see Zhang Xun report received GX 26/8/15 (8/9/1900), AJ, 71, on Haifeng county; SDDC, 131–134, on Chiping.

88. YHTSL, 1:18. Very similar versions of this notice are also seen in Sawara and "Ou-yin," YHT, 1:112, where it was taken from Tianjin, in May; and in SDDC, 315–316, where it is attributed to the Guan county boxers.

89. The best collection of these wall posters is in YHTSL, 1:4–20. See also Zhong-fang, 10; an excellent analysis, arguing persuasively for their

White Lotus inspiration, but less persuasively for their connection to the Boxers, is Cheng Xiao, "Min-jian zong-jiao yu yi-he-tuan jie-tie," *Li-shi yan-jiu*, 1983.2:147–163. Dai Xuan-zhi, 78–89, also acknowledges the clear White Lotus and anti-Qing content of many of these notices.

90. "Tianjin yi-yue-ji," YHT, 2:142.

91. Shanghai Mercury, *Boxer Rising*, xii–xiii.

92. Yun Yu-ding, YHT, 1:48–49; Yu-lu, GX 26/5/19 (15/6/1900), DASL, 1:142–143.

93. MacDonald to Salisbury, 20/9/1900, BPP, *China (3) 1900*, 21.

94. Carles to Salisbury, 15/6/1900, BPP, *China (3) 1900*, 56.

95. Shanghai Mercury, *Boxer Rising*, 17–23; BPP, *China (3) 1900*, 63–65, 74.

96. DASL, 1:147–148, 152, 157–159, 161–164; Dai Xuan-zhi, 104–105.

97. Edict, GX 26/5/25 (21/6/1900), DASL, 1:162–163.

98. Edict, GX 26/5/24 (20/6/1900), DASL, 1:156–157.

99. Chester Tan, 76–92.

100. Liao Yi-zhong et al., 250–264, and Lu Jing-qi, *Yi-he-tuan zai Shan-dong* (Jinan: Qi-Lu, 1980), 67–85, summarize the Shandong situation in 1900. Chester Tan, 83, 88–89, treats Yuan and the southern officials; DASL, 1:141, 154, 155 has the court's orders to Yuan Shi-kai to send troops, and his equivocation. Heeren, 122–127, covers the missionary evacuation; and SDJDSZL, 3:197, summarizes Catholic casualties. The original documentation on Yuan's policy toward the Boxers is voluminous: two volumes of AJ, and CBOC. For key documents see AJ, 32, 49–51, 58–61, 75–77, 106, 150–151, 180, 181, 264, 266–268, 287; CBOC, 130, 140–141, 157–159, 269–271, 275–281, 340–341, 377.

101. Dai Xuan-zhi, 132–135. Surprisingly, there is little agreement on just how many foreigners died in Shanxi. Latourette (514–515) mentions a total of 78 Protestants, but the total of the individual incidents he lists is 94 plus several uncounted groups. Cen Chun-xuan, who succeeded Yu-xian as governor, reported over 150 foreign deaths. (GX 27/5/24 [9/7/1901], DASL, 2:1233.) My estimate takes Arthur Smith's figure (*China in Convulsion* 2:648–649) of 12 Catholics killed in Shanxi and 159 Protestants killed in Shanxi and Inner Mongolia, then subtracts the 40 Protestants Latourette reports killed in Inner Mongolia.

102. Dai Xuan-zhi, 136; Liao Yi-zhong et al., 286–288; Latourette, 515.

103. Chester Tan, 157–161; Dai Xuan-zhi, 135–136; Liao Yi-zhong et al., 265–278.

104. J. W. Lowrie, 1/9/1900, BFM, reel 212; Latourette, 508–510. The latter source puts Catholic deaths at 15,000 to 20,000, but given the flight of most Catholics to well-fortified missions, that figure looks high.

105. Dai Xuan-zhi, 137; Liao Yi-zhong et al., 279–282.

106. Liao Yi-zhong et al., 289–295; Warren to Salisbury, 23/8/1900 and enclosures, BPP, *China (1) 1901*, 193–197.

107. Peter Fleming, *The Siege at Peking* (London: 1959) usefully summarizes the numerous foreign accounts of the siege.

108. Dai Xuan-zhi, 107–108; Chester Tan, 94–95; Sawara and "Ou-yin," YHT, 1:252; Zhong-fang, 18–25.

109. Dai Xuan-zhi, 112–113; Shanghai Mercury, *Boxer Rising*, 111–114.

110. Zhong-fang, 23, 26–27, 29. For other accounts in this same *Geng-zi ji-shi* volume, see 89, 105, 154.

111. Shanghai Mercury, *Boxer Rising*, 15–32 (quote from 32); William Duiker, 127–144; Dai Xuan-zhi, 143–145; Liao Yi-zhong et al., 159–179, 309–330.

112. Yu-lu, GX 26/6/28 (22/7/1900), DASL, 1:366.

113. Chester Tan, 100–103.

114. Dai Xuan-zhi, 146–149; Chester Tan, 104–111; Duiker, 145–176.

115. Cited in George Lynch, *The War of the Civilizations, Being a Record of a "Foreign Devil's" Experience with the Allies in China* (London: Longmans Green and Co., 1901), 84.

116. Accounts of depredations by the foreign troops are legion, but see especially Lynch, *War of Civilizations*; L. Putnam Weale, *Indiscreet Letters from Peking* (London: Dodd, Mead and Co., 1907); and Arthur Smith, *China in Convulsion* 2:522 ff. For a delightful discussion and useful citations of the missionaries' role, see Stuart Creighton Miller, "Ends and Means: Missionary Justification of Force in Nineteenth Century China," 249–282 in John K. Fairbank, ed., *The Missionary Enterprise in China and America*.

117. Chester Tan, 129–156, 215–236.

EPILOGUE

1. Marc Bloch, *The Historian's Craft* (New York: Knopf, 1953), 29, 32.

2. Ibid., 32.

3. James Mooney, *The Ghost-Dance Religion and the Sioux Outbreak of 1890* (Washington: Government Printing Office, 1896); Robert Utley, *The Last Days of the Sioux Nation* (New Haven: Yale, 1963).

4. Peter Worsley, *The Trumpet Shall Sound: A Study of "Cargo" Cults in Melanesia* (New York: Schocken Books, 1968).

5. On the Red Spears, see Elizabeth Perry, *Rebels and Revolutionaries*, 152–207.

6. Pierre Bourdieu, *Outline of a Theory of Practice*, trans. Richard Nice (Cambridge: Cambridge University Press, 1977), 82–83.

7. For Hong's travels, see Franz Michael, *The Taiping Rebellion: History and Documents* (Seattle: University of Washington Press, 1966, 1971), 1:203 (map 2). Michael's work is the standard English-language treatment of the Taiping, but its weakness is illustrated by the fact that his chapter on "The Setting of the Rebellion" contains only three pages of very general discussion of Guangdong and Guangxi. The best treatments in English are Jen Yu-wen, *The Taiping Revolutionary Movement* (New Haven: Yale, 1973) and Philip A. Kuhn, "The Taiping Rebellion," in *The Cambridge History of China*, Vol. 10: *Late Ch'ing, 1800–1911*, Part I, 264–317. On Hong's vision, the key source is Theodore Hamberg, *The Visions of Hung-Siu-Tsuen, and the Origin of the Kwang-si Insurrection* (Hongkong: China Mail, 1854; reprinted San Francisco, 1975); an important recent study is Rudolf G. Wagner, *Reenacting the Heavenly Vision: The Role of Religion in the Taiping Rebellion* (Berkeley: University of California Institute for East Asian Studies, 1982).

8. In addition to Kuhn, "The Taiping Rebellion," see Li Fei-ran, Deng Jie-zhang, Zhu Zhe-fang, and Peng Da-yong, "Tai-ping tian-guo qi-yi qian-ye de Guangxi she-hui," *Tai-ping tian-guo shi xin-tan* (Suzhou: Jiangsu People's Press, 1982); Laai Yi-faai, Franz Michael, and John C. Sherman, "The Uses of Maps in Social Research: A Case Study in South China," *The Geographical Review* 52.1 (1962); and especially Xie Xing-yao, *Tai-ping tian-guo qian-hou Guangxi de fan-Qing yun-dong* (Beijing: San-lian, 1950), a source suggested and kindly furnished to me by Elizabeth Perry.

9. For a general introduction to such millenarian movements see Sylvia L. Thrupp, *Millennial Dreams in Action: Essays in Comparative Study* (The Hague: Mouton, 1962).

10. "Deposition of Li Xiu-cheng," translated in C. A. Curwen, *Taiping Rebel: The Deposition of Li Hsiu-ch'eng* (Cambridge: Cambridge University Press, 1977), 80.

11. Kuhn, "The Taiping Rebellion," 265.

12. "Tai-ping zhao-shu," in Xiao Yi-shan, *Tai-ping tian-guo cong-shu* (Taibei: Taiwan Book Co., 1956), 1 : 115. Cf. Michael's translation, 2 : 34.

13. For a rather different attempt to explain the spread of the Taiping doctrine in the Guangxi hills, an explanation in terms of the appeal of Taiping "dualism" in a polarized society of hostile ethnic groups, see Philip A. Kuhn, "Origins of the Taiping Vision: Cross-Cultural Dimensions of a Chinese Rebellion," *Comparative Studies in Society and History* (1977), 19 : 350–366.

14. In addition to Wagner's *Reenacting the Heavenly Vision*, see Vincent Shih, *The Taiping Ideology: Its Sources, Interpretations and Influences* (Seattle: University of Washington Press, 1967).

15. Hamberg, 49. See also Li Xiu-cheng's statement that except for the six Taiping kings, the others "really followed for the sake of food." (Curwen, 80.)

16. From "Tian-tiao shu," in Xiao Yi-shan, 1 : 73. Other prayers on pp. 69–77. For translations, see Michael, 2 : 115–119.

17. Hong Ren-gan, in Michael, 2 : 4, 7.

18. Hamberg, 45–46.

19. For some of the best examples, see Carlo Ginzburg, *The Cheese and the Worms: The Cosmos of a Sixteenth-Century Miller*, trans. John and Ann Tedeschi (New York: Penguin, 1982); Nathalie Z. Davis, *The Return of Martin Guerre* (Cambridge, Mass.: Harvard University Press, 1983); Emmanuel Le Roy Ladurie, *Montaillou: The Promised Land of Error*, trans. Barbara Bray (New York: Vintage, 1979); and *Carnival in Romans*, trans. Mary Feeney (New York: George Braziller, 1980). For a first attempt in the China field, see Johnson, Nathan, and Rawski, eds., *Popular Culture in Late Imperial China*, though much of the subject of this volume is what Ginzburg (p. xv) terms "not 'culture *produced by* the popular classes,' but rather 'culture *imposed on* the popular classes.'"

20. Marshall Sahlins, *Islands of History* (Chicago: University of Chicago Press, 1985), 138.

21. For an interesting new discussion of shamanistic healing see Arthur

Kleinman, *Patients and Healers in the Context of Culture: An Exploration of the Borderland between Anthropology, Medicine, and Psychiatry* (Berkeley: University of California Press, 1980).

22. The terms and conceptualization here owe much to Scott Lawson, "Prompting an Audience, Summoning a God: Toward a Phenomenology of Possession with Oral-Epic Performance in South India," paper presented at the Association for Asian Studies annual conference, March 1985. Lawson's insightful paper discusses ritual performances of the Siri myth, which involve mass possession by lay actors. They are described in Peter J. Claus, "The Siri Myth and Ritual: a Mass Possession Cult in South India," *Ethnology* 14.1 (January 1975).

23. Here I am thinking especially of Victor W. Turner: *The Ritual Process: Structure and Anti-Structure* (Chicago: Aldine, 1969), and *From Ritual to Theatre: The Human Seriousness of Play* (New York: Performing Arts Journal, 1982).

24. Rees to Cousins, 8 June 1899, in Purcell, 286–287.

APPENDIX

1. See Naquin, "Connections," 339–342. A large number of documents on this sect was published in *Qing-dai dang-an shi-liao cong-bian* 3 (1979).

2. Lao Nai-xuan, "Yuan-liu-kao," YHT, 4:434–438. The original is the Na-yan-cheng memorial of JQ 20/11/3, NYC, 42:6a–12a.

3. Lao Nai-xuan, YHT, 4:431–439.

4. A listing of all articles on this subject would be both excessively tedious and beyond my capabilities. The following are the best that I have encountered. The attack on Lao Nai-xuan was led by Dai Xuan-zhi, in his *Yi-he-tuan yan-jiu*; but the merits of his critique of Lao are offset by the weakness of his argument for the militia origins of the Boxers. Sasaki Masaya, "Giwadan no kigen," part 1, *Kindai Chūgoku* 1977.1:144–180, is a very convincing questioning of both Lao and Dai, though Parts 2 and 3 of this article are much weaker. Fang Shi-ming of the Academy of Social Sciences takes the extreme position that the Yi-he Boxers and White Lotus were actually antagonistic organizations, based largely on evidence (considered below) from Jinshan county in Shandong ("Yi-he-quan [tuan] yu bai-lian-jiao shi liang-ge 'shi-tong qiu-huo' de zu-zhi," *She-hui ke-xue ji-kan* 1980.4:95–100). Finally Xu Xu-dian of Shandong University has contributed a very nicely reasoned consideration of the evidence ("Yi-he-tuan yuan-liu chu-yi," *Shandong da-xue wen-ke lun-wen ji-kan* 1980.1:23–35), concluding that the Yi-he quan were much closer to traditional martial arts than to any White Lotus tradition. Three articles seem to me to make the best case for a White Lotus connection. Li Shi-yu, "Yi-he-tuan yuan-liu shi-tan," *Li-shi jiao-xue* 1979.2:18–23, presents an ingenious attempt to trace the genealogy of the Plum Flower Boxers (another name for the Guan county Boxers of 1898) all the way back to the Kang-xi era, with a link to the 1813 rebels on the way. Lu Yao, from Shandong University, presents one of the most detailed cases for a White Lotus connection, with extensive reliance on

documents from the Beijing archives ("Lun Yi-he-tuan de yuan-liu ji qi-ta," *Shandong da-xue wen-ke lun-wen ji-kan* 1980.1 : 36–61). And perhaps the most copiously documented defense of Lao Nai-xuan, which is a direct response to Sasaki's piece above, is Satō Kimihiko, "Giwadan (ken) genryū: hakkekyō to giwaken," *Shigaku zasshi* 91.1 (January 1982): 43–80. Finally, the only scholar to discuss this subject in English is Susan Naquin, who treats boxing as an integral part of the practices of "meditational sects" (Naquin, "Transmission"), and explicitly includes the Yi-he Boxers among boxing groups closely tied to the sectarians (*Millenarian Rebellion*, 3, 30–32, 106).

5. Jiang Sheng and Liu E, QL 48/12/7, GZD 46730; Hu Ji-tang, Ke-ning-a, and Zhou Yuan-li, QL 44/1/5, GZD 37394. In the documents from 1774, the "he" of Yi-he is given as "合" (united) rather than the later more common "和" (harmony).

6. Guo-tai, QL 39/10/4, GZD 30177. The accusation that Li Cui traveled to Linqing seems highly suspect. His accuser had named a large number of others who allegedly went along—and all who could be located were absolved of any crime.

7. Shu-he-de, QL 39/10/16, in YLSL, 15–16.

8. The first case arose in 1778, and the boxers were allegedly in Guan county, south of Linqing and near the Zhili border. The accuser (a Shanxi merchant trying to call attention to another suit he was bringing against excessive exactions for repair of the Yellow River dikes) had heard that Wang Lun's boxing was called "Yi-he," and thus he mentioned the name. (Hu Ji-tang and Ke-ning-a, QL 43/12/17, GZD 37240; Hu Ji-tang, Ke-ning-a, and Zhou Yuan-li, QL 44/1/5 GZD 37394; YLSL, 23–25, especially Zhou Yuan-li memorial, QL 43/11/25.) The second case was in 1783, and was brought by a village leader who had been beaten up when he cursed some fellow villagers who were late on their tax obligations. The accusations of Yi-he Boxing activities were apparently false, but some of the accused were indeed sectarians and were ordered executed. (Jiang Sheng and Liu E, QL 48/12/7, GZD 46730; YLSL, 25–26.) The third case, in 1786, followed the Eight Trigrams uprising of that year, and involved the landlord of one of the leaders of that revolt. The accused was the father of a military *ju-ren* who indignantly asked to prove his loyalty by assisting in the capture of the rebels. (YLSL, 29–33.) For a recent attempt to link Wang Lun to the Yi-he Boxers, see Lu Jing-qi, "Shandong Yi-he quan de xing-qi, xing-zhi yu te-dian," *Wen-shi-zhe* 1982.4 : 72.

9. Shu-he-chen [*sic*, -de?], QL 39/10/19, cited in Lu Yao, "Lun Yi-he-tuan," 43. Susan Naquin concludes in her book on Wang Lun (*Shantung Rebellion*, 192) that the Yi-he Boxing was unrelated to Wang Lun, and I have her and her careful book to thank for leading me to the documentation cited in note 8.

10. Qing-pu, JQ 19/10/14, YLSL, 72. The second case, another false accusation, is from En county: Chen Yu, JQ 21/6/10, YLSL, 89–90.

11. Yi Ke-shao confession, JQ 19/6/X, YLSL, 69. Yi was a salt smuggler from southwest Shandong, so the clientele of this group was as described above.

12. Hu Ji-tang and Ke-ning-a, QL 43/12/17, GZD 37240.

13. Na-yan-cheng, JQ 19/3/27 and 20/11/25 in NYC 39:3a–8a, 41:17b–20b; YLSL, 53–54, 56–59, 78–80.

14. Liu Yuan confession, Zhang Xu, JQ 19/8/21, YLSL, 71.

15. Song Shu-de confession, [JQ 19?]/12/2, YLSL, 75.

16. Guo Wei-zheng's confession, undated, is in YLSL, 75–76. We shall discuss Guo later in connection with Yi-he Boxing where his name is variously given as 郭維正, 郭維貞, or 郭爲楨.

17. Feng Ke-shan confession, Dong Gao memorial, JQ 18/12/11, JFJL, 24:21b–26b; Song Yu-lin (Yue-long's son) confession, Dong Gao, JQ 18/12/21, JFJL, 28:1a–3a; Liu Yuan confession, Zhang Xu, JQ 19/8/21, YLSL, 70–71 (= GZD 16303, JQ 19/8/16). It may be that these boxing groups were far more difficult to unify than the religious sects which Lin Qing brought together in the Beijing area, or Xu An-guo in southwest Shandong. A certain "sectarianism" is indicated by one of these boxers, describing the fortifying of his village while awaiting Li Wen-cheng's northern march: "We feared that other sects or schools would come out and grab for power. If they came to the village, we were prepared to kill them." (Li Sheng-de confession, JQ 18/12/21, YLSL, 62–63.)

18. Song Yu-lin confession, Dong Gao, JQ 18/12/21, JFJL, 28:2a.

19. Ge Li-ye confession, JQ 20/9/3, in NYC, 38:73a–75a. Na-yan-cheng later attempts to suggest a sectarian nature of this boxing by referring to this group in the memorial cited by Lao Nai-xuan as the "Yi-he *school* boxing and cudgels" (Yi-he-*men* quan-bang).

20. Liu Kun confession, Zhang Xu, JQ 19/2/2, JFJL 34:16b–18b. Liu's teacher was Huo Ying-fang. His confession is paraphrased in Zhang Xu, JQ 18/12/16, JFJL 26:31b–32a. It makes no mention of boxing.

21. It may be significant that in his final confession in Beijing, Ge Li-ye calls Liu Kun a Li Trigram disciple of Song Yue-long, and makes no mention of either boxing or the Old Heavenly Gate Sect. (*Shang-yu-dang fang-ben* 363–65, JQ 20/9/26.)

22. Lü Fu confession, Chen Yu, JQ 19/10/30, YLSL, 73.

23. Li Sheng-de, JQ 18/12/21, YLSL, 62–63. The appearance of this text in a group which so clearly practiced boxing reminds us that Susan Naquin's useful distinction between "sutra-recitation" sects and "meditation" sects (with the latter alone involved in martial arts) is not to be understood in absolute terms. This same source mentions that Song Yue-long's son asked for an explanation of the meaning of some phrases in the text—which suggests how little the boxing specialists knew about the religious tenets of the sects.

24. The confessions from this area give us an unusually clear picture of the rituals of the Li Trigram, and of their recruitment into Xu An-guo's Zhen Trigram. Cui Shi-jun confession, Tong-xing JQ 18/9/15, JFJL 1:23a–32b; Zhang Jian-mu, Wang Pu-ren, and Gao Tian-you confessions, JQ 18/9/30, YLSL, 45–49.

25. See Naquin, *Millenarian Rebellion*, 122 ff., for this side of the story.

26. YHT, 4:433.

27. Wu Jie, "[Jin-shan] Ji-shi lüe," *Jining zhi-li-zhou zhi*, 1:21a.

28. Wu Jie reports JQ 18/8/17 and 8/19, YLSL, 39. These reports form the critical base (and provide the title) for Fang Shi-ming's argument of White Lotus–boxer antagonism; and Lu Yao ("Lun Yi-he-tuan," 45–46) and Satō ("Giwadan [ken] genryū," 59–62) have attempted to answer his argument. Both Lu and Satō argue that the Yi-he Boxers opposed the Jinshan sectarians because the latter had abandoned the Li for the Zhen trigram. There are several problems with this argument. First, it is unlikely that the switch from one Trigram to another was that serious a matter. The White Lotus sects seemed extremely liberal toward name changes and the amalgamation of sects. (See Naquin, *Millenarian Rebellion*, 42–43.) Xu An-guo himself had earlier switched from the Zhen to the Dui trigram. (See his confession in Dong Gao, JQ 18/12/23, JFJL, 29:1a–2a.) More seriously, Lu and Satō's argument relies on the assertion that Jinshan sectarian Wang Pu-ren, whose confession clearly establishes him as a member of the Li Trigram sect, was also a member of the Yi-he Boxers. Wang is held to have been the leader both of the boxers and the Li Trigram, whose antipathy to the sectarians rebels (in the name of the Yi-he Boxers) was motivated by Cui's defection to the Zhen trigram. The only evidence for a connection between Wang and the boxers is Wu Jie's statement, after Wang's arrest, that he "feared" Wang was an Yi-he Boxing leader, because Wang had admitted only practicing boxing, and no sectarian practice. However, Wang's later confession (YLSL, 47–48) clearly establishes that his denial of sectarian membership was false. Most likely, in his attempt to escape the sectarian charge, and aware of the Yi-he Boxers' cooperation with the government in this case, Wang initially tried to pass as only a boxer—until he finally broke under torture at the provincial level. That he was not an Yi-he Boxer is further suggested by the fact that the runner who arrested him was himself an Yi-he Boxer. If Wang was, as suggested, a "big chief" of the boxers, it is unlikely that a member of his organization would have been so diligent in pursuing him. (See Wu Jie, YLSL, 39.)

29. Wu Jie, "Ji-shi lüe," 4:31b.

30. Tong-xing, JQ 18/11/13, YLSL, 51.

31. Liu Wan-quan confession, JQ 19/12/2, YLSL, 75.

Glossary of Names
and Terms

Ba-gua jiao 八卦教

Bai-lian jiao 白蓮教

Bai shang-di hui 拜上帝會

bai-shi chuan-tu 拜師傳徒

Bang-chui hui 棒棰會

bao-jia 保甲

bao-juan 寶卷

Bao-Qing mie-yang 保清滅洋

Bei-di 北堤

Beitaiji 北台吉

Ben-ming 本明

bi-pao 閉砲

bi qiang-dao 避槍刀

bie-hao 別號

cai-zhu 財主

can-jiang 參將

Cao De-li 曹得禮

Cao Ti 曹倜

cha-hua-di 插花地

chang 場

chang-gong 長工

Chang-qiang hui 長槍會

Chang Wu-hua-gui 常五花貴

Chen De-he 陳德和

Chenjiazhuang 陳家莊

Chen Zhao-ju 陳兆舉

cheng yang-jir 撐洋勁儿

Cui Shi-jun 崔士俊

cun-shen yang-qi 存神養氣

Da-cheng jiao 大乘教

Da-dao hui 大刀會

Da-hong quan 大紅拳

da-hu 大戶

Da Liji 大李集

da shi-xiong 大師兄

dao-an 盜案

dao-qiang bu-ru 刀槍不入

Dao-shi 道士

daotai 道台

di-bao 地保

Disankou 第三口

di-zhu 地主

Dong Fu-xiang 董福祥

Dongtuan 東湍

dou-dou 兜兜

dou-du 兜肚

duan-gong 端公

er shi-xiong 二師兄

fa 法

fa-jin 法盡

fei 匪

fei-di 飛地

Feng Ke-shan 馮克善

Feng-shen yan-yi 封神演義

feng-shui 風水

Feng Yun-shan 馮雲山

fu 撫

fu-lu 符籙

fu-Qing mie-yang 扶清滅洋

fu-sheng 附生

fu Zhong-chao mie yang-jiao 扶中朝滅洋教

gan-huo 幹活

Ganji 干集

Gang-yi 剛毅

Gangzi Lizhuang 杠子李莊

Gao Shi-cai 高世才

Gao Xiao-ma-zi 高小麻子

Gao Yuan-xiang 高元祥

Ge Li-ye 葛立業

Ge Wen-zhi 葛文治

gong-fu 功夫

gong-sheng 貢生

Guxian 固獻

Gu Yan-wu 顧炎武

gua-fen 瓜分

Guan-gong 關公

guan-lu 官路

Guang-xu 光緒

guo-jia 國家

Guo Jing-shun 郭景順

Guo Wei-zheng 郭爲正

Han Guang-ding 韓光鼎

Han Lin-er 韓林兒

Han Shan-tong 韓山童

Hao He-sheng 郝和昇

He Hu-chen 赫虎臣

He Shi-zhen 何士箴

Hong-bang 紅幫

Hong-deng-zhao 紅燈照

Hong-men 紅門

Hong-quan　紅拳

Hongtaoyuan　紅桃園

Hong Xiu-quan　洪秀全

Hong-yang hui　紅陽會

Hong Yong-zhou　洪用舟

Hong-zhuan hui　紅磚會

Houjiazhuang　侯家莊

Hu-wei bian　虎尾鞭

Huang Chao　黃巢

Huang Fei-hu　黃飛虎

Huang-lian sheng-mu　黃蓮聖母

Huang-sha hui　黃沙會

hui-fei　會匪

jia-shen fu-ti　假神附體

jian-sheng　鑑生

Jiangjiazhuang　蔣家莊

Jiang Kai　蔣楷

jiang-shen fu-ti　降神附體

Jiang Tai-gong　姜太公

jiang xie-shen　降邪神

Jiang Zi-ya　姜子牙

jiao-chu　剿除

jiao-ji　剿擊

jie　劫

jie hui-shou　街會首

jie-san quan-min　解散拳民

jie-shen　接神

Jietouzhuang　街頭莊

Jinjiazhuang　靳家莊

jin-shi　進士

Jin-zhong zhao　金鍾罩

Jing Ting-bin　景廷賓

ju-ren　舉人

jue-zi　訣字

kan　坎

kan-jia　看家

kan re-nao　看熱鬧

Kang You-wei　康有爲

Lao Nai-xuan　勞乃宣

Lao Tian-men jiao　老天門教

lao-tuan　老團

Li Bing-heng　李秉衡

Li Chang-shui　李長水

Li Cui　李萃

Li Da-du-zi　李大肚子

Li-gua jiao　離卦教

Li Hao-ran　李浩然

Li Hong-zhang　李鴻章

Li Jin-bang　李金榜

Li Ting-biao　李亭標

Li Wei-xian　李維誠

Li Wen-cheng　李文成

Liyuantun　梨園屯

li-zhang　里長

lian-jun　練軍

Liang Qi-chao　梁啟超

liang-quan 亮拳

Lin Qing 林清

Liu Chang-an 劉長安

liu da-yuan 六大冤

Liu De-run 劉德潤

Liu Ge-da 劉疙瘩

Liu Kun 劉坤

Liu Kun-yi 劉坤一

Liulisi 琉璃寺

liu-mang 流氓

Liu Shi-duan 劉士端

Liu Tai-qing 劉太清

Liu-tang quan 六躺拳

Liutitou 劉堤頭

Liu Tian 劉田

Liu Wei-ling 劉維領

Lü Cai 呂某

Lu Chang-yi 盧昌詒

Lü Deng-shi 呂登士

Lü Fu 呂福

Lü Wan-qiu 呂萬秋

Lu-xi-bei 魯西北

Luo Hui-ying 羅會英

Maliangji 馬良集

ma-pi 馬匹

Ma Zhao-lin 馬昭林

mai-zai 買災

man-tou 饅頭

Mao Sui 毛遂

Mao Zi-yuan 茅子元

Mei-hua quan 梅花拳

Ming-zun jiao 明尊教

mu 畝

nao-qi-lai le 鬧起來了

nei-gong 內功

Nian 捻

Nie Shi-cheng 聶士成

niu-gong 牛工

pai-zhuan pai-dao 排塼排刀

Pang Hong-shu 龐鴻書

Pangjialin 龐家林

Pang San-jie 龐三傑

Pei-yi tuan 配義團

Peng Gui-lin 彭桂林

Peng Yu-sun 彭虞孫

pian-fang 偏方

qi-gong 氣功

qi-li 氣力

Qi-wu 齊巫

qian 乾

qian-zong 千總

Qiang-xue hui 強學會

Qing-bang 青幫

Qing-cha men 清茶門

qing-guan 清官

qing lao-shi xia-shan 請老師下山

quan-chang   拳場

quan-jiao   拳脚

quan-jiao   拳教

quan-ya-xiang-cuo   犬牙相錯

Rong-hua hui   榮華會

Rong Lu   榮祿

Ruan Zu-tang   阮祖棠

San-fo lun   三佛輪

San-guo yan-yi   三國演義

Sanmenwan   三門灣

san-yong   散勇

Sen-luo Temple   森羅殿

sha-fu ji-pin   殺富濟貧

Shaliuzhai   沙柳寨

Sha-seng   沙僧

shan-nan xin-nü   善男信女

"Shan-xian zun-zha yi-ban
  tuan-lian zhang-cheng"
  單縣遵札議辦團練章程

shang-fa   上法

Shaobing Liuzhuang   燒餅劉莊

Shao Shi-xuan   邵士宣

Shao Yu-huan   邵玉環

she-chang   設場

shen-dong   紳董

Shen-quan   神拳

shen-shi   紳士

Sheng-ren dao   聖人道

Sheng Xuan-huai   盛宣懷

sheng-yuan   生員

Shi-ba-cun   十八村

shi-ba kui   十八魁

Shifokou   石佛口

shi-po   師婆

Shi Yan-tian   施硯田

shu-tang   書堂

Shui-hu-zhuan   水滸傳

Shun-dao hui   順刀會

Song Jing-shi   宋景詩

Song Yue-long   宋躍瀧

song-zhou xi-quan   頌咒習拳

Sun Bin   孫臏

Sun Shang-wen   孫上汶

Sun Wu-kong   孫悟空

Sun Zhi-tai   孫治泰

tai-bao   太保

Tai-ping dao   太平道

tan   壇

Tang Heng-le   唐恒樂

Tang Sai-er   唐賽兒

tao-fan   討飯

tao-huang   逃荒

ti-tian xing-dao   替天行道

Tian-di hui   天地會

Tian-tiao shu   天條書

Tie-bu shan   鐵布衫

Ting-yong   廷雍

tong-xin   同心

Tong Zhen-qing　童振清

tu-bu　土布

Tu-di shen　土地神

tu-hao　土豪

tuan-min　團民

tuan-zhong　團衆

wa-wa dui　娃娃隊

wai-gong　外功

Wang Cheng-xiang　王丞相

Wang Chuo　王綽

Wang Li-yan　王立言

Wang Lun　王倫

Wang Ming-zhen　王明鎮

Wang Que-zi　王瘸子

Wang Shang-xuan　王尙選

Wangshigong cun　王世公村

Wang Tai-qing　王太清

Wang Zhi-bang　王治邦

Wang Zi-rong　王子容

Wei He-yi　魏合意

wen　文

wen-wu jiao-men　文武教門

Weng Tong-he　翁同龢

wo-wo　窩窩

wu　武

Wu Jie　吳堵

wu-lai gun-tu　無賴棍徒

Wu Meng-tu　吳夢圖

wu-po　巫婆

Wu-sheng lao-mu　無生老母

Wu-wei jiao　無爲教

Wu-wei jun　武衛軍

Wu-ying bian　無影鞭

Xi-liang　錫艮

Xi si　西寺

Xi-you-ji　西遊記

xia-yi　俠義

xiang-tou　香頭

xiang-tuan　鄉團

xiao-jing fu-mu, he-mu jia-xiang
孝敬父母, 和睦家鄉

Xiaoligu　小里固

Xiaolu　小蘆

xie-fa　卸法

xie-jiao　邪教

Xie Wu xia-zi　謝五瞎子

Xin-cheng　心誠

xing-li jiao-ming　興立教名

xing-Qing mie-yang　興清滅洋

Xing-Zhong hui　興中會

xiu-min　莠民

Xu An-guo　徐安國

Xu Bing-de　許秉德

Xu Hong-ru　徐鴻如

Xu Tong　徐桐

Xuan-tian shang-di　玄天上帝

xue-hui　學會

Xue-Kong lou　薛孔樓

xue-quan nian- (song-) zhou
學拳念(誦)咒

xue-quan yun-qi　學拳運氣

Yan Lao-fu　閻老福

Yan Ming-jian　閻明鑑

Yan Shi-he　閻士和

Yan Shu-qin　閻書勤

Yang Bing　楊炳

Yang Chang-jun　楊昌浚

Yang De-sheng　楊得昇

Yang Fu-tong　楊福同

yang-huo　洋貨

Yang Jian　楊戩

yang-jiao　洋教

yang-min　洋民

yang-ren　洋人

yang-sha　洋紗

Yang Shun-tian　楊順天

yang-wu　洋務

Yang-wu ju　洋務局

Yang Xiu-qing　楊秀清

yang-xue　洋學

Yang Zhao-shun　楊照順

Yao Luo-qi　姚洛奇

Yao Wen-qi　姚文起

Yao Xi-zan　姚錫贊

Yihebao　義和保

Yi-he-men jiao　義和門教

Yi-he-men quan-bang
義和門拳棒

Yi-he quan　義和拳

Yi-he quan-jiao　義和拳脚

Yi-he tuan　義和團

Yi-he-ying　義和營

Yi-huo quan-jiao　異伙拳教

Yi-jing　易經

Yimenji　義門集

Yi-min hui　義民會

yi-qi　義氣

yi-xue　義學

ying-shen sai-hui　迎神賽會

Yong-le　永樂

yong-ying　勇營

you guan-chai, mei guan du-zi
有官差, 沒官肚子

you-fei　游匪

yu-bing yu nong　寓兵于農

Yu-huang miao　玉皇廟

Yu-lin jun　榆林軍

Yu-lu　裕祿

Yu Qing-shui　于清水

Yu-xian　毓賢

Yu Xian　豫咸

yu-yi　羽翼

Yuan Chang　袁昶

Yuan-ming-yuan　圓明園

Yuan Shi-dun　袁世敦

Yuan Shi-kai　袁世凱

Yue Er-mi-zi　岳二米子

Yue Jin-tang　岳金堂

Yun-chan si　雲禪寺

yun-qi　運氣

Zeng Guang-huan　曾廣寰

Zeng Guo-quan　曾國荃

zha-dao　鍘刀

zhai-zhu　寨主

zhan-shu　戰書

Zhang Cheng-xie　張成爕

Zhang Fei　張飛

Zhang Guo-zheng　張國正

Zhang Huan-hou　張桓侯

Zhang Jue　張角

Zhang Lian-zhu　張連珠

Zhang Lun-zao　張掄藻

Zhang Luo-di　張洛弟

Zhang Luo-jiao　張洛焦

Zhang Ru-mei　張汝梅

Zhang Shang-da　張上達

Zhang Yin-huan　張蔭桓

Zhang Ze　張澤

Zhang Zhi-dong　張之洞

Zhang Zong-yu　張總遇

Zhao Jin-huan　趙金環

Zhao Lao-guang　趙老廣

Zhao Lao-xing　趙老行

Zhao Luo-zhu　趙洛珠

Zhao San-duo　趙三多

Zhao Shu-qiao　趙舒翹

zhao-xin gu-piao　昭信股票

Zhao Yun　趙雲

zhe-xi　折席

zhen-kong zhou-yu　眞空咒語

zhen-tian-ye　眞天爺

zhen-wu shen　眞武神

zhen-ya　鎭壓

zhen-zhu　眞主

Zhi-he tuan　志和團

Zhongxingji　中興集

zhou　咒

Zhou Cang　周倉

Zhou De-qian　周得謙

zhou-shui　咒水

Zhou Yun-jie　周允杰

Zhou Zhen-jia　周震甲

Zhu Ba-jie　猪八戒

Zhu Hong-deng　朱紅燈

zhu-Qing mie-yang　助淸滅洋

Zhu Zhen-guo　朱振國

zong-tan　總壇

zu-shi　祖師

zu-shi lao-ye zhi shen-wei
祖師老爺之神位

zuo-dao yi-duan　左道異端

zuo-gong yun-qi　作功運氣

Zuo Jian-xun　左見勳

Bibliography

Ai Sheng 艾聲. "Quan-fei ji-lüe" 拳匪紀略 (A brief history of the Boxer bandits). In *Yi-he-tuan* 1:441–464.

Album des Missions Catholiques: Asie Orientale. Paris: Société de Saint Augustin, 1888.

Amano Motonosuke 天野元之助. *Santō nōgyō keizairon* 山東農業經濟論 (Agricultural economics of Shandong). Dalian, 1936.

American Board of Commissioners for Foreign Missions. Papers. Houghton Library. Harvard University. Cited as ABC.

Armstrong, Alex. *Shantung (China): A General Outline of the Geography and History of the Province; a Sketch of its Missions and Notes of a Journey to the Tomb of Confucius.* Shanghai: Shanghai Mercury, 1891.

Atlas des Missions Franciscaines en Chine. Paris: Procure des Missions Franciscaines, 1915.

Bays, Daniel H. "Christianity and the Chinese Sectarian Tradition." *Ch'ing-shih Wen-t'i* 4.7 (June 1982): 33–55.

Beresford, Lord Charles. *The Break-up of China, with an Account of its Present Commerce, Currency, Waterways, Armies, Railways, Politics and Future Prospects.* New York: Harper and Brothers, 1899.

Billingsley, Philip. "Bandits, Bosses and Bare Sticks: Beneath the Surface of Local Control in Early Republican China." *Modern China* 7.3 (1981): 235–288.

Bloch, Marc. *The Historian's Craft.* New York: Knopf, 1953.

Bodde, Derk and Morris, Clarence. *Law in Imperial China: Exemplified by 190 Ch'ing Dynasty Cases (Translated from the Hsing-an hui-lan) with Historical, Social, and Juridical Commentaries.* Philadelphia: University of Pennsylvania Press, 1973.

Bourdieu, Pierre. *Outline of a Theory of Practice.* Translated by Richard Nice. Cambridge: Cambridge University Press, 1977.

Brown, Arthur Judson. Papers. Yale Divinity Library. Yale University.

Buck, John Lossing. *Land Utilization in China, Statistics*. Shanghai: University of Nanking, 1937.

Butterfield, Fox. "The Legend of Sung Ching-shih: An Episode in Communist Historiography." *Papers on China* 18 (December 1964): 129–154.

Cao Ti 曹偶. "Gu-chun cao-tang bi-ji" 古春草堂筆記 (Notes from the Gu-chun cao-tang). In *Yi-he-tuan shi-liao* 義和團史料, 1:267–275.

Cao xian-zhi 曹縣志 (Gazetteer of Cao county). 1716.

Cao xian-zhi 曹縣志 (Gazetteer of Cao county). 1884.

Cary-Elwes, Columbia. *China and the Cross: A Survey of Missionary History*. New York: P. J. Kennedy and Sons, 1957.

Chan, Hok-lam. "The White Lotus-Maitreya Doctrine and Popular Uprisings in Ming and Ch'ing China." *Sinologica* 10.4 (1969): 211–233.

Chang Chung-li. *The Chinese Gentry: Studies in Their Role in Nineteenth-Century China*. Seattle: University of Washington Press, 1955.

Chang-qing xian-zhi 長清縣志 (Gazetteer of Changqing county). 1835.

Chang-qing xian-zhi 長清縣志 (Gazetteer of Changqing county). 1935.

Chao Wei-ping. "The Origin and Growth of the Fu Chi." *Folklore Studies* 1 (1942): 9–27.

Charles, W. R. "The Grand Canal of China." *Journal of the North China Branch of the Royal Asiatic Society* 31 (1896–1897): 102–115.

Chen Bai-chen 陳白塵. *Song Jing-shi li-shi diao-cha-ji* 宋景詩歷史調查記 (Record of an investigation into the history of Song Jing-shi). Beijing: People's Press, 1957.

Ch'en, Jerome. "The Nature and Characteristics of the Boxer Movement—A Morphological Study." *Bulletin of the School of Oriental and African Studies* 23.2 (1960): 287–308.

——. "The Origin of the Boxers." In *Studies on the Social History of China and Southeast Asia*, edited by Jerome Ch'en and Nicholas Tarling, 57–84. Cambridge: Cambridge University Press, 1970.

Chen Zai-zheng 陳在正. "Lun Yi-he-tuan yun-dong shi-qi de Yu-xian" 論義和團運動時期的毓賢 (On Yu-xian during the Boxer movement). Paper delivered at International Conference on the Boxer Movement. Jinan, 1980.

Chen Zhan-ruo 陳湛若. "Yi-he tuan de qian-shi" 義和團的前史 (A prehistory of the Boxers). *Wen-shi-zhe* 文史哲, 1954.3:17–25.

Cheng Xiao 程歗. "Min-jian zong-jiao yu Yi-he-tuan jie-tie" 民間宗教與義和團揭帖 (Popular religion and Boxer placards). *Li-shi yan-jiu* 歷史研究, 1983.2:147–163.

Cheng Xiao and Zhu Jin-fu 朱金甫. "'Yi-he-tuan dang-an shi-liao xu-bian' chu-tan" 《義和團檔案史料續編》初探 (An initial look at "Further Archival Documents on the Boxers"). Paper prepared for conference commemorating the sixtieth anniversary of the First Historical Archives. Beijing, October 1985.

Chi, Ch'ao-ting. *Key Economic Areas in Chinese History as Revealed in the Development of Public Works for Water Control*. London: George Allen and Unwin, 1936.

Chi-ping xian-zhi 茌平縣志 (Gazetteer of Chiping county). 1710. Taibei reprint: 1976.

Chi-ping xian-zhi 茌平縣志 (Gazetteer of Chiping county). 1935. Taibei reprint: 1968.

China, Inspectorate General of Customs. *Decennial Report on the Trade, Navigation, Industries, etc. of the Ports Open to Foreign Commerce, and on Conditions and Development of the Treaty Port Provinces, 1891–1900.* 2 vols. Shanghai: Statistical Department of the Inspectorate General of Customs, 1906.

————. *Reports of Trade at the Treaty Ports in China.* Annual publication. Cited as C:IGC.

Chinese Recorder and Missionary Journal. (May 1868–) Cited as CR.

Chou-bi ou-cun 籌筆偶存 (Retained working notes). Edited by Zhong-guo she-hui ke-xue-yuan jin-dai-shi yan-jiu-suo he Zhong-guo di-yi li-shi dang-an-guan 中國社會科學院近代史研究所和中國第一歷史檔案館 (Institute of Modern History of the Chinese Academy of Social Sciences and China, First Historical Archives). Beijing: CASS Press, 1983. Cited as CBOC.

Claus, Peter J. "The Siri Myth and Ritual: A Mass Possession Cult in South India." *Ethnology* 14.1 (January 1975): 47–58.

Cochrane, Thomas. *Altas of China in Provinces.* Shanghai: Christian Literature Society for China, 1913.

Colquhuon, Archbald R. *China in Transition.* New York: Harper and Brothers, 1898.

Coltman, Robert, Jr. *The Chinese, Their Present and Future: Medical, Political and Social.* Philadelphia: F. A. Davis, 1891.

Cordier, Henri. *Histoire des Relations de la Chine avec les Puissances Occidentales, 1860–1900.* 3 vols. Paris: Germer Baillière, 1901–1902.

Curwen, Charles A. *Taiping Rebel: The Deposition of Li Hsiu-ch'eng.* Cambridge: Cambridge University Press, 1977.

Da-Qing hui-dian shi-li 大清會典事例 (The Qing legal code and precedents). 24 vols. 1899. Taibei reprint: 1963.

Da-Qing jin-shen quan-shu 大清搢紳全書 (Directory of Qing officials). Beijing: Rong-hua-tang 榮華堂, quarterly.

Da-Qing jue-zhi quan-lan 大清爵秩全覽 (Directory of Qing officials). Beijing: Rong-bao-zhai 榮寶齋, quarterly.

Da-Qing li-chao shi-lu 大清歷朝實錄 (Veritable records of the Qing dynasty). Edited by Man-zhou guo-wu-yuan 滿洲國務院 (State Council of Manchuria). Tokyo: 1937.

Dai Xuan-zhi 戴玄之. *Yi-he-tuan yan-jiu* 義和團研究 (A Study of the Boxers). Taibei: Wen-hai, 1963.

Davis, John Francis. *Sketches of China; Partly During an Inland Journey of Four Months, Between Peking, Nanking, and Canton; with Notes and Observations Relative to the Present War.* Vol 1. London: Charles Knight, 1841.

Davis, Nathalie Z. *The Return of Martin Guerre.* Cambridge, Mass.: Harvard University Press, 1983.

De Groot, J. J. M. *Sectarianism and Religious Persecution in China: A Page in the History of Religions.* 2 vols. Amsterdam: Johannes Muller, 1903.

Dong-chang fu-zhi 東昌府志 (Gazetteer of Dongchang prefecture). 1808.

Duiker, William J. *Cultures in Collision.* San Rafael, Ca.: Presidio Press, 1978.

Eberhard, Wolfram. "Chinese Regional Stereotypes." *Asian Survey* 5.12 (December 1965): 596–608.

Edkins, J. "The Books of the Modern Religious Sects in North China." *Chinese Recorder.* Part 1, 19.6 (June 1888): 261–268. Part 2, 19.7 (July 1888): 302–310.

———. "Religious Sects in North China." *Chinese Recorder* 17.7 (July 1886): 245–252.

———. "A Visit to the City of Confucius." *Journal of the North China Branch of the Royal Asiatic Society* 8 (1874): 79–82.

Edwards, E. J. *Man From the Mountain.* Techny, Illinois: Mission Press, n.d. (1968?)

Eliade, Mircea. *Shamanism: An Archaic Technique of Ecstasy.* Translated by Willard R. Trask. Princeton: Princeton University Press, 1972.

Ellis, Henry. *Journal of the Proceedings of the Late Embassy to China.* London: John Murray, 1817.

Esherick, Joseph W. "Number Games: A Note on Land Distribution in Prerevolutionary China." *Modern China* 7.4 (1981): 387–412.

Fairbank, John K., ed. *The Cambridge History of China, vol. 10: Late Ch'ing, 1800–1911, Part 1.* Cambridge: Cambridge University Press, 1978.

———. ed. *The Missionary Enterprise in China and America.* Cambridge, Mass: Harvard University Press, 1974.

Fairbank, John King; Bruner, Katherine Frost; and Matheson, Elizabeth MacLeod. *The I.G. in Peking: Letters of Robert Hart, Chinese Maritime Customs, 1868–1907.* 2 vols. Cambridge, Mass: Harvard University Press, 1975. Cited as I.G.

Fang Shi-ming 方詩銘. "Yi-he-quan (tuan) yu bai-lian-jiao shi liang-ge 'shi-tong-chou-huo' de zu-zhi" 義和拳(團)與白蓮教是兩個"勢同仇火"的組織 (The Boxers and the White Lotus are two 'hostile' organizations). *She-hui ke-xue ji-kan* 社會科學輯刊, 1980.4 (July): 95–100.

Faure, David. "The Rural Economy of Kiangsu Province, 1870–1911," *The Journal of the Institute of Chinese Studies of the Chinese University of Hong Kong* 9.2 (1978): 365–471.

Feng Shi-bo 馮士鉢. "Yi-he-tuan yuan-liu zhi-yi" 義和團源流質疑 (Query on the origins of Yi-he-tuan). *She-hui ke-xue ji-kan* 社會科學輯刊, 1980.4 (July): 101–108.

Feuerwerker, Albert. "Handicraft and Manufactured Cotton Textiles in China, 1871–1910." *Journal of Economic History* 30.2 (1970): 338–378.

Field, James A. Jr. "Near East Notes and Far East Queries." In *The Missionary Enterprise in China and America.* Edited by J. K. Fairbank, 23–55. Cambridge, Mass: Harvard University Press, 1974.

Fleming, Peter. *The Siege at Peking.* New York: Harper, 1959.

Gao-tang zhou xiang-tu-zhi 高唐州鄉土志 (Local gazetteer of Gaotang department). 1906. Taibei reprint: 1968.

Garnett, W. J. "Journey Through the Provinces of Shantung and Kiangsu." Great Britain, Parliamentary Papers. *China,* No. 1. 1907.

Geng-zi ji-shi 庚子記事 (Events in 1900). Edited by Zhong-guo she-hui ke-xue-yuan jin-dai-shi yan-jiu-suo 中國社會科學院近代史研究所 (Chinese Academy of Social Sciences, Institute of Modern History). Beijing: Zhong-hua, 1978.

Ginzburg, Carlo. *The Cheese and the Worms: The Cosmos of a Sixteenth-Century Miller.* Translated by John and Ann Tedeschi. New York: Penguin, 1982.

Great Britain, Parliament. *China, No.3* (1900): *Correspondence Respecting the Insurrectionary Movement in China* (Command Paper 257). London: Her Majesty's Stationery Office, 1900.

————. *China, No. 4* (1900): *Reports from Her Majesty's Minister in China, Respecting Events at Peking* (Command Paper 364). London: 1900.

————. *China, No. 1* (1901): *Correspondence Respecting the Disturbances in China* (Command Paper 436). London: 1901.

————. *China, No. 5* (1901): *Further Correspondence Respecting the Disturbances in China* (Command Paper 589). London: 1901.

————. *China, No. 6* (1901): *Further Correspondence Respecting the Disturbances in China* (Command Paper 675). London: 1901.

Guan-cheng xian-zhi 觀城縣志 (Gazetteer of Guancheng county). 1838.

Guan He 管鶴. "Quan-fei wen-jian-lu" 拳匪聞見錄 (What I heard and saw of the Boxers). In *Yi-he-tuan* 1 : 467–492.

Guan Wei-lan 官蔚藍. *Zhong-hua min-guo xing-zheng qu-hua ji tu-di ren-kou tong-ji-biao* 中華民國行政區劃及土地人口統計表 (Administrative divisions and land and population statistics from the Republic of China). Taibei, 1955.

Guan xian-zhi 冠縣志 (Gazetteer of Guan county). 1934. Taibei reprint: 1968.

Gulick, Edward V. *Peter Parker and the Opening of China.* Cambridge, Mass.: Harvard University Press, 1973.

Gundry, Richard Simpson. *China, Present and Past; Foreign Intercourse, Progress and Resources; the Missionary Question, etc..* London: Chapman and Hall, 1895.

Guo Dong-chen 郭棟臣. "Guo Dong-chen de qin-bi hui-yi" 郭棟臣的親筆回憶 (Personal recollections of Guo Dong-chen). *Shandong da-xue wen-ke lun-wen-ji* 山東大學文科論文集 (Essays in the humanities from Shandong University), 1980.1 : 155–156.

————. "Yi-he-tuan zhi yuan-qi" 義和團之緣起 (The origins of the Boxers). In *Shan-dong Yi-he-tuan diao-cha zi-liao xuan-bian* 山東義和團調查資料選編 (A selection of survey materials on the Boxers in Shandong), 327–338. Jinan: Qi-Lu, 1980.

Hamberg, Rev. Theodore. *The Visions of Hung-Siu-Tshuen, and the Origin of the Kwang-si Insurrection.* Hong Kong: China Mail, 1854.

Harrell, Stevan and Perry, Elizabeth J. "Syncretic Sects in Chinese Society: An Introduction." *Modern China* 8.3 (July 1982): 283–303.

Harvey, Edwin O. "Shamanism in China." In *Studies in the Science of Society*, edited by George Peter Murdock, 247–266. New Haven: Yale, 1937.

He-ze-xian xiang-tu-zhi 荷澤縣鄉土志 (Local gazetteer of Heze county). 1907.

Heeren, John J. *On the Shantung Front: A History of the Shantung Mission of* the *Presbyterian Church in the U.S.A., 1861–1940 in its Historical, Economic and Political Setting*. New York: Board of Foreign Missions of the Presbyterian Church in the U.S.A., 1940.

Hinton, Harold C. *The Grain Tribute System of China (1845–1911)*. Cambridge: Harvard University Press, 1956.

Hobsbawm, E. J. *Bandits*. New York: Dell, 1971.

———. *Primitive Rebels: Studies in Archaic Forms of Social Movement in the 19th and 20th Centuries*. New York: Norton, 1965.

Horikawa Tetsuo 堀川哲南. "Giwadan undō kenkyū josetsu" 義和団運動研究序説 (An introduction to the study of the Boxer movement). *Tōyōshi kenkyū* 東洋史研究, 23.3 (1964): 41–67.

———. "Giwadan undō no hatten katei" 義和団運動の発展過程 (The development of the Boxer movement). In *Kōza Chūgoku kingendaishi 2: Giwadan undō* 講座中国近現代史 2. 義和団運動 (Lectures on modern Chinese history, 2: The Boxer movement), 207–236. Tokyo: Tokyo University Press, 1978.

Hoshi Ayao 星斌夫. *The Ming Tribute Grain System*. Abstracted and translated by Mark Elvin. Ann Arbor: University of Michigan, Center for Chinese Studies, 1969.

Hou Chi-ming. *Foreign Investment and Economic Development in China, 1840–1937*. Cambridge, Mass.: Harvard University Press, 1965.

Hou Ren-zhi 侯仁之. *Xu tian-xia jun-guo li-bing shu: Shandong zhi bu* 續天下郡國利病書：山東之部 (Supplement to "The strengths and weaknesses of the states of the empire": Shandong). Peking: Harvard-Yenching, 1941.

Hsiao Kung-ch'üan. *Rural China: Imperial Control in the Nineteenth Century*. Seattle: University of Washington Press, 1960.

Hu Sheng 胡繩. "Yi-he-tuan de xing-qi he shi-bai" 義和團的興起和失敗 (The rise and fall of the Boxers). *Jin-dai-shi yan-jiu* 近代史研究, 1979.10: 96–163.

Hu Zhu-sheng 胡珠生. "Yi-he-tuan de qian-shen shi zu-shi-hui" 義和團的前身是祖師會 (The predecessor of the Boxers is the Patriarch's Assembly). *Li-shi yan-jiu* 歷史研究, 1958.3:8.

Huang Chun-yao 黃淳耀. "Shan-zuo bi-tan" 山左筆談 (Notes on Shandong). In *Cong-shu ji-cheng* 叢書集成, edited by Wang Yun-wu 王雲五, vol. 3143. Changsha: Commercial Press, 1938.

Huang Ji 黃璣. *Shan-dong Huang-he nan-an shi-san zhou-xian qian-min tu-shuo* 山東黃河南岸十三州縣遷民圖說 (Map illustrating the relocation of people from thirteen counties on the south bank of the Yellow River in Shandong). N.p.: 1894.

Huang, Philip C. C. *The Peasant Economy and Social Change in North China*. Stanford: Stanford University Press, 1985.

Huang Yu-pian 黃育楩. "Po-xie xiang-bian" 破邪詳辯 (A detailed refutation of heterodoxy). (1834) In *Qing-shi zi-liao* 清史資料, vol. 3. Beijing: Zhong-hua, 1982.

Huang Ze-cang 黃澤蒼. *Shan-dong* 山東. Shanghai: Zhong-hua, 1935.

Hunt, Michael H. "The Forgotten Occupation: Peking, 1900–1901." *Pacific Historical Review* 48.4 (November 1979): 501–529.

Hyatt, Irwin T. *Our Ordered Lives Confess: Three 19th Century Missionaries in East Shantung*. Cambridge, Mass.: Harvard University Press, 1976.

Ichiko Chūzō 市古宙三. "Giwaken no seikaku" 義和拳の性格 (The nature of the Boxers). In Ichiko Chūzō, *Kindai Chūgoku no seiji to shakai* 近代中国の政治と社会, 289–310. Tokyo: Tokyo University Press, 1977.

———. "Giwaken zakko" 義和拳雑考 (Miscellany on the Boxers). In Ichiko Chūzō, *Kindai Chūgoku no seiji to shakai*, 311–324. Tokyo: Tokyo University Press, 1977.

Ileto, Reynaldo Clemena. *Pasyon and Revolution: Popular Movements in the Philippines, 1840–1910*. Manila: Manila University Press, 1979.

Isoré, P. "La chrétienté de Tchao-kia-tchoang sur le pied de guerre" (The Christendom of Zhao-jia-zhuang on a war footing). In *Chine et Ceylan: Lettres des missionaires de la Compagnie de Jesus* 1 (1899): 106–113.

James, F. H. "The Secret Sects of Shantung, With Appendix." *Records of the General Conference of the Protestant Missionaries of China, Held at Shanghai, May 7–20, 1890*, 196–202. Shanghai: Presbyterian Mission Press, 1890.

Jen Yu-wen. *The Taiping Revolutionary Movement*. New Haven: Yale University Press, 1973.

Ji-ning zhi-li zhou-zhi 濟寧直隸州志 (Gazetteer of Jining department). 1840.

Jiang Kai 蔣楷. "Ping-yuan quan-fei ji-shi" 平原拳匪紀事 (A record of the Boxer bandits in Pingyuan). In *Yi-he-tuan* 1: 353–362.

Jiao-wu jiao-an dang 教務教案檔 (Archives of missionary affairs and missionary cases). Zhong-yang yan-jiu-yuan jin-dai-shi yan-jiu-suo 中央研究院近代史研究所. Series 5 edited by Lü Shi-qiang 呂實強, 4 vols. Taibei: 1977. Series 6 edited by Lu Bao-gan 陸寶千, 3 vols. Taibei: 1980. Cited as JWJAD.

Jin Chong-ji and Hu Sheng-wu 金冲及, 胡繩武. "Yi-he-tuan yun-dong shi-qi de ge-jie-ji dong-xiang" 義和團運動時期的各階級動向 (Tendencies of social classes during the period of the Boxer movement). In *Zhong-guo jin-dai-shi lun-wen-ji* 中國近代史論文集 (Collected essays on modern Chinese history), edited by Zhong-guo ren-min da-xue Qing-shi yan-jiu-suo 中國人民大學清史研究所, 692–709. Beijing: Zhong-hua, 1979.

Jing Su 景甦 and Lo Lun 羅崙. *Qing-dai Shan-dong jing-ying di-zhu de she-hui xing-zhi* 清代山東經營地主的社會性質 (The social character of managerial landlords in Qing dynasty Shandong). Jinan: Shandong-sheng Xin-Hua shu-dian, 1959.

Johnson, David; Nathan, Andrew J.; and Rawski, Evelyn S., eds. *Popular Culture in Late Imperial China*. Berkeley: University of California Press, 1985.

Johnston, R. F. *Lion and Dragon in Northern China*. London: John Murray, 1910.

Journal of the North China Branch of the Royal Asiatic Society. 1859–. Cited as JNCBRAS.

Kanbe Teruo 神戶輝夫. "Shindai kōki Santōshō ni okeru 'danhi' to nōson mondai," 清代後期山東省における「団匪」と農村問題 ("Militia bandits" and the rural problem in Shandong at the end of the Qing). *Shirin* 史林, 55.4 (July 1972): 61–98.

Kang-Yong-Qian shi-qi cheng-xiang ren-min fan-kang dou-zheng zi-liao 康雍乾

時期城鄉人民反抗鬥爭資料 (Materials of resistance struggles of town and country people during the Kang-xi, Yong-zheng, and Qian-long periods). Edited by Zhong-guo ren-min da-xue Qing-shi yan-jiu-suo 中國人民大學清史研究所. Beijing: Zhong-hua, 1979.

Kataoka Shibako 片岡芝子. "Minmatsu Shinsho no Kahoku ni okeru nōka keiei" 明末清初の華北における農家経営 (Farm management in north China in the late Ming and early Qing). *Shakai keizai shigaku* 社会経済史学, 25.2/3 (1959): 77–100.

King, Clifford J. *A Man of God: Joseph Freinademetz, Pioneer Divine Word Missionary.* Techny, Ill.: Divine Word Publications, 1959.

Kleinman, Arthur. *Patients and Healers in the Context of Culture: An Exploration of the Borderland between Anthropology, Medicine and Psychiatry.* Berkeley: University of California Press, 1980.

Kobayashi Kazumi 小林一美. "Chūgoku hakurenkyō hanran ni okeru teiō to seibo—hansei kyōdōtai no nigenronteki sekai—" 中国白蓮教反乱における帝王と聖母—仮性共同体の二元論的世界 (Ruler and Holy Mother in White Lotus Rebellions in China—the two-dimensional world of counter-community), *Rekishigaku no saiken ni mukete* 歴史学の再建に向けて, 5 (1980): 52–64.

———. "Giwadan minshū no sekai—kindaishi bukai Satoi hokoku ni yosete" 「義和団民衆の世界」——近代史部会里井報告によせて (The world of the Boxer masses—on the report of Satoi to the modern history section), *Rekishigaku kenkyū* 歴史学研究, 364 (1970): 29–34.

———. "Giwadan no minshū shisō" 義和団の民衆思想 (The popular thought of the Boxers). In *Kōza Chūgoku kingendaishi 2: Giwadan undō* 講座中国近現代史2. 義和団運動 (Lectures on Modern China, 2: The Boxer movement). Tokyo: Tokyo University Press, 1978.

———. "Kakei hakurenkyō hanran no seikaku" 嘉慶白蓮教反乱の性格 (The nature of the Jia-Qing White Lotus Rebellion). In *Nakajima Satoshi sensei koki kinen ronshu:* 中嶋敏先生古稀記念論集, 559–580.

———. "Kōsō, kōryō tōsō no kanata—kakyū seikatsu no omoi to seijiteki shūkyōteki jiritsu no michi—" 抗租抗糧闘争の彼方—下層生活の想いと政治的, 宗教的自立の途 —(Beyond rent- and tax-resistance struggles—the thought of the lower classes and the road to political and religious autonomy), *Shisō* 思想. 584 (1973): 228–247.

Kong Ling-ren 孔令仁. "Shi-jiu shi-ji-mo Shan-dong de she-hui jing-ji yu Yi-he-tuan yun-dong" 十九世紀末山東的社會經濟與義和團運動 (Society and economy in late nineteenth century Shandong and the Boxer movement), *Shan-dong da-xue wen-ke lun-wen ji-kan* 山東大學文科論文集刊 (Essays in the humanities from Shandong University), 1980.1 : 1–22.

Kuhn, Philip A. "Origins of the Taiping Vision: Cross-Cultural Dimensions of a Chinese Rebellion." *Comparative Studies in Society and History* 19 (1977): 350–366.

———. *Rebellion and Its Enemies in Late Imperial China: Militarization and Social Structure, 1796–1864.* Cambridge, Mass.: Harvard University Press, 1970.

———. "The Taiping Rebellion." In John K. Fairbank, ed., *The Cambridge*

History of China, vol. 10: *Late Ch'ing, 1800–1911*, Part 1: 264–317.

Laai Yi-faai; Michael, Franz; and Sherman, John C. "The Use of Maps in Social Research: A Case Study in South China." *The Geographical Review* 52.1 (1962): 92–111.

Langer, William L. *The Diplomacy of Imperialism, 1890–1902*. Second edition. New York: Knopf, 1965.

Lao Nai-xuan 勞乃宣. "Lao Nai-xuan zi-ding nian-pu" 勞乃宣自訂年譜 (Chronological autobiography of Lao Nai-xuan). Excerpted in *Yi-he-tuan shi-liao* 1:416–417.

————. "Quan-an za-cun" 拳案雜存 (Miscellaneous papers on the Boxers). 1901. In *Yi-he-tuan* 4:449–474.

————. "Yi-he-quan jiao-men yuan-liu kao" 義和拳教門源流考 (An Examination of the sectarian origins of the Boxers United in Righteousness). 1899. In *Yi-he-tuan* 4:433–439.

Latourette, Kenneth Scott. *A History of Christian Missions in China*. New York: Macmillan, 1929.

Lawson, Scott. "Prompting and Audience, Summoning a God: Toward a Phenomenology of Possession within Oral-Epic Performance in South India." Paper presented at Association for Asian Studies Convention, 1985.

Le Roy Ladurie, Emmanuel. *Carnival in Romans*. Translated by Mary Feeney. New York: George Braziller, 1980.

————. *Montaillou: The Promised Land of Error*. Translated by Barbara Bray. New York: Vintage, 1979.

Leboucq, Prosper. *Associations de la Chine. Lettres du P. Leboucq, missionaire au Tche-ly-sud-est, publiées par un de' ses amis*. Paris: F. Wattelier [ca. 1880].

Lees, Jona. "Notes on a Journey from Tientsin to Chi-Nan Fu." *Chinese Recorder and Missionary Journal* 1.6 (October 1868).

Li Bing-heng 李秉衡. *Li Zhong-jie-gong (jian-tang) zou-yi* 李忠節公(鑑堂) 奏議 (Memorials of Li Bing-heng). Liaoning: Zuo-xin Publication, 1930. Cited as LBH.

Li Chien-nung. *The Political History of China, 1840–1928*. Translated by Ssu-yu Teng and Jeremy Ingalls. Princeton: Van Nostrand, 1956.

Li Fei-ran, Deng Jie-zhang, Zhu Zhe-fang, and Peng Da-yong 黎斐然, 鄧潔彰, 朱哲芳, 彭大雍. "Tai-ping tian-guo qi-yi qian-ye de Guang-xi she-hui" 太平天國起義前夜的廣西社會 (Guangxi society on the eve of the Taiping rebellion). In *Tai-ping tian-guo shi xin-tan* 太平天國史新探 (A new approach to the history of Taiping rebellion). Edited by Nanjing University History Department, 147–173. Suzhou: Jiangsu People's Press, 1982.

Li Hong-sheng 李宏生. "Yu-xian yu Shan-dong Yi-he-tuan" 毓賢與山東義和團 (Yu-xian and the Shandong Boxers). Paper presented at International Conference on the Boxer Movement. Jinan, 1980.

Li Kan 李侃. "Yi-he-tuan yun-dong yan-jiu-zhong de ji-ge wen-ti" 義和團運動研究中的幾個問題 (Several problems in the study of the Boxer movement). *Li-shi jiao-xue* 歷史教學, 1979.2:12–18.

Li Shang-ying 李尚英. "Dui Yi-he-quan yan-jiu-zhong ji-ge wen-ti de tan-tao" 對義和拳研究中幾個問題的探討 (Discussion on several problems in the study of the Boxers). *Xue-xi yu si-kao* 學習與思考, 1982.6 : 55–59.

Li Shi-yu 李世瑜. "Bao-juan xin-yan" 寶卷新研 (A new study of bao-juan). In *Wen-xue yi-chan zeng-kan* 文學遺產增刊, 4 : 165–181. Beijing: Writers' Press, 1957.

———. *Xian-zai Hua-bei mi-mi zong-jiao* 現在華北秘密宗教 (Secret religions in contemporary north China). Chengdu: 1948.

———. "Yi-he-tuan yuan-liu shi-tan" 義和團源流試探 (An Exploration into the origins of the Boxers). *Li-shi jiao-xue* 歷史教學, 1979.2 : 18–23.

Li Wen-zhi 李文治, ed. *Zhong-guo jin-dai nong-ye-shi zi-liao* 中國近代農業史資料 (Materials on the agrarian history of modern China), vol. 1. Beijing: San-lian, 1957.

Li Xing-hong 李行宏 and Qin Ya-min 秦亞民. "Guan-yu 'Da-dao-hui' shou-ling Liu Shi-duan de bu-fen qing-kuang" 關于"大刀會"首領劉士端的部份情況 (On some aspects of the situation concerning the Big Sword Society leader Liu Shi-duan). Manuscript provided by Shan county Cultural Bureau.

Li Zong-yi 李宗一. "Shandong 'Yi-he-tuan zhu-li xiang Zhili zhuan-jin' shuo zhi-yi" 山東"義和團主力向直隸轉進"說質疑 (Questions on the theory that 'the main force of the Shandong Boxers marched into Zhili'). *Jin-dai-shi yan-jiu* 近代史研究, 1979.1 : 303–319.

Lian Li-zhi 廉立之 and Wang Shou-zhong 王守中, eds. *Shan-dong jiao-an shi-liao* 山東教案史料 (Historical materials on Shandong missionary cases). Jinan: Qi-Lu, 1980.

Liang Fang-zhong 梁方仲. *Zhong-guo li-dai hu-kou, tian-di, tian-fu tong-ji* 中國歷代戶口, 田地, 田賦統計 (Statistics on population, land and taxes in China during the successive dynasties). Shanghai: People's Press, 1980.

Liao Yi-zhong, Li De-zheng, and Zhang Xuan-ru 廖一中, 李德征, 張旋如. *Yi-he-tuan yun-dong shi* 義和團運動史 (A history of Boxer movement). Beijing: People's Press, 1981.

Lin Chuan-jia 林傳甲. *Da-Zhong-hua Zhili-sheng di-li-zhi* 大中華直隸省地理志 (Geography of Zhili province of China). Beijing: Wu-xue shu-guan, 1920.

Lin Xue-jian 林學瑊. *Zhi-dong jiao-fei dian-cun* 直東剿匪電存 (Telegrams on suppressing the [Boxer] bandits in Zhili and Shandong). N.p.: 1906. Taibei reprint: Wenhai, n.d.

Litzinger, Charles Albert. "Temple Community and Village Cultural Integration in North China: Evidence from 'Sectarian Cases' (*Chiao-an*) in Chihli, 1860–95." Ph.D. dissertation, University of California at Davis, 1983.

Liu Chun-tang 劉春堂. "Ji-nan ji-bian ji-lue" 畿南濟變紀略 (An account of meeting the emergency in southern Zhili). In *Yi-he-tuan shi-liao* 1 : 306–349.

Liu T'ieh-yun. *The Travels of Lao Ts'an*. Translated by Harold Shadick. Ithaca: Cornell, 1952.

Lu Jing-qi 陸景琪. "Lun Yi-he-tuan yun-dong de zheng-zhi kou-hao" 論義和團運動的政治口號 (The political slogans of the Boxer movement). *Shan-dong da-xue xue-bao* 山東大學學報, 1960.1 (March): 55–69.

—————. "Shan-dong Chi-ping, Ping-yuan yi-dai Yi-he-tuan diao-cha-ji" 山東茌平, 平原一帶義和團調查記 (Investigations on the Boxers in Chiping and Pingyuan counties in Shandong). *Wen-wu* 1976.3 : 1–11.

—————. "Shan-dong Yi-he-quan de xing-qi, xing-zhi yu te-dian" 山東義和拳的興起, 性質與特點 (The rise, nature, and characteristics of the Shandong Boxers). *Wen-shi-zhe* 文史哲, 1982.4 : 72–79.

—————. "Yi-he-tuan yun-dong zai Shan-dong de bao-fa ji-qi dou-zheng" 義和團運動在山東的爆發及其鬥爭 (The outbreak and struggles of the Boxer movement in Shandong). In *Yi-he-tuan yun-dong liu-shi zhou-nian ji-nian lun-wen-ji*, 67–83.

—————. *Yi-he-tuan zai Shan-dong* 義和團在山東 (The Boxers in Shandong). Jinan: Qi-Lu, 1980.

Lu Jing-qi and Cheng Xiao 程嘯. *Yi-he-tuan yuan-liu shi-liao* 義和團源流史料 (Historical materials of the origins of the Boxers). Beijing: Chinese People's University, 1980. Cited as YLSL.

Lu Yao 路遙. "Lun Yi-he-tuan de yuan-liu ji qi-ta" 論義和團的源流及其他 (Discussion of the origins of the Boxers and other matters). *Shandong da-xue wen-ke lun-wen ji-kan* 山東大學文科論文集刊, 1980.1 : 36–61.

—————. "Yi-he-tuan yun-dong chu-qi dou-zheng jie-duan de ji-ge wen-ti" 義和團運動初期鬥爭階段的幾個問題 (Several problems on the initial stages of the Boxer movement). In *Zhong-guo jin-dai-shi lun-wen-ji* 中國近代史論文集, 2 : 661–691. Beijing: Zhong-hua, 1979.

Luo Cheng-lie 駱承烈. "Zhao San-duo, Yan Shu-qin ling-dao de Yi-he-tuan fan-di dou-zheng" 趙三多, 閻書勤領導的義和團反帝鬥爭 (The anti-imperialist struggles of the Boxers led by Zhao San-duo and Yan Shu-qin). Paper delivered at meeting of Shandong Historical Association. Jinan, October 1979.

Luo Dun-rong 羅惇曧. "Quan-bian yu-wen" 拳變餘聞 (Further stories of the Boxer crisis). In *Geng-zi quan-luan zi-liao* 庚子拳亂資料 (Materials on the Boxer unrest in 1900). Edited by Zuo Shun-sheng 左舜生, 98–136. Taibei reprint: n.d.

Lynch, George. *The War of the Civilizations, being a Record of a "Foreign Devil's" Experience with the Allies in China*. London: Longmans Green and Co., 1901.

Markham, John. "Notes on the Shantung Province, being a Journey from Chefoo to Tsiuhsien [Zou-xian], the City of Mencius." In *Journal of the North China Branch of the Royal Asiatic Society* 4 (1869–1870): 1–29.

Martin, Christopher. *The Boxer Rebellion*. London: Abelard-Schuman, 1968.

Michael, Franz with Chang Chung-li. *The Taiping Rebellion: History and Documents*. 3 vols. Seattle: University of Washington Press, 1966, 1971.

Miller, Stuart Creighton. "Ends and Means: Missionary Justification of Force in Nineteenth Century China." In *The Missionary Enterprise in China and America*, edited by John K. Fairbank, 249–282. Cambridge: Harvard University Press, 1974.

Mooney, James. *The Ghost-Dance Religion and the Sioux Outbreak of 1890*. Washington: Government Printing Office, 1896.

Muramatsu Yūji 村松祐次. *Giwadan no kenkyū* 義和団の研究 (Studies on

the Boxers). Tokyo: Gannan-dō 巖南堂, 1976.

Myers, Ramon. *The Chinese Peasant Economy: Agricultural Development in Hopei and Shantung, 1890–1949*. Cambridge, Mass.: Harvard University Press, 1970.

Na-yan-cheng 那彥成. "Na wen-yi-gong zou-yi" 那文毅公奏議 (Memorials of Na-yan-cheng). Edited by Zhang-jia Rong-an 章佳容安. Taibei reprint: n.d. Cited as NYC.

Nan-kai da-xue li-shi-xi Zhong-guo jin-xian-dai-shi jiao-yan-zu 南開大學歷史系中國近現代史教研組 (Modern Chinese History Section, History Department, Nankai University). "Yi-he-tuan shi yi nong-min wei zhu-ti de fan-di ai-guo zu-zhi" 義和團是以農民爲主體的反帝愛國組織 (The Boxers were an anti-imperialist patriotic organization with peasants as the main component). In *Yi-he-tuan yun-dong liu-shi zhou-nian ji-nian lun-wen-ji*, 256–274.

Naquin, Susan. "Connections Between Rebellions: Sect Family Networks in Qing China." *Modern China* 8.3 (1982): 337–360.

――――. *Millenarian Rebellion in China: The Eight Trigrams Uprising of 1813*. New Haven: Yale University Press, 1976.

――――. *Shantung Rebellion: The Wang Lun Uprising of 1774*. New Haven: Yale University Press: 1981.

――――. "The Transmission of White Lotus Sectarianism in Late Imperial China." In *Popular Culture in Late Imperial China*, edited by D. Johnson, A. Nathan, and E. Rawski. Berkeley: University of California Press, 1985.

Neill, Stephen. *Colonialism and Christian Missions*. New York: McGraw Hill, 1966.

Nevius, John L. *Demon Possession and Allied Themes—Being an Inductive Study of Phenomena of Our Own Times*. New York: Fleming H. Revell Co., 1894.

――――. "Shantung Mission, North China." In *Foreign Missionary of the Presbyterian Church*. N.p.: 1872.

Niida Noboru 仁井田陞 et al., eds. *Chūgoku nōson kankō chōsa* 中國農村貫行調查 (Surveys of village customs in China). Tokyo: Iwanami, 1981.

Nong-shang-bu 農商部. *Nong-shang tong-ji-biao, 1918* 農商統計表, 一九一八 (Statistical tables on agriculture and commerce, 1918). Beijing: Ministry of Agriculture and Commerce, 1922.

Norem, Ralph A. *Kaiochow Leased Territory*. Berkeley: University of California Press, 1939.

The North China Herald and Supreme Court and Consular Gazette. Cited as NCH.

Overmyer, Daniel L. "Attitudes Toward the Ruler and State in Chinese Popular Religious Literature: Sixteenth and Seventeenth Century Pao-chuan." Unpublished manuscript, 1983.

――――. *Folk Buddhist Religion: Dissenting Sects in Late Traditional China*. Cambridge, Mass.: Harvard University Press, 1976.

Perry, Elizabeth J. *Rebels and Revolutionaries in North China*. Stanford: Stanford University Press, 1980.

Pi zhou-zhi 邳州志 (Gazetteer of Pi department). 1851.

Pila, Fernand. "Une Province Chinoise en progrès: Le Chantoung." *Bulletin du Comité de l'Asie Française* 40 (July 1904): 331–337.

Ping-yuan xian-zhi 平原縣志 (Gazetteer of Pingyuan county). 1749. Taibei reprint: 1976.

Popkin, Samuel. *The Rational Peasant: The Political Economy of Rural Society in Vietnam*. Berkeley: University of California Press, 1979.

Porter, Henry D. *Mary H. Porter: First Missionary of the W. B. M. I.* Chicago: Women's Board of Missions of the Interior (Congregational), 1914.

———. "The Missionary Invasion of China." *New Englander* 14 (January 1890): 47–63.

———. "A Modern Shantung Prophet." *Chinese Recorder* 18.1 (January 1887): 12–21.

———. "Secret Sects in Shantung." Parts 1, 2. *Chinese Recorder* 17.1–2 (January, February 1886): 1–10, 64–73.

Presbyterian Church in the U.S.A. Board of Foreign Missions. *Correspondence and Reports [on China] 1837–1911*. (Microfilm) Philadelphia: Presbyterian Historical Society. Cited as BFM.

Purcell, Victor. *The Boxer Uprising: A Background Study*. Cambridge, England: Cambridge University Press, 1963.

Qi Chang-fa 亓長發. "Lun Yu-xian" 論毓賢 (On Yu-xian). Paper presented at International Conference on the Boxer Movement. Jinan, 1980.

Qi-he xian-zhi 齊河縣志 (Gazetteer of Qihe county). 1737.

Qi-he xian-zhi 齊河縣志 (Gazetteer of Qihe county). 1933.

Qin-ding ping-ding jiao-fei ji-lüe 欽定平定教匪紀略 (Imperially commissioned account of the suppression of the sectarian rebels). Ed. To-jin 托津 et al. 1816. Taibei reprint: 1971. Cited as JFJL.

Qing-dai dang-an shi-liao cong-bian 清代檔案史料叢編 (Compendium of materials from the Qing archives). Edited by Ming-Qing archives section of the Palace Museum. Beijing: Zhong-hua, 1979. Cited as QDDASLCB.

Qu-zhou xian-zhi 曲周縣志 (Gazetteer of Quzhou county). 1747.

Reclus, Elisée. *The Earth and Its Inhabitants. Asia, vol. 2; East Asia: Chinese Empire, Corea and Japan*. New York: D. Appleton and Co., 1884.

Records of the General Conference of the Protestant Missionaries of China Held at Shanghai: May 7–20, 1890. Shanghai: American Presbyterian Mission Press, 1890.

Renaud, Rosario. *Suchou, Diocèse de Chine*. vol. 1 (1882–1931). Montreal: Editions Bellarmin, 1955.

Richard, L. *Comprehensive Geography of the Chinese Empire and Dependencies*. Translated by M. Kennelly. Shanghai: T'usewei Press, 1908.

Sasaki Masaya 佐々木正哉. "Giwadan no kigen" 義和団の起源 (The origins of the Boxers). Parts 1–3. In *Kindai Chūgoku* 近代中国, 1977.1:144–180; 1977.7:113–134; 1978.5:133–186.

Satō Kimihiko 佐藤公彦. "Giwadan (ken) genryū: hakkekyō to giwaken" 義和団(拳)源流:八卦教と義和拳 (The Origins of the Boxers: The Eight Trigrams Sects and the Yi-he Boxers). *Shigaku zasshi* 史学雑誌, 91.1 (January 1982): 43–80.

———. "Kenryū sanjukyūnen Ō Rin Shinsuikyō hanran shoron—Giwadan ron josetsu" 乾隆三九年王倫清水教叛乱小論―義和団論序説 (A short discussion of the Clear Water Sect Uprising in the 39th year of Qian-long—an introduction to the discussion of the Boxers), *Hitotsubashi ronshū* 一橋論叢, 81.3:321–341.

―――. "1896 nen Santō seinanbu no taitōkai no kyūkyō tōsō ni tsuite— taitōkai shuryō Ryū Shidan no kokyō o tazunete" 1896年山東西南部の大刀会の仇教闘争について―大刀会首領劉士瑞の故郷を訪ねて(On the 1896 anti-Christian struggle of the Big Sword Society in southwest Shandong—a visit to the home of the Big Sword leader Liu Shi-duan). Privately printed manuscript, 1980.

―――. "Shoki Giwadan undō no shosō—kyōkai katsudō to taitōkai" 初期義和団運動の諸相―教会活動と大刀会 (The early face of the Boxer movement—Christian activities and the Big Sword Society). *Shichō* 史潮, 11 (1982):47–74.

Satoi Hikoshichiro 里井彦七郎. *Kindai Chūgoku ni okeru minshū undō to sono shisō* 近代中国における民衆運動とその思想 (Popular movements of modern China and their thought). Tokyo: Tokyo University Press, 1972.

Sawara Tokusuke 佐原篤介 and "Ou-yin" 偶隱. "Quan-shi za-ji," 拳事雜記 (Miscellaneous notes on Boxer affairs). In *Yi-he-tuan* 1:235–300.

Schlesinger, Arthur, Jr. "The Missionary Enterprise and Theories of Impe-rialism." In *The Missionary Enterprise in China and America*, edited by J. K. Fairbank, 336–373. Cambridge, Mass.: Harvard University Press, 1974.

Schrecker, John E. *Imperialism and Chinese Nationalism: Germany in Shan-tung*. Cambridge, Mass.: Harvard University Press, 1971.

Shan xian-zhi 單縣志 (Gazetteer of Shan county). 1759.

Shan xian-zhi 單縣志 (Gazetteer of Shan county). 1929.

Shan-dong da-xue li-shi-xi 山東大學歷史系 (History Department of Shan-dong University). *Shan-dong di-fang-shi jiang-shou ti-gang* 山東地方史講授提綱 (Teaching outline for Shandong local history). Jinan: Shandong People's Press, 1960.

―――. *Shan-dong Yi-he-tuan diao-cha bao-gao* 山東義和團調查報告 (A report on the surveys of the Shandong Boxers). Jinan: Zhong-hua, 1960.

Shan-dong da-xue li-shi-xi jin-dai-shi jiao-yan-shi 山東大學歷史系近代史教研室 (Modern Chinese history section of History Department of Shan-dong University). *Shan-dong Yi-he-tuan diao-cha zi-liao xuan-bian* 山東義和團調查資料選編 (Selections from survey materials on the Shandong Boxers). Jinan: Qi-Lu, 1980. Cited as SDDC.

―――. "'Yi-he-tuan zai Shan-dong' diao-cha ji-lu." 《義和團在山東》調查記錄 Manuscript notes of oral history surveys done in 1960, 1965, 1966, and bound by county, combination of counties, or (in one case: Zhao San-duo) by the leader of a Boxer uprising. Cited as SD Survey, [county or other name].

Shan-dong Huang-he Guang-xu er-shi-qi-ba liang-nian xian-gong-tu 山東黃河光緒廿七八兩年險工圖 (Dangerous sections of Yellow River during 1901 and 1902). Manuscript, Library of Congress.

Shan-dong jin-dai-shi zi-liao 山東近代史資料 (Materials on the modern history of Shandong). Edited by Shan-dong-sheng li-shi xue-hui 山東省 歷史學會 (Shandong Historical Society). Jinan: 1961. Reprinted Tokyo: Daian, 1968. Cited as SDJDSZL.

Shan-dong quan-sheng he-tu 山東全省河圖 (A Map of the Yellow River in Shandong). Manuscript, Library of Congress.

Shan-dong sheng-li min-zhong jiao-yu-guan 山東省立民衆教育舘 (Shandong Provincial Mass Educational Center). *Shan-dong min-jian yu-le diao-cha 1: Er-tong you-xi* 山東民間娛樂調查, 1: 兒童遊戲 (Survey on popular entertainment, No. 1: Children's games). Jinan: Shandong Provincial Mass Educational Center, 1933.

Shan-dong sheng-li min-zhong jiao-yu-guan yan-jiu-bu 山東省立民衆教育 舘研究部 (Research department of the Shandong Provincial Mass Educational Center). *Shan-dong ge-yao* 山東歌謠 (Shandong Songs). Jinan: Shandong Provincial Mass Educational Center, 1933.

Shan-dong sheng-zhi zi-liao 山東省志資料 (Materials for a Shandong provincial gazetteer). Jinan: Shandong People's Press, 1960. Cited as SDSZZL.

Shan-dong shi-fan-xue-yuan li-shi-xi Shan-dong tong-shi bian-xie-zu 山東 師範學院歷史系山東通史編寫組 (Editorial group for a history of Shandong of the History Department, Shandong Teacher's College). "Shandong Yi-he-tuan fan-di ai-guo yun-dong" 山東義和團反帝愛國運動 (The anti-imperialist patriotic movement of the Shandong Boxers). In *Yi-he-tuan yun-dong liu-shi zhou-nian ji-nian lun-wen-ji*, 84–110.

Shan-dong tong-zhi 山東通志 (Gazetteer of Shandong). 1915.

Shan-dong Yi-he-tuan an-juan 山東義和團案卷 (Archives on the Shandong Boxers). Edited by Zhong-guo she-hui ke-xue-yuan jin-dai-shi yan-jiu-suo, jin-dai-shi zi-liao bian-ji-shi 中國社會科學院近代史研究所近代史 資料編輯室 (Editorial section for modern history materials of the Modern History Institute of the Chinese Academy of Social Science). Jinan: Qi-Lu, 1980. Cited as AJ.

Shan-dong yun-he quan-tu 山東運河全圖 (Map of the Grand Canal in Shandong). Manuscript, Library of Congress.

"Shanghai Mercury." *The Boxer Rising: A History of the Boxer Trouble in China.* Shanghai: 1900. New York: Paragon reprint, 1967.

Shek, Richard. "Millenarianism without Rebellion: The Huangtian Dao in North China." *Modern China* 8.3 (July 1982): 305–336.

Shi Nian-hai 史念海. *Zhong-guo de yun-he* 中國的運河 (The Grand Canal of China). Chongqing: Shi-xue shu-ju, 1944.

Shi Si-qun 史思羣. "Lun Yi-he-tuan fan-di-guo-zhu-yi dou-zheng" 論義和 團反帝國主義鬥爭 (An exposition to the anti-imperialist struggle of the Boxers). In *Zhong-guo jin-dai-shi lun-wen-ji* 中國近代史論文集 (Collected essays on modern Chinese history), 642–660. Beijing: Zhong-hua, 1979.

Shih, Vincent. *Taiping Ideology: Its Sources, Interpretation and Influence.* Seattle: University of Washington Press, 1967.

Si-sheng yun-he shui-li quan-yuan he-dao quan-tu 四省運河水利泉源河道 全圖 (Map of irrigation, water resources, and the course of the Grand Canal in four provinces). 1855.

Simon, G. Eng. *China: Its Social, Political and Religious Life.* London: Sampson Low, Morston, Searle and Rivington, 1887.

Skinner, G. William, ed. *The City in Late Imperial China*. Stanford: Stanford University Press, 1977.

Smith, Arthur Henderson. *China in Convulsion*. 2 vols. New York: Fleming H. Revell, 1901.

————. "Sketches of a Country Parish." *Chinese Recorder*, Part 1, 12.4 (July to August 1881): 245–266. Part 2, 12.5 (September to October): 317–344. Part 3, 13.4 (July to August 1882): 280–298.

————. *Village Life in China: A Study in Sociology*. New York: Fleming H. Revell, 1899.

Song Jia-heng 宋家珩 and Pan Yu 潘鈺. "Yi-he-tuan yun-dong-zhong de fu-nü qun-zhong" 義和團運動中的婦女羣衆 (Women in the Boxer movement). *Shan-dong da-xue xue-bao* 山東大學學報, 1960.2 (March): 54–60.

Song Jing-shi dang-an shi-liao 宋景詩檔案史料 (Archival materials on Song Jing-shi). Edited by Guo-jia dang-an-ju Ming-Qing dang-an-guan 國家檔案局明清檔案館 (Ming-Qing archives of the State Archives Bureau). Beijing: Zhong-hua, 1959. Cited as SJSDA.

Song Zhe 宋哲. *Shan-dong min-jian gu-shi* 山東民間故事 (Shandong folk tales). Hong Kong: Wong Yit Book Co., 1962.

Speer, Robert E. *Missions and Politics in Asia*. New York: Fleming H. Revell, 1898.

Spence, Jonathan. *To Change China: Western Advisers in China, 1620–1960*. New York: Boston: Little, Brown, 1969.

Stauffer, Milton T. *The Christian Occupation of China: A general survey of the numerical strength and geographical distribution of the Christian forces in China made by the Special Committee on Survey and Occupation, China Continuation Committee, 1918–1921*. Shanghai: China Continuation Committee, 1922.

Steiger, George Nye. *China and the Occident: the Origin and Development of the Boxer Movement*. New Haven: Yale University Press: 1927.

Stenz, Georg M. *Beiträge zur Volkskunde Süd-Schantungs*. Leipzig, R. Voigtlander, 1907.

Stenz, George M., *Life of Father Richard Henle, S.V.D., Missionary in China, Assassinated November 1, 1897*. Translated by Elizabeth Ruft. Techny, Illinois: Mission Press, 1915.

————. *Twenty-five Years in China, 1893–1918*. Techny, Illinois: Mission Press, 1924.

Sun Jing-zhi 孫敬之. *Hua-bei jing-ji di-li* 華北經濟地理 (Economic geography of north China). Beijing: Science Press, 1957.

Sun Xiao-en 孫孝恩 and Jiang Hai-deng 江海澄. "Shi-lun Yi-he-tuan yun-dong de xing-zhi" 試論義和團運動底性質 (An inquiry into the nature of the Boxer movement). *Shan-dong da-xue xue-bao* 山東大學學報, 1960.2: 22–43.

Suzuki Chūsei 鈴木中正. *Chūgokushi ni okeru kakumei to shūkyō*. 中国史における革命と宗教 (Rebellion and religion in Chinese history). Tokyo: Tokyo University Press: 1974.

————. *Shinchō chūkishi kenkyū* 清朝中期史研究. 1952. Tokyo reprint: Rangen shobo, 1971.

Tan, Chester C. *The Boxer Catastrophe*. New York: W. W. Norton, 1971.

Tanaka Tadao 田中忠夫. *Kakumei Shina nōson no jisshōteki kenkyū* 革命支那農村の実証的研究 (An empirical study of the villages of revolutionary China). Tokyo: Shuninsha, 1930.

Tawney, R. H. *Land and Labor in China*. Boston: Beacon Press, 1966.

Thauren, John. *The Mission Fields of the Society of the Divine Word I: The Missions of Shantung, China; with a General Introduction to China and the Catholic Missions There*. Translated by Albert Paul Schimberg. Techny, Illinois: Mission Press, 1932.

Thrupp, Sylvia, ed. *Millennial Dreams in Action: Essays in Comparative Study*. The Hague: Mouton and Co., 1962.

Tiedemann, R. G. "The Geopolitical Dimensions of Collective Rural Violence: North China, 1868–1937." unpublished mss. 1979.

Tōa Dōbunkai 東亞同文會. *Shina shōbetsu zenshi*, vol. 4: *Santōshō.* 支那省別全誌；4：山東省 (Gazetteer of the provinces of China, vol. 4: Shandong). Tokyo: Tōa Dōbunkai, 1917.

Turner, Victor. *From Ritual to Theatre: The Human Seriousness of Play*. New York: Performing Arts Journal Publications, 1982.

————. *The Ritual Process: Structure and Anti-Structure*. Chicago: Aldine, 1969.

U.S. Congress, House of Representatives. *Papers Relating to the Foreign Relations of the United States*. Cited as FRUS.

Utley, Robert. *The Last Days of the Sioux Nation*. New Haven: Yale University Press, 1963.

Varg, Paul. *Missionaries, Chinese and Diplomats: The American Protestant Missionary Movement in China, 1890–1952*. Princeton: Princeton University Press, 1958.

Wagner, Rudolf G. *Reenacting the Heavenly Vision: The Role of Religion in the Taiping Rebellion*. Berkeley: University of California, Institute for East Asian Studies, 1982.

Wang Tong-zhao 王統照. *Shan-dong min-jian gu-shi* 山東民間故事 (Shandong folk tales). Beiping: 1938.

Wang Xiao-qiang 王小强. "Nong-min yu fan-feng-jian" 農民與反封建 (Peasants and anti-feudalism). *Li-shi yan-jiu* 歷史研究, 1979.10 (October): 3–12.

Wang You-nong 王友農. "He-bei Ning-jin nong-ye lao-dong" 河北甯津農業勞動 (Agricultural labor in Ningjin, Hebei). In *Zhong-guo nong-cun jing-ji zi-liao xu-bian* 中國農村經濟資料續編 (Materials on the Chinese village economy, continued), edited by Feng He-fa 馮和法. 1935. Taibei reprint, 1978. vol. 2: 781–783.

Weale, L. Putnam. *Indiscreet Letters from Peking*. London: Dodd, Meade and Co., 1907.

Wehrle, Edmund S. *Britain, China and the Antimissionary Riots, 1891–1900*. Minneapolis: University of Minnesota Press, 1966.

Wei xian-zhi 威縣志 (Gazetteer of Wei county). 1929.

Willeke, Bernward H. *Imperial Government and Catholic Missions in China During the Years 1784–1785.* St. Bonaventure, New York: Franciscan Institute, 1948.

———. "Documents Relating to the History of the Franciscan Missions in Shantung, China." *Franciscan Studies* 7 (1947): 171–187.

Williamson, Alexander. *Journeys in North China, Manchuria and eastern Mongolia; with some account of Corea,* 2 vols. London: Smith, Elder and Co., 1870.

———. "Notes on the North of China, Its Productions and Communications." *Journal of the North China Branch of the Royal Asiatic Society,* n.s. 4 (December 1867): 33–63.

———. "Notes on the Productions, Chiefly Mineral, of Shan-tung." *Journal of the North China Branch of the Royal Asiatic Society* n.s. 4 (December 1967): 63–73.

Wo-xian jin-dai-shi (1840–1919) 我縣近代史 (Modern history of our county, 1840–1919). Edited by Chi-ping-xian wen-hua-guan 茌平縣文化舘 (Cultural office of Chiping county). Manuscript, 1958.

Worsley, Peter. *The Trumpet Shall Sound: A Study of 'Cargo' Cults in Melanesia.* New York: Schocken Books, 1968.

Wu, Chao-kwang. *The International Aspect of the Missionary Movement in China.* Baltimore: Johns Hopkins Press, 1930.

Xiao Yi-shan 蕭一山, ed. *Tai-ping tian-guo cong-shu* 太平天國叢書 (Collection of Taiping writings). 2 vols. Taibei: Zhong-hua cong-shu wei-yuan-hui, 1956.

Xie Xing-yao 謝興堯. *Tai-ping tian-guo qian-hou Guang-xi de fan-Qing yun-dong* 太平天國前後廣西的反清運動 (Anti-Qing movements in Guangxi before and after the Taiping Rebellion). Beijing: San-lian, 1950.

Xu Xu-dian 徐緒典. "Yi-he-tuan yuan-liu chu-yi" 義和團源流芻議 (My humble opinion of the origins of the Boxers). *Shan-dong da-xue wen-ke lun-wen ji-kan* 山東大學文科論文集刊, 1980.1:23–35.

Yang, Benjamin. "Sung Ching-shih and His Black Flag Army." *Ch'ing-shih Wen-t'i* 5.2 (1984): 3–46.

Yang, C. K. *Religion in Chinese Society: A Study of Contemporary Social Functions of Religion and Some of their Historical Factors.* Berkeley: University of California Press, 1961.

Yi-he-tuan 義和團 (The Boxers). Edited by Jian Bo-zan 翦伯贊 et al. 4 vols. Shanghai: 1951. Reprinted Taibei: Ding-wen, 1973 under title *Yi-he-tuan wen-xian hui-bian* 義和團文獻彙編. Cited as YHT.

Yi-he-tuan dang-an shi-liao 義和團檔案史料 (Archival materials on the Boxers). Edited by Gu-gong bo-wu-yuan Ming-Qing dang-an bu 故宮博物院明清檔案部 (The Ming-Qing archives division of the Palace Museum). Beijing: Zhong-hua, 1959. Cited as DASL.

Yi-he-tuan shi-liao 義和團史料 (Historical materials on the Boxers). Edited by Zhong-guo she-hui ke-xue-yuan jin-dai-shi yan-jiu-suo "Jin-dai-shi zi-liao" bian-ji-zu 中國社會科學院近代史研究所"近代史資料"編輯組. 2 vols. Beijing: CASS, 1982. Cited as YHTSL.

Yi-he-tuan yun-dong liu-shi zhou-nian ji-nian lun-wen-ji 義和團運動六十週年紀念論文集 (Articles commemorating the sixtieth anniversary of the Boxer movement). Edited by Zhong-guo ke-xue-yuan Shan-dong fen-yuan li-shi yan-jiu-suo 中國科學院山東分院歷史研究所 (Modern History Institute of the Shandong divison of the Chinese Academy of Sciences). Beijing: Zhong-hua, 1961.

Yin Wei-he 殷惟龢. *Jiang-su liu-shi-yi xian-zhi* 江蘇六十一縣志 (Gazetteer of sixty-one counties in Jiangsu province). Shanghai: Commercial Press, 1936.

Young, Marilyn Blatt. *The Rhetoric of Empire: American China Policy, 1895–1901*. Cambridge: Harvard University Press, 1968.

Yu-cheng xian xiang-tu-zhi 禹城縣鄉土志 (Local gazetteer of Yucheng county). 1908.

Yu-cheng xian-zhi 禹城縣志 (Gazetteer of Yucheng county). 1808.

Yuan Chang 袁昶. "Luan-zhong ri-ji can-gao" 亂中日記殘稿 (Fragments of a diary from the midst of disorder). In *Yi-he-tuan* 1 : 337–349.

Yun Yu-ding 惲毓鼎. "Chong-ling chuan-xin-lu" 崇陵傳信錄 (A true account of the Guang-xu emperor). In *Yi-he-tuan* 1 : 45–55.

Zhang Xin-yi 張心一. "He-bei-sheng nong-ye gai-kuang gu-ji bao-gao" 河北省農業概況估計報告 (An estimate of the agricultural situation in Hebei). *Tong-ji yue-bao* 統計月報, 2.11 (November 1930): 1–56.

———. "Shan-dong-sheng nong-ye gai-kuang gu-ji bao-gao" 山東省農業概況估計報告 (An estimate of the agricultural situation in Shandong). *Tong-ji yue-bao* 3.1 (January 1931): 20–45.

Zhang Yu-fa 張玉法. *Zhong-guo xian-dai-hua de qu-yu yan-jiu: Shan-dong sheng, 1860–1916* 中國現代化的區域研究：山東省 (Regional studies on Chinese modernization: Shandong, 1860–1916). 2 vols. Taibei: Academia Sinica, Modern History Institute, 1982.

Zhang Yu-zeng 張育曾 and Liu Jing-zhi 劉敬之. *Shan-dong zheng-su shi-cha-ji* 山東政俗視察記 (A survey of politics and customs in Shandong). Jinan: Shandong Press, 1934.

Zheng He-sheng 鄭鶴聲. "Lun 'tie-quan'" 論鐵拳 (On the "Iron fists"). *Shan-dong da-xue xue-bao* 山東大學學報, 1960.2 (June): 44–53.

Zhi-li feng-tu diao-cha-lu 直隸風土調查錄 (Survey of the natural conditions and local customs of Zhili). Edited by Zhi-li-sheng shi-xue 直隸省視學. Shanghai: Commercial Press, 1916.

Zhi-li-sheng shang-pin chen-lie-suo 直隸省商品陳列所 (Zhili provincial commodities exhibition). *Di-yi-ci diao-cha shi-ye bao-gao-shu* 第一次調查實業報告書 (Report on the first survey of industry). Tianjin: 1917.

Zhong-fang 仲芳. "Geng-zi ji-shi" 庚子記事 (A record of events in 1900). In Zhong-guo she-hui ke-xue-yuan jin-dai-shi yan-jiu-suo jin-dai-shi zi-liao bian-ji-shi 中國社會科學院近代史研究所近代史資料編輯室. ed., *Geng-zi ji-shi*. Beijing, Zhong-hua, 1978: 9–78.

Zhong-guo qu-yi yan-jiu-hui 中國曲藝研究會 (Chinese Folk Art Institute). *Shan-dong kuai-shu Wu Song zhuan* 山東快書武松傳 (Shandong clapper ballad: Biography of Wu Song). Beijing: Writer's Press, 1957.

Zhong-guo shi-ye-zhi: Shan-dong-sheng 中國實業誌：山東省 (Chinese Industrial Gazetteer: Shandong province). Shanghai: International Trade Office of the Ministry of Industry, 1934.

Zhou Hai-qing 周海清. "Shan-dong Yi-he-tuan zu-zhi de yuan-liu ji-qi fa-zhan" 山東義和團組織的源流及其發展 (The origins and development of the Shandong Boxers' organization). *Po yu li* 破與立, 1979.6, No. 33 (November): 33–39.

Zhu Fu 祝芾. "Geng-zi jiao-an han-du" 庚子教案函牘 (Correspondence concerning anti-Christian cases in 1900). In *Yi-he-tuan* 4: 363–394.

Index

Agricultural laborers, 21, 25, 27, 104, 144, 148, 208, 232, 234, 235, 238, 246, 275

Agriculture, 207; commercialization, 2, 3, 10, 12; crops, 1–3, 13, 143, 347; irrigation, 2, 10; yields, 9, 10, 11, 143. *See also* Cotton cultivation

Anti-foreignism, 182–183; of Boxers, 252–253, 271, 287–288, 296; of court, 273–274, 286

Anzer, Bishop Johann Baptist von, 80–87 *passim*, 112, 128, 131, 188, 193, 198, 203, 205

Armor of the Golden Bell (Jin-zhong zhao), 136, 227, 228; early history of, 55, 96–98, 105, 141, 358n.42; ritual, 105–107; in Southwest Shandong, 104–109. *See also* Big Sword Society

Army, 137, 381n.27; Anhui, 285; and Beijing Siege, 306–307, 309; Big Swords in, 257, 399n.53; coastal defense, 170, 172, 193; disbanding, 159, 162–164, 170, 171–173, 203; and Guan county Boxers, 157–158; and International Expedition, 308–310; and NW Shandong Boxers, 246–258 *passim*, 264, 266; recruitment in Shandong, 45, 129, 371n.14; Wu-wei jun (Military Guards Army), 285, 286; Yuan Shi-

kai's, 280–281, 286, 304; and Zhili Boxers, 279, 280, 283–286, 288–290

Associations, voluntary, 272–273, 300–301

Bandits, 10, 24, 35–36, 45, 119, 126, 322, 348; 1898–99 increase, 174–177, 192, 196; and Big Swords, 109–112; and Christians, 89–90, 102, 113, 114; highway robbery, 20, 140, 174; on Shandong-Jiangsu border, 6, 13, 18–23, 48, 98–102, 104, 351n.57; on Shandong-Zhili border, 20–21, 138–140

Bang-chui hui (Cudgel and Whip Society), 41

bao-jia, 159–160

Baoding, 279, 282, 283, 305, 310

Beijing, 5, 168, 182, 213; Boxers in, 290–303, 307–310; Siege of, xiii, 303, 306–307, 309–311

Ben-ming. *See* Xin-cheng

Big Sword Society (Da-dao hui), 96, 136, 161–162, 176, 191, 199, 269, 318–320; 1896 uprising, 115–120; 1898–1900 activity, 120, 195, 198, 203, 204; in army, 257, 399n.53; vs. bandits, 104, 109–112; and Boxers, 216–217, 223, 226–228; vs. Catholics, 112–122; invulnerability

rituals, 105–107, 113–114, 327–
328; in Juye, 120, 126–127; leaders,
107–109, 238–239; and officials,
109–112, 368n.58; suppression of,
120–122; in War of Resistance, 107;
and White Lotus, 97–98, 105, 106.
See also Armor of the Golden Bell
Bloch, Marc, 315, 322
Bonds to Manifest Confidence (*zhao-
xin gu-piao*), 170
Boping, 258, 260, 264–265
Border region, Shandong-Jiangsu-
Henan, 18–23, 39, 98–104, 174–
177, 195, 352n.68; Big Sword
Society in, 96, 109–112, 176; sects
in, 40, 333, 335, 336. *See also* Zhili,
Zhili-Shandong border
Bourdieu, Pierre, 321
Boxer Protocol, 311
Boxer Uprising: effects of, 311–313;
foreign reactions to, 286–288, 302–
303, 308–311; and imperialism, 72;
origins, 317–321; spread of, 304–
306; targets of, 68, 287–288, 296,
304–306. *See also* Boxers United in
Righteousness; Spirit Boxers
Boxers. *See* Boxers United in Righteousness; Martial arts; Militia
United in Righteousness; Spirit
Boxers
Boxers United in Righteousness (Yi-he
quan): anti-foreignism, 252–253,
271, 287–288, 296; in Beijing-
Tianjin, 277, 290–303, 307–310;
and Big Swords, 195, 226–228, 294;
court policy toward, 272–275,
301–303; discipline, 295, 307;
foreign victims, 269–270; in Guan
exclaves, 136, 149, 153–166
passim, 238–239, 328; healing,
216–217, 224–225, 234, 294–295;
invulnerability, 243, 252, 267, 279,
294–295; leadership, 236–240,
242, 252, 267, 275, 277, 296, 308;
loyalism, xvi, 163, 226, 247, 250,
252–254, 290, 296, 301, 327,
376n.57, 393n.86–87; and militia,
154–155, 159–164, 166, 230, 244,
253–254, 268–269, 286, 287, 303,
307; name, 154, 165, 328, 377n.63;
non-Christian victims, 258, 261–
266, 280, 400n.70; official policy

toward, 229–230, 255–256, 303–
306; organization, 221, 231, 247,
295–296; in Pingyuan, 230, 234,
238, 241–257; placards, 277, 278,
282, 298–301; and Plum Flower
Boxers, 153–154, 227; and popular
culture, 64–67, 327–331; ritual,
216–219, 275, 290, 292–297, 327–
329, 391n.59; social composition,
224–225, 234–240, 277, 291–292,
395n.120; and Spirit Boxers, 206,
223, 227–228; spread of, 230–235,
266–270, 304–306; suppression of,
310–311; and White Lotus, xiv,
217–222, 244, 295–296, 299–301,
307–308, 315, 320–321, 327; in
Zhili, 232, 271–272, 275–290. *See
also* Boxer Uprising; Militia United
in Righteousness; Spirit Boxers; Yi-
he Boxers
Brandt, Max von, 79
Brooks, S. M., 269–270, 272, 287, 304
Buddhist monks, 277

Cao county, 18, 103, 110, 131; Big
Swords in, 98, 107–108, 114–115,
119, 120, 203
Cao De-li, 107–108, 114–115, 118–
120
Cao Ti, 156–157, 158, 379n.102
Caozhou, 13, 131; banditry in, 18–23,
99, 102, 109–110
Catholics, 142, 192, 214–215, 242; and
Big Swords, 112–122, 126–127;
and Boxers, 242, 243, 280; Church's
political role, 84–86, 91, 94, 113,
121–122, 135, 185, 202. *See also*
Christians; Missionaries; Society of
the Divine Word
Catty (*jin*), 9n
Chang-qiang hui (Long Spears), 101
Chang Wu-hua-gui, 140
Changqing, 10, 208, 209; Boxers in,
206, 216, 223–225, 258, 259, 264,
265, 266
Charm Boxing (Jue-zi quan), 195
Chefoo. *See* Yantai
Chen De-he, 246–249
Chen Zhao-ju, 196, 198, 202, 204
Chengdu riot (Sichuan, 1895), 93, 112,
132
Chengwu, 110, 114–115, 131

Chiping, 207–209, 232; 1898 flood, 177, 223–224; Boxers in, 206, 216, 229–230, 235, 236–237, 258, 260, 265, 267, 270; Christians in, 215; White Lotus in, 86–87, 209–212, 221

Christians: abuse of power, 82, 94, 132, 134–135, 186, 187 194–195, 199, 200, 215, 283, 296–297, 304–306; attacks on, 68, 76, 93–94, 115–119, 145, 152, 163–164, 176, 187–188, 194, 196–197, 202, 241–249, 254, 257–270, 277–284, 374n.37, 387n.143; conversion patterns, 76–79, 85–91, 113, 120–122, 134, 215, 232, 268; defensive measures, 164, 264, 267, 282; former bandits, 89–90, 102, 113, 114; former White Lotus, 85–89, 116, 126, 142–143, 212, 283; in Guan exclaves area, 138–139, 163–164; history of, in Shandong, 76–79, 214–215; and imperialism, 74–76; in Liyuantun, 143–164 passim; poverty of, 90; supported in lawsuits, 83–86, 185, 242, 283. See also Catholics; Missionaries; Protestants

Cixi, Empress Dowager, 168, 170, 188, 191, 200, 273–274, 289, 302, 310

Commercialization, 3, 6, 10–12, 36, 98, 322, 353n.80, 354n.100; limited, in Northwest, 25, 31–32, 208

Confucian temple and estate (Qufu), 13, 80, 81, 116

Conger, Edwin H., 205, 268, 281

Congregationalist missions. See Missionaries, Congregationalist; Pangzhuang mission

Cotton cultivation, 2, 24–25, 32, 70–72, 98, 137, 143, 207–208

Cotton textiles: handicraft (tu-bu) 70–73, 137, 143, 207–208; imports, 69–73, 208, 237, 361n.9

Crop-watching, 65–66

Cui Shi-jun, 338

Da-cheng jiao, 357n.24

Da-hong quan (Great Red Boxing), 142

Da-shi-xiong (Senior Brother-Disciple), 231

Dagu forts, 286, 288–289, 302–303, 308, 311

Dai Xuan-zhi, 148, 160

Daitoulou, 118, 119

Dangshan, 21, 101, 102, 115–116, 117, 176

Dao-guang Emperor, 77

Daoism, popular, 40, 41, 57

Daoist priests (Dao-shi), 55, 104, 141, 146, 277, 355n.6

Denby, Charles, 76

Dezhou, 31, 172, 336–337

Di-bao, 145, 243, 283

Ding Temple (Dingsi), 225, 257

Dong Fu-xiang, 119, 182–183, 200, 292, 302, 306

Dong'e, 177, 208; Boxers in, 261, 266

Dongchang, 15, 31

Dongtuan, 116–117

Dou-dou, 106, 295

Duan-gong, 41, 355n.6

Duan, Prince, 274, 302, 307, 311

Eddy, Sherwood, 92–93

Eight Trigrams sects, 43–44, 46, 97, 213, 295–296; 1786 uprising, 50; 1813 uprising, 44, 51, 55, 61, 149, 211, 333, 336–338. See also Li Trigram Sect; Sectarian religion; White Lotus Sect

Eighteen Chiefs (shi-ba-kui), 136, 147–148, 151, 155, 157, 159, 162–164, 374n.39.

Eighteen Villages. See Guan county, exclaves

Empress Dowager. See Cixi, Empress Dowager

En county, 207, 208, 334–337; Boxers in, 206, 242, 247, 252, 259, 267; missionaries, 70–71, 78, 177, 205, 212, 214–215, 250

Enfeoffment of the Gods (Feng-shen yan-yi), 62, 65, 211, 218, 294, 329

Er-shi-xiong (Second Brother-Disciple), 231

Eternal Venerable Mother (Wu-sheng lao-mu), 40, 98, 213, 221

Exclaves, 99; Guan county, 138–166 passim

Famine, in 1876–78, 15, 211, 214; in 1898–99, 174–175

Fei county, 176, 188

Feicheng, 217; Boxers in, 261, 266, 269–270
Feng county (Jiangsu), 116, 117, 118, 196
Feng Ke-shan, 44, 50, 51, 52, 149, 336–337
Feng-shen yan-yi. See Enfeoffment of the Gods
Feng Yun-shan, 325
Feuerwerker, Albert, 70
Fiscal crisis, 170–173, 181
Foreign Affairs Bureau (Yang-wu ju), 169
Foreign powers: and Boxers, 286–288, 302–303, 308–311. See also Imperialism; Scramble for Concessions; and individual countries
France, 91, 124, 286; and Catholic missions, 77, 79, 80, 146, 155, 180, 244–245, 268
Freinademetz, Joseph, 188
Fu-Qing mie-yang. See "Support the Qing, destroy the foreign"

Gama, Vasco da, 74
Gambling, 46–49, 64, 145, 209, 339
Gang-yi, 132, 288, 290, 303, 307
Gangzi Lizhuang, 242, 246–249, 252, 253, 256
Ganji, 140, 141, 144, 156, 158
Gao Yuan-xiang, 148
Gaoluo, 283–284
Gaomi, 193, 202
Gaotang, 207, 208; Boxers in, 206, 223, 234, 237
Ge Li-ye, 337
Ge Wen-zhi, 337
Gentry, 10, 120, 135, 171, 184, 349n.19, 388–389n.16; anti-Christian agitation, 81, 116, 187; and Boxers, 243, 284; in Guan county, 137, 140, 142, 144–147, 155, 163, 164; ju-ren distribution, 11, 12, 13, 29–37, 319, 347; weakness in West, 28, 30–37, 209–210, 240, 248, 397n.9
Germany, 91; and Boxers, 286, 303; in Jiaozhou and Qingdao, 7, 93, 123, 124, 127–131, 156, 169, 170, 172, 179, 184, 268, 320; military incursions, 184, 188–189, 193, 194, 200, 204–205; railway and mining

surveys, 130, 184–185; support of missionaries, 79, 81, 85, 112–113, 115, 119, 128, 130–131, 132, 189, 198, 204–205; and Yu-xian, 192. See also Society of the Divine Word
Ghost Dance, 316–317
God-worshipping Society (Bai shang-di hui), 322–327
Gong-fu, 55, 105–106, 107, 114, 228
Gong-sheng, 144, 242, 248
Grand Canal, 5–6, 12–13, 31–33, 208; silting of, 14–15, 31, 72, 141, 350n.35
Great Britain, 75, 91–92, 93, 124, 133, 286; in Hong Kong, 183
Gu Yan-wu, 32
Guan county, 136–137, 335; Boxers in, 148–166 passim, 259, 279; exclaves, 138–166 passim, 372n.10; sects in, 55, 59, 97
Guan-gong, 62, 63, 218, 294, 329
Guang-xu Emperor, 130, 167–168, 273–274, 289
Guangxi: Taiping in, 319, 322–325, 327
Guo Jing-shun, 334
Guo Wei-zheng, 336–337
Gutian massacre (Fujian, 1895), 93, 112

Hakka, 319, 322–324
Han Guang-ding, 145
Han Lin-er, 40
Han Shan-tong, 40
Hao He-sheng, 114
Hart, Robert, 92, 183
He Hu-chen, 238
He Shi-zhen, 145–146, 152, 155
Healing: by Boxers, 216–217, 224–225, 294–295; by missionaries, 79, 212; by sectarians, 39, 43, 55, 56, 57, 211–214
Henan, Boxers in, 305–306
Henle, Richard, 82, 123–125, 135
Henninghaus, Augustine, 81–82
Heterodox sects. See Sectarian religion
Heyking, Edmund, 128, 131, 188, 189, 198
Heze, 120, 131
Hobsbawm, Eric, 45, 102
Hobson, J. A., 92, 93
Hong-deng-zhao. See Red Lantern Shining

Hong-quan. *See* Red Boxing
Hong Xiu-quan, 219, 321–326
Hong Yong-zhou, 147–148, 156, 157, 159
Hong-zhuan hui (Red Brick Society), 338
Hongtaoyuan, 163, 164
Hou Chi-ming, 70
Houjiazhuang, 117, 118, 119
Hu-wei bian (Tiger-tail Whip), 46, 336
Huang Chao, 39
Huang Fei-hu, 329
Huang-lian sheng-mu, 298
Huang, Philip C. C., 17–18, 24–26
Huang-sha hui (Yellow Sand Society), 142

Imperialism: in 1890s, 91–92, 131, 180–181; economic impact, 68–73; and missionaries, 74–76, 91–95, 146, 152, 189, 320; threat of partition, 73–74, 124. *See also* Foreign powers; Scramble for Concessions; *and individual countries*
Inner Mongolia: Boxers in, 305
International Expedition (Eight-Nation Expedition), xiii, 132, 191, 218, 309–311
Invulnerability rituals, 53–58, 67, 86, 195, 317, 339; absent in Guan county boxers, 149, 165, 374–375n.46; of Big Swords, 96, 97, 98, 113–114, 327–328; of Boxers, 217–219, 222, 223, 225–228, 279, 294–295, 327–328; of Wang Lun, 44, 54
Iron-cloth Shirt (Tie-bu shan), 106, 109, 227
Italy, 183, 200

Jade Emperor, Temple of (Yu-huang miao), 144, 145, 152
Jaeschke, Paul, 188, 189, 205
Japan, 124, 170, 309–310. *See also* Sino-Japanese War
Jian-sheng, 107, 144, 145, 335
Jiang Kai, 227, 235, 255–256, 257; handling of Boxers, 230, 242–248, 253
Jiang Zi-ya (Jiang Tai-gong), 65, 294, 329
Jiaxiang, 194–200, 202
Jimo, 184, 202

Jin-zhong zhao. *See* Armor of the Golden Bell
Jinan, 10, 11, 94, 208
Jing Ting-bin, 165
Jingzhou, 277, 279, 285
Jining, 12–13, 31, 80–81, 131; Red Boxers in, 194–200, 202–204, 387n.143
Jinshan, 338–339
Journey to the West (Xi-you-ji), 62, 294, 329
Ju-ren, 29. *See also* Gentry
Juye Incident, 123–127, 194; Big Swords and, 120, 121, 126–127; effects of, 127–135, 152, 156, 181
Juzhou, 187, 188

Kang You-wei, 167–168, 173
Ketteler, Baron Clemens von, 303
Kipling, Rudyard, 91
Kong Ling-ren, 238–239
Kuhn, Philip, 137

Laishui, 283–285, 286, 290, 294
Landlordism, 9, 10, 12, 36–37, 162, 347; and Big Sword Society, 108–109, 122; in Liyuantun, 143–144, 373n.29; in Southwest, 21, 23, 103–104, 203; weakness in Northwest, 24–26, 208, 238, 240, 353n.76
Lanshan, 176, 188, 189, 192, 193, 194, 202
Lao Nai-xuan: on Boxer origins, xiv, 46, 48, 217–220, 333–340; Boxer policy of, 254, 290, 404n.60; as Wuqiao magistrate, 277, 279
Lao tian-men jiao (Old Heavenly Gate Sect), 337
Leboucq, Prosper, 89
Legation guards, 182, 287
Li Bing-heng, 129, 132–134, 170; in Beijing (1900), 307, 309–311; and Big Swords, 96, 97, 109, 111, 122; and Christians, 152; and reform, 169; as Shandong governor, 159, 170–172, 179, 180, 181, 268
Li Chang-an, 145–146
Li Chang-shui, 242, 246–247
Li Cui, 334–335
Li Da-du-zi (Big Belly Li), 212–213
Li Hao-ran, 334
Li Hong-zhang, 94, 273, 285, 304, 309

Li Jin-bang, 246
Li Trigram Sect, 51, 55, 141, 212, 235, 244, 334, 336–338. *See also* Eight Trigrams sects
Li Wei-xian, 245
Li Wen-cheng, 44, 53, 337–338
Li-zhang, 238, 242
Liyuantun, 136–166 *passim*
Liang Qi-chao, 168
Liaocheng, Boxers in, 260, 266
Likin, 6, 346n.7
Lin Qing, 44, 50, 53, 338
Lineages, 24, 116
Linqing, 15, 16, 17, 31, 44, 138, 171, 351n.50; missionaries in, 76, 79, 83, 134
Linyi, 281
Liu Bing-zhang, 132
Liu De-run, 126
Liu Ge-da (Pimpled Liu), 176
Liu Kun, 337
Liu Kun-yi, 288, 303
Liu Sect of Shan county, 43, 50–51, 357n.25
Liu Shi-duan, 107, 108, 110, 114–115, 118–120, 191, 204, 370n.92
Liu-tang quan (Six Reclining Boxing), 336
Liu Tian, 227
Liulisi, 225
Liushangu, 152
Liutitou, 116, 117
Low, Frederick, 75
Lü Cai, 114
Lu Chang-yi, 248–249
Lü Deng-shi, 114
Lü Fu, 337
Luo Hui-ying, 401n.77
Luo Sect (Luo jiao), 42–43, 48

Ma-pi, 56, 57, 62
Ma Zhao-lin, 234
MacDonald, Claude, 92, 133–134, 281, 288
Mahan, Alfred, 127
Maliangji, 118
Manchu bannermen, 172
Manchu invasion, 16, 30–31, 207, 209
Mao Sui, 218
Mao Ze-dong, 313
Mao Zi-yuan, 219
Marco Polo Bridge, 182

Martial arts, 65–67, 154, 187, 411n.17; and sects, 38, 41, 43–62, 149, 210–214, 333–340, 357n.24–25, 411n.23; in west Shandong, 45–47, 61, 99, 209–210, 335
Manchuria, 305, 312
Mei-hua quan. *See* Plum Flower Boxers
Militia, 101, 108–109, 137, 146, 306; and Big Sword Society, 111, 118, 119; and Boxers, xiv, 148, 154–157, 159–164, 166, 196–198, 199, 203, 204, 253–254, 268–269; and martial artists, 53, 338; official promotion of, 159–160, 173, 179, 181
Militia United in Righteousness (Yi-he tuan), 154, 160, 241, 253, 254, 257, 270, 277, 291
Millenarianism, 300–301, 316–317, 319; absent in Boxers, 226, 394n.88; in Taiping, 322–323, 325, 327; White Lotus, 40, 59–60, 66, 98, 322–323
Ming restorationism, 57, 101, 226, 300, 376n.57
Missionaries: Boxer attacks on, 267, 269–270, 287–288, 304–306, 406n.101; Catholic, 74–77, 93; Congregationalist, 79, 205, 212, 214–215, 245, 268; defensive measures, 164, 264, 267, 282, 400n.66; early history in Shandong, 76–79; famine relief, 78–79, 103; Franciscans (Italian), 77, 80, 83, 142, 145–147, 152, 159, 180, 205, 215, 267, 244–245; French Jesuits, 77, 83, 102, 115–122 *passim*, 142, 164; and imperialism, 74–76, 91–95, 146, 185, 189, 256, 268, 320, 384n.81; interference in lawsuits, 82–84, 113, 124, 126, 132, 185, 283; Jesuits, 76; Presbyterian, 77, 79, 94, 187; Protestant, 75, 77–79, 85–86, 93, 135, 165, 205; revenge of, 310–311. *See also* Catholics; Christians; Pangzhuang mission; Protestants; Society of the Divine Word
Mobility, 26–27, 232, 240
Motonosuke, Amano, 103
Moule, A. J. H., 92
mu, 9n
Muslim rebellion (1896), 119

Na-yan-cheng, 333, 336, 337
Nangong, 72, 139
Naquin, Susan, 42–43
Nationalism, xiii, 312
Natural disasters, 9, 13, 14, 15–16, 26–27, 207, 347–348; in 1898–1899, 174–175; 1899–1900 drought, 244, 279, 281–282; famine of 1876–78, 15, 211, 214; floods, 12, 18–19, 98, 140, 209; and rebellion, 40, 44, 59, 101, 173–174, 176, 181, 322. *See also* Yellow River, floods
Nian, 17, 59, 69, 101, 116, 137, 174, 176
Nie Shi-cheng, 286, 288, 309
Nies, Francis Xavier, 123
North China macroregion, 3–7
North China Plain: climate, 2; agricultural conditions, 1–3, 17–18, 24–28. *See also* Shandong, Northwest
North Slope region (Shandong), 10–11, 29–30, 319
Northern Cathedral (Beijing), 297–298, 307

Open Door, 312
Opera. *See* Theatre
Opium, 19–21, 99, 101, 322, 366n.19
Opium War (1839–1842), 69, 75
Oral history surveys, xv–xvi; on Big Swords, 108, 366n.13; on Boxers, 148, 149, 153, 220–221, 226, 227, 235, 236, 238, 258, 265; on Christians, 83, 125–126, 215

Pang San-jie, 116–121, 161, 369n.82
Pangzhuang mission, 70–71, 78, 177, 205, 212, 214, 245, 250, 267, 268
Pardonne, Odoric de, 76
Parker, Peter, 75
Patriarch's Assembly (Zu-shi hui), 56–57
Peasants: living standards, 26, 137. *See also* Popular culture; Villages
Peng Gui-lin, 108, 118–119
Peng Yu-sun, 186, 194–199, 203, 386n.117, 123
Perry, Elizabeth, 175
Pingyin, Boxers in, 260, 266–267
Pingyuan, 71–72, 207–208, 210; Boxers in, 206, 223, 227, 230, 234, 236, 238, 241–257 *passim*, 259,

267, 270; Christians in, 215, 242; incident, 246–254
Plum Flower Boxers (Mei-hua quan), 136; anti-Manchuism among, 153; early history, 148–149, 335; in Guan exclaves area, 149–151; and Liyuantun struggles, 151–159, 162, 199; and White Lotus, 52–53, 376n.54; and Yi-he Boxers, 153–154
Poli mission (S.V.D.), 81, 82
Popkin, Samuel, 86, 87
Popular culture, 38–39, 62–67, 326–327; and Boxers, 218–219, 222, 232; and martial arts, 61
Popular religion, 62–67, 86, 149; and Boxer gods, 64–65, 218–219, 222, 294, 327–331; and Taiping, 324–326
Population density, 3, 7–14 *passim*, 207, 346–347n.11
Porter, Henry, 94, 134, 213, 214, 217, 227
Post, China Imperial, 169
Protestants, 77–79, 192, 214–215; and Boxers, 242, 267, 280, 396–397n.3. *See also* Christians; Missionaries
Purcell, Victor, xv, xvi, 393n.86

qi-gong, 225, 327
Qi-wu, 39, 56, 219
Qiang-xue hui (Society for the Study of National Strengthening), 168
Qihe, Boxers in, 260, 266
Qing-bang (Green Gang), 142
Qing-cha men (Clear Tea Sect), 333
Qing court, 180; and Big Swords, 109, 119, 122, 368n.58; "declaration of war," 303–306; and missionary cases, 94, 134, 188; policy toward Boxers, xiv, 122, 168, 190, 200, 272–275, 285–290, 301–303, 307, 310–311
Qingdao (Tsingtao), 7, 184
Qingping, Boxers in, 260, 264
Qiu county, 59, 138
Quan-chang (boxing ground), 231, 234
Qufu, 13

Railways, 2, 182, 184, 206, 279; Boxer attacks on, 284, 287, 288, 300, 305
Red Boxers (Hong quan), 60, 157, 335; in Jining, 194–204, 244

Red Eyebrows uprising, 39, 174, 219
Red Gang (Hong-bang), 142
Red Lantern Shining (Hong-deng
    zhao), 136, 227, 235, 297–298,
    394n.88
Red Spears (Hong-qiang hui), 104–105,
    319
Red Sun Assembly (Hong-yang hui), 57
Reforms: of 1898, 130, 167–168, 180,
    273; post-Boxer, 312; in Shandong,
    169–170
Refugees, famine, 6, 174–175, 179,
    194, 203. See also Mobility
Richthofen, Ferdinand von, 127–128
Rizhao, 187, 188, 189, 192, 193, 194,
    202
Romance of the Three Kingdoms (San-
    guo yan-yi), 62, 65, 218, 294, 329
Rong-lu, 286, 306
Ruan Zu-tang, 111
Russia, 124, 128, 129–130, 170, 183,
    309, 312

Salt smuggling, 19, 48, 55, 99, 101,
    175, 176, 322
San-fo lun, 337
Schlesinger, Arthur, Jr., 92
Scramble for Concessions, 91, 124, 130,
    167, 180–182
Sectarian religion, 5; conversion to
    Christianity, 85–89, 126, 142–143,
    212–215, 283; in Guan county, 137,
    141–142; as heterodoxy, 41–42,
    66; and martial arts, 43–62, 97–
    98, 149, 210–214, 333–340,
    357n.24–25, 41 n.23; in northwest
    Shandong, 209–212, 389n.22, 24;
    and popular religion, 61–64, 211;
    and rebellion, 38–44, 50–53, 57,
    59–62, 63. See also Eight Trigram
    sects; Li Trigram Sect; White Lotus
    sect
Senluo Temple, Battle of, 249–258,
    267, 268, 270
Seymour, Edward, 288, 302
Sha-seng ("Sandy"), 149, 294
Shaliuzhai, 148, 152, 158, 162, 163
Shamanism. See Spirit-possession
Shan county, 18, 103, 131, 176;
    banditry in, 21–23; Big Swords
    in, 98, 104, 107–122 passim, 203;
    Liu sect of, 43, 50–51

Shandong: northwest, 13–17, 24–28;
    peninsula, 2, 7–11, 29–30, 319;
    provincial budget, 170–173;
    regions of, 7–28; southwest, 13,
    18–23, 98–104. See also Border
    region, Shandong-Jiangsu-Henan;
    North Slope; South Hills
Shanxi, 190–191
Shao Shi-xuan (Shao Yu-huan), 196,
    198, 244
Shaobing Liuzhuang, 104, 107
Shaolin Boxing, 225
Shek, Richard, 210
Shen county, 59, 335; Boxers in, 259
Sheng-ren dao (Way of the Sages), 142
Sheng Xuan-huai, 288, 303
Sheng-yuan, 22, 28–29, 144, 151, 155,
    249, 252, 253, 255, 283; military,
    61, 237, 238, 242, 243
Shi Yan-tian, 238, 398n.27
Shimonoseki, Treaty of, 94–95
Shouzhang, 177, 202
Shun-dao hui (Obedient Swords), 46
Silver prices, 101, 171
Sino-Japanese War (1894–95), 73–74,
    91, 172; impact of defeat, 81, 93,
    112–113, 129, 182, 320; indemnity,
    170; and Shandong troop with-
    drawals, 102, 104, 159
Sioux Indians, 316–317
Skinner, G. William, 3–7, 18
Smith, Arthur H., 70–73, 78, 214, 220
Société des Missions Etrangères, 74
Society of the Divine Word (S.V.D.),
    79–88, 93, 115, 123–126, 128, 134–
    135, 185, 187, 188, 194
Song Jing-shi, 17, 59–61, 137, 141,
    143, 359n.50
Song Yue-long, 336–337
Sorghum (gaoliang), 23, 177
South Hills, of Shandong, 11, 31
Spirit Boxers (Shen-quan), 204, 205,
    318–320, 327–331; and Big
    Swords, 217, 223, 226–228, 266;
    and Boxers United in Righteous-
    ness, 206, 223, 226–228; healing,
    222, 223–224; invulnerability,
    222–223, 225–228; leadership,
    224–226, 231, 236–240; loyalism,
    226, 318–319; in mid-Qing, 57–58;
    and officials, 229–230; organization,
    206, 221, 230–235; origins in

Changqing-Chiping, 177, 214, 216–228, 390n.45; in Pingyuan, 241–257; ritual, 206, 216–219, 240; social composition, 234–240; spread of, 231–232; and White Lotus, 58, 217–222, 235. *See also* Boxers United in Righteousness

Spirit-possession (*jiang-shen fu-ti*), 39, 41, 54, 56–58, 62, 67, 219, 340; absent in Big Swords, 106–107, 367n.45; absent in Guan county Boxers, 149, 165; in Boxers, 64–65, 206, 217–219, 222, 292–294, 327–329; and healing, 56–57, 212; in Taiping, 325–327

Spirit-writing (planchette), 61–62

Steiger, George, 160

Stenz, George, 123–126, 187, 188

Sugiyama Akira, 302

sui, 107n

Sun Bin, 218

Sun Shang-wen, 212

Sun Wu-kong ("Monkey"), 62, 149, 218, 294, 329

Sun Yat-sen, 273

Sun Zhi-tai, 247, 250

"Support the Qing, destroy the foreign" (*fu-Qing mie-yang*), xiv, 68, 136, 163, 165, 226, 254, 270, 273, 277, 280, 291. *See also* Boxers United in Righteousness, loyalism

Tael, 21

Tai-bao, 41, 355n.6

Taian, 240

Taiping Rebellion, 59, 69, 101, 219, 319–327; Northern Expedition, 16–17, 137; spirit-possession in, 219, 325–327

Tan (Boxer "altar"), 231, 293

Tancheng, 188

Tang Heng-le, 52–53, 149

Tang Sai-er, 40–41

Tangyi, Boxers in, 260, 266

Tao-hua shan (Peach Flower Mountain), 217

Taxes, 59, 144, 170–171, 209

Telegraph, 169; Boxer attacks on, 284

Temple fairs, 63–64, 150, 232, 277, 330

Theatre, 62, 63–67, 111, 140, 152, 283; and Boxers, 218, 222, 229, 232–233, 328–331

Tianjin (Tientsin), 5, 69, 72, 346n.7; Boxers in, 277, 279, 291–292, 298, 301, 302, 308–309; Massacre (1870), 83

Ting-yong, 285, 305, 310

Tirpitz, Admiral Alfred, 127, 204–205

Tong Zhen-qing, 175–176, 177

Trade, foreign, 68–73, 94, 182, 208

Travels of Lao Can (*Lao Can you-ji*), 102

Triads, 323

Triple Intervention, 182

Tu-di shen, 63

United States, 91, 286; policy toward missionaries, 75–76, 92, 187, 205, 268

Villages, 1; community, 23, 65–67, 87–88, 103, 162, 186, 318; elite, 25, 234, 237–238, 245, 248; openness in Northwest, 27–28, 215, 231

wa-wa dui ("Baby Brigade"), 235

Wang Chuo, 255–256

Wang family, of Stone Buddha Village, 49, 61, 333

Wang Li-yan, 237–238, 267

Wang Lun, 43–44, 50–51, 52, 53, 106, 333–335, 339

Wang Ming-zhen, 238

Wang Shang-xuan, 237

Wang Zhi-bang, 243, 247

Wang Zi-rong, 247

Water Margin (*Shui-hu zhuan*), 13, 39, 45, 65, 294, 329

Waterlogging, 2, 14, 33–34, 207

Wavoka, 316–317

Weber, Max, 127

Wei county (Shandong), 10–11, 30, 134

Wei county (Zhili), 138, 142, 148, 158, 164, 165

Wei He-yi, 146

Weihaiwei, 170

Weng Tong-he, 133

Wenshang, 134

White Lotus Sect (Bai-lian jiao), 40–54, 66, 114; and Big Sword Society, 97–98; and Boxers, xiv, 38, 149, 217–222, 235, 244, 295–296, 300–301, 307–308, 315; Chiping uprising (1882), 86–87, 210–211;

conversion to Christianity, 87–89, 126, 142–143; rebels of 1796–1803, 42; rebels of mid-nineteenth century, 17, 59–63, 137, 141, 322–323; women in, 40, 51–52, 54, 336; and Yi-he Boxers, 46, 53–54, 58, 333–340. *See also* Eight Trigrams Sect; Sectarian religion

Wilhelm II, Kaiser, 123, 127–131 *passim*

Williams, S. Wells, 75

Women, pollution of, 44, 235, 293, 297–298, 307; in Red Lanterns, 136, 227, 235, 297–298; in White Lotus, 40, 51–52, 54, 336

Wu Jie, 338

Wu-sheng lao-mu. *See* Eternal Venerable Mother

Wu-wei jiao, 88

Wu-ying-bian (Shadowless Whip), 106

Wucheng, 31, 142, 147, 215, 281

Wulizhuang, 266

Wuqiao, 277, 279, 280

Xi-liang, 119–120

Xi-you-ji. See Journey to the West

Xiajin, Boxers in, 260, 266, 281

Xian county (Zhili), 277, 279

xiang-tou, 56

Xiaoligu, 163

Xiaolu, 142, 162

Xin-cheng (Ben-ming), 224–226, 234, 236, 257–258, 264–266, 393n.84

Xincheng (Zhili), 277

Xu An-guo, 338

Xu Bing-de, 248, 249

Xu Hong-ru, 41

Xu Tong, 159, 173

Xuan-tian shang-di, 106

Xue-Konglou, 118, 119

Xuzhou, 20, 21, 101, 112, 116, 121

Yamen clerks, 46, 338

Yamen runners, 89, 140, 151, 156, 246–248, 338, 340

Yan Lao-fu, 283–284

Yan Ming-jian, 148

Yan Shi-he, 162

Yan Shu-qin, 148, 155, 157, 159, 162, 164–165

Yang Bing, 149

Yang Chang-jun, 156

Yang De-sheng, 227

Yang Fu-tong, 284, 285, 286, 287

Yang Jian, 218, 329

Yang Xiu-qing, 219, 325, 326

Yang Zhao-shun (Yang Shun-tian). *See* Xin-cheng

Yangzi River valley, 5, 72, 303; riots of 1891, 76, 93–94, 146

Yantai (Chefoo), 7, 11, 69, 73

Yanzhou, 80–81, 99, 112–113, 363n.45

Yao Wen-qi (Yao Luo-qi), 152–153, 155, 162–164

Yellow River, 2; 1898 flood, 172, 173, 177–180, 216, 223–224; flooding, 170, 173, 181; in Northwest, 14–15, 207; in Southwest, 13, 18–19, 98, 116, 174

Yellow Turban rebellion, 39

Yi-he Boxers, 46, 58, 141; and 1898–1900 Boxers, 153–154, 333–334, 340; ritual, 339; and White Lotus, 53–54, 333–340, 410n.8, 412n.28

Yi-he-men jiao, 336

Yi-he-men quan-bang, 334

Yi-he quan-jiao, 337

Yi-he tuan. *See* Boxers United in Righteousness; Militia United in Righteousness

Yi-huo quan, 335

Yihebao, 154

Yiheying, 154

Yin-Yang Boxing, 336

Yizhou, 86–88, 172–173, 185–188, 189, 192–193

Yongqing, 287

Yu-lin jun (Elm Forest Army), 16

Yu-lu, 246, 274, 275, 285, 286, 288, 302, 303, 305, 309, 310

Yu Qing-shui, 236–237, 257–258, 264–266

Yu-xian (governor): in Beijing, 274, 286; and Boxers, 190–191, 197–204, 229, 240, 243–246, 253, 255–257, 258, 264, 265–270, 273–274, 387n.142, 401n.80, 402n.7; in Caozhou, 102, 109–111, 119–120, 191–192, 257; execution, 311; and Germans, 192–193, 198, 202–203; as judicial commissioner, 124, 160–161, 192; as Shandong governor, 168, 172, 173, 180–181, 190–192; in Shanxi, 190–191, 286, 304–305

Yu Xian (magistrate), 229–230
Yuan Chang, 289
Yuan-ming-yuan, 170
Yuan Shi-dun, 248–250, 255–256, 258, 269
Yuan Shi-kai, 248–249, 268–270, 272, 281, 286, 289, 304, 312–313, 381n.26
Yucheng, 208, 215; Boxers in, 206, 225, 227, 237, 257–258, 259, 264, 267
Yue Er-mi-zi ("Rice Grain Yue"), 110, 113
Yue Jin-tang, 177
Yun-chan si, 224
Yun-qi, 105
Yuncheng, 120, 131, 177
Yong-zheng Emperor, 76

Zaoqiang, 275, 277
Zeng Guang-huan, 119
Zeng Guo-quan, 14
Zhai-zhu, 108, 112
Zhang Fei, 294, 329
Zhang Guo-zheng, 160
Zhang Huan-hou, 294
Zhang Jue, 39
Zhang Lian-zhu, 114
Zhang Luo-di, 282
Zhang Luo-jiao, 55, 97, 141
Zhang Ru-mei, 134, 172, 176, 179–180, 184, 192, 383n.64–65; and Guan county Boxers, 161, 162; and militia, 159–160, 173, 196
Zhang Shang-da, 180
Zhang Yin-huan, 133, 173

Zhang Ze, 242, 243, 245
Zhang Zhi-dong, 288, 303
Zhang Zong-yu, 137
Zhangguantun, 229
Zhangzhuang, 258, 261n, 264–265
Zhao (Armor of the Golden Bell teacher), 104–105, 107, 366n.31
Zhao Lao-guang, 155
Zhao San-duo (Zhao Luo-zhu), 148, 150–165, 236, 375n.51
Zhao Shu-qiao, 288
Zhao Yun, 218, 329
Zhejiang, 306
Zhen-wu-shen (Zhen-wu di or Xuan-tian da-di: the True Martial God), 106
Zhenjiang (Chinkiang), 5, 6, 69, 101, 347n.7
Zhifang, 250–252, 253
Zhili: Boxers in, 232, 271–272, 275–291; ecology of, 17–18, 275; Zhili-Shandong border, 20–21, 72
Zhou Cang, 218
Zhou De-qian, 336
Zhou Yun-jie, 108
Zhou Zhen-jia, 225
Zhoucun, 10
Zhu Ba-jie ("Pigsy"), 218, 294
Zhu Hong-deng, 224–226, 234, 236, 241, 244, 247–266 passim, 271, 392n.76, 393n.84, 86
Zhu Zhen-guo, 101
Zhuang, Prince, 307, 311
Zhuozhou, 284, 286
Zongli Yamen, 83, 84, 131, 268, 287, 302
Zuo Jian-xun, 145–146